A
CRITICAL DICTIONARY
OF SOCIOLOGY

A
CRITICAL
DICTIONARY
OF
SOCIOLOGY

RAYMOND BOUDON
and
FRANÇOIS BOURRICAUD

Selected and Translated by

PETER HAMILTON

Routledge

First published in 1982
by Presses Universitaires de France
108, boulevard Saint-Germain, 75006 Paris
Second edition, 1986

First published in English in 1989
by Routledge
11 New Fetter Lane, London EC4P 4EE
and The University of Chicago Press
5801 Ellis Avenue, Chicago 60637

© 1982, 1986 Presses Universitaires de France
© English translation 1989 Routledge and
The University of Chicago

Typeset by Leaper & Gard Ltd, Bristol, England
Printed in Great Britain

British Library Cataloguing in Publication Data

Boudon, Raymond, *1934-*
    A critical dictionary of sociology.
    1. Sociology
    I. Title   II. Bourricaud, François   III.
Hamilton, Peter
301
    ISBN 0-415-01745-9

CONTENTS

EDITOR'S FOREWORD

The *Critical Dictionary of Sociology* is unlike most other sociology or social science dictionaries. Its authors, Raymond Boudon and François Bourricaud, are eminent French sociologists. Both are typical of the cosmopolitan French intellectual class – they are extremely widely read, are rich in what Pierre Bourdieu would call social and cultural capital, are highly conversant with American versions of Anglo-Saxon sociology, speak and write in several languages, and doubtless hold social and political views which are perhaps a little right of centre. They are also the authors of major sociological studies on issues as widespread as stratification, sociological method, and the social theories of Talcott Parsons. So, when they come to write a book like the *Critical Dictionary* their objectives are almost certainly irreconcilable with those of the average compiler of the banal but worthy work which it is the destiny of most works with the title 'dictionary' to be.

The title of the book of course discloses its authors' objectives. But it is 'Critical' in a sense which has very little to do with how that prefix has been commandeered and overworked by essentially left-wing social thinkers since the resurgence of Marxist thought in the 1960s, and indeed it is used by Boudon and Bourricaud in a sense which evokes earlier and more wide-ranging though not unconnected references, whose force has been evident from the Enlightenment right through to the present, the critical rationalism of the *philosophes* and their *Encyclopedie* being one of its earliest forebears.

If the critical rationalism which underlies the *Dictionary* has a long and honourable pedigree it is because it forms a mode of thought which is irreverent in the best sense of that term: it has little respect for conventional wisdom or for intellectual fads and fashions. The authors take a clear and uncompromising line on their subject, and their choice of entries is as much a matter of personal delight in the glorious variety of sociological concepts and theories as it is of a wish to settle certain problems of their 'erstwhile philosophical conscience' as Marx would have said. This gives the *Dictionary* a tough and acerbic edge. Each entry grapples directly with an issue, whether theoretical, epistemological, philosophical, political, or empirical, and provides a strong statement of what Boudon and Bourricaud think about it. The discussions are considered but argumentative; they reveal as much about the views of their authors as they do about the topic under review.

If this means that the *Dictionary* is less a conventionally conceived dictionary

vii

than a collection of original essays, then there is little amiss with its outcome. Sociology is too replete with textbooks, guides, glossaries and, yes, even dictionaries. One more synthetic and weighty edition would have been one too many, and we should be thankful that Boudon and Bourricaud took the bull very firmly by the horns and avoided the temptation (if, in their case, it ever existed) to write a worthy but ultimately lack-lustre excursion through the great and the good of classical and contemporary sociology.

By reaffirming that a non-Marxist style of critique is still possible, Boudon and Bourricaud have performed a great service for a discipline which most would agree has lost its vocation and, more arguably, its claim to represent a distinctive way of approaching the key issues which confront the societies of the twentieth and twenty-first centuries.

In preparing and editing this translation of *The Critical Dictionary of Sociology*, a number of changes have been made to the content and presentation of the entries by comparison with their French originals. In the first place two editions of the French work have now appeared, necessitating some modification and elision of the entries in order to accommodate changes which marked the progress from first to second edition. Second, it was deemed necessary to abridge the *Dictionary* slightly in its English edition, in order that the entries which were included would more adequately reflect issues which would be of greatest interest to English-speaking readerships. Third, the bibliographic references supplied for each entry in its French editions were not all entirely relevant to English-speaking readerships, which has meant that certain French versions of works cited in the texts are not referenced, although their English or original-language editions have always been included within the bibliographies.

Finally, the index (which does not appear in the French editions, where a 'Thematic General Index', cross-referencing terms and names with entries but without page number references, was included) is prepared in such a way as to conform to English-speaking conventions as to the listing of subjects and authors. Although there are good arguments for the French method, it is significantly less helpful in the rapid 'dip-searching' which will most often result from the way a reader will consult the index, and the editor makes no apologies for substituting this Anglicized method of Indexing for the French method of the original work.

Those readers who may have consulted the French editions will, no doubt, wish for some explanation of why the French text has been abridged and certain entries excluded from this translation.

The editor/translator should explain that the decision to exclude was taken relatively early on in the translation work, when he took a certain view about the appropriateness of some of the material for its intended audience. The original intention of the translation was to produce a version of *The Critical Dictionary of Sociology* which could stand muster as a sociology textbook. This meant selecting those articles which were most usable for that purpose, and certainly may well have kept out material which from a purely scholarly viewpoint deserves inclusion. However, the objective was to include the material which best suited an English-speaking readership.

In the main, the articles left out are (although there are some exceptions) on average shorter than the majority of included entries, and constitute the less relevant, less accessible, or more ethnocentrically 'French' discussions in terms of current sociological concerns. This should not be taken to mean that the editor considers distinctively French concerns to be of no interest or relevance for an English-speaking audience – for clearly in many cases they are of vital concern (witness, in this context, the impact of French structuralism on British or American sociology as only one among many examples of French intellectual influence) – but it is to recognize that certain issues, or empirically grounded debates, have a purely French relevance to academic teaching of the subject in France itself which limits their utility for those working in an English-speaking intellectual environment – however Francophile it may be.

In the light of what has been said above, it may be helpful for the reader to know how the translated edition as presented here differs from the two French editions. This will offer those readers who have a particular interest in those entries which have not been included the opportunity of themselves referring to the originals. Thus, below are listed the entries which will be found in the French editions, together with the main reasons for their exclusion from this translated edition.

Consensus

The article covers a concept which has declined as a topic of current interest in the sociological literature – as the bibliography makes clear, the most recent work cited being published (in French translation) in 1972.

Constraint

While an interesting topic, the discussion is very general and adds relatively little to the treatment of concepts which are more effectively handled at other points in the book. The issues it covers are, in fact, better dealt with in 'Conformity and deviance', 'Durkheim', and 'Social control'.

Dependence

Not included as an entry in the second edition, therefore not translated. The issues it covers are mainly dealt with in 'Needs'.

Division of labour

A slightly marginal decision. Again, however, a great deal of the material is duplicated in other entries – notably in 'Anomie', 'Development', 'Durkheim', 'Economics and sociology', 'Needs', 'Methodology', and 'Marx'.

Generation

Although increasingly recognized as an important area of sociological interest, the discussion does not reflect contemporary literature.

Individualism

Although one article which might now be seriously reconsidered for inclusion, it was originally left out because of its length and because it is more concerned with a methodological issue than with the empirical process of individualization itself – so much a concern of contemporary society. The real subject of the entry is *methodological individualism*. However, this subject (as a methodology central to Boudon and Bourricaud's whole approach) is, moreover, handled without any discussion of or reference to certain important contributions, especially those of Steven Lukes and Peter Winch, widely recognized as being definitive contributions to a long-running methodological debate.

Individual

'Structuralism' and 'Action' are both entries which deal with much the same material, but in a more focused way. In some ways this article exhibits the same problems for an Anglo-Saxon readership as 'Individualism'.

Industrial society

A broad-ranging discussion which adds relatively little to what is already covered in 'Capitalism', 'Social change', 'Development', and 'Utopia'. More recent discussion of this concept in the sociological literature has focused quite explicitly on various 'post-industrial society' notions – post-capitalism, information society, post-modernism, etc. – notions which Raymond Boudon and François Bourricaud do not treat directly in the French original other than somewhat peripherally in its last two paragraphs.

Inequalities

Although an important topic in its own right, it is one which Raymond Boudon and François Bourricaud return to in a number of other and in many ways more satisfactory entries. 'Equality', 'Capitalism', 'Elite', 'Measurement', 'Rousseau', 'Social mobility', each quarter the same terrain. As a result it was difficult to find enough distinctively different in terms of the discussions the entry contains to justify its inclusion.

Influence

A topic which has a lengthy entry devoted to it, but which does not manage to illuminate the subject to a corresponding degree.

Institutions

The reader will find that 'Democracy', 'Family', 'Status', 'Values', and 'Functionalism', overlap almost completely with the French original. Although there is a kernel of material here which might be considered of interest in its own right, the entry as a whole is not as central to contemporary concerns within Anglo-Saxon sociology as it could be.

Intellectuals

The material is very adequately covered, in so far as it links to wider *sociological* issues, in the entries 'Elites', 'Ideologies', 'Knowledge', 'Professions'. In the entry itself, the discussion is quite general and, although interesting, not particularly relevant to contemporary Anglo-Saxon sociology.

Liberalism

As with a number of entries, the generality of treatment argues against inclusion, for the more specifically sociological issues are better handled in entries such as 'Democracy', 'Equality', 'Ideologies', and 'The State'. Again, distinctively French concerns are raised which have undeniable importance for the original French audience, but create problems of context and comprehension for the likely readers of this translation.

Models

Complex mathematically, the entry probably suffers too much from its own rigour. In this, the cultural emphasis on mathematics exhibited by French academic institutions is perhaps to blame. It was felt that, although the mathematical arguments will be accessible to graduate students who are particularly interested in mathematical sociology, they risk being impenetrable to those whose concerns are more conceptual or empirical. The entry relies on the admittedly much higher level of mathematical ability of the French Grande Ecole-level student, as compared to his or her British or American counterpart. Conceptually, the entry does not supplant material already covered in 'Explanation', 'Methodology', and 'Measurement'.

Modernization

Although on the surface it may seem one of the best cases for inclusion, the original article was excluded because of very direct overlap with the 'Development' entry and because it does not discuss the wide range of 'anti-modernization thesis' literature of the last ten to fifteen years or so (cf. Roxburgh, Frank, Brenner, Laclau, etc.). Even Immanuel Wallerstein, whose work has demonstrably been at the centre of a considerable international debate about these questions, receives only a bibliographical mention, when most contemporary treatments of the topic do not fail to include discussion of his world-system thesis.

Montesquieu

Certainly an interesting article, but the utility of this philosopher/historian's work (although undoubtedly of historical interest) may not be of central significance in a *Critical Dictionary of Sociology* designed to be relevant to contemporary sociological teaching.

Norms

A very difficult decision, but one forced on the editor because of the partial treatment of the subject. Despite Bourricaud's close acquaintance with Parsonian sociology, the whole treatment of the normative, so central to his work, hardly receives mention (except in the bibliography). The concept of the norm and normatively oriented action has very close links with functionalism and especially the work of Robert Merton – again, it is surprising not to see this mentioned. Rather, there is lengthy treatment of Piaget and, although his work is important, few sociologists would consider it central to the development of *sociological* analysis in this area.

Organization

Much of the discussion here is replicated, in so far as it connects to wider sociological concerns with material contained in the entries 'Authority', 'Bureaucracy', 'State', 'Power', and 'Groups'. In addition, the more empirical references in the entry itself cover studies which are not now in the forefront of research in this area, which risks giving the impression that the entry is outdated.

Pareto

This is an interesting discussion, despite the fact that it overemphasizes certain aspects of Pareto's theories, e.g., the whole logical vs. non-logical action distinction, and devotes almost no attention to Pareto's influence on sociology generally.

Parties

Excluded because the material contained a heavy emphasis on sources now considered largely outdated.

Polyarchy

Based on a concept used by the American political scientist Robert Dahl, it was hard to justify inclusion of an entry on so little-known an idea, despite the intrinsic merits of the entry itself.

Social conflicts

Much of the content of this entry overlaps with that in 'Dialectic', 'Action (collective)', 'Alienation', 'Anomie', 'Conformity and deviance', 'Minorities', and 'Power'. It was difficult to find a distinct justification for its inclusion.

Social movements

A difficult decision. Although the theme is an important one, the entry itself tends to the overgeneral, and does not cover some of the more important concepts and theories in this area – notably of course the fairly recent work of Tilly. Since there is some overlap with other entries (notably 'Action (collective)', 'Groups', 'Social change', 'Prophetism', 'Charisma', and 'Religion') it was excluded.

Socialism

Not especially relevant in a *Dictionary of Sociology*; the more precisely sociological themes are taken up elsewhere in more useful form, notably in 'Marx', 'Capitalism', 'Dialectic', and 'Alienation'.

Totalitarianism

Not a current interest in sociology, although there have been notable contributions to the study of totalitarian regimes, which are well presented in this entry.

Tradition

Much of the discussion mirrors material already well presented in 'Charisma', 'Development', 'Social change', 'Weber', 'Prophetism', 'Culturalism and culture', and 'Theory'.

Typologies

Very similar considerations apply here as do to the entry on 'Models'. Over-complicated in its use of mathematics for the audience most likely to use *The Critical Dictionary of Sociology*.

Values

As a topic, it would be logical to include the entry. But Raymond Boudon and François Bourricaud contrive in their treatment of it to leave aside a number of important issues. Values and value-systems form important elements of the theories of Weber, Durkheim, Parsons, Shils, Merton – all of whom otherwise figure widely in the *Dictionary*. But here the discussion, though it does include Durkheim and Weber fairly peripherally, does not get to grips with contemporary discussions (cf. the resurgence of interest in Weber's Protestant Ethic thesis,[1] or in Durkheim's concepts of the sacred and the profane).

Violence

Although this was an interesting essay in its own right, again the terms of the translation precluded inclusion. The original is somewhat lengthy, and if it had been possible to make the necessary changes, an edited and revised version would have given greater prominence to the Hobbesian problem of order theme around which the best elements of the entry are organized.

The authors of the *The Critical Dictionary of Sociology* have given their approval of the minor changes and abridgements made to the French originals. Although these have – inevitably – led to a slight change in the character of the resulting work, it is felt that the *The Critical Dictionary of Sociology* as presented here remains extremely close in spirit to the original, while at the same time providing a translation which fits much more closely the requirements of an English-speaking sociological audience.

1. See the best recent discussion of the debate, Gordon Marshall (1982) *In Search of the Spirit of Capitalism*, London: Hutchinson.

INTRODUCTION

In the same way that war is a thing too important to be left to soldiers, sociology is something too serious to be abandoned to sociologists and their debates. Is this discipline, which has made an undeniable contribution to the progress of western thought, threatened with an irreversible decline? Its future certainly does not look as rosy as it did. During the period 1950 to 1970 sociology experienced extensive development. The number of students, teachers, and researchers increased rapidly. The opinion of sociologists was sought – if not always followed. They took the roles of experts and consultants. Corporations and public administrations were open to them, not without a certain reluctance, however. The most active had the flattering feeling that they were involved in the great movements and affairs of society. Why then was this rapid rise followed by such a swift decline? If we put on one side the historical events which, in the eyes of the public particularly in France, led to the image of our discipline being linked with the most extreme forms of university discontent, it is possible to see the decline being essentially due to two reverses, each caused by the excessive pretensions of certain sociologists. First, many sociologists sought to present themselves as 'thinkers' – or rushed, with too evident satisfaction, into such an unrewarding role. At the same time, they had not the slightest hesitation in claiming for sociology the status of a 'science', thus giving themselves the right to the same privileges and the same considerations as their colleagues in the exact sciences, without feeling hindered from insistently claiming the traditional mission of general culture and philosophy, namely to provide an answer to the widest questions concerning social organization and the role of man in society.

There was a further point on which the position of the sociologists was clearly untenable: those who do not see themselves as thinkers or gurus are as happy to see themselves as 'counsellors of the Prince' – to say nothing of those who see no problems in espousing both roles. If being a counsellor to the Prince is not possible, many have to content themselves with exercising their expertise at a more modest level. But expertise demands both prudence and patience. A certain modesty fits well with the role. In addition, competence is exercised on behalf of the client, under his control, and for his benefit. Now the expert and his client do not speak the same language. They do not always work for the same reasons.

1

By involving himself in 'applied' projects the sociologist exposes himself to the risk of simultaneously disappointing his clients and inflicting on himself all the torments of a bad conscience.

Finally, the ideological climate has changed. The expansion of the period 1950-70 encouraged unrealistic hopes about our ability to control social change. To the extent that it presented itself as a 'science' of planned change and development, sociology benefited from this brief euphoria. Throughout the 1970s, as the illusions were destroyed, the sociology which seemed to have maintained them naturally lost its status. We have arrived at a point today where the series of internal crises and the mounting scepticism which it encourages have significantly degraded its status. It is no longer capable of scientifically analysing social data or of providing the positive basis for a modern consensus. This depression is, however, as unfounded and excessive as the crisis that it followed.

In our view this dictionary should help sociology take its place once more among the classical disciplines. In addition, it aims to provide the intelligent reader with the means of assessing the importance of the sociological tradition. Reflection on social life is one of the permanent tasks of western thought. This task has been carried out by historians, philosophers, moralists, and jurists. Thucydides, Machiavelli, Montesquieu, de Tocqueville, and Marx have as much to offer among the founders of sociology as Durkheim and Weber. But if it is true that sociology is part of an intellectual tradition which precedes it, and perhaps even goes beyond it, it brings to this tradition analytic tools which historians and philosophers would be wrong to disdain. Sociology can and should contribute to the reflection of man upon his condition. It can, if it first renounces the illusory ambitions which it has nourished for so long. In any event sociology cannot be a substitute for philosophy or for general culture.

Such pretensions have, moreover, been destructive for sociology: they have condemned it, at least in France, to be often little more than sophistry. To avoid its own illusions, sociology should be critical, comparative, and rigorous. It is not essential for sociological critique to limit itself to opposition and denunciation. We see it more as a way of maintaining a suitable distance from data and problems, which allows both the sociologist and his reader to treat them as significant data. Sociology must be comparative; we mean that it constitutes a device for checking the similarities and differences that the observer notes in the variety of situations, circumstances, and products of social activity. Finally, sociology must be rigorous. It is aimed at the constitution, consolidation, and extension of specialized knowledge. This knowledge is above all an ordering or *codification* which rests on explicit and recognized procedures of explanation and analysis.

The work which we present to the public is neither an encyclopaedia nor a glossary: it is a dictionary. The reader will not find a complete exposition of all the concepts which are currently in use in sociology. We expect no lack of critics surprised at the omission of this or that concept. We will also be reproached for not having covered all the domains of sociology: rural, urban, political, etc. Such an enterprise would have been beyond our means. Impractical, even when produced by a team, for its coherence is then necessarily quite weak, such an enterprise would have been absurd for two authors and their sole resources.

In writing this work, then, we have avoided making it an encyclopaedia or glossary or vocabulary. In general, those authors who have attempted that task have been guided by two principles: in the first place, survey the widest range of meanings – however varied they are – for the words selected by the authors of the glossary; in the second place, define the 'proper' use of the word, based on its use by the 'right' authors.

Our ambitions in writing this book were thus neither encyclopaedic, nor normative. In fact, our dictionary pursues objectives which are completely different. It is dedicated to the fundamental *questions* of sociology. These questions can be examined using the format of a dictionary, even if there are good reasons to believe that their more detailed examination requires a more systematic method. Second, we wanted to flush out the *received ideas* which insinuate themselves among the words which are wrongly used. Finally, we sought to illuminate the links between certain fundamental concepts. This is why each entry is accompanied by a list of related entries, and why the dictionary has a thematic index, outlining certain groupings of themes and fields. But we cannot hide the fact that these groupings are outlines only – another book would be necessary to follow their implications through.

If we could sum up our objective in one word we would say that it would be essentially to present a *critical* analysis of the sociological tradition. One reference will help to show what we mean by 'critique': Bridgeman, in a famous passage in his *The Nature of Physical Theory* (1936), puts forward a proposition which condenses, according to him, the reflections common to Mach, Poincaré, and Einstein. The development of knowledge in physics, he said, proceeds along two paths: theory and critique. *Theory* aims to connect observational data. *Critique* has as its object theories themselves: it scrutinizes and analyses the imperfections, uncertainties, and failures, but also the successes; it examines the reasons for failure as well as the reasons for success. Paul Lazarsfeld liked to cite this text.[1] He would say with insistence that critique in Bridgeman's sense was at least as important in the social sciences as in physics, and devoted a large proportion of his time to putting this idea into operation.[2] His prescriptions have very largely guided us in this book. Throughout our reading of the major sociological contributions on this or that problem, we have tried to use the most fruitful paradigms from the point of view of the explanation of social phenomena. At the same time, we have attempted to explain why certain paradigms appear more and more as dead-ends. We hope we have not slid too often from the critical to the caustic mode! But while conscious of the neutrality necessary to scientific debate, we are not prevented from treating certain propositions or concepts with the irony that they deserve. Did not Popper constantly insist on the fact that certain propositions and concepts were the concern of critical rationality, while others were not?

Having adopted this fundamental orientation, our enterprise led to a series of other decisions which needed to be justified.

The references are numerous and undoubtedly sufficient to guide the reader who wishes to acquire an overview of the classical and modern literature. But they make no claims to be exhaustive. We have described and commented upon only the research which appears to us to be of undoubted importance, from a point of view which is essentially our own. More precisely, we have selected and discussed those writings which we have judged to bring, either directly or indirectly, a decisive clarity to the ways in which this or that type of phenomenon can be explained. Our aim is not to inform the reader on the most recent research or the latest refinements of a methodology, but to debate with him the best way of approaching a certain subject or of using a particular method.

As will by now be clear, the dictionary is founded on a body of work, a *corpus*. This corpus is composed of the classical and modern research which constitutes a decisive step in the analysis of complex systems, and in the explanation of the phenomena which they treat. During our attempt to retrace, on the basis of this corpus, the fundamental direction of the sociological tradition, we were often struck by the thought that the classical sociologists were especially useful to our discussion. After a number of detours, the sociology of political mobilization has rediscovered certain intuitions, already present in de Tocqueville's work. For example, political mobilization is more likely to accompany economic growth than recession. Pareto set out some essential propositions on the subject of the relation between knowledge and ideology, and insisted on the continuity of these two phenomena that common sense is more likely to treat as contradictory. Rousseau outlined the basic orientations of all research on inequality. Marx identified the existence of a class structure, fundamental to the understanding of social change, where individual and collective interests are essentially incompatible. Weber and Durkheim showed, each in his own way, that beliefs can be analysed in a scientific fashion. In the field of analytical techniques, modern research often appears to be the elaboration of old intuitions. That is why the references to classical sociology hold a major place in this dictionary.

Once these general orientations had been chosen, it was necessary to draw up a list of rubrics covering the types of entry which the dictionary contains. Such a list would have to be not too long, so that we did not have to cover themes too elliptically. Through trial and error, we established a list of about eighty[3] entries, which could be grouped together under the following headings:

1. Major classes of social phenomena (for example, cycles, ideology, religion)
2. Types and fundamental aspects of social organization (for example, bureaucracy, minorities)
3. Major concepts of sociology (for example, anomie, charisma)
4. Concepts widely used in contemporary sociology (for example, structure, system)
5. Paradigms and theories of a generalizing type (for example, culturalism, functionalism, structuralism)
6. Major theoretical questions (for example, power, social control)
7. Major epistemological questions (for example, objectivity, prediction, theory)
8. We also decided to include a series of entries on the main founders of sociology, with the objective of describing the essentials of their contribution, from

the theoretical and methodological points of view, and evaluating the contemporary relevance of their teachings today.

A number of concepts which are not given an entry to themselves are covered under several headings and can be found by consulting the general index at the end of the dictionary. Thus, the concept of class is discussed within the entries on 'Stratification' and 'Social mobility', and referred to at some length in a number of others.

The theoretical orientation of the work has led us to avoid treating subjects which would require the listing of a wide range of essentially empirical studies. Thus, we have not included entries on particular social institutions or on descriptive categories which define applied sociology. This is why entries on subjects such as judicial institutions, schools, churches, leisure, migration, education, or juvenile delinquency will not be found in the dictionary.

In deciding to produce a dictionary, it is inevitable that the decision to use one word rather than another is in the end rather arbitrary. Of course certain 'entries' are inevitable. A dictionary of sociology without the words group, anomie, or alienation – or even élites and family – is inconceivable. But if it is restricted by certain constraints, the construction of such a work allows a measure of flexibility. That said, we are conscious of the imperfections of our list.

Our main interest is in industrial societies. We would willingly agree that there are no *ontological* reasons to draw a dividing line between sociology, anthropology, or ethnology. It seems to us impossible to state that ancient societies are in all respects more 'simple' than modern societies. Moreover, we are ready to recognize that stratification among the Natchez or Bororo can illuminate the mobility problems of our own societies. But we are more concerned with our societies than with theirs. Hence the anthropologist will not find entries on kinship or myth, even if certain developments relevant to these questions are mentioned in certain of our headings. It is impossible to treat the question of modernization without interrogating the roles of rites and myths in social life.

It is appropriate now to deal with the bases of collaboration between the two authors of the dictionary. They shared entries equally: but while the first version of the entries was prepared by one of them, the final version was a joint responsibility. This work was made possible by the agreement of the two authors on the fundamental orientations of the dictionary. Without any doubt, the competence of each author was exercised in distinct areas. Raymond Boudon, because of his earlier work, was more qualified for the entries relating to methodology and epistemology, i.e. for those on problems of stratification, social mobility, and social change. François Bourricaud felt more at ease in the entries concerning politics, culture, and comparisons of institutions and social systems. But on three equally important dimensions of the diverse field of sociological theory the two authors explicitly shared the same approach.

First, they rejected what Piaget called 'totalitarian realism', that is, the explanation of social facts by the supposed and often imaginary demands of the 'system' or of the 'totality' of which these phenomena are part. According to them, social facts must be interpreted as relations between a plurality of actors or agents. It is on this condition that these facts have a meaning and may be understood. Whatever the ambiguities which attach to terms like action or interaction, their use appears opportune to emphasize the importance of the intentional and strategic dimension in social behaviour.

The second proposition to which the two authors are committed is that social facts, if treated as the products of systems or of processes of action or interaction, are not reducible to interpersonal relations, but should always be treated as emergent phenomena. The price of a product in a competitive market, the appearance of political violence in a social system are emergent effects, in the sense that, although they result from the interaction of microscopic individual actions, they represent macroscopic phenomena, that is, defined at the level of the system. The 'involuntary', 'unexpected', ultimately 'perverse' aspects of social facts are inseparable from emergent effects.

The third proposition, to which the two authors attach a central importance, is that the term general theory carries more disadvantages than advantages in sociology. It is true that every observation is part of a 'frame of reference' within a group of questions which are more or less relevant and linked together. But it is important to be wary of believing that this frame of reference authorizes us to deduce from a few clear and simple propositions a whole chain of universally applicable consequences: to understand a system or a social process is eventually to uncover the presence of a structure, of a schema, or of a theoretical model, but it is also to be aware of the particularities of the system and of the process. To parody Hayek, it is possible to say that *piecemeal theorizing*, partial theories of limited ambition, has contributed much more to our comprehension of social phenomena than the theories which claim to take account of the social systems and processes with the help of a few summary, and for the most part malleable and uncertain, concepts and propositions.

We would like to thank all those who have helped us in our task, in agreeing to read parts or the entirety of the manuscript and to give us their comments (the final manuscript remaining of course our entire responsibility), or in helping us to prepare the text for publication. Thanks to: Pierrette Andrès, Georges Balandier, Philippe Bénéton, Philippe Besnard, Pierre Birnbaum, Bernard Cazes, Rémy Chauvin, Mohamed Cherkaoui, Philippe Cibois, Michel Crozier, Eric de Dampierre, Béatrice Frison-Roche, Alain Girard, Michel Henry, Yves Fricker, Arthur Kriegel, Jacques Lautman, Jacqueline Lécuyer, Annie Morelle, Jean Padioleau, Norbert Parguel, Jean-Daniel Reynaud, Denis Szabo, Alain Wolfelsperger.

1. Lazarsfeld, P. *et al.* (eds) (1972) *Continuities in the Language of Social Research*, New York: The Free Press, p. 3.
2. Lazarsfeld referred as much to methodology as to critique. The two words were synonymous for him and recalled the ideas of Bridgeman. Unfortunately today the concept of methodology tends to describe the techniques of research.
3. *Translator's note*: the 100 or so entries of the original French second edition have been edited down to a list of eighty which are more appropriate to an English-speaking audience.

INTRODUCTION TO THE SECOND EDITION

The generally favourable welcome given to the first edition of this work is perhaps best explained by the fact that the nonconformist perspective we have put forward is not entirely without foundation.

To begin with we have tried to show that sociology represents an essential dimension of thinking about society, and that much sociological theory and research is resistant to critique, so that it renders otherwise opaque phenomena more transparent, in keeping with the task of all scientific theory.

At the other extreme the label 'sociology' also covers theories whose object appears to be to provide a 'scientific' appearance to *generally accepted ideas* which contradict evident facts, are based on vicious circles, and cannot survive their exposure to rational discussion.

In emphasizing this distinction, we have wanted to present a critical work – in the most classical meaning of this term – to our readers. That said, we are very far from indulging in nihilism or relativism, and are opposed to those forms of dogmatism which involve the presentation of a certain number of propositions as scientific (for example, on stratification or social mobility) whose sole function is to consolidate ideological prejudices. But we are as much against the dogmatism of those sceptics and 'pluralists' who treat all theories as if they were 'fairy stories' on the assumption that all that counts is the interest they evoke. We believe, on the contrary, that it is important to distinguish between those theories which enable the better understanding of certain aspects of the social, and those which are no more than chimeras. This is certainly not the place to adopt an eclectic perspective towards the analysis of social facts, and it is certainly not the best way of restoring the prestige of sociology. The 'anything goes' slogan of the philosophy put forward by the avant-garde sciences was a salutary reaction perhaps to the dogmatism of the 1960s and 1970s, but it is surely excessive. Social reality certainly exists: it is not just a product of the imagination. Consequently, sociology is not destined to be in the first instance a literary or aesthetic activity, and the first rule of sociological method is not to please or touch, but to state verifiable propositions which may help us to better understand social phenomena.

We would also like to distance ourselves on one point from a current perspective. We do not believe that there is only *one* sociological tradition, which we should refer to here. By contrast, we believe that there are sociological traditions between which the sociologist should choose. We will use some examples to make our position clear. There is a contemporary cult which idolizes Marx and Durkheim. The devotees of one or the other idol reconstruct the entire history of sociology according to a well-ordered series of stages which led the great man to either the sanctuary or the throne. And it is not only the past of our discipline which has been amputated in such an absurd way. Its future too is mortgaged by the requirements of the cult. The high priests of the cult decide what is in conformity with the spirit and methods of sociology. In the name of tradition they reject heterodox questions and hypotheses.

It is not, however, sufficient merely to recognize the diversity of sociological traditions. It is also necessary to abstain from inventing doubtful convergences between them. Parsons attempted to show that the foundations of sociological theory, as he understood it, were laid by three European sociologists at the beginning of this century: Pareto, Weber, and Durkheim. Let us say on Parsons's behalf that he emphasized that the personal connections between these three thinkers were practically non-existent. He even took especial pains to describe the differences between the intellectual milieux from which they came and in which they worked: Durkheim was marked by the positivism of August Comte, while Pareto and Weber took no notice of it. Pareto was a very great economist, while Durkheim understood little of economics. Weber, for his part, was a historian of juridical and economic institutions, whose reflections on problems of objectivity in history were guided by neo-Kantian theories which were widespread in the German universities of his time. It would have been very surprising if the three 'founding fathers' had shared the same conception of the relations between the economy and religion, of the nature of law and religion, or of the other problems which sociologists classically debate. Enforced convergence is a sort of bed of Procrustes; everything which falls outside its area is cut off, and what is left is not necessarily either the most meaningful or the most instructive. It would perhaps have been easier to have brought out real convergences, notably in relation to method, between Spencer, Marx, Pareto, and Weber than between the three protagonists chosen by Parsons.

If Weber, after all, never cited his contemporary Durkheim once in the thousands of pages which constitute his work, it is perhaps because he thought of Durkheim what he said at the end of his life about the *collective concepts* which haunt sociology and which he believed it was important to reject from the discipline. And it is perhaps as easy to condemn sociology to a sterile eclecticism as to seek a 'synthesis' between the individualist mode of thought of which Weber was the first explicit advocate and the totalitarian realism to which Durkheim was never entirely committed.

Sociology is then more diverse than is often admitted. On the other hand, it is not the result of a 'break' whose origins can easily be established. It is true that Comte's work was influential during the entire nineteenth century, that it inspired a number of intellectuals, thinkers, and sociologists, and that Durkheim expressed in a more academic form ideas which Comte had enunciated in a more prophetic style. But Comte had almost no influence on classical German or Italian sociology, and the break that Comte constituted for the development of French thought has no counterparts in England or Germany. Dare we say that the Comtean 'break' seems to us a misleading notion? Comte tried hard to discredit the philosophy of the Enlightenment. Now it seems absurd to us to consider Montesquieu and Rousseau as relevant only to one or other conception of sociology's prehistory, while Comte or Durkheim, like Moses, would go forward majestically to the Promised Land. In his *History of Economic Analysis*, Schumpeter had no hesitation in introducing Turgot, Cantillon, and even St Thomas Acquinas. Should sociology, whose territory is notably less well defined, react to the risks of market penetration by a sort of haughty protectionism? What advantage is gained from passing silently over the fact that Montesquieu, like Aristotle, is responsible for a rigorous *comparative analysis* of an immense mass of social and political data, or that Rousseau had already applied the now-classic method of the *model* to political analysis?

Who can deny the Machiavellian origins of Pareto's thought or the progressive incorporation of economic ideas from Adam Smith in his *Treatise of General Sociology* onward? Did not Marx himself recognize that he owed the concept of class to the Physiocrats? His ideas on religion are inspired by the Enlightenment philosophers of the eighteenth century. So impressed was he by the concept of the state of nature that he uses it to the point of forgetting it was intended by Rousseau as a useful fiction. The fact that Marx was – as has so often been pointed out – so close to the tradition of the Enlightenment philosophers does not mean that this concept should be banished to the shadows. Weber endlessly repeats, in his *Economy and Society* and his methodological writings, that the mode of thought of the economist and sociologist are essentially the same in the sense that the sociologist too must relate all social phenomena to the individual actions of which it is composed.

Weber supposes that these actions are by definition understandable. They may also be legitimately qualified as rational, if it is admitted that there is no need for the concept of rationality to be defined, in an unnecessarily restrictive manner, on the base of the adequacy of the relationship between means and ends. Rational behaviour is not always of the same type as that of the engineer who is solving a technical problem.

On this point, Weber and Pareto are almost exactly united. The traditional and *Wertrational* actions of Weber and Pareto's non-logical actions are not assimilable with arbitrary, fantasy, or illusion-motivated behaviour. One postulate of both writers is that, on the contrary, all actions which are of direct interest to sociological analysis may in principle be rendered intelligible and understandable if they are related to: 1) the situation of the actor; 2) his actual strategies; 3) the genesis of these two things. The consequence of this postulate is that there is no hard and fast distinction between sociology and economics, history or philosophy.

In the last account it is perhaps a sort of corporate act of defence that brings certain sociologists to 'unify' sociological traditions, and, according to their convictions, date sociology from the beginning, middle, or end of the nineteenth century. The only incontestable point is that the word was born at the beginning of the nineteenth century, almost by chance, in a debate between Quetelet and Comte. The word, but not the *thing*.

Our preferences are, it is clear, rather towards the individualist tradition. It seems to us to have proved it is more fertile than the others. And the defence and the illustration of this thesis are one of the objectives of this book. On a wide range of subjects – whether social movements, crime, organizations, processes of diffusion, socio-economic development, political analysis, and many other subjects – this tradition has given birth to a body of solid research which contributes to our understanding of the social world and to the formulation of theories which stand up to the examination of 'critical rationalism'. We see no reason why sociology should not be subject to this tribunal. Methodological individualism can be applied, as the reader patient enough to follow our examples will easily see, to all types of society and not merely, as another generally accepted idea would have it, to industrial societies alone.

The most illuminating research in the sociology of development is that which reveals chain reaction mechanisms, set off by one or other endogenous or exogenous change, or the reproduction mechanisms which are engendered by the interdependence of actors in a particular context. By contrast, that research inspired by the philosophy of history to find a prime mover for change or reduce long-term developmental change to a few holistic schemas or equations, or even a few fluid concepts (for example, centre-periphery, dependence) often appears rather fragile.

Against such holistic syntheses, Schumpeter showed that the development of England from the thirteenth century could be analysed in a rigorous way on condition that it was accepted that it was the product of a multitude of partial processes which could be precisely identified, but which could not be easily integrated into a global schema.

In opposition to the individualist tradition, the holistic tradition appears incapable of development or progress. It appears to be condemned to a continual reassessment of irremediably tautological concepts which even the most knowledgeable are incapable of making more precise.

Why then is the resistance to individualism in sociology so widespread? The answer is not difficult to find.

First, 'structures' exercise a frequently 'despotic' effect on the behaviour of social actors. That is why certain sociologists have a tendency to see *homo sociologicus* as a totally manipulable subject. They forget that structures are the product of human action, and that their effects are not assimilable to those of mechanical forces. Hence their passionate opposition to methodological individualism.

Second, these same sociologists often find it difficult to conceive that methodological individualism not only does not lead to some form of atomism, the misunderstanding of structures, but is on the contrary the only method capable of explaining analytically their genesis, persistence, and transformation.

In many cases, the corrections and additions of this second edition have been carried out under the influence of friendly criticism. We would like to thank all those who have helped in this way.

A

Action

In a letter to Robert Liefmann dated 9 March 1920, the year of his death, Max Weber wrote,

> If I have finally become a sociologist (as my most recent professional title would indicate) it was mainly so as to bring to a definite conclusion these essays based on collective concepts whose spectre still prowls. In other words: sociology, like all the others, can only come from the actions of one, of several, or of a number of separate individuals. This is why it is bound to adopt methods which are strictly *individualist.*

We decided to make this text the epigraph for the *Critical Dictionary of Sociology.* It casts the salutary shadow of doubt on all the variants of 'holism' or 'totalism' (structuralism, historicism, culturalism, Marxism, etc) which continue, despite Weber's warnings, to take their turns at the centre of the sociological stage.

It is true that to explain a social phenomenon is in all cases to bring it back to the elementary individual actions of which it is composed, whether this phenomenon takes, for example, the form of an *event* of a specific *empirical observation*, or of a *statistical distribution* or *regularity*, or any other form.

Let us take the example of a particular *event.* Following the liberalization of marriage and divorce laws decreed by the Bolsheviks following their coming to power in Russia in 1917, a severe housing crisis developed. Why? Because the new institutions made the couple a fragile relationship, they encouraged each of the spouses to try to ensure that they had available somewhere to live in case the union broke down. Institutional change had modified the field of action and of rationality (see entry 'Rationality') of individuals, and thus their behaviour in relation to housing. The aggregation of these behaviours created an event at the macrosociological level: the appearance of a housing crisis which would oblige the authorities to go back on their decision to make open marriage official policy.

11

Second, a *specific observation*. Why, asks Sombart at the beginning of the twentieth century, have socialist ideologies never been able to take root in the United States? Because, he replies, the United States have been seen by American citizens, for a considerable period stretching as far back as even the distant past, as a frontier land. As a result, a powerful ideology of individual mobility developed. The individual unsatisfied with his current situation is more likely to use a strategy of defection than of protest. Rather than agitating to improve the condition of the group to which he belongs (collective strategy), he tries to change his own situation (individual strategy). By contrast, in societies where the barriers between social classes are more visible, for historical reasons, and thus apparently more difficult to surmount, it is most likely that individuals will be attracted more by ideologies advocating the collective advancement of deprived groups. Thus, different historical structures and traditions correspond with different images, strategies, and actions on the part of individuals. At the macrosociological level, a global effect results from these individual actions: here a response, there a lack of response, to socialist ideologies.

Third, *statistical distributions and regularities*. Why is it so frequently observed that the electorate divides into two roughly equal groups within two-party political systems? Because, suggests Hotelling, if it is supposed that voters situate themselves on a left-right continuum, each of the two parties (even where one, L, is supposed to be 'left-wing', and the other, R, 'right-wing') has an interest in placing itself close to the centre of the continuum if it wants to maximize the size of its vote.

If such is the case, half of the electorate (all the voters situated to the left of L) will feel themselves to be closer to party L than to party R, and the other half (all those voters situated to the right of R) will feel themselves to be closer to R than to L. Macrosociological regularity results from the rationality that institutional structures impose on the parties, as well as the choices offered to voters by the parties. Why do the sons/daughters of workers always have much less opportunity than the sons/daughters of managers to gain entry to the highest levels of the educational system? Because disadvantaged families offer a less favourable cultural environment to their children, but particularly because they are more prudent in their choice, and try less frequently to 'push' a child whose academic performance is below average. Since every educational career is the result of a sequence of directions taken at each of the educational crossroads encountered by the pupil during his or her progress through the school system, differences in the reasons for choices have multiplying effects – or more precisely, exponential effects – which explain the *intensity* of class differences at the highest levels of the school system: such a macrosociological effect is only understandable if it can be referred back to the actions carried out by individuals, and to the rationality of these actions as a function of the resources and conceptions of these individuals on the one hand and the fields of action created by institutional structures on the other.

Events, specific observations, statistical regularities, more generally all categories of social phenomena that sociologists undertake to explain, all result from the aggregation of individual actions, as the quote from Weber clearly indicates. This methodological principle, implicitly or explicitly adopted by the majority of political philosophers and sociologists, from Rousseau to Weber, and including Marx and de Tocqueville along the way, does not in any way imply either compliance with the paradigm referred to by Piaget as *atomistic individualism* or the risk of a reduction to psychologism. If the elementary actions of individuals are alone capable of accounting for macrosociological phenomena, this does not mean that they are the product of a 'free agency' or of an individual liberty which is conceived as absolute. Individual action always occurs within the framework of a system of *constraints* which are more or less clearly defined, more or less transparent to the subject, and more or less rigorous. Action therefore has nothing in common with the Sartrean concept of *engagement*. By contrast, action also cannot be conceived as the simple effect of conditioning produced by 'social structures' (see 'Socialization'). A conception of this type suggests the 'totalitarian realism' to which Piaget refers, or the more widely used notions of 'holism' or 'totalism'. It illustrates the 'spectre of collective conceptions' described by Weber.

To understand (and thus to explain) an individual's action, it is of course generally necessary to have access to information about the socialization of the individual. If I observe – to take the celebrated example used by Jaspers – a mother slapping her child, I should begin my explanation of this act by finding out about the educational concepts internalized by the mother. In certain social contexts, the slap is considered to be a legitimate and efficient educational method. In other contexts it is considered to be wrong and harmful. But data about socialization would be insufficient in themselves to understand the reasons for the action. It is highly unlikely that the mother did not have other methods of persuasion open to her than the slap. So why did she choose this method? Perhaps because it was the end point of a process of escalation after other indirect and more gentle methods had failed. Perhaps because at that moment she was too preoccupied to enter into a difficult process of reasoning with the child. In short, she had other methods available to her, but at the instant *t* the 'logic of the situation' led to her considering the slap the most appropriate. It is also possible that she felt herself unable to weigh the advantages and disadvantages of the slap versus reasoning and, as it were on the throw of a dice, all of a sudden chose the first 'solution'. This example is paradigmatic in its simplicity. Action is never the mechanical consequence of socialization. To understand an action, it is necessary to discern the intentions, and more generally the motivations, of the actor (why should the mother want the child to behave in a certain way?); the means available or thought to be available to the actor, as well as the evaluation of these different means made by the actor, determine the range of possibilities resulting from the interaction situation in which the actor is involved (hence the range of possibilities is generally more open at the beginning than at the end of a process of escalation). Action therefore cannot be reduced to the effects of conditioning. But, on the other hand, it is clear that the 'preferences' of the actor, as well as the means which he has or believes he has available to him, are influenced by 'social structures'. Thus, according to Bernstein, education usually has a more authoritarian character in underprivileged areas because methods of persuasion require more subtle psychological and rhetorical resources than authoritarian methods, and such resources are more easily acquired in more privileged areas.

In avoiding atomism or totalitarian realism, the sociological conception of action as used by such classical sociologists as Marx, de Tocqueville, or Weber also avoids psychologism. As social phenomena are always composites of action they must be referred back by the sociologist to the individual actions which they comprise. He or she will, however, most often describe individual actions according to simplified schema, retaining only the elements which seem most pertinent to the phenomena he or she wishes to explain. In describing action according to highly simplified schemas of action – which otherwise would seem to be pertinent to the task – the sociologist is exposed to the risk of outrageously oversimplifying an essential element of the explanatory process: the analysis of the mechanisms of *aggregation* of individual actions. This is the reason why a work such as Sartre's *Critique of Dialectical Reason* is so rich from a psychological point of view, but so poor from a sociological point of view.

In a general way, the sociologist accepts that the social actor attempts to optimize, and that he operates in a framework of constraints determined both by socialization and by the structure of the situation. If we consider the way in which Weber explained the proliferation of Protestant sects in America at the end of the nineteenth century, this will be clearer. At the time, the nation was populated by individuals with very diverse ethnic origins. Geographical mobility was extensive. Business, exchange, and transactions of all sorts were highly developed. But those transactions which were of a particularly long-term nature (i.e., especially those based on credit and loans) relied upon trust. Now trust can only be developed between people who know each other, or, if they do not know each other, recognize themselves and the person with whom they are dealing as belonging to the 'same world', or between persons capable of exhibiting signs of the honourableness which would be recognized as such. Commercial travellers and other sellers of goods and services who were not able to count on the first two solutions (because of the ethnic heterogeneity and geographical mobility of the population) found themselves encouraged to have recourse to the third: in declaring their membership of a Protestant sect they were provided with a reliable method of acquiring, at low cost, a qualification of honourableness which was indispensable to their business activities. Weber's analysis is extremely ingenious. It shows a system effect which is fairly complex. It includes important and unexpected effects or repercussions (for example, the suggestion that the development of commercial and economic exchange does not necessarily mean, by contrast with a widely used evolutionary thesis about religious belief, a weakening of traditional religious values). However, it does rely upon a deliberately simplified model of *homo sociologicus* (sociological man) whose logical status is not that different to its close cousin from economic theory, which Popper described as *homo oeconomicus* (economic man). It shares with this conception two essential elements – first, being of an a priori character, second, being made up of several simple principles (socialization effects, limited rationality, optimization).

The explanation of a social phenomenon always implies that the individual actions of which it is comprised can be accounted for. But what is it that 'accounts for' an action? It is possible to follow Weber on this point. To account for an action, he said, is to 'understand' it (*Verstehen*). This means that the sociologist must be able to put himself in the position of the actors in whom he is interested. To 'understand' the action of the mother slapping her child or the American commercial traveller who attends Sunday church services is to be able to conclude 'If I was in the same situation, I would undoubtedly have done the same thing'. Naturally, to be 'in the same situation' as the actor it is usually necessary to know about his or her socialization, about the givens of the situation in which the actor is located, about the structure of the situation in which the actor moves. The relation of understanding which *may* be created between observer and actor is not immediately given. It generally supposes that the observer will both inform himself and distance himself from the actor: to *understand* the action of the other, the observer must be conscious of the differences which distinguish his situation from that of the actor observed.

The celebrated Weberian concept of *understanding* has two important consequences. The *first* is that an observer, on condition that he has the necessary information, can always in principle explain the behaviour of an actor. However great the cultural distance between an observer and an actor, the first is able in principle to 'understand' the second. Such a proposition implies in turn that the logic of individual action includes some elements which do not vary according to cultural context. It is possible, if necessary, to use the classic concept of *human nature* to characterize these invariant elements. It is because there is a nature common to all that a Frenchman of the twentieth century can *understand* the suicide of an Eskimo. A fourteenth-century monk and an American commercial traveller of the nineteenth century belong to different social contexts. But if it is in principle possible to understand their actions, it is very necessary that they should conform to these invariant elements. Cultural or temporal distance is never sufficient to render the action of the other opaque to the observer. If the latter feels that he cannot 'understand' the actor, if he feels that his action is 'irrational', it is generally because the observer is ill-informed, or because he projects inadequate data, probably taken from his own situation, on that of the actor.

The *second* important consequence results from an elementary remark: it is possible to believe that the action of the other has been *understood* even if the interpretation that has been given is erroneous. Its 'understanding' is thus an essential stage of sociological analysis. But it is only one stage. The sociologist who is content to reconstruct the subjectivity of the actors in whom he is interested risks making his analysis arbitrary and projecting his own subjectivity onto the actors with whom he is concerned. Hence sociologists of development who live in societies where the number of children is inversely correlated with income are sometimes inclined to assume that this is the case everywhere, and to conclude that in developing countries high birth rates are evidence of a submission by the population concerned to a dominant, and irrational, cultural tradition. In the same ways educational sociologists, who owe their social position to the educational qualifications which they possess, sometimes aver that individuals with limited educational aspirations display irrational behaviour and are moved by obscure and alienating social forces. The sociologist must, therefore, guard against his own presuppositions. But the most effective protection is for the sociologist to verify that his microsociological analysis is quite compatible with the macrosociological data that he is able to observe. This second stage of analysis is generally in conformity with the classical epistemological schemas of a Popperian type. Thus, the micro-sociological analysis leads to a theory T, this theory T contains inferences, $a,b,c,d...n$. The theory is acceptable if $a,b,c...n$ are congruent with empirical observation. The greater the number and distinctiveness of the inferences $a,b,c,d...n$, the more credible is theory T. It would be easy to demonstrate that this is the method followed by authors as different as Marx, de Tocqueville, and Weber. The fact that the atoms of sociology may be composed of individual actions and that the observer may maintain an 'understanding' relation with social actors which has no counterpart in the natural sciences does not imply, as Weber demonstrated, that the methods of sociology are fundamentally different from those of the natural sciences (see 'Objectivity'). A statistical regularity will remain both obscure and uncertain (cf. the problems of demographic forecasting) to the extent that it cannot be linked to the individual actions of which it is composed. It is difficult, for example, to understand why development is accompanied in one place by an increase in birth rates, in another by a decrease, and in yet another by stability, or to understand a rise or a decline in crime or suicide rates, if such data are not related to composites of action which are 'understandable'. Thus Lipset, in his classic study *Revolution and Counterrevolution*, poses the question why American cities have generally much higher crime rates than comparable Canadian cities, although the former have much larger police forces. He resolves this enigma by showing how it is the result of a group of historical factors.

In Canada, the British Crown was an important factor in the development of colonies. The authority of the State was, from the beginning, direct and percep-tible. In the United States, the State was distant and the new colonies were set up under a system of virtual self-government. In Canada the law thus appeared as an external and hence more constraining and redoubtable force. In the United States it was seen more as a sort of contract than as a constraint. Psychologically it was thus easier to operate outside the law if it seemed as if doing so did not mean run-ning too great a risk. Once such a theory had been elaborated, it was necessary for Lipset first to verify that it was acceptable from the point of view of historical analy-sis. Then, it was necessary to show that the theory accounted for a number of other differences between countries belonging to the British tradition. It is clear that the reconstruction of individual actions as proposed by the sociologist is only valid and credible if two conditions are satisfied.

First the reconstruction must be compatible with the empirical data available. The *premisses* of the theory must in other words be considered as acceptable.

Second, the theory must lead to *inferences* or *conclusions* which are compatible with empirical data, and which are themselves as carefully collected, distinct, and numerous as possible. The fact that the concept of action may define the atom of sociological analysis should not condemn sociology to subjectivism in any way. A sociological theory can undergo the procedures of 'critical rationality', in the sense that Popper gives to the term, in absolutely identical fashion to the ways in which they are applied to natural sciences, which implicitly define the concept of scientific knowledge.

The Weberian theory of action is a means of concluding a famous debate, begun in Germany by Droysen and Dilthey, which has continued up to the present day (cf. the debate about positivism of which Adorno and Popper were the principal protagonists at the end of the 1960s): does the relationship of understanding which may be created between observer and observed in the social sciences, and which has no counterpart in the natural sciences, indicate a radical opposition between the modes of knowledge appropriate to these two orders of reality?

Correctly interpreted, the response of Weber and the majority of sociologists is negative: the potential provided to the observer to understand action does not mean that he can dispense with the need to subject his interpretation to a critical rationality whose ways and means are not fundamentally different in the natural or the social sciences. Weberian *understanding* has little in common with the 'hermeneutic' approach. It in no sense implies an intuitionist epistemology, as Albert has suggested.

Action (collective), Beliefs, Causality, Dialectic, Ideologies, Knowledge, Marx, Objectivity, Theory, Utilitarianism, Weber.

Bibliography

ALBERT, H., 'Theorie, Verstehen und Geschichte' in ALBERT, H., *Konstruktion und Kritik*, Hamburg, Hoffmann & Campe, 1972, 1975, 195-220. — APEL, K.O., *Die Erklären-Verstehen Kontroverse in transzendental pragmatischer Sicht*, Frankfurt, Suhrkamp, 1979. — ARON, R., *La sociologie allemande contemporaine*, Paris, F. Alcan, 1935; Paris, PUF, 1950. — BERGER, P. and LUCKMAN, T., *The social construction of reality*, London, Doubleday, 1966, Penguin 1967. — BLUMER, H., 'Society as symbolic interaction', *in* ROSE, A.M. (ed.), *Human behavior and social processes. An interactionist approach*, Boston, Houghton Mifflin, 1962, 179-192. — BOUDON, R., *La logique du social. Introduction à l'analyse sociologique*, Paris, Hachette, 1979. — BOURRICAUD, F., *L'individualisme institutionnel. Essai sur la sociologie de Talcott Parsons*, Paris, PUF, 1977. — CROZIER, M. and FRIEDBERG, E., *L'acteur et le système. Les contraintes de l'action collective*, Paris, Le Seuil, 1977. — DILTHEY, W., 'Die Entstehung der Hermeneutik (1900)', in DILTHEY, W., *Gesammelte Schriften*, Leipzig, Teubner, 1914-1958, 12 vol.; Stuttgart, B.G. Teubner, 1957, 12 vol.; Stuttgart, B.G. Teubner/Göttingen, Vandenhoeck & Ruprecht, 1961-1974, 17 vol., V, 317-331. — DROYSEN, J.G., *Historik. Vorlesungen über Enzyklopädie und Methodologie der Geschichte*, Munich, R. Oldenbourg, 1937, 1974. — ELRIDGE, J.E.T., *Max Weber: the interpretation of social reality*, London, M. Joseph, 1970, 1971. — LIPSET, S.M., *Revolution and counter-revolution*, Garden City, Doubleday, 1970. — PARSONS, T., *The structure of social action*, Glencoe, The Free Press, 1937, 1964. — PIAGET, J. *Etudes sociologiques*, Geneva, Droz, 1955. — RAUB, W. and VOSS, T., *Individuelles Handeln und gesellschaftliche Folgen. Das individualistische Programm in den sozialwissenschaften*, Darmstadt/Neuwied. Luchterhand. 1981. — SCHUTZ. A., *in* BRODERSEN, A. (red.), *Alfred Schültz. Collected papers. II. Studies in social theory*, La Haye, Martinus Nijhoff, 1964. — WEBER, M., *Gesammelte Aufsätze zur Religionssoziologie*, Tübingen, J.C.B. Mohr 1920, 1963-1972, 3 vol., I, 207-236. — WIPPLER, R., 'Nicht-intendierte soziale Folgen individueller Handlung', *Soziale Welt*, XXIX 1978, 155-179. — WRIGHT, G.H. (von), *Explanation and understanding*. London, Routledge & Kegan Paul, 1971.

Action (collective)

Several types of groups and groupings are classically identified by sociology. A collection of individuals sharing a common characteristic (such as car owners, persons between the age of 40 and 45, etc.) may be described as a *nominal group* or *social category*. Those sharing a common *interest* can be described as a *latent group*, as in Dahrendorf's usage. Hence, the group described as consumers is constituted by that set of individuals having an interest in the quality of consumer products. The term *organized group* is used to describe a group endowed with means of collective decision-making (the oil producers' cartel, OPEC, for example). By convention, the term *semi-organized group* can be used about latent groups 'represented' by those organizations which claim to defend their interests (e.g., the latent group of school children's parents). The range of semi-organized groups naturally includes numerous forms which are distinguished from each other by the nature of the relationship between latent groups and their 'representative' organizations. Thus, the French Communist Party (PCF) does not represent the French working class in the same sense as the French *Parlément* represents the citizens of the French State, because many of those who vote for the PCF are not workers and many workers do not recognize the PCF as their 'natural' party. Another example may be given: that where the interests of a latent group are defended by an organization without any mandate from the group's members. Having provided these definitions, the problematic of the collective theory of action can be dealt with in terms of two questions: Under what conditions is a latent group able to undertake action designed to promote the common interest of its members? By what processes and under what conditions can a latent group transform itself into a semi-organized or organized group?

It is often assumed to be normal that a latent group, provided it does not encounter any obstacle or resistance and that it has sufficient 'consciousness' of the common interest, will act 'naturally' in advancing its interests. Such a proposition is implicit in Dahrendorf's work. The development of industrial societies is accompanied by a growth in the number of latent groups, according to Dahrendorf, who would seem to be correct on this point. Such latent groups are aware of their interests, and such awareness leads 'normally' to collective action aiming to advance the common interest. The sole obstacles which might prevent this collective action are, on the one hand, a delay in the appearance of an awareness of common interest, and, on the other hand, a resistance which derives from divergent or contradictory interests of other groups. Since the network of latent groups and of organized interest groups tends to become increasingly dense and complex as industrial societies develop, a resulting chronic state of conflict occurs, as well as a reciprocal limitation of group influence as the power of each limits the power of the others. Dahrendorf's theory restates to a large extent the theory developed by Durkheim in his preface to the second edition of *La division du travail social*. Durkheim saw that competition between groups whose interests are both legitimate and at least partially in opposition was a basic means of avoiding too great a concentration of power in modern societies, and saw hope in that for the future. Marx's position on collective action is more equivocal. As a general rule Marx admits that social classes (another typical example of a latent group in Dahrendorf's sense) have a variable awareness of consciousness of their interests, class consciousness leading 'naturally' to collective action. But at the same time Marx recognized that in certain circumstances collective action may be hindered by the existence of a contradiction between common and individual interests.

The famous examples of the 'smallholding peasants' in *The Eighteenth Brumaire of Louis Bonaparte* and of the competition between capitalists referred to in *Capital* are sufficient to illustrate this point. The problems of field boundary disputes for peasants and the necessity for capitalists to invest lead both to relegate their class interests in favour of their individual interests.

Some writers, and notably Olson and Hirschman, have raised questions about the basis of the sequence: common interest – consciousness of common interest – collective action, a sequence generally assumed to be self-evident. Let us consider the latent group formed by the consumers of a clearly defined product: meat, for example. Furthermore, let us suppose that the quality of this product should decline in an obvious way and increase in price at the same time. Every consumer will clearly be aware of these changes. Moreover, he will have no trouble in recognizing that these changes affect not only himself but the whole latent group of consumers. Will he as a result involve himself in some form of collective action? The answer to this question must be qualified to a certain extent: in some cases involvement will occur, while in others it will not, despite being in the interests of the actor. This is in part due to the fact that the consumer has the option, as Hirschman says, of recourse to *defection* rather than *protest*. He may, for example, choose to substitute other products for meat. Alternatively, while protest is in general terms costly ('loss' of time, etc.) it may also be ineffective (if I am the only one to protest, I have little chance of being heard; if there are a lot of us, my voice will only make a marginal and negligible contribution to the effectiveness of collective action.) Lastly, he may defect rather than protest because the eventual benefits of collective action will be available to the consumer, whether or not he participates in collective action. In other words, although each consumer considered as an individual might have, hypothetically, a clear consciousness of the deterioration of his own conditions, and of those of his fellow consumers, the logic of the situation is as likely as not to lead him to inaction rather than to action.

The existence of the possibility of defection may often be used to explain why collective action does not appear when it would be expected to develop. In general terms, the probability that discontent will manifest itself as protest is reduced as defection appears less costly and more effective. In the case of France, for example, the possibility of defection to the *grandes écoles* has probably contributed to a limitation of the protest of French 'élites' concerning improvement in the quality of university education. Similarly, in the USA the quality of the private secondary educational system, developed principally on the East coast, offers possibilities of defection to families dissatisfied with the quality of state or 'public' schools. As a result there has been a tendency for élites to ignore the system of public education.

In both cases the strategy of defection appears to be much more appropriate than the strategy of protest: even if the latter were to be effective its results would only appear long after the individual could hope to benefit himself.

While the possibilities of 'defection' are limited, the appearance of protest – in other words, collective action – cannot in any event be guaranteed, even where the 'consciousness' of common interest is present. This conclusion is drawn from two situations which frequently occur: 1) where the 'cost' (in the widest sense of the term, to include both psychological and social costs as well as economic costs) of participation in collective action may be significant, while the marginal effectiveness of participation is virtually nil; 2) where the eventual benefits of collective action acquired by an individual do not depend upon his participation. This 'logic' explains, for example, the rationale of the 'closed shop', according to Olson. Unions provide *collective* benefits (wage increases, job security, etc.) clearly desirable to those for whom they are produced. Why should it be necessary in such a situation to resort to a coercive method such as the *closed shop* to ensure that workers belong to the union? Olson's answer is that in the absence of coercive measures, where involvement can only be encouraged by indirect means, each person would be likely to wonder whether his contribution would have more than negligible marginal effectiveness, and particularly whether he would in any case acquire the benefits of union action.

It is thus impossible to accept that a latent group, even where it has a 'consciousness' of common interests, must in all circumstances develop collective action designed to advance those interests. The existence of a common interest and the 'consciousness' of that interest are both necessary but not sufficient conditions for the appearance of collective action. In order that collective action should occur, other conditions must be fulfilled.

1) There is a probability of collective action occurring where the number of individuals forming the latent group is very limited. In this first case, the marginal contribution of each individual is significant. The effectiveness of collective action and in consequence the benefits that it can produce are dependent upon the participation of every individual. In this case, we are concerned with an oligopolistic latent group, for which the oligopolies of economic theory provide a perfect example.

2) A second example, already encountered above, is that where collective action is assured by the existence of coercive measures. To this case must be added the example of means of *indirect pressure*, illustrated by the teachers' and research workers' unions in France. These unions do not have the capacity to coerce. But the fact that educational and research institutions allow union officers to play an important role in the career development committees which oversee personnel in these fields puts them in a position to be able to procure desirable individual benefits for their members (promotion, insurance against job loss where there is no established post, etc.). This particular example describes a general illustrative case. The gift of 'parallel' individual benefits is a method frequently used by purveyors of collective benefits such as unions,

political parties, and professional associations in order to increase membership where otherwise it would be lost. The party political 'machine' is another
illustration. Like unions, political parties are officially producers of *collective*
goods and benefits. The individual goods and benefits that they are able to
distribute (positions in the party hierarchy, 'seats' in the political system) are
clearly limited in number. A frequently used expedient to increase size of
membership and the number of activists is the creation of a discreet but effective party 'machine' enabling the distribution of individual benefits in return
for party loyalty.

3) A third illustrative case is provided by the situation where collective action is
facilitated by an *asymmetry* between the interests and resources of participants.
Let us consider the example of a latent group where one member has much
greater influence than the others. It may be in his interests to take on all the
costs of collective action. Thus, in the fifth century BC Athens assumed the
greater part of the costs of defence of the cities belonging to its alliance. If I
have less to lose and more to gain than my neighbours by participating in an
action intended to produce a collective good, I may, even if I am not an altru-
ist, behave as if I were: I have a personal interest in helping to create a benefit
or good whose collective nature means that it will be made available to my
neighbours as soon as it is created.

4) A fourth illustrative case is that of the *fragmented latent group*. Let us suppose
that a latent group (once again, in other words, a group of individuals with a
common interest) is of considerable size but is divided up into small units. At
the level of each unit we encounter the case of the oligopolistic form of latent
group. Collective action is therefore likely to occur at the level of each of these
units and as a result to implicate the whole of the latent group, notwithstanding its large scale. Perhaps such a 'federal' structure goes some way to
explaining why printers played as important a role as heavy industry workers
in the history of the French unions in the nineteenth century. While they were
numerous when considered all together, and therefore constituted a latent
group of significant scale, printers were dispersed in a large number of workshops each comprising very few persons. Solidarity and collective action could
thus be more easily expressed. The 'federal' structure also explains why the
unionization of printers developed through a process of self-organization,
while industrial unions were often organized by *entrepreneurs* (to use the term
employed by Schumpeter) who did not come from the working class.

5) A fifth illustrative case is provided by what can be termed the *'external' organization* of latent groups. The recent history of consumer groups is typical in this
respect. A large-scale latent group, the consumer group is made up of atomized individuals. Each of its members is thus subject to a system of incentives
which is more likely to lead him into non-involvement than into participation
in eventual collective action even where defection is impossible (as is the case,
for example, for a consumer faced with a producer in a monopolistic situation,
or with producers who have *all* reduced the quality of their products because
of competition). It is for such reasons that the interests of consumers have

generally been expressed by 'external' entrepreneurs (cf. the case of Ralph Nader in the USA; Esther Rantzen in the UK, etc.). See also on this point the classic analysis of Michels (*Political Parties*), perhaps the most celebrated of Max Weber's disciples, on the role of the intellectuals in the birth and development of socialist parties in nineteenth-century Europe. It should be noted in this respect that the capture by an 'entrepreneur' of the market constituted by a latent group is made easier if the group members have no opportunity for defection. The fact that consumer associations developed earlier in the USA than in France, for example, can perhaps be explained by the greater industrialization of food production in the former. As the resulting reduction in quality was uniform, the consumer had no opportunity to change his supplier. Defection was ineffectual.

In general terms, the existence of numerous atomized latent groups constitutes a significant potential market for intellectuals (see the importance accorded by de Tocqueville to 'publicists' in democracies) whose position guarantees access to the 'means of mass communication'. Naturally, the 'action' of intellectuals may be and often is reinforced by the creation of associations, parties, or other types of organization claiming to represent the interests of this or that latent group. But there is no guarantee that these associations can be any more than an 'individual' interpretation of the interests of the groups that they claim to defend. This is because a large-scale, atomized, latent group is usually incapable of collective action, even to control the initiatives of the organizations which prosper through the defence of its interests. As to the control exercised by electors when their representatives come to review their mandates – in the case where the members of the representative organization of a latent group are designated by the members of the latent group – this is often of limited effectiveness, as shown by both theoretical analysis and empirical observation. This is because, on the one hand, group members choose between candidates or politicians chosen by the representative organization or, on the other, control through elections can take place only at given intervals. These remarks, which are Michels' fundamental theorems in *Political Parties*, also include an advisory corollary: theories which present the great latent groups and the 'social movements' which are thought to direct them as the privileged carriers of social change and the central forces of history should be viewed with utmost suspicion. The Marxist tradition is not mistaken in this case, i.e., it anticipated and then interpreted in its own style Michels' analysis: for Lasalle the socialist intellectuals, for Lenin the party have the duty to express the interests of the working class, to enlighten and guide it. Michels' theorem, alongside Lasallism and Leninism, takes on the colouring of a practical, political recommendation: both intellectuals and party can and should rely on the support of the working class, but it is the former who have the task of defining the objectives and means of political action.

6) A sixth illustrative case is given by those latent groups whose members are linked together by a relationship of loyalty. It is clear that the development of

loyalty depends on both the size of the group and what Durkheim would have called its 'density'. It would be difficult to imagine this attitude developing within a large atomized group. By contrast, it appears frequently in the case of moderate-sized groups characterized either by face-to-face relations or by a high 'density' of mutual relations (face-to-face relationships at the level of subgroups).

7) A seventh rather obvious case, but which should none the less be included, corresponds to that where the costs of individual involvement in collective action are either nil or 'negative'. In this case, the internal obstacles to collective action described at the beginning of this article disappear. For example, during the upheavals of May 1968 in France, the middle-level management of certain enterprises saw that the general contestation of authority allowed them to question the power of top management without the normal risk to careers that this would entail. For a time, they were involved in 'collective action'. The case of *desperados* – 'nothing to lose, everything to gain' – is an illustration typical of this seventh form.

Another example is provided by most situations where involvement in collective action is not only entirely without risk but attractive in itself (enjoyment of being among friends, pleasure of demos, etc.).

The often violent character of collective action movements has encouraged certain authors to provide irrationalist interpretations of them. Le Bon's *La Psychologie des foules (The Psychology of the Crowd)* represents a sort of caricature in which the individual is described as if he were dissolved within the fused mass that the crowd represents. Nevertheless, it is incontestable that examples of fusion of this type do exist. As Simmel noted, harmony, mobilization, and fusion are moreover more likely to appear in principally *negative* themes. The Roman crowd in Shakespeare's *Julius Caesar* is mobilized *against* Caesar, then *against* Brutus. As soon as a positive theme is proposed to the emotions of a crowd, the antipathies, qualifications, and 'if-buts' come into their own. The individual rediscovers his authority. Modern sociology of collective violence has tended for its part to suggest that it is only rarely part of an irrational explosion, but must, rather, generally be analysed as a 'rational' response, in other words as a well-adapted response to certain types of situations (see, for example, Tilly, *From Mobilization to Revolution*). What is true of crowd collective violence movements is true of organized groups as well: party members have a greater chance of being heard on a negative issue than on a positive issue. But what must above all be noted is that it is very doubtful that all phenomena of collective action can be reduced to this model. Even if they are less extreme than those of Le Bon and certain theorists of social movements, theories such as those of Durkheim and Dahrendorf raise considerable difficulties because they tend to treat latent groups as units capable of 'consciousness' and 'action', without qualification. Now, if this *model* is acceptable for organized groups, more precisely for those organizations which claim to express – or are recognized as able to express – the interests of latent groups, it is less acceptable for the latent groups themselves and for the complex and diverse entities that semi-organized groups represent, except in a conditional way. The analysis of these *conditions* is precisely the fundamental basis of the theory of collective action.

Action, Durkheim, Groups, Marx, Utilitarianism.

Bibliography
BRINTON, C., *The anatomy of revolution*, New York, Vintage, 1958. — COMMONS, J.R., *The economics of collective action*, New York, Macmillan, 1950. — DAHRENDORF, R., *Soziale Klassen und Klassenkonflikt in der industriellen Gesellschaft*, Stuttgart, Ferdinan Enke, 1957. (Tran.), *Class and class conflict in industrial society*, Stanford, Stanford University Press, 1959. — DEUTSCH, K.W., 'Social mobilization and political development' *American political science review*, LV, 3, 1961, 493–514. — HIRSCHMAN, A.O., *Exit, voice and loyalty. Responses to decline in firms, organizations and states*, Cambridge, Harvard University Press, 1970. — LE BON, G., *Psychologie des foules*, Paris F. Alcan, 1895; Paris, PUF, 1939, 1963; Paris, Retz, 1975. — LENIN, V.I., *What is to be done?*, Moscow, Progress Publishers, 1971. — LUKÁCS, G., *Geschichte und Klassenbewusstsein. Studien über marxistische Dialektik*, Berlin, Malik 1923. *History and Class Conflict*, London, Merlin Press, 1971. — MICHELS, R., *Zur Soziologie des Parteiwesens in der modernen Demokratie*, Leipzig W. Klinkhardt, 1911. — OLSON, M., *The logic of collective action*, Cambridge, Harvard University Press, 1965. SMELSER, N.J., *Theory of collective behaviour*, London, Routledge & Kegan Paul 1962; New York, The Free Press, 1963. — TILLY, C., *From mobilization to revolution*, London, Addison-Wesley, 1978.

Aggregation

'Aggregation of preferences' is used to describe the methods which allow us to draw a 'collective' preference from a set of 'individual' preferences: majority rule is one of these methods (cf. 'Elections'). The notion of aggregation is often given a larger meaning and it can describe not only preferences but also individual actions. On the other hand, aggregation effects – also called composition effects – can result from the application of one aggregation 'rule', but also from the mere coincidence of preferences or of individual actions.

Several illustrations of the four cases defined above can be given. Criteria such as that of majority or unanimity can aggregate preferences with a rule. Merton's self-fulfilling prophecy is an aggregation effect which comes from 'coincidence' of preferences: anyone who draws out their money because they fear a bank failure contributes in effect to the bank's bankruptcy. Individual actions can themselves be aggregated by rules, any organization is by definition made up of a set of rules which is supposed to generate some desirable effects, i.e., creating some product in the best possible conditions. But aggregation effects can also happen outside of rules and result in the actors, for instance belonging to a certain category, being all exposed to a similar modification of their environment: thus, too rigorous a limitation of redundancy regulations may encourage managers to take on fewer workers and consequently increase the number of jobless. A 'collective' effect has been produced by the aggregation of uncoordinated actions which goes against the desired objective of protecting jobs.

The notion of aggregation defines a fundamental question for sociology, that of the relationship between individual actions and preferences on one hand and the collective effect they have on the other. One of the main postulates of individual-orientated sociology is that the 'social structures' described by sociologists must be explained as aggregational effects as far as possible.

This point has been widely examined in 'action' and here the fact that aggregation effects often have an 'emergent' character will be examined. 'Emergent' because phenomena undesired by individuals and a result of actions and preferences aiming at completely different objectives appear at the collective level.

Most of the classical sociologists insisted on this point. Simmel explains that 'forms' like 'politeness', 'good manners', are the result of the aggregation of multiple individual actions. In a society where the division of labour is strong and where transactions are a common event, each of the partners to the exchange feels instinctively that it is not in his interest to cheat his partner, as he might bitterly regret it. Because everyone tends to do the same there is a gradual 'formation' of norms, for instance the norms defining a notion like that of 'clean living'. When there is deviance, it is criticized. The law follows, in some cases, to formalize what appears to be first a 'collective feeling'. But this 'collective feeling' is itself the result of numerous individual perferences and actions. It is an aggregational effect. Spencer also emphasizes that 'aggregates' can be understood only through their elements and that the whole can be explained only through its parts, even if it is more than its parts.

Schelling showed, through a whole series of very obvious didactic models, the fact that aggregation of 'micromotives', i.e., individual actions and preferences, often leads to emergent 'macrophenomena', with no relation whatever to actors' motives. Many of these models deal with the omnipresent phenomenon of social segregation.

When looking at this 'segregation' phenomenon an immediate interpretation is to take this 'collective' phenomenon for the result of the direct expression of preferences: blues and reds live in different districts because 'they don't like each other'. A variant of this explanation would be 'blues don't want to live near the reds that they despise, and they have the power and the resources to stay together'. In these two common explanations, segregation (a collective phenomenon) is seen as the result of the 'explicit preferences' of either both groups' individuals or of individuals in a particular group. In the latter case, the explanation must be taken further and show that the blues, whose preferences are sufficient to generate a collective effect, really have the power to satisfy their preferences.

Another kind of explanation, often seen in sociology and not only to explain aggregation, is to explain collective phenomena as the 'direct' result of unconscious preferences: the blues and reds don't realise they hate each other, but 'deep down' they do; this is why they live apart. Although this kind of explanation might sometimes express a certain truth, it is always highly suspect a priori as it is always possible to apply it automatically to whatever phenomenon.

This phenomenon exists because, either everybody, or the most powerful, want it.

Objection: but they say they don't want it and there is no evidence that they do.

Answer: it is because these are such deep-rooted mechanisms that they are not conscious of them.

Following other writers, Schelling emphasizes that there is a third type of explanation. This kind is as important if often unrecognized, not only by 'common sense', but also by social scientists. It is to show that individuals who do not desire segregation, either consciously or unconsciously, can under certain conditions provoke it.

In order to show that it was not a meaningless paradox or a 'curiosity', but on the contrary was a fundamental point, one of Schelling's theoretical models will be closely analysed. Imagine twenty blue pawns and twenty red pawns placed anywhere on a sixty-four square chess board. Imagine that the blue pawns have 'no dislike' for the red pawns, but they feel more akin to the blue ones. Vice versa, red pawns have no dislike for blue pawns but prefer the reds as they feel closer to them. So as to make it clearer, or more exactly so as to transform the hypotheses into a model, pawns of both colours will be said to be happiest in an environment where they would not be in a minority. Thus, a red pawn placed in a central square of the chess board with five out of eight neighbouring pawns of his own colour would be completely happy. Similarly, a blue pawn on a side square of the chess board would be satisfied if three out of his five neighbours were blue. As for one in a corner, he would be happy if two of his neighbours were the same colour. Again, pawns have a very understandable preference and one which is, after all, easy to forgive: they'd rather not be in a minority. In the same way as a small number of tennis fans might feel uneasy in a crowd of football addicts, blues prefer not to be in a minority although they don't dislike reds and even are happy with them, provided they don't feel 'swamped'. Imagine that gradually the pawns, dissatisfied with their social environment, move around and look for the nearest square where their preferences will be satisfied. In theory, this model will have a very large number of solutions. In other words, the described process can lead to many states of equilibrium corresponding to very diverse configurations. (In the present context, a configuration is in 'equilibrium' when everyone is happy with his environment and no longer wishes to move.)

Some of these equilibrias are associated with a segregation phenomenon: If all the blues are together and all the reds too, there will be an 'equilibrium' as we defined it. However, it must be noted that many theoretical states of equilibrium 'do not correspond' to a segregational configuration. It is possible to place pawns on the chess board in such a way that the reds are all surrounded by $n/2+1$ red pawns (or $(n+1)/2$ reds if the number of squares taken as the environment is an odd number), and the same goes for the blues. In that case, there would not be segregation, although such a configuration corresponds to an equilibrium, since everyone's preferences would be satisfied.

But, as Schelling showed using the simulation method, among the possible theoretical states of equilibrium, those coupled with a segregation effect are much more likely. A marble thrown on a track going up and down can 'in theory' stop either at the top or at the bottom of a slope. The two situations correspond to two cases of mechanical equilibrium. But it is obvious that it is more likely to stop at the bottom. In the same way here, the model will be more likely to lead to segregational effects. 'Most' of the reds (blues) will have 'almost all' their neighbours red (blue) even if neither one nor the other demanded as much.

There are several lessons to be learned from this model. First, it outlines an 'explanation model' quite distinct from the two previous ones. In these two first ones, the collective effect – the segregation effect – is supposingly translating actors preferences directly either consciously or 'unconsciously'. On the contrary here, the collective effect has an 'emergent' character in relation to preferences. Actors simply want 'not to be in a minority' in their environment. From the moment they all have this preference, the result is – with a strong probability – a collective effect which goes much beyond those preferences and is a caricature of them. Here, the aggregation provokes an 'overshooting' effect, way beyond the aim.

This explanation mode is of crucial importance in sociology. Many reproduction effects (cf. 'Reproduction') can be explained in this way: actors do not want, consciously or unconsciously, the reproduction of such or such a structure. But, influenced by simple preferences, and by all means easy 'to understand' in the Weberian sense, they can generate a reproduction effect. Also, when everyone wants to better themselves and succeed, the result might be that everyone remains in the same relative position (Hirsch). Many 'transformation' effects come not from a will for transformation but from the aggregation of 'small decisions' following much humbler motives and situated at the scale of the actor. If everyone consumes less, for easily understandable reasons (when tax rates increase for instance), they can contribute to the creation of a deep recession. This is of course a common example and very unlikely to be challenged since such aggregational effects are accepted in the field of economics. Curiously however, it is not so easily admitted that there is no reason for these effects to be restricted to this domain: in reality, they appear as soon as there are diverse actors and they are indispensable to the analysis of the most varied subjects. Social change theories which do not consider them are often condemned either to a naive 'naturalism', seeing change as the result of 'laws' which appear from nowhere, or to an equally naive 'voluntarism' (cf. 'Social change'). This does not imply that some collective phenomena, some institutions, or some structures are not the result of an action of will.

Many 'structures' that sociologists are led to observe and study can be explained 'naturally', i.e., such as the phenomenon dear to Sartre of the queue at the bus stop. The structure of the queue does not mean that people like queuing. It is not the direct expression of their conscious or 'unconscious' preferences. It shows the reality of the aggregation effect: by standing after the last person arrived I also am ahead of those who will follow. In so doing I accept that those in front of me have the right to choose some of the seats I might have preferred myself but I also endow myself with the right to choose a seat those who follow me might have liked. The solution of the waiting queue is seen by all as an acceptable compromise; each person accepts it on condition that others do too. This is why the 'cheat' – the one 'who thinks the others are soft' – will be told off, unless he makes the others 'fight for themselves' and start a rush. In any case, the waiting queue is a simple example of aggregation effect or of 'shape' in Simmel's sense.

The concept of aggregation effect thus describes both a reality and a method. It helps to explain collective structures and phenomena which cannot be interpreted as the direct result of actors' preferences and which cannot be explained scientifically as being God's will. It also prevents an *ad hoc* hypothesis, which is often used when a collective effect cannot be seen to be the result of explicit individual preferences, consisting of making it the result of 'unconscious' preferences or of the action of evil spirits taking over the social actors' will. Whatever these spirits are called – reflected-conscience, false conscience, 'habitus' – they represent tautological hypotheses the explanatory power of which is more or less the same as that of opium's *vis dormitiva.*

When a collective phenomenon directly reflects preferences which are obviously clear, the social sciences are not needed. When a collective phenomenon is 'puzzling' and the social sciences attempt to explain it with 'unconscious' motivations the reality of which cannot be proven except by the collective phenomena being studied, this is not acceptable. But the social sciences have proved to be useful every time they have managed to explain puzzling collective phenomena, making them the aggregational effect of 'understandable' individual actions, preferences, and motivations.

Ricardo's 'law of comparative costs' was said by Samuelson to be one of the most important discoveries of economics. And, if its structure is analysed, it corresponds clearly to the third kind of pattern. The law states that, within a regime of international exchange, a country benefits – under some conditions – from importing some categories of goods, 'even if it can manufacture them cheaper itself'. Ricardo's law changes a mystery (why should a country A buy goods B that they could produce cheaper than their partner?) into an aggregational effect of rational behaviours: the country A imports B goods because, 'in spite of all appearances', it benefits from doing so.

Suppose, to take Ricardo's own example, that eighty hours of work in Portugal are needed to produce x bottles of wine and 120 in England, and that ninety working hours in Portugal, 100 in England, are needed to produce y metres of cloth. Portugal can therefore produce the cloth, like the wine, at a lower cost than England. In spite of that it 'benefits' from buying the cloth from England, where its comparative advantage is weaker. In a regime of protected economy x bottles of wine allow Portugal to buy $80/90$ y metres of cloth; in England y metres of cloth can buy $100/120$ x bottles of wine. However, in a free market, Portugal can offer England x bottles of wine in exchange for y metres of cloth; the latter will accept because at home England can get only $0.83x$ bottles of wine for the same quantity of cloth.

Similarly, the greatest successes in sociology are those explaining puzzling collective phenomena, demonstrating that they can be taken for the aggregational effect of 'non-puzzling' motivations, which are also called 'understandable' or 'rational'. Such is Weber's reasoning when he studies the strength of Protestantism in the US (cf. 'Action') and Michels' when he studies the iron law of oligarchy, and Popkin's, a contemporary example, when he studies 'reproductive' mechanisms inherent in the Asian mode of production.

Popkin wonders why in traditional 'Asian villages' innovation is so rare. It is because collective decisions are taken unanimously. Why? Because everyone is in a very close interdependent relation with others and gains enormously from being able to veto collective decisions which might be prejudicial to him in his own life since these villages are self-sufficient. This explanation does not take into account the 'origins' of the unanimity rule often found in such a context and deals only with its 'function'. The unanimity rule is rarely used in the process of collective decisions since there are risks of blockage and it is costly in terms of time: it implies an endless period of 'palavers'. It cannot therefore be used in social systems where time is short and expensive. But such is not the case here. 'Asian villages', like many traditional rural societies, have an extremely high rate of underemployment; so the cost of unanimous decision-making is not very high. But the result of this system of collective decision-making is that any proposal for innovation for what-ever collective or individual benefits – even where it is able to induce a 'set' of co-operative structures – might be vetoed: if x proposes to improve his harvesting methods, he might be prejudicial to his neighbour who has a right of cutting hay on his field and, being so poor, will refuse to agree to long-term benefits in view of his immediate loss. The system structure thus generates an aggregational effect which here takes the shape of 'blockage' or of 'reproduction'.

Aggregational effects can have many different forms (differentiation, reproduc-tion effects, etc.). Although it is useful to isolate typical effects, it must be said: 1) that these effects can only be idealized models; 2) that it is a waste of time to privi-lege one situation over another. Neither the continuous model of change through 'differentiation' nor the discontinuous model of change through accumulation of 'contradictions' for instance can pretend to have all the answers. The 'relativist' position of traditional German sociology which prides itself only on defining typical models or patterns is the most trustworthy. Spencer himself, who proposed the differentiation pattern, had clearly studied this model as typical and not universal. Spencer clearly saw that some patterns in fact led to de-differentiation (although he does not use this very word) and that discontinuous as well as contin-uous processes could be observed. It is only in Durkheim's reading in the *Division of Labour* that Spencer's differentiation process becomes the 'ultimate' example of change.

The notion of aggregation sometimes has a 'logical' meaning which bears some relation to its sociological meaning. Since Condorcet, it has been well known that by aggregating transitory preferences, an intransitory collective preference can be obtained. Condorcet's paradox is only one of the paradoxes generated by an aggregational operation. When a series of anthropometric measurements is taken from a set of subjects and an average measure is calculated, the 'average man' so derived can appear to be so far from perceived reality as to be virtually a monster. The case of calculated correlations of collective units is another case of paradox: in theory it is logically possible, even if manual workers tend to vote for a 'more' specific party than other social classes, that a ward could show results less favour-able to the said party although a large number of manual workers were part of it. It is also known that if a historical observation of salary patterns brings out irregular variation in relation to age with a maximum observed in such-and-such an age group, this does not imply, as is often believed, that individual salaries go down after this particular age.

Action, Dialectic, Elections, Rationality, Reproduction, Social Change, Spencer.

Bibliography

ARROW, K.J., *Social choice and individual values*, New York, Wiley, London Chapman & Hall, 1951, 1963. — BAUDELOT, C., *L'évolution individuelle des salaires en France 1970–1975*, coll. de l'INSEE, series M, october 1983. — BOUDON, R., *La logique du social. Introduction à l'analyse sociologique*, Paris, Hachette, 1979; *La place du désordre. Critique des théories du changement social*, Paris, PUF, 1984. — COLEMAN, J.S., *The mathematics of collective action*, London, Heinemann (Educational Books), 1973. — HANNAN, M., *Aggregation and disaggregation in sociology*, London, Lexington Books, 1971. — HIRSCH, F., *Social limits to growth*, Cambridge, Harvard University Press, 1976; London, Routledge & Kegan Paul, 1977. — HOMANS, G., *The nature of social science*, New York, Harcourt Brace & World, 1967; 'Steps to a theory of social behavior', *Theory and Society*, 12, 1983, 1-45. — POPKIN, S.L., *The rational peasant. The political economy of rural society in Vietnam*, Berkeley, University of California Press, 1979. — SAMUELSON, P., Illogisme de la doctrine néo-marxienne de l'échange inégal, *Commentaire*, V, 17, 1982, 52–62. — SCHELLING, T., *Micromotives and macrobehavior*, Toronto, Norton, 1978. — 'Dynamic models of segregation', *Journal of Mathematical Sociology*, 1, 2, 1971, 143–186. — SIMMEL, G., *Die Probleme der Geschichtsphilosophie*, Leipzig, Duncker and Humblot, 1905. — SPENCER, H., *A study of sociology. Introduction by Talcott Parsons*, Ann Arbor, University of Michigan Press, 1961.

Alienation

The Latin word *alienatio* has a legal sense (the transfer or sale of a good or right), a psychological sense (dementia, insanity), a sociological sense (dissolution of the link between the individual and others), and a religious sense (dissolution of the link between the individual and the gods). In German, the word *Entfremdung* (literally, to become estranged from or a stranger to) covers a range of meanings, but to a large degree these parallel those of the Latin *alienatio*.

However, the modern history of the concept of alienation begins undoubtedly with Rousseau:

> these articles [i.e. the articles of association of the social contract] are reducible to a single one, namely the total alienation by each associate of himself and all his rights to the whole community . . . since the alienation is unconditional, the union is as perfect as it could be, and no individual associate has any longer any rights to claim . . . since each man gives himself to all, he gives himself to no one . . . each one of us puts into the community his person and all his powers under the supreme direction of the general will. (*The Social Contract*, trans. Maurice Cranston, pp. 60–1).

The abandonment of natural liberty is an act of alienation which may be freely consented to, in a situation where it is reciprocated, because it guarantees the advantages of civil liberty to the individual. But Rousseau's feelings on the consequences of this act of alienation are equivocal: the model can never be found in any real society, because it is difficult to imagine any institutions ensuring that the 'general will' should prevail over individual wills, particularly those of the rich and powerful. The act of alienation founding the social pact thus turns upon a more or less extreme dispossession of a larger or smaller proportion of the society's members. Rousseau's worries resurface with different emphases in the work of the German romantic philosophers, in Hegel and Feuerbach. For Marx, the notion of alienation is used mainly to describe the dehumanization resulting from the development of capitalism. In *Economic and Philosophical Manuscripts of 1844* the concept of alienation is used abundantly: capitalist society alienates the producer from the product of his labour; it places him in competition with those whose interests he shares, and therefore alienates him from his fellow workers; whereas the farmer perceives directly the meaning of his work (to derive his means of subsistence from nature), the industrial worker's labour is stripped of its meaning; in the end, the division of labour deprives the worker even of his own humanity. Alienated labour 'alienates his spiritual nature, his *human essence*, from his own body and likewise from nature outside him'. Subsequently, and notably in *Capital*, the concept of alienation is used with greater parsimony, and in many cases avoided altogether. But the themes of the young Marx's writings are constantly evoked: capitalism unleashes cumulative processes which slip beyond the control of individuals, liberating social forces which they are incapable of mastering and dispossessing the majority of them of the product and meaning of their labour.

> The capitalist reproduction process thus reproduces itself the separation between the worker and his conditions of work. It even reproduces and drags out as a result the conditions which force the worker to sell himself in order to live, and place the capitalist in the position to buy his labour in order to enrich himself.

The autonomous and alienated character that capitalist production imprints in general on the conditions and product of labour in relation to the worker, develops a most pronounced antagonism through the machine. It is because of this that it gives rise at first to a brutal revolt of the worker against the means of labour.

> In sum, the introduction of machines increases the division of labour within society, the task of the worker in the workshop is simplified, capital is accumulated, man has been increasingly fragmented. (*Economic and Philosophical Manuscripts of 1844*)

These Marxian themes were subsequently taken up by a number of authors. For Fromm, capitalist society alienates the individual through its capacity to make difficult the realization of certain fundamental needs, such as the need for creative activity, the establishment of social relations with others, the need for stable roots, the need for self-identity, and the need for self-orientation (need to have a frame of references and understandings). This image reappears in a variety of forms in the work of Marcuse, C. Wright Mills, and Habermas. Each author puts the emphasis on different themes, on the subtle conditioning and repressive mechanisms which characterize industrial societies (Marcuse), on the fact that social structures deprive the individual of the chance of realizing his own desires and force him to realize the desires of others (Habermas), on the feelings of absurdity which result from the complexity of social systems whose operation individuals cannot understand (Mannheim). It is not difficult to extend this list.

The notion of alienation is quite clearly dependent on postulates which are essentially utopian in character. In other words it can only appear once the decision is taken to compare existing societies, whether capitalist or industrial, to an utopian society where man is able to satisfy his basic needs, where the social order is such as to be freely accepted by all, where social institutions are intelligible, transparent, and acceptable, and where in the last analysis the only constraints experienced by the individual are those to which he freely consents (cf. 'Utopia'). The gap between this democratic model and real societies constitutes a measure of the intensity of alienation, according to C. Wright Mills. By comparison with many of his successors Rousseau has the advantage of having demonstrated that it was practically impossible for a real society to conform to such a model, although the model would inevitably serve as an utopian point of reference (cf. 'Rousseau'). By contrast, Marx, Marcuse, Mills, and Habermas condemn themselves to a 'realist' interpretation of Rousseau's utopia from the point at which they make of alienation a characteristic of a particular form of social organization, in other words capitalist societies or what these authors term industrial societies (because for orthodox Marxists socialist industrial societies are not afflicted by alienation). It is not difficult to draw the conclusion from such an assumption that by changing the form of society one can hope to create utopia.

How can we explain the success of the notion of alienation – a notion which, moreover, has today become current in everyday usage? A primary reason for its popularity resides in the fact that one can use the term with facility to cover phenomena that anyone can observe (the subdivision of work tasks, the sense of powerlessness felt by the individual in the face of complex social systems, etc.). As Pareto would have said, although theories of alienation reach beyond experience, they are at the same time founded on observations that anyone can make. A second reason is undoubtedly to be found in the fact that it can at least cover, if not explain, a range of highly varied phenomena from psychosomatic problems produced by 'modern life' to major social upheavals (cf. Marx's allusion, cited above, to the destruction of machinery by the Luddites or Marcuse's interpretation of the crises of the 1960s). By contrast, it may equally be used to explain the resignation of the oppressed. A third reason perhaps lies in the fact that the notion of alienation recalls the Judaeo-Christian myth of the fall of man, providing it with a lay meaning which is better adapted to modern society. Thanks to the concept of alienation the fall of man can, in one sense, be seen on any street corner as part of everyday life – as Henri Lefebvre has put it.

As a sort of conceptual nebula, the notion of alienation has been given a range of meanings which have been made all the more difficult to classify since the nebula is refracted by a group of related notions, such as Hegel's *Entaüsserung* (objectification) or *Verdinglichung* (reification) which derives from Marx and Marxist thought. Certain of these variations are usable by the sociologist while others lead to confusions which render them useless. It was perhaps because he was aware of these problems that Marx dispensed with the vocabulary of alienation in his mature works. However, there is nothing to prevent the use of this vocabulary to describe the feelings of political impotence which may affect the citizen, the boredom of the assembly-line worker, the fact that the employee must sell his labour power, or the terrible conditions experienced by workers in 1848. Understood in this restricted sense, the concept of alienation is useful and encourages empirical research. On the other hand, it is hard to see how a sociology with intellectual ambitions could use theories which, in going beyond the writings of the young Marx such as those of Marcuse and other sociologists, conceive of industrial societies as alienating man so profoundly that he is quite incapable of becoming aware of his misery. The question arises as to how the sociologist, alone among his contemporaries, is able to tear himself away from the wall of the cave to gaze upon and proclaim the truth! At its extremes, the conception of alienation is indistinguishable from one of its most celebrated variants – the notion of 'false consciousness' and its functional alternatives (in other words all those ideas which support – occasionally explicitly but more often implicitly – the notion that the observer is a better judge of the feelings of the subject than the subject himself). By giving the impression that it provides a way of illuminating the way for the blind, it contains the worst of all forms of totalitarianism. You believe you are happy. It is only the product of your false consciousness. You feel that you are free. That is an unmistakable sign that you are alienated. As C. Wright Mills noted, the notion of alienation derives from the need to encounter 'real' democracy. In the end it leads to the justification of totalitarianism.

Alienation constitutes a sort of counterpoint to anomie, as a number of writers have noted. The two notions are derivations of the same residue, to use Pareto's words: the feeling that the individual will find it more difficult to give meaning to his existence in an industrial society than in other types of society. But the concept of anomie has remained within the confines of academic sociology. The notion of alienation is equally concerned with disillusion and with progress and the 'disenchantment of the world' spoken of by Weber. But it has the immense advantage of indicating the way to redemption and salvation.

Anomie, Capitalism, Dialectic, Marx, Needs, Utopia.

Bibliography

AXELOS, K., *Marx, penseur de la technique. De l'aliénation de l'homme à la conquête du monde*, Paris, Minuit, 1961. — FROMM, E., *The sane society*, New York, Holt, Winston & Rinehart, 1955; London, Routledge & Kegan Paul, 1956. — GABEL, J., *La fausse conscience. Essai sur la réification*, Paris, Minuit, 1962. — HABERMAS, J., 'Zwischen Philosophie und Wissenschaft. Marximus als Kritik', *in* HABERMAS, J., *Theorie und Praxis, Sozialphilosophische, Studien*, Neuwied, Luchterhand, 1963. Trans. *Theory and Practice*, London, Heinemann, 1976. — ISRAEL, J., *Alienation. Från Marx till modern sociologi. En makrosociologisk studie*, Stockholm, Rabén & Sjögren, 1968, Trad. French., *L'aliénation, de Marx à la sociologie contemporaine. Une étude macrosociologique*, Paris, Anthropos, 1972. — LEFEBVRE, H., *La vie quotidienne dans le monde moderne*, Paris, Gallimard, 1968. — LUDZ, P., 'Alienation as a concept in the social sciences', *Current sociology. La sociologie contemporaine*, XXI, 1, 1973, 5–115. — LUKES, S., 'Alienation and anomie', *in* LASLETT, P. and RUNCIMAN, W. (ed.), *Philosophy, politics and society*. Oxford, Blackwell, 1962, 1972, 3 vol., III, 134–156. — MARCUSE, H., *One dimensional man. Studies in the ideology of advanced industrial society*,

London, Routledge & Kegan Paul, 1964. – MILLS, C. (Wright), *White collar. The American middle classes*, New York, Oxford University Press, 1951, 1956. NISBET, R., 'Alienation', *in* NISBET, R., *The sociological tradition*, New York, Basic Books, 1966, chap. VII, 264–312; London, Heinemann, 1967. – SEEMAN, M., 'On the meaning of alienation', *American sociological review*, XXIV, 6, 1959, 783–795.

Anomie

The concept of anomie, which seeks to express the vague notion of the breakdown of social rules (or normlessness) in a precise way, is one of the most widely used of sociological concepts. However, its content varies considerably from writer to writer. There are differences between its use by Durkheim and its use by Merton, although Merton (at least in some of his statements) indicates that he is following Durkheim. In Durkheim's work itself, it is not absolutely clear whether anomie has the same meaning in *The Division of Labour* and in *Suicide*, the two works which make use of the notion. Although Parsons claims to be basing his usage of the concept on Merton, he does not give it the same meaning. In fact, the notion of anomie is best seen as a set of concepts. Why should the same word cover a group of very different concepts? Two hypotheses can be advanced. The first is essentially epistemological: in the same way as the notion of magnetism is used in physics, the notion of anomie is implicitly considered by many sociologists as an entity which can be observed only through its diverse manifestations. One sociologist may, then, be interested in manifestations of 'anomie' which are quite different from those of concern to another sociologist, while at the same time being under the impression that they are both concerned with the same entity.

The second hypothesis comes from the sociology of science: perhaps anomie is to Marxist sociology what alienation is to Marxist sociology: alienation and anomie describe in two different theoretical frameworks the idea of a fundamental deregulation or breakdown of relations between the individual and society (cf. 'Alienation'). Most sociologists, from Durkheim to Merton, agree in their assessment that these phenomena of deregulation are not exclusively a result of class struggle. Such a negative agreement is perhaps the main reason for the longevity of a notion with such varied meanings.

In *The Division of Labour*, Durkheim particularly associates the notion of anomie with the failures of the system of division of labour which characterize those societies described as, in his words, 'industrial'. 'Partial ruptures of organic solidarity', exemplified by bankruptcies, show 'that certain functions are not adjusted to each other'. Class struggle, or in Durkheimian terms 'the antagonism of labour and capital', is another manifestation of anomie (note that this proposition implies as a corollary that 'alienation' in the Marxist sense is no more than a manifestation and consequence of anomie for Durkheim).

Another example of 'anomie' is the increasing specialization of scientific research which leads to a growing atomization, representing for Durkheim yet another rupture of organic solidarity. These three examples have one thing in common: they all describe phenomena which appear to be incompatible with the image of society as organism which filters through the Durkheimian notion of 'organic solidarity' (cf. 'Durkheim').

In *Suicide* the notion of anomie takes on a rather different meaning, perhaps more precise as a result of the fact that this time it is immersed in a set of two conceptual dichotomies. The first dichotomy opposes the concepts of *egoism* and *altruism*. The idea of egoism as employed by Durkheim covers the popular notion of individualism to a certain extent: egoism is more evident in a society where individuals have a greater tendency to regulate their behaviour according to their free will, than on the basis of collective norms and values. The average propensity of individuals to *egoism* or to its opposite, *altruism*, varies with societies, cultures, and situations.

A society with 'mechanical' solidarity (in other words one where the division of labour is limited, and where solidarity is the result of similarity rather than complementarity) is in this sense more 'altruistic'. Collective norms play a more important role in the determination of individual behaviour in traditional societies than in modern societies. Other examples of this distinction are given by the observation that Protestantism is more conducive to 'egoism' than Catholicism; and the fact that bachelors find it easier to be 'egoists' than fathers of families.

The second dichotomy places the concepts of anomie and 'fatalism' in opposition. Anomie exists when the actions of individuals are no longer regulated by norms which are clear and constraining. In such a situation, they are likely to set themselves objectives which cannot be achieved, to abandon themselves to the whim of their emotions, to give way to despair. Fatalism occurs when norms are so rigidly defined that they give the individual almost no autonomy in the selection of ends and means. Like egoism and altruism, anomie and fatalism vary in significance according to society, culture, and situation. 'Oppressive discipline' encourages 'fatalism'. By contrast, the 'world of industry and commerce' is essentially anomic in the sense that the norms to which actors are subject provide them with considerable autonomy. At a collective level, this autonomy leads to the 'breakdown of organic solidarity' (crises) and on the individual level it exposes the social actor to risk, uncertainty, and eventually to failure and confusion. In the same way, one of Durkheim's favourite examples – the institution of divorce – increases the autonomy of the partners, and its use indicates and implies the displacement of morality towards the 'anomie' end of the axis fatalism – anomie.

Behind the typologies of egoism/altruism, anomie/fatalism, one of Durkheim's fundamental institutions can be seen, namely the assumption that increasing complexity of social systems leads to a growing individualism of the systems' members and, therefore, the growing effects of 'deregulation'. It is also possible to discern an ideological position in all this. Durkheim wanted to see, as the conclusion to *The Division of Labour in Society* demonstrates, a society where individuals would be guided by a system of values and norms – in other words a morality – which would encourage and invite them to be satisfied with their position in the system of the division of labour: the idea of anomie evokes, at its base, Durkheim's attachment to the arguable and simplistic model which assimilates society with organization, and even society with organism.

In Merton's case, his perspective is microsociological rather than macrosociological, the latter being Durkheim's point of view. In every society, one can observe values that are more or less shared by all of its members (thus, in the American society which is of particular interest to Merton, 'social mobility' is positively valued). Values, which can be internalized to varying degrees, are the foundation on which individuals base their objectives. In order to attain these objectives, individuals have available to them means which are also determined by social norms. Some of these means are legitimate. In every society, individuals operate with a certain autonomy which allows them to adopt attitudes which contrast with socially valued goals and means. By combining the range of possible attitudes, four fundamental modes of 'adaptation' are possible. The *conformist* is the individual who sticks to positively valued objectives and means. The *innovator* is someone who achieves positively valued objectives by negatively valued means (cf. the social 'success' of the criminal). The *ritualist* is someone who scrupulously respects socially valued means, but is indifferent to ends (i.e., the civil servant who keeps his department running efficiently without any concern for the aims of the organization). Finally, the behaviour of the person who *withdraws* is characteristic of the individual who avoids goals and means which are positively valued. This typology has led to numerous discussions and critiques. It contains a problem in that goals and means cannot be defined in themselves, as the example of social mobility shows: it can be either a means or an end. It is true that in his discussion of the typology Merton suggests some distinctions which lead to a considerably more complex typology which goes further than the four previous types. Thus, individuals may *want* to pursue socially valued goals by legitimate means, but not be *able* to do so. In the American lower middle class, mobility is highly valued, but the resources to achieve it are often lacking. There is in such a case *anomie* in one sense: the social structure encourages an element of the population to innovate (which may take the form of individual 'deviance' or of collective revolt) or to withdraw (cf. 'Crime').

But anomie in a second sense may also exist: when legitimate means are not accessible, social actors may be encouraged to contest goals and means (the case of 'rebellion', or, as it might be better described, 'protest', would fall into this category). Extending Merton's analysis further to discuss an example which he does not employ, it is possible to use anomie in another sense when there is doubt and uncertainty about socially valued goals. This takes us back to one of the senses of anomie found in Durkheim and also in Parsons. Hence, for Parsons, the Weimar Republic is a good example of anomic society in the sense that its institutions and the values that it put forward were incapable of awakening a feeling of legitimacy. Evidently, the variables used by Merton would enable many other definitions of anomie to be given. This analysis serves as a demonstration that, while Merton's typology furnishes a good heuristic device (which would explain its success), it also contributes to an atomization of the notion of anomie into a multitude of possible meanings. The diversity of empirical measures of anomie which have been proposed (cf. Besnard) reflects the many meanings of a concept whose unity is, at the end of the day, essentially *negative*: in the Mertonian sense, anomie appears as soon as one goes beyond the situation where social actors have legitimate means at their disposal, which they accept as such, for attaining goals defined according to values which they have internalized. This is not so far away from Durkheim, for whom anomie increases to the extent that 'fatalism' – a notion which describes *over*integrated societies – diminishes.

Like the notion of alienation, that of anomie proposes to measure real societies alongside an ideal model characterized by a successful 'integration' of the individual in society, in certain of its meanings. But it also includes more useful meanings: it is true that certain social systems have such a structure that social actors are incapable of defining objectives which are both desirable and realizable, or that certain organizations set out to achieve objectives which are incompatible. For example, it is not certain that a university can be at one and the same time – by contrast with the demands of both public opinion and the political system since the university protests of the 1960s – a centre for the production of new knowledge *and* a centre for the provision of a wide range of professional courses. The relative incompatability of these two objectives may introduce an incapacity on the part of their members, taken collectively, to put them into operation, a consequent dissatisfaction and thus the appearance of *withdrawal, innovative,* or *ritualistic* behaviours.

The notion of anomie may thus cover a specific situation, in certain cases. But the probability is that it will decrease to the extent that it is applied to more complex systems. Applied to an organization, the notion of anomie can be defined clearly, and may thus be of practical use. An organization is always defined in relation to its objectives. It is thus possible to measure the degree of anomie of the organization, for example, by the reciprocal of the extent to which the organization's members have the capacity to achieve set objectives. In a case such as this, Merton's categories may be easily applied. Things are not so simple when the level shifts from organizations to societies. Societies are not defined in relation to objectives. That is why it is much more difficult to provide a precise definition of the notion of anomie in such a case. How can the *adaptation* of a system's elements or the *integration* of the system itself be assessed, unless it is in relation to some supposed ends of the system? Even in its most analytic versions, the notion of anomie may still retain some traces of teleology (cf. 'Teleology').

Alienation, Conformity and Deviance, Crime, Durkheim, Role, Suicide.

Bibliography

BESNARD, P., 'Merton à la recherche de l'anomie', *Revue française de Sociologie*, XIX, *1*, 1978, 3–38. — BOUDON, R., 'La crise universitaire française: essai de diagnostic', *Annales*, XXIV, *3*, 1969, 738–764. — CHAZEL, F., 'Considérations sur la nature de l'anomie', *Revue française de Sociologie*, VII, *2*, 1967, 151–168. — CLINARD, M.B. (ed.), *Anomie and deviant behavior; a discussion and critique*, New York, The Free Press, 1964. — DURKHEIM, E., *Suicide. The Division of Labor in Society, op cit.* — LACROIX, B., 'Régulation et anomie selon Durkheim', *Cahiers internationaux de Sociologie*, XX, *55*, 1973, 265–292. — MERTON, R.K., 'Continuities in the theory of social structure and anomie', *in* MERTON, R.K., *Social theory and social structure; toward the codification of theory and research*, Glencoe, The Free Press, 1949, rev. eds. 1957, 1961, 161–194. — NISBET, R., *The sociological tradition*, New York, Basic Books, 1966. — PARSONS, T., 'Durkheim's contribution to the theory of integration of social systems', *in* WOLFF, K.M. (ed.), *Emile Durkheim et al. Essays on sociology and philosophy*, New York, Harper, 1964, 118–153.

Authority

We talk about the authority of a *person*, of an *institution*, or of a *message*, in order to signify that we have confidence in them, that we welcome their advice, suggestions, or commands with respect, that we look upon them favourably or at least without hostility or resistance, and that we are ready to defer to them. Authority is thus a relation that must be analysed from the point of view of those who transmit the message or command (the person or institution), and from the points of view of those who receive it.

In taking the first of these points of view, Max Weber's classic analyses of the three forms of *legitimate* power come immediately to mind. In the first place, a message can be said to be *authoritative* if it conforms to tradition. This latter can be understood as a practice, a way of doing, being, or feeling which is expected ('it has always been like that'). It may also be understood as a heritage to which we are accountable, and which we cannot give up without renouncing ourselves and losing our identity: we are concerned here with traditional authority. In the second place, the authority of the message or command comes from the fact that it conforms to a procedure or a code, to a system of rules, which can be explained or proved on request. This is what Max Weber called rational-legal authority. Finally, a message or a command may have effect because it is invested with a charm or with a grace (charisma) which makes it literally irresistible. This is the authority of the prophet or hero.

The authority relation is unstable to the extent that it may shift from one type to another. Such shifts occur more frequently in cases where, as in our own societies, the three types exist simultaneously. The authority that we recognize in many rules is strictly traditional. We have followed them for so long that we have decided not to question them any more. There are also watchwords and slogans that we accept with enthusiasm. However, most attention is placed – and perhaps this is currently a little excessive – on rational-legal authority. There are two reasons for this. First, this type of authority is so much in evidence in the context of the professions and formal organizations which are so apparent in the modern world. Second, its basis can be found in the rationalist conception of legitimacy which our civilization is so fond of claiming as one of its principal characteristics. It is tempting to conclude that authority (in the general sense) *tends* to be confused with the ideal-type of rational-legal authority. But in fact this is no more than a tendency which is itself in conflict with a number of others, even if it does not produce tensions which are particularly severe.

In fact Max Weber was aware of such tendencies, particularly in relation to bureaucratic authority which he believed belonged to the rational-legal type. Bureaucratic hierarchies are not closed systems. They derive from a system of political power to which they are subordinate, in pure Weberian theory. If the Government absorbs the administration, the latter risks losing its efficiency, because it loses autonomy – for example, in the recruitment of civil servants. If the government, on its side, allows itself to become 'bureaucratized', it will tend to confine itself to management tasks and no longer exercise its executive functions. Authority erodes in two ways: in becoming routinized or arbitrary. A society in which there is only rational-legal authority would be as utopian as one in which all violence or injustice were absent.

Even if the three Weberian types of authority are present in our society, we should not avoid the hypothesis that one of these types – in this case the rational-legal – holds a predominant position over the other two. In order to appreciate the relevance of a Weberian analysis, it will be helpful to generalize it in order to see if it can be applied to the whole of society or only to specific sectors. Legal rationality takes the form of a code or syntax, in other words a system of relatively explicit and coherent prescriptions. Rational-legal authority is characterized by its capacity for self-justification, its ability to furnish its reasons for an action or decision to any properly formulated request.

An examination of the professions emphasizes this point in a most opportune manner. The professional (doctor, lawyer, teacher) must be able to justify the use that he makes of his authority, particularly in front of his peers. It is justified according to two criteria: his recognized competence and his morality – understood as the conformity of his professional conduct with the imperatives of his professional code of ethics.

Professional authority may thus be called rational-legal since it is based on competence and knowledge. It may then be interesting to look at the ways in which it resembles and differs from the legal rationality of the Weberian bureaucrat.

The common element in the two cases consists of a specific authority, one which is, in other words, limited. The jurisdictional competence of the civil servant is circumscribed. So is that of the professional, especially since his skill is only practised in the realm of knowledge and technique – even if this realm is of a decisive and literally vital importance for the professional's client. Second, this authority is delegated in the case of the civil servant and subject to certification in the case of the professional. Third, authority is not exercised for the profit of the person on whom it is conferred or even for the institutions which have accredited him. Both carry out service activities: but the services provided are not commodities. Weber insisted on the clear differences between the civil servant's salary, the worker's wages, and the capitalist's profit. In addition, it is quite clear that a doctor's fees cannot be assessed according to criteria of the marginal utility of his services.

However, there is a fundamental difference between bureaucratic authority and professional authority. The one is more *hierarchical* and the other is more *fiduciary*. In bureaucratic systems strictly conceived the civil servant is not elected; he is appointed. Even if he is elected, as happens in Switzerland and the USA, his competence is defined territorially. It is very likely, for instance, that I will pay my taxes to an official whom I have not chosen. But I am the *patient* of Dr X or the *client* of lawyer Y: it is I who have chosen them. It is true that in a 'free' or 'private' medical system the 'free choice' of a doctor by the patient is largely illusory; this is explained by a group of social determinants which do not have a great deal to do with the choice of a friend, a mistress, or a spouse. Nevertheless, the fact that I can leave Dr X's clientele is of considerable significance. I do not have this option with my tax collector, whom I must put up with for as long as I live in a particular area. Second, when I leave the practice of Dr X and join that of Dr Y this establishes a certain element of competition between these practitioners. Lastly, it is particularly significant that the right of 'desertion' negatively symbolizes the importance of a highly personalized relationship – the *confidence* which I have in my doctor.

Confidence is not a psychological epiphenomenon. In the case of medical practice, the success or failure of a cure largely depends on the nature of the link between patient and doctor. It is crucial in the case of psychoanalysis and psychotherapy.

Bureaucracy, Organization, Role, Status, Weber.

Bibliography

ADORNO, T.W. *et al., The authoritarian personality*, New York, Harper, 1950, 1964. — ASCH, S.E., 'Effects of group pressure upon the modification and distorsion of judgments', *in* GUETZKOW, H., *Groups, leadership and men*, Pittsburgh, Carnegie Press, 1951; New York, Russell & Russell, 1963. — BARNARD, Ch. I, *The functions of the executive*, Cambridge, Harvard University Press, 1938, 1962. — BOURRICAUD, F., *Esquisse d'une théorie de l'autorité*, Paris, Plon, 1961; 2 ed., Paris, Plon, 1969. — de GRAZIA, S., 'What authority is not', *American Political Science Review*, 1959, *53*, 321–331. — EYSENCK, H.J., *The psychology of politics*, London, Routledge & Kegan Paul, 1954, 1957. — JOUVENEL, B. de, *De la souveraineté: à la recherche du bien politique*, Paris, M.T. Génin, 1955. — LEWIN, K., 'Group decision and social change', *in* SWANSON, E., NEWCOMB, T., and HARTLEY, L., *Readings in social psychology*, New York, Holt, 1947. — LIKERT, R., *New patterns of management*, New York, McGraw-Hill, 1961. — MORENO, J.B., *Who shall survive? Foundations of sociometry, group psychotherapy and sociodrama*, New York, Beacon House, 1934. — PARSONS, T., *The social system*, New York, The Free Press, 1951. — PIAGET, J., *La formation du jugement moral chez l'enfant*, Paris, F. Alcan, 1932; Paris, PUF, 1969. — SENNETT, R., *Authority*, New York, Knopf, 1980. — SHILS, E.A., 'Authoritarianism: "Right" and "Left" *in* CHRISTIE, R. and JAHODA, M. (eds), *Studies in the scope and method of 'The authoritarian personality'*, Glencoe, Free Press, 1954, 24–49. — WEBER, M., *Economy and society*, London, Owen, 1962. — WHITE, R.K. and LIPPIT, R., 'Leader behavior and member reaction in three "social climates"', *in* CARTWRIGHT, D. and ZANDER, A. (ed.), *Group dynamics*, Evanston, Row, Peterson, 1953; London, Tavistock, 1960, 1968.

B

Beliefs

In many cases, the behaviour of social actors depends on beliefs: even if I do not run the risk of any moral or social sanction in abstaining from going to vote, and even if I am conscious that my vote cannot change the outcome of the poll, I will none the less go and vote if I *believe* that it is 'appropriate' to do so. In this case the behaviour is governed by a *normative* belief. It can equally be governed by *positive* beliefs: I am going to vote because I believe that the poll is going to be very close. The distinction between *positive* and *normative* beliefs is essential. The first constitutes judgements which can have different methods. It can take the form of statements affirming the *existence* or the *non-existence* of an event, or, more generally, of a state of affairs, its possibility or its impossibility: it can, with greater or less precision, associate a probability with the event or state of things considered. A general characteristic of positive beliefs is that their validity is *in principle* controllable by confrontation with reality. To be sure, it is necessary to underline this restriction, because a positive belief can take the form of an estimated statement bearing on a more or less distant and more or less clearly dated future. In contrast, the validity of normative beliefs is in essence impossible to demonstrate, in truth difficult to define. It should however be noted that, as Pareto said, normative and positive beliefs are sometimes inextricably linked. Thus, the whole statement 'It is vital to choose policy *A* rather than *B*, because *B* would lead to consequence *b*, but consequence *b* is undesirable' draws a normative conclusion from two statements, of which one is positive and the other normative.

Another important distinction: that which opposes normative beliefs and value judgements. The former deal with questions of procedure, in the wide sense of the term; the latter affirm the existence of principles which regulate action. Thus, according to Parsons, the ideal of personal *accomplishment* is a fundamental and constant value of American culture. But this value may, according to conjecture, correspond to different norms. Different normative prescriptions in the field of

41

education are associated, according to the period, with the value of accomplishment: at the end of the nineteenth century socialization was defined as an apprenticeship of puritan values; in the second half of the twentieth century as an apprenticeship of autonomy and responsibility. But in both cases, the educational norms are seen as being subordinate to a constant value: to prepare children for personal accomplishment.

These distinctions thus summarily introduced, the principal questions raised by the sociological tradition regarding beliefs can be gathered under several principal titles: the sensitivity of *beliefs* compared with reality; the more or less systematic character of beliefs; the role and function of beliefs in the determination: 1) of the *objectives* of individual action and of social action; 2) of the most appropriate *means* for the realization of these objectives; the relationship between social structures and beliefs; the role of interests in the determination of beliefs – in other words, the full significance of the utilitarian theory of beliefs.

On the first two points, we can be content with brief notations. Beliefs can be more or less sensitive to the influence of experience: if I believe that an event will occur and it does not, the belief will easily be abandoned. If I believe that social equality is bound to increase, I may not let myself be discouraged by proofs to the contrary. Beliefs are thus unequally sensitive to experience according to their contents, the nature and precision of the judgements which express them, and also according to the personality and the social role of the actor. Thus Milton Friedman reports that he has always been struck by the absence of dogmatism and the openmindedness of businessmen, as he has been struck, conversely, by the dogmatism of many intellectuals. It is because, he explains, the beliefs of the former lead to actions for which the sanction is immediate (preface to W.E. Simon, *A Time for Truth*, New York, Berkeley Books, 1979). On the other hand, it should be noted that beliefs are, according to the individual case, more or less isolated or more or less narrowly associated with other beliefs. In the two earlier examples we are dealing with singular beliefs expressing themselves with the aid of a simple proposition ('It is necessary to vote', 'the poll will be closed'). But very often, singular beliefs belong to what it is convenient to call systems of belief. The 'Catholic' believes in a collection of normative and positive propositions. It is the same for the 'liberal'. If I believe that it is necessary to vote for such a party, this belief is likely to be connected with other beliefs, belief in the relevance of its programme, in the efficacy of its leader, possibly belief in a *Weltanschauung*, even in an ideology.

More complex and more interesting, and better explored by sociological tradition, are the questions relative to the role, functions, and social determinants of beliefs. As authors as diverse as Durkheim, Weber, and Pareto have frequently mentioned, beliefs play a fundamental role in social life. They can fix the goals of individual and collective action. They can give direction to the search for means. *Goals*: thus the positive valuation of equality imposes itself on the governments of liberal societies. *Means*: when the objectives pursued by a social actor are complex, the choice of means is generally not the act of a rational selection in a universe of possibilities; it results more from the positive valorization of a certain type of means, from the belief that such a type of means is preferable to others. If I pursue a simple objective (for example to address to X an urgent message), it will not be difficult for me to decide the means best adapted to the object aimed at. If I aim at a complex objective (for example 'to succeed' in life), the means that I will use will themselves be determined by beliefs. Thus Baechler (*The Suicides*) remarks that one can 'choose' a general existential strategy of *dependence* or of *domination*. The same distinctions can be made concerning collective action. Generally a government will simultaneously pursue objectives which are more or less complex. The more complex are the objectives, the slighter is the chance that the rational model of selection of means can be fittingly applied. The means will themselves be selected according to beliefs which, in this case, will have a function of economy of thought: in the cases where the action is pressing and where we have neither the time nor sometimes the means to weigh and examine the consequences of different possible choices, the decision is likely to rest on beliefs or on stereotypes.

Hirschman's studies on development are a good illustration of that proposition. According to the circumstances, the solution to the problem of the underdevelopment of north-east Brazil during the period studied by Hirschman is conceived by the élite as a problem of *engineering* (building of dams, etc.), as an *economic* problem which can be resolved with the aid of the installation of appropriate mechanisms of incentive, or as a *legal* problem, the 'solution' of which is stated in more or less overall terms (limited measures from which one expects a chain reaction or plans for 'agrarian reform'). Between the goal and the chosen means a paradigm is interposed by which the reformer *believes* that he defines the category of means within which the solution to the problem posed has the best chance of finding itself. Of course, the *manner* in which the problem is posed, that is to say the objective as it is pursued, depends also on beliefs bearing on the ends of collective action (it is better to make the population stay in the *sertao* than to let it move towards the south). Similarly, the reformers of the French university at the end of the nineteenth century hesitated between two paradigms, that of 'public service' and that of enterprise. The 'choice' in the case of such an alternative is certainly guided by the partial anticipations that one can formulate of the advantages and disadvantages of each type of solution. But these anticipations cannot but contain deficiencies. This can only be because the paradigms are largely indeterminate. There are a thousand ways to define the organization of a public service. Leaning towards such and such a solution is thus inevitably partly the product of beliefs which the actors will have a tendency to demonstrate as well founded with the help of *derivations* (Pareto) which bring into play the pseudo-deductive resources of rhetoric (for example, the education of the citizens is a national obligation, it can *therefore* only be conferred upon the State). Generally, these two examples – and the numerous others which we might present – demonstrate the close interdependence in all processes of individual or collective action between value judgements (for example 'to stabilize the population in the *sertao* is a political imperative'), normative beliefs which bear on the procedures and of which the criteria are those of agreement (the objective cannot be obtained by, for example, coercion), and positive belief (the problem can be treated by the regularization of the water course).

As soon as individual and collective objectives are complex, their pursuit thus generally implies adhesion to *beliefs*. This statement is sufficient to disqualify the view according to which entirely impartial experts can exist who are capable of indicating the best methods of managing companies. These beliefs naturally do have some relationship with reality. It was not a priori unreasonable to think that the construction of dams in the north-east of Brazil, in a region where rainfall is very irregular, could cause a chain reaction and rescue the region from underdevelopment. But if this paradigm seemed indispensable for a time, it is also because engineers occupy an important place in the Brazilian élite. Their prestige and their influence were themselves due to complex reasons which are naturally not explained only by the diffuse influence of 'Saint-Simonism' in Brazil. An equally important fact: the social movements of protest against the underdevelopment of the north-east were extremely sporadic. This circumstance is explained in its turn because, in the prolonged dry periods, the peasants had an alternative to collective protest: individual *exit* to temporary employment in the coastal developments. With others, such a circumstance made it easy for the problem of the north-east to be seen to be of a technical nature.

This example demonstrates that beliefs depend upon what we sometimes call, in rather a vague term, social structures. The engineers' influence and their powerful position, combined with the absence of popular movements allowed them to impose the belief that the problem was of a purely technical nature. But it would be inappropriate to gather from this example the idea that beliefs mechanically reflect the interests of ruling classes, as the Marxist theory of ideologies would have it. The construction of dams in the north-east did not produce the anticipated development, but it set off complex social and economic effects which tended to deprive the engineers of their influence, to give to other factions of the élites the chance to express themselves, and finally provoked, to use Kuhn's language, a change of paradigm, a *paradigm* shift. But, because of the vested interests of certain actors in the paradigm in process of becoming obsolete, and also because of the ambiguity of the arguments that can be opposed to a paradigm, a change of paradigm is always a long and complex process (cf. 'Knowledge'). Rather than saying that beliefs depend on social structures, it is thus preferable to say that they are, in a complex manner, affected by the systems of action and interaction in which social actors find themselves situated.

The theories which claim to establish generally applicable relationships between structural data and beliefs are in effect often belied by observation. Thus Bohek and Curtis, reviving a widely held cliché, advanced the idea that urbanization, because it isolates individuals from each other and dissolves community groups and the traditions of which they are the bearers, exercises a destructive effect on collective beliefs. To which we can say in opposition that, in certain cases, the city can have an inverse effect. The concentration of council housing and workers' quarters has encouraged rather than inhibited the development of certain social and political movements and, consequently, the diffusion of the collective beliefs that these movements exert themselves to promote. The collective manifestations of Polish Catholicism during the course of the events of 1980 appear to have been favoured rather than inhibited by urban concentration.

Another example: certain authors contend that intellectuals, because their number is growing, are exposed to a process of proletarization, are threatened with being stripped of their influence, and as a result are sure to develop attitudes of opposition towards society (Touraine). Others, basing their reasoning on the development of higher education and the growing demand for intellectuals from that sector, predict a growing embourgeoisement of the intellectuals (Lipset).

It is true that during the first half of the nineteenth century the over-production of intellectuals was relatively greater in France and in Germany than in England (O'Boyle). This explains perhaps in part the greater turbulence of French and German intellectuals in 1848. But other examples contradict the notion that we should give general relevance to this relationship. Even though the Second Empire did not experience an over-production of intellectuals, it refused all positions of influence to radical intellectuals compromised during 1848 and 1851. The distrust of the Bonapartists for the nonconformist thinkers ended in the constitution of a sort of ghetto for intellectuals. Perhaps this explains their participation in the Commune. It is thus difficult to enunciate propositions with a general relevance on the relationship between the number and the place of intellectuals in social structures and their beliefs. The revolt of the intellectuals in 1848 was possible not only because many had lost their social position, but because the events of 1848 offered them the opportunity and the possibility of expressing themselves. In the United States a large number of intellectuals trained in the traditional 'left-wing' disciplines (social sciences, social work, urban planning) were recruited by the unions, by programmes fighting against poverty, and by organizations for the defence of civil rights. They constituted a category the very existence of which contradicted at once both the thesis of embourgeoisement and that of radicalism. Even though employed in the higher education sector, they had the chance of staying mainly directed 'to the left'; often they chose their field of studies because they wanted to 'change society'; their left-wing leanings had been 'reinforced' by the university environment; they were harnessed to tasks the ultimate goal of which was to correct social injustices. Even though leaning to the Left, even though belonging to a group which had been growing in numbers for a long time, they were employed by the 'technostructure'. They had thus little chance of showing attitudes of revolt. By contrast, intellectuals, even if they are employees of the State, can develop more radical attitudes of opposition if they are confined, or have the impression of being confined, in ghettos cut off from civil society. Once again it is necessary, in order that this opposition shall manifest itself, that the circumstances or the environment give it the occasion to do so. In a socially turbulent period these attitudes could take a radical form. In periods of calm, they will seek to express themselves through the conduit of certain organizations (unions, political parties) and will take a more reserved form.

To analyse a phenomenon of belief it is thus indispensable to replace it in the context of the *singular* system of interaction in which it appears rather than to seek to establish general relationships between social structures and beliefs. In the decade which started in 1945 many French intellectuals were communists or fellow travellers of the Communist Party. At the same time, few American intellectuals felt attracted by Marxism. Neither 'structures' nor 'cultural differences' explain this contrast. Before the war, many American intellectuals were Marxists. Marxism was very well accepted even in Hollywood studios. But the American Communist Party, relatively powerful before the war, was discredited in 1945 when it espoused the aggressively anti-western line of Moscow. Thus it lost, according to Bell, a large part of its influence over the unions, whose evolution towards *market-unionism* was confirmed. In the decade before, the communist movement acquired sympathy in unionist quarters. But in 1945 Marxism no longer appealed to any large organization. Thus the intellectuals felt confusedly that in sinking their wish for social justice in Marxist dogma they ran the risk finding themselves stuck up a blind alley. Conversely, the French Communist Party was at its hour of greatest glory in 1945. It had participated in the national resistance movement against the occupiers. A powerful union obedient to the communist cause played an important role in social life. In addition, the Right appeared to be no longer legitimate. Thus there existed on the market of ideologies no expression apart from Marxism of the need for 'totalization' which could, before 1939, be satisfied by belonging to traditionalist ideologies (Bourricaud). In 1945–50, to admit to communist sentiments had an entirely different sense in France than in the United States. Similarly, left-wing intellectuals felt many more affinities for the Communist Party than for the Socialist Party under the Weimar Republic. The essential reason for this is that the social democracy of the period saw itself as determinedly working class, leaving no hope of influence and of promotion to anyone who was not a worker. In addition, after having signed the Treaty of Versailles, it managed the country without flair, in an atmosphere of general hostility to new institutions. And if, at the same time, a number of Jewish intellectuals affiliated themselves to the communist movement, it is less because of the universalism of the Judaic tradition than because ancient practices tended to distance them from the university *establishment*, which in the main tends to the Right.

There is naturally no question of drawing from these comments a utilitarian interpretation of beliefs. In overworking the expression, one can say that we are chosen by our beliefs rather than that we choose them. But we must immediately add that a belief only has a chance of affirming itself if it gives meaning for the actor situated in a given situation. This meaning can coincide with the interests of the actor only in certain cases and in certain limits. In the 1970s, the logic of the two-tier majority poll, united with the existence of the Communist Party, contributed to convincing the First Secretary of the French Socialist Party to demonstrate Marxist beliefs at the time when the Communist Party showed a wish for 'opening up'. But the 'problem' to which a belief responds is not always so clearly defined as that which consists of maximizing the size of a parliamentary group. This is why beliefs must generally be analysed starting from their function of adaptation and from their meaning for the subject rather than from their utility. They are instituted at the meeting point of a personal history, personal projects, and the situation of the actor.

Structures determine the fields of action within which social actors move. These fields of action mean that certain beliefs constitute responses which are more or less well adapted than others. Adherence to Marxist dogma was a poorly adapted response for the American intellectual of 1945 who wished for social progress. In Brazil, the 'technical' paradigm ceases to be a fitting response from the moment when the constellation of factors which carried it modifies. According to Laqueur, the social reformism of the social democracy of Weimar had little chance of tempting the Jewish intellectual. Another example: as Feuer has shown, when a scientific theory is unsettled by observations which it appears to have difficulty in integrating, the members of the scientific establishment often continue to believe in it: it is generally possible to imagine a complementary hypothesis which permits the rendering of a theory compatible with the facts. Among the members of the establishment, many have rested their reputation on work done within the framework of the theory in question. The arrival of a new theory is likely to make this work obsolescent. On the other hand, young or fringe researchers can find in the questioning of the theory the occasion to establish their reputation. The situation encourages them to develop a negative belief with regard to the theory.

If beliefs must be seen as responses to the situations of interaction, we must not underestimate their inertia. During the periods when the Russian proletariat was animated by social movements and showed its combativeness, Lenin developed a vision of the Party integrated with the masses. In the periods when the combativeness fell back, he proposed that the Party be seen as the advanced guard and guide of the masses. But when the Bolshevik Party had taken power, at a time when it was defined as the guide of the masses, this interpretation took on the value of destiny. At the individual level, everyone has experienced the difficulty there is in abandoning a belief, even when one has serious doubts about its validity. This happens because beliefs are often held in systems which constitute general guides of evaluation and of action. From this spring the difficulties and the pains of conversion. That which is true at an individual level is also true at the collective level. Because the modernization of England was developed from an economic sub-system, Anglo-Saxon intellectuals often tend, even today, to think that economic development is the licensed driving force of modernization. Because the modernization of France has been brought about by political shake-ups French intellectuals tend to see political change as the source of all progress. One of the essential reasons for the inertia of beliefs resides in the fact that a belief has a tendency to dissipate only when it is replaced by another. Lucien Febvre has shown once and for all that disbelief in God developed only with the appearance of belief in nature.

Even though beliefs must be understood and analysed as responses to interactive situations, it would be excessive to treat them in all cases as dependent variables. This essential point has been raised by Weber in his classic work on Protestantism and the spirit of capitalism: the religious values expressed by Protestantism played an essential role in the development of capitalism. Without doubt we must be wary of a too-literal interpretation of Weber's thesis. A plausible partial interpretation of this thesis is that the Protestant movement had created a sort of cultural shock where hierarchies were shaken up at the same time as the

value of the individual was reaffirmed, and that this shock facilitated the legitimation of activities which, like financial, commercial, and industrial activities,
were hit by a relative *atimia*. By way of counter-argument it can be noted that at
the end of the nineteenth century, at a moment when Russia had a notable economic development, the entrepreneurs, shopkeepers, and industrialists endeavoured to show by their offerings and their devotions that their activities, which
were perceived as going against the characteristic values of a society which had
remained largely rural, were not the acts of lost souls. Whatever interpretation one
makes of Weber's thesis, from it comes the idea that beliefs can play the role of
independent variables, that is to say, appear as cause rather than as effect, not only
in individual development but in social change. To take a more simple example
than Weber's an example borrowed from Gerschenkron, it is because they were
Saint-Simonians and believed that progress came by industrialization, that the
Pereira brothers thought up a type of bank entirely unprecedented in England,
business banks, to which they gave the objective of financing large industrial
projects. Naturally the implementation of the project was greatly aided by the
authoritarian and centralized character of political power under the Second
Empire.

A tradition which goes back to the philosophy of Enlightenment has it that
beliefs should be essentially the representations of a distorted reality under the
influence of interests (Marxist tradition) or tensions (Freudian tradition). It is true
in certain cases. Generally, beliefs are more, as Durkheim would say, guides of
'selected' evaluation and action or, according to the situation, constructed by the
social actors according to their personality, their situation, and their environment.
The Durkheimian paradigm has not only the advantage of being better applied
than others to observable reality, it has furthermore the advantage of eliminating
simplistic visions of the relationship between beliefs and social reality, and the one
in particular which wishes to see belief as an irrational manifestation (cf.
'Rationality').

Ideologies, Knowledge, Objectivity, Rationality, Social Symbolism, Utopia.

Bibliography

BELL, D., *The end of ideology. On the exhaustion of political ideas in the fifties.* Glencoe, The Free Press, 1960,
ed. rev. 1965. — BERGER, P. and LUCKMANN, T., *The social construction of reality*, London, Doubleday,
1966; London, Penguin, 1967. — BLUMER, H., 'Society as symbolic interaction', *in* ROSE, A.M. (ed.),
Human behavior and social processes, Boston, Houghton Mifflin, 1962, 179-192; London, Routledge Kegan
Paul. 1962. — BORHEK, J.T. and CURTIS, R.F., *A sociology of belief*, New York, Wiley, 1975. — BOURRI-
CAUD, F., *Le bricolage idéologique. Essai sur les intellectuels et les passions démocratiques*, Paris, PUF, 1980. —
CAZENEUVE, J., *Les rites et la condition humaine*, Paris, PUF, 1957. — DOWNS, A., *An economic theory of
democracy*, New York, Harper, 1957. — FEBVRE, L., *Le problème de l'incroyance au XVI* siècle: la religion de
Rabelais*, Paris, A. Michel, 1968. — FESTINGER, L., RIECKEN, H.W., SCHACHTER, S., *When prophecy fails*,
Minneapolis, University of Minnesota Press, 1956; *When prophecy fails. A social and psychological study of a
modern group that predicted the destruction of the world*, New York, Harper & Row, 1964. — GEERTZ, C.,
'Ideology as a cultural system', *in* APTER, D.E. (ed.), *Ideology and discontent*, Glencoe, The Free Press,
1964, 47–76. — GERSCHENKRON, A., 'Economic backwardness in historical perspective', *in* GER-
SCHENKRON, A., *Economic backwardness in historical perspective. A book of essays*, Cambridge, The Belknap
Press of Harvard University Press, 1962, 5–30. — HIRSCHMAN, A.O., *Journeys toward progress. Studies of
economic policy making in Latin America*, New York, The twentieth Century Fund, 1963; New York,

Doubleday, 1963, 1965; New York, Greenwood Press, 1963, 1968. — LAQUEUR, W., *Weimar: a cultural history, 1918-1933*, London, Weidenfeld & Nicolson, 1978. — O'BOYLE, L., 'The problem of an excess of educated men in Western Europe, 1800-1850', *Journal of modern history*, XLII, *4*, 1970, 471–495. — SELZNICK, P., *The organizational weapon: a study of bolchevik strategy and tactics*, New York, McGraw-Hill, 1952.

Bureaucracy

This term designates a relatively original form of administration, but it has been given a great variety of diverse meanings, which have extended its usage beyond the field to which it was initially intended to refer. Max Weber, who did more than any other writer to introduce the term to the technical vocabulary of sociology, gave it a relatively narrow meaning while many others – notably those of a Marxist inspiration – saw in bureaucracy a general form of power which was increasingly predominant in capitalist societies. It should be noted that a whole tradition of writing about bureaucracy – which has included a strong French element, from de Tocqueville to Michel Crozier – has been devoted to analysing historical experience and cultural traditions as the source of a propensity, which can be observed in a number of countries, for all public administrations and even some private ones to be organized in the bureaucratic mode.

The Weberian type of bureaucracy is one characterized by a specific number of systematically defined traits. Each bureaucrat is employed within a status hierarchy, and imperatively co-ordinated by the supervision exercised by his superiors. The bureaucrat carries out duties defined in terms of both his technical and jurisdictional competence. His competence as a bureaucrat is specific: it consists of a package of rights and obligations, which are founded on both his capacity to carry them out and on an explicit set of orders from the hierarchic authority which has recruited him and which monitors his performance. Bureaucratic recruitment is based on *universalistic* criteria. At least in principle the bureaucrat is not employed because he is the relative, client, friend, or associate of whoever engages him, but because of attributes common to all candidates for the job who, strictly speaking, must be distinguished only by their publicly recognized aptitudes: the bureaucrat is recruited through examination or on the basis of educational qualifications. Similarly, he is promoted on the basis of rules which, in theory, prevent or at least limit favouritism. In addition the bureaucrat's income cannot be considered either as profit or reward. It is a salary which does not depend upon the services which he provides to his employer – the State – but which is designed to ensure that he can live an honourable and decent life, in accordance with the obligations of his *rank*.

Taken together, these traits make the bureaucrat a quite novel individual. They guarantee his independence, as much *vis-à-vis* his superiors as his subordinates, at the same time as they place him strictly under the control of the rules which determine the functioning of the administration to which he belongs. From the moment he takes up his post he cannot be removed from it save in exceptional circumstances and only then through specific administrative or legal processes.

His superior can only recruit, promote, discipline, move, or dismiss him according to specific procedures and in return for indemnities laid down in his employment contract. His subordinates are not protégés to whom he can extend a helping hand. Moreover, he does not depend upon the public, who cannot do anything either to further his career or to deprive him of his post, protected as he is by a shield of rules designed to guarantee his position. Teachers (who in France and some other countries are civil servants), for example, are not recruited by the mayor or town council of the borough, *commune*, or country in which they teach: if the mayor's son is a dunce, the teacher cannot be dismissed because he has given him bad marks. But although the bureaucrat is protected against the arbitrary whims of his superiors, he can exercise his powers *vis-à-vis* the public only within strictly defined limits – if he exceeds them, he is exposed to the risk of all sorts of legal actions.

Weber saw clearly that the guarantees from which the bureaucrat benefits do not derive only from the recognition of the rights which he is justified in claiming, either as an individual or as a citizen. They are the strict counterpart of the bureaucracy's functional exigences. In effect, the bureaucracy is presented to us as a *machine* in the service of the State or the civil power. Bureaucracies are instruments of the power of the citizenry – or of the State. In order that a bureaucratic organization can contribute to the maximization of such power, two sets of conditions must be fulfilled. First, the bureaucrats must know how to do what they have been recruited for: by comparison with a coterie of favourites or amateurs, bureaucracy is administration by experts. A second condition which ensures the efficiency of a bureaucracy is that the bureaucrats obey orders: they must execute these orders whether or not they understand or agree with the ultimate ends of the policies they are putting into effect. These two sets of conditions can be realized simultaneously only if the bureaucrats' functions are specific, universalistic, and carried out unemotionally – *sine ira et cum studio*.

While the Weberian ideal-type of bureaucracy is relevant, its field of application is limited. In other words, there are many forms of public administration which conform to this type, but also many which do not. Quite clearly, not all organizations are necessarily of a bureaucratic type, despite the fact that a propensity towards bureaucratization is discernible in the majority of modern organizations. Such a tendency is explicable in terms of the advantages that the collectivity draws from the correct operation of efficient and disciplined bureaucracies. Certain armies and administrations are, or have been, bureaucracies in the Weberian sense. Thus, the military fights those – often civilians – who are designated as enemies by their political masters. Tax officials collect taxes: even if, as individual citizens, they disagree with the government's fiscal policies. The cohesion of the French State, for example, was for a long period based on the existence of a disciplined corps of civil servants, who were able to ensure the regular provision of public goods, even when weakness and inconsistency in political institutions made such provision difficult. It may even be suggested that services such as armies, tax assessment and collection, police forces (at least in certain of its aspects) can be managed by only bureaucratic means. Elected officers, for example, would be unlikely to have their orders obeyed – except where they could count on exceptional circumstances or on the good will of their troops, motivated either by public spiritedness or by the most ardent fanaticism.

Those activities which come closest to the exercise of state power lend themselves most readily to bureaucratic organization. Yet even those activities which produce 'public goods' administered by the State are not necessarily best adapted to bureaucratization. De Tocqueville remarked on the fact that in America many activities for which the State has responsibility and finances are carried out by public servants elected for short periods and subject to the control of the electorate. Education is financed by local boards, and its management, personnel, and curricula are not subjected to uniform regulation. As a result, agents of a public service such as education are subjected to much closer scrutiny by the service's users than would be the case in France, for example, where the user is prevented from interfering with the service's organization.

Bureaucracy is not simply a general instrument available to political leaders: it is a *centralized* instrument, even if, as the history of government administration demonstrates, the degree of centralization varies over the long term. In French terms, the civil service was more centralized under Napoleon than under Louis-Philippe, or in the Fifth as opposed to the Third Republic. The periphery's demands were less haughtily ignored during the Orleanist regime (1830–48) and the opportunist regime of 1871–1940 than during the Bonapartist or Gaullist regimes. Centralization simultaneously affects both the recruitment and management of personnel placed under the authority of a standardized set of rules, or at least rules based on the same spirit and principles. The more centralized a bureaucracy is, the more likely it is to attempt rigorous codification of the proliferating and confused mass of laws, decrees, regulations, etc., in order to give them an overall coherence.

Ultimately, the centralized bureaucracy is supplied by a single treasury, its expenditures set out under the constituent headings of a single budget. If, then, the criteria which characterize a centralized administration are taken in their strictest sense, and if in addition centralization is treated as one of the necessary conditions of bureaucracy, it has to be recognized that bureaucracy is only one among many possible ways of organizing public administration.

Why then has the centralized bureaucracy become widespread as a general organizational form in modern societies? Weber gives two answers to this question. First, bureaucracy provides a powerful 'multiplier effect' to the power of political leaders. It allows them to mobilize and direct an increasing mass of human, physical, and financial resources. This power increase cannot be understood simply as a *mobilization* effect through which an increasingly wide range of resources is made available to the government. It is also accompanied by an increasingly intensive exploitation of the physical environment and its resources. Bureaucracy is doubly effective because it increases the efficiency of the administrative system, and hence the control it exerts over society. In addition, it often appears beneficial to the public, or at least to those sections which are assured of a supply of public goods.

If bureaucratic organization is considered as a means for political leaders to increase their power, it may be readily understood why they should seek to 'bureaucratize' their power so as to avoid the sanction of electoral control. This is the idea developed by Michels in his study of the 'iron law of oligarchy'. The consolidation of positions at the summit of the party organization, the substitution of co-option for election, and the nomination by political leaders of the middle level of party officials – these are characteristics of the process of bureaucratization of political parties, even those with socialist or revolutionary objectives. This theme, proposed by a number of sociologists whose ideas were influenced by Machiavelli, such as Pareto, Michels, and Mosca, was also taken up by Trotsky and his followers in their critique of the Stalinist regime. Whatever the relevance of the Trotskyist critique of Stalinism, co-option and control of the summit over the base of the party constitute highly effective means for political leaders to protect themselves against electoral risks and democratic competition.

Alongside 'bureaucratization' as the strategy by which pseudo-democratic leaders seek to elude the control of their electors, a place must also be allotted to 'bureaucratization' as long term process affecting both public and private sector organizations which tends to insulate both offices and office holders from being affected by the short term and usually primarily financial pressures that provide the organization with its resources. The bureaucratization of employees' occupations in the capitalist enterprise is the form by which certain limitations are imposed on the employer's rights to hire, fire, promote, or discipline personnel.

The bureaucratization of the enterprise is the result of a whole set of legislative and regulatory measures which, through their application, tend to shackle hierarchical authority to a greater or lesser extent. This long term trend is, at least in part, the result of a combination of essentially independent factors. The demand from enterprises for an increasingly qualified labour force is transformed into an upgrading of qualifications gained outside of the enterprise itself, either conferred by professional associations or, as in the highest levels of the organization, by academic institutions. But it also proceeds from an encounter with the strategy of unions seeking to limit the direct personal authority of the boss, and through the strategies of those parties and politicians who, whether because of their ideological affinities or through their interest in electoral gain, side with the unions in opposing the 'divine right' of the bosses.

The bureaucratization of public administration, of private enterprises, of unions and political parties, share a number of common features, which Max Weber sought to designate in a comprehensive and synthetic manner when he used the term 'rational–legal'. This form of power is characterized by a general suspicion of all that is arbitrary in any order, and by the desire to substitute 'the administration of things for the government of persons'. But such a pretention encounters so many obstacles that it leads to a wide variety of 'dysfunctions'. The famous Mertonian analysis of anomie is illustrated by the consideration of the 'side effects' generated by the objective of introducing a 'rational–legal' order within organizations, and by extension into all domains of social life. The rigorous formalization of statuses, their minute segmentation and stratification, the multiplication of guarantees given to the diverse strata and their occupants, simultaneously render the tasks of co-ordination and control both indispensable and extremely difficult. Crozier has coined the term 'bureaucratic vicious circle' to describe how bureaucratic control and surveillance mechanisms become increasingly cumbersome as their scope extends, and yet increasingly more necessary as their efficiency declines. They are hardly calculated to provide a high level of motivation to employees of such an organization, who are more inclined to follow strategies of safety rather than strategies of initiative. Bureaucratic organizations are subject to the greater costs resulting from a low level of involvement and commitment, even if the risk of 'defection' (or exit, in Hirschman's terms) by their members is reasonably well controlled, to the extent that the organization succeeds in covering its minimal requirements for security. The risk of what Merton calls 'retreatism' is particularly difficult to resist. Whilst the bureaucratic organization seeks to legitimate itself by offering its employees security (especially in respect of employment), it also mobilizes the commitment of politicians in emphasizing the disinterestedness, and ultimately the 'humanitarian' nature of the public goods that it places at the disposal of individuals.

It is possible to ask the question, are western societies exposed to the risk of an increasingly rapid and widespread bureaucratization? De Tocqueville was already writing about the 'immense and tutelary despotism' which democratic societies tended to produce. He well understood that this risk varies in accordance with national traditions. Nowadays bureaucracy is frequently denounced as 'the French disease'. But whatever its seriousness, and the extent to which it is diffused within society, this 'disease' cannot be said to apply to all aspects of our social life. No society is entirely bureaucratic or even bureaucratizable, especially when the fundamental options of that society are decided according to the procedures of democratic competition, and when enterprises continue to allot a major role to the demands of both management and decentralized innovation.

Anomie, Capitalism, Organization, Power, State, Weber

Bibliography

ARONSON, S.H., *Status and kinship in the higher civil service*, Cambridge, Harvard Univ. Press, 1964. — ARROW, K.J., *The limits of organization*, New York, W.W. Norton & Co., 1974. — CHAPMAN, B., *The profession of government; the public service in Europe*, London, Allen & Unwin, 1959, 1966. — CROZIER, M., *Le phénomène bureaucratique*, Paris, Seuil, 1963. — CROZIER, M. and FRIEDBERG, E., *L'acteur et le système: les contraintes de l'action collective*, Paris, Seuil, 1977. — DAHL, R., 'The concept of power', in *Behavioral Science*, 1957, 2, 201-215. — DOWNS, A., *Inside bureaucracy*, Santa Monica, Rand Corp., 1964; Boston, Little, Brown & Co., 1967. — EISENSTADT, S.N., *The political systems of Empires*, Glencoe, The Free Press, 1963, 1967. — ETZIONI, A., *A comparative analysis of complex organizations: on power, involvement and their correlates*, New York, Free Press, 1961. — GRÉMION, P., *Le pouvoir périphérique: bureaucrates et notables dans le système politique français*, Paris, Seuil, 1976. — GOULDNER, A.W., *Patterns of industrial bureaucracy*, Glencoe, Free Press, 1954, 1967. — HIRSCHMAN, A.O., *The strategy of economic development*, New Haven, Yale Univ. Press, 1958. — KINGSLEY, J.D., *Representative bureaucracy: an interpretation of the British civil service*, Yellow Springs, Antioch College Press, 1944. — LEFORT, C., *Eléments d'une critique de la bureaucratie*, Geneva, Droz, 1971. — MARCH, J.G. and SIMON, H.A., *Organizations*, New York, Wiley, 1958. — MERTON, R.K., *Social theory and social structure*, Glencoe, The Free Press, 1949. — MICHELS, R., *Zur Soziologie des Parteiwesens in der modernen Demokratie*, Leipzig, W. Klinkhardt, 1911. — ROSENBERG,

H., *Bureaucracy, aristocracy and autocracy. The Prussian experience 1660-1815*, Cambridge, Harvard Univ. Press, 1958. — SELZNICK, Ph., *Leadership in administration: a sociological interpretation*, Evanston, Row Peterson, 1957. — WEBER, M., *Economy and Society*, vol. 1., Part 1, London, Owen, 1962.

C

Capitalism

The term capitalism has a very long history; but from the beginning it has often had ideologically negative connotations. Since these have been imposed by socialist thinkers, who associate capitalist society with the idea of the pitiless 'exploitation' of the 'proletariat' by private owners, certain writers (notably Aron and Parsons) have preferred to take over an expression used by Comte and Spencer and speak of *industrial society* rather than capitalist society.

When is it correct to speak of *industrial society*? And when to speak of *capitalism*? While they are closely linked, these two terms are by no means synonyms. In effect, the capitalist process is the basis of the industrialization process, since historically it is the capitalist societies which were also the first to industrialize. The rallying-cry 'catch up with the capitalist societies', so often proclaimed by the leaders of socialist societies, also suggests that capitalist organization possesses something in common with all industrial societies, and thus with socialist societies as well. These characteristics have to do with the high level of productivity (and the conditions which are connected with it, notably the relation between labour and fixed capital among the factors of production), and the close link between science, technology, and production. They also include phenomena such as mass consumption, the 'standardization' of products and of the needs which they are designed to fulfil. These characteristics are not independent: capitalism is a 'system'. Complex relationships exist among technology, production, productivity, the size and distribution of incomes among the different categories of the population, and the scale and nature of public and private consumption.

These relations can take different forms. For example, income distribution is more or less unequal, the substitution of labour by capital can produce very different effects (desired or unexpected) on the volume of production, productivity rates, average income, and the range over which incomes vary. The different values assigned to these variables mean that it is possible to distinguish sub-categories of

55

'capitalist' and 'socialist' within the category of industrial society. Such distinctions are far from easy to make, but we hold the two forms of capitalist and socialist organization to be distinct, even if they share a common origin and, in part at least, a common inspiration.

Let us begin by asking ourselves what are the characteristics of *the capitalist form of the industrialization process*. In answering this question we are inclined to emphasize traits which concern the hierarchy of social groups and the articulation of social institutions. Spencer contrasted industrial society – where, to give it a Saint-Simonian ring, the 'producers' are dominant – and military society – where warriors are one but not the only dominant group – alongside the agents of an oppressive and repressive state power. Saint-Simon himself prophesied the emergence of the 'producers', to whom he opposed nobles, clerics, and landowners. In this respect capitalist society, like any industrial society, is characterized by the rise of shopkeepers, industrialists, wage-labourers, and the managers of commerce and industry – in brief, those persons active in sectors that, since Colin Clark and Fourastie, have been termed secondary and tertiary. But a hierarchy placing 'producers' at the pinnacle of social stratification can persist only if it is supported by institutional mechanisms which guarantee certain prerogatives to the capitalist.

As Marx saw clearly, the advent of capitalism is characterized by the emancipation of producers, who are liberated from certain cultural, economic, and political constraints. Within the pre-capitalist economic order manufacturers were shackled by the corporations and guilds of the feudal system. But the relaxation of such restraints, particularly as they affected the recruitment of workers, their training, and work disciplines, meant that a contract of 'formal freedom' (to use Max Weber's expression) could be passed between employers and employees. This relation, enshrined in the wage, is one of the characteristic institutions of capitalism, not only in the form in which it has appeared in Europe since the beginning of the modern era, but today even in the developing countries. The creation of a 'labour market' – a contentious term, since it implies that labour is as much a commodity as any other – appears to be one of the essential conditions for economic take-off. It is the reason why the liberation of the serfs and agrarian reform are seen as pre-conditions of 'capitalist accumulation'. Some historians (cf. Paul Mantoux using the case of England in the eighteenth century) have gone so far as to argue that an 'agricultural revolution', characterized principally by the expropriation of common land, the rights of new landowners to enclose in fields such land and thus abrogate the traditional rights of '*vaine pature*' or common grazing, constituted a prior condition for the industrial revolution. In the political sphere emancipation was manifested through the dissolution of the old society of 'orders'. In some cases this dissolution required a prior revolution which transformed subjects into citizens, and sometimes it developed gradually through the generalization of rights whose exercise was essential to the growth of economic life. In such cases it was limited to changes in the rights of property, taxation, and civil law.

But in either of the two cases – a French-style revolution or a reform of the sort dreamt of by the exponents of 'enlightened' despotism – economic emancipation is indissociable from the profound transformation of political society. The elimination of those obstacles which seek to preserve the wealth of a privileged minority, by limiting access to certain positions or occupations and consequently discouraging entrepreneurial individuals, constitutes a liberty of establishment in its widest sense – the universally recognized right to enter into a contract, to buy and to sell, in conditions which are equal for all. Realization of these conditions is not a simple matter, and the resistance of the 'privileged' to reform can lead to prolonged and violent revolution, as occurred in France from 1789 to 1815. Finally, within the cultural domain it is necessary that the more or less 'static' notion of 'natural' and well-regulated needs gives way to the concept of an appetite seeking legitimate satisfaction by the possession and enjoyment of a new and growing range of goods and services. This development of an appetite challenges the traditional hierarchy of values in which the activities of production are subordinated to moral and religious ideals.

This three-part emancipation ensures neither the philosophical liberty of capitalist man nor the rightness of the choices he must make as an economic actor, however. It is even possible to argue that the elimination of traditional constraints is accompanied by an increase in *anomie*. Such a pessimistic vision of capitalist society is reinforced by the equally unfavourable perception engendered by the increased inequality that capitalist organization is held to produce. The first phase of capital accumulation is generally accompanied by an uprooting of the peasantry. As they join the ranks of the proletariat, they find themselves doubly disadvantaged – by a marked lowering both of their *living standards* and of their *style of life*.

Is this 'brutal deterioration', to which doctrinaire socialists have devoted so much attention, linked merely to an initial and brief phase of capitalism? The sufferings inflicted on workers in the first phase of industrialization are often presented – at least implicitly – as the counterpart of 'take off' and of subsequent economic progress. In fact over the long term, it is incontestable that improvement does occur in the standards of living of all categories of the population, and particularly in those of industrial workers. But, if it seems unlikely that capitalism is really a machine for 'pauperizing' the masses, some reservations are in order to restrain the optimism of *laissez-faire* liberals of the Manchester School.

First, living standards improve at a very unequal rate in relation to different periods and categories of the population. Even where improvement is very rapid, pockets of poverty persist. Today, capitalism remains a system characterized by its capacity to *exclude* a larger or smaller proportion of the population. It leaves on the margins of proletarian society many different *minorities* who can pick up only the scraps from the table – and only after, one might say, the table has been laid. But even if the standard of living of the lowest categories of the population is currently higher than that of the proletariat in the reign of Louis Philippe (i.e., the 1830s and 1840s), there still exists a significant difference between the better and worse-off categories of the population, which is only very slowly disappearing and which is only partly due to differences in productivity. These inequalities are denounced as injustices since in the view of egalitarian ideology *all* inequality is an injustice.

Although it is possible to argue that today's poor will be compensated in the long term, that their present condition is a *stage* on the way towards a better condition, the argument is neither solid or convincing. The inequalities suffered by a 'sacrificed generation' cannot be compensated for by benefits for a subsequent generation. In addition, there is no convincing proof that individuals badly treated today will find themselves (or their descendants) compensated at some future date.

Capitalist organization is presented as radically and incurably unjust for at least two reasons. It is said to be a *class society*, a society founded on *profit*. Class division is a direct result of capitalist accumulation. Displaced peasants, ruined artisans, all find themselves packed into the factories of industrialists. These 'proletarians' are directly confronted by 'capitalists'. The two classes will be embroiled in a fight to the death, which can result only in the expropriation of the means of production from the hands of the owners of private property. Capitalist society is thus a 'zero-sum society' in periods both of crisis and falling production and of prosperity and rising production, because the *totality of net product*, even when it increases, will be confiscated by the capitalists.

Such an extreme conception of class struggle in capitalist societies is untenable. First, how can it account for the persistence of intermediate groups (peasants, family farmers, executives) whose extinction was predicted by the first socialist theoreticians? Then, what meaning can be given to the rise of technicians, managers, and professionals, who are neither proletarians nor capitalists, since they are not the owners of capital? Capitalist society has evolved along different lines to those set out in the model which interprets all conflicts as a fight to the death between two classes, one defined as the carrier of labour power, the other as holder of the means of production. The need to reconcile empirical data with this allegedly 'scientific' model is satisfied by the contention that the multiplicity of intermediary groups is only an *apparent* reality which takes in the naïve 'empiricists', while the 'deep structure' continues to be made up of the opposition between 'dominating' and 'dominated' groups (or even exploiters and exploited) which is fundamental to the capitalist regime. This first dogma is supported by a second, according to which profit and exploitation are synonymous. Capitalist organization may thus be denounced as a form of institutionalized theft, more or less adeptly hidden by the mystifications of morality and law.

This orthodox socialist interpretation is opposed by a number of revisionist interpretations which emphasize the institutional evolution of capitalist societies. The concept of property has developed considerably since the time when it was defined as the absolute right to enjoy and dispose of goods as the owner saw fit. Property ownership is no longer vested solely in physical individuals and frequently has an impersonal character, as in the corporate board. In addition, many shareholders of modern corporations are content simply to draw their dividends and never participate in the affairs of the company.

Does this mean that *ownership* and *control* of the corporation are separated? This has been the 'revisionist' thesis, from the end of the nineteenth century up to Burnham and Galbraith. But the 'technostructure' is far from being as independent from the shareholders as these writers would imply. Even if they are not its owners, the managers of the technostructure are often obliged to act as representatives of the owners and their capital: their logic is that of profit.

Profit has been presented by the socialists, and most notably by Marx, as a form of *overwork* extorted by the capitalists. Since in this view net economic product is no more than the sum of the work performed by the proletariat, capitalist profit is nothing more than the other face of workers' exploitation. This notion constitutes part of the received wisdom of anti-capitalist ideology, extending even beyond socialist thought. However to the extent that profit can derive from sources other than the exploitation of wage labour, in particular from 'natural advantages' accruing from a reorganization of productive resources, profit or its anticipation should be recognized as an irreplacable regulator of the capitalist system, if not of all industrial organization. It enables an evaluation of the efficiency of different productive combinations. Through it one can see whether resources have been properly utilized or whether a different use of the same resources would have generated greater net product.

Profit is by no means the only criterion used for the optimization of the factors of production in capitalist society. It can be defined only in relation to the production unit itself. When defined as the maximization of the firm's monetary resources, it may be challenged as a management criterion not only by employees but by the capitalists themselves, who may prefer to 'consume' their dividends rather than continue to invest them in the enterprise. Company profit does not constitute, therefore, the sole criterion in a capitalist regime for deciding the best use of resources.

Since profit cannot be defined globally, at the level of the whole society, in a capitalist society, but in the context of units of production which are more or less in competition and more or less autonomous *vis-à-vis* political and administrative authorities, a close link is evident between profit and property. It is true that the aggregate profits realized by individual firms affect the volume of consumption, savings, and investment in society, through the variation in money supply and rates of interest. But these profits are created in production units where the executives plan on the basis of their anticipation of the consequences of their decisions for *their* firm's accounts – whether they are owners or managers makes no difference.

In fact the thesis of a 'managerial revolution' in which the capitalism of the property owners has been replaced by that of a 'technostructure of executives and managers' is much more relevant to the discussion of ruling-class development than to debates about the nature of the industrial enterprise. The nature of industrial growth suggests that investment decisions are mostly based on predictions of future profit. Disinvestment decisions, to get out of a particular industrial sector or firm which no longer appears viable, are similarly taken on the basis of the accounts of the business, by shareholders themselves or by creditors.

Capitalism without property owners is as inconceivable as capitalism without entrepreneurs. Schumpeter insisted on the importance of individual risk and initiative in capitalist society. Such individualism appears just as necessary to everyday management of the enterprise, for its results can be attributed to an executive or management team. The problems of centralized planning derive from location of the production unit in an organization which is too vast and complex, so that it becomes difficult to monitor production through its various phases, to identify clearly success and failure, and to check the whole process.

Another way of characterizing the capitalist regime is to observe that the State does not exercise the ultimate responsibility in the management of the economy. And it is not only the State or the public authorities alone which can deprive the capitalists of control of their enterprises. The substitution of union leaders or representatives of the employees for capitalist owners constitutes another eventuality, although one linked to the first. But two important questions in relation to this point should be posed. On the one hand, are the new managers obliged to submit to the logic of decentralized profit (in which case little has effectively changed)? Or, on the other hand, has the arrival of new managers led to a radical change in the management of the enterprise? In this case the 'logic of profit' has been replaced by one of a completely different type, which must be defined. In this case it must be asked whether the conditions of economic progress continue to be maintained, particularly where they affect the relation between consumption, savings and investment, and the balance in resource use between public and private sectors.

Schumpeter identified a number of 'protected strata' within capitalist society, at least in its mature phase, such as peasants, small shopkeepers, white-collar workers, remnants of the nobility and traditional élites, who acted as a buffer between proletariat and capitalists. He also pointed to the value conflicts which would be key features of modern society. Today, it is usual to consider that the rules of capitalism underpin all institutions in contemporary society, even if they are not obliged to measure themselves against market forces. Schools, hospitals, bureaucracies, etc., may all be labelled 'capitalist'. Such expressions are helpful where they draw attention to the constraints on efficiency imposed on the directors of such institutions, since they affect both funding and expenditure. It is thus possible to use conceptions of profitability while recognizing that it is rare to use such conceptions as decisive factors even in the most extremely 'capitalist' societies. Public 'goods' such as health, education, etc., are rarely exposed to the full logic of profit and its 'maximization'. Daniel Bell has described a series of 'cultural contradictions of capitalism' which express the difficulties faced by attempts to extend the principles of private enterprise to the management of the 'public good' in our society. Because it varies over such a massive cultural and political range, capitalism does not constitute a single sociological type of society, but is rather more useful as a concept which describes a form of organization of the economic sub-system.

Alienation, Marx, Needs, Religion, Social Stratification, Weber.

Bibliography

ARON, R., *Dix-huit leçons sur la société industrielle*, Paris, Gallimard, 1962; *Trois essais sur l'âge industriel*, Paris, Plon, 1965. — BAECHLER, J., 'Essai sur les origines du capitalisme', *Archives européennes de Sociologie*, IX, 1968, 205–263. — BELL, D., *The cultural contradictions of capitalism*, London Heinemann, 1976. — BRAUDEL, F., *Civilisation matérielle, économie, capitalisme, XVᵉ–XVIIIᵉ siècle*, Paris, A. Colin, 1979, 3 vol. — BURNHAM, J., *The managerial revolution; what is happening in the world now*, New York, The John Day Co.,

1941. — CLARK, C., *The conditions of economic progress*, London, Macmillan & Co., 1940; New York, St Martin's Press, 3rd ed, 1957, — GALBRAITH, J.K., *American capitalism: the concept of countervailing power*, 1952; rev. ed: Boston, Houghton Mifflin, 1956; London, Hamilton, 1952; *The new industrial state*, Boston, Houghton Mifflin, 1967. — GORZ, A., *Stratégie ouvrière et néo-capitalisme*, Paris, Seuil, 1964. — MANTOUX, P., *La révolution industrielle au XVIIIe siècle: essai sur les commencements de la grande industrie moderne en Angleterre*, Paris, Société nouvelle de Librairie et d'Edition, 1906; Paris, Editions Génin, 1973. — MARX, K., *Capital*. — PERROUX, F., *Le capitalisme*, Paris, PUF, 1948, 1969; *L'économie du XXe siècle*, Paris, PUF, 1961; 3rd edn 1969. — POULANTZAS, N., 'The problem of the capitalist state', *New Left Review*, vol. 58, nov.-déc. 1969, 67-78. — SAINT-SIMON, C.-H. de, *Œuvres 1868–1875*, Paris, Anthropos, 1966, 6 vol., t. II and III — SCHUMPETER, J., *Capitalism, socialism and democracy*, New York, Harper & Brothers, 1942; London, Georges Allen & Unwin Ltd., 1976. — SMITH, A., *An inquiry into the nature and causes of the wealth of nations*, London, W. Strahan & T. Cadell, 1776; Oxford, Clarendon Press, 1976. — SOMBART, W., *Der moderne Kapitalismus*, Leipzig, Duncker & Humblot, 1902–1927, 3 vol. Trad. — SPENCER, H., *The principles of sociology: quarterly serial*, New York, D. Appleton, 1874–1875; 1891, 3 vol.; *Principles of sociology (selections)*, London, Macmillan, 1969. — ULLMO, J., *Le profit*, Paris, Dunod, 1969. — WALLERSTEIN, I., *The modern world system, capitalist agriculture and the origins of the European world economy in the sixteenth century*, New York, London, Academic Press, 1974. — WILDAVSKY, A., *Revolt against the masses and other essays on politics and public policy*, New York, Basic Books, 1971.

Causality

The notion of causality has had a bad press from the epistemologists, as Herbert Simon once remarked. They prefer to substitute the idea of interdependence or functional relation. The major problem is a definitional one. Although cause is conceived as prior to effect, the two are often observed simultaneously. Cause is also difficult to reconcile with the ideas of classical logic about implication (necessary conditions, sufficient conditions, necessary *and* sufficient conditions). For example, the increase in the English birth rate between 1840 and 1870 is the *cause* of the increase in population during the period. But it is not a *necessary* condition (since the increased population could have occurred as a result of decreased mortality rates). Neither is it a sufficient condition (since its effects could have been counterbalanced by an increase in the mortality rate).

Yet, despite the epistemological critique of the concept of cause, it is widely used in the social sciences. Bad weather (*e1*), for instance, was the cause of a poor harvest (*e2*), which caused prices to rise (*e3*). When such a proposition is set out, it is not assumed that the state of affairs *e1* is the necessary or sufficient condition of *e2* nor that *e2* is the necessary or sufficient condition of *e3*. All that is meant is that, *in the situation observed, e1* provoked *e2*, and *e2* provoked *e3*. In other words, if the weather had been different, the harvest would have been better, and demand would not have exceeded supply to such an extent as it did. The states of affairs, *e1, e2,* and *e3* are interrelated. Moreover, they are interrelated in an asymmetric way: it is virtually certain that the link can only be expressed *e1 → e2*, and that *e2 → e1* has no meaning. There is no way in which the bad harvest could have led to the bad weather. In other words, establishing a causal relation', *e1 → e2*, means demonstrating: 1) that *in the situation concerned* a modification of *e1* would lead to a corresponding modification in *e2*; 2) that the reverse relation *e2 → e1* seems to be either logically impossible (as in the case where *e2* occurs after *e1*) or empirically falsified (such as in the example of the rise in the British population between 1840 and 1870 (*e2*) which was due to an increase in the birth rate (*e1*): it is unlikely that, in this example, *e2* could ever have been the cause of *e1*).

The concept of causality is most often used in a probabilistic way in sociology. When, for example, it is possible to establish a causal relation *e1 → e2* by a range of observations under comparable conditions showing that the appearance of *e1* favours, or makes more likely, the appearance of *e2*. For instance, it is easy to understand that a child brought up in a disadvantaged family situation, where the parents had a limited education, might be less well-prepared for school work than a child coming from an advantaged background. In order to establish a causal relationship, we will try to show that the characteristic 'disadvantaged family background' leads to the appearance of the characteristic 'low educational attainment'. In a case like this we would create a sample of school pupils classified according to the two criteria (disadvantaged/advantaged background, high/low attainment) and examine the distribution of these two characteristics in the sample. A table of the type set out below would be obtained (Table 1). As can be seen, when the pupil comes from an advantaged background, educational attainment is high in 366 out of 600 cases, against 128 out of 400 when family background is disadvantaged. The characteristic *x* is neither the necessary condition of good attainment (32 per cent of pupils from disadvantaged backgrounds show high attainment) or the sufficient condition of high attainment (39 per cent of pupils from advantaged backgrounds do badly). But *y* does appear *more frequently* when *x* is present. The two criteria are statistically linked. It is possible to measure the strength of the link by a number of methods, the simplest being to use what is termed a *regression coefficient* of *x* against *y*. In this method, a statistical index of correlation is calculated by taking the proportion of cases where attainment is high and background is advantaged and subtracting the proportion of cases where attainment is high and background is disadvantaged. Where the total equals 1 correlation is perfect, and we can say that background is the necessary and sufficient condition of high attainment. In this example, the correlation coeffecient is 0.61−0.32=0.29. Thus, an advantaged background favours high attainment. It does not determine it.

Table 1 Relation between social background and educational attainment

	Family background		
	Advantaged (X)	Disadvantaged (−X)	Total
Attainment			
High (Y)	366	128	494
Low (−Y)	234	272	506
Total	600	400	1000

Some refinement of the analysis can be introduced. For example, the introduction of new variables (multivariate analysis) allows us to ask questions like 'do high attainment pupils from disadvantaged backgrounds experience more parental attention or pressure? Let us now call advantaged/disadvantaged background $x1$ and $x-1$, define a new variable called strong/weak parental interest in the child's education, $x2$ and $x-2$, and examine the distribution of the sample's characteristics in relation to the three criteria (see Table 2).

Using regression coefficients again, we can see that advantaged families show more frequent interest in the child's schoolwork $[f(x2,x1)=420/600=0.7; p(x2,x-1)=160/400=0.4]$. It is also possible to see that, quite independently of background, the parents' interest is the 'cause' of high attainment $[p(y,x2)=348/580=0.6; p(y,x-2)=84/420=0.2]$. Finally, we can also see that when parents have the same level of interest, attainment is independent of background: whatever the background, the proportion of cases of high attainment is the same.

Table 2 Influence of family background and parental interest on attainment — first type of possible structure

	Family background			
	Privileged (x1)		Underprivileged (x−1)	
	Strong interest (x2)	Weak interest (x−2)	Strong interest (x2)	Weak interest (x−2)
Attainment				
High (Y)	252	36	96	48
Low (−Y)	168	144	64	192
Total	420	180	160	240

Let us imagine that, for the same variables, the results are as follows (see Table 3):

Table 3 Same variables as in Table 2 – second type of possible structure

	Family background			
	Privileged (x1)		Underprivileged (x−2)	
	Strong interest (x2)	Weak interest (x−2)	Strong interest (x2)	Weak interest (x−2)
Attainment				
High (Y)	294	72	80	48
Low (−Y)	126	108	80	192
Total	420	180	160	240

Once again family interest in education depends on family background. Once again, attainment, when all family backgrounds are held constant, depends on interest $(p(y,x2)=374/580=0.64;p(y,x-2)=120/420=0.29)$. But by contrast with the previous case, when the parents have the same level of interest, background remains influential: $p(y,x1,x2)=294/420=0.70;p(y,x-1,x2)=80/160=0.50$. When the level of interest is strong, the proportion of cases of high attainment is 0.7 in privileged families and 0.5 in underprivileged. Thus $p(y,x1,x-2)=72/180=0.4$ and $p(y,x-1x-2)=48/240=0.20$: when interest is weak, the proportion of high attainment is 0.4 in the privileged families and 0.2 in the underprivileged families. Hence in this case background makes interest more or less likely and interest makes high attainment more or less likely. But holding interest constant, background makes higher attainment more likely. More precisely, holding interest constant background is responsible for an increase in the proportion of cases of high attainment of the order of 0.2: when interest is strong this proportion goes from 0.5 to 0.7 depending on whether the background is privileged or underprivileged. The analysis can be summarized in the causal schema below:

The arrow going from $x1$ to y indicates that the influence of background on attainment is not extinguished (by contrast with the previous example) by the fact that interest in education may appear more frequently in privileged backgrounds. The relation $x1 \rightarrow y$ may be provisionally interpreted as translating the fact that privileged families tend to ensure better cultural preparation for their offsprings' education. In the previous hypothetical structure the factor $x1$ appeared to have no effect on attainment.

Finally, we will consider a third hypothetical distribution (see Table 4).

Once again, the family's interest in education depends on background, and attainment, all backgrounds constant on interest. It may be immediately seen that,

Table 4 Same variables as in Table 2 – third type of possible structure

	Family background			
	Privileged (x1)		Underprivileged (x−1)	
	Strong interest (x2)	Weak interest (x−2)	Strong interest (x2)	Weak interest (x−2)
Attainment				
High (Y)	336	54	80	48
Low (−Y)	84	126	80	192
Total	420	180	160	240

by contrast with the first example, for a given level of interest, background exercises an effect on attainment. Thus if interest is strong, the proportion of cases of high attainment is respectively equal to 0.8 and to 0.5, depending on whether background is privileged (*x1*) or underprivileged (*x−1*). In comparing the two proportions, it may be seen that, when interest is strong, background is responsible for an increase in high attainment equal to 0.8−0.5=0.3. If we consider the case where interest is weak, the proportion of high attainment cases is 0.3 and 0.2 depending on whether background is privileged (*x1*) or underprivileged (*x−1*). This time background is responsible for an increase in the rate of high attainment equal to 0.3−0.2=0.1. In the case of this structure, which is differentiated on this point from the earlier one, background exerts an influence on attainment at similar levels of interest, but this influence is stronger when interest is strong. The intensity of influence of background on attainment thus depends on interest, while in the previous case it was independent. Moreover it is easy to see that the intensity of the influence of interest on attainment is dependent on background: it is equal to 0.5 when the background is privileged (*x1*) and to 0.3 when the background is underprivileged (*x−1*). To express the difference from the previous case in another way: *x1* has an influence on *y*, *x2* has an influence on *y*, but, on the other hand, *x2* reinforces the influence of *x1* on *y* and *x1* the influence of *x2* on *y*. Family interest stimulates the child, the cultural level of the family helps preparation for school, but interest has a greater influence when cultural preparation is better and cultural preparation has a greater effect when interest is greater. This structure can be summarized in the schema below which indicates the effect (termed the interaction effect) of the combination of *x1* and *x2* on *y*.

The examples above show in an 'intuitive' way the methods of 'causal' analysis in sociology. In these examples, a variable *y*, whose 'causes' are being sought, has been considered to be 'dependent' (in this case, educational attainment which has been reduced to two categories: high and low). Then the hypothesis was advanced that this variable is influenced by other variables which are termed 'independent', in the example, *x1* and *x2*. But these variables are themselves interlinked. Thus, in the three examples, *x1* influences *x2*. The problem of causal analysis consists of 1) determining the network of causal relationships underlying the 'independent' variables and the 'dependent' variable; 2) measuring the strength of the relationship linking pairs of variables. Thus, in the first example, there is a network of two relationships: *x1−x2*, and *x2−y*. It is possible to measure the strength of the influence *x1−x2* for example via the amount *p(x2, x1)−p(x2, x−1)* and the influence of *x2* on *y* by the difference *p(y,x2)−p(y,x−2)*. In the second example, there is a network of three relations *x1→x2*, *x1→y*, and *x2→y*. It is possible to measure the intensity of the influences on these relations by $p(x2,x1)-p(x2,x-1)$, etc. However, there is a complication here because $x1$ has a direct influence on y and an indirect influence which results from the two relations $x1 \rightarrow x2$, and $x2 \rightarrow y$. In the third case, the problems of measurement are more complex. It is impossible to describe *the* influence of $x2$ on y because it differs according to its sub-populations $x1$ or $x-1$. When there is an interaction between two independent variables there is no sense in comparing their respective influences on the dependent variable. (To take another example which has been the point of much bitter and ultimately pointless discussion: the existence of interactions between environmental and genetic factors on a dependent variable, for example, test performances, makes it definitively impossible to measure *the* respective influence of these two types of factors.)

In the earlier examples, dichotomous variables were considered – those defined by two categories; of course other types of variables could be used. More than the three covered above are easily conceivable. There are also other types of causal analysis, far less boring than those discussed up to now. There are many specialist technical studies of causal analysis and its statistical measurement, to which the reader is referred in the bibliography.

But it is important to be wary of automatic methods. Causal analysis is useful to the sociologist only when he can *understand* the results, in the Weberian sense of the term. That is to say, when he can recover the logic of the behaviours responsible for the causal relations. In the hypothetical examples given above the network of relationships is just about intelligible. It would be easy to imagine elementary processes responsible for the same influences as were observed. In fact it is very likely that in the case used above it would be possible to find a structure of the second or third type: the ambition nourished by the parents concerning the child's education and the cultural level of the family each play their part in the attainment level. A mutual reinforcement effect (interaction) between the two factors could easily be observed in a concrete situation. On the other hand, if a structure of the second or third type was observed between the variables described above, it could easily be understood and interpreted. But of course such a situation almost never occurs in attempts to understand the complexity of real social contexts. Thus it would be useless or at least insufficient to research the causal links between a group of variables $x1, x2, \ldots y$, and to measure the influences corresponding to the relations $xi \rightarrow xj$, if we are incapable of formulating precise hypotheses on the processes underlying these relationships, or to decide between hypotheses which are ultimately contradictory. What is true of complex networks of relationships is also true of simple correlations. Certain sociologists of crime have tried to prove the dissuasive influence of prison sentences by showing that there is a negative correlation between the severity of prison sentences and the frequency of certain types of crimes: the more severe the penalty the fewer the crimes. But even such apparently simple correlations are hard to interpret. The penalty may reduce the frequency of the crime or it may be a result of other factors in the judicial system, where the overcrowding of prisons may be proportional to the frequency of crimes, which may lead courts to hand out shorter sentences. As long as the ambiguity remains, the existence of the correlation is a datum which has little interest for the sociologist. *A fortiori* it is unnecessary to measure its strength.

One method for reducing ambiguities in relation to causality is the *panel* method, which consists of repeated observations over a certain period. Applied to the problem described above, it would consist of the observation of the two variables, penalties and incidence of crimes, at regular intervals and to see whether there is any variation in the incidence of crimes in t according to the severity of sentences in $t-1$. The problem comes back in the end to the analysis of a network of causal relationships between $2n$ variables if the frequency of crimes and the severity of sentences are observed at n points in time.

But the interpretation of a causal relation can be satisfying only when it is shown to be the consequence of 'meaningful' microsociological behaviours, in Weber's sense. In certain cases these behaviours can be easily understood (thus the simple hypotheses on the behaviour of economic actors which explain why a bad harvest is usually followed by price rises). In other cases, the analysis of microsociological behaviour is more complex.

In general terms causal analysis rests on a paradigm: it supposes that the phenomenon that is to be explained is the result of a certain number of causes. This approach is sometimes appropriate. The demographic evolution of a population depends on its birth and death rates, and as a result the causes which influence these rates. It is important to note, however, that in cases such as these analysis is frequently complicated by the presence of phenomena of circular causality: the growth of the population may in certain cases (e.g., in highly urbanized societies), create conditions of overcrowding which influence the birth rate and thus the growth of the population. The presence of circular causality does not prevent the use of methods of causal analysis: as has been seen, by using repeated observations over a period of time, it is possible to substitute the circular relation $x \rightarrow y$ by the non-circular relations $xt \rightarrow yt+1 \rightarrow xt+2-yt+3$. But it is possible to go further and ask if the causal language itself is always appropriate. Let us take a simple example. In his widely discredited book on *Inequality in America*, Jencks attempts to show that, contrary to certain assumptions, the 'intelligence' level has a slight influence on social status, even in a society like that of America, where academic qualifications play an important role in the mechanism of the job market. He explains this result by arguing that social status is a complex result of a group of causes (intelligence level, chance, 'relations', but also psychological variables – ambition, for example). Certain of these variables, such as intelligence, are apparently easily observed. The others are less easily accessible. Their influence can only be measured, if at all, on some global level, by differences with the influences of observed variables, such as intelligence. In fact it may not be right to conceive of social status as the result of a group of causes which either add to it or detract from it. To make concrete this proposition, consider an example. Let us imagine that at a given moment 400 and 600 persons appear on the job market with, respectively, high and low intelligence levels, and that there are 200 high status jobs and 800 low status jobs available. In this case, even if the intelligence level is hypothetically the key criterion of social status, those with high intelligence have only a 1 in 2 chance of obtaining a high status job. The influence of intelligence on status measured by coefficient of regression will thus be 200/400—0/600=0.5. The weakness of the correlation is due not to causes which are difficult to observe but to structural conditions which govern the job market. If the structural conditions were other than that, the influence of intelligence level on status could be greater, even in the case where intelligence played less of a role in the attribution of status. In such a case *the 'dependent' variable* – social status – *cannot be expressed as a simple function of other variables characterizing the individuals observed.* It is in fact a complicated function of a variable (intelligence level) and of two distributions (distributions of intelligence levels and statuses). It is difficult to speak of 'causes' of the attribution of status in such a case.

To summarize, statistical methods of causal analysis are all founded on a paradigm which consists of *designating a dependent variable, as a function which is more or less simple but easily expressible in a mathematical language of a certain number of variables* (themselves ultimately simple functions of other variables). This paradigm is often useful. But it would be inappropriate to accord it too general a remit. The appearance of a relation between two variables is always the result of the behaviour of actors acting in systems of interaction with a given structure. But if there is no problem in unpacking the relationship between bad harvest and price increase and no difficulty in declaring that the first is the cause of the second, it is much more difficult to explain a relation such as that which appeared between educational level and social status, and dangerous to see in the first variable one of the causes (among others) of the second. This form of expression implies that a group of individual variables $x1,\ldots xn$ exists which are linked by a simple function – linear, for example – which, if they were all observable, would enable exact prediction of status.

The remarks above which apply to the statistical analysis of causality, also apply to what is sometimes referred to as the *singular* analysis of causality: to research the 'causes' of an event, to conceptualize it as the result of a group of causes or factors is to start off by adopting a paradigm which may be unnecessarily rigid. This paradigm is adequate for simple events (a fire was the cause of a panic), but less useful for more complex events. It is perilous to talk about the 'causes' of the First World War. Trevor-Roper has shown that the causal link which Weber thought he had established between Protestantism and capitalism summarized in a rather doubtful way a complex process which can only be understood by analysis of the behaviour of multiple categories of actors (intellectual, political, ecclesiastical, economic, élites) situated in changing systems of interaction.

To summarize, the explanation of a state of affairs e can only be treated as causal propositions of the type, $a, b, \ldots, \rightarrow e$ (singular causality) or the explanation of a variable y by functions $y=f(x1, x2, \ldots, xn)$ of a simple (for example linear) form, in cases which, even if they may frequently occur, are none the less specific. If we try to learn the epistemological lesson provided by social science practice, the concept of cause appears less contestable in principle than philosophers of science would think and less universal in its applicability than sociologists or historians frequently suppose.

Action, Determinism, Experimentation, History and Sociology, Theory, Weber.

Bibliography

ALKER, H., *Mathematics and politics*, New York/London, Macmillan, 1965. — BLALOCK, H.M. Jr., *Causal inferences in non-experimental research*, Chapel Hill, University of North Carolina Press, 1964. — BLALOCK, H.M., AGANBEGIAN, A., BORODKIN, F.M., BOUDON, R., CAPECCHI, V. (ed.), 'Causal analysis, structure, and change', *in* BLALOCK, H.M., AGANBEGIAN, A., BORODKIN, F.M., BOUDON, R., CAPECCHI, V. (ed.), *Quantitative sociology. International perspectives on mathematical and statistical modeling*, New York/London Academic Press, 1975, 1-258; BLALOCK, H.M. Jr. and BLALOCK, A. (ed.), *Methodology in social research*, New York/London, McGraw-Hill, 1968. — COLEMAN, J.S., *Introduction to mathematical sociology*, Glencoe, The Free Press, 1964; London, Collier Macmillan, 1964. — DOGAN, M. and ROKKAN, S., *Quantitative ecological analysis in the social sciences*, Cambridge, MIT Press, 1969. — GOLDBERGER, A.S., and DUNCAN, O.D. (ed.), *Structural equation models in the social sciences*, New York/London, Academic Press, 1973. — GOODMAN, L.A., 'A brief guide to the causal analysis of data from surveys', *American journal of sociology*, LXXXIV, *5, 1979, 1078-1095.* — GRANGER, G.G., 'L'explication dans les sciences sociales', *Information sur les sciences sociales*, X, 2, 1971, 31–44. — LAZARSFELD, P.F., 'Interpretation of statistical relations as a research operation', *in* LAZARSFELD, P.F. and ROSENBERG, M. (ed.), *The language of social research. A reader in the methodology of social research*, Glencoe, The Free Press, 1955, 1962, 115–125. — LAZARSFELD, P.F., PASANELLA, A.K., ROSENBERG, M., *Continuities in the language of social research*, New York, The Free Press/London, Collier Macmillan, 1972. — MALINVAUD, E., *Méthodes statistiques de l'économétrie*, Paris, Dunod, 1964; Paris, Bordas, 1978. — SIMON, H.A., 'Causal ordering and identifiability', *in* HOOD, W.C. and KOOPMANS, T.C. (ed.), *Studies in econometric method*, New York, Wiley, 1953, 49–74 *in* SIMON, H.A., *Models of man. Social and rational. Mathematical essays on rational human behavior in a social setting*, New York, Wiley/London, Chapman & Hall, 1957, 10–36, and *in* LERNER, D. (ed.), *Cause and effect*, New York, The Free Press, 1965, 157–189 London, Collier Macmillan, 1965. 'Spurious correlation: a causal interpretation', *Journal of the American statistical association*, XLIX, *267*, 1954, 467–479. — SIMON, H.A., *Models of man. Social and rational. Mathematical essays on rational human behaviour in a social setting*, New York, Wiley/London, Chapman & Hall, 1957, 37–50; 'On the definition of the causal relation', *Journal of philosophy*, XLIX, *16*, 1952, 517–528 *in* SIMON, H.A., *Models of man. Social and rational. Mathematical essays on rational human behavior in a social setting*, New York, Wiley/London, Chapman & Hall, 1957, 50–61. — WEBER, M., *The Methodology of the Social Sciences*, Free Press, New York, 1949.

Charisma

The term charisma was popularized by Max Weber. Initially, he used the word charisma in its rather technical meaning, as given to it by religious historians. Charisma is the charm or gift which attaches itself to certain figures in the sight of and chosen by God. Such persons are vested with a *power* (*pouvoir*) which is clearly very different to the power surrounding rational-legal bureaucracy or that accorded to a traditional monarch succeeding through primogeniture.

Charismatic power is marked out by its 'extraordinary, superhuman, and supernatural' character. The person who possesses it is an 'envoy of God', a hero – a 'mighty warrior', or a leader (*Führer*). What characterizes the charismatic leader is not so much what he does as the way in which it is carried out – his style. In addition, charismatic phenomena can be properly dealt with only by a value-free sociology. Even if, in terms of his own values or in the light of well-founded predictions, the sociologist is led to condemn it as criminal or absurd, the programme of the charismatic leader should be understood as an original type of action, having its own logic and capable of being embodied in an institutionally *legitimate* system, notwithstanding the typical problems posed by such institutionalization.

This feature of the notion of charisma – on which Max Weber was most insistent – is the most often neglected in its current usage. It is often said that a 'like-able' and 'charming' (in the ordinary sense of this term) person has charisma. In everyday language charisma, popularity, attractive personality are treated as synonyms. Yet these terms are separated by differences of meaning which for good reasons should be maintained. A popular, pleasant individual – even one who is continually in our thoughts – is not necessarily someone with whom we would share the most personal of commitments. In the case of a popular person, we would not be ready to let him decide our course of action in our place. Such a person is popular in most cases because he *demands* nothing from us – which is not at all the case with the charismatic leader, who on the contrary is a very demand-ing master, as is clearly suggested in Jesus's injunction to the rich young man: 'sell all your possessions and follow me'. To this rather negative qualification another more positive qualification can be added: the individual for whom we have a liking is popular because he has an affinity with us (he is 'one of the boys') and because he reflects a favourable image of ourselves with which we feel capable of identifying without having to haul ourselves up to the ideal of an inaccessible model. This is a situation clearly very different to the *distance* maintained by the charismatic figure from his disciples and his lieutenants, as exemplified by John the Baptist's remark-ing of Jesus that 'I am unworthy to unloosen his shoes'.

Charisma is no more reducible to pure *suggestion* than it is to *popularity*. It is true that it can often be associated with demonstrations of enthusiasm, with trance-like states such as described by Gustave Le Bon in his *Psychology of the Crowd*. Prophets, demagogues, 'mighty warriors', appear to take possession of their audience, to substitute their own wills for those of their disciples and followers. But even supposing that the enthusiasm which takes over the disciples during such a 'great mass' may be to a certain extent forced, simulated, or feigned, it is hardly reason-able to reduce the *conversion* of the disciple to a sort of bewitchment produced by the infection of strong feelings. That would be to go back to the old Voltairean prejudice which deliberately confuses the prophet with the con-man and the faith of disciples with ignorance and stupidity.

It is true that charisma is connected with exuberant symbolism. The peremp-tory character of the charismatic message ('sell your possessions and follow me') or, by contrast, its deliberately sensible and concrete nature ('the land of milk and honey') is based on the more or less suspect use of the imaginary. But charismatic metaphors are not the product of an unrestrained imagination. They are guided by a more or less conventional rhetoric, through which the charismatic figure seeks to safeguard his role, and which nourishes the faith of his disciples. In the process of *certification* which establishes the charismatic figure, a form of social make-believe is resorted to which, if not always unique, is sometimes decisive. Certainly, success of a *miraculous* nature bolsters the prestige of the charismatic leader. It helps to persuade the disciples that his *programme* – to which he demands that they devote themselves entirely – is not a chimera, that in a certain sense the Kingdom is of this world.

Charisma may be defined as a highly asymmetric power-relationship between an inspired guide and a cohort of followers who see in him and his message the

promise and anticipated achievements of a new order, to which all adhere with
greater or lesser conviction. For the charismatic leader, the message is a vocation.
This message is not simply the description of a possible or desirable order. It is an
injunction to devote himself – ultimately with fanaticism – to its realization. His
legitimacy, affirmed subjectively to himself and others, is something tested not
merely as a belief but also as a matter of urgency. *Ich kann nicht anders*, as Luther
said to the ecclesiastical judges: 'I can neither think nor do otherwise.' In addition,
the relationship of the charismatic leader with his disciples is not at all of the same
order as that which unites the democratic leader with his electorate or the sociometric 'star' with his peers. In both these cases, the leader wants to be recognized
as more visible, more sought after, and more appreciated than anyone else. By
contrast with the popular politician or the sociometric 'star', the charismatic leader
does not derive his legitimacy from the favourable opinion others have of him, but
from the vocation to which he has devoted himself. To a certain extent he is
completely independent. In the last analysis he has neither predecessor nor successor.

Charismatic power is thus personal power. It will often also appear to be arbitrary to those who escape or resist its attraction. Faced with a leader whose
charisma we do not recognize, we are likely to take an attitude which is not indifferent but hostile or contemptuous: he is a con-man or crank. In order to authen-
ticate his call, the charismatic leader has no alternative but to insist on the
radically personal nature of his message. 'The Pharisees and the High Priests
speak . . . but I say unto you . . . etc.'. The charismatic leader seeks to legitimize
himself by opposing tradition, or at least by opposing a *certain* tradition. Max
Weber observed that while the Jewish prophets attacked the established order and
announced its overthrow they also declared their humble allegiance to the law.
They were thus led to distinguish between a compromised tradition which they
denounced and a living tradition, associated with the word of God, with which
they identified themselves. Ultimately, what authenticates the prophet's message is
his conformity to the law, his submission to the word of God.

The extreme personalization of charismatic power makes its institutionalization
problematic. Three conditions at least must be fulfilled in order to institutionalize
or legitimize charismatic power. First, it is necessary that a relatively stable hierarchy is established in the 'emotional community', as Max Weber puts it. Now the
charismatic leader occupies a quite central position in such a group. Relations
between members of the community are mediated through him. As a result, free
and direct (if not exclusive) access to the leader is highly valued by his lieutenants.
His favour becomes the prize in a competition which he has great difficulty in
controlling. Since everyone's status in the group depends on his intimacy with the
leader, there is a resultant risk of meteoric promotions or crashing downfalls, of
purges which may sometimes be bloody, and of consecrations which are often
ephemeral. Such unpredictability has its echoes in the totally irregular manner by
which the 'emotional community' provides for its own maintenance and subsistence. The Gospels, for example, display in several places a calm disdain for the
requirements of the domestic economy. The 'emotional community' has as much

difficulty in organizing its adaptive relations with its external environment as it has in establishing stable relationships among its members. In the end, because it is built around a charismatic leader, his disappearance threatens it with the gravest of crises. A variety of measures can be envisaged which tend to reduce this danger. But the death of the 'founding father' always means for the 'emotional community' either the normalization (in Weber's terminology, *routinization*) of the charisma from which it originated or a more or less extreme crisis which is liable to end up in a new charismatic upheaval.

What types of groupings are likely to form themselves into 'emotional communities'? In this context it is possible to distinguish three principal situations. Giving the word its widest sense, the religious sect constitutes the first type of environment which is favourable to the growth of charisma. The issues around which sects tend to crystallize touch upon the most general problems of the human condition, with the most fundamental meanings which we attach to life, death, sickness, and suffering – what Max Weber called *theoridies* or problems of meaning (*Sinngebung*). Those political parties which constitute 'secular religions' in Raymond Aron's sense – a term which applies only to those which propose explicitly and deliberately and in the most fundamental of senses to 'change the conditions of existence' – come close to the great sectarian programmes, if not in their structures at least in their ambitions. But while they were characteristic of the large totalitarian parties of the first half of the twentieth century, the 'emotional communities' are more likely to thrive today in the marginal or breakaway organizations which claim to represent the pinnacle of morality and devote themselves to achieving progress towards certain objectives to which they are attached with a fundamental conviction. Moreover, such 'ghettos' or groupuscules can be seen as expressions of secular religiosity, although they are not at all hierarchical or totalitarian like the Hitlerian or Stalinist parties.

All 'emotional communities' raise questions about their own *authenticity*. How sincere is the attachment of the charismatic leader and his disciples to the movement with which they declare themselves to be identified? In this respect concern about deception, the traditional rationalist suspicion about charisma, is a precondition which still retains all its relevance. Second, we should ask ourselves what the 'emotional community' can teach us about the state of society: is it a limited rebellion which is doomed to collapse and which, even when it produces major disturbances, leaves the normative system intact? Finally, the predictive value of the emergence of certain types of charismatic movement for understanding the future state of society poses questions about the relationships between charisma and different forms of social movement.

Authority, Minorities, Power, Prophetism, Religion, Weber.

Bibliography

ARON, R., *L'âge des empires et l'avenir de la France*, Paris, Ed. de la Défense de la France, 1945, 1946. – EISENSTADT, S.N., *Max Weber on charisma and institution building, Selected papers*, Chicago, The Univ. of Chicago Press, 1968. – LE BON, G., *Psychologie des foules*, Paris, F. Alcan, 1895; Paris, Retz, CEPL, 1975. – OTTO, R., *Das Heilige. Ueber das Irrationale in der Idee des Göttlichen und sein Verhältnis zum Rationalen,*

Breslau, Trewendt & Granier, 1920. Trans.: *The idea of the holy: an inquiry into the non-rational factor in the idea of the divine and its relation to the rational*, Oxford Univ. Press, 1950, 1967. – SCHOLEM, G.G., *The messianic ideology in Judaism and other essays in Jewish spirituality*, New York, Schoken Books, 1971, 1974. – SHILS, E., 'The concentration and dispersion of charisma: their bearing on economic policy in under-developed countries', *World Politics*, 1958, *11*, 1–19; 'Charisma, order and status', *American Sociological Review*, 1965, *30*, 199–213. – WEBER, M., *The Methodology of the Social Sciences, Economy and Society*, London, Owen, 1962.

Community

That all members of society possess something in common is a vague idea, which can be used in many contexts through analogies. Members of society are like a large family – they are descended from the same Father, they live the same sort of life, they are like the parts of a body. It is Aristotle who, in connection with what he holds as the model of political organization – the city, while speaking about the community, uses the term in a technical sense for the first time. He shows how this concept links with that of *totality*, and reproaches Plato for having taken them both in a *realist* sense, as if the link which assures a number of individuals of their unity is a thing or a substance and not a system of attributes and relations.

Unfortunately, sociologists have often lost sight of this precious criticism; and when the term community comes into the technical vocabulary of sociology, in the title of Tönnies' famous book, it is condemned to be found lastingly associated with the most awkward confusions. To characterize the classic, if not vulgar, conception of community, we shall point out some features borrowed from Tönnies. For him, community is opposed to society, as if men could establish their relationships only in two types of situation. To *society* (*Gesellschaft*) based on the strict individuality of interests, which suggests the Hobbesian conception of the conflict of all against all, is opposed *community* (*Gemeinschaft*) established through the substantial, but often unconscious identity of wills which derives from sharing the same origin and the same destiny. This romantic antithesis between 'the icy waters of selfish motives', to echo the *Communist Manifesto*, and the warmth of the primary group, where social relations are personalized, assumes historicist and evolutionist tinges. The community is the good old days, this world we have lost (Peter Laslett) of which we have been deprived by machines, money, profit. Society is the future promised us by big industry, production, and 'mass' consumption. Thus under-stood, the society-community opposition acquires an evident ideological con-notation. It is true that it cannot be reduced to the capitalism-socialism opposition, except at the price of a caricatural simplification. Politically, it is 'over-determined', since the 'community' in the manner of Tönnies can feed reactionary dreams about the pre-industrial order, as do the socialist utopias about a classless society.

Once rid of its ideological connotations, Tönnies' theory is reduced to a list of groupings where community relations would be predominant, and consequently to an interpretation, open to critique, of the functioning of these groupings. These refer to family community, territorial or residential community, linguistic community. Anthropologists, such as Redfield, have recognized in Indian villages of Mexico, Guatemala, or the Andes, communal units where the pre-Columbian culture would have survived as in a kind of glasshouse, although dominated and marginalized by the colonial society. Redfield does not borrow these views only from Tönnies, but also from the Durkheimian conception of a segmented society unified by the constraints of mechanical solidarity. As to the nature of the integration prevailing in the segmented societies or the village communities, it would be caused by very complex historical processes, through which local 'cultures' have been exposed to the shock of violent and dominating imperialisms. For the colonized populations, the village community has constituted at the same time a ghetto, a kind of shelter, and refuge. Therefore it is not possible to build up an adequate theory of community on the experience of groupings such as village communities.

It would be no more rational to elaborate on the notion of community in the case of the family community or the political community. Aristotle had very well perceived that what the members of a family have in common is not of the same nature as what the citizens of a republic have in common. Moreover, relations between parents and children, husband and wife, brothers and sisters often reveal something quite different from the imminent identity of individual wills. By making the family a community, one refuses to see that familial sociability is an 'emerging effect', caused, as Freud has understood it well (*Totem and Taboo, Group Psychology and the Analysis of the Ego*), by compromises between wills at first opposed, which accept submission to the same law once everyone has learnt there is no chance of subjecting all the others to one's own law. It is possible to refer to blood community between parents and children; but between spouses it is a matter of *alliance*, whether the spouses choose each other or they belong to groups linked by connections of matrimonial exchange.

The community does not constitute a primitive and simple social relation. It is complex, since it associates in a very fragile way heterogeneous feelings and attitudes; it is learnt, as it is only through a socialization process, which, strictly, is never completed, that we learn to take part in interdependent communities. It is never pure, since communal links are associated with situations of calculation, conflict, or even violence. That is why it seems preferable to refer to 'communalization' (*Vergemeinschaftung*) rather than community, and to find out how some 'diffuse solidarities' are constituted and maintained.

One area where the process of communalization is best perceived is the 'emotional community' (*Gemeinde*), which is so important in Weber's religious sociology. The congregation around an exemplary prophet (ascetic or guru), or again around an ethical one – who announces God's worst punishments if the most sacred rights and duties keep on being violated by an unfaithful people, weaves a network of very strong relations among those receiving this message and following this inspiration. Jesus's disciples and Buddha's form communities – or, as Weber says using a neologism stressing the dynamic aspect of this process, a *communalization*. The regrouping of the faithful in closed units of monks subject to the discipline of a closed order or on the contrary in the dispersal of hermits in the desert, not to mention the begging bonzes of the Buddhist tradition or the girovagues denounced in the Benedictine rule, shows the multiplicity of forms which may be taken by the religious communities' organization. Similarly, then, this organization is part of a process of education, through which the prophet's or guru's pupils or disciples can in turn become masters, miracle workers ('mystagogues', in Weber's term), and sources of inspiration for a wider and wider lay public. It can lead to very diverse institutional forms, which go from the closed and more intolerant sect to the congregation and parish, or even to the bureaucratic hierarchy characterized by the modern papacy.

Religious communalization is thus inseparable from a double process of organization. By organization, we mean a more or less marked distinction between the 'soul healing' virtuosos and the various publics with more or less differentiated salvation needs. By institutionalization, we refer to the elaboration of a legitimacy of rites and beliefs which make the faithful members of a same 'family'. Therefore, communalization is no more a blind and instinctive process than the community is an undifferentiated magma.

Max Weber's analysis will be useful to us on a second point. Far from affecting only the area of relations characterized chiefly by the affective, the imaginary, or the spiritual (meant in the vague term of religious spirituality) it applies too to the economic order – and this in two ways. First, many communities – or communalizations – have some economic aspects, either because they explicitly aim for strictly economic objectives, or, while not doing so, they are however subjected to an economic constraint of solvency. Second, there are economic groups which are communities in the full meaning of the term. The fact that the family is a production unit, that in our own societies, as a household, it forms a consumption unit, that its members are nearly everywhere interested in the transmission of a patrimony, attests that its functioning can and must, partially at least, be analysed from an economic point of view. Now, family groups can be described as communities for at least two reasons. First, their members show some solidarity vis-à-vis the outside world, partly because of their common status – the family is collectively given a position on the stratification ladder the more univocally as family unity is more clearly bound. Second, the members of a family enjoy a certain number of possessions, goods, and services which are, in the economic sense of the term, indivisible. They live in the same house, and, insofar as they share meals, take holidays together, they are engaged in a system of collective consumption. One must add that economic groups such as enterprises, where the requirements of industrial discipline, the search for profit, create conditions favourable to the proliferation of very keen conflicts between leaders and executants, capitalists and salaried workers, these constitute communities too, although in a very ambiguous and narrow sense – in so far as the survival of the enterprise forms a common aim for all the personnel's categories. When the survival of a group becomes for its members an objective opposed in their eyes to the individual objectives which they feel they have the right to pursue, one can say this group constitutes a community, or is in the process of communalization.

By observing the scientific community, one can perceive the nature of the objectives that some communities propose to or impose on their members. This not only influences the increase or the diffusion of knowledge. It is also based not only on a value system but on a deontology. It states certain rules or procedures which it enforces if necessary with possibly very forceful sanctions. Whoever plagiarizes his colleagues without naming them, whoever 'fiddles' his data takes the risk of being excluded from the 'Scientists' Republic'. The condition of admission – and correlatively the exclusion risks – make these communities relatively closed groups, as their members must pass a probation period before admission and can be ostracized if they did not conform to certain ethics. On the contrary, territorial communities are, or rather have become, thoroughfares or transit places, containers where anonymous people are in transit; they tend to become the emptiest form of coexistence. Yet even in this case, the community is something other than an ecological niche. Coexistence can become unbearable with neighbours whose contiguity alone is a 'nuisance'. Migrations, more or less costly, lead to the reconstruction of communities easier to live in – and livelier. In an aphorism which suggests the Weberian concept of 'elective affinity', according to Goethe, coexistence alone is not enough to define the community. One must add two more features. Lazarsfeld and Merton talk of homophily to designate a community of interests and tastes which goes beyond adhesion to common values. To be a community, the members of the group must also care for what they profess to be their common tastes and interests, accept to participate in its management, by sacrificing some of their time and resources. The community implies directly or indirectly a minimal participation in the communal business. That is why a 'dormitory town' cannot, unless by mistake or misuse, be called a 'community'.

We still need to know what are the bases of homophily and participation. To render an account of the force of the 'primary group', Shils insists on the presence of three main elements. There must be first a network of interpersonal interactions showing both resilience and plasticity. There must be also some 'sacred ties' which may be the object of symbolic identifications. Finally, the group must fit smoothly into the society at large in which it is enveloped. Under these conditions, each of these groups will be able to form a community, without the ensemble itself – society – being, so to speak, 'communalized'.

Alienation, Development, Durkheim, Rousseau, Utopia, Weber.

Bibliography

ARISTOTLE, *The Politics*, Harmondsworth, Penguin, 1957. – DURKHEIM, E., *The Division of Labour in Society*, op cit. – FREUD, S., *Totem und Tabu*, Leipzig, Vienna, H. Heller, 1913. *Massenpsychologie und Ich-Analyse*, Leipzig, Internationaler psychoanalytischer Verlag, 1921. – FRIEDRICH, C.J., 'The concept of community in the history of political and legal philosophy', in FRIEDRICH, C.J. (ed.), *Community*, New York. Liberal Arts Press, 1959, 3–25. – LASLETT, P., *The world we have lost*, London, Methuen, 1965, 1971. – LAZERSFELD, P. and MERTON, R.K., 'Friendship as a social process', in GOULDNER, A.W., *Studies in leadership: leadership and democratic action*, New York, Russell & Russell, 1965. – POLSBY, N.W., 'The sociology of community power: a reassessment', *Social Forces*, 1959, *37*, 232–236. – REDFIELD, R., *The little community and peasant society and culture*, Chicago, Univ. of Chicago Press, 1960. – ROSSI, P.H., 'Power and community structure', *Mid-west Journal of Political Science*, 1960, 4, 390–401. – SCHULZE,

R.O., 'The bifurcation of power in a satellite city', in JANOWITZ, M. (ed.). *Community political systems*, New York, Free Press, 1961. – SHILS, E.A. and JANOWITZ, M. 'Cohesion and disintegration in the Wehrmacht in World War II', *The Public Opinion Quarterly*, 1948, XII, 280–315. – TÖNNIES, F., *Gemeinschaft und Gesellschaft*, Leipzig, R. Reisland, 1887. – VIDICH, A.J. and BENSMAN, J., *Small town in mass society: class, power and religion in a rural community*, Princeton Univ. Press, 1968. – WEBER, M., *Economy et society*, op cit. Part II, chap. 3. – WIRTH L., *The Ghetto*, Univ. of Chicago Press, 1928, 1956.

Comte, Auguste

Comte (1798–1857) is acclaimed as the 'founder of sociology'. It is true that he invented the word. But does his work constitute one of the 'epistemological breaks' from which can be dated the birth of a discipline or of a completely original way of thinking about social facts? There are indeed scientific revolutions (Kuhn), but it is less sure that there are such discontinuities in the history of social science. In any case, the insistence on making Comte the founder of sociology is bound to arouse suspicion. By establishing themselves as the descendants of Comte are sociologists not refusing above all to regard themselves as the children of the Enlightenment and the contractualist tradition? In fact, the debates on the '*coupure*' (break/break-through) are pleas for affiliation: to cite Comte as the great ancestor means above all that one challenges the Hobbes-Locke-Rousseau descent.

Comte could lay claim to a dual merit. He could have discovered the specificity of the social; he could have established the supremacy of sociology over all other branches of knowledge. As to the specificity of the social, he illuminates it by the importance he gives to the notion of *consensus*. It is true that he borrows the concept from biology, but he transforms it fundamentally. Compared with biological philosophy, consensus is understood as the *agreement* between the different organs which form the human being, and also as the relationship between the latter and his environment or, as Auguste Comte says, his '*conditions d'existence*'. When one goes from biology to society, consensus, while retaining features acknowledged by biological philosophy, acquires radically new ones.

First, social consensus is based on common ideas and beliefs. Durkheim will define it later as a 'collective conscience'. Second, social consensus is not a phenomenon happening by itself, like the biological equilibria which condition our survival and of which we are not conscious. Comte compares it with the principle of *social cohesion*, which he names 'government' and which would be described in modern vocabulary as 'cybernetics'. In Comte's work, 'government' is not reduced to politico-administrative activities dealt with by publicists and constitutionalists. It is a completely general function through which the diversity of interests and opinions is made compatible with the demands of 'co-operation' (a term Comte prefers to 'division of labour' inherited from Adam Smith, where the social dimension would not be marked sufficiently). The governmental function is practised both as a temporal power and a spiritual one. *Social consensus* which ensures the pre-eminence of the 'whole over the parts' uses both the means of physical constraint and those of moral education – in the wider sense that Durkheim will later give this term

The Comtean conception of social order is on many points a precursor of that developed by Durkheim. Both conceptions are characterized by an orientation Piaget calls '*le realisme totalitaire*'. Society is presented as a 'whole', or a self-constituting (autonomous) system whose life and survival, up to a point, would not owe anything to the intentions and strategies of actors and to the comprehension these actors have of their intentions and strategies. What is neglected by sociology, and what is so opportunely asserted in the contractualist tradition, although Comte pretends to believe that it knows only selfish individuals, is the *problematic* character of consensus. Comte repeats after Aristotle that the social state is the *natural* state of man. But this pun makes him disregard what Hobbes and Rousseau had each well perceived in his own way: social order is not a *given* such as the order which governs the relationships of one living species with its living conditions.

About the place of sociology within the system of the sciences, Comte developed views which could not help but seduce sociologists. But they face two series of difficulties. First, they are based on a conception of science which arguably lays stress on the rigour which would preside over scientific development. Moreover, they imply a fixed hierarchy of the various phases through which human development is expressed, and subordinate them all to the development of scientific ideas. The *loi de trois états* (law of the three stages) renders an account of the passage which would lead human knowledge and institutions from the theological age to the positive age going through the 'metaphysical transition'. In a strict sense, the law of the three stages cannot be described as evolutionist. Comte never fails to stress that progress is only the development of order. History is only the actualization of invariant traits written in human nature, which evolve without transforming – '*evolue sans se transformer*'. But development is subject to *laws*, and it is the first task of sociology to establish these laws. Combined with the idea that humanity 'constitutes an immense and unique social unity', the law of the three stages leads Auguste Comte to make progress a march toward a fixed conclusion, although never reached, through a series of necessarily determined stages. Against Condorcet and the philosophers of the Enlightenment, Comte holds for the existence of a definite end to the march of humanity. In this respect, one should compare his views to Hegel's on the 'end of history' and to John Stuart Mill's on the 'stationary state'. Moreover, Comte believes in the chain of necessarily determined stages; the result is that the laws of social dynamics can be applied in an identical way to all societies.

Since sociology is the science of social dynamics, in that sense, as it makes clear the actualization of order in progress, it is the queen of sciences. In truth, this primacy must be understood with caution. Auguste Comte holds to a differentiated conception of science. Contrary to what is suggested by a commonplace but false interpretation, there is no unique model of positive knowledge for Auguste Comte. Mathematics and physics are not the only forms of knowledge. In his mind, there is no question of applying to sociology the methods of these sciences. No superstition of the quantitative can be found in his work. Moreover, he challenges the probabilist schemas for the analysis of social facts. He conceptualizes the system of sciences as a progression of disciplines from the most abstract and the most simple knowledge (mathematics and astronomy) towards the most complex and the most concrete (biology and sociology). Each discipline has its own field and, from the simplicity as from the complexity point of view, distinguishes itself as much from its predecessor as from its successor. Therefore, sociology is not a science like geometry. But sociology is the only one able to render an account of the way in which sciences born before it and of which it is the crowning achievement are constituted.

The supremacy of sociology is one of the weakest positivist dogmas. It originates in the search Comte never abandoned, even if he increased his relativist leanings for a science able to 'integrate' human experience in its diverse aspects. This ambition underpins Comte's conception of a system of sciences, the constitution of which provides 'the end point, never before reached', *'le terme defini, quoique jamais atteint'*, of the development of our knowledge. But sociology does not only allow the human mind to reflect on itself and its own movement, by the knowledge of its products and its operations. It also conveys the solution to the crisis of western civilization which concerned Comte right from his early youth. Comte never ceased to consider himself a social reformer. Sociology for him was a kind of positive gospel, which he had been given the mission to preach.

This prophetic obsession is not peculiar to Comte. It can be found in those Marx has called the utopian socialists; and Schumpeter explained the glory of Marx himself at least as much by the vehemence of his prophecies and the intensity of his commitment to the socialist movement as by the quality of his scientific analyses. By a remarkable paradox, Comte has, despite his claim to the pontificate, a conception of social reform which could almost be described as 'cautious'. Comte does not hold the slightest illusion about the subject of social intervention. Social facts being the most complex of all facts, the destabilization of a social system is consequently not at all difficult to bring about; on the other hand, it is very difficult to control effectively and to re-stabilise a social process. In other respects, his distinction between temporal and spiritual power was his security against the confusion between social reform and the taking of power. He understood very well that this reform implies a revision of fundamental notions and a refinement of morals, which both require a lot of time and patience. Although he showed a marked tendency to dogmatism, Comte, unlike other social reformers, did not succumb to the terrorist and totalitarian temptation. Moreover, the characteristic dislike which he always showed towards the 'pedantocracy' cautioned him against the intellectuals' pretension to take themselves for the avant-garde of the historical movement. He has always recognized the importance of common sense and feeling in the keeping of social consensus — even if his final pretension to assuming the pontificate of humanity is a cruel testimony against the impossibility of reconstructing a consensus via ritual alone.

Comte's synthesis broke up rapidly. The fusion between knowledge and feeling, on which Comte based the religion of humanity, was very quickly seen to be a work of pure imagination. The fusion between an empiricist point of view, reducing science to the 'legality' of pure observable statements, and the ambition to construct a system of knowledge summarizing and co-ordinating the totality of human experience of the past, present, and future, was rapidly perceived to be impracticable. The synthesis between statics (order) and dynamics (progress) has proved an undertaking far beyond the abilities of the new science – sociology – of which Auguste Comte himself claimed to be the founder. Therefore, sociologists today call themselves 'positivist' in a sense which has almost nothing to do with Comte's variant. When one refers to the positivism of contemporary sociologists, one is satisfied with stressing their conviction that the knowledge of social facts is subject to the same methodological requirements as any other data of experience. This proposition involves a series of very diverse consequences regarding the nature of social facts and the way they can be understood.

The positivist orientation is generally advanced to explain the distance sociologists claim to maintain between the collective values and preferences in force in the societies they study and their own values. In fact, this axiological neutrality originates far more directly in Weber's legacy than in Comte's. In the first case, positivism, widely credited among sociologists, is a variety of relativism very different from the historicism or evolutionism of Comte himself. Moreover, the contemporary sociologist's positivism can be characterized as the respect of facts and of observation. But among many of them it is associated with a scientism, notably 'quantitative', for which Comte felt only mistrust or contempt. Comte has taught sociologists that sociology is, or must be, a science. But he failed to make them agree with either his conception of science of his conception of sociology.

Durkheim, Historicism, Marx, Teleology.

Bibliography

COMTE, A., *Cours de philosophie positive*, Paris, Bachelier, 1830–1842; Brussels, Culture et civilisation, 1969, 6 vol.; *Discours sur l'esprit positif*, Paris, Carilian-Gœury & Dalmont, 1844; Brussels, Culture et Civilisation, 1969; *Système de politique positive, ou Traité de sociologie, instituant la religion de l'humanité*, Paris, L. Mathias, 1851–1854, 4 vol.; Brussels, Culture et Civilisation, 1969, 4 vol.; *Catéchisme positiviste, ou sommaire exposition de la religion universelle*, Paris, 1872; Paris, Garnier-Flammarion, 1966. – ALAIN, *Idées, introduction á la philosophie*, Paris, P. Hartmann, 1939; Paris, Flammarion, 1967. – ARBOUSSE-BASTIDE, P., *La doctrine de l'éducation universelle dans la philosophie d'Auguste Comte comme principe d'unité systématique et fondement de l'organisation spirituelle du monde*, Paris, PUF, 1957, 2 vol. – ARNAUD, P., *Politique d'Auguste Comte, extraits*, Paris, A. Colin, 1965; *Sociologie de Comte*, Paris, PUF, 1969. – ARON, R., *Les étapes de la pensée sociologique*, Paris, Gallimard, 1967. – DELVOLVÉ, J., *Réflexions sur la pensée comtienne*, Paris, Alcan, 1932. – GOUHIER, H., *La jeunesse d'Auguste Comte*, Paris, Vrin, 1933–1941, 3 vol. – LENZER, G. (ed.), *Auguste Comte and positivism. The essential writings*, New York, London, Harper, 1975, introduction, XVII–LXVIII. – LÉVY-BRUHL, L., *La philosophie d'Auguste Comte*, Paris, Alcan, 1900. – LITTRÉ, E., *Auguste Comte et Stuart Mill*, Paris, Baillière, 1866. – MAURRAS, Ch., *Romantisme et révolution*, Paris, Nouvelle Librairie nationale, 1922, 1925, 89–127. – MILL, J.S., *Auguste Comte and positivism*, London, N. Trübner, 1865; Ann Arbor, Univ. of Michigan Press, 1961. Trad., *Auguste Comte et le positivisme*, Paris, G. Baillière, 1868; Paris, F. Alcan, 1885. – MISES, R. von, *Kleines Lehrbuch des Positivismus*, Chicago, The Univ. of Chicago Press, 1939. Trans. *Positivism: a study in human understanding*, New York, Dover Publications, 1968. – NEURATH, O., 'Foundations of the social science', *International Encyclopedia of Unified Science*, II, 1, 1952. – SCHLICK, M., *Fragen der Ethik*, Vienna, J. Springer, 1930. Trad. angl., *Problems of ethics*, Englewood Cliffs, Prentice Hall, 1939; New York, Dover Publications, 1962. – SIMON, W.M., *European positivism in the nineteenth century: an essay in intellectual history*, Ithaca, Cornell Univ. Press, 1963.

Conformity and Deviance

Any social act is based on a minimum of conformity. But conformity must not be confused with conformism. Both propositions are easily understood as soon as the interaction process is studied carefully. 'I' and others direct their actions respectively according to the 'expectations' that each has of their partner's reactions to these actions. 'I' defines his own initiatives at least partly from the 'others' 'anticipated' reaction. These expectations are not arbitrary. Most of the time they are accurate. The other behaves like 'I' expected. The root of this conformity is found in a norm controlling 'I' and 'other', even if the same behaviour is not forced upon them. In other words, the demand for conformity is only one aspect of the normative character of a social act. But how is this demand satisfied, how is conformity ensured or restored?

There are several forms of conformity. First, to follow Durkheim's lectures it is possible to distinguish, 'a conformity by resemblance from a conformity by divergence'. Durkheim contrasts primitive and traditional societies, which he characterizes by the fusion of the individual with the group to which he belongs, with modern societies which are characterized by the value of the individual contributions of their members, and by the autonomy to which this fact gives rise. Conformity takes totally different forms in both contexts. In the first, it is synonymous with resemblance and even identification. Anyone behaving singularly is penalized because he is seen as a threat to group unity and solidarity. In the second context, freedom for everyone to follow their own interests and enter into a contract with any other is accepted as legitimate − so long as the content of that contract is lawful. The social demand for conformity is no longer a matter of the individual identifying as closely as possible with a social 'model'. It is a question of accepting and respecting (in a moral sense) the rules of the game so as to build up a 'reciprocity' between the costs and benefits of different actors. This regime of solidarity that Durkheim qualified as 'organic' is fragile: how can societies rewarding 'individualism' protect themselves against the members' 'selfishness' and how do they succeed in promoting a minimum of conformity? Durkheim not only makes a distinction between these terms but he also sees them in opposition to each other. For him individualism does not mean a lack of consultation or co-operation: on the contrary, it rests on them. Selfishness, by contrast, means first the destruction of common references and the loosening of primary links (familial and local); only the interests and the attitudes of the individual are a reference for him.

In an individualistic society, organized according to the principle of the division of labour, conformity and difference condition each other. But how can a discipline, according to Durkheim, be accepted by all, and under what conditions can a common law prevail over specialism and dispersion? The answer associated with the utilitarian tradition has to be rejected here. As soon as individuals do their sums, the utilitarians say, 'they realize that their true interest is to co-operate': the produce of their work is increased with a collective organization of efforts, each producer's share is increased, and his labour is reduced. Discipline appears like a cost that any individual is ready to accept so as to draw the maximum advantages from solidarity. It is easy for Durkheim to show that any discipline, even if, and maybe because, it only imposes very vague obligations, is not the product of an official negotiation between abstract protagonists, as the utilitarian tradition, where individuals are simply different parties of an exchange or contract, sees it. There is in discipline, at least in that which ties us to our constitutive obligations, otherwise sacred ones, something categorical which opposes transaction and selfish motives. The contrast cannot be said to shape discipline, but the opposite can be said. Conformity cannot be reduced, however, to the immersion of the individual in the collective conscience. Collective conscience is far from being unified and coherent. Beliefs and passions which constitute it are not all of the same legitimate value, so to speak; they are not uniformly adhered to. Durkheim himself, when proclaiming the normality of crime, showed the narrow link between conformity and deviance. Crime is not 'normal' only because a crime rate is found with impressive regularity in every society. Each society has its own list of crimes, and such acts taken here as criminal might be tolerated, even approved, elsewhere. Beyond relativism however, Durkheim acknowledges that scandal, which cannot be separated from crime, violence done to the certainties and 'strong feelings' of 'collective conscience', fulfils, or rather 'can' fulfil, a positive function by creating new social and cultural forms, thanks to the upheaval that goes with it. Socrates' or Jesus's 'crime' has nothing to do with a murder committed by a brute or a maniac. Essential changes in history have come through revolutionary movements or by out-of-the-ordinary personalities seen as 'deviant', 'shocking', or even 'monstrous' and 'criminal' in their times. Durkheim's thoughts on crime can be compared to Weber's views on charisma (cf. Charisma). In the same way as crime is not an anticipation of the law to come, a charismatic figure is not a prophet. Although there can be a promise and a revelation in what is strange and paradoxical, prophets and demagogues are not only revealed by the fact they speak 'against' traditional authority. They also bring with them a new legitimacy. They reject old ties (keeping some of the previous law that they re-affirm and validate), but they offer new ties, a living and original faith. What is routine today was charisma yesterday; what is conformity today was paradox, scandal, crime – in short, deviance – yesterday. Therefore, it is not possible to reduce conformity to conformism.

First, several variants of conformism must be examined, according to their extension and their modality. Conformism can extend to all aspects of social life, or on the contrary be restricted to a mostly symbolic domain. 'Soft' (weak) or 'hard' variants can be distinguished. The Soviet Union – at least under Stalin – and Germany under Hitler are the perfect models of total conformism. A number of 'dogmatic beliefs' very articulated and very extended, on the historical mission of values (egalitarian on one side, élitist on the other), are proclaimed as absolute. What is proclaimed to justify one of the greatest denials of justice, i.e. obscurantism, is a very general model or project, at the end of which history would be suspended. In both cases a party formed which not only identifies itself with the State but takes its place to the point of corrupting the essential functions of the state organization, and redirecting them to the party's ends.

In the 'liberal' regimes, conformism, although present, is of a radically different nature. It does not refer to an official doctrine reinforced by a bureaucracy; it sneaks in and is dispersed. This conformism too produces a form of censure; but it does not shut down newspapers, does not condemn 'dissidents' to prison, exile, or psychiatric hospital. Marcuse referred to it as 'repressive tolerance'. Conformism in 'liberal' regimes presents three particularities and should not be mistaken for totalitarian conformism. First, it remains implicit and likes presenting its dogma as 'scientific' evidence, as in the diverse ideologies followed in the educational or economic domains. Second, the promotion of conformism is not 'directly' assumed by the State. The 'black lists', stifling by silence, are the equivalent of the concentration camps. Third, censure, as far as knowledge is concerned, is more an inhibition mechanism than a repression mechanism. It restricts the horizon of possibilities our minds could extend to. It does not forbid us to think in a particular way, it simply prevents us from taking it seriously. Censure is surveillance not punishment. As it is not strictly centralized, it works in added 'cumulative slants' which lead to a consensus on 'negative beliefs' rather than on 'dogmatic beliefs'.

Conformism does not always ensure conformity of norms in practice. In reality, totalitarian conformism is a resource for those in power. By trying to establish or re-establish a spiritual unity, totalitarian governments attempt to insure themselves with the perfect docility of the governed. For the latter to believe in the dogma is less important than their obedience or at least their passivity. As for liberal conformism, it is a consequence, an emergent effect rather than a strategy deliberately worked out by the 'ruling class'. In so far as it is defined, by Marcuse, as a 'repressive tolerance' its legitimacy can be questioned. Neither in the liberal nor in the totalitarian variant is conformism constituted as an adequate solution to Durkheim's problem of conformity. Within conformity there is a need for 'autonomy' which prevents it from being reduced to violence, constraint, or selfishness. To understand this dimension, the nature of the normative process must be studied, and in particular the way it distinguishes conformity from deviance. Everyone accepts that some social norms cannot be followed because they are extreme, others because they are so vague. Some norms (word of honour and duty to pay a gambling debt) are so strict that they place individuals in the position where suicide may appear a better solution than would breaking one's word or repudiating the debt; it is the situation Durkheim refers to as altruistic suicide, when the subject gives up his own life for a self-image which is more precious to him than his biological existence. It may happen that other norms, in professional or economic context, have to be violated, at least in spirit, because they have become changeable, volatile, or even contradictory. In the first case, conformity was only possible if one agreed to sacrifice oneself to the norm. In the second case, if it is so difficult to conform to the norm, it is because we don't know exactly what it is demanding. There can also be a split between 'values' (strong preferences but not clear in their content or their mode of realization) and the 'norms' which dictate the way to do things, to think, even to feel, the realization of which is controlled by the network of sanctions available to the group's rulers. It is not enough for conformity to be ensured that individuals agree with some common 'beliefs' or 'feelings'!

But if action needs a sanction procedure, a reference authority, and executory power for it to happen, and if its strictness depends on these conditions and consequently on their compatibility, then deviance is likely to happen, either because norms are too (or insufficiently) explicit, or because the sanctions are too (or insufficiently) hard, or because the referee is too (or insufficiently) tolerant. Take a situation where the system of norms and the system of values are placed in strict contradiction: anything prescribed by the authorities would be devalued by collective conscience. How could this situation of perfect unlawfulness be able to subsist? The authorities would have to act in two ways: first, they would have to clear the ground and decide, in a very loose way, on the area where private interests would be left completely free. Moreover, they could count only on naked force to force individuals to do what 'they' decide. A state of unlawfulness makes the central power of that society experience a very notable reduction of their ability to be obeyed just 'for what they are' and the corresponding necessity to act quickly and in the strongest possible way. For the authorities, a state of deviance, by taking away their legitimacy, leads to group atomization, without any effective focus for unity, to exacerbation of each camp's forces – in short, to a de-socialization or a return to the state of nature. How can an individual behave when faced with contradictory indications about what he must do (to avoid sanctions) or what he must prefer? If we remain in the extreme case of perfect unlawfulness, the individual could react either by opting out (total passivity) or by aggression (hyperactivity). In any case, the individual cannot accept the situation he is given; he can only refuse it, either by attempting to change it or by getting away from it. Faced with two contradictory situations, the individual might reject both – and keep to himself. Opting out of a society which is seen as illegitimate but is too strong to be challenged can be called 'escapism' and might take different forms. It can be strictly individual ('to live happily let's go away') or, on the contrary, spread to the behaviour of a whole group trying with more or less success to get away from the pressures of a hostile world, pretending to be part of it for instance. Keeping it secret is an efficient protection for those who have to protect themselves from repression but still persevere in their own way. The secret might well be known eventually: it is 'Punch's secret' which is made a lot of so as to increase its importance. The escapist can also take refuge in the accomplishment of rites he alone knows the meaning of and which bring him security. It is the case of Bouvard and Pecuchet, Flaubert's two scribes, who find peace again in going back to their writing that they had left for a while to get into the outside world.

After the escapist, we could describe the rebel. It is possible to distinguish the rebel from the revolutionary according to the intensity of the contestation and the aim of the movement through which he attacks norms or value systems. The revolutionary violently attacks rules and their principles whereas the rebel attacks one or the other without understanding their links: 'I am a rebel, society's unfairness disgusts me', but it is enough for me to express my disgust, in the loudest possible manner, without making my hands dirty, 'because THEY are all as bad'. Different kinds of rebellions can be defined according to their target. Sometimes, the rebel unloads his anger on social objects felt as presently unacceptable (people or rules). Sometimes, rebellion moves by a series of symbolic substitutions which follow the rules of equivalence and opposition (as we see in racial prejudice for example, 'Arabs and blacks, it is all the same, they are all foreigners', meaning non-French).

Up until now we have treated the situation generating deviance simply as a contradiction between norms and values. Such an hypothesis refers to an extreme case, useful because it clearly shows the acute problems of an unlawful society and clearly describes, although only in outline, the reactions of the individual caught in that situation. But these analyses unfortunately show deviance as if, by nature, it was the result of a choice – explicit or conscious – of strategy through which the individual decides to reject, oppose a long-standing order he wants to change, or maybe simply destroy. But what is known of the two phenomena which make up the two largest sources of criminality, i.e., juvenile delinquency and 'gangs', forces us to reject a strictly strategic conception of deviance and to complicate our initial model. To start from the conflict between a value system and a norm system is to suppose that one or other is coherent when taken by itself. It seems well established that the tendency to commit a crime – or more generally to become deviant – does not depend so much on the opposition of the individual to the norms as on their ambiguity. Juvenile delinquency (for instance that of young Whites in a Baltimore district) is notably higher than average in residential areas where rival ethnic groups live, where the turnover of inhabitants is high, and where the percentage of tenants (more mobile) is higher than that of owners (less mobile). If the last two criteria are looked at together and treated as the representation of geographical mobility, and if that is added to the first one regarding cultural and racial diversity, it becomes clear that delinquents are more likely to be found among the 'marginals', i.e., individuals belonging simultaneously to different groups who no longer have a legitimate, explicit, or clear point of reference. Then marginality appears as a 'subculture' used as a protection by the deviant individual. This 'subculture' is represented by a group, the 'gang' for instance, which is created by the disorganization of the 'natural' social background – like the family, the area, and clubs or leisure associations. For the Chicago sociologists, delinquency is sometimes explained as a process of social disorganization. The white adolescent from a working-class background living in slums is pulled between the norms and values of his parents, of the school (where middle-class culture prevails personified by the school teacher), of groups (gangs), and of peer groups, the composition of which varies all the time according to street meetings. Not only does marginality emphasize the multiple references an individual might follow (and in the light of which people can judge behaviour); these references do not have the same value. A young boy often humiliated by being seen as 'greenhorn' can't wait for adult status; similarly, if our society is seen as ordered in a clear way, those with low status will look up to those with a high one. Wanting to be seen as a 'man' when you are a boy, and especially if the boy already has some attributes of the adult condition, is a desire for promotion aiming to become real through actual belonging to the group taken previously as a reference, as a more or less accessible ideal. The 12-year-old boy smoking in spite of parental prohibition, appears less as a sign of delinquency than as a call to be treated, or at least accepted, as an adult, 'having a right' to this status. This is why this pretence is most often treated with indulgence and seen as a very minimal form of deviance. But it could become delinquency (if marijuana replaces the cigarette) or even become 'criminal' (if the subject uses the black market to get hold of the forbidden drug). Whatever the seriousness of the deviant act, it comes out as self-affirmation, through the search for real and symbolic advantages of a condition seen as desirable but which is not accessible to the 'deviant', either temporarily or permanently. If there is a case for describing delinquency as 'substitute' behaviour (in the same way as one smokes to look 'big', one can steal and kill to be seen as 'tough', and be admitted to the prestigious society of the 'underworld'), it remains the case that this substitution fortunately confines itself to the symbolic and imaginary, and above all that it is efficiently controlled – and precisely by those of our partners who we are most keen should recognize our change of condition. It is not because the boy smokes in front of his father that he will be treated as an adult by him. He might even be 'given a lesson'. But he might try to get his pretensions accepted by his peer group. But this recognition remains unsatisfactory since the legitimation does not come from those who had provoked this pretension and still refuse to admit it. It is simply 'a small consolidation'.

Any demand for legitimation from a marginal (individual or group) is not necessarily criminal. Merton's analysis of the phenomenon shows this clearly and calls it 'anticipated socialization'. Abnormal and deviant behaviour in relation to the 'present status' of an individual might be judged as normal in relation to his 'future status'. What is forbidden today might be lawful and inevitable tomorrow. It is in fact the capacity to assume the integrity of the status which decides the legitimacy of the pretension and, without this capacity, 'anticipated socialization' will end in failure.

The success of anticipated socialization depends on conditions linked to the 'environment' and conditions linked to the commitment to it. It is not enough to claim the importance of 'social background', the fact that it provokes very different situations must be acknowledged. A society will without fail generate deviance if actors are placed in a permanent contradiction between its values and the norms according to which their behaviour is sanctioned. But this contradiction might be felt for more or less time by only small groups which lack influence and who at first will protect themselves rather than organize effective resistance. If, in some cases, it results in deviance, the 'social context' might slow it down and even stifle it, when it is not given means of expression. In a first developmental phase, deviance is felt subjectively by the deviant as an uneasiness, and by others as a tension or a lack of harmony. For deviance to explode, some sort of 'help' must be offered to the marginal within his social context: loosening of repressive controls allowing the individual to 'try his luck' and 'lead his own life', encouragement for the young deviant from the actual realization, through new acts and situations he had been dreaming of and that until now he thought impossible, the wonder of not being the only one and therefore not 'a monster', which might lead him to see himself as a 'chosen one'.

Not only does society create the 'contextual' conditions for deviance (in submitting the individual to intense contradictory pressures, in leaving him to find out his duties and even his identity, in brandishing in front of him privileges he will never be able to obtain), but it also provides the opportunities, by a kind of 'demonstration effect', showing that others 'do well' in a way the said individual was refused – if he did not refuse it to himself. From this perspective, the subject tries to 'take off' so as to get away from parents' and friends' judgement, to dive into the anonymity of a large town, to take up a vagrant life – even forming a society with his peers with whom he no longer is ashamed of what he is. It may be that we could say that our societies are as tolerant as they are repressive.

Anomie, Beliefs, Crime, Role, Social Control, Socialization, Suicide.

Bibliography

ASCH, S.E., *Social psychology*, New York, Prentice Hall, 1952, 1962. – CHILTON, R., 'Continuity in delinquency area research', *American Sociological Review*, XXIX, 1, 1964, 71–83. – COHEN A.K., *Delinquent boys. The culture of the gang*, Glencoe, The Free Press, 1955; London, Routledge & Kegan Paul, 1956. *Deviance and control*, Englewood Cliffs, Prentice Hall, 1966. – DURKHEIM, E., *The Division of Labour in Society; Suicide; Moral Education*, Glencoe, Free Press, 1961; London, Routledge & Kegan Paul, 1952. – FOUCAULT, M., *Surveiller et punir: naisance de la prison*, Paris, Gallimard, 1975. Trans: *Discipline and Punish*, New York, Pantheon, 1977; London, Allen & Unwin, 1977. – FREUD, S., *Totem und Tabu*, Leipzig and Vienna, H. Heller, 1913. *Massenpsychologie und Ich-Analyse*, Leipzig, Internationaler Psychoanalytischer Verlag, 1921. – KATZ, E. and STOTLAND, E., 'A preliminary statement of a theory of attitude, structure and change', in KOCH, S. (ed.), *Psychology: a study of science*, New York, McGraw-Hill, 1959, vol. 3. – MARCUSE, H., *One-dimensional man*, Boston, Beacon, 1964; London, Routledge & Kegan Paul, 1964. – MERTON, R.K., *Social theory and social structure; toward the codification of theory and research*, Glencoe, The Free Press, 1949. – PARSONS, T., *The social system*, New York, The Free Press, 1951. – SHERIF, M., *The psychology of social norms*, New York, London, Harper & Brothers, 1936; New York, Harper & Row, 1966. – SUTHERLAND, E.W., *White collar crime*, New York, Dryden Press, 1949; New York, Holt, Rinehard & Winston, 1961.

Crime

As in the chapter on suicide, the contribution of Durkheim is essential to the chapter on crime. It is contained in the celebrated pages of the *Division of Labour* and the *Rules* where Durkheim puts forward a series of propositions: 1) We do not disapprove of an act because it is criminal, but it is criminal because we disapprove of it. Socrates, a criminal in Athenian eyes, is not one in our eyes. 2) Crime is a 'normal' phenomenon, because the feeling of aversion evoked by those acts defined as criminal in a given social context cannot be developed with the same intensity in all individuals. 3) 'Punishment is above all destined to act upon honest people', in whom it reinforces the feeling of solidarity, rather than on criminals. Sanctions can have a certain dissuasive effectiveness; but, the feeling of aversion with regard to a reprehensible act not being strongly felt by certain individuals, they cannot claim to eliminate crime. 4) There is only crime where there is a legal sanction. But, there can only be legal sanction for acts which are well defined by law. Certain behaviour can excite strong disapproval without being considered criminal, if it does not correspond to easily identifiable acts. ('The bad son and even the most hardened egotist are not treated as criminals.')

It is perhaps not exaggerated to contend that the sociological theory of crime, as it has been latterly constructed by the accumulation of successive contributions, has been largely guided by the questions that Durkheim posed. Why, asks Merton in his theory of deviance, is the feeling of aversion with regard to disapproval of acts unequally distributed? Durkheim seems to suggest that the distribution is problematical. But we observe the relationship between certain types of crimes and offences and the variables of social position. Theft is most often the act of individuals belonging to the underprivileged classes. The 'white-collar criminality' to which Sutherland gave its name is most often the act of the middle and upper classes. According to Merton, this lack of aversion for acts considered as reprehensible may not only be due, as Durkheim advances, to an insufficient conformity to social values, but may also be the result of an excess of conformity. In American society and in others social success is highly valued. But the means of success are unequally accessible to individuals. The objective of success, if it is sufficiently inwardly digested by the individual, may cause him to have recourse to means which themselves are the object of a negative valuation from the moment that the normal means appear to him to be beyond his reach. Naturally, other types of 'solution' to the contradiction exist. For the individual, the first consists of repressing his will to succeed ('I content myself with what I have', 'do not aim too high and you will not be disappointed'). Even though it is uncomfortable and exposed to diffuse social sanctions, on the evidence this is very common. The other solution is that of 'retreat', illustrated by the character of Charlie Chaplin, resigned to being 'Mr Nobody . . . to have no pretension to virtue or to distinction'. Rebellion, the third type of response, is translated by a dispute with cultural objectives. It is only possible in exceptional circumstances. As for 'innovation' (submission to cultural goals and utilization of deviant means), it is the 'solution' which corresponds with punishable and criminal behaviour. Naturally, this 'solution' is not chosen following rational deliberation. Ohlin remarks that we frequently observe a feeling of injustice in the young delinquent. He writes 'delinquents tend to be people who wait for the chance to show themselves off to advantage to present itself, in as much as they are convinced of their potential capacity to satisfy formal evaluation criteria, institutionally established' (Cloward and Ohlin). If the opportunity does not present itself, they can have the feeling that the 'system' is at fault, and that, despite the way it is presented on the surface, it in fact rests upon immorality, extortion, blackmail, nepotism, and social pressures. He thus feels justified in turning to means which are disapproved of. But in order for the deviant to become confirmed in his vocation, it is necessary that mechanisms of reinforcement are put in place. Ohlin remarks that the delinquent who commits his first larceny generally feels himself guilty of offending against established norms. But this first act can put him in contact with other delinquents. The misdemeanour, which caused a feeling of shame, thus becomes a means of personal affirmation. It may gain for its author the approbation and esteem of the members of the delinquent group. Durkheim, even while considering crime as normal, presented the criminal as an individual who only slightly experiences the sentiments of aversion raised by certain acts. With Merton and the authors who were inspired by him, for example Clinard, Cloward, and Ohlin, Durkheim's hypothesis is completed by an inverse hypothesis: the criminal persists in pursuing a socially valued objective. And if he innovates as regards the means, the innovation can seem legitimate to him. It can be interpreted by him as a response to a situation which he perceives as unjust. Furthermore, it may be the source not only of social success but of approbation from the members of the 'in-group'. Sutherland suggests that the criminal should be seen as a normal man. Merton suggests that criminal behaviour is to be seen as a form of conformity.

Crime is, despite everything, a rare event: it bears a risk of sanction; those who experience a sentiment of 'relative deprivation' can seek refuge in ritual and retreat and are very likely to do so if they have acquired a minimal social status which they run the risk of losing by engaging in 'innovation'; finally the 'innovation' which deviance represents has every likelihood of coming to nothing if it does not meet with favourable circumstances, as we are reminded by an anecdote of Sutherland's. Two young delinquents commit a larceny and are pursued by the police. The first, who has long legs, escapes. Covered with cold sweat at the thought of having risked prison, he settles down and becomes honest. The other is caught, thrown in prison, and there enters into contact with thieves and begins a criminal career. *The Professional Thief* by Sutherland, an admirable autobiographical account dictated to the sociologist, illustrates the role of 'differential associations', that is to say delinquent pseudo-organizations, in the confirmation of criminal careers. Sutherland's thief starts with several casual thefts. As a result of his larcenies he meets an older delinquent who initiates him into picking pockets. But picking pockets is not very profitable, although it brings in more than individually committed thefts. It calls for a minimum team of two people. The first steals the desired object and immediately passes it to the second. The thief thus progressively discovers more and more complex techniques of thieving. At the same time, he discovers that the remuneration, not only material but symbolic, to which he can lay claim is a function of the complexity of the deed. In the milieu that he has started to penetrate, punishable offences are socially hierarchized. The shoplifter is the object of general contempt. Picking pockets, even though considered slightly better, is thought the act of seedy and incapable people. Burglary, which assumes knowledge, organization, and a precise execution, belongs in a higher level of the hierarchy. Before being permitted to progress to a higher level, the thief is put through a severe apprenticeship and possibly fails the test. His status and rewards will be according to the level to which he has been capable of raising himself. Sutherland's story not only demonstrates the role of 'differential associations' in the reproduction of the criminal phenomenon (he writes 'the efforts of repression tend to eliminate the professional thief, but leave the entire equipment in place'); it also confirms Merton's hypothesis. Having become a delinquent by chance, the thief is drawn into a professional career in which he tries to climb the ladder, each rung climbed giving him additional status, power, and prestige.

The 'differential associations' of which Sutherland speaks in addition do not always take a 'professional' form. The classic study by W.F. Whyte of Cornerville, the Italian quarter of an American town, analyses in detail the process by which an 'adolescent gang' is formed into a structured sub-system. The offences that they commit, in the main not serious, bring them a certain income, but above all they furnish the gang with common objectives, which presuppose decision-making, organization, and a system of authority. The gang gradually transforms into a hierarchical association. The lieutenants, proud to serve the chief, take advantage of the authority he delegates to them. The chief, wishing to preserve his authority, only borrows money from his lieutenants in small sums and strives to return it as quickly as possible. The subordinates seek favours from the hierarchy from which they can expect support. The delinquent sub-system or 'subculture' is formed starting from the feeling of rejection. Once constituted, it renders possible the search for status. Philip Robert, relying on the observation of adolescent gangs, makes similar remarks. Very often the group at first takes the form of a disparate assembly resulting from a 'feeling of rejection, often latent'. When an incident occurs, the assembly takes on a structure. 'A carelessly thrown stone which breaks a pane of glass is sufficient for several young people to cover the clumsiness with collective lies. They have soldered their sympathy into an attitude of defense which creates cohesion.' Once constituted, the 'gang' has appreciable resources available for the use of its members: it is capable of giving them security and consideration. The loyalty which it engenders is naturally reinforced by the fact that the more strongly constituted the gang, the more it reinforces segregation with regard to the surrounding milieu, and the more likely it is to set in train a 'labelling' reaction. We should also note that, as indicated by Cloward and Ohlin who go even further than Merton on this point, deviant subcultures can take the form of either violence or retreat, such as that studied, for example, by Becker in his monograph on marijuana smokers (*Outsiders*).

Durkheim maintained that there is a crime only where there can be a sanction of a disapproved-of act, and he added that acts considered as reprehensible depended on the general evolution of morals. At a general level, the thesis is acceptable. But certain writers, following Sellin, have underlined the fact that the law, if it depends on morals, is under the relative influence of social groups. At the same time, the feeling of disapprobation aroused by a crime can be very weak among those who do not see the individual consequences of the act in question very clearly and whose experience and social position do not permit them to put themselves in the place of the offender. Homicide and theft are the object of general reprobation. But it is not the same, for example, for certain forms of 'white-collar criminality'. In 1961, twenty-nine electrical equipment companies came before the courts for violation of American anti-trust law. Even though the crime affected the taxpayer as well as the consumer, it is very unlikely that either felt a strong feeling of reprobation. This is why the accused were able to repeat one after the other during the trial that they did not have the impression of having acted in a reprehensible manner. 'White-collar criminality' is often stigmatized from the time when the latent groups whose interests have been injured give birth to pressure groups. The feeling of reprobation aroused by fraudulent publicity would by itself have been insufficient to exalt it to a crime without the presence and action of consumer associations. The relationship between morality, law, and crime is thus more complex than as stated by Durkheim. It is necessary to insert between these three terms an intermediate variable, that is to say the relative influence of organized or diffused social groups. It is equally necessary to see that the feelings of reprobation with regard to a given act can vary according to social groups. Balzac's *Paysans* thought it normal to mix a few sheafs of straw with the gleaned ears of grain and a few green branches with the logs. During the Depression, unemployed ex-miners took advantage of uneconomic pits abandoned by mining companies but remaining the property of those companies. When the owners wished to indict the 'thieves' they got no support from the legal authorities. The prohibition of betting, because gambling is not − except in certain countries − the object of very marked reprobation, can have counter-productive effects. In the State of New York where lotteries were forbidden, one could, according to Sellin, easily get in contact with a bookmaker, give him a three-figure number which he would note on a paper with the address of the punter. The winning combination corresponded to the three last figures of the overall total of the cheques put in during the day, information published daily by a financial publication. Naturally, most of the bookmakers who practised this clandestine lottery were 'honest', but others were not. Prohibition was not only inoperative but also police and law officers charged with the task of applying the law put little effort into it. In addition, it invited corruption and encouraged the settling of scores. As for the bookmakers, they considered the fines that were occasionally inflicted upon them to be part of their general expenses. Generally, the hypotheses which issue directly from the Durkheim-Merton tradition are applicable to direct attempts against the person and property. But they are less useful where other forms of criminality are concerned. In the case of prohibition, criminality was engendered by a gap between the law and public opinion regarding betting. When a practice harms individuals only marginally and collectively (contravention of anti-trust laws, fraudulent publicity), it sets off only a slight collective reaction. In this situation, the legislators or the actions of representative groups (for example consumer associations) are often in advance of 'morals'.

The development of sociological research has contributed to a better understanding of criminal phenomena at the microsociological level. At the macrosociological level, hypotheses such as those of Merton are effective guides. But a fundamental problem posed by Tarde is still imperfectly resolved: that of establishing the relationship between microphenomena with relative overall data, be it the evolution of criminality over time or the differences in the structure of criminality in space on the other hand. In each case one thing is sure: it is altogether insufficient to seek to explain the evolution of levels of criminality by putting them in relation with variables defined at the level of overall societies (for example the degree of 'anomie'). An official American report of 1969 notes that, between 1947 and 1967, most of the indicators which are generally taken as positively connected with urban criminality had become more favourable: progress in the schooling of the black population, lowering of the level of unemployment, a clear increase in the average family income of the Blacks and a relative one in the average level of the Whites, fewer people living below the legal poverty lines. Despite this, criminality in the towns went up during the same period. Why? Cohen and Felson put forward an interesting hypothesis to resolve the enigma: the favourable effect of the above indicators had been neutralized, and more, by another evolution. Attacks, whether against goods or people, are easier for the delinquent when the target is less protected. But various factors (longer journeys to work and length of journey to the work-place, the disappearance of small local shops and the development of supermarkets on average creating a greater distance between the point of sale and the home of the consumer, the nuclear family, the distance of home from school, the development of female employment, etc.) all mean that individuals are alone longer and the home more often unguarded. A statistical analysis made of a collection of ecological units seemed to confirm the hypothesis. Voluntary homicide, rape, assault and battery, robbery, and aggravated robbery are more frequent as the indicator that measures the time passed at home compared with time passed away from home decreases. The same crimes and offences grow with the population aged 15 to 24 years old. The growth in criminality in the period thus perhaps results in part from how much the structural evolutions indicated above have the effect of making more frequent or more easy the coming together of delinquents and non-protected targets. Similarly, we have been able to confirm in France a proposition established by monographic studies on delinquent gangs, namely that certain ecological structures, such as large blocks of flats, can encourage the development of delinquency: they make the formation of gangs easy; they also induce certain types of offences such as the theft of cars and motorbikes, which permit escape from a desolate environment.

Despite these results, we are today far from being able to relate macrosociological data and microsociological processes in an entirely satisfactory manner. Thus, the classic debate on the dissuasive effect of punishment appears still open. Certain people suggest the application to criminal behaviour of a model of economic inspiration, and compare the punishment, balanced by the probability of being caught, to a price. But it is not sufficient to establish the presence of a negative correlation between levels of criminality and the gravity of sanctions in order to verify the dissuasive effect of the punishment. The interpretation of this correlation can be ambiguous. There is nothing to show that it does not result from a relationship of causality emanating possibly just as much from the crime to the sanction as from the sanction to the crime. It is in effect possible that a high level of criminality in a legal jurisdiction can provoke an effect of clogging up the courts and the prisons and lead the law enforcing agencies to give lighter punishments. It is also possible that the frequency of certain offences, as long as they do not go beyond a certain level of gravity, creates a more tolerant attitude. For more serious offences, the effect might be the opposite: a greater frequency of these offences may bring about greater severity. Longitudinal panel studies always allow for the nuancing of the hasty interpretations which have been presented of the observable correlations at the aggregated level between the level of criminality and the severity of sanctions (and/or probability of arrest). A study made of a population of American towns in 1964 to 1970 (Greenberg *et al.*), using a panel model (which allows the study of the influence on criminality in t of the levels of arrest in $t - 1$, the levels of arrest being defined by the relationship between the cases ending in an arrest and the total number of cases known to the police in a given year of a given type of offence), showed up a negligible influence on the level of arrests on the levels of criminality. Such a study does not indicate that the dissuasive effect does not exist (it is possible that an increase in the level of arrest would be accompanied by a lowering of the severity of the sentences given). But it demonstrates: 1) the complexity of the relationship between criminality and repression due to the recip- rocal character of the causality; 2) that the 'anticipated cost' of crime is only one of the parameters of criminal behaviour. To which it must be added that the influ- ence of the cost, as more generally the influence of the institutions of repression and the social structures, depends on the type of criminality: the crime of passion and the crime of Raskolnikov are perhaps similar statistical entities, but they are certainly distinct criminological entities. As in the case of suicide, the analysis of criminal phenomena cannot, contrary to what Durkheim appeared to believe, be considered as relevant to only one sociology.

Anomie, Community, Conformity and Deviance, Durkheim, Groups, Suicide.

Bibliography
BECKER, H.P., *Outsiders. Studies in the sociology of deviance*, New York and London, The Free Press, 1963. – CLINARD, M.B. (ed.), *Anomie and deviant behavior. A discussion and critique*, New York, The Free Press, 1964; London, Collier Macmillan, 1964. – CLINARD, M.B., 'White collar crime', in *International Encyclo- pedia of the Social Sciences*, New York, The Macmillan Company and the Free Press, 1968, 483–490. – CLOWARD, R. and OHLIN, L.E., *Delinquency and opportunity. A theory of delinquent gangs*, New York, The Free Press, 1960; London, Routledge & Kegan Paul, 1961. – COHEN, L.E. and FELSON, M., 'Social change and crime rate trends: a routine activity approach', *American sociological review*, XLIV, 4, 1979, 588–608. – DURKHEIM, E., *The Division of Labour in Society*, New York, Macmillan, 1933. – GREENBERG, D.F., KESSLER, R.C., and LOGAN, C.H., 'A panel model of crimes rates and arrest rates', *American socio- logical review*, XLIV, 5, 1979, 843–850. – KELLENS, G., LASCOUMES, P., 'Actualités bibliographiques: moralisme, juridisme et sacrilège. La criminalité des affaires: analyse bibliographique', *Déviance et société*, I, 1, 1977, 119–133. – MERTON, R.K., 'Social structure and anomie', *American sociological review*, III, 5, 1938, 672–682. Reproduced in MERTON, R.K., *Social theory and social structure; toward the codification of theory and research*, Glencoe, The Free Press, 1949, rev. ed. 1957, 1961, 131–160. – OHLIN, L.E., *Sociology and the field of corrections*, New York, Russel Sage Foundation, 1956. – ROBERT, Ph., 'La formation des bandes délinquantes', in ROBERT, Ph., *Les bandes d'adolescents*, Paris, Editions Ouvrières, 1966, 183–198. – ROSE-ACKERMAN, S., 'The Economics of corruption', *Journal of public economics*, IV, 2, 1975, 187–203. – SELLIN, Th., *The sociology of crime and delinquency*, New York/London Wiley, 1962. – SZABO, D., *Crimino- logie et politique criminelle*, Paris, Vrin/Montreal, Presses de l'Université de Montréal, 1978. – TARDE, G., *La criminalité comparée*, Paris, F. Alcan, 1886. – WHYTE, W.F., *Street corner society*, Chicago, The Chicago University Press, 1943, 1965.

Culturalism and Culture

Culturalism: a term which belongs to anthropology (cultural anthropology and culturalism could be held to be, if not synonymous, at least very closely related terms) but is transposable to sociology. The culturalist perspective is based on a collection of propositions which tend to appear in combination. According to the authors and the contexts studied, the accent can be placed on one or other of these propositions. As with structuralism and functionalism, culturalism can be seen at once as a paradigm, that is to say as a framework of thought starting from which have been developed fertile theories and research, and like a *Weltanschauung*, that is to say like an ideological representation of societies.

First proposition: the structure of personality is very dependent on the characteristic culture of a particular society, by culture it being understood the fundamental value system of that society. Thus, according to Kardiner, there is a 'basic personality' corresponding to each socio-cultural society. 'Ego is a cultural precipitate', he wrote. According to McClelland, certain societies give a supreme value to *achievement* (a concept which signifies simultaneously performance and success, which we generally talk about as *accomplishment*). In these societies, the *need for achievement* tends to be a fundamental component of the personalities of the members who belong to it. As a corollary to this first proposition, culturalists tend to accord a decisive role to the socialization by which the fundamental values of a society are transmitted from one generation to another in their analyses of social systems. *Second proposition:* each society tends to constitute a single cultural totality. Societies which are similar from the point of view of their degree of economic development can be, as common sense and immediate experience tend to admit, profoundly different from a cultural viewpoint. The Germans are culturally different from the English; as Linton remarks, a traveller who, disembarking in Norway, asks a porter to change a bank-note is almost certain to see the porter return with the change. In Italy, he is almost certain never to see it again. *Third proposition,* which completes the above: the value system of societies tends to be characterized by the dominant or modal values (which does not exclude, to use Kluckhohn's terminology, the existence of *deviating* values and *variable* values). Thus, according to Ruth Benedict, the Zunis of New Mexico attach vital importance to the measure, harmony, and unity of man with the universe: they constitute an Apollonian society. The Kwakuitl of the north-west coast of America are, conversely, immersed in a climate of constant competition where everyone tries to demonstrate their superiority, and to beat their competitors, possibly by violence: they constitute a Dionysian society. For Parsons, Americans attach more importance to 'achievement' and less to the 'maintenance of cultural models' than do the Germans. According to Margaret Mead, 'Americans see the world as a vast malleable space, controlled by man, in which one builds what one wishes. . . . The important sentiment is to be able to control the environment' (*Anthropology: A Human Science,* p. 123). For the English, the world is a 'natural place to which man adapts himself, within which he does not attribute to himself any control over the future, but only the foresight of experience of the cultivator or gardener. . . . Man is seen as the minor associate of God'. *Fourth proposition:* the culture of a society tends to organize itself in a collection of coherent, mutually complementary elements: 'the second ambition of anthropology is totality. It sees social life as a system of which all aspects are organically connected,' writes Lévi-Strauss (whom one would not class as an anthropologist, but who does not differ from them on that point) in *Structural Anthropology,* p. 399. This proposition is illustrated by Benedict's attempt to sift out *patterns of culture* and to classify them. *Fifth proposition:* man lives in a symbolic universe created by himself. All reality is symbolic to him. Judgements, evaluations, and perceptions are all relative to the cultural system to which he belongs. According to Herskovits, who mirrors Cassirer on this point, all 'reality' being perceived through a cultural system, culture is the measure of everything.

There is no question of denying what culturalism brings to the social sciences. But it is also necessary to be aware of its limitations. The first objection, the most obvious without doubt, is that, at least in complex societies, it is only at the price of a great over-simplification that we can admit the idea of common values and imagine that these values are more or less administered to all by way of socialization. In fact, individuals are never exposed to the culture of a society as such. That 'culture' is largely no more than a simplification and a rationalization produced by certain social actors, such as priests, intellectuals, or, according to the case, some fraction of the élite. As for individuals, they undergo complex processes of apprenticeship the contents of which depend upon their environment, which is variable. That is why culturalists are obliged to introduce the idea of subculture to characterize the value systems appropriate to sub-groups. *Bildung* was an essential value in Germany at the end of the nineteenth century, not for Germans in general, but for intellectuals and state servants who, since the reforms of the Prussian state at the beginning of the nineteenth century, enjoyed considerable social weight. In the United States, towards the end of the nineteenth century, the Americans of New England and those of Illinois experienced an intense feeling of 'cultural distance' one from another. The former reproached the latter for their lack of culture, prosaicness, and materialism. The latter accused the former of conformity, inefficiency, and lack of enterprising spirit. The historical reasons for these differences are too obvious for it to be necessary to go into them. Chicago developed after Boston, starting with a wave of immigration which was not only ethnically different but found itself confronting a different situation precisely because it was more recent. In Colombia, the *Bogotanos* were traditionally, on this point, convinced of the cultural difference which separated them from their co-citizens of the Medellin region, from which they forged, in course of time, a mythological arsenal which permitted them to acknowledge a contrast which, even today, strikes foreign observers as much as the natives: the Spanish colonists who came to Medellin in the sixteenth century were mainly of Basque origin, in so far as they were not in the majority Jewish. These myths make it possible to explain the spirit of enterprise, the taste for money, the materialism, the lack of culture, and the relative absence of national sentiment which the Medellin population is said to show. Concerning complex societies, one should thus recognize the existence of local subcultures and of subcultures which correspond to particular social groups. The idea of class subculture is classic in this respect. Numerous studies have shown that in underprivileged classes the education of children is often of a more authoritarian nature than in the privileged classes. One more frequently observes in the former a *fatalistic* representation, and in the latter a *voluntarist* representation to become individual. Except perhaps in the case of the most simple societies, the totalist or holistic conception, according to which all the members of a society would participate in a single culture, that is to say a common value system, represents an extreme over-simplification. To tell the truth, the only 'common' cultural elements are perhaps, in the case of complex societies, the most superficial ones. A Frenchman can be without doubt more easily distinguished from an American by his gestures or his costume than by the degree of his 'need for achievement'.

From an historical viewpoint, it is necessary to note, in parenthesis, that the holistic conception of societies is principally of German origin. However, it was developed at a time when German intellectuals, for complex historical reasons which have been well analysed by Ringer, untiringly developed the theme of the specificity of German culture.

On the other hand, culturalism has a tendency to utilize a debatable represent-ation of the mechanisms of socialization: it presupposes that the values and other elements of the 'cultural system' are faithfully digested by the individual and constitute a kind of programme which will come to regulate his behaviour mechanically (cf. 'Socialization'). Thus McClelland admits that, in a society where *achievement* is a fundamental value, individuals normally experience a *need for achievement*. Thus to cultural *value* corresponds an individual *need*. In this way culture would be capable of acting as an extension of nature and of producing quasi-instinctive behaviour which is largely beyond the control of the individual subject to it. To which one can object that many kinds of behaviour must be analysed not as the product of conditioning but as the result of something uninten-tional. In addition, even when this behaviour is inspired by the interiorization of values, these furnish only flexible indications in the general case which are suscept-ible to multiple interpretations. In addition, socialization must be seen not only as a mechanism of interiorization but as a process of adaptation to changing and varying situations, processes marked out with arbitrations and compromises effected by the subject between the norms which impose themselves upon him, the values and beliefs to which he subscribes, and his interests such as he conceives them to be. This is why, as Durkheim points out in the celebrated pages of *Rules*, deviation from collective norms and values is a normal phenomenon in every society. More generally, numerous observations demonstrate that it is dangerous to exaggerate the influence of values transmitted by the socialization of behaviour. When the environment of a system modifies, we often see on the contrary, a rapid adaptation of behaviour to the new circumstances. Epstein shows this clearly in the case of India. From the moment when the irrigation programme launched by the government on the eve of the Second World War allowed a certain number of villages to pass from a subsistence-level economy to that of a market economy, certain peasants adopted entirely new behaviour, creating capitalist-type enter-prises such as milling or repair of agricultural tools. The 'cultural resistance' to change, even if it does exist beyond dispute in certain cases, must not be overesti-mated. Very often, this resistance is only 'cultural' in the spirit of the observer, and must rather be attributed to the fact that a change is likely to run counter to the interests of the social actors, interests which the actors see very clearly, but which the observer may miss. Contrary to a current perception among culturalists, values and attitudes interiorized by the individual must thus be seen as parameters rather than as determinants of action.

Let us, in the third place, come on to the question of the coherence of 'cultural systems'. First, we must reject the proposition according to which all reality is symbolic. If we understand by that that all experience is mediated by a symbolic system, such as language or science, this is a truism. It is a false proposition if the symbolic and the imaginary are taken to be synonymous and if culture is reduced to a projective system. Next, we must note that it is indispensable for the needs of analysis to distinguish the different elements which compose the cultural system of a society: structures, techniques, institutions, norms, values, myths, and ideologies all form part of the cultural system, if we understand by this that they are all the product of human activity. But it is preferable to reserve the description 'cultural' for the entirety of artefacts and mentefacts (that is to say the products of art and the mind/spirit). A birth rate, even if it results from the aggregation of behaviour partly guided by 'culture', is not, in itself, cultural information. It is thus necessary to put the cultural pseudo-evidence according to which everything in societies is 'culture' back in its proper place. Apart from culture, what must be called social reality also exists. The fact that between t and $t + 1$ the birth rate is maintained while the death rate goes down represents a structural change rather than a cultural one.

This reservation having been made, what are we to think of the culturalist assumption relating to the coherence of cultural systems? Without doubt we can admit that in simple societies cultural elements have a tendency to present a certain degree of coherence. Murdock perhaps is right when he affirms that the rules of residence tend to dominate many other aspects of a cultural system: according to whether they are, for example, matrilocal or patrilocal, the norms and customs regulating the relationships between two individuals connected by a given family relationship, the manner of designation of the parents, the rules of relationships, etc., tend to be different. Starting with the rules of residence, it is possible, at a statistical level, to predict the particular form that the other types of rules are likely to take. But in the case of complex societies, it is unwise to exaggerate the 'coherence' of cultural systems. In the United States, free enterprise ideology has a strong collective value. Despite this, the interference of the State in the game of individual actors is more and more affirmed, and in addition accepted. Many times it has been claimed that industrialization presupposes (in so far as it does not cause) the process of nuclearization of the family. This is true in the United States, but in Japan, until a recent phase, industrialization appears to have been effected more in harmony with the extended family than against it. As Ezra Vogel has shown, the rural Japanese family, through the intermediaries which it has at its command in the city, finds a job for the young migrant with an employer. The family and the intermediaries support the migrant if there are difficulties with his employer. The employer who has negotiated the recruitment with the family cannot easily sack him. If despite everything this is what happens, the family takes the migrant back until a new arrangement is found. Another example: it is repeated, unduly generalizing a celebrated thesis of Weber, that industrialization presupposes the diffusion of individual values, but Russia experienced a remark-able industrialization at the end of the nineteenth century, even though the 'dominant values' were those of rural societies where community-type institutions held an essential place, and though Russian intellectuals were in agreement that industrialization was incompatible with the tradition and structures of Russia. The introduction of modern techniques in a traditional society 'necessarily' implied (or caused) an erosion of traditional values. Linton stresses, in counter-argument to this corollary of the Comtian law of three stages, that technical advances can happily co-exist with magic itself.

> I found myself in Cairo at the moment when the model T Ford started to replace donkeys. . . . On the radiator caps were very often suspended neck-laces of big blue pearls which previously were hung round the necks of donkeys to repel the evil eye.

The simple fact that the different elements of a cultural system coexist certainly presupposes a minimum coherence between them. But we must be wary of inter-preting this coherence in an over-restrictive manner. It is certainly easy to imagine cultural elements which are mutually incompatible. A state cannot be both theo-cratic and atheist at the same time. If a projected law is contrary to the constitution, the law will be rejected or the constitution modified. But situations where the idea of compatibility or incompatibility between two cultural elements can be clearly defined are particular rather than general. Observation shows us that magic is not incompatible with technical things, that industrialization is not incompatible with the persistence of the family structures characteristic of rural societies, that an ideology can remain alive even if it is abundantly contradicted by the facts and in practice. Culturalists often tend, together with the functionalists, whom they some-times wish to oppose, to exaggerate the 'coherence' of the elements which compose the cultural system.

This exaggeration perhaps largely results, in the case of 'archaic' societies, from the fact that the anthropologist does not have access to the historic processes responsible for the state of a society such as he can observe it at a given moment. In this case, he has few resources other than to analyse the 'coherence' between the elements of the system, namely to demonstrate that they are linked by relationships of reciprocal implication. According to the situation, he will thus suggest that a particular element (cf. the rules of residence of Murdock) or a domi-nant characteristic (cf. Benedict's types of culture) tends to imply, and thus explain, others. Possibly the 'synchronic' perspective to which he is condemned will suggest to the analyst that he is dealing, as Lévi-Strauss puts forward not with-out imprudence, with 'societies without a history'. If complex societies are concerned, a methodological perspective of this type is of limited interest. It is understood that Germany and England constituted two different cultural systems at the end of the nineteenth century: 'disciplined' working class in one, aggressive in the other; cult of the State in one, cult of enterprise in the other; veneration of the *Bildung* here, utilitarian ideology there. But the best way of understanding the difference between the two systems does not consist of analysing the coherence of each. We are hardly any further forward when we declare with Parsons that Anglo-Saxon societies give more value to *accomplishment* than to 'the maintenance of cultural models' and that the relative hierarchy of these values is inverse in the Germany of the end of the nineteenth century and of the beginning of the twentieth century. A proposition of this type is not only descriptive rather than explanatory; it tends, furthermore, to cheapen the distinction that it is appropriate to introduce between the hypothetical 'common values' and the representations that the élites develop of common values. This is a distinction which Parsons does not perhaps sufficiently stress, even though he is aware of the fact that, in a country such as America, there is no integrated élite and that each segment of the élite has its own sub-system of values (thus the accomplishment of the businessman is not that of the academic). The difference between the German and English 'cultural' systems can be explained in a much more convincing manner if we analyse them as the result of two different processes occurring at one historical time. The industrialization of Germany, which was later, was more abrupt. The workers in industry were often ex-agricultural workers who had to submit to the iron discipline which ruled over the domaines of the *Junker*. This circumstance cannot fail to have had an effect on working-class 'culture'. In Prussia, the monarchy played an essential role in modernization. In England, modernization was to a large measure set off starting with the free play of interests. This difference induced contrasting ideas about the role and the place of the State, as one sees, for example, in the celebrated critique that Hegel presents of English economists in his *Principles of Right Wing Philosophy*. In Prussia the civil servants, recruited on the strength of a diploma, constituted an important fraction of the ruling élite starting from the time of the reforms of Baron von Stein. The attachment of the civil servants and the academics to the *Bildung* intensified with the process of galloping industrialization which was started in 1860, threatening their influence. Their opposition to the English utilitarian ideology had, in fact, every chance of being stimulated by the logic of the situation. Jean Stoetzel in another context (*Youth without Chrysanthemum or Sabre*) clearly showed that the static image that Benedict gave of Japanese culture was an excessive over-simplification.

The comments that Balandier aptly sets against the ambitions of cultural anthropology apply nearly literally to sociology of culturalist inspiration:

> It does not take into account the incidence of *situations*, concrete and historic conditions, on social and cultural systems. Such a direction leads to the idealization of the societies considered, in not taking sufficient account of the reticences of individuals and antagonisms or conflicts of interest. It can appear as an 'anti-history'.

Like structuralism, culturalism claims to be able to erase without damage the fundamental category of action, without which cultural phenomena themselves are unintelligible (cf. 'Structuralism'). How can we understand the santification of the *Bildung* in pre-Hitlerian Germany and the cult of *achievement* in the United States if not by situating these phenomena in the context of historical processes, and in interpreting them as the response of social actors placed in interactive systems with distinct structures?

Beliefs, Conformity and Deviance, Socialization, Social Symbolism, Structuralism.

Bibliography

BALANDIER, G., 'Sociologie, ethnologie et ethnographie', in GURVITCH, G. (ed.), *Traité de sociologie*, Paris, PUF, 1958–1960, 2 vol.; 3ᵉ éd. mise à jour, 1968, 2 vol., vol. I, 99–113. – BENEDICT, R., *Patterns of culture*, Boston/New York, Houghton Mifflin, 1934; London, Routledge & Kegan Paul, 1935; New York, Penguin Books, 1946; New York, The American Library, 1946. – BENEDICT, R., *Chrysanthemum and the sword*, Boston, Houghton, Mifflin, 1946; London, Secker and Warburg, 1947. – CASSIRER, E., *An essay on man: an introduction to the philosophy of human culture*, New Haven, Yale University Press, 1944, 1956. – DUFRENNE, M., *La personnalité de base. Un concept sociologique*, Paris, PUF, 1953, 1972. – GERSCHENKRON, A., *Economic backwardness in historical perspective. A book of essays*, Cambridge, The Belknap Press of Harvard University Press, 1962. – HERSKOVITS, M.J., *Man and his works: the science of cultural anthropology*, New York, Knopf, 1948. – HYMAN, H.H., 'The value systems of different classes', in BENDIX, R. and LIPSET, S.M. (ed.), *Class, status and power. A reader in social stratification*, New York, The Free Press, 1953; London, Routledge & Kegan Paul, 1967; *Class, status and power. Social stratification in comparative perspective*, 2ᵉ ed. London, Routledge & Kegan Paul, 1966, 488–499. – KARDINER, A., *The individual and his society. The psychodynamics of primitive social organization*, New York/London Columbia University Press, 1939, 1961. — LÉVI-STRAUSS, *Anthropologie structurale*, Paris, Plon, 1968. – LINTON, R., 'Cultural and personality factors affecting economic growth', in HOSELITZ, B.F. (ed.), *The progress of underdeveloped areas*, Chicago, The University of Chicago Press, 1952, 73–88. – LIPSET, S.M., *Political man*, London Mercury Books, 1963. – McCLELLAND, D.C., *The achieving society*, Princeton. D. Van Nostrand Co., 1961; New York, The Free Press, 1967. – MEAD, M., *Anthropology. A human science. Selected papers, 1939–1960*. Princeton/New Jersey/Toronto/London, D. Van Nostrand, 1964. – PARSONS, T., 'A revised analytical approach to the theory of social stratification', in BENDIX, R. and LIPSET, S.M. (ed.), *Class, status and power. A reader in social stratification*, New York, The Free Press, 1953; *Class, status and power. Social stratification in comparative perspective*, London Routledge & Kegan Paul, 2nd edn. 1966, 92, 129. – RINGER, F.K., *The decline of German mandarins. The German academic community, 1890–1933*, Cambridge, Harvard University Press, 1969. – SCHEUCH, E.K., 'Society as context in cross-cultural comparisons', *Social science information/Information sur les sciences sociales*, VII, 5, 1967, 7–15. – STŒTZEL, J., *Jeunesse sans chrysanthème ni sabre. Etude sur les attitudes de la jeunesse japonaise d'après-guerre*, Paris, Plon, 1954. – VOGEL, E.S., 'Kinship structure, migration to the city, and modernization', in DORE, R.P. (ed.), *Aspects of social change in modern Japan*, Princeton, Princeton University Press, 1967, 91–111.

Cycles

Cyclic phenomena generally result because a process, in developing, causes a negative feedback to arise, which ends in a reversal of the earlier observed tendency. The new tendency can afterwards be reversed by the appearance of a new effect of retroaction.

Let us imagine that in a given society at a given period t, a shortage of doctors occurs. A political campaign supported by the press thus starts. The publicity given to the deficit and the fact that doctors' earnings are normally high in a situation where the demand for medical care exceeds the supply encourage a certain number of students to undertake medical studies. To clarify the idea, let us imagine that the number of medical candidates would have been equal to N if the deficit had not been brought to the attention of the public, and that the effect of publicity takes the number to $N + \Delta N$. Let us suppose furthermore that an annual recruitment of $N + \Delta N$ doctors suffices to fill the deficit. The following year, in $t = 1$, the deficit is still present because the doctors who successfully complete their studies are always on average N number by year. It is thus possible that the campaign denouncing the gap in medical provision will continue: the statistics are known only after a time delay. In addition, the deficit continues to be as perceptible in $t + 1$. In consequence, a new increase in candidates is likely to occur. Let us suppose that in $t + 2$ the number of candidates is equal to $N + 2\Delta N$ and that the same cause creates the same effects in subsequent periods. In this hypothesis, the number of candidates continues to grow until the moment when the group which started its studies in t arrives on the job market, that is to say, if one supposes that the study of medicine lasts seven years on average, in $t + 7$, $N + \Delta N$ new doctors will appear on the market, a number which by hypothesis will suffice to fill the deficit if it was maintained at that level in the periods following. But, the number of new doctors is in reality going to continue to grow for a certain number of years. If we accept the simplifying hypotheses of the model, $N + 2\Delta N$, $N = 3\Delta N$, etc., new doctors will appear on the market in $t + 8$, $t + 9$, etc. At a given moment, a negative retroactive effect is likely to appear. In effect, starting from $t + 8$, the average earnings of new doctors have every chance of diminishing. The statistics are going to show, in addition, an excess of medical services. A new political campaign has thus a chance of developing. One can easily imagine the themes: reinforce the difficulty of medical studies in such a way as to produce fewer and better trained doctors. Briefly, there is every chance that we observe the appearance of a *dissuasive* effect symmetrical to the effect of *incentive* which appeared in t. For reasons exactly symmetrical to the earlier ones, it is possible that the dissuasive effects stay active during an overlong period. The result is that, starting from a certain moment, a new deficit is likely to appear.

This example is, to be sure, a simplification. Cyclic phenomena never present themselves with that purity in social life. But it shows up one of the essential reasons for the appearance of cycles, namely the further distant the future the less clearly social actors perceive it. In $t + 1$, the deficit is *potentially* reabsorbed. But this fact will become visible only in $t + 8$. In $t + 1$ the deficit is as apparent as in t.

Economists have contributed very largely to drawing attention to this type of phenomenon. Thus, the famous theorem of the spider's web (*Cobweb theorem*) introduces the hypothesis that producers have a tendency to estimate the comparative prices of tomorrow starting with those of today. As a consequence, they tend to produce *in excess* the products which they think ought to be the most advantageous and in insufficient quantities the products which they think ought to be less profitable. The result is that the former sell at a lower price and the latter at a higher price than expected. A process with a similar structure has been observed with regard to vaccination campaigns in the developing countries. Initially, a high proportion of young mothers had their newborn babies vaccinated. Consequently, the illness disappeared. The vaccination of newborn babies thus tended to be neglected; the illness thus reappeared, causing a return to prudence in the following period.

Naturally the gap between anticipation and reality is not the only cause of the appearance of cyclic phenomena. In very many cases, cycles are produced by the fact that a tendency hits a platform which causes the reversal of the tendency. Here one thinks of the models developed by Malthus (population growth comes to an end on the limitation of natural resources, which provokes higher mortality and possibly a lower birth rate, the two factors causing a decrease in population) or by Ricardo (oscillation of wages round subsistence level). These theoretical models appear to have some pertinence where the explanation of certain historical phenomena is concerned. Thus, LeRoy Ladurie has applied a neo-Malthusian model to rural Languedocian society from the fourteenth century to the middle of the fifteenth century: population growth causes the subdivision of the land and pauperization, which causes a demographic contraction. Other writers, such as Bois, whose work deals with another province, Normandy, have given a much more complex interpretation of the cyclical phenomena which appear at that epoch. Briefly summarized the analysis is as follows: the growth of the population causes the ploughing of new land, which is less and less fertile. Consequently, productivity goes down. The lowering of productivity is even further accentuated by other factors. Thus, cultivation develops at the expense of pasture, resulting in a relative rarity of manure. Following the lowering of productivity, an increase in relative agricultural prices appears. But it is accompanied by a lowering of the real wages of the peasants. As for seigneurial tithes, their volume may grow or at least remain stable. Over a certain period, the diminution of the level of tithes, which is implied by the pauperization of the peasants, being compensated, and sometimes more, by the number of units upon which the tithes are levied, the tendency to weakening of the level of the rate of the portion deducted in advance continues to encourage the reproduction of the peasant population and, consequently, the formation of even less viable units. But a ceiling is eventually reached, above which the volume of seigneurial tithes cannot be maintained if the rate of the tithe is not raised. This circumstance, added to the growing pauperization, has the effect of stopping the growth of the population. Thus we observe an inversion of all the earlier tendencies: the rate of tithes increases, the working of the land and production retract, productivity increases, relative agricultural prices go down, the level of the tithe goes down.

The gap between anticipation and reality and the effects of reaching a ceiling are two major causes of the appearance of cyclic phenomena. But there are certainly other cases to take into account. Certain phenomena put in motion, in a quasi-natural manner, *overshooting* effects which in their turn put in motion a reaction in the opposite direction. When a social state E is seen as undesirable, it tends to give rise to the appearance of ideologies and of utopias preaching its reform. But in order for the ideologies in question to be effective, they must simplify and exaggerate the criticism. First, because, as Simmel and Weber noted, it is easier to achieve a high level of agreement on negative propositions of rejection than on positive propositions; and second, because a message is assured of a larger diffusion in proportion to how simple it is. But if the ideology is effective, it is likely to lead to excessive measures which set off a return of the pendulum. Thus we observe ideological cycles where the growth of the power of the State over civil society is alternatively recommended and denounced. In taking the analyses of Pareto further, we equally draw the conclusion that ideologies, by their intrinsically excessive character, have a tendency to contain their own contradictions. The excesses of the artificial vision of society developed by the philosophy of the Enlightenment (as well as the practical consequences the Revolution drew from this philosophy) instigated the development, for example by Bonald and de Maistre, of a traditionalist vision which itself bears an excessive aspect. After Bonald and de Maistre, the vision of social *engineering* reappeared with the Saint-Simonians. We can discover in the analysis of ideological phenomena another phenomenon with a cyclic effect, foreseen by Tarde in his analyses of fashion: when a product (or an attitude) is adopted by the élite, it has a tendency, in certain circumstances, to become diffused and to lose its function of distinction in the eyes of the élite (Simmel's *Vornehmheit*), who will have thus a tendency to abandon it for another product (or another attitude). This type of phenomenon explains for example the fact that 'structuralism' takes and holds an important place in the teaching of philosophy in the *lycées*, at the moment when a declared scepticism is developing concerning it among the intellectual élite.

The existence of partial, linear processes has given place to a metaphysical side-slip: the evolutionary theories of history. The existence of partial, cyclic processes has given birth to another metaphysical side-slip, that of cyclical theories of history, illustrated, for example, by Spengler and Toynbee and, in a more careful manner, by Sorokin and Pareto (cf. the final sub-title of his *Treatise* – after having shown that 'suppleness' and 'crystallization' of societies mutually succeed one another, Pareto explains precisely, 'Here there is a particular case of the general law of social phenomena, which have an undulating form'). But, as Collingwood remarks, in order to discover cycles in historical evolution considered in its totality, in practice it is sufficient to want it to happen: it is open to anyone to view the eighteenth century as a period of decadence when the social order of the seventeenth century disintegrated or as a period of renaissance paving the way for the conquests of the nineteenth century; the seventeenth century as a flowering of the sixteenth century or as a period of decline. Incontestably, partial cyclic processes exist – we have presented several examples above – as do partial evolutive processes. The proposition according to which *Change* or *History* is cyclic is purely metaphysical.

Determinism, Diffusion, History and Sociology, Historicism, Social Change.

Bibliography

ALLEN, R.G.D., *Mathematical economics*, London, Macmillan, 1957. – BOIS, G., *La crise du féodalisme*, Paris, Presses de la Fondation nationale des Sciences politiques, 1976. – COLLINGWOOD, R.G., *Essays in the philosophy of history*, Austin, Texas University Press, 1965, 1967. – GRAS, A., *Sociologie des ruptures: les pièges du temps en sciences sociales*, Paris, PUF, 1979. – LE ROY LADURIE, E., *Les paysans de Languedoc*, Paris, SEVPEN, 1966, 2 vol.; Paris, Flammarion, 1969, 2 vol.; Paris/La Haye, Mouton, 1974, 2 vol. – SCHELLING, T., *Micromotives and macrobehavior*, Toronto, Norton, 1978. – SCHUMPETER, J., *History of economic analysis*, London, Oxford University Press, 1954, 1972. – SOROKIN, P.A., *Social and cultural dynamics*, New York, American Books, 1937–1941, 4 vol. Abridged version, 1 vol. Boston, Extending Horizons Books, 1957; Boston, Porter Sargent, 1957, 1970. – SPENGLER, O., *Der Untergang des Abend-*

landes: Umrisse einer Morphologie der Weltgeschichte, Munich, C.H. Beck, 1919–1922, 1973. (Trans) *The Decline of the West.* – TARDE, G., *Les lois de l'imitation. Etude sociologique,* Paris, F. Alcan. 1890, 3rd rev. edn, 1900, Paris/Geneva, Slatkine Reprints, 1979. – TOYNBEE, A.J., *A study of history,* London/New York/ Toronto, Oxford University Press, 1934–1961, 12 vol.

D

Democracy

The term democracy belongs to the vocabulary of ideology, but it also has an analytic content, which is attested to by the position it holds in the vocabulary of philosophers, political scientists, and sociologists.

The first question to address concerns whether the word is being used with the same meaning when it is said that the Athens of the fifth century BC was a democracy and when we talk about the great western democracies of today. The Athenian regime was characterized by the direct nature of popular government. It was a citizens' assembly, never exceeding 20,000 persons, which took direct decisions on public affairs. The citizenry was confined to free men, and excluded slaves and aliens resident in the city. It is also true that the magistrates – as shown by the example of Pericles, who contrived to be re-elected a number of times – exercised in fact a greater influence on the affairs of the State than would be apparent at first sight from the way they were elected. They were not, as Rousseau would have us believe, simple clerks or minor officials, but in many cases 'demagogues', or in other words, *political entrepreneurs*. Despite these reservations, Athens was a direct democracy, where the citizens, as a body which was only a minority of the population, exercised sovereignty.

Benjamin Constant has identified a radical distinction between this form of democracy and that which is observed in the political institutions of modern Europe. Our democracies are representative and pluralist. They are less likely to involve the reign of a very hypothetical general will than to organize or engineer the mechanisms of control through which those who 'govern' are held in more or less firm check by the 'governed'. This political regime is linked to a social structure characterized by an advanced division of labour, by the existence of a civil society, where the 'middle classes' give legitimate expression to their interests and opinions. By employing this distinction between direct and representative democracy, Benjamin Constant was aiming to discredit the absolutism which he detected in the Rousseauist conception of a general will, with its Roman and Spartan overtones, and to promote by contrast a practical and reasonable conception of British-style democracy. The conception used by Constant, who used the British and American models as his points of reference, can be called liberal while the position he imputed to Rousseau can be termed radical.

This conflict has as much to do with the principles of political organization as it does with the modalities of institutional arrangements. Viewed from the perspective of the value hierarchy whose realization they propose, democracies are obliged to arbitrate between the three components of the French slogan – *Liberty, Equality, Fraternity* – if the term is held to refer to a solidaristic collectivity. *Liberal democracy* gives priority to liberty, understood as independence from and non-interference by the authorities in the sphere of private interests – except in the case where it is duly debated and recognized by official judgement as in the public good. Equality, understood as the absence of privilege, is valued to the extent that it appears as a favourable condition for the realization of personal independence and autonomy or for the meritocratic social order which is naturally linked to them. Fraternity, the existence of a politically solidaristic community, is valued to the extent that it results from the respect and esteem which free and equal individuals have for each other, rather than for any fusion or assimilation which may be held to be suspect or illusory.

According to the scale of values which characterize *radical democracy*, it is equality which has priority. Liberty is devalued because of its aristocratic origins. Instead of being linked to co-operation and contract, fraternity is seen as synonymous with public-spiritedness; it is the unity of a political body, where differences are tolerated only where they pose no threat to the solidity of a homogeneous social tissue. To put it in the style of Montesquieu would be to say that the spirit of liberal democracy is *moderation*, whereas the spirit of radical democracy is the *virtue* which assures the predominance of collective obligations over all forms of private and personal interest.

Liberal democracy relies on the balance of power, by checks and balances, in its mode of institutional organization; radical democracy tends towards simplicity and the concentration of power. Liberals recommend pluri-cameralism, a multiplicity of electoral institutions; while radical democrats propose the single assembly, through which the government is no more than an executive committee, which can be abolished at any moment. The downside of radical democracy is what de Tocqueville, while visiting the USA during Jackson's presidency, described as the 'tyranny of the majority'. The downside of liberal democracy is the multiplicity of processes, guarantees, and regulations, with the paralysis of central power simultaneously accompanied by the over-representation and excessive protection of acquired interests.

Democratic societies display national traditions which are more or less strongly individualized but at the same time share a similar co-tradition, which particularly stresses religious inspirations (Judaeo-Christian in the case of Europe and North America). Moreover, each national tradition is itself complex and combines in a more or less successful way the liberal and the radical perspectives. For example, in the French tradition the Montagnarde convention is the model for radical democrats; the Orleanist compromise and the constitutional laws of 1875 are the favoured precedents for liberal democrats. In the USA it is possible to distinguish a Jeffersonian tradition, extended by the administration of President Jackson and Roosevelt's New Deal. The complexity and heterogeneity of these traditions has been increased by the fact that the concepts of radical democracy were established in the nineteenth century, before socialism, with its concern for establishing central and egalitarian state control over the relatively decentralized initiatives of entrepreneurs, had become one of the main axes of thought about political organization. Hence there are radical democrats who are in favour of a socialist economic organization of society and other radical democrats who see in socialism an insupportable extension of the 'tutelary despotism' of bureaucracy.

If we look for the common points among the different democratic institutions and ideologies, for what constitutes, in spite of their diversity, their co-tradition or common 'spirit', we will find an affirmation of individualism and a suspicion of government. The affirmation of individualism is expressed with striking clarity in the Gettysburg Address: 'The government *of* the people, *by* the people, *for* the people'. It is reinforced by Lincoln's implicit concept of the 'people'. It is not the State nor even the nation, much less the bodies which make them up, but the entirety of citizens, each judging according to his own principles and conscience which is right for the Republic. The result is that political leaders should only be agents or commissaries of the sovereign collectivity.

This ideology of control, which has a double meaning in that the governors must be accountable and the governed are the masters, is embodied in institutions which are very different, and are not wholly political. Functionaries and civil servants, whether they have a post on the basis of election or nomination by a higher authority, are responsible for any abuse or excess of power, of which they might be found guilty before a judicial system, either civil or administrative. Control over those who govern is exercised through the electoral system, which invests them with power for a limited period, and which may be withdrawn at the end of their tenure of the post. The radical model is equivalent where those who govern are subject to an imperative mandate, and when they can be dismissed without notice by a general assembly.

The control of the governed over those who govern appeared to be an arguably hypothetical state of affairs to those sociologists who studied representative mechanisms. The famous Iron Law of Oligarchy, on which Michels and Mosca drew so heavily, points to the very limited circulation of political élites, and the efficiency of the strategy through which elected representatives become established in their posts and are less easy to dislodge the more that their services are unique and unsubstitutable. 'Representatives' and their 'machines' thus constitute a 'screen' which prevents the sovereignty of the governed from expressing itself. Radical democrats always claim to be able to break these mediating links and give the 'power to the people'.

The confiscation of political power by professional politicans has struck a number of writers, and notably Schumpeter, who even suggested that democratic regimes are mainly characterized by the preponderance of politicians within them. They constitute a fraction of the élite of western societies, specialized in the functions of mediation and power broking. In this context, even if they can be seen as professional intermediaries or persuaders, they are not professionals in the same sense as lawyers or doctors who, even if their power over their clients is channelled through a process in which it is reinforced by influence, may plead a technical competence which is certified. They are at the frontier of several groups such as top civil servants, businessmen, intellectuals – and especially journalists. But politicians are distinguished from the other leading groups through the ways in which they are recruited and by nature of the competition between them. They are more dependent on the public in general than any other élite group because of their need to be elected or re-elected.

But election, the decisive mechanism of their investiture, poses a whole series of logistical problems. It involves consulting a group of respondents – the body politic – and assessing the likely vote of each member. This procedure contains three sorts of problems. First, do the electorate have the minimum level of *competence* or will their lack of information or analysis expose them to a fatal error? Do they have the minimum level of *morality*, or 'virtue' as it was called in the eighteenth century, to distinguish between their self-interest and the common good? And third, election also poses a logical problem. It involves the *aggregation* of individual choices to construct a collective choice which will have the property of binding each and everyone. To the extent that electors are unanimous in their support for a policy or a candidate, it is unnecessary to worry about the singular intentions of each individual who, behind the facade of unanimity, may pursue his or her own ends. But as soon as any cleavage appears between a majority and a minority, it is appropriate to ask with what right the will of the greatest number is confounded with the will of the majority? The problem is aggravated when the majority is not absolute but relative, which often happens when the electoral body is presented with more than two choices. It is particularly apposite to inquire whether the coherence of this will, once the policy has been chosen and the candidate elected, is really the expression of the majority, or if it is no more than a compromise consented to by an accidental majority, made up of a coalition of individuals whose strategies and preferences are in fact very diverse.

From this analysis of 'majority decisions' it is possible to draw a pessimistic assessment of both liberal and radical democracy, and of the capacity of democratic institutions to 'function' according to their principles. But the term 'democratic' is not applied only to governmental institutions. In general it applies to any society where, whatever the leaders call themselves, the exercise of power occurs under certain conditions concerning the definition of collective objectives and the involvement of group members in their definition and realization. From this perspective, strongly supported by social psychologists of the Lewinian tradition, any society will be labelled democratic in which collective objectives are based on at least a minimum of *consensus* and where status is attributed on functional criteria and not merely according to hierarchical rules. Certain social psychologists refer to a 'democratic' mode and form of organization. Although officers are not elected by their men, teachers by their pupils, or doctors by their patients, it is possible even so to refer to a 'democratic' army, school, or hospital, if classical discipline – obey without question – is replaced by processes of discussion and decision-making where, to the fullest extent that is possible, collective constraints are negotiated and legitimated. Election thus changes its meaning. It is no longer aimed at the expression of a quite hypothetical 'general will'. Rather, it contributes, or is thought to contribute, to the establishment of a 'climate' of information and of mutual understanding, where solidarity may develop – or at least tolerance between members of society – and where the risks of abuse and exploitation by those who govern are methodically controlled. Thus interpreted, democracy is a mode of government of any organization where the guarantees of expression and participation to all categories of interest and opinion, *reduce the distance* between governors and governed.

One paradoxical observation is worth emphasizing. First, all modern regimes describe themselves more or less explicitly as democracies, but challenge such a description when it is applied to opposing regimes. For the Soviets, and western communists who consider the regime 'positive in global terms' despite the Gulag, Soviet communism is the sole authentic democracy, and 'bourgeois democracy' is an imposter. Hitler himself presented national socialism, not at all as a democracy – a regime necessarily compromised in his view, but as the sole authentic expression of the 'profound' will of both God and the people. Franco described his system as 'organic democracy'. Two considerations follow from this paradox. First, all modern regimes seek to legitimize themselves by invoking their service of a cause or of the people who identify with this cause. On the other hand, those who govern never dare to invoke, at least explicitly, a right to govern which would be connected to the divine right – or natural right – of their person. Hitler described himself as at the service of the German people. The communist party is the 'vanguard of the proletariat', itself the 'vanguard' of humanity. There is in a very wide sense a general democratic sensibility diffused within modern political culture, which is perceptible even among the bitterest enemies of democracy. But the reason for such ambiguity is, on reflection, hardly a mystery. It proceeds from the gap in any regime between the ideal of legitimacy and the institutions in which it is embodied – a gap which varies in width from one historical situation or regime to another. It is at its widest when extermination camps are called labour camps – either in Hitler's Germany or Stalin's Soviet Union. More generally it depends on the historical conditions in which the democratic regime was created. De Tocqueville drew attention to this point. If America was in his view the model for peaceful and responsible democracy, it was because the 'Revolution' which preceded it had not been disfigured like the French Revolution, first by the Jacobin Terror and then by Bonapartist despotism.

Development, Elections, Power, Rousseau, Schumpeter, State.

Bibliography

ARON, R., *Démocratie et totalitarisme*, Paris, Gallimard, 1965. – BARRY, B., *Sociologists, economists and democracy*, New York and London, Collier-Macmillan, 1970. – CONSTANT, B., *Écrits et discours politiques*,

Paris, J.-J. Pauvert, 1964. – DAHL, R.A., *A preface to democratic theory*, Chicago, The Univ. of Chicago Press, 1956; *Who governs? Democracy and power in an American city*, New Haven, Yale Univ. Press. 1961. – DOWNS, A., *An economic theory of democracy*, New York, Harper, 1957. – FINLEY, M.I., *Democracy, ancient and modern*, New Brunswick, Rutgers University Press, 1973; London, Hogarth, 1985.; – LIPSET, S.M., *Political man: the social bases of politics*, Garden City, Doubleday, 1960; London, Heinemann, 1983. – LOWI, T., *American government. Incomplete conquest*, New York, Rinehart & Winston, 1977. – MARSHALL, T.H., *Citizenship and social class*, Cambridge. The Univ. Press, 1950. – MONTESQUIEU, C. de, *L'Esprit des lois*. – ROUSSEAU, J.-J., *La contrat social, The Social Contract*, Penguin Classics, 1963 – SARTORI, G., *Democratic theory*, Detroit, Wayne State Univ. Press, 1962. – SCHUMPETER, J.A., *Capitalism. socialism and democracy*, New York, Harper, 1942, London, G. Allen & Unwin, 1976. – TOCQUEVILLE, A. de, *De la démocratie en Amérique, Democracy in America*, Viking, 1957.

Determinism

A social system is said to be subject to determinism if knowing its state in t, we can predict its state in subsequent 'moments' $t + 1, \ldots, t + k$, etc. But two types of situation must be immediately distinguished. It is possible that no elements enabling the observer to predict the state of a system in $t + 1, \ldots, t + k$, etc, are available to him, although the future state of the system is contained in its present state. It can be said, in this case, that the system is objectively determined, but seems subjectively to be undetermined. Although the trajectory of a falling leaf is entirely determined, it is difficult to predict where it will fall, as generally the characteristics of the forces determining its trajectory are not known. One knows only that it is very likely, or at least that there is some probability (the value of which can eventually be determined) that it will fall within a given circle. When a system is such that, even while assuming an omniscient observer, the state of the system in $t + 1$, $\ldots, t + k$, etc., can only be known starting from the knowledge of its state in t, the system will be said to be either objectively undetermined, or abstracted from the 'general law' of determinism. The question whether there are indeed objectively undetermined systems raises thorny philosophical questions which are beyond the present discussion. The main difficulty raised by philosophical discussions relevant to determinism lies no doubt in the fact that they must introduce the fiction of an omniscient observer. Now, one may wonder whether this notion does not carry an internal contradiction: how can a non-omniscient observer take the place of an omniscient observer? One can imagine an omniscient observer knowing more than such an observer on this or that subject. But the notion of an omniscient observer supposes that he is informed about subjects the nature of which the real observer might be unable to conceive.

Sociology inherited from its birth a determinist vision of social systems – perhaps more exactly from its institutionalization in the nineteenth century, at a time when physics was considered the queen of sciences and when a Laplacian conception of the world reigned supreme (knowing the state of the world in t, it is possible for the omniscient observer to predict its state in $t + 1, \ldots, t + k$ etc.). In other words, many sociologists will admit that the indetermination of social systems can only be subjective; the state of a social system in $t + 1, \ldots, t + k$, etc., is entirely contained in its state in t. Some errors of prediction can of course be noted but these errors are conceived as resulting from the ignorance the sociologist might have about the intensity of the social 'forces' (as Marx would have said) at play in such or such system.

One may wonder if the recent evolution of sociology does not lead to the substitution of this Laplacian vision by a more complex one where: 1) the determination of social systems would be considered as objectively variable and as liable to variation by degree, some social systems being objectively more predictable and more determined, others less so, even for an observer who is not omniscient but provided with relevant data; and 2) the more or less determined character of the system would be conceived as resulting from the structure of the system itself.

To illustrate this non-Laplacian conception of social determinism, one may resort to a simple example borrowed from genetic theory: let us imagine that two social actors in an interaction situation have a choice between two strategies A and B. Four 'solutions' are possible: AA (the first chooses A, the second A), AB (the first chooses A, the second B), BA, and BB. Let us suppose now that the first actor prefers AA to all combinations, and the same goes for the second actor. Let us suppose, furthermore, that each knows the other's preferences. In this case, the future of the system is entirely determined. The sociologist observing such a situation would not, in other terms, incur any risk if he asserted that both actors will choose A and that the combination finally realized, to the exclusion of all the others will be the AA combination. Let us imagine now that the preferences of the two actors are as follow: the first prefers AB to BA, BA to AA, and AA to BB; the second prefers BA to AB, AB to AA, and AA to BB. Both then consider AA and especially BB as undesirable, but do not agree about the relative preferability of AB and BA. The first wishes to choose A as long as the other chooses B; the second would like to choose A as long as the other chooses B. What is going to happen? Each is aware that to obtain his favourite combination, he must play A, but each sees also that if the other plays A, the combination achieved will be AA which neither considers desirable. Actor 1 might try and give a convincing sign to actor 2 that he will not play anything other than A. But actor 2 might do the same. In such a system, it is very difficult to predict what is going to happen. The future of the system is not contained in the present. At the very most it is possible to assume that, if the stakes are important, the two actors will do everything to avoid the realization of the combinations AA and BB which they both agree to judge undesirable. But it is difficult to predict which of the two combinations AB or BA will be finally realized. One might indeed imagine cases where 'psychological' data would enable the 'omniscient' observer to limit uncertainty. Thus, if actor 1 is timid and actor 2 domineering, BA will be more likely to be realized than AB. But, if we suppose that actor 1 and actor 2 are psychologically entirely indistinct from each other, the omniscient observer is unable to reach a conclusion. The system is objectively undetermined.

More generally, some systems of action have such a structure that: 1) actors' behaviours can be easily predicted; 2) actors' behaviours have no impact on the structure of the interaction system. In this case, the system's behaviour can easily

be anticipated by an observer provided with relevant data. The system is objectively determined. Actors' behaviour can be anticipated without difficulty especially
in two cases: either when the interaction system allows them to realize their objectives, or when, without enabling them to realize their objectives, it incites them to a
particular course of action. Thus, Michel Crozier's *The Bureaucratic Phenomenon*
describes an interaction system where some actors, because of their position within
the organization, can choose the most favourable interpretation of their role to
their interests and that which best conforms to their preferences, and impose this
interpretation on the others, while other actors are constrained by the context to
interpret their own role in a way which does not satisfy them, without however
being able to choose a more favourable interpretation or to lead the others to
change their behaviour. Thus, the maintenance workers of Crozier's Monopoly,
who move from workshop to workshop to repair broken machines, can choose to
not let themselves be harassed and allow the production workers to suffer from the
sudden stoppages in the work and the financial repercussions which result.
Despite the unfavourable situation created for them by the maintenance workers,
the production workers cannot try to modify the 'selfish' interpretation the former
'naturally' adopt for their role, because, if they tried to bring pressure to bear on
the maintenance workers, not only would it be unlikely to be effective, but it would
lead to tension harmful to the workers' solidarity. This tension would compromise
the advantages of solidarity which, if union mediation were to take place, it would
offer to everyone. As the system is moreover defined in such a way that none of the
actors outside the system formed by the maintenance and production workers
benefits from changing the situation, the result is that we are dealing with an
almost entirely predictable and determined system. The system's structure is such
that the actors' behaviours are easily predictable. As, moreover, the actions of one
or the other have no effect on the system's structure, it tends to reproduce itself
from t to $t + 1$ or $t + k$.

Predictable and determined systems often have a 'reproductive' character. But
it is not necessarily so. Some systems are such that: 1) the actors' behaviour is easy
to predict; 2) the effects of the actors' behaviour on the system's structure are also
predictable. In this case, the system's future is itself predictable. Its future may be
held to be included in its present.

Sociology's history itself offers many examples of subjective indetermination
where one or other sociologist either proved unable to predict the future of a
system because he lacked the necessary information or was led to make erroneous
predictions (cf. 'Prediction') because of inadequate information. Consider, for
example, the numerous disappointments resulting from development policies
based on the injection of physical capital or the failures suffered by some fertility or
birth-control programmes (cf. 'Development'). Such examples do not necessarily
imply the existence of an objective indetermination. Thus, failure of some birth-
control programmes has sometimes led to a return to the field, which has shown
that hypotheses about the rationality of actors used by those programmes were not
taking into account particular and relevant features of the socio-economic context.

But it is especially important to stress that there can be an objective indetermination in social systems. This indetermination appears in a first instance when the structure of a system is such that it gives at least some of the actors included in the system sufficient autonomy that they can effectively choose between contrasting options, and when the actors have no predictable preferences regarding these options. A situation of this kind may arise for example if: 1) some actors are indifferent to the possible end results; 2) they are unable to determine the actions most in agreement with their preferences (cf. 'Rationality'); 3) their choice is subject to the 'paradox of information' (to acquire an optimum amount of information, one must know its value; but one cannot decide on the value of information one has not acquired yet). Given these three hypotheses, the actor will act in an objectively risky way. Buriden's donkey (second instance) certainly 'will choose' one of the two sacks of oats, but his choice can only be risk-laden. In a situation of this kind, the system is partially undetermined. Indeed, the system's future evolution depends on the actors' choices (choices which might eventually have irreversible consequences) and the system indeed presents possibilities of choices. But these choices themselves are not predictable. The state of the system in $t + 1$ cannot then be determined from its state in t. It is not worth supposing that the choice made by the actor always depends, even when he is indifferent about the options offered to him, on variables present in the 'structure of his personality'. It is true that, in some cases, the actor's tastes or ambitions can enable him to decide between the options. But there are also cases of real indifference: when, for example, two options A and B offer both advantages and disadvantages, these advantages and disadvantages are not clearly comparable, and their probabilities of being realized are not easily appreciated by the actor. Thus, union leaders cannot avoid having as one objective the maintenance and potential increase of their membership. This objective being established, any number of means (in different historical circumstances) can be used to achieve it: offering trade union members services they would appreciate, attempting to control entry into the trade or profession, etc. In some cases, these might be unequally effective and costly. In other cases, the leaders might find themselves in a position of indifference towards the possible means, so that the strategy finally adopted is broadly unpredictable. Naturally, once a strategy is chosen, it is likely to be irreversible; its full implementation is not immediate but spreads over a certain period. Consequently some actors will be more or less deeply involved in its defence and will oppose it being challenged. Moreover, a change of strategy might imply collective costs superior to the advantages to be provided by a new strategy. These considerations help to explain, for example, why societies directly comparable from an economic point of view have highly contrasted traditions of trade unionism. More generally, they explain the 'relative autonomy' of institutions in relation to each other, as well as of the institutions in relation to the 'structures'.

The fact that there are structures placing actors in a situation of indifference is evidence that sociologists sometimes find difficult to accept. The reason lies no doubt in an epistemological misinterpretation. One sometimes tends to consider situations of indetermination as not being worth mentioning by the observer. But if he does not take into account the objective indetermination caused by some structures, the sociologist is powerless to explain them. Thus to explain why the industrial revolution has been linked to different forms of trade union action, one must show that some structures and historical contingencies offer options towards which the actors feel (and have the right to feel) indifferent. The use of statistical instruments by some sociologists is very instructive in this respect. When a sociologist observes a correlation, possibly a very weak one, between two variables X and Y, he often remembers only the existence of the correlation (that is to say the fact that it is not null) and forgets to consider its weak absolute value. But to give an explanation of a correlation is not only to explain why it is not null, but also why it is situated in such or such system of values. Now, sometimes, a correlation is weak because it arises from structures giving the actors some possibilities of choice between options towards which they are likely to perceive themselves as indifferent.

Second instance: some systems have a structure that generates a demand for *innovation*. This case is found, for example, when a sequence of political actions conceived within the framework of the same 'paradigm' generates a diffuse feeling of failure and gives the impression that the 'paradigm' is inadequate. One must then resort to another 'paradigm'. But the 'choice' finally made may be difficult to predict. More precisely, it may be difficult to predict which of a finite group of possible paradigms will finally be chosen. Thus, as Hirschmay has pointed out, the Colombian 'agrarian problem' was first approached for a long period within the framework of a juridical paradigm inherited from the Spanish tradition until most of the participants became convinced that the objective summarized by the proverb *morada y labor* could not be achieved by improvement of the legal system. There then occurred a *paradigm shift* in Kuhn's words; the achieving of the fixed objective was then attempted through improvements of a fiscal kind. But the form of the new paradigm, if understandable a posteriori, was hardly predictable a priori. Generally speaking, when a system generates a demand for innovation, a range of situations may occur. Thus, in the England of the eighteenth and nineteenth centuries, the competition established between entrepreneurs in the textile industry gave birth to a demand for technical innovation. But it could be predicted that new looms would be invented and that inventions guaranteeing an increase in productivity would be retained. The existence of a demand for innovation is therefore not enough to make a system unpredictable and undetermined. But there are also cases where the effect of a demand for innovation does not allow us to include anything much a priori about the content of innovation. Generally speaking, when a system involves a demand for innovation, the greater or lesser predictability of innovation is a function of the characteristics of the system. Hence the corollary that the evolution of some systems may not be easily predictable even by a thoroughly informed observer.

The twin conclusions that some social systems: 1) determine areas of possibilities towards which some actors might be indifferent; 2) generate a demand for innovations, the content of which might be imperfectly predictable, introduces an objective indetermination; to which must be added the fact that indetermination increases as the observer situated in t tries to predict the evolution of the system in a period further from t. Whereas some social systems involve an objective indetermination, all systems oppose to the observer a subjective indetermination which becomes greater as the distance increases between t, the 'moment' of the prediction, and $t + k$, the 'instant' about which the prediction is made. This subjective indetermination results simply from the fact that the actions of actors in a social system almost always entail consequences which go beyond the actors' intentions and the observers' ability to anticipate. Naturally, one must also take into account the fact that the observer is not always able to distance himself sufficiently, and therefore tends sometimes to fall into the particular form of socio-centrism which consists in projecting into the future elements borrowed from the situation he is in at the 'moment' t.

Evolutionary processes which have a social component (the development of sciences, technology and, generally, speaking knowledge) have for a long time confirmed sociologists in the idea that the social systems displayed a Laplacian type of determinism. Furthermore, the belief in universal determinism seemed to them a condition of any science. The incontestable fact that some processes are easily predictable (cf. the 'heavy tendencies' of economists), linked with the epistemological malaise caused by the idea of an objectively indetermined system (even if this indetermination is partial), was to make many sociologists more Laplacian than Laplace. Even today, a sociologist who observes a weak correlation between two phenomena will tend either to consider the weakness of the correlation as the result of errors of observation or to accept without discussion that the correlation would be at its maximum if it was possible to observe all the factors acting on the independent variable. The two interpretations are in agreement over a fundamental question: they both dismiss the possibility of objective indetermination. But the existence of an objective indetermination is not an obstacle to scientific explanation. As the examples summarily developed above are enough to demonstrate, one can *explain* that some situations define possible 'solutions' towards which actors are indifferent. In the same way, one can *explain* that some structures entail demands for innovation the content of which may, in some cases for reasons that can be analysed, be difficult to predict. Contrary to Thom's thesis, the view that determinism is an essential postulate of scientific explanation may, in the social sciences at least, inhibit rather than help explanation.

Causality, Historicism, Knowledge, Prediction, Social Change, Theory.

Bibliography

ARON, R., *Introduction à la philosophie de l'histoire. Essai sur les limites de l'objectivité historique*, Paris, Gallimard, 1938, 1981. – AYERS, M.R., *The refutation of determinism: an essay in philosophical logic*, London, Methuen, 1968. – BOUDON, R., 'Les limites des schémas déterministes dans l'explication sociologique', in BUSINO, (ed.), *Les sciences sociales avec et après Jean Piaget. Hommage publié à l'occasion du 80ᵉ anniversaire de Jean Piaget*, Geneva, Droz, 1976, 417–435; 'Déterminismes sociaux et liberté individuelle', in BOUDON, R., *Effets pervers et ordre social*, Paris, PUF, 1977, chap. VII, 187–252. – GURVITCH, G., *Déterminismes sociaux et liberté humaine. Vers l'étude sociologique des cheminements de la liberté*, PUF, 1955. – MATERNA, P., 'A formulation of the determinism hypothesis', *Theory and decision*, VI, *1*, 1975, 39–42. – MONOD, J., *Le hasard et la nécissité. Essai sur la philosophie naturelle de la biologie moderne*, Paris, Le Seuil, 1970. – NAGEL, E., 'Determinism in history', *Philosophy and phenomenological research*, XX, *3*, 1960, 291–317. *in* GARDI-

NER, P. (ed.), *The philosophy of history*, Oxford, Oxford University Press, 1974, 187–215. – POPPER, K.R., *The poverty of historicism*, London, Routledge & Kegan Paul, 1957, 1963. New York, Basic Books, 1960; New York, Harper & Row, 1961, 1964; London, Ark, 1986. – PRIGOGINE, I. and STENGERS, I., *La nouvelle alliance*, Paris, Gallimard, 1979. – TAYLOR R., *Action and purpose*, Englewood Cliffs, Prentice Hall, 1966. – THOM, R., 'Halte au hasard, silence au bruit', *Le débat*, 3, 1980, 119–132.

Development

This expression and the related terms 'underdevelopment' and 'developing country' appear within the framework of the new world 'order' and the international organizations set up following the Second World War. They were supplemented by a term which had much currency in left wing circles, and was destined to have a great future, the concept of the Third World. Formulated by A. Sauvy on the model of a French juridical expression which has its roots in the French revolutionary period, the 'Third Estate', which rose up against church and aristocracy, the term suggests that an international 'class division' of societies exists within the new world order. The opposition 'development/underdevelopment' or 'developed countries/developing countries' suggests a linear evolutionist process. The notion of the Third World, by introducing the implicit hypothesis that the dialectic of class struggle has spread over the entire planet, both revives and modernizes Marx's historicist vision.

The notion of development itself, the task given to international experts of determining the appropriate measures to promote and accelerate the process of development, involved both an incentive and a temptation: to search for a *general* explanation of development and underdevelopment. Many writers therefore tried to explain why the structures of underdeveloped countries included processes of reproduction of blocked development. Thus the 'theory' of the vicious circle of poverty, for example, put forward by Nurkse then revived by Galbraith about thirty years later, is based upon the following propositions: 1) low productivity leads to a low income; 2) when income is low, the ability to save is negligible; 3) when savings are negligible, capital accumulation is impossible; 4) when investment is negligible, productivity is inevitably stagnant. This logical circle is a paradigmatic example of a reproductive process and can easily be translated (and has indeed been translated by Samuelson) into mathematical terms: income is a function of invesment, investment is a function of saving, saving a function of income. Thus we have a theory which, from a formal point of view, recalls the famous reproductive processes described by Malthus and Ricardo. But, unlike the classical theorists, the theorists of underdevelopment see the reproductive processes they think they have made clear within an evolutionist framework. These reproductive processes are therefore considered as blockages or *bottlenecks* which must be analysed and reduced.

A second theory – or, to be more precise, a second group of theories – argues that market limitations are the main factor of stagnation: supposing that there is an ability to save, it is still necessary for the holders of a 'surplus' of income to be encouraged to convert this surplus into savings, rather than conspicuous consumption, for example. Now, the encouragement to save and invest implies solvent demand. It is difficult to imagine an entrepreneur trying to tap savings in order to build a factory to produce agricultural equipment if he is also able to predict that no one will be able to afford to buy these tools.

A third group of theories stresses the perverse mechanisms generated by what is traditionally called the '*demonstration effect*': when there is an income 'surplus', it tends to be consumed rather than saved, because of the irresistable attraction of the western way of life for the upper classes of underdeveloped countries.

A fourth group of theories focuses on the lack of *working or 'overhead' capital* on the principle of blockage: because of the lack of sufficiently developed means of transport and communication, markets are condemned to be limited and local. Consequently, surpluses of income cannot be tapped for savings and investment: with low general productivity leading moreover to a low average income, the state's income is insufficient to enable development of the means of transport and communication.

These bottlenecks are again reinforced by additional mechanisms, according to development theorists. The infrastructure of most developing countries being composed of tight and relatively isolated communities, as a result of the lack of working or overhead capital in particular, capital goods (for instance, agricultural equipment) and non-food consumption goods (for instance, clothes) are the object of craft production for local markets. The productivity increase of such craft enterprises is blocked not only by the above factors but also because the division of labour in the village community is intimately linked to social and family structures. As Hoselitz suggested, in a passage inspired by classical theorists such as Tönnies and Redfield, in 'traditional' societies, productive activity has not only economic objectives; it is also considered by the members of traditional societies as containing ritual elements, elements which increase social cohesion. The multiplicity of these 'dimensions' of any social act is the root of problems met when one tries to modify these behaviours.

Other theories put forward make the hypothesis of a demographic vicious circle of a neo-Malthusian type: an increase in income would cause an increase in population which would absorb the 'surpluses'. The ability to save would therefore remain stagnant, in spite of economic development.

Evolutionism and what can be called reproductionism are indissolubly linked in these development theories. The identification of bottlenecks leads to the explanation that underdeveloped societies appear to be 'blocked' societies. At the same time, it points to the levers (aid to governments with the view to facilitating the formation of working or overhead capital, technical help, development of investments, etc.) helping to set underdeveloped countries on the path to what is considered to be a 'normal' type of evolution. This is why the many variants of the *bottlenecks* theory do not contradict openly evolutionist theories, such as the economic *take-off* theory, introduced by Rostow in *The Stages of Growth* as a process caused by the elimination of bottlenecks. Thus, the appearance of enterprises directed towards wider markets and characterized, as Marx would have said, by a process of extended reproduction is introduced by Rostow as one of the main mechanisms of growth of the industrialized countries (cf. the role of milk production in Denmark or of textile production in eighteenth-century England). Once the bottlenecks are reduced, cumulative effects appear which lead societies into evolutionary processes.

Looked at together, these general theories of development seem to be incompatible with each other – the first point which it is important to note. The theory of the 'vicious circle of poverty' suggests that underdeveloped countries are characterized by the lack of savings because of inadequate income. The theories based on the 'demonstration' effect assume, on the contrary, that surpluses are diverted into conspicuous consumption. The neo-Malthusian theories certainly admit that income can increase, but they assert that this increase is checked by the population increase to which it leads. According to some theories, one of the main factors in economic stagnation is the weakness of contacts and exchanges with industrialized countries. Others see in the exchanges with industrialized nations one of the causes of blocked development (demonstration effect, concentration of production equipment on raw materials aimed at the markets in industrialized societies). Second, these theories are often incompatible with historical data or incontrovertible facts. As Bauer has observed, both Gross National Product and output per capita increased faster between 1920 and 1953 in Latin America than in the United States. This does not mean that poverty does not exist in Latin America. But such data are clearly incompatible with the theory of the vicious circle of poverty. Against the neo-Malthusian theories, demographers have shown that population growth is due mainly to lower mortality rates which result from the spread of hygiene. Against the demonstration effect, historical data seem to indicate that in traditional societies which have limited contact with the industrialized society most sumptuary or conspicuous consumption is no less important than in societies exposed to the influence of the West. If endogenous blocking mechanisms characteristic of traditional societies are responsible for underdevelopment, it can be concluded that change could only be exogenous. But how then can we explain the spectacular development of nineteenth-century Japan at a time when this country had virtually no contact with the external world? The creation of appropriate infrastructures (social capital) would be a necessary condition of development. But history demonstrates that infrastructures often accompany rather than precede development. Thus, Colombia had one of the highest growth rates of the world at the turn of the century. And yet the means of transport between the main towns of this country were at that time quite rudimentary. The same applies to Argentina. The development of the particular form of social capital represented by the means of communication seems to have followed, rather than preceded, the take-off of this country at the turn of the century. It was the restriction on markets which was mainly responsible for stagnation. But the same Colombia, at the beginning of the century, had a modern industrial base (sugar industry, mining industry) at its disposal, while the entire population numbered only a few million inhabitants and the markets were sharply segmented by the geography and the rudimentary character of the means of transport and communication. The intricacy of social and economic structures would be such that the system of division of labour and productivity would be ineluctably blocked. However, the irrigation programme launched by the Indian Government on the eve of the Second World War has made some important sectors of Indian agriculture move from the stage of subsistence economy to the stage of exchange economy.

The theory of the demonstration effect attributes changes in the structure of consumption to contacts with industrialized societies. But these contacts can also affect production (cf., in India, the increase in productivity as a result of the adoption of Japanese methods of rice cultivation). It is true that demonstration effects can occur and may have negative consequences. The adoption by some developing countries of education systems inspired by those of industrial societies has in some cases started a brain drain effect and/or increased the distance between élites and the rest of the population. But there is no reason why contacts between industrial societies and developing societies should either have exclusively negative consequences or be doomed to affect only the structure of demand for goods and services. Markets are often limited and the demand for some products is low. But it is not so for all products. Capital formation is undoubtedly an essential aspect of economic development. But Solow has shown that in the United States between 1909 and 1949 only 13 per cent of the increase of production per capita and per hour was due to capital accumulation. Denison has likewise shown that the economic growth of the United States after the Second World War could not be explained merely by the increase of physical capital.

Incompatible with one another, not easily reconcilable with the facts, the reproductionist theories of bottlenecks also seem to be ethnocentric. The theories giving importance to the demonstration effect find their source of inspiration in the fact that American households amassed considerable debt during the years following the Second World War. This fact itself is explained by a demonstration effect ('Keeping up with the Joneses'). The importance given to infrastructures is partly a consequence of a doubtful interpretation of the 'development' of England in the eighteenth century. Indeed, like Japan, England had certain cost-free infrastructures at its disposal (cf. the importance of coastal sea traffic). But this advantage is not enough to explain England's development. The development of industrialized societies has indeed in many cases been accompanied by the birth of highly mechanized, complex industries. But the increase of productivity and income does not always, nor in every actor, imply the formation of a complex industry.

It seems inevitable that the theories of development which appeared after the Second World War are akin to a patchwork quilt. Composed of partially incompatible propositions, they often form questionable generalizations built up from particular processes observed in specific historical and geographic contexts. They are often affected, to use Piaget's words, by an unquestionable 'sociocentrism': traditional societies are supposed to be set, belatedly, on the evolving path whose direction is dictated by the historical development of industrialized societies. There are considerable risks and temptations involved in the notions of development and underdevelopment themselves (as in the notion of the Third World) in so far as they classify under a single category societies which are extremely diverse. Neo-Marxist ideologies see the fact that societies of the Third World are 'declassed' as a unifying principle so important that the difference between these societies can only be considered as secondary. 'Development' ideologies generated from the new world order following the Second World War are also, in a way, searching for the 'laws of history'. While it is true that there is growing interdependence between nations, some changes – such as the increasing demand for fossil fuels by industrialized societies, which comes naturally to mind – create systems of interdependence which involve a considerable number of societies and simultaneously generate consequences which are similar in many ways. But the tendency to generalization of development theories is not only an effect or a reflection of a growing international interdependence. It is also a consequence of the persistence of the historicist and evolutionist paradigms inherited from the nineteenth century (cf. 'Historicism'). Interdependence or not, studies which endeavour to analyse the economic and social changes in various societies suggest the extreme diversity and, hence, the great unpredictability of the processes of change. It is possible to understand the development of Colombia at the turn of the century only if one makes it the result, in Cournot's terms, of the coincidence of an independent series of causal factors, as Hagen has shown: if Colombia's geography had been different, its development would have been changed. The loss of social status by the Japanese Samurai class in the Tokugawa era is a crucial element in the explanation of the processes of social change in Japan in the nineteenth century. Hirschman has shown through a multiple series of field studies that the secondary effects (*linkages*) of changes which occur in one part of the social and economic structure depend very much on the context in which these changes appear. Some of these changes cause chain reactions. Others seem in retrospect to be little more than damp squibs. In India, the irrigation programmes launched on the eve of the Second World War have upset the social structures of villages which did not have access to flooded land and reinforced those of the 'wet' villages, contrary to what was intuitively expected, but for reasons which can be analysed and understood a posteriori.

These remarks are not intended to suggest that social change is contingent or that it is always unpredictable. Rather they suggest that a society at a given time always tends to form a singular system, despite possible 'structural' concomitants and common historical traditions. Consequently the same cause can bring about the same effects, but also contrary ones, according to the system in which it is applied. It also follows that the coincidence of independent series of causal factors plays an incontestable rôle. Here, foreign investment will lead to the formation of an 'enclave' and will have negative effects on 'development'; there, it will provoke a positive mechanism of chain reactions. This explains why wholly contradictory ideologies of change and development can easily be understood to be equally based on 'the facts'.

Of course, it would be an exaggeration to see 'theories' of development as simply ideological products. We have here, to use Pareto's words, 'theories based on experience but which go beyond it'. The mechanisms of the vicious circle of poverty described by the theorists can occur and, occasionally, they describe the *structure* of real processes. Demonstration effects are sometimes to be observed and can have major consequences. Generally speaking, there is no doubt that the models built by development sociologists and economists constitute an imposing body of work, which has increased in size over time. No doubt equally these models have considerably increased our ability to comprehend the processes of change and development, exactly in the same way as Marxist theory has contributed to our comprehension of the history of industrial societies. But, most often, the mechanisms evoked by the theorists of development must be conceived as models, describing in a simplified way more complex processes. Furthermore, the models must be seen as having a limited validity and significance: a limited validity because they lead to simplifications; a limited significance because they can be held as suitable approximations of reality only within narrow and well-defined spatio-temporal boundaries. Like the Marxists of the nineteenth century and the neo-Marxists of the twentieth century, development theorists have a marked tendency to look for the 'laws' of change, to conceive them as strict, as translating linear processes of evolution, unless they are reproductive or repetitive, and as having a general application.

Even when they admit that there are specific models of development, they insist on finding generalities hidden behind specificities. In exactly the same way, Marx and Lenin attempted to compare Prussian or Russian cases with variants of the model of English industrialization. The obsession with generality arises on one hand from the 'rôle constraints' imposed on sociologists and especially the development economists, as we indicated earlier, but also because of the nomothetic character generally attributed to these disciplines and accepted by those practising them, and lastly from the permanence of historicist ideology in all its various forms (cf. 'Historicism'). To these causes, another must be added which is no less important, namely that *in some areas* and *from some points of view*, societies do indeed undergo linear developments comparable from one to another. Technologies are modernized and are diffused; hygiene tends to increase. But the linear evolution of some 'heavy tendencies', to use the economists' term, does not guarantee growth, or development or modernization. The improvement of hygiene may help to reduce infant mortality, but it *may* also contribute, if it leads to over-population, to increased mortality simply because this effect depends on the evolution of birth rates and resources, which in their turn are broadly independent of the evolution of mortality.

We have dealt in the pages above with economic development. A wide literature also exists which deals with what is sometimes called political development: it is devoted to the analysis of the reciprocal relation between modernization and political change. The sequence modernization → mobilization → participation has an essential place in it. But the historicism which is found in theories of political development has almost immediately been confronted by historical experience. Where political 'developmentalists' expected social differentiation, growing mobilization and political participation, a process of de-differentiation and demobilization, and the emergence of authoritarian regimes has often been observed.

The claim to generality of the theories of development (and more generally speaking of social change) would only be a problem if their political translation – which is generally also a betrayal – was not sometimes responsible for the new 'pyramids of sacrifice' as described by Berger. For some theorists of development, development involves a modification of individual's attitudes and values. It is likely, as Weber maintained and as did, later, McClelland, Hagen, and Parsons (cf. 'Socialization'), that some value systems are more favourable to development than others. This was also the belief of the Red Guards during the Chinese cultural revolution.

Historicism, Social Change.

Bibliography

BADIE, B., *Le développement politique*, Paris, Economica, 1978, 1980. – BAUER, P.T., *Dissent on development. Studies and debates in development economics*, London, Fakenham & Reading, 1971. – BERGER P.L., *Pyramids of sacrifice, political ethics and social change*, New York, Basic Books, 1974; London, Allen Lane, 1976. – CARDOSO, F.H., *Cuestiones de sociologia del desarrollo de America latina*, Santiago, Editorial Universitaria, 1968. – DENISON, E.F., *The sources of economic growth in the United States and the alternatives before us*. New York, Committee for economic development, 1962. – EISENSTADT, S.M., 'Breakdown of modernization', *in* EISENSTADT, S.M. (ed), *Readings in social evolution and development*, Paris/London/New York, Pergamon, 1970, 421–452. – GALBRAITH J.K., *The nature of mass poverty*, Cambridge, Harvard University Press, 1979; Harmondsworth, Penguin, 1980. – HAGEN, E., *On the theory of social change. How economic growth begins*, Homewood, The Dorsey Press, 1962; London, Tavistock, 1964. – HIRSCHMAN, A.O., *Journeys toward progress. Studies of economic policy-making in Latin America*, New York, The twentieth Century Fund, 1963; New York, Doubleday, 1963, 1965; New York, Greenwood Press 1963, 1968; 'A generalized linkage approach to development with special reference to staples', *in* NASH, M. (ed.), *Essays on economic development and cultural change: in honor of Bert F. Hoselitz*, Chicago, The University of Chicago, 1977, 67–98 (*Economic development and cultural change*, XXV, suppl., 1977). Reprinted in HIRSCHMAN, A.O., *Essays in trespassing. Economics to politics and beyond*, Cambridge, Cambridge University Press, 1981, 59–97. – HOSELITZ, B.F., *The progress of underdeveloped areas*, Chicago, The University of Chicago Press, 1952. – HOSELITZ, B.F. and MOORE, W.E., *Industrialization and society*, Paris/La Haye, Mouton, 1963. – LERNER, D., *The passing of traditional society: modernizing the middle East*, Glencoe, The Free Press/London, Collier-Macmillan, 1958, 1964. – NURKSE, R., *Problems of capital formation in underdeveloped countries*, Oxford, Blackwell, 1953. – REDFIELD, R. 'The folk society', *American journal of sociology*, LII, 4, 1947, 293–308. – ROSTOW, W.W., *The stages of economic growth. A non-Communist manifesto*, Cambridge, Cambridge University Press, 1960, 1971. – TÖNNIES, F., *Gemeinschaft und Gesellschaft*, Leipzig, R. Reisland, 1887.

Dialectic

The official history of the notion of dialectic in the modern sense of the word starts with Kant. But, it is mainly from Hegel and after him Marx especially that it comes into a considerable fortune and takes on a meaning which directly concerns the social sciences.

For Hegel as for Marx, the notion of dialectic and the notion of contradiction are without doubt polysemous. But in both cases, they indicate – beyond the two authors' differences as summed up by the traditional opposition between Hegel's idealism and Marx's materialism – an intuition of fundamental importance in the analysis of social phenomena, namely the concept that social agents can contribute, simply because they are pursuing an objective, to provoking a state of affairs distinct from – and possibly contradictory to – the desired objective. In the dialectic of the master and the slave in *The Phenomenology of the Mind* the master wishes to be recognized as master by the slave. But, doing so, he recognizes the slave's humanity, and consequently the identity of the master and of the slave. The law of the tendency of the profit rate to decline, which appears in the third volume of *Capital* is another classic example. Being in competition with one another, it is in the capitalists' interest to try constantly to improve their businesses' productivity. But, while doing so, they flatten the base upon which profit is formed (according to Marxist theory), since by doing so they reduce the role of labour in the factors of production. Up to a point they therefore contribute to the destruction of capitalism. Likewise, the capitalists of *The Poverty of Philosophy*, concerned with bringing down the cost of production in order to hold out against competition, have spinning done in workshops rather than at the farm as it used to be in the past. Almost unknowingly, then, they thus create a proletarian class, whose interests are, according to Marx, fundamentally opposed to theirs. The logic of the competitive situation in which they are placed in relationship with one another forces them to invest as protection against one another. Thus they contribute to the development of both industry and proletariat. Unwillingly they increase and arm the mass of their opponents.

Far from being, as Gurvitch thinks, a vast conceptual cover for odd notions such as those of 'reciprocity of perspectives', 'reciprocal involvement', 'circular causality', the notion of dialectic is therefore, in Hegel and especially Marx, a fundamental intuition: that is to say that some interaction systems incite social actors to adopt behaviours generating unintentional and possibly, from their point of view, undesirable consequences. The structure of these systems is sometimes such that, even if the actors are aware of the counter-productive effects of their actions, they cannot easily correct them: the capitalist in a competitive situation who renounced the idea of improving productivity would be condemning himself to ruin, unless by some miracle his rivals were taking the same decision at the same time.

In Hegel and Marx – as later in Sartre – the notion of dialectic is unfortunately carried beyond this fundamental intuition. Both authors saw in contradictions (in the dialectical sense) the driving force of social change and history. Hegel, then Engels, claimed to universalize the 'laws' of dialectic and extend them to nature itself. Now, it is obvious today that 'contradictions', while they have an important role in the analysis of social change, constitute only a particular case. Change does not necessarily arise from *contradictions*. Contradictions are not necessarily generating change. Moreover, Hegel and Marx adopted an excessively determinist view of change and history. Thus, the examples of the *Poverty of Philosophy* and of *Capital*, briefly mentioned above, analyse social change as a mechanical game of 'contradictions'. But the mechanical and inexorable character of this game is the consequence of two questionable hypotheses: 1) one assumes that the structure of the interaction system which rules the relations between capitalists is constant; 2) the system of interaction between capitalists on one hand and proletarians on the other is assumed to be a constant sum game. But, from the moment when a signi-

ficant trade union movement develops, the second proposition is no longer acceptable, since the power of the unions is able then to divert part of the productivity
increase for the benefit of the working class. Likewise, the first hypothesis is no
longer valid from the moment when a concentration occurs which enables capitalists to initiate agreements. In both cases, the mechanical game of contradictions is
broken up by the appearance of social innovations (union power, agreement, etc.).
Reciprocally, one can describe an evolutionary process as a series of contradictions
only by ignoring the capacities for *innovation* of social systems.

Divergent evaluations of Hegel's and Marx's dialectic come precisely from the
fact that this notion: 1) sums up an intuition which has considerable relevance
(social action frequently leads to consequences contradictory to the actors' objectives); 2) is interpreted by Hegel and Marx as the principal driving force of history.
Concerned mainly with the second aspect, Karl Popper (*What is Dialectic?*)
includes dialectic in his justified condemnation of the notion of the law of history.
Concerned mainly with the first aspect, Louis Schneider (*Dialectic in Sociology*)
interprets Marx's 'dialectic' as the particular expression of an institution present in
the whole history of sociology.

If the history of the modern notion of dialectic is linked especially with Hegel's
and Marx's names, this is due mainly to the political success of Marxism, because,
without even using the word, the 'contradictions' of social action had been noted
by many eighteenth-century authors. In the *Fable of the Bees*, Mandeville wonders
whether the harmonious functioning of societies assumes virtuous citizens, that is
to say respectful of the general interest. Do human societies, as the societies of
bees, imply that individuals should be concerned by the common good? No,
answers Mandeville, in a famous theorem: private vices make public virtue; greed,
vanity, inconstancy are the driving force of commerce and maintain the inventive
spirit. So much so that the poor now live better than the rich of the past. For Rousseau in *Discourse on Inequality* and the *Social Contract* natural freedom leads to undesirable consequences.

Without moral and social constraints, individuals are incited not to keep to
their agreements. But doing so, they deny themselves the benefits which could be
brought to them by co-operation. It is thus in their interest to accept constraints
freely and to exchange their natural freedom for civil liberty, which involves other
undesirable consequences (cf. 'Rousseau'). Adam Smith's famous 'invisible hand'
prefigures too the notion of a contradiction in the dialectic sense of the term: by *selfishly* pursuing their own interest, social agents can occasionally provoke desirable
and seemingly *altruistic* consequences (by competing with each other, grocers serve
the consumer's interests). Similar effects have been noted by Montesquieu.

The notion of 'invisible hand' in Adam Smith, the notion of 'dialectic' in Marx
have at the same time and indistinctly an analytical dimension and an ideological
one. Sharing Mandeville's optimism, Adam Smith considers the 'invisible hand' as
essentially benign: the unintentional effects of the aggregation of individual actions
are generally speaking positive and desirable. They move in the direction of the
common good, the general interest, and social progress. The game of dialectic
contradictions is likewise conceived by Marx as the mechanism which leads

human history towards a happy end. 'Invisible hand' and 'dialectic' testify to the characteristic climate of the second half of the eighteenth century and part of the nineteenth century. The progress which is evidenced by the development of science and technology cannot any longer be attributed to the effect of providence in a period when 'incredulity' was spreading. One must therefore imagine lay substitutes for the notion of providence. 'Invisible hand' and 'dialectic' represent these substitutes. Of course, 'dialectic' was a more acceptable representation of providence from the moment when the industrialization of European societies gave birth to intense class conflicts. This is why it was destined for greater fortune.

In modern sociology the term 'dialectic' itself is avoided, no doubt essentially because of the mishaps due to its political use. Thus we find the fundamental intuition contained in this notion under various names: composition effects, aggregation effects, emergent effects, perverse effects, counter-finality (Sartre), anti-intuitive effects, etc. 'Dialectic' effects made obvious by sociological research are countless. For instance: Merton's 'self-fulfilling prophecy' (believing in a banks' insolvency, customers withdraw their deposits, which actually provokes the bankruptcy they feared); the effects of Calvinist ethics on the development of capitalism according to Weber (the Calvinist seeks economic success on this earth, hoping to find in it a sign of his salvation in the next world; doing so he unwittingly promotes the accumulation of capital); the effects of the democratization of society caused by the élites' efforts to defend their privileges (at the beginning of the nineteenth-century, Mill demonstrates that the *Magna Carta* was the result of the nobles' desire to establish their position by limiting royal power, but turned to the peasants' advantage with the improvement of their living conditions – 'The limitations of the royal power ... turned to the advantage of the whole community, as if they had originated from a high spirit of patriotism'; cf. also, in the same vein, de Tocqueville's classic analysis in the second volume of *L'Ancien Régime* about the effects of the nobles' reaction against royal power at the beginning of the Revolution).

Today the notions of 'emergent effect', 'composition effect', 'unintentional consequences', as used by modern sociology, are in general divested of any reference to the idea of progress. 'Contradictions' are not entrusted with the progress of history. Occasionally, one finds these notions associated rather with an ideology of reproduction (assuming then the 'invisible hand' to be ensuring no longer progress but rather the fixity and perenniality of 'social structures'). But most modern sociologists agree that composition effects have a social significance and are variable indications. They can generate social transformations or on the contrary block them. They can be desirable or undesirable for all, desirable for some and undesirable for others, include desirable and undesirable aspects, be desirable at first, undesirable later, be cumulative or not (cf. 'Social change'). Thus the development of school demand and competition after 1945 has led to productivity gains advantageous for all, without anyone ever having sought this result. According to Denison, the development of school attendance largely explains the economic growth of industrial societies during the period following the Second World War. At the same time, this development has caused such a scholastic inflation that individuals must make an excessive scholastic investment in relation to what their socio-professional status will be later, and the diploma tends to become an increasingly necessary and decreasingly adequate condition of social mobility. In this case, unintentional positive and negative effects seem to be inextricably combined.

One last point needs to be stressed. Modern sociologists have not only purged the fundamental intuition contained in the notion of dialectic of the ideological contamination which in Marx makes it a lay substitute for the notion of providence. They are aware also of the fact that, while it is necessary in sociological analysis to take into consideration anonymous 'social forces' and unintentional effects such as the effects of composition, simultaneously one must consider the capacity for voluntary intervention on these social forces which any social system has at its disposal – or more accurately which some of the actors belonging to the social system have at their disposal. Men not only 'make history without knowing it', they have also the ability to convert their will into history.

Action, Historicism, Marx, Rationality, Rousseau, Social Change, De Tocqueville.

Bibliography

BOUDON, R., *Effets pervers et ordre social*, Paris, PUF, 1977, 1979. – DUBARLE, P. and DOZ, A., *Logique et dialectique*, Paris, Larousse, 1972. – ELSTER, J., *Logic and society*, New York, Wiley, 1978. – GURVITCH, G., *Dialectique et sociologie*, Paris, Flammarion, 1962. – MANDEVILLE, B., *The fable of the bees*, London, J. Roberts, 1714. – MERTON, R.K., 'The unanticipated consequences of purposive social action', *American sociological review*, I, 6, 1936, 894–904. – MILLAR J., *An historical view of the English government*, London, J. Marumànn, 1812. – POPPER, K.R., 'What is dialectic?', in POPPER, K.R., *Conjectures and refutations*, London, Routledge & Kegan Paul, 1963, 3rd rev. edn, 1969, 312–335. – ROUSSEAU, J.-J., 'Discours sur l'origine et les fondements de l'inégalité parmi les hommes', in ROUSSEAU, J.-J., *Œuvres complètes*, t. III: *Du contrat social. Ecrits politiques*, 109–238. –SARTRE, J.-P., *Critique de la raison dialectique*, Paris, Gallimard, 1960. – SCHNEIDER, L., 'Dialectic in sociology', *American sociological review*, XXXVI, 4, 1971, 667–678. – SMITH, A., *An inquiry into the nature and causes of the wealth of the Nations*, London, W. Strahan & T. Cadell, 1776. London, Ward Lock, 1812; Oxford, Clarendon Press, 1976.

Diffusion

The term diffusion is used to describe the process by which an item of true or false information (a rumour for example), an opinion, an attitude, or a practice (for example, the use of a new agricultural technique or method of birth control) is distributed through a given population.

In the simplest cases, the process of social diffusion may exhibit a form broadly similar to that of processes observable in the world of medicine or biology. Thus let us suppose that a rumour spreads through a large and homogeneous population. In such a case, the increase at any moment of the number of persons aware of the rumour is likely to be strongly proportional to the number n of persons already aware of it: $dn/dt = kn$. Such a process develops exponentially (see diagram). It is this type of process that Tarde was concerned with when he discussed 'geometric progression' in his *Lois de l'imitation* (*Laws of Imitation*).

Now let us suppose that the population is of limited size. In this case the increase at any moment of the number of persons aware of the rumour is proportional both to the number of persons already aware of the rumour, and able as a result to inform others, and to the number of persons who remain unaware, and in consequence who are capable of being informed about it: $dn/dt = kn \ (N-n)$ where N represents the total population, n the number of persons aware of the rumour, and k a constant. Such a process develops logistically (see diagram). While n is small (few persons are informed), the speed of the process dn/dt is low; it thereafter increases uniformly and attains its maximum value when $n = N/2$; then slows down uniformly and tends towards zero as $N-n$ tends towards zero.

Thus the curve representing the process (variation of n in terms of t) has a characteristic S shape. The logistical process is a fundamental one in epidemiology (the growth of the number of contaminated subjects is proportional to the number of contaminating agents and to the number of non-contaminated and consequently vulnerable subjects). Some social processes look roughly like logistical processes. Likewise some studies on the adoption of agricultural innovations indicate that processes of a logistical type are evident (cf. Hambling and Miller). In other cases, the processes of diffusion do not follow the hypothesis of contagion introduced in the first two examples. Let us suppose that a message is 'diffused' repeatedly through the radio waves or in the press and that this message is not likely to be transmitted 'along the grapevine' as would be the case in a population of individuals having little contact with each other. In this case, the increase at each 'instant' of the number of informed persons is likely to be proportional to the number of persons not yet informed: $dn/dt = K \ (N-n)$. In this case, the 'instantaneous' speed of the process (derived at each instant from the curve representing the process) is at its maximum when $n = 0$, then regularly decreases, and tends towards zero in proportion as n tends towards N (see diagram on page 127).

The three ideal cases just described assume populations of homogeneous individuals. In the first two cases, one supposes moreover a network of homogeneous *relations*, each individual being as likely to be informed by any of his compatriots.

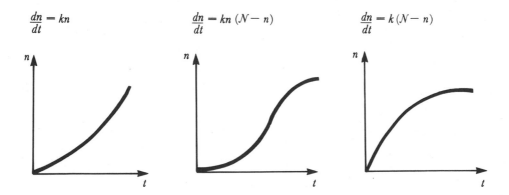

Figure 1   Three simple models of diffusion

Such hypotheses, acceptable in some epidemiological applications, are more rarely valid in sociology (cf. Cherkaoui, however), where social structures and their effects on the processes of communication and consequently of diffusion must be taken into account. Thus, in a survey on the diffusion of medicines in medical circles, Coleman and his colleagues have observed that the global process followed a complex pattern which could not be reduced to any of the three models referred to above. They then had the idea of dividing the population of doctors they had surveyed into two categories: general or family practitioners on the one hand and doctors practising in hospitals on the other. They demonstrated then that the process of diffusion in the first category followed the pattern $dn/dt = K(N-n)$. In this case, the institutional position of doctors means that they are informed about new drugs through advertisements and information in the specialized publications or journals they receive. As to the effects of 'contagion', that is to say information spread through interpersonal relations or contacts, they are limited. At each 'instant', the number of doctors using the new product increases thus *grosso modo* in proportion with the number of doctors who have not yet adopted it. In the hospital milieu, by contrast, interpersonal relations play an important role. It is easy and advantageous for a doctor to consult his colleagues before using a new drug. The process of adoption of the new product then has the structure of a process of contagion: the increase at each 'instant' of the number of adopters is proportional to both the population of the adopters and the population of the non-adopters: $dn/dt = Kn(N-n)$.

It is possible, but to our knowledge still unproven, that many fashion phenomena follow composite patterns like this. It is proved that in many cases, a particular fashion begins its development within relatively limited social categories. New clothes or styles are often reserved to a social élite because of their price. Within this élite the process of diffusion probably looks like a 'contagious' process (second pattern). Later, financially more accessible copies of the new garment come on the market. They are adopted less because they follow a process of interpersonal 'contagion' than because they are 'diffused' in shop windows and magazines. The process corresponding to the period of wide diffusion is then likely to follow an elementary process of the third type. But the global process is complicated in this case by the fact that as the new garment or style becomes more common, it loses its function of social distinction from the viewpoint of the élite. This effect having been foreseen by the manufacturers, a new product is then launched. The process of diffusion of the first product continues to develop, but an overlap occurs: its successor begins to take its place on the market. The combination of these processes generates cyclic phenomena at the level of aggregation, as the life cycles of the successive products partially overlap.

As authors such as Pareto, Tarde, and Sorokin have suggested, it is likely that not only fashion clothing phenomena, but some cultural or conceptual phenomena follow processes of a similar structure to the one just described and take on in consequence a cyclic form.

In the above examples, we have assumed that the innovation or information the diffusion of which we were studying was accepted as soon as it was known. More precisely, the first two models, of a 'contagious' type, imply that the encounter between informer and non-informed person is effective. In other words, that transmission occurs. In the third pattern, we assume the source of information to be effective. More complex versions of these models involve the introduction of probabilistic hypotheses. One might assume for example that the effectiveness of the encounters, or in other words, the resistance to change or to information obeys a certain distribution (n_1, n_2 . . ., subjects who must have respectively m_1, m_2, . . ., encounters before they are convinced and converted). One might combine this hypothesis with hypotheses connected with the effects of social structures on the probabilities of encounters taking place. Such patterns, sometimes taking the shape of patterns of simulation, have been successfully used in the field of agricultural innovations. Thus, Hagerstrand has succeeded in reproducing accurately some data relating to the diffusion of an agricultural innovation in Sweden, by assuming a simple distribution of the resistance to change and a structuration of probabilities of encounter as a function of geographical distance.

The three patterns above and the different variants which can be deduced from them do not exhaust the range of the elementary models of diffusion. The arms race, the increase in educational demand, the generalized search for an increase in productivity do not arise from either a phenomenon of contagion (patterns 1 and 2) or a phenomenon of stimulation from an external source (pattern 3). In all these cases, diffusion is the result of competition among the actors, as it is to each one's interest to be better armed, better educated, or more productive than his neighbour. The similarity of behaviours is therefore a result of the structure of the system of interdependence linking individuals and the strategies which it imposes on them or at least which it encourages them to follow. In other cases, the similarity of opinions or behaviours is simply a result of the similarity of the situation or of interests:

> One sees in all this first part [of the Revolution], the complete unity which exists in the whole body of the third estate; because class interest, class relations, the conformity of position, the uniformity of grievances in the past, the discipline of corporation, all hold strongly together and make the most dissimilar minds work together, even those who least agree about the final direction to follow and the objective to be achieved in the future.
>
> (De Tocqueville, *L'Ancien Regime et la Revolution*, II: 177)

These examples suggest a general comment, namely that the analysis of a process of diffusion requires an adequate theory of the microsociological processes which underpin it. Only in some cases can the simple hypothesis of contagion, or, in Tarde's words, of 'imitation', be introduced. This reservation applies to the phenomena of consumption themselves: if consumers are as passive as some sociologists claim, this does not explain, as Lindbeck notes, the failure of a large proportion of products launched on the market. In fact, the adoption of a new product or an innovation by an individual is rarely passive. Numerous studies show that the process of adoption or rejection is preceded by an exploratory period during which the individual gets support and advice from some information networks: the family or close circle of associates in industrial societies (Katz and Lazarsfeld), 'local networks' in traditional societies (Lin and Burt). In both contexts, the recourse to the immediate social environment is an easy way to reduce the uncertainty and the risks attached to the adoption of an innovation.

Just as we tend sometimes to interpret the phenomena of diffusion on the basis of microsociological hypothesis of passive imitation, so we sometimes observe that the *phenomena of non-diffusion* are interpreted using a hypothesis of passive *resistance to change*. Thus, several observers interpret the failure of certain campaigns for the spreading of methods of contraception or of new agricultural methods in developing countries using notions such as 'resistance to change' or the 'burden of tradition'. Now, in many cases, a more detailed analysis demonstrates that the so-called 'burden of tradition' only expresses the disappointments and the presuppositions of the observer, and that the actors themselves have good reasons for 'resisting change'. Thus, in the case of India, the alleged 'resistance' to birth control can often be explained by the problems a decrease in the number of births would cause for farmers. Likewise, Epstein has observed that the 'Japanese method' of rice cultivation (which ensures noteworthy productivity gains compared with the traditional methods used by Indian farmers) rapidly spread in some villages but was rejected in others. Through a thorough field study she was able to account for this difference. Starting in the 1940s, the Indian administration developed an irrigation programme which had positive effects. It contributed to the modernization of agriculture and to a rise in the peasants' standard of living, and finally led to a transition from a subsistence economy to a cash economy. But its global effects were differentiated according to the types of villages they affected. In 'wet' villages (those with a high proportion of irrigated or irrigable land), modernization led to a rise in the peasants' standard of living but preserved the complex links between agricultural organization and social organization, or, if one wants to use Marxist language, between relations of production and social relations. The 'dry' villages, for their part (villages with little irrigated or irrigable land), could hardly benefit directly from irrigation. But the economic changes occurring around them prompted the peasants from the dry villages to look for an activity outside the village, to develop enterprises for the treatment of grain, etc., leading in total to a considerable increase in the links between these villages and the surrounding area. Consequently, traditional social relations within the village were affected and were as if overlaid by the new social relations resulting from the village's integration with its environment. Now, the transition from the Indian method to the 'Japanese' method for rice cultivation implied in particular an obliteration of the personal links of clientilism between peasants and untouchables, as well of the internal hierarchies of the untouchable group. In Dalena, a dry village, the farmer could easily undertake to reorganize the teams of labourers responsible for the planting and harvesting of rice. In Wangala, a wet village, such a reorganization was practically impossible, the members of the labourers' teams being tied to the farmers by complex and often hereditary relations of clientilism. The effects of the development of irrigation on social relations are such that the fields of action of the Wangala or Dalena peasants have an utterly different structure. The 'Japanese' method therefore spread easily in dry villages where these social relations were highly distended, but did not spread easily in 'wet' villages. These examples demonstrate that the analysis of the processes of diffusion (or non-diffusion) requires that the fields of action within which the actors move must be accurately described.

The methodological principles which are brought out by the above analysis have a general application. Thus, in a brilliant study, Daniel Bell investigated why the revelation of the horrors of Stalinism led, from the 1940s, to the fierce rejection of Marxist ideology by American intellectuals, who had up to that time, been rather fond of it. The question is all the more relevant as the same revelations did not generate the same rejection in other countries. According to Bell, the revelation of the Gulag was 'effective' because it coincided with two phenomena. It occurred at a time when American unionism, which had for a period taken a political and ideological stance, seemed to have turned towards a position which favoured negotiation and *market unionism*. At the same time, the alignment of the American Communist Party with Moscow had radically limited its appeal. Thus the Marxist ideology was evicted from all the political or union institutions which mattered in the political life of the country. From then on, the allegiance to Marxism was devoid of the meaning it might have had in previous times. The situation of the French intellectuals of 1945 was evidently quite different: the Communist Party was important, its participation in the Resistance made it legitimate, the union movement based itself partly on Marxist ideology: the intellectual allegiance to Marxism therefore still had some significance. The *fields of action* of the American intellectual and of the French intellectual of 1945 (as also their counterpart of 1980) are entirely different. That is why the rejection of Marxist ideology has been diffused at different rhythms in France and in the United States (cf. 'Beliefs').

One could find similar illustrations in Kuhn, who demonstrates how the diffusion of new scientific paradigms is retarded by the importance of paradigms established in the structuration of the researchers' field of action (cf. 'Knowledge').

Tarde's *laws of imitation* explain the phenomena of social diffusion from the hypothesis of *imitation* and the phenomena of non-diffusion from the complementary hypothesis of *custom*. Modern sociology has substituted for this simple and mechanical sketch a much more complex one: the diffusion or non-diffusion of a rumour, an attitude, a practice is conceived as the aggregate effect of a multitude of individual *actions*; these individual actions depend on the individual's field of action; the individual's fields of action are partly determined by structural circumstances. Therefore the analysis of a phenomenon of diffusion or non-diffusion implies a knowledge of these individual fields (of action). Only in simple and extreme cases can the phenomena of diffusion or non-diffusion be reduced to effects of imitation or contagion, or be conceived as the result of tradition, custom, or 'resistance to change'.

These remarks also enable us to avoid the general argument between *diffusionists* and *functionalists*. This argument, which has become a major one in the area of anthropology, occurs in less obvious forms in many sociological debates. It leads back to the general question: should change be conceived as 'fundamentally' exogenous or endogenous? The permanence of the debate sufficiently demonstrates that such a question is wrongly expressed and should not receive a general answer. Of course, an innovation cannot be adopted if its receptive environment is not ready for it. In the Middle Ages, the plough with a metal ploughshare had not been adopted in the regions with a population of low density despite its advantages in terms of productivity, because it required that the peasants could form eight-oxen teams. In regions where shoes are unknown, the spade is very unlikely to become implanted as an agricultural tool. But the fact that the adoption of an innovation depends on conditions internal to the system of reception does not imply that change *is* or is *necessarily* endogenous. Innovations are sometimes caused by the internal *needs* of a system. But sometimes, too, they are adopted because: 1) they are available; 2) they lead to advantages (for example, productivity gains); 3) they find favourable internal conditions. In this second case, one cannot be satisfied with the assertion that the adoption of the innovation arises from internal needs or necessities of the system.

Beliefs, Cycles, Knowledge.

Bibliography

BAILEY, N.T.J., *The mathematical theory of epidemics*, London, Charles Griffin, 1957. – BELL, D., 'The mood of three generations', in BELL, D., *The end of ideology. On the exhaustion of political ideas in the fifties*, New York, The Free Press, 1960, rev. ed. 1965, chap. XIII, 299–314; London, Collier Macmillan, 1965. – CHERKAOUI, M., *Les changements du système éducatif en France, 1950–1980*, Paris, PUF, 1982. – COLEMAN, J.S., KATZ, E., and MENZEL, H., *Medical innovation. A diffusion study*, New York, Bobbs-Merrill, 1966. – EPSTEIN, T.S, *Economic development and social change in south India*, Manchester, Manchester University Press, 1962. – HÄGERSTRAND, T., 'A Monte-Carlo approach to diffusion', *Archives earopéennes de sociologie*, VI, *1*, 1965, 43–67. – HAMBLIN, R.L. and MILLER, J.L.L., 'Reinforcement and the origin, rate and extent of cultural diffusion', *Social forces*, LIV, *4*, 1976, 743–759. – KATZ, E. and LAZARS-FELD, P.F., *Personal influence. The part played by people in the flow of mass communication*, Glencoe, The Free Press, 1955, 1965. – LIN, N. and BURT, R.S., 'Differential effects of information channels in the process of innovation diffusion', *Social forces*, XXXIV, *1*, 1975, 256–274. – LINDBECK, A., *The political economy of the new left: an outsider's view*, New York, Harper & Row, 1971. – RAPOPORT, A. and REBHUN, L.I., 'On the mathematical theory of rumor spread', *Bulletin of mathematical biophysics*, XIV, 1952, 375–383. – SIMMEL, G., 'Die Mode', in SIMMEL, G., *Philosophische Kultur. Gesammelte Essais*, Leipzig, Klinkhardt, 1911, 29–64 (*Philosophische-Soziologische Bücherei*, Band XXVII). – SOROKIN, P.A., *Social and cultural dynamics*, New York, American Books, 1937–1941, 4 vol.; abridged version in 1 vol., Boston, Extending Horizons Books, 1957; Boston, Porter Sargent, 1957, 1970. – TARDE, G., *Les lois de l'imitation. Etude sociologique*, Paris, F. Alcan, 1890: Paris/Geneva, Slatkine Reprints, 1979. – WOLF, E.R., 'The study of evolution', *in* EISEN-STADT, S.N. (ed.), *Readings in social evolution and development*, London/Paris, Pergamon, 1970, 179–190.

Durkheim, Emile

Durkheim's (1858–1917) sociological theories, notably those which deal with the division of labour, suicide, and the elementary forms of religious life, are occupied by an obsessive question, close to the classic Hobbesian question about social order, reformulated in a new manner: by what mechanisms are individuals integrated into society? Under what conditions are their activities compatible with the maintenance of a coherent social order? Under what conditions do they feel solid-

arity one to the other? Under what conditions and by what mechanism is the autonomy of the individual compatible with the existence of a social order?

But if this *persistent* interrogation of Durkheim rediscovers questions posed by
Hobbes and by Rousseau, the answer which is given is entirely different.
Durkheim sets against the philosophical fiction of the *Social Contract* a response
drawn from the positive science of custom, which sociology seems to him to have
to be.

One of Durkheim's essential contributions is to have shown in a definitive way
the limits of artificialist and voluntarist conceptions of the social order. In *The
Division of Labour in Society*, he is opposed to Spencer and generally to those who
attempt to explain the growing complexity of the system of division of labour starting from the socially and individually advantageous effects which it brings about.
According to Durkheim, division of labour develops in a continuous manner
throughout history, not because it is useful, but as a mechanical process, the structure of which evokes the Darwinian theory of evolution. Using a modernized
language compared with that of Durkheim, we can sum up the process described
by *The Division of Labour* in a simple fashion. From the moment when the 'social
density' and 'rural density' of societies begin to grow (that is to say 'the number of
persons who, at a given volume, are effectively in communication'), the system of
what we would today call social roles becomes more and more differentiated,
causing constant change in the system of norms and values. These changes
provoke, in their turn, an effect of positive retroaction on the 'social and moral
density'. The initial growth of moral and social density thus gives birth to a self-
perpetuating process of evolutionary aspect: the fundamental form of solidarity
evolves in a constant sense; the mechanical solidarity, or that of resemblance,
which characterizes traditional societies, progressively gives place to organic or
complementary solidarity. The place of repressive law, characteristic of mechanical solidarity, diminishes in consequence, as the place of co-operative law
increases. But at the same time the evolutionary process sets off a constant
development of individualism and of 'egoism'; the consequence of the development of organic solidarity, individualism exerts a dissolving effect upon solidarity
itself. In the language of systems analysis, the evolutionary process described by
The Division of Labour thus engenders negative retroactive effects, effects which,
according to Durkheim, constitute the fundamental explanation of the social and
economic crises of his epoch.

Nowadays *The Division of Labour* still retains a certain historic and methodological importance. Durkheim endeavours in it to take the great evolutionary
tendencies into account (the development of individualism, etc.) starting from a
process whereby he attempts to exclude all hypotheses of a teleological nature.
The fact that it is possible to retranslate this process in the language of systems
analysis suffices to show the path followed from Comte to Durkheim. Without
doubt, Durkheim's analysis remains summary and unlikely to carry in its train the
unconditional agreement of historians in the long term. The evolutionary model
that he puts forward is too rigid and too close in its logical simplicity to the models
Darwin used to explain the evolution of the species. But, by way of a schematic

approximation, it has a certain explanatory power. It is important to emphasize the debt Durkheim owes to Spencer, despite the polemic in which he engaged against Spencer's theories. Durkheim's theory of the division of labour is much more compatible with the Spencerian theory of differentiation than Durkheim would like to admit.

Suicide takes up and develops one of the essential conclusions of *The Division of Labour*. The evolutionary process which Durkheim had described in his doctoral thesis led him, as we have seen, to distinguish two polar types of society. On one hand, societies of mechanical solidarity, where the individual sees himself as the same as others and consequently has only a rough consciousness of his individuality. On the other hand, societies of organic solidarity corresponding to an advanced stage of evolution, where the individual has on the contrary a tendency to attribute an essential uniqueness to himself. In societies of mechanical solidarity (similar to Tönnies' *Gemeinschaft*), the individual is an indivisible whole. In societies of organic solidarity (close to Tönnies' *Gesellschaft*), the individual, conversely, tends to feel himself as being isolated in the social body. The fundamental hypothesis of *Suicide* is that the balance of personality (as we would say today) or the 'happiness' of the individual (as Durkheim says) depends on the intensity of the 'ties' between the individual and society: these ties must be neither too close nor too stretched. To demonstrate this proposition, Durkheim utilizes an index, that of suicide rates. Starting from a statistical analysis which is still a model on the methodological level despite the criticisms which have been made about it, he shows that the rates of suicide tend effectively to go up when individuals find themselves in social contexts bearing normative constraints, particularly when they are either very strong or very weak.

As for Durkheim's third major work, *Elementary Forms of Religious Life*, it deals with the symbolic aspects of social integration. Religion is seen by Durkheim as a phenomenon which, over and above its particular manifestations, is of a universal nature. In order to grasp its nature, he thus chose to analyse the form of religion which, from within the evolutionary perspective which is his own starting from *The Division of Labour*, seemed to him the simplest, namely, Australian totemism, seen as an 'elementary form of religious life'. Sometimes, doubtless in order to make a thoroughly 'modern' writer of Durkheim, we try to erase the evolutionary dimension of his thought. In which case, we do not see how one can declare that one religion is simpler or more elementary than another. Having decided that Australian totemism represented this elementary form, Durkheim undertakes to define religion. If it is defined by the belief in a transcendent god or by belief in the supernatural, religion ceases to be a universal phenomenon, because numerous religions exist which imply neither a transcendent god nor a belief in supernatural forces. In addition, the idea of the supernatural implies that of nature, and the opposition of natural facts to supernatural facts presupposes the development of positive thought. The ideas of the supernatural and of transcendescence must thus be considered as outmoded ideas corresponding to particular forms of religion and not as concepts capable of serving as a definition of the essential nature of the religious fact.

Durkheim finds this essence in the opposition between sacred and profane, common to all religious systems: 'A religion is a system of solidarity of beliefs and practices relative to the sacred things, that is to say, separated, forbidden.' Thus the problem consists of explaining why all societies experience this distinction, whether we are dealing with Australian societies or modern societies (the flag). If we explain the practices of the Australians by making totemism derive from another form of religion, such as the cult of ancestors or the cult of animals, we preclude ourselves from explaining the religious phenomenon of its generality. Thus it is necessary to give another reason: it is, according to Durkheim, because the totem symbolizes 'a kind of anonymous and impersonal force, which is to be found in each of these beings [the animals], without any possibility of it being confused with any one amongst them.' The impersonal force of which the totem is the symbol is also to be found among the Melanesians 'under the name of *mana*, an idea which is the exact equivalent of the *wakan* of the Sioux and of the *orenda* of the Iroquois.'

Thus it must be explained what leads societies to conceive of this anonymous and diffuse force, the symbols of which they consider to be sacred. For Durkheim, only one interpretation is possible, because the only real force which goes beyond individuals and takes for them the form of an anonymous and diffused force is society itself: 'A society has all that it needs to arouse in [men's] minds, solely by the action which it exercises upon them, the sensation of the divine: because it is for its members that which a god is to his believers.' All society thus implies a moral authority of the collective over the individual, an authority which it exercises not by the constraints that it practises, but by the respect which it inspires. The acceptance of constraints presupposes that these are seen by the members of the society as being founded upon an authority which inspires in them a feeling of legitimacy, and therefore of respect. This respect is the source of the sacred, consequently it explains the phenomenon of religion. Thus, religion, far from being capable of interpretation in the manner of the artificialists as a 'phantasmagoria' (cf. religion is the opium of the people), must be seen as a kind of projection of the norms and values upon which reposes the integration of the individual with society. This implies that religions are destined to evolve with social structures. Thus, Durkheim notes that, at the time when he was writing, the development of the division of work and of individualization and the intensification of competition between nations tended to render sacred science, the individual, and the flag. At this point, we come back to a question posed in *The Division of Labour* and *Suicide*: how can respect for the individual and individualist religion be compatible with the existence of social order? Durkheim's response to this question is ambiguous and circular: the individual can only achieve 'happiness' by acting in a realistic manner, that is, in accepting his role and his place in the system of the division of labour. This is why the social conflicts of his time seemed to him to express a transitory state which preceded the appearance of a morality which would lead each individual to admit that 'happiness' could be attained by the individual only if he accepted the need to keep to his role and his place in society.

The passion which Durkheim brings to the problem of social integration and to what we now call socialization explains, of course, his constant interest in the problems of education (*Moral Education, The Evolution of Educational Thought in France*).

Durkheim strove in his major works to find a narrow way between two opposing poles: on one hand, artificialist, voluntarist, and atomist conceptions of the social order, for which he felt merely antipathy, and, on the other hand, the holistic and organicist ideas, for which he showed more sympathy. It is not certain that he altogether found his way through. Several of his fundamental concepts, 'society', 'collective conscience', for example, appear to be afflicted with an irremediable obscurity. *Anomie, egoism, altruism, fatalism*, the classic quartet of concepts stand out for their originality and their utility to be sure, but also for their impreciseness. The sociological literature on the 'exact interpretation' of the ideas of anomie or of egoism is almost boundless. Perhaps it indicates by its existence that these concepts are irremediably blurred. Perhaps the haziness itself comes from the ontological primacy which Durkheim always wished to accord to society compared with the individual. The choice of words bears witness to the ambiguity. *Egoism*: this word, borrowed from morality and generally used to qualify the behaviour of an individual (compared to another or to others), is promoted by Durkheim to the rank of an essential characteristic, not of individuals, but of social systems. Thus, indicators of egoism can be presented, that is to say a *demonstrative* type of definition can be resorted to, but a more precise definition cannot be achieved. How could it be otherwise, from the moment that we use a moral idea, essentially defined at the level of the individual, to characterize an entity of a completely different nature? Elsewhere we will note that, of the four concepts, certain of them, such as egoism, derive from concepts defined at an individual level, while *anomie* is primarily a concept defined at the collective level. The major difficulty therefore comes from the holistic conception which he has of *society*, conceived as an undifferentiated entity. This conception is responsible for the vagueness which surrounds Durkheimian ideas. Another difficulty rests in his conception of the individual as the single medium (to use anachronistic language) of collective norms and values. This is perhaps why Durkheim has been called to the rescue when structuralism and neo-Marxism (at least in its strictly economic variants) found themselves discredited towards the end of the 1960s. Reference to Durkheim enabled a scientific authority to be given to the viewpoint according to which the individual is solely the materialization of 'structures'. Even though it is possible, as Alpert has demonstrated, to retranslate many passages of Durkheim's work in interactionist language, the principal source of its obscurities rests perhaps in the fact that Durkheim, unlike Marx, de Toqueville, or Weber, always wished to avoid giving the individual the status of an active subject. His closest intellectual inheritor, Halbwachs, had, however, to show that the principal uncertainties and weaknesses or errors of *Suicide* arose from Durkheim's refusal to consider the motives of suicides when taking account of the aggregated statistics of suicide. Is Durkheim's refusal of the sociology of action in itself an excessive reaction against the excesses of voluntarism and artificialism? Is it the product of a naturalist epistemology inspired by the statistical regularity which certain social phenomena obey, or of a methodological rigidity which leads him to make of the rules of induction, such as codified by Stuart Mill (cf. *The Rules of Sociological Method*), the canon of scientific method? It is difficult, and perhaps useless, to decide between these hypotheses.

Anomie, Crime, Suicide.

Bibliography

DURKHEIM, E., *De la division du travail social*, Paris, F. Alcan, 1893; Paris, PUF, 1960, 1967. – DURKHEIM, E., *Les règles de la méthode sociologique*, Paris, F. Alcan, 1895; Paris, PUF, 1950, 1963. – DURKHEIM, E., *Le suicide, étude sociologique*, Paris, F. Alcan, 1897; Paris, PUF, 1960. – DURKHEIM, E., *Les formes élémentaires de la vie religieuse*, Paris, F. Alcan, 1912; Paris, PUF, 1967. – DURKHEIM, E., *L'éducation morale*, Paris, F. Alcan, 1925; Paris, PUF, 1963. – DURKHEIM, E., *L'évolution pédagogique en France*, Paris, F. Alcan, 1938; Paris, PUF, 1969. – DURKHEIM, E., *Leçons de sociologie. Physique des mœurs et du droit*, Paris, PUF, 1950, 1969. – DURKHEIM, E., *Textes*. I: *Eléments d'une théorie sociale;* II: *Religion, morale, anomie;* III: *Fonctions sociales et institutions*, Paris, Minuit, 1975. – DURKHEIM, E. *The Division of Labour in Society*, London, Macmillan, 1984. – *The Rules of Sociological Method*, London, Macmillan, 1982. – *Suicide: a Study in Sociology*, Glencoe, Free Press, 1951. London, Routledge & Kegan Paul, 1952. – *The Elementary Forms of the Religious Life*, London, Allen and Unwin; New York, Macmillan, 1915. – *Moral Education: a Study in the Theory and Application of the Sociology of Education*, Glencoe, Free Press, 1961; London, Collier Macmillan, 1961. – *The Evolution of Educational Thought*, London, Routledge and Kegan Paul, 1977. – ALPERT, H., *Emile Durkheim and his sociology*, New York, Columbia University Press, 1939; New York, Russell & Russell, 1961. – ARON, R., *Les étapes de la pensée sociologique*, Paris, Gallimard, 1967, 1974. – CHERKAOUI, M., 'Changement social et anomie: essai de formalisation de la théorie durkheimienne', *Archives européennes de sociologie*, XXII, 1, 1981, 3–39. – HALBWACHS, M., *Les causes du suicide*, Paris, F. Alcan, 1930. – LUKES, S., *Emile Durkheim: his life and work. A historical and critical study*, New York, Harper & Row, 1972; London, Allen Lane, 1973. – MADGE, J.H., *The origins of scientific sociology*, New York, The Free Press, 1962, 1967; London, Tavistock, 1963. – NISBET, R.A., *The sociology of Emile Durkheim*, New York, Oxford University Press, 1974; London, Heinemann, 1975. – PARSONS, T., *The structure of social action*, Glencoe, The Free Press, 1937, 1964.

E

Economics and Sociology

The history of the relationship between economics and sociology is complex and ancient. In *Discourse on Political Economics*, which he wrote for Diderot and d'Alembert's *Great Encyclopaedia*, Jean-Jacques Rousseau discusses the many themes which today are considered relevant, for some to economics, and for others to sociology. The fundamental work of Adam Smith on *The Wealth of Nations*, generally considered as the starting point of economic science, also goes beyond the frontiers of economics such as they are commonly fixed today. Marx and Pareto, but also to a certain extent Max Weber, Schumpeter, and the Durkheimian Simiand, are considered to be both sociologists and economists. It is only with the development and the success of so-called neo-classical economics that economics became institutionalized as a discipline almost completely independent of sociology. But this independence has been questioned anew by the economists themselves, following the 'crisis of economics' which followed the political and social leaps which occurred in industrial societies at the end of the 1960s. Must we, from this tormented history of the relationship between economics and sociology, conclude that the two disciplines are at once complementary and opposed on essential points?

Economics is distinguishable from sociology, to be sure, by its object. Its essential interest is the production and the circulation of goods and services. The objects which interest sociology are more diverse. But the two disciplines doubtless owe the reciprocal autonomy which is generally conceded to them less to the distinction between their objects than to the differences which traditionally separate some of their fundamental principles. Economics – this proposition being above all true of neo-classical economics – sees the economic subject, *homo oeconomicus*, as rational. In other terms, its assumes that his behaviour can be seen as the result of a calculation by which he seeks to maximize his 'pleasure' and to minimize his 'pain' or, to use language which conforms more to the usage of modern sociology, to make choices which accord with his *preferences*. In contrast, *homo sociologicus* is often, implicitly or explicitly, seen as irrational, that is to say as capable of being moved by neutral, indeed negative, forces, compared with his interest and his preferences. Thus, Tarde considers that the two principal motivating forces of human action are imitation and custom. The former pushes men to adopt such or such a type of behaviour not because it is profitable to them or conforms to their preferences, but because it is new. The latter explains why traditions can be preserved even when they are of no benefit and have no significance for those who observe them. Similarly, Pareto sets 'logical' actions (that is, as we would be more likely to say today, 'rational' actions), which are the subject of economics, against 'non-logical' actions (in our language, 'irrational' actions), which define the field of studies of sociology. Again similarly, Weber makes a distinction between *Zweck-rationell* actions (rational compared to the ends) and *Wertrationell* actions (that is, actions resulting from submission to supreme values), *affektuell* actions (emotional or passionate actions), and *traditionnell* actions. If the economist can content himself with considering the first type of action, according to Weber it is to be recommended that the sociologist takes into account the four types of action, and principally the second. Let us however note the difficulty of introducing too clear-cut distinctions: if *homo oeconomicus* is defined by a congruence between choice and preferences, *Wertrationell* actions can be explained by that model. The difference between sociologists and economists on that point is perhaps more one of custom or of practice than of doctrine: economists often consider values as *data*, while sociologists seek to *explain* them.

On the other hand, while economists generally obey the principle of methodo-logical individualism (i.e., considering that an economic phenomenon is analys-able and comprehensible only as the result of individual behaviour), sociologists sometimes deny this principle and follow a holistic approach (i.e., postulating that individual behaviour must fundamentally be seen as the consequence of social structures which are thus put forward as primary in the order of explanation). But, as in the above cases, care must be taken not to exaggerate the contrasts: econo-mists are well aware that behaviour obeys constraints and that these are fixed by structures.

The two dichotomous criteria above (rationality/irrationality, individualism/holism) determine a typology with four elements (cf. the table on page 141). Type 1 describes the axiomatic in human behaviour, above all used by the economists and sometimes employed by certain sociologists. The three other types are more char-acteristic of particular forms of sociology. Type 2 is represented by certain forms of Marxist or neo-Marxist sociology. Thus, numerous analyses belonging to this movement of thought see 'social structure' as essentially characterized by the exist-ence of two classes, the 'dominant' class and the 'dominated' class. The interests of individuals belonging to the dominant class are supposed to be convergent; with the result that in serving their own individual interest they serve at the same time their class interest. In addition, the dominant class, having control of the 'social structure' and being capable of imposing collective norms and values which conform with its interests, the members of the dominated class have no other solution except resignation. But type 2 can also be illustrated by more credible theories.

	Individualism	Holism
Rationality	Type 1	Type 2
Irrationality	Type 3	Type 4

This is the case with all the theories which see the rationality of the actor as a function of the logic of his situation (the data of the situation being themselves seen as depending on the 'social structures'). Thus, for Oberschall, the Black movement of the 1960s takes a non-violent form in the south and a violent form in the north of the United States because the *situation* of the leaders is different in each case. In the south, they can count upon the support of the Protestant clergy and must avoid choosing forms of action which would be likely to antagonize them. In the north, it is more a case of attracting the attention of journalists and politicians, and of convincing them of the existence of the 'Black problem'. The difference in the *situation* of the Black leaders, in the north and in the south, is evidently the product of 'structures' which themselves result from history.

Type 3 can be seen as characteristic of Tarde's sociology. In effect, this author explicitly declares: 1) that social phenomena can only be seen as the consequence of individual actions; 2) that above all the sociologist must be concerned 'with irrational actions', that is to say those which cannot be seen as resulting from the interests of the actors. The 'programme' thus outlined by Tarde has been put into operation by several modern sociologists. Thus, for Berger and Luckman, the sociologist must see social behaviour as the result of – or more exactly as guided by – collective images. But these images have sense and existence only in so far as they allow the actor to interpret his own situation and to confer significance on his projects. As with Tarde, we are dealing with an axiom which is at once 'individualist' and 'irrationalist'.

Type 4 can be seen as characteristic of the so-called structuralist sociologist. In this case, the actor is practically omitted from the analysis and is given the status of a 'structural support'. Thus, for Foucault, the history of the science itself can be explained, not by starting from the activity of the thinkers, but by the overbalancing of 'epistemic structures' which periodically modify the representations that men make of the world (in fact, the 'theory' of Foucault is only a caricature pushed to absurd lengths of the commonplace statement according to which scientific paradigms *can* be affected by extra-scientific representations). For Althusser, social structures impose roles on individuals which they are destined to carry out with servile fidelity.

At this point, it should be noted that the types which have just been summarily described are, to be sure, ideals, that they are rarely represented in a pure state, and the distinctions holism/individualism, on one hand, and rationality/ irrationality, on the other, must be seen as relative. In effect:

1) The best sociologists go beyond the opposition of holism/individualism. Thus de Toqueville, like Marx in many of his analyses, considers that social structures do not determine the behaviour of actors but the constraints which demarcate and structure their field of action. According to the situation, the constraints are such that they hardly leave the possibility of choice to the actor. Thus, the capitalist in a situation of competition is, according to Marx, condemned to invest or to perish. The constraints which result from the situation of competition leave only, in this case, an appearance of autonomy. But Marx also knew that the situations of forced choice must be held to be not the general case but the particular case, albeit important. Thus, the political actor or the trade union leader can find themselves confronted with complex decision-making situations, where none of the options defined by the 'structures' impose themselves with certainty. This is why (cf. *The Eighteenth Brumaire*) history can occasionally go backwards. This is also why the 'laws of history' are only 'tendential'. Besides, since the behaviour of actors can affect the 'social structures', in the complex models of action utilized by authors such as de Tocqueville and Marx, the result is often a circular relationship of cause and effect between 'structures' and individual actions, which in principle does not permit structures to be considered as 'primary' in the order of explanation.

2) Modern sociology, similarly to modern economics on its side, tends to shade the over-harsh opposition introduced by Pareto and Weber, the former by his distinction between 'logical actions' and 'non-logical actions', the latter by his distinctions between *Zweckrationell* actions, on one hand (= Pareto's logical actions), and, on the other hand, *Wertrationell, traditionell* and *affectuell* actions (= Pareto's non-logical actions). Today the tendency is to admit that the idea of rationality is readily definable only in particular cases. When the actor has to take a decision in conditions of uncertainty, when he is placed in a strategic type of situation, it can be difficult, both for the observer, as for the actor himself, to determine the line of action which most closely conforms to the interest or the preferences of the latter. Certain situations are, in other terms, of such a structure that the idea of *Zweckrationalität* is not defined (cf. 'Rationality'). On another hand, economists recognize, at least since the work of Hayek, that the social actor generally acts under conditions of limited rationality, that is to say that generally he has at his command only a small part of the information which would be necessary for him to act 'in full knowledge of cause'. Being unable to determine the consequences of the lines of action which are open to him, he will thus be constrained to trust his intuition, that is to say his beliefs or, as Pareto would say, his 'feelings', which are likely to be suggested to him by one or another of his 'reference groups'. This is why the 'economic' theory of democracy, as developed by writers such as Downs and Buchanan-Tullock, accords an important place to beliefs and ideologies: being unable to choose between alternative courses of action starting from a rational examination of their consequences, the actor will decide according to the

feeling they inspire in him. A radical policy of redistribution will be likely to be approved by an actor endowed with a 'feeling for' the Left because it will seem to him to conform to his feelings and beliefs, and it is put forward by a party in which he has confidence.

3) More generally: a) modern economics tends, in some of its aspects, to move aside from the classical model of a rational *homo oeconomicus* and to see him more as an example or a heuristic fiction; b) modern sociology tends for its part to reject too blunt a distinction between rational behaviour and irrational behaviour; c) if certain aberrant forms of neo-Marxism and structuralism are put on one side, it can be said that modern sociologists tend to see the relationship between structures and action in accordance with the complex model used, for example, by de Tocqueville and Marx; d) sociologists and economists tend nowadays to think that the validity of a particular axiom is a function of the problem being considered. In certain cases, the rational model of action can lead to a satisfactory theory. Thus, it permits of the presentation in an acceptable fashion of certain criminological data (Ehrlich), past variations of the demand for education or of social mobility (Boudon). In other cases, it will be insufficient or plainly out of place. In certain cases, a holistic schema (supposing behaviour *determined* by the structure) will lead to a satisfactory analysis (as when a situation is being dealt with where the actors are effectively in a position of forced choice). In other cases, it would lack relevance.

The types contained in the table on page 141 must thus, if we examine sociology and economics such as they are today, be thought of as schematic. It is no longer possible to distinguish the two disciplines by making them correspond to one or another of these types. Despite everything, the above typology usefully describes the traditional opposition between economics and sociology. Even if this traditional opposition is – as we have tried to suggest – today outdated in the actual practice of the two disciplines, it would be going too far to say that it has completely disappeared out of mind, because it is profoundly anchored in history. In fact, it has its origin in what is conventionally called the history of ideas. The intellectual – and perhaps ideological – basis of economics comes from the philosophy of the Enlightenment, a movement of ideas in which the individual is presented as the *ultima ratio* and society thought of as a contract of association founded on reason and calculation, and destined to serve as well as possible the interests of the individual. It appears, in effect, beyond doubt that the thinking of the founders of economics, and notably of Adam Smith: 1) is impregnated with the principles of the philosophy of the Enlightenment; 2) defined a paradigm or a 'programme' (Lakatos) within which and in the continuation of which classical and then neo-classical economics developed. The 'archaeology' of sociology, to take up an analogy of Michel Foucault, is, on the contrary, research from the viewpoint of the romantic reaction against the philosophy of the Enlightenment which, for reasons which it is not difficult to analyse, followed the French Revolution and the Napoleonic wars. Comte, following Bonald and Joseph de Maistre, stresses the importance for the social order of tradition and authority, which he sets against reason and contract – we would say against the consensus – ideas which the philo-

sophers of the Enlightenment had brought to the forefront. In the same way,
Durkheim fought against the resurgence of the philosophy of the Enlightenment
and of utilitarianism, which lasted longer in England than on the Continent.
Unlike Spencer, who sought to explain the division of labour by the advantages of
co-operation, he put forward the celebrated idea of the precontractual base of
contract: a contract can only be agreed between individuals who share common
values and traditions. The result of this is that co-operation and contract cannot be
explained by their advantages, but must be explained by the uphill slope, by the
existence of values rendering solidarity possible. To the idea, coming from the
philosophy of the Enlightenment, of freely consented-to obedience, Weber
opposed the celebrated categories of charismatic authority, of rational authority
(which does not in any way correspond to the conception of the philosophers of the
Enlightenment, but describes the form of authority characteristic of bureaucratic
organizations), and of traditional authority. Briefly, it is not difficult to show that
many of the classical concepts and conceptions of sociology must be understood
from the starting point of a reaction against the principles posed by the philosophy
of the Enlightenment.

The historical anchorage of the two disciplines, sociology and economics, in two
movements of antithetical ideas partly explains their relative autonomy and also
the obvious ideological distance which frequently distinguishes their representatives. It also doubtless explains why the two disciplines have been and often are
put forward as more distinct in their manner of thought and analysis than they are
in reality, and why the founders of sociology have all, be it Durkheim, Weber, or
Pareto, sought to define the discipline in a negative manner by contrast with
economics.

Despite this, sociology and economics are condemned to cohabit for the reason
that, in reality, the behaviour of social actors is, because of the situations with
which they are confronted, more or less 'rational' or 'irrational' and that the
causation between structure and behaviour is most often complex and circular.
None of the four types defined above can therefore claim generality. This is why
movements of opposition between the two disciplines are followed by movements
of reconciliation. Look at, for example, the movement which has been confirmed
since the beginning of the 1970s which in France is described by the expression
'sociological economics'. Carrying on the work of Downs and Olson, this movement, of which the most representative figure is perhaps that of Gary Becker,
endeavours to apply the individualist and utilitarian axiom characteristic of
economics, to phenomena traditionally within the jurisdiction of sociology (ideology, divorce, crime, discrimination, social movements, education, etc.). Look at,
in contrast, the movement of 'radical economics' which developed at about the
same time. It concerns a movement of complex ideas which certainly carry principally a criticism and a rejection of neo-classical economics, but also a project, that
of the integration with economic analysis of some aspects of sociological thinking.
Thus the 'radical' economists suggest that a certain number of economic phenomena (for example, the persistence of underdevelopment or of inflation) must be in
part explained by the mechanisms which Tarde described under the name of

imitation and that we would be more likely to call – following Duesenberry, himself a non-radical economist – a demonstration effect (an example of a demonstration effect: the élites of underdeveloped countries choose for themselves as a reference group, and imitate, the élites of developed countries, and thus divert to consumption resources which would be more advantageously employed in investment). Similarly, the 'radical' economists Bowles and Gintis consider membership of a class of decisive importance – a classical sociological concept – in their analysis of preferences in the matter of education. Symmetrically, many sociologists stress the importance of 'economic' types of modes of thought in the analysis of social phenomena.

Are these movements precursors, as Kuhn would say, of a paradigm shift? Will the historian of ideas of the twenty-first century describe the separation between economics and sociology as a transitory episode? Will he stress the fact that, even at the hour of its greatest glory, neo-classical economics was only ever representative of a small part of the production of economists; based on the fact that, even then, educational economists and sociologists, development economists and sociologists are hard to distinguish one from the other in their ways of thinking and of analysis? Who knows?

Action, Development, Rationality, Socialization, Utilitarianism.

Bibliography

ATTALI, J., *Analyse économique de la vie politique*, Paris, PUF, 1972. – BARRY, B., *Sociologists, economists and democracy*, New York, Collier-Macmillan, 1970. – BECKER, G., *Human capital*, New York, Columbia University Press, 1964; *The economics of discrimination*, Chicago, The Chicago University Press, 1957, 1971. – BUCHANAN, J. and TULLOCK, G., *The calculus of consent*, Ann Arbor, University of Michigan Press, 1962, 1965. – COLEMAN, J.S., *The mathematics of collective action*, London, Heinemann Educational Books, 1973. – DOWNS, A., *An economic theory of democracy*, New York, Harper, 1957. – EHRLICH, I., 'Participation in illegitimate activities: a theoretical and empirical investigation', *Journal of political economy*, LXXXI, *3*, 1973, 521–565. – EICHER, J.C., LEVY-GARBOUA, L., *et al., Economique de l'education. Travaux français*, Paris, Economica, 1979. – HIRSCH, F., *Social limits to growth*, Cambridge, Harvard University Press, 1976; London, Routledge & Kegan Paul, 1977. – JENNY, F., 'La théorie économique du crime: une revue de la littérature', *Vie et sciences économiques*, 73, 1977, 7–20. – KARABEL, J. and HALSEY, A.H. (ed.), 'Education, *human capital* and the labor market', in KARABEL, J. and HALSEY, A.H. (ed.), *Power and ideology in education*, New York, Oxford University Press, 1977, 307–366. – NISBET, R., *The sociological tradition*, New York, Basic Books, 1966; London, Heinemann, 1967. – OLSON, M., *The logic of collective action*, Cambridge, Harvard University Press, 1965. – PARSONS, T. and SMELSER, N.J., *Economy and society*, New York, The Free Press, 1956; London, Routledge & Kegan Paul, 1956. – ROUSSEAU, J.-J., 'Discours sur l'économie politique', *in* ROUSSESAU, J.-J., *Œuvres complètes*, t. III, *Du contrat social. Ecrits politiques*, 239–278. – SCHUMPETER, J.A., *History of economic analysis*, London, Allen & Unwin, 1954, 1972. – SIMIAND, F., *Le salaire, l'évolution sociale et la monnaie. Essai de théorie expérimentale du salaire*, Paris, F. Alcan, 1932, 3 vol. – SMITH, A., *An inquiry into the nature and causes of the wealth of Nations*, London, W. Strahan & T. Cadell, 1776; London, Ward Lock, 1812; Oxford, Clarendon Press, 1976. – TULLOCK, G., *Toward a mathematics of politics*, Ann Arbor, University of Michigan Press, 1968. – WEBER, M., *Economy and society*.

Egalitarianism

Egalitarianism is an ideology which, among the values falling within the formula of legitimacy in force in western industrial societies, gives to equality in one or other of its meanings a preponderant place. De Tocqueville sees in the march towards equality of conditions a long-lasting tendency which he ventures to qualify as 'providential'. Even better, he distinguishes the forms that this tendency takes. The legal status of individuals became equal with the end of feudalism. Therefore individuals were recognized as being equally capable of entering into contracts, of buying and selling, of marrying. Afterwards, or concurrently, came a process of equalization of political rights. To all men, then to all adults of both sexes, the right to vote would be given. Third, our societies becoming more productive and richer, the extreme disparities between abundance and penury are gradually diminished – or rather it is seen that they must be diminished. To this very optimistic tableau, a last feature can be added. The inequalities of participation in public benefits such as education, health, and in the diverse amenities of life in society, will themselves also be progressively reduced, to the point where at the limit all the members of the modern city would be able to lay claim to the enjoyment of the same cultural treasure.

This philosophy of history has for a long time furnished egalitarian ideology with a manifestly exaggerated confidence in the conditions of its own realization. However, even deprived of the support that the belief in an indefinite progress brought to it in the nineteenth century, today egalitarianism still constitutes one of the dominant values of our society. It is therefore necessary for us to understand simultaneously why the exigencies of equality impose themselves so strongly and what kinds of resistance they provoke.

As clearly seen by Aristotle, the requirements of equality take two forms which are not easily reconcilable. On one hand, it calls for arithmetical equality. Envisaged in this way, it states that all men must be treated in the same way. But on another hand, it states that the return that they take from the exchange must be in proportion to their contribution. It would not be just that he who has not worked should receive as much as he who has made great efforts. It is true that the gospel parable of the worker of the eleventh hour reminds us that divine justice is not bound by the same criteria as human justice: grace, which does not come without mystery, elects the just without other men being able to see any connection other than the divine will between the *works* of those who are vindicated and the *salvation* which is accorded to them. As soon as a more strictly naturalist conception of the human condition and life in society is affirmed, the demands of equality define themselves in relation to three references: that of merit, that of need, that of solidarity.

The first conception, which we could call *meritocratic*, claims to establish a rigorous connection between the contributions of individuals – their accomplishments – and their status. It depends upon an enhanced social mobility to eradicate privilege, once equal conditions for all have been instituted in the competition between members of a society. Once everybody is on the same footing, the hypothesis is that the winners can only be 'the best'. The meritocratic ideal which is recorded both by the liberal tradition and by the socialist tradition is associated with a criticism of heritage and praise for competition and examinations as normal means of promotion. Thus purified of the unfair promotion of particular individuals, the mechanisms of social mobility and of competition distribute people among roles and status according to criteria of assignment that are supposed to maximize the efficacy and the satisfaction of each. On one hand, the meritocratic ideal disqualifies hereditary transmission and rigidities of all kinds which block initiative and penalize talent. On the other hand, in making of competition and of examinations – or publicity of those merits which are approved of in the market of success – a normal means, it can be invoked to legitimize the hierarchy of status and of material and symbolic remuneration.

Meritocracy thus accepts possibly very strong disparities in the hierarchy of status. These disparities can be appreciated from two points of view. First, what obliges us to show justice towards the producers whose production and productivity are situated below the level which covers their subsistence needs? The question addresses itself at once to the meritocratic logic and to the productivist logic. The first, confronted with unqualified individuals, has nothing to offer them. The second foresees nothing concerning individuals who do not produce 'added value'. None the less, it is necessary to take into account, in default of their merits and their efficacy, their 'needs'. This argument is at the centre of debates which, ever since the first industrial revolution, concerned the fate that society should reserve for 'the poor' and 'the unemployed'. An inequality of income which would exclude insufficiently productive or involuntarily inactive individuals from the enjoyment of the goods and the services reputed to be necessary for the maintenance of human life would appear to be morally unacceptable. At the limit, it is the responsibility of government to take from those who have too much in order to give to those who have not enough, in order to put an end to an inequality which is an injustice.

As for giving a strict definition to the idea of 'needs', it cannot be counted upon. Thus the determination of norms which would preside over an equitable redistribution is inevitably contentious. It offends by imprecision as far as the definition of the threshold of intervention is concerned, but also as to the scale and the methods of transfer. The difficulties are even further aggravated if the needs thought not to be satisfied are defined not with regard to the possible beneficiaries but with regard to the real or supposed capacity of a technically advanced society to satisfy the said needs. It can in effect appear 'scandalous' that in societies where a majority of the citizens have every chance of squandering money, a minority receive in fact only the minimum of education, of culture, and of health. This theme is constantly and with conviction underlined in the various socialist traditions.

To appreciate the power of egalitarian ideology, a third reference must be considered. Up to this point, this ideology appears to us to be nourished by a consciousness of what is due to our merits, and of what, beside any merit, is due to each man because of his 'needs'. In both cases, the egalitarian demand latches on to the individual. But it has another source, which has been particularly underlined by classical thinking even though today it is less obvious. *Civisme*, or virtue, that is to say the bond which links private individuals to the body politic, is only possible if an excessive inequality of riches (of patrimony as well as of income) does not put too great a distance between citizens, does not break up all solidarity. The sumptuary laws exist to check the envy and resentment which the ostentatious display of luxury inspires in underprivileged individuals. This theme, which has been abundantly developed by Montesquieu and Rousseau, is today taken up by Rawls, who expects individuals to become envious beyond a certain degree of inequality in the sharing out of primary goods, although in the 'original situation' they are not.

The demands of egalitarianism, when they are not hierarchized, are thus strongly divergent. The meritocratic ideal accommodates a great inequality in income and in status if this appears to be founded on the value and social utility of our contributions and on the effort that these have cost us. 'Enrich yourself, but by work and by saving', according to Guizot's command, which is much quoted but generally out of the context of its further explanations regarding the ways and means of enrichment. The meritocratic ideal, even when refined, can come into conflict at the same time with the demands of *civisme* and of philanthropy which both lay stress, even if for different reasons, on the solidarity between the members of the same community. Inversely, if for fear of breaking that solidarity, the links have to be loosened between individual contributions and returns, if the most productive and deserving individuals have to accept that part of the production attributable to their industry be transferred to other less diligent individuals, this egalitarianism of redistribution or, at the outside, of confiscation contradicts the meritocratic ideal.

In so far as the meritocratic ideal exalted by the positivist tradition is today decried by all those who see in it only an ideology which permits the hiding from view of the inequalities and the mechanisms of reproduction, the criteria of equality find themselves changed. In the positivist tradition, equality is understood as the equality of opportunity, or more precisely as the absence of privilege and of handicaps; the *starting conditions* given to competitors must be equal. Also this form of egalitarianism attacks first the diverse means of inheritance, not only patrimony but the various advantages that the privileged enjoy from the cradle. Today it is not only equality of beginning which is claimed, but also equality of results. It is no longer only the privilege of birth which is scandalous, it is the very existence of gaps between the performance of different competitors which is held to be suspect. It is true that this gap, even though it partly depends upon conditions which are hard to control by the political authorities, can be seen as tolerable by the upholders of utilitarian ideology if it contributes, by judicious redistribution, to the improvement of the condition of the most underprivileged.

In order to understand clearly the ambiguity of the egalitarian ideal, it is insufficient to emphasize that each of its expressions is likely to clash with the others. It must also be noted that it is possibly in opposition to other requirements, which are also well known and time honoured by our value system. A strict equality of result, before or after redistribution, can be obtained only by means of an extremely restricting social organization, which the ideologies of solidarity seek to legitimize by invoking the general interest. The egalitarianism of results leads to sometimes dramatic reduction in individual liberties. It does not only limit the liberty of those to the detriment of whom the transfer of resources is operated. It also institutes a kind of *supervision* over those for whose benefit it takes place. Not only must there be very detailed controls determining the categories 'having rights' and the conditions on which their rights can be exercised, but these rights often have an obligatory nature in the sense that the individuals for whom they have been created have absolutely no latitude to renounce them. The obligation to attend school until an age fixed by law, the ban on working above the legal number of hours are probably justifiable, the one for considerations of public utility (it is advantageous for the country that the young go to school until 16), the other by considerations involving the conditions of fair competition in the labour market. But in both cases, the imposition of a uniform rule as far as the amount of work or the duration of schooling are concerned is accompanied by a diminution of the field left to the initiative of certain individuals, and by correlation in the extension of what de Tocqueville called the 'immense and supervisory despotism' of public administration. Our value system is not entirely lacking in all counterweights to egalitarianism – even though we are justified, with de Tocqueville, in observing an age-old tendency towards a greater equality of conditions. This counterweight is given to us by the attachment to the private domain inside which 'the coalman is the master in his own home'.

Democracy, Needs, Social Mobility, Social Stratification, De Tocqueville.

Bibliography

BARKER, E., *Greek political theory: Plato and his predecessors*, London, Methuen & Co., Ltd., 1918, 1964. – BOUDON, R., *Effets pervers et ordre social*, Paris, PUF, 1977, chap. 6, 157–186. – BOUGLÉ, C., *Les idées égalitaires, étude sociologique*, Paris, F. Alcan, 1899, 1925. – BOURRICAUD, F., 'Cotradition et traditions chez Tocqueville', *The Tocqueville Review*, 1980, II, 1, 25–39. – DARRAS, *Le partage des bénéfices, expansion et inégalités en France*, Paris, Editions de Minuit, 1966. – HALÉVY, E., *La formation du radicalisme philosophique*, Paris, F. Alcan, 1901–1904, 3 vol. – HOMANS, G.C., *Social behavior: its elementary forms*, New York, Harcourt, Brace & World, 1961; London, Routledge & Kegan Paul, 1961. – MERTON, R.K., *Sociale theory and social structure*, Glencoe, The Free Press, 1949. – MONTESQUIEU, C. de *L'esprit des lois*. – NOZICK, R., *Anarchy, state and utopia*, Oxford, B. Blackwell, 1974. – RAWLS, J., *A theory of justice*, Oxford, Clarendon Press, 1973. – ROUSSEAU, J.-J., *Le contrat social*. – STEPHEN, L., 'Social equality', *International Journal of Ethics*, vol. 1, 1890–91, 261–288. – TAWNEY, R.H., *Equality*, London, Allen and Unwin, 1931, 1964; New York, Barnes & Noble, 1965.

Elections

The election is a procedure by which the members of a group (whatever its principal outcome) will be in a position to designate their leaders and to effect a collective choice as to the conduct of their common affairs. The election is one of the characteristic institutions of modern regimes. It is practised, with variable degrees of efficacy and sincerity, nearly everywhere in the contemporary world. Soviet citizens elect the ministers of the Supreme Soviet, as German citizens during the Hitlerian Third Reich returned theirs to the Reichstag. The absence of elections is an oddity in today's world, to the point that the leaders who deprive their co-citizens of them generally invoke temporary circumstances, regrettable and altogether independent of their will. The election is not only a nearly universal practice in usage in contemporary political societies – it being, to be sure, only in countries with a one party system, or even a dominant party, with censorship, dictatorship of the proletariat, that this practice does not have the same sense as in regimes with multiple, competing parties, with public liberty constitutionally guaranteed to the opposition by way of the press, television, and meetings. In addition, there are numerous non-political associations whose affairs are conducted by means of elections. It is finally a remarkable tendency that bureaucratic organizations, which, in the name of hierarchic principle, have for a long time forbidden this method of appointment of their leaders – to say nothing of capitalist enterprises, where the right to vote was strictly limited to the owners of authorized capital, in directing themselves toward co-management or self-management, give a growing place to the election.

This century-old movement which, parodying de Tocqueville, we could qualify as 'providential', has encountered all sorts of resistance. It appeared, at first sight, to contradict the old precept that 'all power comes from God'. But the metaphysicians and the theologians of sovereignty have more or less easily accommodated it. The Jewish tradition saw in the law the expression of the divine will. Can we not discover in law, the expression of the will of the electors, the characteristics of generality, of *impartiality* recognized in the divine will? This requirement of impartiality, which obliges the elector to come to a decision, as Rousseau says, in the 'silence of passion', gives to the political election a character which distinguishes it from others. The citizen does not state his personal preferences, he comes to a decision on the common good or the general interest. He does not say what seems to him to conform to his own interest, he declares what conforms to the interest of the body politic. Reduced to essentials, the criticism which the conservatives, from Hobbes to Maurras, make of the election as a procedure for appointing governors is that the electors are *individuals*, but that it is never possible to treat them as *citizens*, sufficiently detached from their private interests to prefer the general interest, regarding which, incidentally, they can only be imperfectly informed.

All the same, the election is not challenged in all its aspects by conservative criticism. It can enlighten the holders of sovereignty about the intensity of feeling, the configuration of interests, in brief about the opinions of their subjects. Thus it constitutes a lifelike survey of opinion. When the king of France convokes the Estates General, he invites his good people to name representatives, but also to express their grievances. The electoral base of consultation is very large, since in the parishes nearly everybody votes. But the Estates are no more than a consultative assembly in the mind of the king. It is the forcible coup of Mirabeau and of the Third Estate which made of an assembly a deliberative and constituent power. On the other hand, when the election concerns the 'intermediary bodies' (corporative, professional, municipal, or regional assemblies) it does not arouse any objection from the conservatives. The monarchy of the *Ancien Régime* left the towns, the trades, the orders, and the estates to organize themselves in elected bodies. The election of their governors appeared as a privilege which guaranteed the autonomy of these bodies – their capacity to govern and administrate themselves by themselves. Finally, suffrage appeared less as a right than as a responsibility attached to a competence or to a status, as, for example, that of head of a family, a category of which, in the case of the Third Estate's members, the right of suffrage was often limited. Suffrage appeared as an appropriate means of consultation, and also of decision-making, when it concerned the government of societies or of non-political bodies – on condition of not constituting an arm of war against the legitimate holders of the sovereignty. The enumeration of opinions, the division of the assembly into a majority and a minority thus become common and legitimate procedures, even more so because they are very commonly employed in religious orders.

Rokkan has shown how, at the end of a long history, suffrage has become universal and, if one can say so, equalized. The universalization happens because of the progressive inclusion of categories of electors formerly excluded. Universal suffrage has been practised in the United States since Independence, in most of the states of the Union. But it was instituted in England only after the First World War. Again, even in countries which, like France, introduced it quite early (it was instituted in 1848) it became universal only with the vote for women, which, in France, was obtained only in 1945. In addition, the condition of a minimum age, recently lowered, excludes a proportion of the population.

On the other hand, the principle of equality (*one man, one vote*), even if it has only belatedly been proclaimed by the American Supreme Court, has imposed the equality of electors: 'Votes are counted not weighed' – which means that they all have the same weight, whatever the status and the quality of the elector. The multiple vote, the family vote, the right recognized up until 1945 of students and ex-students of Oxford and of Cambridge to vote in the electoral constituency of their *alma mater* without prejudicing the vote that they continued to give in the constituency of their residence are no longer more than amusing curiosities. Similarly, the multiplication of electoral colleges according to a weighting which deliberately favours a certain category is a way of violating the principle of *one man, one vote*. The electoral law introduced in Prussia by Bismarck and that which Nicolas II applied to the Douma of the Empire are good examples of this. Everyone votes, but in separate colleges, the number elected by each college being neither equal nor proportionate to the number of electors registered in those colleges. The strict equality of the number of senators in the federal American Constitution constitutes a different situation, because the senators are not supposed to represent the population, but the member States of the Union, themselves treated on an egalitarian basis. It is true that equality before the suffrage can also be put in check by the cutting-out of electoral boundaries so that an elector of the Lozere 'weighs' ten times more than an elector of Seine-Saint-Denis. (The American Supreme Court obliges the competent authorities to establish a strict equality, as far as the number of registered electors is concerned, between the constituencies, and to update the electoral boundaries after each census.) Does the principle of the equality of electors disqualify as unfair all electoral systems except the proportional system? The argument invoked by the 'proportionalists', that all electors have an equal right to be represented according to the criterion of number is contested by those who maintain that equality of suffrage does not imply the right to a proportional representation of electors. In effect, the vote enables a distribution of opinion, which has every chance – except in the case of unanimity – of taking the form of a division between majority and minority. A proportional election cannot cancel out that effect, even if, in order to respect this principle, it was agreed to make the electors vote not for a candidate (voting for a single candidate), but for a list of candidates whereby the probability would be greater that all the parties, if not all opinions, would be represented. In effect, those elected could not – unless they took the risk of incoherence or insignificance – construct their policies proportionally. It would be necessary for them to decide – in the majority – whether to keep certain items or whether to dispose of them. Proportional election does not dispense with resorting to the majority rule. It only transfers the job of applying it from the electorate to the elected.

Rokkan stresses a third aspect of suffrage: secrecy. In France, the guarantees regarding the secrecy of the vote became altogether effective only with the Third Republic. Under the parliamentary monarchy of the restored Bourbons and of Louis-Philippe, where the right of suffrage was reserved to several hundreds of thousands of electors, the better his vote was known to the authorities, the easier it was to corrupt the elector. The authoritarian Empire utilized the law of security to get rid of the 'unruly' from the polling booths. Whether it concerned corruption or repression, the authorities attached the greatest importance to knowing the vote of the elector, in order to buy him or intimidate him. Subsequently, the legal system retained violation of the secrecy of the vote which appeared as one of the conditions of its 'genuineness', as one of the causes of annulment.

From this historic evolution, recalled in broad outline, two principal tendencies stand out. First, the vote appeared more and more as the constitutive exercise of sovereignty. A government which does not have its origins in regular elections is suspected of being illegitimate. On the other hand, the vote is the act of an individual who freely expresses his preferences concerning the composition and the policies of the governmental authorities. In reconciling these two propositions, we are led to define the election as the procedure by which individual preferences are aggregated in a collective decision capable of imposing itself as common law on all the members of the group, to bind them, whether or not they approve of the majority opinion. This definition raises two kinds of problems, one logical, which comes from the difficulty of *aggregation* of the individual will, the other really sociological, which concerns the *legitimacy* of the majority decision.

The first problem has been dealt with by Condorcet who gives a classic analysis of it. When the electors have to choose between two – and only two– candidates or programmes, Condorcet does not raise any difficulty. To be truthful, it could be pointed out (but Condorcet does not do so) that, even in that situation, individual preferences are affected by unequal intensity, and it is not impossible that the majority should be composed of 'lukewarm people' in the face of a minority, numerically weak, but 'passionately' hostile or 'passionately' in favour of the other policy or the other candidate. (It is, incidentally, to face up to this risk that, in affairs that are likely gravely to affect the interests of certain categories of electors, the guarantee of qualified majorities – absolute, two thirds, etc. – is offered to them.)

As soon as the electors have to choose between more than two candidates or two policies, two risks appear. The first is that a majority prefers A to B, B to C and . . . C to A. At the individual level, such an *intransitive* ensemble of preference is nearly inconceivable. A subject who prefers A to B and B to C is very likely also to prefer A to C.

The interesting point in Condorcet's paradox is that it shows that an ensemble of transitive individual judgements can result in an intransitive collective opinion. This would be the case if an electoral body of sixty people showed the following preferences:

23 prefer A to B and B to C;
17 prefer B to C and C to A;
2   prefer B to A and A to C;
10 prefer C to A and A to B;
8   prefer C to B and B to A.

In studying this ballot in detail, we note a majority of thirty-three persons in sixty prefers A to B and that a majority of forty persons prefers B to C. But from this it does not result that a majority prefers A to C. On the contrary, the preference A > C is expressed by only a minority of twenty-five persons. None of the candidates can thus be held to be collectively preferred to the others. The collective choice is *indeterminate*, at least if we insist on effecting the detailed study by comparing the options by pairs, because we can also consider that option A has received a relative majority of the votes. But this study eliminates the difficulties raised by Condorcet at the price of an elimination of the distinction between the second and third level of preferences.

A more ordinary example, but one which also illustrates the difficulties raised by the application of the majority rule, can be associated with Condorcet's paradox. Let us suppose that our electoral body of sixty persons show the following preferences:

23 prefer A to C and C to B;
19 prefer B to C and C to A;
16 prefer C to B and B to A;
2   prefer C to A and A to B.

In this case, the collective preferences are transitive: a majority prefer C to B, B to A, and C to A. C can thus be held to be collectively preferred. But it must also be noted – this is a second paradox – that C is that of the three options to which the first place is least often given. When all is said and done, should the study by pairs be preferred to the study of the first level of preferences? To be honest, the question is unanswerable, because if the second method implies, compared with the first, a loss of information, it must be seen that the first treats by paralipsis information which would be essential, and would eliminate all difficulty, but is hardly accessible, namely the intensity of preferences.

The interest of this second 'paradox' is that at the same time it draws attention to an essential point: there are *several* ways – and in fact a considerable number of ways exist – to study a ballot and to apply majority rule. The question is therefore: what is an adequate method for aggregating the individual preferences and transforming them into a collective order? Arrow has furnished a response which brings out the narrowness of the limits within which majority rule is valid. An acceptable rule of aggregation must first permit the definition of an effectively applicable order of collective preferences, whatever individual preferences are. The rule, on the other hand, must reflect the preferences of the individual. In the third place, individuals do not give opinions except on the options which are effectively submitted to them. The aggregation must therefore not be susceptible to their preferences on 'non-pertinent alternatives'. Conditions 4 and 5 affirm that collective order cannot be imposed and specify that it cannot be imposed by a referee.

This purely logical thought process allows us to appreciate the risk of perverse effects appearing, of which we have analysed two examples. It thus permits it to be emphasized that, in many cases, the majority principle does not sift out the general will. Therefore it still needs to be explained how such a contestable rule is considered to be the source of an obligation which makes a *law* out of the collective decision and *citizens* out of individuals. We can link up this transmutation to two series of causes. First, in the western political tradition, whether it is envisaged in its Greek sources or in its Jewish sources, that which assures the legitimacy of the law and distinguishes it from an order, pure and simple, is its impersonality. It can be linked to a divine source or apprehended as consubstantial (as a real presence) to the will of those who are subject to it. In no case can it be founded on caprice or the interest of an individual or of a faction. From this negative demarcation, which determines what is not the law, what it cannot be, no logical necessity results which says that the majority should have *the right* to command the minority. Liberals, such as Benjamin Constant and de Tocqueville, have emphasized that majority despotism was as insupportable as tyranny by one individual alone.

In order to explain the legitimacy which is attached to one majority procedure, it is thus necessary to take into account not only the religious or philosophical 'derivations' with which it is associated, but also the breadth of its jurisdiction. If the ruin or prosperity, life or death of the individuals who compose the minority depend on the result of a single vote, it is to be expected that they will be likely to challenge the majority verdict. If, on the contrary, a demarcation is installed between individual interests and what the majority can decide, the wishes of those who have won the election will be accepted by those who have lost it, so much the more so if the result does not bring into play their *vital* interests – in the strongest sense of this term. If, besides, the losers have the chance and the hope of becoming the winners again before the Greek calendes, they will bear their misfortune patiently. If their defeat in an election does not forbid them, even during the time when they are in the minority, to be winners in other elections, this diversification of the stakes permits them to put themselves in the hands of the principle of alternation. Finally, if the policy followed by the majority is *reasonably* crowned with success and achieves *approximately* the objectives which it has promised, the more or less rapid rallying of a smaller or larger fraction of the minority becomes probable. This is thus the nature of the relationship between government and opposition which explains the nature of the relationship between the majority and the minority – these relationships condense an historic experience and incarnate strategies elaborated by political art. Even if the election is very far from always bringing out the general will *stricto sensu*, the majority can legitimately decide for the political body, under the double reservation that the minority is not, or does not feel itself to be, oppressed, and that the policy implemented is practicable. These two criteria make us become aware of the institutional fragility of majority rule.

Action (collective), Aggregation, Democracy, Rousseau

Bibliography

ARROW, K.J., *Social choice and individual values*, London, Blackwell, 1984; New York, J. Wiley & Sons, 1951, 1963. – BASTID, P., *L'avènement du suffrage universel*, Paris, PUF, 1948. – BLACK, D., *The theory of committees and elections*, Cambridge Univ. Press, 1958. – BOIS, P., *Paysans de l'Ouest; des structures économiques et sociales aux options politiques depuis l'époque révolutionnaire dans la Sarthe*, Paris, Flammarion, 1971. – BUCHANAN, J.M. and TULLOCK, G., *The calculus of consent: logical foundations of constitutional democracy*, Ann Arbor, Univ. of Michigan Press, 1962. – CHARNAY, J.P., *Le suffrage politique en France: élections parlementaires, élection présidentielle, référendums*, Paris, Mouton, 1965. – DAHL, R.A., *A preface to democratic theory*, Univ. of Chicago Press, 1956. – DUVERGER, M., *L'influence des systèmes électoraux sur la vie politique*, Paris, A. Colin, 1950. – FAVRE, P., *La décision de majorité*, Paris, Presses de la Fondation nationale des Sciences politiques, 1976. – GOGUEL, F. and GROSSER, A., *La politique en France*, Paris, A. Colin, 1964, 501–551. Reproduced in GUILBAUD, G. Th., *Eléments de la théorie mathématique des jeux*, Paris, Dunod, 1968, 39–109. – MOULIN, L., 'Les origines religieuses des techniques électorales et délibératives modernes', *Revue internationale d'Histoire politique et constitutionnelle*, Nouvelles séries, 1953, *3*, 106–148. – ROKKAN, S., *Citizens, elections, parties: approaches to the comparative study of the process of development*, with CAMPBELL, A., MOULIN, L., 'Les origines religieuses des techniques électorales et délibératives modernes', *Revue internationale d'Histoire politique et constitutionnelle*, Nouvelles séries, 1953, *3*, 106–148. – ROKKAN, S., *Citizens, elections, parties: approaches to the comparative study of the process of development*, with CAMPBELL, A., TORSVIK, P. and VALEN, H., Oslo, 1970; 'Mass suffrage, secret voting and political participation', *Archives européennes de Sociologie*, 1961, *1*, 132–154. – SEYMOUR, C., *Electoral reform in England and Wales: the development and operation of the parliamentary franchise, 1832–1885*, New Haven, Yale Univ. Press, 1915; Newton Abbot, David & Charles, 1970. – SIEGFRIED, A., *Tableaux politiques de la France de l'Ouest sous la IIIᵉ République,* Paris, A. Colin, 1913; Geneva, Slatkine, 1980. – STOETZEL, A., 'Comment reconnaître la volonté générale?', *Revue française de sociologie*, XVII, *1*, 1976, 3–11.

Élite(s)

Should the word be written in the singular or in the plural? Pareto is one of the rare sociologists to emphasize the impossibility of making a choice in this respect. The idea of élite implies, according to him, an evaluation of success, by which social actors display their activities. Since to evaluate is the same as comparing and one can only compare the comparable, one cannot speak of the élite except from inside a sphere of a given activity: 'Let us thus form a class of those who have the highest marks in the sphere where they deploy their activity and give to this class the name of *élite*.' There are then as many élites as there are spheres of activity. But, beside this idea of the unshakeable plurality of élites, Pareto also takes up the Machiavellian opposition between the governing and the governed classes. For the great Italian sociologist, there thus exists at the same time *a* ruling élite in the singular and non-ruling *élites* in the plural.

Other authors prefer to write the word exclusively in the singular and to speak of a 'ruling élite', like Bottomore, or 'power élite', like C. Wright Mills. To further complicate matters, certain of them employ the word 'class' where others, with an identical meaning, prefer the word 'élite'. 'Ruling élite' and 'ruling class', 'governing élite' and 'governing class' are nevertheless expressions which are often interchangeable. As for the idea of 'dominant class', it suggests the existence, over and above the 'apparent' diversity of élites, of a convergence of their interests, of a complicity of their members, of a collaboration between the *power* of one and the *influence* of the other.

Pareto's conception is certainly one which, by its care not to erase essential distinctions, is the most congruent with observation. Its principal traits are taken up in a celebrated article by Aron. But it also contains some imprecisions and difficulties which it is worth commenting on. The *first* is that it is not very explicit regarding the criteria which permit of distinction between members of élites and it hardly lays any stress on the ambiguity of these criteria: there can be a contradiction here between the judgement of equals (pairs) and the judgement of the public. That physician, that economist, or that ethnologist can enjoy considerable prestige in the eyes of the 'public', even if his work is the object of dubious judgement from his equals. In the *second* place, it seems evident that different branches of activity are unequally valued and in consequence are not incommensurate, contrary to what Pareto suggests. With all due respects to Edgar Poe, draughts players do not inspire the same terror before the sacred monsters as the great chess players arouse. In the history of music Offenbach does not occupy the same place as Mozart.

This *second* objection leads to an important question: does the unequal valuation of 'branches of activity' indicate the existence of a common value system? A subsidiary question: can this common system of values (if it exists) be considered as the indirect proof of the existence of a dominating class, having the capacity of imposing on the whole of society the hierarchy of values which belongs to it? If one asks oneself why draughts are less valued than chess or Offenbach than Mozart, it really seems that we can reduce these differences to hierarchies in general values. Draughts is seen as a game based on cunning, speed, the internalization of 'classic' moves of a not only finite but also limited number. Conversely, chess is seen as putting into operation a capacity for exceptional deduction and anticipation. On one hand cunning, deductive intelligence on the other. The second 'quality' being in general more valued than the first, the chess player is more esteemed than the draughts player. This statement is without doubt true. Certainly an institutional element must be taken into account, namely that chess championships are organized on a world scale and enjoy media publicity. The latter is perhaps only the consequence of the former. Beethoven is more esteemed than Offenbach because the former created new sound combinations and rhythmic structures, while the latter succeeded perfectly only in a minor genre. These analyses, which it would be possible to define and to multiply – elementary analyses for all that – appear to indicate that we can disclose a common value system behind the hierarchization of spheres of activity. Because the values belong not to the order of nature, but to that of culture, the temptation is great to make of them the product of 'arbitrariness' and to see in the existence of a dominant class the foundation of that arbitrariness. The pre-eminence of opera over operetta and, as a consequence, the fact that a composer of operetta, however prestigious he may be, would be unable to lay claim to the same level of respectibility as the composer of opera does not rest upon any intrinsic reason. 'Great' music is thus only great because it is preferred by a section of social actors, to whom it serves as a sign of recognition. Finally, the hierarchization of works, like that of 'spheres of activity' only reflects the hierarchization of their publics. The fact that this hierarchization is seen as being of universal relevance indicates both the existence and the capacity for domination of a 'class' of society, the dominant class.

A certain interest must be recognized in this theory. It has been popularized notably by Bourdieu and his disciples who, from their neo-Marxist perspective, generally prefer the expression 'dominant class' to that of 'élite'. But it is equally important to see the very narrow limits of it. First of all, it can be questioned whether the 'dominant class' is effectively capable of imposing a consensus on the dominated class: Margot is not always convinced of the superiority of *Fidelio* over *Tosca*. The preferences of the dominant class are not always capable of establishing hierarchies between élites. Tennis courts assuredly 'attract a better class of person' than bicycle tracks. But the champion cyclist can be a candidate for the status of 'superstar' just as much as the tennis champion. Hitchcock, whose audience is without doubt more popular than that of Resnais, is not considered to be a minor figure. The detective film is not altogether a minor art. An important discovery has recently revealed that French workers have a weakness for bananas and the middle classes for endives. However no myth classes the endive among the food of the gods. Briefly, it seems clear that phenomena such as the development of the media, 'mass' arts such as the cinema, audio-visual techniques, popular sport, etc., have largely contributed to the mixing up of the scales of traditional values. It is sure that, up until a late stage in the nineteenth century and at the beginning of the twentieth century, success for the middle classes was equivalent to canonization. But the coming of 'mass' culture has obscured the hierarchies. The children of the middle classes sometimes prefer Asterix to Corneille. To establish the existence of a 'dominant class' starting from a hierarchy of prestige and of branches of activity is thus a debatable enterprise from two points of view. On one hand, it has an element of sophistry (the existence of the dominant class is 'demonstrated' starting not from observation, but from a deductive process). On the other hand, the premises upon which the deduction is founded contradict a factual proposition: that is to say, if *partial* hierarchizations really exist (at the level of social perception) between activities and spheres of activities, it is assuredly impossible to claim that the hierarchies pertaining to one group can be imposed upon others. Hyper-realism in painting (which applies to painting the rule seen as 'popular', that of the faithful reproduction of reality, and abolishes the distinction between painting and the 'popular' *art* of the photo), the canonization of popular history, music which is described precisely as 'pop' (which is not of 'popular' origin but which wishes to be attached to a 'popular' musical culture) seem to indicate that in the matter of hierarchy of values, the dominant class is not always who we believe it to be. Overall we might ask if the attenuation of the phenomena of stratification in industrial societies, the extension of education, and the corresponding appearance of phenomena such as 'mass' culture and 'mass' sport do not bring a new vigour to Pareto's theory. It is impossible, except at a local level, to establish a hierarchization of forms and spheres of activity which would be more or less recognized by all. *A fortiori*, it is impossible to demonstrate that this hierarchization corresponds to the preferences of a 'class'.

Let us now come onto the discussions which relate to the ruling élite (or élites). We have already said that if all sociologists agree in distinguishing within the élite (élites) a subgroup corresponding to the part of the élite (élites) having an influence or a direct power over the social system, they would not be in agreement on the singular or plural nature of this subgroup. Among those who refer in the singular to the ruling élite, all ideological nuances are represented. According to certain variants of popular Marxism, power is held by the holders of capital or, in more modern language, by the economic actors in charge of the biggest capitalist enterprises. According to others, the 'real' power is held by the managers of multinational companies. Did not Marx himself uphold, in his esoteric statements on the question, that the national State was enslaved to the interests of the capitalist bourgeoisie? For certain neo-Marxists, the political apparatus of liberal societies is enslaved to the interests of international capitalism. According to popular liberalism, the State always has the capacity of exercising a function of arbitration between divergent interests. According to this vision, the 'true' holder of power is thus the politician. Thus, popular liberals and popular Marxists are in agreement in disclosing in the complexity of the system of social roles a particular class of actors who would be the 'authentic' depositaries of power. We can summarize the two positions which have just been evoked by speaking of popular monism.

It is important to distinguish popular monism from what might be called academic monism. In this last variant the plurality of ruling élites is recognized. But one should endeavour to show at the same time that the interests of different 'fractions' of the ruling class are convergent and that these fractions have the capacity to advance on the back of the ruled class towards agreements intended to promote their own interests. This position is for example that of Mills. Mills is against both popular Marxism which denies all 'real' power to politics, and popular liberalism which wishes economic man to be subordinate to politics. But he wishes that the groups of the power élite which he distinguishes (in the case of the

America of the 1950s: political élite, economic élite, and military élite), despite the frictions which can arise between them: 1) should have a common interest in the maintenance of a 'system' which favours them equally; 2) should be able to co-operate in order to maintain their undivided hold over the mass of their subjects. A variation of academic monism consists of observing that factions of the ruling class, even if they do not communicate much among themselves ('it appears', writes Lewandowski, 'that one rarely sees a businessman, *a fortiori* the world of business, telephone his orders to a politician on a "strictly political problem"'), not only have common interests but see themselves as belonging to the same world. Without communication being necessary, agreement and complicity will thus spontaneously be established. This effect results from: 1) the existence of a dominant class and a dominated class; 2) the social system inculcating in its participants a clear and distinct idea of the class they belong to; 3) this inculcation being even simpler if the system mainly recruits the future members of the dominant class from the dominant class, and the members of the future dominated class from the dominated class. The membership of a class being to a large extent inherited, then confirmed by the family and by the school, individuals are from infancy endowed with a 'reference group', which imposes itself upon them as evidence. This is why the members of the dominant class would sing together without there being need of a conductor. Thus the conspiracy theory of society is no longer necessary: the principal agents of socialization produce effects of complicity between members of the same class, rendering understanding and conspiracy unnecessary. As in Belise's argument, the fact that bankers, politicians, generals, and bishops do not constitute an organized pressure group, far from being the sign of the relative autonomy of élites, would on the contrary be the unmistakeable sign of their collusion. Finally, it is sufficient, to 'demonstrate' the 'theory', to establish that the educational level (indicator of the anticipated socialization in one class or another) of members of the 'dominant class' tends, whatever group of the dominant class is envisaged, to be higher than the educational level of different groups of the dominated class. This demonstration presents hardly any difficulties.

The American variant (illustrated for example by Mills) and, even more, the French variant (illustrated for example by Bourdieu and Lewandowski) of monism encounter obvious objections. Because, if Mills had had the wisdom to emphasize that the collusion he described between fractions of the élite was *on one hand* conjunctural, his French opposite numbers made of it a structural given. The evolution towards the complexification of industrial societies tends certainly to call for an extended training of those who hold the responsible posts. Sincerity, eloquence, and a capacity to define and formulate 'big plans' are the qualities always appreciated in the politician. But his chances of success are increased if he is equally able to show a real capacity to analyse technical dossiers. The fact that in France the *École Nationale d'Administration* is a nursery where a large part of the 'ruling faction of the dominant class' is educated is certainly not created by historical necessity. But it represents the particular form taken by a general evolution in industrial societies. The fact that the socially recognized capacity to exercise responsibilities in various areas today depends more on formal qualifications perhaps indicates a tendency by the ruling class to reinforce its socio-professional and cultural homogeneity. But cultural homogeneity is one thing, corporative interests and emotions are another. Cultural homogeneity does not appear to be more capable of leading to class consciousness than does homogeneity of 'positions in the production system'.

Certainly, societies exist which are dominated by a *ruling caste*. In this case, birth is sufficient to determine if an individual will belong to the élite and hence have an influence, to a variable degree, on a given aspect of social life. The fact that industrial societies lay great emphasis on formal qualifications, added to the fact that the access to formal qualification is unequal as a result of birth, is evidently insufficient to yield the conclusion that these societies are subject to a ruling caste.

Societies also exist which are subject to a *ruling class*, to which recruitment is open, but which exercises a more or less direct (and more or less effective) control over the most important aspects of social life. But the existence of a ruling class in this sense presupposes: 1) a high degree of political centralization; 2) a capacity on the part of the ruling class to limit the access of all interest groups to the 'password' or, more subtly, to create conditions such that these interest groups have an overwhelming interest in cultivating the goodwill of the ruling class. Thus the association of Soviet writers has an obvious interest in keeping the ear of the political authority. The leaders of the USSR Communist Party thus form a ruling class in the most incontestable sense of the term. It is difficult to claim that journalists in liberal societies all have, and in all situations, an essential interest in serving the power in office, or that they represent only Her Majesty's Opposition. It is equally difficult to claim (inevitable consequence of a coherent monism that the followers of that doctrine generally avoid evoking) that the union leaders of liberal societies have no desire other than to try to please the bosses or the government in power. One of the rare authors who has faced up to this consequence, Ralph Miliband, discards it in affirming that the unions have a power incomparably weaker than management's. (But, despite Lindblom, who agrees with Miliband on this point, it is hard to see how this power can be measured.) Having ousted union leaders from the élite, he can, thanks to this epicycle, preserve the thesis according to which: 1) a dominant class exists; 2) its interests are opposed to those of the dominated class. Which raises a supplementary difficulty. Supposing a dominant class exists, from which is drawn the élite, in the singular, and a dominated class, why is it also necessary that the interests of the former are necessarily opposed in every case to those of the second? Supposing that we wish to place the union leaders in the dominated class, how can we reconcile the opposition between the dominant class and the dominated class with the fact that union-management conflicts most usually bear elements both of co-operation and of conflict, far from generally taking the form of a relationship of total opposition?

In the case of liberal industrial societies, it is hard to affirm that they submit to either a ruling class or caste. It appears more reasonable to consider that a plurality of ruling élites is to be observed there. These élites can maintain co-operative relationships, conflictual relationships, or relationships which include inseparable elements of co-operation *and* conflict. The kind of relationships that they maintain at a given juncture is a question which arises not from deduction but from observation. A military élite engaged in the politics of colonial 'pacification' can have some difficulty in accepting without hanging back the inauguration by the political authorities of a policy of decolonization. Similarly, the process of the recruitment of the élite (élites) varies from one society to another and from one conjuncture to another. Even though France and the United States are both liberal industrial societies, the recruitment of élites is effected differently, as a result of the contrast between the two countries from the viewpoint of 'administrative centralization' and of the organization of the educational system.

It is true that at a level of extreme generality élites can be seen as collaborating in the direction of social systems. This point has been put forward since Saint-Simon proposed it in 1807: intellectuals, organizers, and priests collaborate in the functioning of society. It was raised by Mannheim in his distinction between 'organizing and directing élites' and diffused élites who deal with spiritual, cultural, and moral problems. It was again raised by Parsons, and, following him, by Suzanne Keller: the four functions of the Parsonian theory determine four types of élites, whose collaboration assures the direction of social systems. It is in effect possible that Marcuse or Habermas has contributed to the 'integration' of American society or of German society by expressing new cultural needs and that thus they may have rendered signal service to the political élites of their countries. But the difficulties of this functionalist conception are so evident and have so often been described that it is pointless to stress them here. The intellectual monism of Mills and of his followers picks up the essence of the functionalist theory (the collaboration of factions of the élite in the maintenance of the 'system'). It differs from it in as much as it introduces the supplementary hypothesis that the different functions of the élite have an interest in the maintenance of the system because it places them in a dominant position. Unfortunately for the theory, it is not unusual to observe conflicts between factions of the ruling élite. Functionalism, in its 'classic' form, as in its neo-Marxist form, decidedly cannot come to terms with the idea of social conflicts. Applied to the question of élites, assuming in everyone the will to serve the 'system', it is led to neglect an essential aspect, that of the rivalry between the élites and factions of élites which the Machiavellian tradition (Mosca) has so aptly stressed. In liberal, industrial societies where the right to free speech is more widespread than in any other known form of society, the élite system is more complex and heterogeneous than ever before. The political or intellectual entrepreneur, the journalist who puts forward a skilful defence (that is to say a defence carried on in the name of the public interest) of the particular interests of one group or another can from one day to the next gain access to fame and to the 'élite'. Since the interests of this group are likely to clash with the interests of other groups (who will equally be defended by political or intellectual entrepreneurs), inevitable rivalry and conflict will result. The 'cultural homogeneity' of the advocates of the different groups will no more contribute towards reconciling them than would the fact that they all had an opposable thumb. In industrial societies, as in other types of society, the methods of recruitment of élites, the profile and the resources which it is necessary to have at one's disposition in order to have a chance of gaining access to the élite, the fragmentation of the homogeneity of élites depend on the 'social structure' and also on elements of contingency. According to the international climate, the élites of industrial societies seem to be crystallized in the form of a military-industrial complex, an economic-industrial complex, or, if the climate is towards 'crises of civilization', an intellectual-political complex. In classical China, the power of the mandarins was based upon culture and on financial property. In the ideal type of 'oriental despotism' put forward by Wittfogel, the power belongs to the adminstrative élite. In both cases, the mode of recruitment, the profile, the homogeneity of the élites must be explained starting from the properties of the social system concerned. It is the same in the case of industrial societies. We cannot hope to produce an acceptable theory of élites in these societies if we interpret them as systems of the same degree of complexity as agrarian societies.

Authority, Democracy, Social Stratification, Weber.

Bibliography

ARON, R., 'Classe sociale, classe politique, classe dirigeante', *Archives européennes de sociologie*, I, 2, 1960, 260–282. – BIRNBAUM, P., *Les sommets de l'Etat. Essai sur l'élite du pouvoir en France*, Paris, Le Seuil, 1977. – BOTTOMORE, T.B., *Elites and society*, London, Watts, 1964. – BOURDIEU, P., *La distinction. Critique sociale du jugement*, Paris, Minuit, 1979. – DAHL, R., 'A critique of the ruling elite model', in URRY, J. and WAKEFORD, J. (ed.), *Power in Britain*, London, Heinemann, 1973, 282–290. – KELLER, S., *Beyond the ruling class: strategic elites in modern society*, New York, Random House, 1963. – LEWANDOWSKI, O., 'Différenciation et mécanismes d'intégration de la classe dirigeante. L'image sociale de l'élite d'après le *Who's who in France*', *Revue française de sociologie*, XV, 1, 1974, 43–73. – LINDBLOM, C., *Politics and markets*, New York, Basic Books, 1977. – MILIBAND, R., 'The power and labour and the capitalist enterprise', *in* URRY, J. and WAKEFORD, J. (ed.), *Power in Britain*, London, Heinemann, 1973, 136–145. – MILLS, C. (Wright), *The power elite*, New York, Oxford University Press, 1956, 1967. – MOSCA, G., *Elementi di scienza politica*, Roma, Fratelli Bocca, 1896. (Trans) *The ruling class*, New York/Toronto/London, McGraw-Hill, 1939. – PARETO, V., 'Forme générale de la sociéte' et 'L'équilibre social dans l'histoire', in PARETO, V., *Traité*, chap. XII and XIII, 1306–1761. – PARSONS, T., BALES, R.F., and SHILS, E., *Working papers in the theory of action*, Glencoe, The Free Press, 1953. – PUTNAM, R.D., *The comparative study of political elites*, Englewood Cliffs, Prentice Hall, 1976. – SULEIMAN, E., *Elites in French society: the politics of survival*, Princeton, Princeton University Press, 1978. – WITTFOGEL, K., *Oriental despotism. A comparative study on total power*, New Haven, Yale University Press, 1957.

Experimentation

Take a variable y which is taken to depend in a certain way on variables such as $x1$, $x2$, $x3$, etc., so that $y = (x1, x2, x3,$ etc.). Experimenting on this system is the same as creating situations such as $x1$, $x2$, $x3$, etc., which have variable values from one situation to another. If the experimental programme (cf. Fisher) is well planned, it will allow us to define the influence of each of the 'independent' variables i.e., $x1$, $x2$, $x3$, etc., on the dependent variable y. Alternatively, the experiment may consist of the transformation of the structure f of the system linking y, $x1$, $x2$, $x3$, etc., in order to study the effect of a change from f to f' on y.

It is rare in sociology, except in laboratory experiments carried out by social psychologists, to be able to manipulate either the variables of a system or the structure of the system itself. This explains why two alternatives or substitutes for experiments, corresponding to the two cases mentioned above, are often used. The first of these substitutes is a type of analysis said to be 'causal' or 'multivariate'. It consists of systematic comparisons which, according to Durkheim's expression in *The Rules*, function as 'indirect experimentation'. Let us take the simplest case. Suppose n situations are observed and each of these situations can be associated with a value of $x1$, $x2$, $x3$, and y. If it is noted, for instance, that for each increase of $x3$, there is an increase of y, whatever the values of of $x1$ and $x2$, then, under certain conditions, it will be possible to draw conclusions about the effect of $x3$ on y by comparing each of the situations. It is this kind of operation which is used by Durkheim when he shows, in *Suicide*, that, all other things being equal, suicide rates vary in direct proportion with the number of Protestants in a population. Thus the French-speaking *cantons* of Switzerland, like the German-speaking ones, and the German provinces had, according to the suicide statistics available to Durkheim, suicide rates which increased in direct proportion to the number of Protestants living in them. In its simplest form, causal analysis coincides with the traditional procedures proposed by J. Stuart Mill (differences method, concomitant variation method, residual method). But it is generally used in sociology in more complex and general forms (see 'Causality').

The second alternative for experimentation is what can be called 'analysis through simulation' in a specific meaning of this concept (which is also used in other ways) and which might be preferably called quasi-experimental analysis. Suppose that in a specific situation, the form of f in $y = (x1, x2, x3,$ etc.) had been established. This model can be used to establish the distribution of y in an hypothetical situation where, for instance, $x1$ and $x2$ would be distributed differently from the observed situation. F can also be modified, i.e., either the functional form linking the independent variables $x1$, $x2$, $x3$, etc., to the dependent variable y, or such and such parameters expressing the relations between independent variables and dependent variables. These quasi-experimental manipulations allow us to explore the behaviour of the system under different conditions from the effectively observed conditions. The applications of these quasi-experimental manipulations are obvious. Suppose, for instance, that we have good reasons to think that an institutional modification resulted in the transformation of the system $y = f(x1, x2, x3,$ etc.) into a system $y = f'(x1, x2, x3,$ etc.). The behaviour of the second system will only have to be studied and compared to that of the first to establish the effect of the institutional change on the distribution of y. Or suppose we are asking the reasons for the different distribution of y in two societies and that a difference d between the societies is supposed to bear a relation to the difference observed. If it is possible to prove that d provoked a substitution, f', for the relation system f and that the difference between f and f' clearly reflects the difference in the distribution of y, the question will have been answered.

To illustrate these abstract notions, it will be useful to examine in some detail a simple example of the application of the quasi-experimental method as it has just been described.

   In an interesting study made of a sample of French schoolchildren in 1962, as they were finishing their primary school studies (within the French system then operating the equivalent of junior or primary school in the UK and USA), Girard and Clerc have shown that these pupils' orientation depended on their social background, their age, and their school performance. To clarify these points the results corresponding to two groups differentiated in terms of social backgrounds are described here: sons of senior executives and sons of manual workers. The first table (page 165) shows that on average manual workers' sons are older and their academic achievement is lower than that of senior executives. The second table (page 166) shows the percentage of children entering the first form of *lycées* according to their social background, their age, and their achievements. The second table demonstrates that when children are young and have a good academic standard, they are sent to the first form of *lycées* in similar proportion whatever their original social class. As age and standard become less favourable, the difference between the two groups increases.

   How does one interpret these tables? The first table shows mainly the effects of the social background on 'aptitudes': pupils with a working-class background are less prepared for the kind of demands that the school makes on them; they have repeated classes and their marks are generally lower. The second table shows the differences in 'motivations' or 'attitudes': working-class families send their children to a *lycée* only if their markets are good and they have not repeated a class. As for the executives, it is only when both age and achievement are unfavourable that they hesitate to send their children to the *lycée*.

   Suppose we want to find out which aspects (aptitude or attitude) are most important in the inequality between social groups in schooling. In other words, are the inequalities observed between the social groups as far as the first form entrance is concerned essentially due to the fact that the cultural environment is less favourable in the manual classes (i.e., it does not prepare children as well to face school activities), or are working-class families less keen to take risks if their children's performance is mediocre? Answering this question is not without theoretical or practical importance. If schooling differences are mainly due to the children not being prepared in the same way by their families, a relevant policy for equality would attempt to help children from deprived backgrounds by offering them compensatory teaching. If, however, differences are due mainly to the difference in motivation of families, correcting them can be either by finding mechanisms encouraging deprived families to be more ambitious for their children, or by reducing the family influence in the process of school orientation.

   In Girard and Clerc's survey, 93 per cent of sons of senior executives and 46 per cent of manual workers' sons went to the *lycée*. To answer the question posed above, it is possible, from the given data, to make a simple simulation exercise: we can ask what percentage of manual workers' sons would have been sent to the *lycée* if – hypothesis 1 – the cultural and cognitive handicap for working-class pupils had been suddenly neutralized, and if – hypothesis 2 – the motivations of working-class families had been the same as for senior executives' families. According to one or the other of the hypotheses, decreasing the inequalities between manual

Table 1 School achievement and age at conclusion of primary education, France 1962 (from Girard and Clerc, Table X, p. 849)

Achievement	*11 and under*	*11*	*12*	*13*	*14 and over*	*Total*
			Age of pupil			
			Sons of manual workers			
Excellent to good	2.4	16.4	13.9	2.4	0.1	35.2
Average	0.5	11.7	16.7	5.7	0.6	35.2
Below average to poor	0.1	4.6	14.7	8.5	1.7	29.6
Total	3.0	32.7	45.3	16.6	2.4	100.0
			Sons of senior executives			
Excellent to good	20.2	32.7	7.9	1.0	*	61.8
Average	5.0	13.3	8.1	1.6	0.3	28.3
Below average to poor	0.7	4.1	3.4	1.3	0.4	9.9
Total	25.9	50.1	19.4	3.9	0.7	100.0

Numbers insufficient for percentage.

workers' and senior executives' sons as far as first form *lycée* entrance is concerned, we will be able to conclude that the 'cognitive handicap' factor in relation to the 'motivation factor' is more or less important. The quasi-experimentation in this case consists of creating the two fictitious situations corresponding to the above two hypotheses.

a) In the situation corresponding to the first hypothesis, 'aptitude' differences (cognitive environmental effect) are supposed to be wiped out between the sons of each class (manual workers' and executives' sons are assumed to be equally distributed in terms of ages and performance) but 'attitude' differences (motivation) are still operative. If such had been the case, as the following calculations show, 68 per cent of manual workers' sons would have gone to the *lycée* (against 46 per cent). To obtain this result, you just multiply and add up in the correct way the data given in the second half of Table 1 and the data from the first half of Table 2. The sum of the multiplications:

A. $(20.2 \times 0.79) + (32.7 \times 0.90) + (7.9 \times 0.79) + (1.0 \times 0.45) + (5.0 \times 0.69) +$
$\ldots + (0.3 \times 0.14) + (0.7 \times 0) + \ldots + (1.3 \times 0.03) + (0.4 \times 0.8) = 68$

does indeed represent the percentage of manual workers' sons who would have gone into the first form if their distribution in terms of ages and performance had been the same as that of executives' sons.

(b) In the second fictitious situation, 'aptitude' differences operate but 'attitude' differences are wiped out (workers' sons and executives' sons of similar age and performance are sent to the first form in the same proportion). Calculations show that, had that been the case, 82 per cent of manual workers' sons would have been sent to the *lycée* (compared with 46 per cent in fact and 68 per cent if aptitude had been the same). To obtain this result, the first half of Table 1 and the second half of Table 2 are used to calculate the sum of the multiplications:

B. $(2.4 \times 0.98) + (16.4 \times 0.95) + (13.9 \times 0.98) + (2.4 \times 0.69) + (0.5 \times 0.90) +$
$\ldots + (5.7 \times 0.86) + (0.1 \times 0) + \ldots + (8.5 \times 0.59) = 82$

This value does represent, as is easily seen, the percentage of manual workers'

Table 2 Rate of entry to sixth grade of *Lycée*** as a function of social origin, educational achievement, and age, France 1962. (Source as Table 1; Table XII, p. 854)

Achievement	Age of pupil				
	11 and under	11	12	13	14 and over
	Sons of manual workers				
Excellent to good	79	90	79	45	*
Average	69	57	45	11	14
Below average to poor	*	18	9	3	8
	Sons of senior executives				
Excellent to good	98	99	98	69	*
Average	90	99	90	88	*
Below average to poor	*	85	52	59	*

*Number insufficient for percentage.
**Lycée *represents the highest level of secondary education – the most academic, preparing students for* baccalauréat *at 18/19 (university entry qualification).*

sons who would have entered the *lycée* first form if their family motivations had been distributed in the same way as those of the senior executives' families in regard to age and performance.

It can be concluded from the quasi-experimental comparison between the actual situation and the two fictitious ones that attitude differences (motivation) between the two social classes play a slightly stronger part than aptitude differences. The inequality between the two groups is far less a question of the relative cognitive handicap resulting from belonging to a deprived background than a question of 'prudence' in the working classes. In other words, inequalities between the two groups are due mainly to the lack of educational aspirations in working-class families compared with the senior executives' families. It is not a surprising result in itself: it seems obvious that a well-off family will try to protect their child from ending up with a lower social status than they started with. Even if that child is average or poor in educational achievement, the family will attempt to keep him in the school which is ostensibly the most socially rewarding. But quasi-experimentation allows us to show that this influence, in a way commonplace, of social position on motivation is a slightly stronger inequality factor than the 'aptitude' differences produced by cultural background.

The quasi-experimental methods can supply a very useful basis for 'comparative analysis'. In a very interesting study, Perrenoud compared schooling inequalities in France (in Paris) with those in Geneva at the beginning of the 1960s using Girard and Clerc's data concerning first form *lycée* entrance that we have just used and comparable data from Geneva. The comparison reveals slightly less inequality in Geneva than in Paris. Using the quasi-experimental method we have just explained, Perrenoud showed that the difference was essentially due to a difference between 'institutions': more authoritarian, more meritocratic, giving less attention to family wishes, the system of Geneva was effectively neutralizing the strength of social group differences in relation to attitudes and motivations. Its narrower liberalism was providing greater equality in return. This of course is not the result of a deliberate move, but of history.

The previous examples show the virtues of quasi-experimentation in sociological analysis. Knowing that a variable y depends on some variables $x1$, $x2$, $x3$, etc., it is often useful to find out a sociological interpretation, the influence of each of the elements of the observed system f on the phenomenon y being studied. The near-experimental method is in fact studying the effects on y of the sociologically significant modifications f', f'', etc., of f. Applied to the previous examples, this method enables us to say that in France, in 1962, aptitude differences produced by social background are not the main reasons for inequalities in schooling. Also, it enables us to show the importance of 'institutional' structures in a field where sociologists tend to concentrate exclusively on the cultural effects of social class.

In general, quasi-experimentation plays a major role in the analysis of complex relational systems, the behaviour of which can hardly be analysed in an intuitive fashion. If a system f includes a large number of variables or has a complex structure (for instance a non-linear relational system), it can be difficult to find out, intuitively, the effect of a structural change f yo f' (or a structure difference f/f').

Quasi-experimentation enables us to 'observe' the behaviour of the system f', to compare it to that of f and thus find out the transformational effects $f - f'$ or of the difference f/f'. See the works by Orcutt in the field of demography for an illustration of these remarks. See as well the effects of paradoxical systems brought out by Boudon in the field of social mobility. One of these effects is : in a meritocratic system where social status depends heavily on school achievement, the schooling equalization (f/f') in regard to social background does not necessarily mean an increase of mobility between generations. In order to prove this anti-intuitive effect, it is virtually essential to use the quasi-experimental method.

Finally, the distinction made here between two types of substitutes in quasi-experimentation can be applied in general to comparative analysis. In the case of the Geneva/Paris comparison described above, the research strategy consists of comparing the effects of the two structures f and f' on the phenomenon to be explained (in this example: schooling differences). In other cases the comparison is essentially a question of studying the co-variations between variables. The first kind of strategy can be illustrated by de Tocqueville's comparison between France and England during the *Ancien Régime*, to use a classic reference, the second by Durkheim's *Suicide*.

Finally, contrary to a widely spread idea in the nineteenth century, which is still accepted by Durkheim in *Rules*, scientific research cannot be exclusively defined by the notion of experimentation and its substitutes. Such a notion is misleading in the case of natural sciences, if only because some of them deal with singular phenomena. It is misleading in at least the same degree in the case of the social sciences.

Causality, Durkheim, Social Mobility, Theory.

Bibliography

ALKER, H., *Mathematics and politics*, New York/London, Macmillan, 1965. – BLALOCK, H.M. Jr., *Causal inferences in non-experimental research*, Chapel Hill, University of North Carolina Press, 1964. – BLALOCK, H.M., AGANBEGIAN, A., BORODKIN, F.M., BOUDON, R., CAPECCHI, V. (ed.), 'Design, measurement, and classifications', in BLALOCK, H.M., AGANBEGIAN, A., BORODKIN, F.M., BOUDON, R., CAPECCHI, V. (ed.), *Quantitative sociology. International perspectives on mathematical and statistical modeling*, New York/London, Academic Press, 1975, 259–472. – BOUDON, R., *L'inégalité des chances. La mobilité sociale dans les sociétés industrielles*, Paris, A. Colin, 1973, 1978. – DURKHEIM, E., *Rules of Sociological Method*, Chicago, University of Chicago Press, 1938. – FISHER, R.A., *The design of experiments*, Edinburgh/London, Oliver & Boyd, 1935, 1951. – GERARD, A. and CLERC, P., 'Nouvelles données sur l'orientation scolaire au moment de l'entrée en sixième: âge, orientation scolaire et sélection', *Population*, XIX, 5, 1964, 829–864. – GUETZKOW, H. (ed.), *Simulation in social science. Readings*, Englewood Cliffs, Prentice Hall, 1962. – ORCUTT, G., GREENBERGER, M., KORBEL, J., RIVLIN, A.M., *Micro-analysis of socio-economic systems. A simulation study*, New York, Harper, 1961. – PERRENOUD, P., *Stratification socio-culturelle et réussite scolaire*, 1st ed. in *Cahiers Vilfredo Pareto*, 20, 1970, 5–75; 2nd ed., Geneva/Paris, Droz, 1970. – PRZEWORSKI, A., and TEUNE, H., *The logic of comparative social inquiry*, New York, Wiley, 1970.

F

Family

The family is one of the characteristic institutions of human society, but there is no reason to believe that all institutions are originated and explained in the family, that all relations of subordination, co-operation, solidarity have their 'matrix' in the relationships between parents, children, spouses, and relatives.

It is often said that the family constitutes a *'fait social total*' ('total social fact'). Marcel Mauss's formula, as famous as it is obscure, has at least two meanings. The *'totalité*' which the social fact would constitute can be understood as a closed totality. One cannot see in this case that the formula applies to the family, whose principle according to Lévi-Strauss would be supplied by the scriptural saying, 'You will leave your father and mother', an unbreakable rule dictated to every society so that it will be established and endure. If, on the contrary, the 'totality' he refers to is nothing more than the whole of the relations maintained by members of the family organization within and outside this organization, the family can confidently be called a *'fait social total*'. It constitutes indeed a system of relations between spouses, parents, and relatives and between the system they constitute and the other sub-systems of society (especially economical and political ones). Therefore it is indeed an open group and in no way a closed totality.

To quote Lévi-Strauss again, the family group derives its origin from marriage. It includes the nucleus made by the husband, the wife, and the children born from their union, as well as, eventually, 'other relatives' who are bound to this nucleus. The family bond is a legal bond, bringing about economic, religious, or other obligations, especially 'in the form of sexual rights and taboos'. Finally, the family bond is inseparable 'from psychological feelings such as love, affection, respect, fear . . .'.

One of the most evident aspects of family organization is the set of rules it introduces in sexual life. It is no doubt in this respect that the family appears as a social fact: the bond it establishes between a certain number of adults and children of opposite sexes cannot be reduced to 'instincts' such as sexual desire or pleasure, or even to feelings of gratitude and tenderness. In *Le discours sur l'origine de l' inégalité*, Rousseau thus characterized the life of savages as 'being driven by the physical side of love, their relations are peaceable'. Moved by 'pity and commiseration' adults and especially women give infants all the necessary solicitude so that in their first years the totally dependent creatures small children are can first survive, then become grown people. Finally, as the savage man is not yet fixed to the land and as private property does not exist yet, the group he forms with a female and his offspring is mobile and unstable.

Can we then refer to a family? This is possible neither according to Lévi-Strauss's definition – from which we started – nor according to Rousseau's text. The latter refers to family (*Discours*, 2nd part) only after the first revolution, 'which formed the original base of the family, and involved a form of property'. The family *sensu stricto* is thus missing from the state of nature; it appears only with the revolution which marks the transition to civil society and the institution of property. It is true that the sexual life of the uncivilized man is not reduced thereby to satisfaction of sexual impulses. It includes, however rudimentary they might be, the obligations tied to the rearing of children.

This interpretation seems to be confirmed by numerous ethnographic studies, and that is probably why Lévi-Strauss likes to present Rousseau as one of the fathers of modern anthropology. The Andaman, Fuegians, Nambikwara, Bushmen live a little like Rousseau's savage man. Their small semi-nomadic groups are more or less without political organization; most of them ignore agriculture, weaving, pottery, and the construction of permanent dwellings. The family, mainly monogamic, constitutes their sole form of social organization. However these primitive people differ on one essential point from Rousseau's natural man: they practise matrimony and are bound to the rule of exogamy.

One understands best the transition from nature to culture by comparing sexual life before and after the first 'revolution' referred to by Rousseau. The functionalist anthropologists, and the sociologists who followed them, have tried to interpret the presence in all known human societies of the 'nucleus' constituted by two individuals of opposite sex and their children as the social 'response' to a biological 'need' derived from the extreme dependence of man's children. From this has been drawn the thesis that the 'nuclear family' is a universal institution – a thesis open to several criticisms. First some data invalidate the universality of the nuclear family. There are societies such as the Nayars', where the parental couple have none of the responsibilities of rearing and training towards their children. Men make war, women make love with as many lovers as they like, children are entrusted to the wife's brothers, at least to those discharged from their warlike duties. Neither the father nor the 'biological' mother exerts any influence over the education of their children left in the care of their mother's brothers. Among the possibilities offered by nature, which has the minimal requirement of the presence of adults with infants, the Nayar culture (to use a convenient language but one tinged with an awkward realism) would have chosen a definite category of adults, the mother's brothers. This choice would be explained by other aspects of the social structure, especially the soldierly character of the Nayar society and the great autonomy it leaves to women.

The relativity of sexual and parental roles has struck anthropologists. The inversion of the relation of authority between the biological father and the mother's brother, according to whether the rule of descent is patri- or matri-lineal, has been the object of endless comments. Moreover, in many matrilineal societies, the one we call the father is not for the native the child's 'procreator' in the sense we give this word. As, on the other hand, the child belongs to his mother's lineage, he is brought up near and by his uncles. The disciplinary responsibilities being exerted by the mother's brother, the role of the 'big brother' falls to the biological father, who has only casual and occasional relations with his natural children.

Even if the persistence over a possibly very short period of a 'nucleus' formed by the mother and her youngest children is practically universal (except for a few cases regarding populations of limited size), the composition of the 'nucleus' is as important as its own existence. Therefore alliance and marriage throw more light on the functioning of the family than do the biology of reproduction or the psychology of feelings. Such at least is the thesis developed with remarkable continuity by French sociologists who, from Durkheim to Lévi-Strauss, place in the centre of their analysis the prohibition of incest, and exogamy.

These two rules have an obvious social character. Let us admit that the prohibition of incest is a universal rule. The content of the rule, the degrees of kinship prohibited vary with societies. These define the rule, specifying its content and penalizing infractions. A prohibited spouse in one society can be allowed in another. The sexual relationship which is tabooed here is tolerated or even prescribed elsewhere. The diversity of the rules about matrimonial union furnish inexhaustible repertory to ethnological relativism. In the medley of rules one can look for some principles which introduce order and simplicity in a diversity inextricable at first sight. The famous case of parallel cousins (prohibited spouses) and cross-cousins (prescribed spouses), which constitutes one of the great purple passages of structuralist anthropology, illustrates the application of some of these principles. First, the role of exogamy does not reveal itself here only as an interdiction, it is paired with a counterpart: by renouncing my parallel cousin, I acquire a cross-cousin. Indeed, I cannot remain a bachelor without incurring the hardships, humiliations, and servitudes attached to the pitiable condition of the man without a brother-in-law. This very elementary pattern, which rests, in addition to the rule of exogamy, on the assimilation (incidentally fictitious according to biology) between half-relatives and parallel relatives, can be complicated by taking into consideration a certain number of other independent variables regarding the system of descent (patri- and matrilineal, uni- or bilateral), of residence (patri- or matrilineal), the number of exogamic groups (parity or disparity of these groups), the direct or indirect, immediate or deferred character of the exchange.

By reflecting on the rules governing the union, even in the case where they not only prohibit certain spouses to the individual but go as far as prescribing him others, one sees that the family is subject to a law of fission which obliges us to look for a wife outside the family 'nucleus' where we were born. This almost universal feature is especially visible in our societies where the prohibition of incest is paired with the freedom formally recognized as ours to choose as spouse and individual of the opposite sex who is not related to us in a prohibited degree. But, even in the societies where the individual is strictly assigned his spouse, marriage shows, with the mutual dependence of the families, the impossibility of any one family constituting a closed unity, because it is an alliance between groups giving and taking women. In no case therefore is it possible to consider the family 'nucleus' as a self-maintained totality: each generation, with the obligation to exchange women, is obliged to set up new families with the 'remains' of the old families which have broken through the effect of the exogamic principle (Lévi-Strauss).

Through the rules of alliance, society and its organization appear to come first regarding the family organization. In comparison with this interpretation, any attempt to make the 'family cell' the primitive social fact seems eminently suspicious. Aristotle had already challenged with very sound arguments the thesis which confuses family and city. The latter is of another nature than the family (*yevos*) and the village (*xwfiy*). A common order, which could be imposed on all citizens, cannot be based on domestic activities (including both family activities such as reproduction and the education of children, but also economic activities in the modern sense). Hegel in *The Philosophy of Right* has the same argument. It is in relation to the particularity of domestic ties and interests at work in civil society that he stresses, no doubt excessively, the 'concrete universality' of the State.

In modern societies, two features are generally attributed to the family organization, which, although seemingly opposite, contribute one and the other to complicating functioning. With the conservative tradition one can deplore the weakening of the family tie. In a 'normal' regime, the family should establish, according to Auguste Comte, a subordination of ages and sexes. This double subordination is strongly threatened today. Indeed young people leave their fathers' homes earlier. More and more they pursue different activities from those he used to pursue. Moreover, the inheritance laws, which since the French Revolution have radically limited the freedom to make one's will and have instituted equal sharing between heirs, have changed the meaning of the family patrimony. This no longer constitutes a value which incarnates the status and honour of the family taken jointly from generation to generation. The equal share, ensuring the heir's independence, reduces their solidarity. At the same time as the subordination of children to parents weakens so the solidarity of children among themselves grows less. The notion of head of the family tends to disappear, whether it is the father or the 'associated heir' (Le Play).

Women's 'liberation' contributes too to weakening the hierarchic aspect of the family organization. This emancipation arises from multiple causes: the less and less unequal access of women to various orders and forms of education, the divorce legislation, the development of family planning. At all events, the subordination between sexes is also threatened today by the subordination between generations. Should we make the assumption, as some feminists believe, that women, presented by anthropologists as the medium of matrimonial exchange, will eventually be replaced in this role by men, who, in a kind of sexual bimetallism, will become alternately with women the 'most precious goods', the circulation of which ensures the regularity of the main social operations?

The slackening of the bond between spouses, parents, and children and a certain devaluation of patrimonial values do not prevent the status of an individual's family from constituting for him a highly important capital and a fairly reliable indicator of his present and future position in the stratification system. The most recent data attest that we choose our spouse not among all the eligible sexual partners (that is to say lawful with respect to the taboo of incest), but in a restricted subgroup of individuals invested with status equivalent or congruent to ours. The family status of my future spouse, that is to say the status of the family from which he/she is descended, constitutes for him/her an 'asset' which he/she is bound to use in his/her matrimonial strategies. The pretension to hypergamy is justified by the advantages offered to his/her eventual spouse by the fact of marrying a person 'descended from a good family'. This pretension is the more understandable as such a person is likely already to hold a 'good situation' or to have the greatest expectations of reaching one at the time of his marriage.

Another reason influences us to choose our spouse from a given category rather than in an aleatory way. It is that the family remains for many of our contemporaries a place of contacts and interactions. It is not only spouses who remain for one another privileged interlocutors, even if the separation of their place of work and their communal place of residence reduces the time they spend together; the parents-in-law, the brothers- and sisters-in-law, possibly some cousins, are also relations and contacts. Thus the status of each individual is affected not only by the status of the spouse, but also by the status of the spouse's relatives, which he cannot, even if he would like to, repudiate or ignore. It is in my interest, if I have ambitions of mobility, to choose my spouse *well*, that is, to choose someone of my rank or of a superior rank.

It is thus false to say that in our societies the choice of a spouse is entirely free – subject to the prohibitions of incest only. Marriage is not a market of pure and perfect competition, and individuals with the advantage of a status derived from belonging to their family of origin (where they have been brought up) and a procreation family (where they will bring up their children) will endeavour to preserve or improve this advantage by marrying 'well' or giving 'good' spouses to their own children – if they can.

It is indeed right to consider with some scepticism the conservative theses about 'social reform' through the regeneration of the 'family cell'. Le Play himself seems to have seen their problems. Indeed, the 'moralization' of relations between sexes and generations can be accomplished only providing that the old conception of patrimony and 'family honour' is given back its full strength. Now, the idea of a stem-family becoming established around the head of the family by the institution of an 'associated heir' supposes a patrimony structure not easily compatible with the essentially fiduciary character of the financial assets which are given such a high position in the composition of modern wealth. There is a tendency for capital to be resistant to longlasting immobilization; it is unlikely to become 'frozen,' as was the case with inherited property, especially when it was managed in order to ensure the perpetuation of the patrimony and not with a view to the best profit from the invested funds.

The ideological followers of Le Play see in the 'extended family' a kind of *Gemeinschaft* which would ensure to men 'the privilege of living amongst themselves' (Lévi-Strauss). But this intimacy is frustrated by the rule of exogamy, which, for each generation, obliges the boys to take a wife outside their father's home, and the girls to marry boys who are not their kin. But as do all ideologists, the theorists of the family *Gemeinschaft* generalize and push undeniable observations to absurd lengths. The family, even if it imposes on grown children departure and dispersion, or at least alliance with strangers, establishes between parents and children a tie the strength of which has no equivalent in any other social relationship.

Moreover, there are grounds to call the theorists of the 'extended family' ideologists. The expression of 'nuclear family' is understood in different ways by anthropologists and sociologists. Among the former, the nuclear family is said to designate the cell constituted in the most primitive relations system by both parents and their infants. One can question the universality of this situation and wonder whether it admits variants, when, for example, the biological father is substituted in his social role by the mother's brother. When sociologists refer to the nuclear family, they refer to a completely different situation. They do think of the parental couple and their children, but they take their stand in the context of industrial societies where the extended family has broken up into a number of more or less important autonomous homes.

It is easy to draw excessive consequences from these observations about the decline of the extended family. First, one will exaggerate the freedom of spouses in their choice of partners. Then, one will over-emphasize the slackening of solidarities between blood relatives and relatives by marriage. Finally, one will idealize the nuclear family by seeing in it an imperative condition for the cultural and economic development of society. The nuclear family would be the stage of perfection of human civilization regarding the relations between ages and sexes. This conception is adhered to by Auguste Comte and opposed by Frederic Engels. In the high days of the sociology of development, the nuclear family was seen as a strict condition of economic 'modernization'. Indeed, it make individuals, their resources, and their talents more mobile, at the same time as it ensured the anchoring of the younger generations within those of the traditional values which remained compatible with the new state of modernized society.

By making the family the authority of socialization above all, one is led to consider the sometimes difficult relations between school and the family institution. Moreover, the analysis of modernization by sociologists has proved to be fallible on two points. First, the relation between the nuclear family and economic modernization is doubtful. The case of Japan, but also that of the Chinese of the diaspora in south-east Asia, suggests that traditional bonds and extended family can coexist with fast development and an excellent control of economic mechanisms. But it does not follow that one can, on the contrary, present the persistence of the extended family as a condition particularly favourable to the primitive stage of capitalist accumulation. The support of parents and relatives, which can be relied upon by an individual exposed to the risks of poverty, unemployment, and under-qualification, contributes to reducing some of the stresses generated by industrialization and urbanization. But other tensions can arise from them: the extended family can in the political order lead to factionalism and regionalism, as we see in the Arab world.

The thesis according to which the family (in its 'nuclear' form) constitutes a reserve of cultural traditions has been highly respected for a long time. It is drawn from Freud's teaching (in *Totem and Taboo*, but also in *Civilization and its Discontents*). It understands culture in a clearly psychological sense, since it is interested above all by *attitudes*, especially towards authority, co-operation, and competition, which it asserts have been learnt and fixed during the very first years of life as a consequence of conflicts experienced by the young child with his father, mother, brothers, and sisters. The stock of attitudes constituting a culture would also be reproduced through the socialization of successive generations.

Robert Bellah has fully demonstrated the weakness of this thesis. It was enough that he should recall the fact that it assumes a correlation between social structures and cultural contents. This correlation is, however, not proved because the aggregates between which correlations are sought are residual categories. Let us take, for example, the diversity of cultural contents, religious beliefs and symbols, and let us wonder what relations they maintain with the social rules of which they are at first sight the impressions and reflections. Let us take the case of the father-son relation: Christians refer to God as a father. Jesus is called God's son. We are brothers in Jesus Christ and Jesus himself is our brother. However, our society is far less paternalist than that of the Chinese for whom the father-son relation is at the centre of social life, while it is very toned down in the religious symbolism of the Chinese, for whom the submission to a transcendent principle is far less stressed than the relation of immanence and fusion of the individual in a universe which supports him while absorbing him. We can no longer treat authoritarian ideologies such as Fascism as simple projections in the symbolic imagination of the relations of authority learnt from infancy in the nuclear family. As for the possibility of making of authoritarian ideology the projection on to political society of the relations of authority in the extended family, it constitutes a scarcely more satisfactory answer. Indeed, the family thus understood includes a great variety of activities. It is almost confused with the whole of society in an undifferentiated *Gemeinschaft*. Is it any better, then, to say that culture, religion, politics are only projections of social relations as a whole? No more than that God or the king is an image of the father. Are we trying to identify a type of family organization (nuclear, extended, patriarchal) which would be the most favourable to economic 'development', demographic expansion, political 'stability'? For all that one should start by saying what one means by such terms and which particular features of the family organization one is retaining. One would then perceive that recourse to this 'structure', taken as a whole, even if one tries to prop it up with a rudimentary typology, does not have a great explanatory value. One would fall down again on some holistic difficulties pointed out many times in this *Dictionary*. It is no more reasonable to make of the family the 'primary institution' from which one can render an account of the genesis and the functioning of all the other institutions than it is to treat the 'relations of production' as the highest authority from which would derive all intelligibility.

Authority, Causality, Conformity and Deviance, Culturalism and Culture, Methodology, Religion, Sociobiology.

Bibliography

ADORNO, T.W. *et al., The authoritarian personality*, New York, Harper, 1950; New York, Science Editions, 1964. – COSER, R.L. (ed.), *The family: its structure and functions*, New York, Saint-Martin's Press, 1964; London, Macmillan, 1974. – ENGELS, F., *Der Ursprung der Familie, des Privateigentums und des Staats*, Hottingen/Zurich, Schweizerische Genossenschaftbuchdruckerei, 1884. – GOODE, W.J., *World Revolution and family patterns*, New York, Free Press of Glencoe, 1963. – HÉRITIER, F., *L'exercice de la parenté*, Paris, Gallimard/Le Seuil, 1981. – LASLETT, P., *The world we have lost*, London, Methuen, 1965, 1971. – LEÑERO-OTERO, L. (ed.), *Beyond the nuclear family model; cross cultural perspectives*, London/Beverly Hills, Sage Publications, cop. 1977. – LE PLAY, F. *L'organisation de la famille selon le vrai modèle: signalé par l'histoire de toutes les races et de tous les temps* (1871), Tours, Mame, 1875. – LÉVI-STRAUSS, C., *Les structures élémentaires de la parenté*, Paris, PUF, 1949; 2nd ed., Paris/La Haye, Mouton, 1968; 'The family', *in* SHAPIRO, L. (ed.), *Man, culture and society*, New York, Oxford University Press, 1956. – MICHEL, A., *Sociologie de la famille et du mariage*, Paris, PUF, 1972, 1978. – MORGAN, L.H., *Ancient society; or researches in the lines of human progress from savagery through barbarism to civilization*, Calcutta, Bharati Library, 1877; Cambridge, The Belknap Press of Harvard University Press, 1964. – RADCLIFFE-BROWN, A.R., *Structure and function in primitive society*, London, Oxford University Press, 1942. – SCHNEIDER, D.M., 'The nature of kinship', *Man*, 217, 1964. – SEGALEN, M., *Sociologie de la famille*, Paris, A. Colin, 1981. *The Sociology of the Family*, Cambridge University Press 1987. – TILLION, G., *Le harem et les cousins*, Paris, Seuil, 1966. – TODD, E., *La troisième planète: structures familiales et systèmes idéologiques*, Paris, Seuil, 1983.

Function

The notion of function has been borrowed by sociologists from the language of biology (cf. the glycogenic function of the liver in Claude Bernard's work) and from the language of organizations (cf. function of management, public function). A certain number of epistemological difficulties are derived from this origin: does the notion of function not involve an assimilation of any social system with an organism or an organization? Is it not leading to the introduction of explanation of a teleological type giving too great a role to final causes?

It is true that the temptation of organicism is not always absent from sociology. The extreme functionalism which is justly criticized by Merton tends to let in the idea that every institution has a function relating to society as a whole. It is unquestionably a proposition which is both debatable and vague (what exactly does the notion of 'society as a whole' mean?). It is equally true that sociologists have not always avoided the temptation of seeing societies as *systems of roles*, i.e., as organizations, networks, or super-organizations composed of more elementary organizations. Such a conception is flawed in that it omits a fundamental distinction. Every society includes not only organized social sub-systems, but also *non-*

organized sub-systems of interdependence in the sense that each agent is free to act in terms of his *preferences* rather than in terms of explicit norms. The two types of sub-systems maintain close relations with each other (cf., for example the relation between the system constituted by educational institutions and the system designated by the expression 'labour market'). But it is important to keep the distinction in mind. Every social system includes mechanisms of control which enable, in a variable way according to each case, the correction of undesirable effects which can result from the aggregation of individual preferences unrestrained by norms. Thus, in a social system where educational institutions are under state control, the State can, if necessary, influence the structure of demand for education by initiating institutional changes which generate effects of incentive or dissuasion. Possibly, it will try to produce coercive effects. But it is important to see that the State's abilities to regulate are closely circumscribed, in liberal societies even more than in others. More importantly still, in many cases it cannot use regulatory procedures of a normative kind. Societies cannot thus be conceived as organized groups of organizations if it is accepted that organizations are systems of roles with which systems of normative constraints are associated. No more can societies be reduced to the model of the organism, despite the almost constant attraction of such a model. A few simple remarks are sufficient to illustrate the problematic nature of the analogy: as Merton indicated, there exist in every society, a-functional institutions or phenomena and dysfunctional phenomena, or, in other words, phenomena 'functional' in relation to some groups but dysfunctional in relation to others. To portray a society as an organism makes the task of explaining the conflicting aspects of social life very difficult and condemns one to considering every conflict as a pathological symptom.

Does it mean that one must forego the notion of function? Such a conclusion seems excessive. For if the notion of function implies that of system, it does not imply that all social systems belong to that particular category of systems which involve living organism, nor that they can be reduced to the model of human organizations.

Let us come now to the main logical objection which has been directed to the notion of function. Hempel and Nagel have attempted to show that explaining a social phenomenon by its function is at best tautological, at worse teleological. It is indeed not very enlightening to explain why men continue to wear cuff-links by the hypothetical function of maintaining traditions, as it amounts to saying that a tradition is maintained because it is maintained. Indeed it is trifling because it is teleological to 'explain' the persistence of inequalities by their hypothetical function of 'reproduction' of social systems. Perhaps Hempel and Nagel thought of examples of this kind when they attempted to persuade sociologists to abandon the notion of function. But their criticism, by seeking to be formal and general, denied itself the possibility of distinguishing the illegitimate uses, tautological or teleological, of the notion of function from its legitimate uses.

It is easy to produce many examples where the notion of function is neither teleological nor tautological. Why, wonders Merton in a classical text, do political parties frequently create 'political machines'? The analysis is based on the example of the political machine of the American Democratic Party, but has a general bearing. Merton observes that the *function* of this 'machine' is to attract and to keep the electors from the lower classes by providing them with services of social assistance and insurance which were not provided by the State when the author made his analysis. The existence of the machine is thus explained by its function: to respond to a demand which was not satisfied another way. As is easily seen, such an explanation is neither teleological nor tautological. As a matter of fact, it can easily be retranslated by eliminating the word and concept of function: 1) every party tries to maintain or increase the number of its electors; 2) a party may hope to keep certain electors if it provides them, beyond the promises of collective goods included in its electoral programmes, with individualized services; 3) it is exposed to competition from agents producing similar goods; 4) thus it will act as a rational economic agent and will try to propose goods it can produce at the least cost and for which there is a demand in the portion of the electorate it hopes to attract. That is why in the 1980s the machine of the French Communist Party (PC) provides some kinds of goods and individual services ('popular' travel, provision of housing with reasonable rent in municipalities with a communist majority, etc.) very similar to those proposed by the political machine of the American Democratic Party of the 1950s (services connected with what is called in France '*la sécurité sociale*'). In such a context, to speak of the function of the PC's machine or the Democratic Party's machine is, one can see, to use a convenient linguistic abridgement. The notion of function as used by Merton in this case is only summarizing the coincidence between an offer (from the party) and a demand (from the real or potential electors), supply and demand being easily explicable from the interests of the two categories of actors.

Merton's example illustrates concretely the general precept formulated by Durkheim in *Les Règles de la méthode sociologique*. The sociological analysis of an institution must always, declares Durkheim, analyse at the same time the causes which gave it birth and the function which helps to maintain it. Translated into another language, this precept asserts that the sociologist must strive to explain an institution from the structure of the interaction system in which it appeared and in which it is maintained. Thus one can explain that the rule of majority decision-making is frequently kept in deliberative assemblies because it represents the simplest compromise between two contradictory 'imperatives' which cannot but appear in all cases: to avoid blocking the decision-making apparatus, which would be bound to happen if the agreement of too large a number of members was required, an excessive number of members must bow to a collective decision they see as undesirable. This analysis made, one can speak of the causes and functions of the rule of the simple majority. But these terms express only the fact that such a rule represents a convenient solution to the problems presented by the determination of collective will. Likewise, to declare that (in some circumstances) the unanimity rule or the right to veto are dysfunctional, simply amounts to asserting that, in the circumstances considered, the requirement of unanimity would involve excessive decision costs and that the right to veto entails the risk of imposing an undesirable decision on an excessive number of members. To explain that a rule is dysfunctional means in this case an explanation of why individuals belonging to a given interaction system would normally tend to reject it if it was proposed to them. Of course, a 'functional' analysis of this kind must be heedful of the structural characteristics of the system considered. Thus, the right to veto can be 'functional' if it is exercised in a decision-making group of limited size and 'dysfunctional' when the size of the group reaches a certain threshold (cf. Buchanan and Tullock).

The example above suggests an important methodological remark, that is that the absence of historical information on the *genesis* of an institution is not in all cases an insurmountable obstacle to its explanation and its analysis. Historical information certainly always constitutes an irreplaceable supplement. Sometimes it is indispensable. But an institution is not always doomed to remain obscure and unintelligible because we are ignorant of everything about its origin and its genesis. This essential methodological proposition constituted in some way the basis of functional analysis – even if it is not always explicitly used by its practitioners.

Custom tends to reserve the term of 'functional analysis' precisely to explanations accounting for the existence of an institution in the absence of historical information on its genesis or of *reference* to the historical information available. A classic example of functional analysis in this sense is provided by Lévi-Strauss's *Les structures élémentaires dé la parente*. Dealing with peoples who do not write, the ethnologist knows nothing about the genesis of the institutions he observes. Nevertheless, some of these institutions, in this case the set of rules defining incest in such or such society, can be made understandable if one succeeds in elucidating their functions. One can, for example, advance the hypothesis that their *function* consists of ensuring a circulation of women among the component segments of these archaic societies. From this hypothesis, Lévi-Strauss has shown that the groups of rules observed in such or such society can be considered as solutions specific to this general problem. In the same way, one can analyse the rules of formation of collective decisions from their *functions*, that is, as understandable responses to a problem of social organization in the wide sense of the term. In the same way still, when Parsons asserts that in the case of industrial societies, the institution of the extended family is dysfunctional and the nuclear family functional, he means only that it is not easy to conceive of observing in the same society both a strong social and geographical mobility and a lasting establishment of the individual near his original family. In this sense, the 'nuclear family' institution can be explained by its *function*: making the individual mobility characterizing the structure of industrial societies possible. Such an analysis obviously does not settle the historical question of the evolution of the family institution. But plausible hypotheses about this evolution are thus made possible.

However, it is important to note that, if the functional analysis is a justified approach, its results can lead to delicate problems of interpretation: when one has demonstrated that a particular institution, a set of rules prohibiting incest for example, could be explained by its function or functions, there remains the problem of knowing how these rules have been imposed: creation of a 'social engineer' or a 'constitutionalist'? Result of a process of cultural selection obeying a plan of Darwinian type? Obviously functional analysis cannot in itself decide between the different hypotheses conceivable. On the other hand, functional analysis includes a risk against which one must be warned: when it has been demonstrated that an institution B represents a response adapted to a set of structural data A, one can be tempted to summarize the analysis by a proposition of the kind 'A implies B' or 'if A, then B'. Merton's notion of a 'functional substitute' indicates that such a summary is always dangerous: the institutions C, D, etc., can equally be responses adapted to data A. Therefore, one knows well today that industrial development does not *imply* the nuclearization of the family, either necessarily or generally. In such an example, by calling upon historical and comparative data, one is able to specify the importance of conclusions drawn from functional analysis. Thus, one cannot entirely explain the correlation industrialization/nuclear family in the United States if one does not take into account the fact that this country was originally a settlement: geographical mobility was therefore and still is no doubt perceived as more natural, that is more easily acceptable by individuals, than in the societies of the old world or in Japan.

The above considerations show, in our opinion at least, on one hand that the notion of function does not imply necessarily either an organicist image of societies or a methodology welcoming explanations of a teleological kind, and on the other hand that the notion of 'functional analysis' describes a legitimate approach to research, with clearly definable objectives and principles. According to context, 'functional analysis' can find a more or less accessible and always useful support in historical and comparative information. Reciprocally, an historical analysis always includes in some way approaches relating to functional analysis. The methodological adage stated by Durkheim in the *Rules* maintains therefore all its importance: functional analysis and genetical analysis (analyses of 'causes', according to Durkheim) are two complementary approaches, the association of which is always to be recommended when possible.

Functionalism, Sociobiology, Structuralism, System.

Bibliography

BOUDON, R., 'Remarques sur la notion de fonction', *Revue française de Sociologie*, VIII, 2, 1967, 198–206. – BOURRICAUD, F., 'L'idéologie du grand refus', *in* CASANOVA, J.C. (ed.), *Mélanges en l'honneur de Raymond Aron. Science et conscience de la société*, Paris, Calmann-Lévy, 1971, 2 vol., I, 443–472. – BUCHANAN, J. and TULLOCK, G., *The calculus of consent*, Ann Arbor, University of Michigan Press, 1962, 1965. – DAVIS, K., 'The myth of functionalism as a special method in sociology and anthropology', *American sociological review*, XXIV, 6, 1959, 757–773. – DURKHEIM, E. *Rules of Sociological Method*, ch. 5. – HEMPEL, C.G., 'The logic of functional analysis', *in* GROSS, L. (ed.), *Symposium on sociological theory*, New York/Evanston/London, Harper & Row, 1959, 271–307. – LÉVI-STRAUSS, C., *Elementary structures of kinship*. – MERTON, R.K., 'Manifest and latent functions', *in* MERTON, R.K., *Social theory and social structure; toward the codification of theory and research*, Glencoe, The Free Press, 1949, first edn, 1957, 1964, chap. I, 19-84. – NADEL, S.F., *The theory of social structure*, London, Cohen & West, 1957. – NAGEL, E., 'A formalization of functionalism', *in* NAGEL, E., *Logic without metaphysics*, Glencoe, The Free Press, 1957, 247–283. – RADCLIFFE-BROWN, A.R., *Structure and function in primitive societies. Essays and addresses*, Glencoe, The Free Press, 1952; London Cohen & West, 1959.

Functionalism

Nowadays, this term belongs less to sociology's technical vocabulary than to the polemical repertoire of sociologists. Nevertheless, whatever misuses have been made of the term, as a symbol or as a term of derision, it represents a way of analysing the organization of social phenomena which, reduced to its purest form, makes a positive and original contribution. Functionalism is also a doctrine which draws out aspects of interaction and interdependence characteristic of social action and of its often unintended or unexpected consequences. Economic analysis has for a long time illuminated several relationships which can be referred to as 'functional', for example, between price on one hand and supply and demand on the other, or also between the level of prices and the rate of interest (or the rate of exchange, if one takes into account the economy in an international environment). In that case, the notion of function brings to mind the idea of an adjustment between global entities which could also be expressed by the term 'function' in its mathematical sense.

But it is important to consider how these functions result from the aggregation of microscopic behaviour. The market, in the form of true and perfect competition, constitutes a typical situation of interdependence. Each actor in the exchange relationship is provided with a stock of limited resources and with a scale of preferences. He is ready to give up a small proportion of his resources in return for a small proportion of resources that another actor would be willing to agree upon. This is feasible only if the said resources (goods or services) that B is ready to transfer to A 'interest' the latter because they appear to him complementary to those he already possesses, and because they allow him to enter new transactions, which increase the total value of his stock. The interdependence between A and B is fixed by the rate of substitution that they have both agreed for the value of goods and services to be exchanged. The interdependence results from the nature of the relationship between resources and the preferences of the possible parties to the exchange. But relationships are restricted to making some value correspond with other values, or else limiting the variations of certain values to the variations of others. Except in the most naive versions of Manchester School liberalism, economists refrain from asserting that these relationships by themselves, and without condition, must be interpreted as the expression of an equilibrium or of an optimum point. Demographic analysis also depends on some functional relationships (between the sizes of age groups or between the phenomena of fertility and of marriage rate).

In sociology functional analysis together with functionalism have had some widely varying connotations. The word functionalism first appeared in the 1930s. It was initially used by anthropologists and ethnologists such as Malinowski and Radcliffe-Brown. Each of them had his own functionalist doctrine, the differences consisting mainly in the essentially normative nature that Radcliffe-Brown saw in the social order whereas Malinowski saw in it the satisfaction of our 'needs' (in terms of feeding, protection against aggression of physical environment, biological reproduction, and sexual pleasure). The functionalist inspiration was to be welcome in the USA in the 1940s, in particular at Chicago University, where Radcliffe-Brown and Malinowski were appointed to teach. It was to contribute to a conception of society which represented it as systemic, as well as essentially harmonious, where conflicts are treated as if they were harmless tensions which are no more than a preparation for an increasingly comprehensive and satisfying social order. Combined with other influences, and particularly that of Durkheim, whose authority had been claimed by Radcliffe-Brown but rejected by Malinowski, functionalism is the label under which the early work of Talcott Parsons and Robert Merton is known. But these two latter authors do not give the same meaning to the word function. Merton attempted a disassociation of the concept of function from that of ends. He succeeded by making a distinction between 'manifest functions' and 'latent functions'. Recalling classical anthropological analysis of ritual, he observed that if the desired effect of certain rites is not attained (for example, the cure of someone ill or favourable weather), it does not mean that the execution of the rite has not produced any effect or that the attained effect (so different from the one expected) was not itself desired and even intended. So Merton is able to illuminate certain phenomena whose results, without conforming to the initial expectations of the actors, derive from their initiatives and intentions, or rather from the manner in which they combined among themselves and from the diverse constraints to which their action is subject. Therefore, the conception of function remains unaffected by criticisms of functionalism. Indeed, in the examples of functionalism which he discusses, Merton applies his method not to society as a whole but to clearly specified segments of the social structure. More generally, the latent function of a practice or an institution must be understood less through its precise contribution to the function of society as a whole than in the operation of the practice or institution itself. So, the latent functions of the political 'boss' must be understood less in relation to the functioning of American society than in relation to the needs for security of 'underprivileged' voters and to the strategy of a candidate in search of votes. To look for the 'latent function' of a rule or of a custom is not to look for its ends – the place that it should occupy in the social system – it is to look for its meaning, the way its sense is constituted and how it persists. One must add that a rite or a practice has several latent functions, according to the social context on which the observer, or even the social actor himself, focuses.

The conception of functional analysis defended by Parsons in his first writings (at least until the mid-1950s) is called 'structural-functionalism'. It looks for the establishment of a link between the normative system (which, at that time, Parsons did not always clearly distinguish from the system of values) and the 'situation', that is to say the environment described as an ensemble of stable and consistent constraints in which the system of action is placed. For example, different professional ideologies are presented as 'solutions' to a 'situation' characterized by the asymmetry of power and competence between the professional and his client: the normative system is presented as functional in the way that it solves the problems arising from the situation. Two problems result from this position. First, one is tempted to exaggerate the congruence between the 'structure' (situation) and the 'function' or functional solution. Second, one is tempted to present the first as virtually the imprint of the second, which reduces the congruence between the two to tautology. So Parsons gave up the term 'structural-functionalism', which he banished from his vocabulary after 1960.

Functional relations are of two kinds: they refer to the interaction that is established between the self and the other in terms of role, but they can also describe some aspects of interdependence, some social situations in which the individual becomes totally anonymous. In a situation of interaction, when the self plays a part *vis-à-vis* the other, the functional connection is provided by a set of rules, or more generally by some mutual expectations. But the self does not expect that the other should act in the same way as himself. There can be some complementarity between the expectations and the behaviour of the self and the other. But this complementarity is not always achieved. If complementarity is the condition of agreement, as in the situation of exchange and division of labour, interaction establishes a functional connection only if it is 'normative' or 'normal'. If it is not, the interaction engenders oppositions and conflicts or even weakens and ceases by a process of gradual withdrawal of all or a number of the actors. In an interdependent situation, the reference is no longer the role but the context in which the role is played. It is no longer a question of a functional connection between the self and the other, mediated by the role, but of a global regulation of an often statistical nature.

So, without being a functionalist, it is possible to look for functional connections, which can take the form either of interaction or of interdependence. One should add that these functional relationships are not always mechanisms of regulation or cybernetic control. In the simplest interactions, sanction creates a regulatory mechanism because, whether internalized by the actor or represented to him by an institutional authority, it calls the deviant to order. At the level of global and macroscopic interdependence some mechanisms, like a rise in prices when a surplus of global demand occurs, return the latter to a level of effective supply. More crudely, the elimination of an excess of mouths to feed could maintain a strict functional relationship between the level of population and the level of subsistence. But these situations, which are hardly satisfactory, are not the most frequent. Except in the very short term, supply is not strictly inelastic, and then there are many ways to act without transgressing the normative principles which define the situation.

Functionalism has been denounced as a conservative ideology. But this would be an application of Dr Pangloss's philosophy to the field of sociology. Yet, as Merton pointed out, if there is a right-wing functionalism, there is also a left-wing functionalism, too. It is not difficult to find some of Marx's texts to be as bluntly functionalist as the most functionalist texts of Parsons. This is why, especially for contemporary neo-Marxists who ask 'what's the purpose of the school – or the hospital, or the police?', it is possible to talk about an 'inverted hyper-functionalism'. Indeed, the systemic nature of social reality is affirmed in a naive way, and not in a counter-intuitive fashion which can produce emergent qualities whose effects are both unforeseen and in some cases unwelcome. Finally, it is a superficial conception of the notion of system (following the confusion between interdependence and interaction) which distorts functional analysis and devalues it as a functional *ideology*.

Conformity and Deviance, Function, Social Control, Structuralism, System, Teleology, Theory.

Bibliography

BOUDON, R., *La crise de la sociologie*, Geneva, Droz. 1971. – BOURRICAUD, F., 'Contre le sociologisme: une critique et des propositions', *Revue française de sociologie*, 1975, XVI, 583–603. – DAHRENDORF, R., 'Out of Utopia: toward a reorientation of sociological analysis', *American Journal of Sociology*, 1958, *64*, 115–127. – DAVIS. K., 'The myth of functional analysis as a special method in sociology and anthropology', *American Sociological Review*, 1959, XXIV, 757–772. – DURKHEIM, E., *Rules of Sociological Method* New York, Free Press, Collier Macmillan, 1964; London, Macmillan, 1982. – GOULDNER, A.W., 'The norm of reciprocity: a preliminary statement', *American Sociological Review*, 1960, XXV, 161–178. – HEMPEL, C.G., 'The logic of functional analysis', *in* GROSS, L. (ed.), *Symposium on sociological theory*, New York, Harper, 1959, 271–307. – MALINOWSKI, B., *A scientific theory of culture and other essays*, Chapel Hill, The Univ. of North Carolina Press, 1944. – MERTON, R.K., *Social theory and social structure*, Glencoe, The Free Press, 1949. – PARSONS, T., 'The present position and prospects of systematic theory in sociology', 1945, in *Essays in sociological theory*, New York, The Free Press, 1954; London Collier Macmillan, 1964. – RADCLIFFE-BROWN, A.R., *Structure and function in primitive society*, London Cohen & West, 1952, 1959. – VAN DEN BERGHE. P.L., 'Dialectic and functionalism: toward a theoretical synthesis', *American Sociological Review*, 1963, XXVIII, 695–705. – WRONG, D.H., 'The oversocialized conception of man in modern sociology', *American Sociological Review*, April 1961, 183–193.

G

Groups

Men live in groups: this is a platitude which has been traced back as far even as Aristotle, who said that man is, according to the usual translation of his famous phrase, a political animal and, according to another, perhaps less equivocal translation, a social being. Usually this is recognized, but there are also many completely unacceptable interpretations. The fact is that there is indeed a group effect, as diverse observations or experiments show. In explaining how an individual can be brought to change his opinion or attitude, one realizes that the group to which he belongs bears an influence on the speed and direction of this change. Asch used these hypotheses to develop a range of well-known experimental situations. In general, the subject of Asch's experiment aligns himself with the positions that he identifies with the group, and this identification, which can be motivated by the search for security, can push him to take a 'risk' with his perception of a given situation. For example, in one such experiment, a line can be perceived to be systematically lengthened compared to an ambiguous standard of reference, if the line has been apparently agreed to be bigger than the reference, according to the consensus of the group in which the subject is placed. But it would be unacceptable to conclude from such facts that the individual is somehow 'dissolved' in the group. Indeed, such formulas go much further than the observed facts. In addition, they make reference to notions such as hypnosis or suggestion in connection with which Durkheim, in his critique of Tarde, showed that where hypnosis or suggestion occurs the relationship established between the parties concerned cannot be considered social. It is only in extreme and exceptional cases that the effect of the group is accompanied by the submergence of the individual into the group of which he is a member.

Therefore, one must distinguish many sorts of groups, as has been done by Gurvitch and Von Wiese. Some of these distinctions may seem arbitrary. This is the case when the number of accepted criteria is too large. In any case, the size of the group, the quality of relationships between members, the intensity of fusion which is established between themselves or, on the contrary, the distance that separates them, the duration, the continuity or discontinuity of their contacts, all must be taken into account. Crowds and masses are different, and each of these types designates different social situations. In the crowd at a football match those who are watching are involved in relations of interaction. Some whistle, some clap their hands; and, on both sides, a solidarity is established, while at the same time a differentiation appears between the supporters, according to the intensity of their enthusiasm. Things happen differently in a queue: very often relationships build up around problems of simple ecological coexistence, which come from the limited nature of territory. In the case of the mass of viewers watching TV or the mass of readers reading a newspaper, they are very unlikely to meet. Besides, their relationships happen only through the mediation of a TV programme or of a printed page. Their only common factor is to be the reader of the same newspaper or viewer of the same programme. Communication between them is organized not through their mutual interactions but through the relationship of each of them in particular with the journalist or with the 'producer' of the TV show.

One cannot reduce the range of groups to an opposition between different forms of 'seriality', as Sartre did: the practically-inert group versus the group in fusion. Other significant oppositions exist between types of groups such as those formed by individuals waiting for the bus to St Germain-des-Prés and the rioters marching towards the Bastille. Far less can one confuse the social group with a particular institutional form. But, even if one agrees with Aristotle who sees in the city, the social form which fits best the requirements of human sociability, one must admit that the city is one of the innumerable types of groups identified by history and anthropology. To resolve these problems, two approaches appear to be available. The first is a comparative approach. But it tends to confuse the collectivity which results from the gathering or coexistence of individuals with institutions which regulate this coexistence. A second direction is also conceivable: instead of studying the diversity of groups, the sociologist will take an interest in the attributes which define the group as an essential unity. The first procedure has the mark of evolutionism and historicism. The underlying question in studies of the first category concerns the nature of the transition, which leads from some groups known as 'undifferentiated' – such as the 'horde' – to the complex organizations of modern society. The second is more concerned with the constituent elements of interaction in the group and tries to bring out the essential relationships.

The observation of groups and in particular of 'small groups' has exercised an overwhelming temptation for the sociologist looking for a readily perceptible object. Historically, this study started with some entirely circumstantial inquiries by sociologists interested in social problems – such as the housing problem – or adaptation of immigrants into social sources such as education. The early studies of the Chicago School were carried out on the behaviour of such groups in the deprived suburbs of the large metropolis of the Mid-West. Independently, some anthropologists, and in particular Malinowski who had lived for several years with Trobriand Islanders in the South Pacific, observed primitive populations. These researchers, whose 'interests' were undoubtedly very different, agreed quite unconsciously about the need to appeal to the method which has been called since then 'participant observation'. The first rule of this method is that sociologists and anthropologists must not be satisfied in studying the society 'from a distance', reading documents, or somebody else's reports. They must understand the people they are observing, speak their language or dialect, and know how to interpret their gestures. It is only under these conditions that it is possible to understand the life of a group.

The contention that direct observation of small and compact groups constituted the main route for a sociological survey remained implicit in this procedure. At first glance, the advantages of this method were numerous. Instead of losing oneself in some ill-established diachronic successions or in arbitrary comparisons, the reality of the group would be immediately revealed to the observer. Besides, the reduced numbers of such groups allowed the researcher, up to a point, to know each of its members, and to have precise and detailed information available about each of them. So, the sociologist and the anthropologist, instead of turning towards the historian to illuminate uncertain origins and questionable links were, in some way, defining the proper object of such research: the prime social fact is the group.

These orientations were developed in many ways. First, they were applied to the study of organizations and in particular of companies. The first studies in industrial sociology started from the observation of small groups. In the well-known Hawthorne survey, a team of workers in a workshop was studied using participant observation. In turn, psychologists discovered in the group the 'milieu' of action in which one could provoke some changes, affecting actors' personalities in a quasi-experimental way. This idea was presented with some ingenuousness by Moreno who believed that he created in that procedure an authentic 'sociometrical revolution'. All that was necessary was to adapt interactions of the type desired to the 'milieu' of work and home. Therefore, one might organize society according to the hierarchy of the preferences that its members express for each other.

The idea of group dynamics, supported by psychologists, influenced by Kurt Lewin's work, is very close but more subtle. One does not look any longer for the coincidence between the ideal and effective structures of interaction. It would be a matter of leading actors through the learning of their roles, and through the discovery of the situations in which these role games are introduced, thus leading them to recognize some rules, which are capable of minimizing their interpersonal tensions and optimizing the effect of co-operation. Therefore the group is no longer an observatory: it becomes a laboratory, where the understanding of the procedure of interaction and of the 'rules of the game' allows actors to change their social 'milieu'.

The theoretical orientations which have led towards the constitution of the group as a sociological object are various and, up to a point, contradictory. A positivist and behaviourist tendency has already been noticed. The group appears as a suitable object for observation. The processes of dissent and solidarity, aggressive gestures, denial or agreement, frequencies of verbal interventions of each person, length, place in the exchange of gestures and words can be recorded in the most neutral and objective way. Bales has drawn up a guide-book allowing a trained observer to code the events that are happening in an interacting group. This theory is limited because Bales analyses only task-oriented groups: a task is proposed to the members, whose 'situation' finds itself 'structured' through the observer who himself proposed the task and not through the organizational context, as was the case in the General Electric factory at the Hawthorne Plant. Moreover, only volunteers participate in the Balesian groups, whereas the workers observed by Roethlisberger and Dickson's team were motivated not by willingness to take part in a group but by the need to earn their living.

Research has also been focused on a second category of groups. They tend to establish, for the benefit of their members, a diagnosis of the difficulties which they have in trying to take up, fulfil, and modify a given role, taking into account the reactions and expectations of other members. These 'diagnostic' groups can go beyond the actor's analysis *in situ*, in the acting out of his roles. Some psychologists, more or less influenced by Freud but whose orthodoxy is in other respects somewhat questionable, attempt to make individuals aware of the conflicts and impulses of their subconscious by immersing them in some 'relaxing' or traumatizing situations that the experience of the group might give them. This therapeutical presentation, whose benefit was mostly cathartic, was proposed in the 1930s by Moreno who saw in *psychodrama* (a kind of projective game played by group members under the control of an audience and of a producer) a course of treatment allowing the individual to express his desires in their objective and imaginary dimension. Freud has been a continuing influence on studies concerning small groups, but his impact has varied in intensity. Freud proposed above all a theory of personality, from its genesis to its structure. It might be tempting to search for analogical equivalents of the ego, super-ego, and id in the life of a group. The two latter examples of the 'psychological mechanism' may be of interest for the analysis of the group. Indeed, one can imagine that the group functions as a 'super-ego' for each individual; or, on the contrary, in certain situations of an 'orgiastic' type, it functions to uncover and express some of the most primitive impulses of the 'id'. Freud insists on the importance of the function of 'identification' through which a form of solidarity is established among the group's members who are assimilated by each other, either through the normative constraints of the super-ego or by the 'instincts' and impulses of the id.

A third category of research dedicated to group dynamics studies the way in which the group starts by being a mere collection of individuals and subsequently becomes a 'milieu of action', which defines its members' expectations, performances, and level of satisfaction. These studies have been called *psycho-sociological*. Indeed, the observers are interested by the way the rules of the game (or norms) are formed because, once constituted, they give to the group a consistency and authority which is possibly in conflict with each individual's interests and feelings. But for the individuals, the setting-up of the group and the elaboration of its norms are inseparable from the initiation into their roles. The dynamic of the group and the taking of roles are the two sides of a single process. The research procedures of this third category of researchers are different from the other two. First, they implicitly stress the relationship between role and person, which is different from the first category, and, second, they do not, contrary to the second tradition of research, attempt to plumb the depths of the individuals' 'subconscious' but always assume them to be either already socialized, or in the process of being socialized.

Group research makes it possible to identify a small number of common features of all processes of interaction – such tendencies are perceptible even in the work of those in opposing research traditions, such as Bales and Homans. The former established some propositions of a very wide generality: 1) the rate of participation is very unevenly distributed in discussion groups; 2) two criteria are enough to identify an individual who is a *potential* leader: the high number of his initiatives and propositions, and the way they are positively received by the other members of the groups; 3) leadership is a collectively exercised function; in every discussion group, several individuals are potential leaders; 4) recognized leaders specialize in differentiated roles: the man with ideas, the friendly man (the sociometric star), the man in whom one has confidence (because he is taken as a loyal person who will sacrifice his time and be able to give some useful and unselfish pieces of advice); 5) leaders who exercise their function as a body, that is to say in coalition, will be recognized even more as loyal, capable, and worthy of confidence, since there has been consensus on the group's priorities.

Homans drew out of his research a complete set of propositions on what he calls 'the elementary forms of social behaviour': these propositions cover competition, influence, and authority. These forms of behaviour are described as 'elementary' for two reasons. First, they are observable always and everywhere, as individuals find themselves in interactive situations. Consequently, they could easily be linked to a few highly generalized psychological laws which express conditions through which intelligent human beings (able to learn and subject to the law of decreasing marginal utility) can be put in exchange relations. 'The elementary forms of social behaviour' are built around the conditions of fair exchange. These conditions are even more difficult to define since actors involved in the exchange relationship have been linked not only to the intrinsic values of the goods and services but also to the relative values, defined through qualities, statuses, and the roles of actors in the exchange process and individuals reputed to be similar and comparable. However, 'envious comparison' influences the exchange process. Moreover, envious comparison is built on a set of partially arbitrary substitutions between criteria of pertinent exchange in the group to which the subject belongs and criteria in use in the reference group to which the subject strongly wishes to belong or that he considers as the one and only authority capable of defining the rules of the exchanges in which he is taking part.

The concept of group dynamics has allowed some propositions to be established about the most satisfactory and efficient forms of leadership. The Lewinian studies have emphasized the excellence of domestic leadership, described not through the absence of a leader, but through the educational and participative direction the leader tries to insist upon. Moreover, these propositions are presented in a restrictive way, because they can be checked only if the task proposed to the group is clearly understandable by every member, if its objectives or goals are approved by them, and if the results do not create any problems of distribution which could set the actors in violent opposition to each other.

Finally, the problem of the relationship between actors and norms, and the nature of such norms, is perhaps best demonstrated by group studies. Two complementary notions are fundamental to this approach. First, the notion of *involvement in the role* (or else of motivation). The performance of the role is transformed to the extent to which the acting subject feels himself committed to it. As for the factors which act on commitment, it is possible to distinguish the nature of the constraints affecting the actor and the manner in which he lives out the role. The performance will be different according to whether it is a fatiguing or boring activity, or a 'gratifying' activity which allows the subject to express and fulfil himself. Since the 'heroic period' of Hawthorne's survey, industrial sociologists studying factors modifying worker productivity have examined the link between the quality of performance (his productivity in the sense we are not concerned with here) and the actor's *involvement*. This notion must not be mixed up with that of identification. The actor is not his role – or only in the imaginary sense, like Sartre's waiter who plays at being a waiter. The distance between the actor and his role is one condition of an efficient performance. Goffman's observations on a surgical operation team suggest that the surgeon who is in control of himself can save a compromising situation, overcome a failing of his team or his assistants – or even one of his own mistakes – by keeping cool and mastering his reactions in face of a situation whose consequences could be simply terrifying. Role-distance helps the actor to keep cool and reinforce his control of the situation. That is why those standing at the top of the hierarchy very often show signs of detachment, trying to give themselves and others the feeling that they can cope and take on their responsibilities.

In thinking about these notions of commitment, of involvement, and distance, it is important to consider norms not as a set of rigid and unequivocal constraints, but as a text on which actors elaborate as in a kind of *Commedia dell' Arte*. But the actors' latitude is not boundless. The waiter can play his part as if he was a tight-rope walker. He can, if need be, sway his shoulders, as if he was a market porter, or charge forward as if he was an infantryman. But he cannot move among his customers giving out blessings. Even supposing he were physically able to play the part of a priest as well as performing his task, he would not be funny and the audience would think he was mad. The role is not a game in the sense of 'acting-out', where the actor does anything that comes to mind. The actor is subjected to rules, which he can execute with more or less witty eloquence and freedom. But he is not the one who has set up these norms, nor is he capable of completely defining the situation according to his wishes and his mood of the moment. His interpretation of norms and situation must be *negotiated*; it takes into account the way in which 'the others' on their side execute or are expected to execute their own work as actors. The role game is situated within two boundary limits: the first of virtuosity and irony towards oneself and the spectators; and the second that of 'competence', that is to say, the ability to meet others' expectations in conforming to the rules.

The study of groups reveals some characteristic dimensions of the process of interaction. First, it makes us sensitive to the resources and difficulties of our relationship with 'the other'. It lets us catch sight of the hidden part of the social iceberg, the way norms are really established and lived out; routine, worries, and diversion very often prevent us from seeing norms other than as strategies.

The study of groups also helps the construction of theoretical models, which expose the variables which change the functioning of the social system. (Hence, the 'clinical method' is opposed to the 'experimental method'.) The problems encountered by this undertaking are those with which any experimenter is confronted. The experimenter must clearly identify his variables, give himself a suitable model of their interdependence, perceive and if possible measure the effects that he attributes to these variables on the functioning of the group. But in the case of the sociologist, the inherent difficulties of experimental method are greatly complicated. First, the variables that are supposed to be identified and understood in their interrelationships are strategic variables. Indeed, the inter-action rests on a system of expectations, that is initiatives and responses. In so far as responses can be intentionally distorted, to confound the expectations of those who have taken the initiatives, the experimenter never fully masters the game. A doubt always hovers over the relation between the way things have happened *in vitro* and the way they would have happened *in vivo*. Second, the demarcation points of elements of the social system are far less stringent than those of mechanical systems. Economists have drawn attention to 'externalities' (positive or negative) which affect the 'purity' and 'perfection' of markets and which indirectly involve agents who were not directly concerned by the exchange process in the exchange itself in ways which either penalize or favour them. Sociologists find themselves in a similar situation with the phenomenon of 'envious comparison'. Let us suppose that a manager gives a rise in wages to a particular category of workers. This rise will appear generous to the employer who compares the former salary to the new one. It might appear derisory to the employees, if they compare their rise to the one given to a certain category of workers with whom they identify. Hence, if the sociologist attempts to estimate the effect of wage increases on productivity, he will have to start by describing what is understood by 'increase' – which is seen differently by the employer and the wage-earner. These problems were already anticipated in Hawthorne's survey, where the researchers explained quite clearly that the level of satisfaction of workers is not only fixed by the level of satisfaction in the group, but also by their place in their family, and even by the opinion that they have of their private situation and the way they live out their stations as members of a 'class' in the wider society.

It is not, then, possible to deal with groups as if they were physical units, easy to locate in social space. By making such assumptions, the small-group sociologists of the period 1940-50 can be seen as committing the 'fallacy of misplaced concreteness'. Society is not a juxtaposition of small groups, which would constitute its atoms. Effects of composition and aggregation can only be imperfectly understood through the related elements which comprise such processes. An industrial group is no more a collection of workshops than the *Wehrmacht* or the Red Army is reducible, except to the statisticians, to a given number of brigades or gangs. It is possible to know everything about the functioning of the assembly line and the electrical workshop of General Electric without understanding why this multinational is flourishing. The study of groups allows us to understand how men live out their roles and the norms which define those roles – even if the description of the way they are lived out allows us to understand only partially the past and future, and even if other constraints than these roles and norms are imposed on the other actors in the situation. Understanding the functioning of small groups does not absolve the sociologist from the responsibility of understanding the larger social entities in which such groups are placed. The problem for the sociologist is not to engage in an absurd debate about whether the chicken or the egg came first – the global society or the limited group. It is to choose, in relation to his hypotheses, the most pertinent level at which they can be stated and validated.

Action, Action (collective), Conformity and Deviance, Experimentation, Role, Socialization, Status.

Bibliography

ARISTOTLE, *The Politics*, London, Penguin, 1962. – ASCH, S.E., *Social psychology*, New York, Prentice-Hall, 1952, 1962. – BALES, R.F., *Interaction process analysis: a method for the study of small groups*, Cambridge, Addison-Wesley, 1950; Folcroft, Folcroft Editions, 1970. – BION, W.R., *Experiences in groups, and other papers*, New York, Basic Books, 1971; London, Tavistock, 1961. – BLAU, P.M., *Exchange and power in social life*, New York, Wiley, 1964. – CARTWRIGHT, D. and ZANDER, A. (ed.), *Group dynamics: research and theory*, Evanston, Row, Peterson, 1953; London, Tavistock, 1968. – FREUD, S., *Massenpsychologie und Ich-Analyse*, Leipzig, Internationalen psychoanalytischen Verlag, 1921. Trad.: 'Psychologie collective et analyse du moi', in *Essais de psychoanalyse*, Paris Payot, 1962. – GOFFMAN, E., *Encounters. Two studies in the sociology of interaction*, Indianapolis, Bobbs-Merrill, 1961; *The human group*, London, Routledge & Kegan Paul, 1951. – GRAFMEYER, Y. and JOSEPH, I. (ed.), *L'Ecole de Chicago*, Paris, Editions du Champ urbain, 1979. – GURVITCH, G., *La vocation actuelle de la sociologie*, Paris, PUF, 1950; 1969, 2 vol. – HARE, A.P., *Handbook of small group research*, New York, Free Press, 1962. – HARE, E.P., BORGATTA, E.F., and BALES, R.F., *Small groups: studies in social interaction*, New York, Knopf, 1955; rev. ed. 1965. – HOMANS, G.C., *Social behavior: its elementary forms*, New York, Harcourt, 1961; London, Routledge & Kegan, 1961. – JENNINGS, H.H., *Leadership and isolation: a study of personality in interpersonal relations*, New York, London, Longmans, Green & Co., 1943, 1950. – LE BON, G., *Psychologie des foules*, Paris, F. Alcan, 1895; Paris, Retz, CEPL, 1975. – LEWIN, K., *Field theory in social science: selected theoretical papers*, (ed.) CARTWRIGHT, D., New York, Harper, 1951; London Tavistock 1952. – MAISONNEUVE, J., *Psychosociologie des affinités*, Paris, PUF, 1966; *Recherches diachroniques sur une représentation sociale: persistance et changement dans la caractérisation de 'l'homme sympathique'*, Paris, CNRS, 1978. – MORENO, J.L., *Who shall survive? Foundations of sociometry, group psycho-therapy and sociodrama*, New York, Beacon House, 1943. – MOSCOVICI, S., *L'âge des foules*, Paris, Fayard, 1981. – PAGES, M., *La vie affective des groupes. Esquisse d'une théorie de la relation humaine*, Paris, Dunod, 1968. – ROGERS, C.R., *On becoming a person, a therapist's view of psychotherapy*, Boston, Houghton Mifflin, 1961; London, Constable, 1967. – RŒTHLISBERGER, F.J. and DICKSON, W.J., *Management and the worker: an account of a research program conducted by the Western Electric Company, Hawthorne Works, Chicago*, Cambridge, Harvard Univ. Press, 1939, 1961. – SARTRE, J.-P., *Critique de la raison dialectique*, Paris, Gallimard, 1960. – SHERIF, M. and CANTRIL, H., *The psychology of ego-involvement, social attitudes and identifications*, New York, Wiley; London, Chapman & Hall, 1947. – SIMMEL, G., *Grund-fagen der Soziologie*, Berlin, G.J. Göschen, 1917; Berlin, W. de Gruyter, 1970. – TARDE, G., *Les lois de l'imitation. Etude sociologique*, Paris, F. Alcan, 1890; Paris, Geneva, Slatkine, 1979. – THIBAUT, J. and KELLEY, H.H., *The social psychology of groups*, New York, Wiley, 1959. – WHYTE, W.F., *Street corner Society: the social structure of an italian slum*, The Univ. of Chicago Press, 1943, 1965.

H

Historicism

Historicism in the sense given to it by Popper (the search for laws of social change or, more ambitiously, of history) is probably a temptation or a *Weltanschauung*, that is to say a *vision*, as old as thought itself. However it was in the nineteenth and beginning of the twentieth century that it was especially dominant in the social sciences. It is usually associated with the names of Hegel, Comte, Marx, Mill, and Spencer, and with certain intellectual movements, Marxism of course, but also social Darwinism for example, and the evolutionism of Morgan and Lévy-Bruhl.

Historicism can be narrowly defined as the doctrine or vision according to which social change or historical development follows unconditional laws of succession, giving a direction or meaning to history. In this case historicism and evolutionism are practically synonymous. Difference remains however in that the reference to biological evolution (defined by the progress of complexity) is more direct in the second case than the first. In the widest sense, historicism coincides with the family of theories which see social change as subservient to evolutionary laws, to cyclical laws, to rhythmic regularities, or to reproductive laws. Hence certain sociologists represent social change as, in certain contexts, proceeding according to the rhythm of a long period of stability followed by a short period of crisis. Others, such as Sorokin, put forward the notion that a regularity can be observed in the alternation of dominant cultural values, periods of 'rationalism' alternating with periods of 'irrationalism'. More precisely, Sorokin conceptualized cultural change as following a three-phased rhythm: an 'ideational' phase, characterized by the importance of supersensory of 'spiritual' values; an 'idealist' phase characterized by the importance of abstract ideas; and a 'sensate' phase characterized by the principle that the true level of reality is that which is presented to the sense organs. Others take the view that while they may appear to change, societies are characterized especially by the permanence of self-reproducing structures. In the widest sense, then, historicism is a feature of all theories which aim to uncover *laws* of social change or regularities within the general range of social change. Another sense, which only partly overlaps with the above, is that historicism is a doctrine which assumes that the future of a society is entirely contained within its present state, in such a fashion that an 'omniscient' observer could deduce the development of a system from time t to $t + k$, from exhaustive observation of its state at t (see 'Determinism'). Historicism in the first two senses generally involves the hypothesis that societies obey a Laplacian determinism. Thus the developmental laws which Marx claimed to have proved are based on the assumption that the state of a system in time t determines its development from t to $t + k$. But other historicists, such as Sorokin, are content with describing the regularities they claim to have observed, rather than being concerned to 'prove' that they result from a necessary succession of conditions, each automatically triggering the next. Historicism in the narrow sense shares with the wider forms of historicism such as cyclical theories of history (e.g., Vico, Spengler) the postulate that historical change follows absolute laws founded in the nature of things. It is distinguished by the form which it imparts to these laws, of a tendency towards a determinate end. Thus Comte thought that human individuals are endowed with a tendency to seek continually to perfect their nature. From this tendency he deduced a 'law of succession' (the law of the three stages) whose existence he had 'verified' empirically by 'historical observation'. According to Mill, the 'progressive nature of the human spirit' is founded on a fundamental 'impulsive force': the 'desire for increased material comfort'. According to Marx, 'history is the history of class struggle', this struggle leading of necessity to the replacement of one class by another up until the disappearance of class society. For Lévy-Bruhl, the mental history of humanity is marked by the passsage from pre-logical to logical mentality.

These few examples are sufficient to indicate historicism's diversity: for certain historicists, the unconditional laws of evolution are inscribed within human nature itself. For others they derive from tendencies which are inexorably inscribed within social organization, or in certain structural properties of social organization (for example, relations of production in Marxist evolutionism). Despite such diversity, of which the foregoing examples provide no more than a glimpse, historicism has an underlying unity: the postulate of a necessary and thus 'natural' succession. Let us note, incidentally, that, in contrast to what has sometimes been suggested, historicism is far from being a doctrine of the past. The sociology of modernization and development includes a number of theories which seek to 'prove' that social systems are subject to certain developmental and ultimately reproductive laws, for example, the law of the vicious circle of poverty, which claims to explain why a poor society will remain so unless external intervention occurs (cf. 'Development'). Other theories (Spencer, Parsons) try to show that change in industrial societies and, in a general manner in all non-'traditional' societies, is characterized by a 'typical' process, that of 'differentiation'. Originally the idea of differentiation came from an analogy between the development of the embryo and social development, suggested by Spencer. The analogy inspired Smelser's study of 1959 of industrial development in eighteenth-century Britain. There is little doubt we have the same faith in *progress* today as in the nineteenth century. Historicism is assuredly more varied and more discreet at the end of the twentieth century than at the end of the nineteenth. If proof were necessary, all we would need to note would be the numerous historicist theories which have emerged in recent decades – if we focus only on evolutionary variants of historicism, the work of Lenski, Boulding, and Wallerstein would immediately come to mind.

Does the concept of an unconditional law of history which underpins the historicist theories of change have any meaning? This is the fundamental epistemological question raised by historicism in all its forms. Now the answer is most likely in the negative. This will be clearer if we look at a famous example of the 'law of succession' (to use Comte's terminology) in the natural sciences, that of the biological theory of evolution. Apparently this theory proves that laws of succession exist not only in the human and social world but also in the natural world. It shows that organisms tend to evolve from simpler to more complex forms. But three reservations should immediately be introduced.

First, the law of evolution is supposed to result from elementary mechanisms which can be verified by observation and experiment, at least in theory. Hence according to the 'neo-Darwinian' theory of evolution, evolution results from 1) the existence of chance mutations; 2) 'natural' selection of these mutations under environmental pressure; 3) the existence of chance effects which can create stable combinations of elements and consequently natural entities which are more complex than the elements of which they are composed.

Second, evolutionary laws are not absolute but *conditional*. They assume that certain givens remain constant or do not vary outside certain limits (thus a nuclear war would certainly have dire consequences for the 'laws of evolution').

Third, and this point is critical, laws of 'evolution' constitute only very general indications. More precisely they propose to account for a given situation: the progressive appearance of more 'complex' species. But they do not, and do not aim to, deduce the evolution of any ecological system from t to $t + k$. They merely explain why species *may* be observed to be more complex at $t + k$ than at t. As to the details of the evolution of an ecological system between t and $t + k$, it depends upon 'historical' events that can be observed but that are almost impossible to deduce: thus a species threatened by predators may be protected from extinction by the existence – clearly contingent – of an ecological niche which allows it to survive. The theory of evolution does not indicate in any way that it would or should be possible to present the history of a species as the result of the endogenous laws of development of a closed system.

With certain historicists none of these restrictions is taken into consideration. With others one at least is omitted. In the case of Comte and Mill, neither the first nor the rest are respected. 'The positive theory of human nature' by which Comte sees men obeying a tendency to try to perfect their nature can only be proven on the basis of observation of historical 'progress'. Comte's statement that 'a law of succession, even if it has been revealed with the fullest possible authority by the method of historical observation must be definitively accepted unless it has been rationally reduced to the positive theory of human nature' reveals a worthy epistemological concern. Comte clearly saw, as this text reveals, the importance of the first restriction cited above. The reasons for progress cannot be derived from its observation. It is also necessary to explain why human behaviour creates the aggregate effect which is called progress. But at the same time, Comte made himself incapable of responding to the condition he himself had posed to the extent that the 'positive theory of human nature' simply pointed out the need to perfect the said nature. Moreover, the fact that the elementary mechanisms responsible for the 'law of succession' are situated at the level of 'human nature' considered as a primitive and absolute given confers on the famous law of the three stages the undesirable status of unconditionality. We should note that it is not entirely unhelpful to contemporary concerns to look carefully at the weaknesses of Comtean historicism, archaic as it may appear. In fact the same critiques, probably more accentuated, could be addressed to many modern historicists, especially those of a phenomenological persuasion (Sartre, Merleau-Ponty) for whom the nature of man is to be inhabited by historicity, and by consequence to be obsessed, as Alain Touraine would say, by the passion for history.

Marx's historicism, like that of Spencer, whose work, as Louis Schneider has shown, presents a number of similar aspects, is much more subtle and interesting. In Marx what we have termed above the first reservation is undoubtedly covered. Steeped in Mandeville, Adam Smith, and Ricardo, Marx clearly saw that history is the result of men pursuing their *individual* objectives and generating complex *collective* effects which are often unexpected and sometimes undesirable ('men make history but do not know that they make it') – effects which Marx conceptualized as escaping the control of individuals in most cases (a point which might be contested). In pursuing their own ends individuals set in motion forces which overtake them and hence become perceived as 'natural' (see 'Dialectic', 'Marx'). Taking as an example the famous law of the tendency of the rate of profit to fall (Book III of *Capital*): each individual capitalist cannot avoid attempting to increase his productivity. If he does not do so others will. By so doing he contributes to the erosion of the basis on which profits are created. In effect, increases in productivity imply a substitution of 'fixed' capital (machines, etc.) for 'variable' capital, in other words human labour. Now profit is the result, according to Marx, of exploitation of the worker. As a result, capitalists cannot prevent themselves from producing a reduction in the rate of production which is prejudicial to their class interest, since it ultimately implies the collapse of capitalism itself. This is a specific example but it is typical of Marx's reasoning. By contrast with Hegel, the obscure 'labour of negativity' has nothing mysterious about it in Marx's work. It results from mechanisms which are as clearly conceptualized in their own field as are those of the 'neo-Darwinist' theoreticians of evolution. By contrast with the elementary mechanisms postulated by Comte, Mill, or Sartre, these mechanisms introduce hypotheses which can in principle be subjected to observation and verification. On the other hand, and this point is of essential importance, Marx considers social change to be an 'emergent' effect, in other words a phenomenon which results from the constituents of behaviour directed towards individual ends but generally not explicitly sought in its own right by social actors. This is quite different from the approach of Comte or Mill, who see evolution as resulting from what is directly inscribed in the aspirations of individuals (see 'Teleology'). It is worth noting that when Marx departs from this individualist paradigm (cf. the notion of 'class consciousness') it is often because he has good *empirical* reasons to do so. Certain situations encourage the use of individual strategies (cf. the smallholding peasantry of the *Eighteenth Brumaire* or the capitalists in *Capital*); others encourage collective strategies (industrial workers). Depending on the system of interaction or interdepence in which actors find themselves, recourse to collective strategies is more or less likely; in Marxian language, 'class consciousness' is more or less active (cf. 'Action (collective)').

The unacceptable character of Marx's historicism derives from the fact that the second and third reservations referred to above are not covered. Biological laws of evolution are only conditional, as we have seen. They assume conditions which are more or less constant. But it is necessary to make some effort to imagine a situation where these conditions are not evident. These laws are, it should be repeated, extremely general, and insist on little more than the fact that the less complex comes before the more complex. They do not even affirm the proposition that the more recent species is necessarily more complex. Finally, they do not even imply that evolution can be described and deduced in its detailed manifestations. This last reservation derives from the fact that ecological systems are generally open rather than closed, or more precisely that they have no necessary reason to be closed. Now the evolution of a system can generally be satisfactorily predicted or deduced only when it is closed. Even in the case where it is closed, its 'output' can create changes in its functioning state. Now these changes will be more or less predictable, and are more likely to be less easily predictable in the case where elements of the systems are capable of innovation, as is the case with human actors. Analysis of the 'laws of change' of human social systems requires an equal if not greater prudence than that shown in the field of the evolution of species by Darwin and the Darwinians. However the least that can be said is that such restrictions are rarely found in historicist theories in general, and in Marx, the first 'modern' historicist, in particular. Although Marx was greatly impressed by Darwin's thought, to the point of sending him a signed copy of *Capital*, he did not show the same prudence as his model. This is particularly clear if we consider the 'law of the declining rate of profit'. It loses its value if it is supposed that capitalists act *in concert* rather than on their own. Development of cartels is of course rather unlikely in the situation of perfect competition which Marx postulates. But it becomes highly likely when technological and productive development create production structures of an oligopolistic form. This is a system which creates changes in its own functioning state and where it is inappropriate to consider this state as stable. Marx was not unaware of the phenomena of technical innovation or of cartels. However, he did not draw the proper conclusions from them: profit is likely to decline only if it is supposed that competition is constant and continuous. The tendency of profit to decline in certain sectors may be compensated by drawing off high rates of profit in new sectors (cf. the development of services with low rates of productivity). In short, Marx postulated a system with a constant structure (perfect competition) immersed in a stable environment, while the structure of the system is in fact variable and the functioning of the system creates 'spillover effects' which affect this environment, and thus in turn affect the system itself. In the language of cybernetics, Marx employed the postulate that only closed systems exist. Now social systems should be considered as open systems (characterized by exchanges with their environments), except in those cases where they can be defined in very precise spatio-temporal limits. It is unrealistic, *a fortiori*, to interpret history as a single process developing within a closed system. Of course it is possible to observe *directed* processes, in other words following a 'law of succession' (the progress of scientific and technological knowledge is an example which springs immediately to mind). But such processes are without exception partial, isolatable, and their 'linearity' is conditional in all cases. Neither the progress of science nor the destruction (or survival) of capitalism can be held to be *necessary*, that is *unconditionally* guaranteed.

The critique of narrowly conceived historicist theories just outlined applies equally, *mutatis mutandis*, to all historicist theories. All see social systems as closed systems functioning under constant conditions.

We should also note the existence of a diffuse line of thought, which Mannheim represents and which has its roots in Hegel, and which might be termed 'absolute historicism': since men's ideas are influenced by the historical conjuncture in which they find themselves, history cannot be analysed 'externally'. Thus it is only via the 'interior' that its 'meaning' or 'direction' can be understood. History and the unfolding of its meaning are thus intimately linked. Such a vision requires a *sceptical* or *mystical* attitude towards the possibilities of knowing and understanding social change.

Finally, it is important not to confuse historicism in the sense given to it by Popper (the search for historical laws) with what is called in the German tradition 'historism', and which is its opposite. Historism takes to its extreme limits the banal idea that 'culture' and its human institutions in all their forms (language, art, religion, law, State, etc.) are subject to perpetual change: in view of such flux the historian is obliged to study only concrete and singular phenomena, and to renounce all quests for structural regularities. Max Weber, who reacted violently against historism, also knew how to avoid the pitfalls of historicism.

Cycles, Determinism, Development, History and Sociology, Marx, Reproduction, Social Change, Teleology, Weber.

Bibliography

ALBERT, H., 'Theorie, Verstehen und Geschichte', in ALBERT, H., *Konstruktion und Kritik*, Hamburg, Hoffman & Campe, 1972, 1975, 195–220. – BERLIN, I., 'Historical inevitability', in BERLIN, I., *Four essays on liberty*, London, Oxford University Press, 1969, 51–81. reprinted in GARDINER, P. (ed.), *The philosophy of history*, Oxford, Oxford University Press, 1974, 161-186. – BOULDING, K.E., *Ecodynamics. A new theory of societal evolution*, London, Sage, 1978. – CAMPBELL, D.T., 'Variation and selective retention in socio-cultural evolution', *General systems*, XIV, 1969, 69–85. – GRAS, A., 'Le temps de l'évolution et l'air du temps', *Diogène, 108*, 1979, 68–94. – HABERMEHL, W., *Historizismus und kritischer Rationalismus*, Fribourg/Munich, Karl Alber, 1980. – HOBHOUSE, L. T., *Social development: its nature and conditions*, London, Allen & Unwin, 1924. – LENSKI, H., 'History and social change', *American journal of sociology*, LXXXII, *3*, 1976, 548–564. – LÉVY-BRUHL, L., *La mentalité primitive*, Paris, PUF, 1922; Paris Retz, 1976.

– MARSHALL, T.H., *Citizenship and social class, and other essays*, Cambridge, The University Press, 1950. – MARX, K., *The Communist Manifesto*, New York, Russell Russell, 1963. – MEINECKE, F., *Die Entstehung des Historismus*, Munich/Berlin, R. Oldenbourg, 1936, 2 vol. Trans, *Historism: the rise of a new historical outlook*, rev. ed. London, Routledge & Kegan Paul, 1972. – MORGAN, L., *Ancient society or researches in the lines of human progress from savagery through barbarism to civilization*, Chicago, Ken, 1877; Cambridge, The Belknap Press of Harvard University Press, 1964. – NAGEL, E., 'Determinism in history', *Philosophy and phenomenological research*, XX, 3, 1960, 291-317. Reprinted *in* GARDINER, P. (ed.), *The philosophy of history*, Oxford, Oxford University Press, 1974, 187–215. – NISBET, R., *History of the idea of progress*, New York, Basic Books, 1980. – SMELSER, N.J., *Social change in the industrial revolution. An application of theory to Lancashire cotton industry, 1770–1840*, London, Routledge & Kegan Paul, 1959, 1967. – SOROKIN, P.A., *Social and cultural dynamics*, New York, American Books, 1937–1941, 4 vol. Abridged version 1 vol., Boston, Extending Horizons Books, 1957; Boston, Porter Sargent, 1957, 1970. – SPENCER, H., *On social evolution. Selected writings*, Chicago, Chicago University Press, 1972. – TROELTSCH, E., *Der Historismus und seine Probleme. Erstes Buch: Das logische Problem der Geschichtsphilosophie*, Tübingen, J.C.B. Mohr, 1922. – WEBER, M., *Die 'Objectivität' sozialwissenschaftlicher und sozialpolitischer Erkenntnis*, Tübingen/Leipzig, J.C.B. Mohr, 1904. Reprinted *in* WEBER, M., *Gesammelte Aufsätze zur Wissenschaftslehre*, Tübingen, J.C.B. Mohr, 1922, 1968, 146–214.

History and Sociology

'The book I am now publishing is not a history of the Revolution . . . . It is a study of this Revolution', wrote de Tocqueville in the first lines of the preface to his *Ancien Régime*. And he continues: 'The French in 1789 made the greatest effort ever of any people, in order, as we might say, to cut in two their destiny, and to separate by an abyss what they had been until that time from what they would henceforth be.' But this effort did not provide the desired results. 'I had always thought that they had been much less successful in this singular enterprise than was believed outside, and that they would to begin with have believed themselves.' When de Tocqueville wrote that *L'Ancien Régime* is not a history but a study (more precisely, a *sociological* study), he means that his objective is not to analyse in the most precise fashion possible the complex series of events which together make up what we call the Revolution, but to answer one question: why did the Revolution, despite the intentions of the revolutionaries, lead to a society which in many of its forms, and in particular in its administrative centralization, was similar to that of the *Ancien Régime*?

History and sociology maintain a complex relationship made up of differences and similarities. In many cases it is difficult to make a rigorous distinction between studies from one discipline or the other. We should be suspicious of hard and fast distinctions. The proposition put forward here is that it is an exaggeration to assume that sociology is essentially a nomothetic science, seeking to uncover general laws, while history would be an essentially descriptive discipline. It is simplistic to see history as a science of the singular and sociology as a science of the general. Such broad distinctions may perhaps have didactic virtue. But they are too crude to describe the similarities and differences between sociology *as it is* and history *as it is*. Such crude distinctions do, however, have a practical and somewhat polemical function: they enable the sociologist to mark out a territory within frontiers which are all too often uncertain and contested. But if it is difficult to separate the two disciplines by clear differences, it is equally true that, from an ideal-typical perspective, they tend (contradicting the opinion of certain historians such as Braudel, who would deny any specificity to sociology) to be distinguished, from the viewpoint of methods and objectives, by a certain number of traits.

The *first* of these traits is that exemplified by de Tocqueville in the preface to *L'Ancien Régime et la Révolution*. Very frequently – if not always – a sociological research project begins by attempting to understand the reasons for a macrosociological phenomenon. Why, asks de Tocqueville, does the Revolution lead to the reproduction of a certain number of traits characteristic of *ancien régime* society? Why, asks Durkheim, do suicide rates appear to increase throughout the nineteenth century in all societies which have come to be known as industrial societies? Why, Durkheim also asks, does individualism tend to be a basic value of industrial societies? Why, asks Sombart at the beginning of the twentieth century, is there no socialism in the United States? Why does the process of diffusion often take the form of an S-curve? Why do the children of manual workers have less chance of entering higher education? Why have Germany and Japan experienced such spectacular development in the twentieth century? There would not be any problem in multiplying such examples many times over. It would be clear that the majority of sociological research is inspired by a question relating to a macrosociological phenomenon, such a phenomenon taking the form of a particular state of affairs (the USA is the only industrial society which has not experienced an important socialist movement in the twentieth century) or of a statistical regularity (growth of suicide rates, S-curve of diffusion), of an evolutionary tendency (growth of individualism) or developmental differences (why, asks de Tocqueville, has urbanization taken different forms in France and England?), of a reproductive tendency (why do certain underdeveloped countries continue to be characterized by high birth rates, which appear to be undesirable from both a personal and a societal point of view?). In short, *the sociologist is more likely than the historian to isolate this or that macrosociological phenomenon in the historical flux*, and to attempt to establish the reasons for its existence. De Tocqueville's work is paradigmatic in this respect. If his work on the *Ancien Régime* is, as he said himself, less a work of history than what has generally come to be seen as a work of sociology, it is mainly because he tried to answer a finite list of questions which can be simply stated: reasons for the persistence of French administrative centralization despite the Revolution, reasons for the differences between Britain and France in the rate of urbanization, in the development of agriculture, and in the production of intellectuals, for example.

The *second* trait which characterizes sociology – at an ideal-typical level – is its generalizing ambition. This ambition does not mean that sociology should be a nomothetic discipline, exclusively concerned with the establishment of general laws, analogous to those of physics, for example. The examples above indicate, on the contrary, that the sociologist may interest himself in or be interested by the analysis of *particular phenomena* (why has socialism not appeared in the USA? (Sombart), why were French political thinkers more radical than their English counterparts in the second half of the eighteenth century? (de Tocqueville)) or *particular subjects* (cf. the 'monographic' studies such as *Street Corner Society* by W.F. Whyte). The generalizing ambition of sociology *may* take the form of the search for general laws, but it does not necessarily take that form. In fact, it may take one of three distinct forms, the last being undoubtedly more fruitful than the others.

The Search for General Laws

Despite sociologists' declared intentions, it is not clear that this activity is in prac- tice either the most frequent or the most productive. A general law can be defined as a proposition with the form $y = f(x)$, more generally $y = f(x1, x2, etc.)$. Thus we are dealing with conditional propositions which can be more precisely set out as follows: if x is in the state S then y is ('always' or 'most often' according to whether it is a deterministic or probabilistic law) in the state T. Hence, according to Durkheim, suicide rates (y) are a function of anomie $(x1)$: an increase in anomie leads to an increase in the suicide rates. In the same way, the suicide rate (y) is a function of egotism $(x2)$. For Gurr, political violence (y) is a function of the level of relative frustration $(x1)$, beliefs $(x2)$ of individuals relative to the justice of their claims and to the usefulness of engaging in open rebellion, of the difference $(x3)$ between their capacities of coercion and organization and those of the authorities, as well as chance or random factors E: $y = f(x1, x2, x3, E)$. For Davies, the prob- ability of collective violence is a function of the relative frustration, which tends to reach a critical level when a long period of improvement is followed by a brief period of sharp recession. For de Tocqueville, 'it frequently happens that a people who put up without complaint with the most oppressive laws, violently reject them as soon as their load is slightly reduced'.

These examples show that it is not difficult to establish a list of sociological propositions which have the more or less classic form $y = f(x1, x2, etc.)$, to which the sociologist would give the widest generality. Noting the introduction of chance or random factors such as those referred to by Gurr, or de Tocqueville's prudent qualification ('frequently'), indicates that the law referred to is considered to be of a probabilistic form. These examples are borrowed from the fields of the sociology of suicide and of political mobilization. It would be possible to find numerous other examples in other fields, (sociology of crime, of education, of development, etc.). Thus the sociology of the development largely consists of the search for development 'factors' (x).

Much sociological research leads to propositions of the form $y = f(x)$. But the putative laws of sociology are most often valid only in specific situations, that is in given contexts or periods. Hence, Durkheim's law according to which suicide rates are a function of anomie and egotism appears to be 'verified' in the nineteenth century, but not in the twentieth. The development of variables that Durkheim considered to be indicators of anomie and egotism (divorce rates, relative import- ance of the professions, development of belief systems valuing the individual, etc.) would, if a general validity was accorded to Durkheim's law, lead to the expect- ation of an increase in suicide rates in the twentieth century. But this did not happen. The regular upward trends of the nineteenth century have been replaced by much more complex and nationally variable movements in suicide rates.

Similarly, looking at the 'laws' of political mobilization put forward by de Tocqueville, Gurr, and Davies, it is clear that they are not all true at the same time. In other words they are not general but applicable to particular contexts: *in certain cases but not all*, political violence occurs after a long period of improvement which is followed by a sudden and brief period of deterioration (Davies). In other cases, it accompanies a period of improvement encouraging an 'inflation' in the number of attempts to create change by comparison with what is possible (de Tocqueville, Durkheim). In other cases (cf. Hirschman's 'tunnel effect'), it accompanies a change when some members of society suddenly realize that their conditions are not improving at the same rate as others. As it is possible to multiply the number of examples, there can be no law of political mobilization of the form $y=f(x)$, even in the prudent (i.e., probabilistic) form used by de Tocqueville or Gurr. As Tilly has shown, it is not even possible to accord the status of law to the proposition that political violence is a function of discontent, which is extremely vague and capable of application to the most diverse set of circumstances. Statistical analysis of the cycles of political violence in France over a century does not show a significant correlation between political violence and the different indicators which can be used to measure social discontent, dissatisfaction, or relative frustration. On the contrary, the analysis shows that political violence appears in periods of political crisis and upheaval. As a result of the virtually tautological character of the two variables which are related, it would be difficult to confer the status of 'law' on this proposition. However lightweight this statistical result might appear to be, it is not without interest. It serves to reveal an important methodological proposition: it is not possible to establish a general law – non-tautological – about political violence, because its appearance depends upon a complex constellation of factors and circumstances which cannot be reduced to a formula of the type $f(x)$.

According to the structure of this constellation, a high level of 'frustration' could for example have a *mobilizing* effect, as the hypotheses of de Tocqueville, Davies, and Gurr would indicate. But it can also have a *demobilizing* effect, as seen in Lazarsfeld's study of unemployed workers in Marienthal, for example. To express the same proposition in another way: a law of the form $y = f(x)$ is in virtually every case of *local* rather than *general* application. The 'laws' of Durkheim and de Tocqueville are applicable to a plurality of situations. But they are not *generally* true. A considerable epistemological complication resides moreover in the fact that very often it is difficult to specify the exact conditions under which a sociological 'law' is valid. From this point of view, the sociologist is placed in a more uncomfortable position than the physicist who, when he establishes a *local* law, can also specify the conditions under which it is valid.

To conclude, it can be said that: 1) the ambition of sociologists to establish laws of the form $y = f(x)$ describes one of the particularities of sociology by comparison with history; 2) this ambition comes up against an obstacle: the *local* character of the laws thus established; 3) the local character of sociological 'laws', linked to the problems of specifying the conditions of validity, means that the proposition that sociology is distinguished from history by its *nomothetic* character must be modified.

The Search for Evolutionary Laws
This is one of the other ambitions of sociology, evident right through from Comte and Marx to contemporary sociology, by way of Durkheim and Spencer. It is illustrated, for example, in Durkheim's *The Division of Labour in Society*. In this case, the concept of law has a significance completely different from that of the section above. It is no longer the relation of two phenomena *x* and *y*. An evolutionary law is a statement indicating that a system is required to move through a series of conditions which can be determined in advance. Marx thought that the stages of British economic development of the eighteenth and nineteenth centuries prefigured the stages of development of all nations. Considerably later, Rostow took up a similar schema and showed that the processes of economic growth are required to go through a series of stages which may be shortened or prolonged according to the case, but whose order is presented as unchangeable and as begun by certain common factors which may vary only slightly from one situation to another. To simplify a little, the development of societies has an invariant character similar to the developmental invariants discovered by Piaget in the development of personality. In fact, it is possible to submit this second ambition of sociology – to establish the existence of evolutionary laws – to a similar form of critique to the first (although the concept of law does have a different meaning in the two cases). It is possible to observe evolutionary processes which are repeated in many different contexts. It is clear, for example, that the dairy industry has played a similar role in Danish economic development to that played by textile manufacture in the British case. It is equally true that *certain* causes never fail to have the same effects. Hence the organization of railway systems poses organizational and management problems which can be resolved only by highly differentiated large-scale enterprises (Chandler). As soon as a rail network is developed this type of enterprise will appear. But evolutionary 'laws', like the conditional 'laws' referred to above, are generally only of local application. The processes of economic development of Germany, Russia, and Japan at the end of the nineteenth century do not follow the same formula, and in no way follow a British model, in contradiction to the argument put forward by Marx. By the same token, if it is true that *in certain cases*, as Durkheim suggested, the extension of the division of labour is accompanied by the reinforcement of *individualistic* values, it is not always true in every case. We know better today that Parsons's famous evolutionary 'law', according to which modernization produced an inevitable 'nuclearization' of the family, is only true in certain contexts. In Japan, economic development appears to have occurred with the extended family rather than against it.

The local and partial character of the evolutionary 'laws' advanced by sociologists serves to emphasize the relativity of the trenchant distinction between sociology and history which many of the pioneers of the discipline wanted to make.

The Search for Structural Models
Sociology's ambitions to be a generalizing science often take a third form, perhaps the most productive: that of the search for what we call structural models. Rather than using an abstract definition to describe this concept, we will try to illustrate

and define it implicitly using several examples. Sombart, as we have seen, was, around 1900, inquiring as to the reasons for a particularity about America: alone among the industrial nations the USA had not experienced any significant socialist movement. Why? Briefly, Sombart's answer is as follows. For many decades the country had been a *frontier* nation; when an individual was unhappy with his social position, he could expect to seek another *elsewhere*. Given the structures and the attitudes which such structures induced, the *individual* strategy of defection, or *exit* as Hirschman described it, was the normal response of the individual to a situation which he judged to be unsatisfactory. The alternative to the *individual* strategy of defection is the *collective* strategy of protest (*voice* in Hirschman's terminology): if I am not satisfied with my position, I can take part in collective action which is intended to produce an improvement in the position of the group or category to which I belong. But when both types of strategy are equally practical, the collective strategy is generally more costly and uncertain than the individual strategy. Moreover its effects are often delayed. In order for a collective strategy to develop, it is necessary for each individual to see his individual strategy as impractical. Now socialism is essentially a legitimating ideology for collective strategies which are intended to improve the position of 'underprivileged' groups. So that it will be successful in finding an audience, socialism must show that for 'underprivileged' groups the individualistic strategies of social mobility are ineffective or impractical. Such was the case, according to Sombart, in countries such as France or Germany, which had only partly ridden themselves of a legal stratification system inherited from the Middle Ages. Such was not the case in the USA which had never experienced such a stratification system. Thus the particularity of the USA on this matter is explained by the fact that in the nineteenth century the 'yield' on the two types of strategy tended to be perceived differently by members of underprivileged groups in the USA and, for example, in France and Germany, this difference itself being the product of differences in the stratification systems of the countries concerned.

Sombart's analysis presents, from the epistemological viewpoint, a certain number of characteristics which are worthy of mention: 1) the sociologist is concerned to explain a particular fact; 2) the explanation takes the form of a model based on several simple propositions: a) an individual dissatisfied with his position has two types of strategy available to him; b) he tends to choose the one whose 'yield' appears better to him; c) the relative yield of the two strategies depends on the structures involved. Properly understood this model will explain a *particular* state of affairs such as the absence of socialism in the USA in the nineteenth century. But at the same time it also furnishes a *general* schema which can be applied to the analysis of numerous other particular phenomena on condition that they are properly understood in each case. Hence Hirschman noted that the absence of social movements in the north-east of Brazil during a long period in the history of that country is due in part to the fact that the peasants had a strategy of *exit* to the coastal sugar cane industry available to them. Another example is that the public secondary schools of the American East Coast appear more run down than those of the West Coast because the network of private schools is much denser, for historical reasons, in the East than the West, and provides the élites with the possibility of using an *exit* strategy. In France the *grandes écoles* serve to weaken many universities because they offer students from the élites the possibility of *exit*. The model of *exit/voice* was identified and described initially by Hirschman, but many other writers have used it implicitly.

The development of contemporary sociology's treatment of political violence – the other area referred to above – demonstrates a movement in research strategies: in recent work there is less concern with establishing laws than with outlining structural models. There is a tendency nowadays to counterpose the idea of a more or less direct relation between frustration and violence with a concept of violence as an emergent effect which can appear in certain types of structures of interaction: for violence to appear, there must be a 'market' of discontent available for exploitation. The wider is this market, the greater is the preparedness of certain sectors of its 'environment' (public opinion, political power, intellectuals) to understand the reasons for violence and to legitimate it by using the resources which are available. Whether there are entrepreneurs ready to inspire and guide collective action, the nature and quantity of resources available to these entrepreneurs, etc., will condition whether violence will appear, and in which forms. Such a general model, properly delimited, enabled Oberschall, for example, to explain the differences in form taken by Black civil rights movements in 1960s America. In the South the Protestant churches were more involved in the social tissue than in the North. They had a positive attitude towards black élites. Religious organizations represented an important source of legitimation for those entrepreneurs who wished to promote civil rights, as they sought collective strategies of action enabling them to conserve and use this precious source of resources; in order not to weaken their credit with the churches, they emphasized the importance of non-violent forms of action. In the northern states the entrepreneurs did not have the same resources available. Working in a looser social framework, being more isolated, their problem was to attract the attention of public opinion, of intellectuals, journalists, and politicians. In a situation where the structure was different, a different rationality was in operation. In the North, collective action took a violent form.

The examples cited above illustrate the third form of sociology's generalizing ambition. The construction of a structural model such as Hirschman's is clearly distinct from that of establishing either conditional general laws or evolutionary laws. It does not involve the search for regularities at the level of the phenomena themselves, but rather the schemas which are applicable, with certain appropriate modifications, to realities which may be highly differentiated from the phenomenal perspective (hence, at the level of appearances, there is little in common between the rejection of socialism in the USA and the weakness of certain French universities). That is why it is possible to describe these types of activities as *structural models*.

It is perhaps at this level that it will be possible to identify the true specificity of sociology in relation to history. The entity which is known as sociological theory can be shown without too much difficulty to be essentially composed of all the implicit or explicit structural models elaborated in the analysis of a wide range of phenomena. Even when the sociologist analyses a particular phenomenon (whether it is a delinquent gang, an historical episode, or a particular characteristic of a certain society), his or her objective is rarely to account for this object in its particularity but rather to interpret it as the particular realization of more general structures.

Determinism, Durkheim, Knowledge, Marx, Objectivity, Social Change, De Tocqueville.

Bibliography

BRAUDEL, F., *Ecrits sur l'Histoire*, Paris, Flammarion, 1969, 1977. – CHANDLER, A.D., *The visible hand, The managerial revolution in American business*, Cambridge, Harvard University Press, 1977. – DAVIES, J.-C., 'Toward a theory of revolution', *American sociological review*, XXVII, *1*, 1962, 5–19. – GURR, T.R., *Why men rebel*, Princeton, Princeton University Press, 1970. – HIRSCHMAN, A.O., *Exit, voice and loyalty, Responses to decline in firms, organizations and states*, Cambridge, Harvard University Press, 1970. – HIRSCHMAN, A.O. and ROTHSCHILD, M., 'The changing tolerance for income inequality in the course of economic development', *Quarterly journal of economics*, LXXXVII, *4*, 1973, 544–566. – JAHODA, M., LAZARSFELD, P.F., and ZEISEL, H., *Die Arbeitslosen von Marienthal; ein soziographischer Versuch über die Wirkungen langdauernder Arbeitslosigkeit. Mit einem Anhang: Zur Geschichte der soziographie*, Leipzig, S. Hirzel, 1933. Trans. *Marienthal; the sociography of an unemployed community*, Chicago, Aldine, 1971; London, Tavistock, 1972. – OBERSCHALL, A., *Social conflict and social movements*, Englewood Cliffs, Prentice Hall, 1973. – PIAGET, J., 'La situation des sciences de l'homme et le système des sciences', *in* Unesco, *Tendances principales de la recherche dans les sciences sociales et humaines*, Paris/La Haye, Mouton, 1970–1978, 3 vol., vol. I, *Sciences sociales*, 1–65. – SOMBART, W., *Warum gibt es in den Vereinigten Staaten keinen Sozialismus?*, Tübingen, J.C.B. Mohr, 1906. Trans *Why is there no socialism in the United States?*, London, Macmillan, 1976. – TILLY, C., TILLY, L., and TILLY, R., *The rebellious century 1830–1930*, Cambridge, Harvard University Press, 1975; London, Dent, 1975. – TILLY, C., *From mobilization to revolution*, London, Addison-Wesley, 1978.

I

Ideologies

The term ideology was coined by Destutt de Tracy at the end of the eighteenth century. He was aiming to define a science of mental phenomena, which he saw as the necessary corollary of the materialist philosophy of Holbach and Helvetius and the sensate philosophy of Condillac. Such a science should, in its author's view, provide a rational foundation to the critique of intellectual traditions which characterized the *Zeitgeist* of the second half of the eighteenth century. A famous reference by Napoleon to the '*idéologues*' (ideologists) of his time gave a pejorative sense to the term. For Marx the term refers to the 'false consciousness' which results from the class position of social actors: the reality of social relations appears deformed to them by virtue of their interests and more generally by the one-sided perspective to which they are condemned as a result of their position in the production system. Mannheim made Marx's viewpoint more systematic, and tried to avoid the uncertainty to which it led by developing the concept of the *freischwebende intelligentz* (the free-floating intelligentsia): according to Mannheim, intellectuals held a position which is essentially detached or 'floating' in respect of the different classes which make up what has come to be called the 'social structure'. Thus there is a guarantee in principle of the possibility of an objective viewpoint through which the realities of social relations, as well as the illusions of ideology and false consciousness, can be revealed. (It should be noted that Mannheim would progressively abandon this optimistic position developed in *Ideology and Utopia*.) With Lenin the concept of ideology returned to a more positive connotation: ideologies are part of the panoply of antagonisms of the class struggle. Lenin thus distanced himself from the Marxian use of the concept of ideology. For Marx, social theories developed by the proletariat – or more properly, in the name of the proletariat – bear the stamp of truth, whereas those of the bourgeoisie were held by him to be more typical of ideology and false consciousness. For Lenin, whose cynical point of view creates many fewer difficulties than that of Marx,

207

ideologies are the doctrinal weapons with which social classes arm themselves.

The multiplicity of meanings of the term ideology, and the difficulties created by the Marxian conception, explain why the concept is used relatively little outside the Marxist tradition of thought. It is rarely found in the work of Durkheim, Weber, or Pareto, for example. But, if the word is avoided by many sociologists, the issues covered by the obscure word are classically important to sociology.

In all social systems it is observable that social actors believe in the truth of certain propositions – and, as Pareto neatly observed, persist in attempting to 'prove' them through rhetorical devices – which are either normative propositions, and thus by definition unprovable, or positive propositions which are either incapable of proof, are unproven, or are false. These beliefs, which naturally vary from one social system to another and ultimately from one group of social actors to another within the same social system, are a phenomenon which can be observed in any society. They are often called values when they have a normative character. When values, or more usually beliefs, are integrated within a system whose elements are interconnected in a relatively fluid manner, they are described as *world views*. The term is more likely to be *religion* if the system includes notions of the sacred or transcendence. Ideology is used to describe a system of values, or more usually beliefs, which makes on the one hand no appeal to ideas of the sacred or transcendent, and on the other hand deals with some particular aspect of the political and social organization, of societies, or, more generally, of their destiny.

These considerations help us to understand why the classical sociologists avoided the concept of ideology. Ideologies are only a particular case which is difficult to distinguish with any rigour from the more general phenomenon of beliefs. In general terms the analysis and explanation of ideology are based on the same principles and are of the same nature as the analysis and explanation of other forms of belief. Thus Pareto's theory of derivations covers religious beliefs as well as ideologies. The same is true of Durkheim's theory in *The Elementary Forms of the Religious Life*. At the same time it is possible to see why the concept of ideology appeared in the Age of Enlightenment, and played a crucial role in the analysis of the social upheavals of the nineteenth century. The birth of 'modernity' was contemporaneous with a questioning of the traditional social order and the attempt to replace it with a 'rational' social order. That is why a multiplicity of social doctrines emerged at the end of the eighteenth and nineteenth centuries. These doctrines were a response to social demands of both diffuse and specific type (that is, coming from specific social groups) which resulted from the questioning of traditional social structure. They reflected the political passions of diverse social groups, and provided the raw material for the more or less coherent systems of 'ideas' – more precisely, of beliefs – which were ideologies.

But the distinction between ideologies and beliefs is, it is worth restating, more of degree than of substance. More precisely, ideologies are a species of the genus which is constituted by beliefs. It is thus necessary to introduce a number of considerations which concern the sociological interpretation of belief (see 'Beliefs'). As has been known since Durkheim, any action, whether it is the most ordinary individual action or collective action, implies support for normative propositions (in other words, values and norms). Such normative propositions result in certain cases from the existence of a system of social constraints: I know that if I adopt a certain type of behaviour (for example, criminal behaviour) I could get into serious trouble. But they are also very often the result of beliefs: even if there is no sanction which inclines me to prefer behaviour A to behaviour B, it may happen, and will in practice frequently happen, that I adopt A without hesitation, because I am convinced that A is preferable to B. Interests and beliefs are in most cases, moreover, indissoluble elements of action. Hence, it is not simply because of opportunist considerations but because of essential beliefs about basic egalitarian values that the governments of liberal societies have, since the Second World War, practised systematic policies of income redistribution. In a general sense, individual and collective action is guided by beliefs whose chance of influencing the social actor is greater the better adapted they are to his situation. Thus, unconditional belief in the virtue of egalitarianism has – as de Tocqueville suggested in *Democracy in America* – more chance of appearing well-founded, and as a result, of being expressed, in a context of prolonged economic growth than in a period of depression or recession. Belief in the myth of a class struggle has a greater chance of survival in a historical context where union power is perceived as illegitimate by many sectors of the population, than in a context where the main unions are generally considered to be the legitimate representatives of workers' interests.

But beliefs are not simply the normal ingredients of *Wertrationalität* (rational orientation to an absolute value), to use Weber's terminology. In other words they do not only contribute to determining the ends to which action is oriented. They also intervene at the level of the selection of means (cf. Weber's *Zweckrationalität*). If the actor has but a simple objective in mind, he may draw up a list of the means available to him to achieve it and choose that which is most effective and least costly. But such a rational schema stops being realistic as soon as the objective becomes more complex. In this case, the choice of means must often be analysed as the product or effect of beliefs. Consider the problem of reducing inflation or unemployment. Several 'theories' of unemployment or inflation may appear on the market and lead to conclusions about the effectiveness of a given range of policies. In most cases, an actor's support for one or other of these theories will be the result of his political convictions, that is, his beliefs or his particular *Weltanschauung*, at least as concerns his critical analysis of the theories in question. Hence, an actor with left-wing political sympathies will more readily support a theory linking inequality to inflation, with the former a cause of the latter, than an actor with the opposing sympathies. But his support is likely to be founded less on the intrinsic virtues of the theory, than on its emotional value. It matters little to him whether the upper classes generate, through a demonstration effect, over-consumption on the part of the other classes; he can only be impressed by the idea that inflation is the consequence of the vice of social inequality which he regards as so fundamental. By contrast an actor with right-wing sympathies, who considers inequalities as 'normal', will find it hard to accept that they may be the result of an undesirable phenomenon. The 'instinct of combination' (Pareto) would lead him to reject such a relationship. In short, then, as soon as objectives reach a certain level of complexity the 'choice' and the evaluation of means are generally not simply the product of rational evaluation, but equally, and in variable proportion according to case, the product of beliefs. To use Pareto's terminology, the evaluation of means is in part the product of 'sentiments', although these sentiments may be rationalized, for obvious reasons, in the form of 'derivations'. (The form of the 'derivation' has the great advantage of providing 'sentiments' with a pseudo-objective value and grounding. Thus I clearly have a greater chance of attracting attention and convincing if I try hard to demonstrate that inequality is the cause of inflation than if I stick merely to hostile outbursts against the one or the other.) Of course the exact mixture of beliefs and rational critique depends as much on the complexity of the objectives as on the experience, knowledge, and situation of the actor.

To summarize, the sociological theory of action has amply demonstrated that the objectives chosen by the actor and the means on which he relies are dependent, to varying degrees according to the case, on *beliefs*. Downs himself, who tried to apply the model of *economic man* to political phenomena, was not merely obliged to recognize but also showed that even the rational voter could not escape beliefs and ideologies. If he was to make a considered and informed choice between the political manifestos which were on offer to him, he would require access to the information on which such a choice could be made. Candidate A puts forward policy *a* and announces that it must lead to consequence *X*. Candidate B puts forward policy *b* and announces that it must lead to consequence *Y*. Even if the voter is certain that he prefers *X* to *Y* he cannot in any general sense be assured that *a* leads effectively to *X*. Only experience will tell. Since policies *a* and *b* cannot be carried out simultaneously if they are incompatible, the voter will find it difficult to determine, even a posteriori, which of the two policies is the best way to reach the desired goal of *X*. Unable to make a rational choice in the classic meaning of the term, the voter has an interest in supporting the party whose principles are closest to his own. Through a sort of paradox, the 'economic' (that is, 'rational') theory of democracy advanced by Downs leads to the conclusion that the voter will support the party whose 'sympathies' or ideology appear to be closest to his own 'sentiments' in Pareto's terms.

As a normal ingredient of action, beliefs tend, as one of Pareto's principal *leitmotiven* suggests, to be presented and experienced as objective truths rather than as subjective phenomena. The actor who wishes to persuade himself of the truth of his beliefs tends to accept at face value any 'theory' (any 'derivation' in Pareto's terms) which 'proves' their validity. This is why any belief carries with it the risk of intolerance. It is also why political opinions are rarely, in democratic societies, presented as or perceived to be opinions, but rather as truths which the adversary fails or refuses to see because he is prejudiced, blind, corrupt, or untrustworthy. Finally, it is why political opinions are generally based on theories which claim to be either proven or at least scientific, through the rhetorical processes analysed by Pareto and Perelman.

In the early 1960s a debate about the 'End of Ideology' thesis developed. Had the disbanding of the Fascist ideologies, the regular economic growth of western societies, not shown that societies could develop to the satisfaction of the majority of their populations more through calling on the services of their experts and using their technologies than by recourse to doctrinaire politicians and ideologies? Were we seeing the 'end of ideology'? Two observations can be made about this thesis: 1) experts could not replace prophets and technology evict ideology without value-consensus. If this was the case the expert could hope to define the most appropriate ways in which values could be realized; 2) but, as the previous analyses tend to show, even in this case it could only be a *pretension*: the uncertainty about which methods to use to realize collective ends when those ends are complex – as they generally are – is enough to ensure that ideologies are indispensable. It becomes very likely that the expert will be tempted to base his action and authority on 'derivations' or 'theories' to legitimate the 'scientific' routes to social reform which he advocates. Such theories will be addressed to a restricted audience, formulated in a language which is more sober, 'factual', and scientific than that used by the 'prophet'. But they are also based on a complex mixture of observations and beliefs. Using another expression of Pareto's, the theories which impress the expert are very likely to belong to the category of 'theories based on experience but which go beyond it'. The theories (current in the USA in the 1950s and in France in the 1960s) which saw the key to social consensus in the democratization of work relations are an example. They were based on observations and quasi-experiments carried out by scientific techniques. Their outcome was propositions which could be made without too much difficulty into legislative programmes rather than general plans for social reform. As a result they were likely to impress civil servants and politicians or, in more general terms, the 'decision-makers'. *Busing*, the policy which consisted of transporting children around so that each school would have the optimum social mix, in order to increase the chances of those from the lowest social groups, was put into operation on the basis of a famous study. This research project directed by Coleman had shown that the variable 'social composition of the class' was the only one which appeared to have significant effect on the educational achievement of children underprivileged by social or ethnic origin.

When 'common values' disintegrate or appear to be disintegrating, experts lose their monopolistic roles. The expert competes for his audience with another type of *intellectual* who, addressing himself to a wider public than the 'decision-makers', of either 'enlightened opinion' or 'popular majority', creates a different sort of 'product' made in a different way because of the needs of its 'market'. Ideology may thus appear more overtly. It is no longer a matter of proposing legislative programmes, but of the denunciation of the fundamentally dissolute character of social structures. Thus the side effects of economic growth helped to create at the end of the 1960s a return to social critique and a resurgence of overt ideology.

In short, the debate about the 'end of ideology' as well as history's comment upon it, showed the main function of ideologies: to offer – in the case of societies where the social order is of a *non-traditional* type – a justification for the values which are assumed to form the basis of consensus and social order. The existence of such a function makes the evolutionist thesis of an 'end of ideology', recurrent since Marx, quite doubtful. Perhaps even more doubtful is the idea that certain periods arc characterized by the relative absence of 'total ideologies' (Lipset). For, even in periods of 'consensus', when the intellectual and the prophet tend to find themselves less in demand than the expert, political action and decision-making are great consumers of ideology. Because it is less obvious does not imply that ideology is not present.

Beliefs, Knowledge, Marx, Rationality, Religion, Social Symbolism.

Bibliography

ARON, R., *L'opium des intellectuels*, Paris, Calmann-Lévy, 1955, 1968; Paris, Gallimard, 1968. – BELL, D., *The end of ideology. On the exhaustion of political ideas in the fifties*, New York, The Free Press, 1960, rev. ed 1965; London, Collier Macmillan, 1965. – CRANSTON, M. and MAIR, P. (ed.), *Ideology and politics – Idéologie et politique*, Brussels, Bruylant, 1980. – DOWNS, A., *An economic theory of democracy*, New York, Harper, 1957. – DUPRAT, G. (ed.), *Analyse de l'idéologie*, Paris, Galilée, 1980. – DURKHEIM, E., *The Elementary Forms of Religious Life* – GEERTZ, C., 'Ideology as a cultural system', *in* APTER, D.E. (ed.), *Ideology and discontent*, Glencoe, The Free Press, 1964, 47–76. – LIPSET, S.M., 'The end of ideology', *in* LIPSET, S.M., *Political man: the social bases of politics*, New York, Doubleday/London Heinemann, 1960, 1963, 439–456. – MANNHEIM, K., *Ideologie und Utopie*, Bonn, F. Cohen, 1929. Trans. *Ideology and utopia. An introduction to the sociology of knowledge*, New York, Harcourt Brace/London, Routledge & Kegan Paul, 1954. – MARX, K. and ENGELS, F., *Die deutsche Ideologie*, Vienna, Verlag für Literatur und Politik, 1932; Berlin, Dietz, 1953. Trans. *The German Ideology*, London, Lawrence & Wishart, 1968. – PARETO, V., *Traité.* – PERELMAN, C., *L'empire rhétorique. Rhétorique et argumentation*, Paris, Vrin, 1977. – PLAMENATZ, J., *Ideology*, London, Pall Mall, 1970. – SHILS, E., 'Ideology: the concept and function of Ideology', in *International Encyclopedia of the Social Sciences*, New York, The Macmillan Company and The Free Press, 1968, VII, 66–76.

K

Knowledge

The area of sociology called 'sociology of knowledge' is not a field of sociology, like the sociology of leisure or of education, for instance. It is more like a scientific programme, in Lakatos's sense, i.e., a set of questions and of methodological directions, aiming to study the social 'determinants' of knowledge and particularly of scientific knowledge. In a wider sense – so wide that the question could be asked of whether the field is still defined – the sociology of knowledge aims to place under its laws the 'determinants' of beliefs and of ideologies as well as those of knowledge. The programme's content and the description of its results will be looked at rather less closely than its nature, i.e., we will look mainly at the very notion of 'social determinants' of knowledge and at the way in which this 'determination' is interpreted. The post-Popperian epistemological debate will form the basis for this discussion: we believe that it permits us to clarify the essential question of 'determinants' of knowledge as posed by Durkheim.

Although the scientific programme of the sociology of knowledge was first established by Mannheim, it had already appeared in Durkheim's work in *The Elementary Forms of Religious Life*. The French sociologist put forward the thesis that some fundamental scientific concepts (like the concept of 'force') or some operative procedures (like those of classification) are a direct consequence of social experience. It is the social experience of moral prohibitions and of the sacred which would have given man the first concept of a force superior to that of the individual. The existence of social groups and their differentiations and hierarchies, would have suggested to man the notions of gender and species, and more generally the concept of logical order and classification. What Durkheim proposes is in fact a de-spiritualization and a socialization of the famous 'a priori' forms of understanding seen by Kant as the conditions for the possibility of knowledge. In more modern language, interrogating reality is only possible from within paradigms, without which experience can only be a 'rhapsody of sensations' (Kant). For Kant, these

213

paradigms are timeless data. For Durkheim, they are a consequence of social experience and vary according to what sociologists now call the evolution of social 'structures'. On this point, as on others, Durkheimian sociology can be attacked for its imperialism: there are no reasons why the immediate data of social experience should be the origin of logical categories, any more than psychic experience, for instance, should be taken as their origin.

If the postulates of Durkheimian sociology on knowledge are provided with rigorous conditions and limits for their validity, they remain acceptable. In the natural sciences, the appearance of an evolutionary paradigm can probably be understood only if it is linked to the social upheavals of the end of the eighteenth century and the beginning of the nineteenth century, and to the appearance of the ideology of progress which accompanies such upheavals. In the social sciences, Bentham's utilitarianism, the birth of political economy with Adam Smith and Ricardo are obviously linked to the development of industrial capitalism in England. However, two warnings, already implicit in Durkheim's own work, must immediately be added to these propositions: first, that 'collective' experience can only offer extremely vague directions to the activity of acquiring knowledge paradigms of the most general nature; second, that the intuitions of the sociology of knowledge must fit in with the pretensions to objectivity which go hand in hand with knowledge and act as a basis for it. Collective experience can suggest the paradigm 'P' or some elements of P (using Durkheim's example again, the concept of *force*). Within the paradigm P are formulated theories T, T^1, etc. These theories may be incompatible. T and T^1 might explain a disjointed set of facts but fail to explain other disjointed sets of facts. In such a case, it will not be possible to decide between the two incompatible theories T and T^1. Neither one nor the other will be held unconditionally true. In spite of this, T and T^1 can matter to the scientific community only if one or the other be credible in terms of their objectivity (because they report on a set of experimental data). It is not because the exactitude of one theory cannot be proved that it has to be the mere product of social factors. In other words, the fact that knowledge depends on 'social structures' is never enough to define either the content of specific theories or the validity or the degree of credibility of these theories.

The debate started by Durkheim began again in the 1960s (although Durkheim's name was not directly mentioned), as an epistemological-sociological confrontation between Popper, Kuhn, Lakatos, and Feyerabend, which can only be roughly summarized here. For Popper, scientific knowledge advances only through an 'internal' logic: a theory T appears incompatible with experimental data. This falsification entices the scientist to create a theory T^1 capable of explaining those data already explained by T as well as those *incompatible* with T. The Popperian theory of scientific discovery is almost completely a-sociological, although quite complex: the scientist's activity is explained exclusively by the rules of the scientific game. Kuhn and following him, Feyerabend and in some ways Lakatos, with their use of a 'theory of scientific revolution', bring sociology into the debate. The scientific community corresponding to a discipline works 'normally' (i.e., Kuhn's 'normal science') with paradigms (Kuhn) or programmes (Lakatos), which are, in the ideal situation, the objects of consensus and a collective belief among the scientific community in their fecundity and validity. Let us suppose that new experimental data are found which are incompatible with the paradigm. According to Popper, such a case questions the validity of the paradigm. According to Kuhn and Lakatos, it is a far more complicated process: first, because the lack of compatibility between data and theory could be an ambiguous notion. Let us suppose (Lakatos would interpret it) that a physician of the Newtonian era discovers that the trajectory plotted for a given planet changes when a theory T is applied. T can, however, be retained by adding a causal hypothesis: the change could occur because of the existence of an unknown planet. However the astronomer, brought in to verify this hypothesis, does not find a planet. It could be because the planet is too small. A stronger telescope is built to test the new hypothesis. Still no planet. Is it sufficient to discard T? No, it could be that cosmic dust hides the planet. A satellite is launched to test the new hypothesis; no cosmic dust. It could be that the satellite's recording equipment was disturbed by a magnetic field, etc. In short, it could take years, centuries, for a 'fact' to appear which justifies a rejection of T. Many other reasons could prevent the Popperian process of 'refutation' or 'falsification' coming into operation in a mechanical fashion. A scientific community can work only in the context of one or several paradigms. Without a paradigm, it is, for instance, impossible to decide on which observations or experiments are pertinent. For T to be rejected, not only must T's credibility be reduced by the accumulation of non-compatible data, and this incompatibility must be accepted, but there must also be a candidate T^1 better placed than T. Even if all these conditions are fulfilled, it does not automatically mean that T^1 simply takes T's place: many scientists have a personal interest in retaining of T. In other words they have to consider the costs of 'taking T away' and 'bringing T^1 in' which will vary according to the case and are complex and multi-dimensional (i.e., the learning of a new scientific language, leaving behind a familiar representation of the world, the obsolescence of published works, etc.). So, the odds are that many will attempt to keep T alive by attempting to reduce the incompatibilities between T and T^1 using random hypotheses whose verification (or rejection) could take a long time. Because there are interests linked to social position, Feuer's theory, according to which scientific progress often goes through a generational conflict, seems to fit: clearly the costs of rejecting and bringing in T^1 are lower for a young scientist, for structural reasons, than for a 'recognized' one. The costs are minimal when a scientist is both young and marginal in relation to the existing scientific institutions, as in Einstein's case – the starting point of Feuer's theory – when he developed the theory of relativity.

The work of Kuhn, Lakatos, and Feuer uses more examples from the history of science than Popper whose sources are more in the realm of a priorist epistemology. They give a more realistic account of development of scientific knowledge. More precisely, they provide a general theory which includes the Popperian theory as an extreme, pure, and special case. These works sometimes run the risk of an over-sociological conception of knowledge, a risk avoided by Kuhn, Lakatos, Feyerabend, and Feuer, but not by some of their followers. Pushing some of Kuhn's and Lakatos's remarks to the limit, it could be tempting to conclude that the belief in a paradigm is not the result of objective 'interest' (a loose term is here purposely chosen) but an act of faith and that this act of faith is itself determined by 'social factors'.

If we suppose that D and D^1 are two sets of experimental data such that D is not part of D^1 and D^1 not a part of D, it would be impossible to decide in many cases between two theories T and T^1, one of them explaining D but D^1 with difficulty and vice versa (cf. Feyerabend's notion of 'incommensurable' theories). Is it not irrational to believe in T or T^1 given these two difficulties and is this irrationality itself explained in the end by 'social factors'? Going a step further, it could be tempting to erase completely the difference between scientific theory and ideology and to see in scientific conflicts oppositions which would be 'deeply' and 'in the last analysis' ideological, religious, or political. Only Feyerabend seems to suggest this step forward, but by continually referring to the intelligent reader's critical sense. He does not in fact deny the base of science's pretension to objectivity. Although 'incommensurable' theories are often found, it does not follow that scientific theory is culturally arbitrary. If theories are maintained through the actions of social actors, it does not mean that the validity of theories is reduced to what Pareto would have called – talking about ideologies – their 'social useful-ness'. If beliefs, *Weltanschauungen*, and ideologies are an inspiration in the production of paradigms and theories, this does not mean that scientific theories can simply be treated as ideologies. The methodological anarchy argued for by Feyerabend was only an attempt to reduce the slowing down effect that social factors and more specifically scientific organizations can generate on the production of new theories or paradigms. The purpose is to 'free' the scientist from the institutions' grip not simply in order to improve the 'quality of life' in laboratories but to increase the scientist's activity and his inventiveness. Feyerabend's methodological anarchy therefore implies a belief in scientific objectivity. It must be said again that this belief is not incompatible with the fact that, here and now, it could be impossible to decide between T, T^1, T^2, and that eventually the choice made by a scientist in favour of a particular theory would be influenced by his interests, or by the compatibility that he thinks he finds between this theory and his religious beliefs.

Thus, what could be called historical epistemology, but can also be termed sociology of knowledge or sociology of science (such as the epistemological concepts, of Kuhn, Lakatos, Feyerabend, or Feuer, impregnated with historical or sociological considerations), is no doubt an important area of research. It completes a more classical tradition, started by Merton and represented by works such as Ben David's, questioning in particular the social conditions of the institutionalization of modern science and the differentiation process of scientific institutions (cf. Lécuyer's excellent review article which gives a complete and detailed picture of the results of the sociology of science, as it developed from Merton's famous thesis on the relationship between puritanism and the development of the sciences in eighteenth-century England). Historical epistemology is different because it endeavours to consider simultaneously the epistemological, historical, and social aspects of the development of scientific knowledge. It completes – and

perhaps amends – the traditional sociology of science and the sociology of knowledge, which sometimes tend to disregard epistemological aspects of the production of knowledge so as to emphasize the relationship between social factors and
modes of knowledge.

Arguments about what is called here historical epistemology are almost exclusively limited to the natural sciences. The case of the human and social sciences is
only referred to in a very marginal way by Kuhn, Lakatos, or Feyerabend.
However it could be argued that debates about historical epistemology could be a
source of inspiration for the sociology of knowledge in the field of the social
sciences. The debate might even suggest that differences between natural and
social sciences are not as strong as is frequently asserted. When de Tocqueville
attempts to explain why French agriculture is less advanced than English agriculture at the end of the eighteenth century, why French intellectuals, unlike their
English counterparts, enjoy abstract thinking so much, why France has so many
more small towns than England, and when he explains these differences by
administrative concentration in France, he is clearly inspired by 'irrational' beliefs
and preferences, in short, by values. His admiration for the Anglo-Saxon world is
incontestable. His admiration could be partly explained by his biography, even
by his class position. But de Tocqueville's theory would not have lasted so long if it
had been just the expression of a belief. Its survival is due to its 'fecundity', to its
explanatory power, i.e., it accounts for a large number of observed data concerning
the differences between France and England, with the help of premises which are
considered widely to be acceptable. In the same way, Durkheim would not have
started the research which led him to *Suicide* if he had not been preoccupied with
the idea – perhaps ideological – of the integration of individuals within society.
But this preoccupation alone could not have ensured the survival of the work. If
Suicide has become a classic, it is because it allows us to explain a considerable
range of data on suicide here again with the help of plausible premises. In the
social sciences as in the natural sciences, ideologies, beliefs, and values are indispensable ingredients of research.

Institutions and social structures watch over the birth and the fall of paradigms
as well as over the conflicts between paradigms and theories. In the sociology of
development (see 'Development'), it is clear that theories which were famous in
their times, like the theory of demonstration affect or the theory of the vicious
circle of poverty, became accepted because: 1) notions of development and underdevelopment had at that time considerable political influence; 2) economists
played a major role in the institutions in charge of analysing and promoting
development. Today these theories are widely contested. A scientific revolution of
the Kuhnian type has eroded their credibility. Why? For complex reasons and
because of complex processes (Kuhn's revolutionary processes are always
complex), but mainly because these theories were not compatible with irrefutable
factual data: how is it possible for instance to reconcile the theory of the vicious
circle of poverty with the fact that several countries, like Japan in the nineteenth
century or Colombia in the twentieth century, among many examples, experienced considerable development despite the fact that their relations with the

outside world had been extremely limited? Those who contributed to the fall of the 'economistic' theory of development could have been motivated either (as Max Weber puts it) by a *Gesinnungsethik*, or ethic of conviction, or by an ethic of responsibility, or *Verantwortungsethik*, which is implicit in the role of a scientist or a research assistant. Their main motivation in that case might even have been to break the economists' monopoly on the subject of development. But such 'social factors' cannot be used to reduce the debate to a fight where the strongest wins. It is not because they were stronger that the theory's critics won. After some time, they were seen as the strongest because they were right. This is why 'theories' of a neo-Marxist inspiration, like that of Habermas, pretending to introduce a simple link between cause and effects, interests and knowledge (see 'Objectivity'), must be looked at with great care. Pareto had in this case put forward a much more subtle and more productive theory. For him, 'social unity' and the 'truth' of a theory are two essential qualities. They have complex and possibly contradictory relationships with each other. But on no account must they be seen as the same thing.

These considerations have shown that it is not always easy to prove that one theory should be preferred over another, or that when a proof is found it generates automatic consensus. In the natural sciences, and even more so in the social sciences, the choice between incompatible theories can be difficult, even at some stages impossible. But if we take such propositions to confirm the radical generalization that scientific theories only reflect social bargaining, the possibility of any distinction between science, ideology, and fantasy is taken away from us.

Beliefs, Determinism, Ideologies, Objectivity, Prediction, Theory.

Bibliography

BEN-DAVID, J. and ZLOCZOWER, A., 'Universities and academic systems in modern societies', *Archives européennes de sociologie*, III, *1*, 1962, 45–84. – FEUER, L.S., *Einstein and the generations of science*, New York, Basic Books, 1974. – FEYERABEND, P., *Against method. Outline of an anarchistic theory of knowledge*, London, NLB, 1975, 1976. – HABERMAS, J., *Erkenntnis und Interesse; mit einem neuen Nachwort*, Frankfurt, Suhrkamp, 1968, 1973. Trans. *Knowledge & Human Interests*, London, Heinemann, 1972. *Technik und Wissenschaft als Ideologie*, Frankfurt, Suhrkamp, 1968. *Towards a Rational Society*, London, Heinemann, 1969. – KUHN, T.S., *The structure of scientific revolutions*, Chicago, University of Chicago Press, 1962, 1970. – LAKATOS, I. and MUSGRAVE, A. (ed.), *Criticism and the growth of knowledge*, London, Cambridge University Press, 1970. – LÉCUYER, B.P., 'Bilan et perspectives de la sociologie de la science dans les pays occidentaux', *Archives européennes de sociologie*, XIX, 2, 1978, 257–336. – LEMAINE, G. and MATALON, B., 'La lutte pour la vie dans la cité scientifique', *Revue française de sociologie*, X, *2,* 1969, 139–165. – MANNHEIM, K., *Essays on the sociology of knowledge*, London, Routledge & Kegan Paul, 1952, 1964; *Ideologie und Utopie*, Bonn, F. Cohen, 1929. Trans. *Ideology and utopia. An introduction to the sociology of knowledge*, New York, Harcourt, Brace/London Routledge & Kegan Paul, 1954. – MERTON, R.K., *Science, technology and society in seventeenth century England*, New York, Howard Fertig, 1970. – MERTON, R.K. (ed.), *The sociology of science: theoretical and empirical investigations*, Chicago/London, University of Chicago Press, 1973. – MERTON, R.K., 'Sociology of knowledge', *in* GURVITCH, G. and MOORE, W.E. (ed), *Twentieth century sociology*, New York, Philosophical Library, 1945, 366–405. – POPPER, K.R., *Logik der Forschung*, Vienna, Julius Springer, 1935. (Trans) *The logic of scientific discovery*, New York, Harper, 1959. Payot, 1973; London, Hutchinson, 1968.

M

Machiavelli, Niccolò

Machiavelli (1469–1527) is the man of 'politics first of all'. But he did not seek to elucidate or found this primary object upon philosophical arguments. He did not bother with the reflections of Aristotle on the relationship between the good life and the political life. He no more saw in the city the only framework within which human activity can find its complete blossoming than he anticipated the developments of Hobbes, who sees in the State the only insurance against the risk of dog eating dog universally. Nowhere does he evoke the war of all against all, to which men would be condemned if they were not protected against their murderous impulses by the effective arbitration of political authorities. He is as indifferent to the views of Aristotle as he is to those of Hobbes.

What interests Machiavelli is less the city than the 'government' of the city. It is not the political phenomenon in 'general' which holds his attention. Even if he accords historical comparison a very great significance, his information remains limited. In no way has it the amplitude of that of Aristotle or of Montesquieu. There is hardly a society known in his time to which the latter does not make allusion: England, Spain, Germany, Italy, but also Turkey, China, and Persia. As for Machiavelli, he is interested in the Italy of the Medicis, the Borgias, and of Julius II. Rome, as he finds it in the history related in Livy, constitutes the other pole of his reflection. But it is not all of Roman history taken in its successive double movement of grandeur and decadence which holds his attention. He concentrates on the republican phase of Rome. Montesquieu envisages all its aspects, all the connections under which political events can present themselves to the observer: civil legislation, penal (code), constitution, finances, commerce, religion, currency. Machiavelli's field of interest is extremely restricted. He speaks with hauteur of his indifference with regard to the economy, his contempt for those who weave wool or cotton, for traders and bankers. He concentrates his reflections upon politics, war and diplomacy, that is to say on the art of governing the State.

The success or failure of such enterprises depends upon calculation, ruses, the mastery of oneself. It is their 'strategic' character which holds Machiavelli; it is thus 'action' as a combination of means and of ends which he sets out to study. He asks himself questions about effective action, that which aims for the success of the actor. But it would be to misinterpret Machiavelli to see in him only the inheritor of Callicles or of Alcibiades. The success or failure which counts for him is not that of an individual, of his vanity, or of his '*libido dominandi*'. It is the success of the enterprise to which that man has decided to sacrifice everything. Cesare Borgia had only one ambition, that of founding a State.

Because he claims to illuminate the sense and the conditions of such enterprises, Machiavelli is a theoretician of strategic action. Even this would be to say too much: Machiavelli limits his field to political strategy and in two types of situations. One broadly corresponds to what one might call the situation of normal legitimacy. This is described in the *Discourse on the First Decade of Livy*. The second concerns the institution of a new aristocracy or legitimacy. This is dealt with in *The Prince*. For Machiavelli, political action is strategic; it aims not at the narcissistic satisfaction of the actor but the creation or the consolidation of States.

In fact, Machiavelli envisages these two situations in a single frame: that of the national State. *The Prince* is dedicated to the study of the conditions which, thanks to the creation of a national Italian State, would permit the driving out from the peninsula of all foreigners, Swiss, French, Spanish. In the *Discourse*, Machiavelli asks himself why the Roman Republic before the civil wars benefited from an exceptional cohesion and good citizenship. Neither the Roman Empire – except during the period of the Antonys – nor even less the Germanic Holy Roman Empire, despite their size and weight, inspired respect in Machiavelli. He is indifferent to the dream of an universal State which, finally, did not seem to him a more adequate political organization than the ancient or medieval city.

Of what nature are the resources of politics to reach their ends? They are remarkably constant throughout the ages. There is a *homo politicus* whose attributes have a sort of universality. This is why Machiavelli is justified in comparing the conduct of the heroes of antiquity with those of his contemporaries. Political maxims constitute the treasure or the wisdom of nations. But the constancy and universality of these maxims do not depend only on the existence of a common basis of human passions, but also on the premise that the political institutions which ruled the Rome of Scipio and Florence before the Medicis contain a definition of the totality of the constraints to which governments are subjected.

The universality of maxims of political prudence depends on all societies being heterogeneous and conflictual. 'In every Republic, there are two parties, that of the men in high places and that of the people; and all the laws which are favourable to liberty are born only because of their opposition' (*First Decade*, I, 4, Paris, Pleiade, 1958, p. 390). Machiavelli is a pluralist. One finds no trace in him of the conception according to which political societies with a strong consensus are closed communities with little to differentiate between them. The republican Rome of Scipio, where public spiritedness was so strong, did not owe the success of its government in the war against Carthage to some unknown Franciscan purity of standards. It is to be credited to the wise ordering of its political institutions, to the mixed regime which combines aristocratic principles and popular principles. In this respect, Machiavelli continues in the vein of Polybius and anticipates the Montesquieu of the *Considerations*. 'Globally', popular power and aristocratic power are mutually limiting. Besides, each power is differentiated. Aristocratic power does not reside only in the Senate. It is incarnated in the dictator or in consuls. An analogous differentiation is observable in popular power which is simultaneously initiative (the electoral meetings) and capable of veto (the tribunals). The regulation of the political system does not proceed from the action of a single organ or of a single magistrature. It is a consequence of diffuse and unforeseen effects.

The functioning of mixed or moderate regimes rests on counterweights. But these mechanisms do not cause compensations which necessarily assure the balance of the system and its perpetuation to arise. Those regimes which are submitted to multiple regulation are far from being self-regulated. They can become corrupt (but also mend their ways). Above all, they can be submitted to intelligent intervention. To a large extent, political wisdom consists of the installation of conditions in which political interventions are possible and effective. The Machiavellian conception of political action has its place both in institutional regularity and in individual initiative.

The creation of new states is the act of princes such as Cesare Borgia who, despite the appreciable advantage of being the son of a pope, had to build his principality with his own hands. Nevertheless, if the initiative of an individual is necessary, it is not enough. It is not sufficient for the prince to want to succeed, he must also understand and master the constraints to which his willpower is submitted. It is not sufficient to undertake, to want, and to know. It is also necessary that 'Fortune' crowns the enterprises of the prince. This is what Machiavelli emphasizes in chapter VIII where, after having analysed the strategy of Cesare Borgia, he concludes that the Duke of Valentinois, irreproachable for the wisdom of his schemes and the justness of his decisions, finally failed, not at all by his own fault but because of the premature death of the Pope his father and his own illness.

Fortune limits the strategic capacity of the politician. But he is submitted to other constraints as well as those of chance. He must take into account the strategy of other men who may surpass him in skill and in perspicacity. One finds hardly any trace of élitist romanticism in Machiavelli. The opposition of the mass/élite is implicit, but Machiavelli does not give value to princes in order to devalue the people, to the aristocratic chiefs to depreciate the popular chiefs. There are weak and stupid hereditary princes. There are people who aspire to the princedom from greed or from vanity. There are peoples, such as that of republican Rome, who, taken together, are devoted to the common good, that is to say to the State, its grandeur and health.

Machiavelli is often the synonym not only of realism but of cynicism. Is this assessment well founded? There is no doubt that Machiavelli's maxims are blunt. 'For a prince, it is much safer to make himself feared than liked' (*The Prince*, chapter XVII). Next Machiavelli praises 'the inhuman cruelty of Hannibal, which together with his infinite virtues always rendered him venerable and terrible in the eyes of his soldiers' (ibid.). What Machiavelli recommends to a prince is first of all to acquire a means of dissuasion. He must make himself feared, as this will assure him two happy results: the fear which he inspires will give weight to his proposals, and in particular to his threats. It will lead his enemies to think twice before crossing swords with him. In the well-known conclusion of the process of dissuasion called the 'show down' the player who inspires fear will have an inestimable advantage. At the end of the 'game of the iron arm' (the equivalent in American would be without doubt playing 'chicken'), his adversaries, for the very reason of the fear he inspires, hesitate to challenge him to carry out his threats. Thus the players can spare themselves the proof of strength with all its risks not only for the weak but also for the strong.

Machiavelli does not consider the 'friendship' (or popularity) that a prince has known how to gain among the people, or among other princes, as a very solid resource. A popular prince will be acclaimed by his subjects. Foreigners will applaud him. But he should not take all these protestations of support, of friendship, or of admiration at face value. 'Men are . . . changeable, afraid of danger, avid to gain' (ibid.). Positive feelings of attraction are not sufficient to guarantee the length of the engagement.

The power of a prince is not founded on the love of his subjects but on the fear which he comes to inspire in them. But if it is advantageous for a prince to be feared, if it is hazardous to count on the friendship of subjects, it can be fatal to be hated, which will be the infallible result if the prince 'takes the possessions and riches of his citizens and subjects – and their wives' (ibid.). Machiavelli, who is so in favour of cowardice, does not exaggerate the advantages that it confers on a prince. Citizens or subjects, however self-centred, may prefer death or the risk of death to a life where they will be despoiled of their riches and humiliated in their homes. The famous *'propter vitam causam vivendi perdere'* defines a bottom line of which it is dangerous for a prince to be unaware. Machiavelli is not at all inclined to explain the vigour of resistance to oppression in terms of intensity of idealism. He imputes it to the attachment, as it were instinctive, of men to their patrimony, to their wives, and to their children. In modern style one would say that the 'civil society' (understood in the sense of Hegel), that is to say the ensemble not only of economic activities but also of domestic activities, constitutes the private sphere within which the prince is well advised not to seek to sow trouble.

Machiavelli's prince is not a tyrant. Not only does he not use his power for egotistical ends, but he recognizes as natural, and consequently legitimate, the limits of his own power. Besides, the Machiavellian conception is as foreign to the modern conception and practice of totalitarianism as it is to the ancient conception of tyranny. One may distinguish the Greek or Sicilian tyrants from the modern tyrants (Hitler or Stalin) by the preponderant place held in the second example by ideological control. The moderns do not merely want to be obeyed. In turning more or less absurd catechisms into dogmas, they claim to subdue the spirit of their subjects. The prince of Machiavelli has no such ambitions. It is true that he may consider it useful to lie. A complete blackguard like Pope Alexander VI, 'who did nothing but cheat everyone' (chapter XVIII), took on engagements that he knew he would not honour. But he was careful enough to produce only plausible lies. Thus, this cynic anticipated the highly moral Abraham Lincoln, according to whom one can lie some of the time to everybody, or for a long time to some people, but certainly not for a long time to everyone.

The capacity of rulers to 'cheat' their subjects is limited by the credulity of those they rule, which is not infinite. But the resources of a prince when he seeks to abuse the people or other princes is not restricted to what nowadays we would call propaganda. Rulers can also count on religion, 'so useful for commanding armies, to comfort the people, to support good people and embarrass bad people' (*Discourse* I, chapter II). The 'utility' of religion is to be found when, in leaning on its maxims, rulers acquire a prestige which gives lustre to their power. Thus they increase their chances of being obeyed and they can obtain the obedience of those they govern without having to seek to make themselves feared by them. This substitution which, among the resources of rulers, replaces fear by respect is advantageous because it dispenses with the necessity for the rulers to have recourse to force, with all its attendant dangers.

Machiavelli never reduced power to force. 'The prince may govern by law or by force' (chapter XVIII). And he adds that if 'the first is appropriate to men, the second is appropriate to animals', in order to clarify that 'since very often laws are insufficient, it is necessary to have recourse to force'. Thus are underlined at the same time the heterogeneousness of the resources at the disposition of rulers and the ultimate nature of recourse to force, which constitutes absolutely the last authority of politics. But force itself may assume two aspects. It is violence, but it is also guile. 'Since a prince must know how to use animals well, he must choose from them the fox and the lion . . . . He must be a fox in order to know the snares, and a lion to stand up to the wolves.'

Force is a mixture of violence and cunning. It therefore implies moderation. Machiavellian politics are no more extremist than they are totalitarian. In interior order, it in fact reposes upon that which, with Augustin Renaudet, one might call a 'constitutional pact', by which certain rights are recognized as owed to the subjects, such as liberty and the right to own property. Is Machiavelli a theoretician of moderate regimes, a precursor of Montesquieu? Like Montesquieu he has a strong feeling of the complexity of political organizations. Montesquieu, obsessed by the fear of despotism, hoped that thanks to political art 'power stops power'. Machiavelli is inclined to think that it is the very distribution of the resources and the interests of the State which contributes to this braking or this tying up. While for Montesquieu 'moderation' depends essentially on the liberty of private individuals being recognized as the principle of free regimes, for Machiavelli it is by reference to the effectiveness and stability of the State that mixed regimes must be assessed.

In the exterior order, Machiavelli certainly breaks with the medieval concepts which sought to subordinate temporal powers to ecclesiastical authority. But he appeared to be in no way susceptible to the claims of a possible empire or universal state. Even if it seemed to him absurd to imagine obligations of a strictly contractual type between states, he does not judge it unreasonable to imagine a balance between the competing pretensions of princes.

The 'disarmed prophets' are promised failure. The founders of the city are recruited from among the 'armed prophets'. Those to whom it falls to conserve and transmit the work of the founders can to a certain extent count upon the authority of traditions. Even when they lean on respected customs and laws, states, like all human things, are menaced with corruption. In order to maintain cohesion and discipline among the governed, the rulers must master the centrifugal forces and, if possible, make them work towards political reinforcement; to achieve this rulers need discernment, courage, and a sense of opportunity. Politics is thus an art requiring the intelligent intervention of the prince, the legislator, or the magistrate. This art is even more delicate because political matter, with which the prince learns to make constraints for others and resources for himself, is composed of heterogeneous ingredients. In every case, whether the Florence of the Medicis or the Rome of the Scipios, what defines the specificity of political action is the place held by force in its various combinations. Ultimately, what defines politics is the ability to perceive the relationships of force and above all the ability to understand that the relationships of force are also the relationships of will.

Machiavelli seized the specificity of politics, which he detached from theology, from ethics, and from philosophy. One might almost say that *homo machiavelicus* is no more than the substratum to which are attached a certain number of attributes thanks to which we can evaluate the strategic behaviour made into objectives by the pursuit of the common good. The ambiguity of 'virtue' according to Machiavelli comes from the ambiguity of this common good. Is *homo machiavelicus* good? Is he bad? Certainly, he is not an egotist. He is only worth that which 'the common good,' to which he sacrifices himself or to which he is sacrificed by the prince, is worth. Machiavelli is not content only to separate politics from other logics and domains of social action. He also tends towards *autonomization*, that is to say towards removing it from the judgement of other authorities. Can one define the common good exclusively in political terms? Can the *'raison d' Etat'* constitute the supreme or even unique criterion of life in society? Machiavelli does not provide a clear answer to these questions, which he affects not even to ask.

Action, Action (collective), Democracy, Power, Prophetism, State.

Bibliography

MACHIAVELLI, N., *Il Principe* (1513), *Discorsi spora la Prima Deca di Tito Livio* (1513–1520), *Dell'arte della guerra* (1521), in *Tutte le opere di Niccolò Machiavelli*, text: est. by F. FLORA and C. CORDIE, Milan, Mondadori, 1949–1950, *The Prince*, London, Dent 1958. – BENOIST, C., *Machiavel*, Paris, Plon, 1907, 1937. – CASSIRER, E., *The myth of the state*, New Haven, Yale University Press, 1946, 1966. – GRAMSCI, A., 'Note sul Machiavelli, sulla politica e sullo stato moderno', in *Opere* di Antonio Gramsci, Turin, Einaudi, 1947–1966, 9 vol., t. 5. – GUILLEMAIN, B., *Machiavel. L'anthropologie politique*, Geneva, Droz, 1977. – LEFORT, C., *Le travail de l'œuvre: Machiavel*, Paris, Gallimard, 1972. – MEINECKE, F., *Die Idee der Staatsräson in der neueren Geschichte*, Berlin, R. Oldenbourg, 1925. – MESNARD, P., *L'essor de la philosophie politique au XVI° siècle*, Paris, Boivin, 1936; Paris, Vrin, 1969. – MOUNIN, G., *Machiavel*, Paris, Club Français du Livre, 1958. – NAMER, G., *Machiavel ou les origines de la sociologie de la connaissance*, Paris, PUF, 1979. – RENAUDET, A., *Machiavel: étude d'histoire des doctrines politiques*, Paris, Gallimard, 1942; revised edn,

1956. – RITTER, G., *Die Dämonie der Macht; Betrachtungen über Geschichte und Wesen des Macht-problems im politischen Denken der Neuzeit*, Stuttgart, H.F.C. Hannsmann, 1947. – STRAUSS, L., *Thoughts on Machiavelli*, Glencoe, The Free Press, 1958.

Marx, Karl

'Literary critics and historical critics often search for the "thought" of an author, of a man of state. This research supposes that there exists one single thought. This is sometimes true, but much more often false.' This remark of Pareto (*TSG*, p. 1793) can be better applied to Marx than to any other sociologist. Which is the true Marx? That of the *Manuscripts of 1844* which stresses the alienation of man in society and notably in capitalist society? That of the *Manifesto* which offers us an evolutionary vision of history? That of *Capital*, a work of scientific economy in which Marx (1818–83) wishes to be the worthy successor of Smith and of Ricardo? Many commentators have been aware of the diversity of Marx's work. Nearly all have chosen to favour certain texts at the expense of others. As for Raymond Aron, he proposes to close the debate, to abandon the youthful works to the 'gnawing criticism of mice' as Marx wished, and to retain as a priority the texts which Marx himself considered important (The *Manifesto*, the *Grundrisse*, and, above all, *Capital*). The principal difficulty of this position arises because the major work, *Capital*, offers only outlines of analysis on the principal questions of Marxist theory. More generally, it is not certain that by excluding the works of his youth one obtains a noticeably more homogeneous collection than that which one obtains by including them. Thus, the *Manifesto* offers an evolutionary vision where the development of the human species appears to obey an implacable determinism. In contrast, the third book of *Capital* seeks to bring out the laws of the development of capitalism, but in order to make clear immediately that these laws are only tendencies. The expression indicates not only that cyclic or uncertain phenomena arise to impose themselves on tendencies (or 'trends' to talk like economists), but also that these tendencies are combatted by opposing tendencies: the contradictions of capitalism condemn the system to crises, but Marx confines himself to describing with precision the process of degeneration. If the third volume of *Capital* had been the only book to have reached us, perhaps Marx would have passed neither for an evolutionary, nor for a determinist, nor even for an author who saw in class war the motor of history, because the contradictions described by the third volume are after all to a large measure internal to the capitalist class. In the third volume, as it has reached us, the proletarians are the passive spectators of a process punctuated by crises by the action of capitalists. On another classic interpretational debate: it is easy to show certain texts making of the 'superstructure' the mechanical product of the 'infrastructure'. But other texts show clearly that Marx was aware of the circular character of the liaison between the two 'authorities'.

Do these difficulties of interpretation demonstrate that it is necessary to give up talking of the 'thought' of Marx? This would assuredly be to go too far. Because the work of Marx, beyond the contradictory character of its specific developments, contains two principles of unity. The first resides in a vision of the world, more exactly in a vision of the society of his epoch, a vision which one finds from his youthful work to his last works. Close to Rousseau on this point, Marx considers that man in society and notably man in capitalist society is dispossessed of his being. The personality of the proletarian is 'dismembered'; the capitalist obeys social forces which he does not master; he is a 'servant of capital'; he cannot but constantly disrupt production. Individuals become 'simple personifications of economic categories, supports where the relationships of classes and particular class interests are crystallized'. To this image of the fall is opposed that of redemption in the communist society where the division of work is abolished, where according to the *Anti-Dühring* of Engels there will be 'neither porters nor architects'. According to a famous text in *The German Ideology*, in a communist society, 'it is possible for me to do one thing today and another tomorrow, to hunt in the morning, to fish in the afternoon, rear stock in the evening, to do literary criticism after dinner, according to my mood, without ever becoming a hunter, fisherman, shepherd or critic'. As Nisbet quite rightly remarks, the description of communist society is not very far from the state of nature according to Rousseau. The difference is that Rousseau considered the state of nature as imaginary, as an ideal point of reference, and judged that the abandonment of natural liberty could have as a compensation a major advantage, that is, to know the acquisition of civil liberty (even though civil liberty was always considered by Rousseau as precarious and slavery as a constant menace). For Marx, on the contrary, it is impossible to adapt oneself to the fall. Thus all Marx's work is a search for redemption. In *Capital*, the hope for redemption ensues from the unstable character – necessarily unstable – of the capitalist system. The crises of capitalism cannot but become closer to one another and increase. Even though they do not imply the crash of the system (the tendential laws are fought by the laws of the inverse sign), they allow for hope. That is why Marx is, according to the happy expression of Rubel, a 'tireless warrior for subversion'. In 1857, the year when, starting with the United States, an economic crisis developed throughout the world which has remained historically celebrated, he writes 'Even though I am myself in financial trouble, never since 1849 have I felt so good than I do now, faced with this crisis' (letter to Engels, 13 November 1857). In *Manifesto*, the hope of redemption flows forth out of a model which makes of the history of humanity a battle between classes devoted to eliminating each other to the point where only one is left and so, consequently, the system of division into classes is conclusively abolished.

The second principle of unity of Marxist work resides in the individualist character of his methodology. Here again, Marx is an inheritor of *Aufklarung* and of Rousseau. The idea of the reconciliation of the spirit with itself in which Hegel saw the meaning and the sense of history seemed strange to Marx – because the 'absolute Spirit' is presented by Hegel in a romantic and substantial manner which must shock an *Aufklarer* – but all the same essential. If there must be a reconciliation, it can only be between the individual and himself, of man with his own nature (once more one finds here a conception close to that of Rousseau). As for the alienation itself, it is also the act of the individual (cf. 'Alienation'). More exactly, alienation is the necessary effect of certain structures or social formations which, even though they are the product of human action, have the effect of rendering man a stranger to himself and the results of his actions out of line with and possibly the reverse of his intentions, desires, or needs. Even if the word alienation has been abandoned in the mature works – without doubt in part to mark the distance from the metaphysical character of the Hegelian *Entfremdung* – the idea is present in all of the works, whether the word is present or absent. In secularizing the idea of alienation, Marx returns to the 'invisible hand' of Adam Smith. More exactly – and it is perhaps what explains Marx's enthusiasm for economics – Adam Smith's work and the English economists generally permit him to give an analytic content to the idea of alienation. But, at the same time, Marx reverses Smith's model (even though the 'invisible hand' of Adam Smith did not always have a benign influence) and by doing so contributes to its generalization. When individuals are plunged into certain structures of interaction and interdependence, the product of their interaction can take the form of a collective evil and possible individual evils undesirable for all or for certain individuals. Thus, capitalists can be called alienated (the word alienation is practically absent from *Capital*, but the idea exists under other names) in the sense that the situation of competition in which they find themselves in regard to one another leads them to step up their productivity and, in a general manner, continually to overthrow the conditions of production and, in doing this, to produce a chain reaction of 'contradictions' and of crises which it would be, according to the evidence, in the interest of capitalists to avoid. But in the hypothesis where a capitalist in particular tried to act in a manner calculated to avoid these crises (by abstaining from investing for example), he would not know how to avoid provoking his own elimination from the system. Thus, the competitive structure imposed by the capitalist system of production generates 'social forces' which dominate the individual. These forces are, and seem to him to be, exterior to him. They lead to unsought social consequences. But they can only exist through individuals. Men alone make history, even if they do not know that they are doing so, even if the history that they make is not that which they would wish to make. *Capital* is at once a magisterial and an eclectic work, where the language and the individualist methodology of Rousseau and political economy are utilized by Marx to construct a secular version of the Hegelian process of reconciliation. Marx's 'invisible fist' alienates man from himself. But the structures which generate alienation are themselves unstable and fragile, in such a way that, on the horizon of history, can be seen the profile of the reconciliation of man with himself.

Smith's methodological individualism and Hegel's philosophical problematic are constantly combined in Marx's work, starting at least from *The Poverty of Philosophy*. They constitute the thread and the texture of the work. The development of factories, the separation between agriculture and industry, the progress of the division of labour are analysed in *The Poverty of Philosophy* as the emerging effects of situations of interdependence where each person attempts to pull the maximum

advantage out of his social situation and his resources. Nobody wishes that industrial work should be autonomized in contrast with agricultural work, nobody
wants the change represented by large industries, nobody wants to create an
exploited class. But each person, in following his interest, contributes to the
production of these results with all the consequences they carry, in particular the
ever-increasing 'dismembering' of the person of the worker. Exploitation is not the
effect of a plot by the powerful. It is the emergent effect of behaviour induced
by the relations of production characteristic of the system. From *The Poverty of
Philosophy* onwards, the double principle according to which: 1) history results
from the existence of emergent effects engendered by the aggregation of individual
actions; 2) the appearance of emergent effects in a system modifies the conditions
of functioning of that system and, in doing so, sets off an evolutionary process, is
applied to the division of labour. In *Capital* the same double principle is constantly
used, but Marx's ambitions have been amplified in the meantime. From now on
he is concerned to explain not only the development of the division of work but to
study the evolution of capitalist societies in all their aspects, economic and social,
as well as legal, and also, even though Marx is less explicit on this heading,
cultural. To these two principles is added – although its application is nuanced – a
third principle, that is to say that the conditions of production represent a kind of
primum mobile determining the totality of social relationships and, at the same time,
the variables which result from the *superstructure*. A fundamental ambiguity must
however be noted in this respect: if the conditions of production are determinant,
they engender effects which themselves contribute in their turn to modify production conditions. A materialist and to an even greater extent an economic interpretation of Marx which was too literal would thus contradict one of the major
elements of Marxist thought, namely the cybernetic character – as we would say
today – of the processes analysed in *Capital* and elsewhere. On this point, Marx
again follows the teachings of Malthus, Smith, and Ricardo whose static and
dynamic models practically always involve the giving of evidence regarding the
effects of retroaction (feedback). But whereas these writers tend to conceive the
processes of social change as being of an essentially cyclic nature (the apparition of
'feedback' effects in a system provoking a return of the system to an anterior state –
cf. Ricardo's iron law of wages or Malthus's iron law regarding population), they
are seen by Marx as profoundly *evolutionary* (the appearance of a *feedback* effect
producing as a general rule a transformation of the fundamental data of the
system).

The scientific importance of Marx's work is perhaps essentially there: in the
demonstration of an original paradigm of analysis of historic processes. This
paradigm is characterized essentially by two characteristics: 1) it presumes that the
historian can work with the same principles and generally the same mental tools as
the economist (individualist methodology, analysis of social phenomena aggregated as the effects of the composition of individual actions); 2) he refuses,
however, to give a general scope to the type of figure that the class economist tends
to highlight (balanced reproductive processes, cyclic processes of return to a
balance by the appearance of negative *feedback*). To be more exact, since the repro-

ductive or cyclic processes which characterize the capitalist economy in certain of its aspects must be understood, Marx comes back to this point time and again, not as if to an absolute law, but as if to conditional laws attached to certain phases in the evolution of the capitalist system, because this is really the primary ambition of *Capital*, the subtitle of which announces that it is a *criticism (critique) of political economy*: to show that the capitalist system engenders the processes of transformation which tend constantly to modify the laws of its functioning. Adam Smith, like Ricardo, clearly disclosed the existence of and analysed the logic of certain inbred evolutionary processes (cf. Smith's theory of the division of labour). But they had not, according to Marx, drawn from these observations all the consequences attached to them. Briefly, Marx's most authentically original contribution is the ambition to apply the mode of thought which we would today describe as *individualistic* which was developed by Rousseau and by Smith and Ricardo by the analysis not of social regularities but of *historical processes of transformation*. The analysis of the birth of factories in *The Poverty of Philosophy* is paradigmatic on this point. This *innovation*, of which the long-term effects must be considerable, is produced by the aggregation of individual actions which obey a short-term rationale. In the same way, the appearance of the middle class in the sixteenth century is interpreted in the same work as the result of the complex effects of a multitude of causes (the growth in the means of exchange, the increasing commodities in circulation) on the rationality of individuals. Here, the 'war' of the classes takes a complex form, that of an effect of the system which contrasts with the realistic conception presented in *Manifesto*. In *The Poverty of Philosophy*, there is a class 'war' in the sense that certain exogenous changes produce changes in the situation of the actors with the result that some of them are advantaged (the merchants) and others disadvantaged (feudal lords who cannot adjust their income to keep up with inflation). The *war* is thus purely metaphoric since the two antagonists never meet. In *Manifesto*, this war is, on the contrary, presented as a frontal clash, like a duel the issue of which is controlled by the law of the strongest, the strongest being in the event defined in a circular manner as the way of the future.

One of the principal sources of the difficulties of interpretation raised by Marx's work resides in the fact that it is at the same time the work of both a scholar and a militant. The militant wished to mobilize his potential troops against the adversary, in such a manner as to reduce the 'historical birth pangs'. The scientist was aware of the complexity of the social processes and of the fact that this complexity itself rendered the consequences of social action difficult to foresee. The militant wished that the proletariat would mobilize itself against the capitalists, perhaps because he was not entirely convinced that the internal contradictions of capitalism would be sufficient to render its destruction inevitable. He wanted the proletariat to eliminate the middle class in the same way as the middle class had eliminated the feudal class. But the scholar had clearly seen the importance of the downfall of private income from the land in the process of the degeneration of feudalism, and realized that it was due to an accumulation of exogenous factors. Thus, not only was the war between the middle class and the feudal class not clothed with any character of necessity, but there had not even been a war. In the language of contemporary ecology, one would say that the substitution of the feudal class by the bourgeois class could be translated, according to *The Poverty of Philosophy*, rather as a process of *ecological succession* (the milieu creates the conditions favourable to the development of a species and conditions unfavourable to the development of another species), rather than as a process of rivalry, of competition, or of conflict. The militant wanted history to roll out in an inexorable fashion to its presumed end. The scientist acknowledged himself incapable of any conclusion regarding the net effect of the tendential laws which are to be found in the capitalist system.

Marx attached considerable importance to what he considered to be his scientific discoveries in economics. Despite the fact that the discussion of this point is beyond the scope of a dictionary of sociology, one cannot exclude the possibility that he was partly right. Morishima has raised the definite kinship between Marx's economic theory and certain modern theories such as that of Leonieff. These discoveries are evoked by Marx here and there, but above all in a note in the third section of the third volume of *Capital* devoted to the tendential lowering in the rate of profit. It is true that this law, provided that it is considered as a conditional *model* of application rather than as a law, is a brilliant application of the individualistic methodology that Marx borrowed from the economists. Much less convincing, having no place at all in individualistic methodology, is the theory of value and of exploitation. Here Marx is carried away by his passions towards circular reasoning, founded on rhetoric rather than on logic. The whole argument reposes, to put it simply, on a series of postulates, of which the hardest to accept, perhaps, is the postulate according to which the *real* costs of production would correspond only to the manipulation and transformation of the base matter, the costs of co-ordination and more generally of the organization of work being supposed non-existent. This postulate can have only one possible foundation: the view according to which *real* work is defined by an immediate or mediate intervention (in the case of transformation industries) by man upon matter. Briefly, the entire theory regarding value and exploitation rests upon a classic rhetorical distinction, of which Pareto highlighted the ample usage made in the construction of the *derivations*, namely the distinction between work and *real* work. Once this distinction has been established, it becomes easy to show that *real* work is not paid for at its *value*. This theory, probably because it rests, to speak like Pareto, on the logic of feelings, has passed to posterity without difficulty. When Marxist parties talk of *workers*, they implicitly oppose work and *real* work. As for the sociological theory of stratification, it is founded on the same distinction when it gives its name to the Marxist tradition: the lower middle class is *bourgeois* because, not manipulating matter and its work not being *real* work, it is paid from funds collected in the name of profit. It is *lower* because, as statistics demonstrate, the part of the profit that it receives *per capita* is modest. But to come back to Marx: the theory of value and of exploitation, when one unites it with the other analyses, models, and theories of *Capital*, provokes a striking effect of contrast. The mode of thought here is different; the logical connection between this theory and other developments is elusive: neither the theory of the development of factories nor the fundamental mechanism described in the law of the falling rate of profit, namely the effect of the incitement to investment due to competition is, to restrict oneself to the examples already given, directly attached to the theory of value and exploitation. Furthermore, one can note that the rhetorical process (the distinction between *work* and *real* work) which 'founds' the Marxist theory of value is used all the time by Marx. To limit it to another example: *law* appeared to Marx to be an ideological construction characteristic of merchant societies and, more specifically, capitalist societies. But the *demonstration* rests upon a distinction between law and *real* law, the *real* being defined as that which affirms the existence of the private individual and of his capacity to make contracts. From this premiss, one deduces without difficulty that the law (that is the *real* law) is characteristic of societies where economic exchanges have attained a certain level of development, which is less important in traditional societies, and that it expresses the destruction of community links in merchant societies.

Marx's contribution perhaps resides above all, as has been indicated above, in the development of an original and fruitful paradigm of analysis of historical processes. But Marx's declared attachment to the scientific ethic added to his political passions explain by their combination why the work is so diverse and contradictory. The militant never manages to pervert the scientist, even if he suggests debatable theories to him, nor does the scientist furnish the militant with sufficient data for him to base his action on science. It is perhaps for that reason that Marx declared to Lafargue, if one is to believe the story of Engels, that he was not a Marxist ('one thing that is certain is that I myself am not a Marxist', Engels to Bernstein, 3 November 1882): he never believed that the purity of the engagement was sufficient to guarantee access to the truth.

Alienation, Dialectic, Historicism, Methodology, Reproduction, Schumpeter, Spencer.

Bibliography

COHEN, G.A., *Karl Marx's theory of history: a defense*, Oxford, Clarendon, 1978 – GIDDENS, A., *Capitalism and modern social theory: an analysis of the writings of Marx, Durkheim and Max Weber*, London, Cambridge University Press, 1971. – HENRY, M., *Marx*, Paris, Gallimard, 1976, 2 vol. – ISRAEL, J., 'The principle of methodological individualism and Marxian epistemology', *Acta sociologica*, XIV, 3, 1971, 145–150. – Marx: *Economic and Political Manuscripts of 1844*. – Marx: *Theses on Feuerbach* (1845). – Engels: *The Condition of the Working Class in England in 1844* (1845). – Marx: *Wage Labour and Capital* (1847). – Marx and Engels: *The Manifesto of the Communist Party* (1848). – Marx: *The Eighteenth Brumaire of Louis Bonaparte* (1852). – Marx: The Preface to *A Contribution to the Critique of Political Economy* (1859). – Marx: *Wages, Price and Profit* (1865). – Marx; *The Civil War in France* (1871). – Marx: *Critique of the Gotha Programme* (1875). – Engels: *Anti-Dühring*: Herr Eugen Dühring's Revolution in Science (1878). –   All the above writings by Marx are contained in Marx and Engels, *Selected Works*, Lawrence and Wishart, London. – MORISHIMA, M., *Marx's economics. A dual theory of value and growth*, Cambridge, Cambridge University Press, 1973. – NISBET, R., *The sociological tradition*, New York, Basic Books, 1966; London, Heinemann, 1967. – PARSONS, T., 'Social classes and class conflict in the light of recent sociological theory', *in* PARSONS, T., *Essays in sociological theory*, Glencoe, The Free Press, 1949, rev ed 1954, 323–335; London, Collier Macmillan, 1964. – SCHAFF, A., 'The marxist theory of social development', *in* EISENSTADT, S.N. (ed.), *Readings in social evolution and development*, London/New York/Paris, Pergamon, 1970, 71–94.

Measurement

In many cases, the sociologist asks himself questions the very nature of which implies the definition of measurements. Thus, Durkheim puts forward the hypothesis that the propensity to suicide grows with egoism (cf. 'Suicide', 'Durkheim'). To test this hypothesis, he is led naturally to compare contexts and situations in which 'anomie' is more or less intense and to verify that the propensity to suicide does vary with the degree of egoism. This verification supposes in its turn that a 'measurement' of egoism and a measurement of the propensity to suicide have been established. For the second variable, Durkheim makes use of the suicide rates as established by the official statistics. For the first variable, he uses various 'indicators' of egoism, these being the various variables that he postulates as being linked to the variable 'egoism' which itself is not observable: thus, members of the professional classes and those who work in industry and commerce appear to him to be more at risk from egoism than those who work in agriculture whose behaviour is more influenced by collective standards. Having introduced these hypotheses, Durkheim seeks to prove that the rates of suicide effectively vary with the value of the indicators of anomie. In the same way, the sociologist who wishes to establish that 'socio-professional status' depends on the level of education must construct a 'measurement' for socio-professional status and for the level of education. He is able, according to the solution that he considers to be the most sociologically judicious, to 'measure' the level of education either by counting the number of years of schooling or by simply identifying an ordered set of levels of educational attainment (such as, for example, primary, partial secondary, completed secondary, and higher education). Similarly, he is able to measure socio-professional status be endeavouring to establish hierarchical groups of occupations (for example, senior management and the professions, middle management, skilled worker, semi- or unskilled worker). Let us observe the way that the preceding examples allow us to distinguish between types of variables or levels of measurement: when we measure the level of education by the length of schooling, we have a *quantitative* or *metric* variable; when we are happy to distinguish between ordered levels, we have an *ordinal* variable. Finally, certain variables are said to be *nominal* when they share observed elements that do not belong to any ordered grouping. For example, sex is a nominal variable that is dichotomous. These distinctions are important in a number of aspects. The intensity of the relationship between two variables will, for example, be measured with the aid of specific statistical instruments for each level of measurement.

The need to define measurements, even if they are ordinal, is derived from the very nature of certain concepts. The very notions of social status, of anomie, or of the level of schooling imply that it might be possible to organize social status into a hierarchy and distinguish the levels of anomie or lower or higher levels of schooling. There is little point, therefore, in debating abstractly the possibility and utility of measurement in the social sciences in general and in sociology in particular. If it is true that the questions that the sociologist asks do not involve all the problems of measurement, it is equally true that some of these questions may involve some unavoidable measurement problems.

Having said this, it is necessary to emphasize that the sociologist who undertakes to define a measurement is hardly ever in a situation as simple as that of the carpenter who measures the length of a table. The suicide rates established by the official statistics are always erroneous. Because of the existence of customary social taboos, a certain number of suicides are reported as accidents. In some cases, it is impossible to decide upon the voluntary or involuntary character of a death. The criminality rates such as they are shown in the statistics do not include crimes or offences that are not reported to the police. An even greater difficulty: the bias in figures in the statistics is not spread uniformly. Women commit suicide by drowning more frequently than men. But a family can more easily pretend that suicide by drowning is an accident than it can with a suicide by hanging. Certain crimes and offences tend not to be reported (petty theft, assault) with the effect that the apportionment of criminality by type of crime and offence as presented in the official statistics gives rise to a distorted picture of real criminality. Numerous social phenomena are, in summary, measured with the aid of record-keeping methods which, not being sociologically neutral, result in a systematic distortion that is not always easily rectified.

A further type of difficulty: when we have defined a measurement, such as, for example, an ordinal measurement corresponding to a set of hierarchical categories, it is not always easy to decide upon the localization within this set of all the objects that we would have classified in it. Is it necessary, for example, to classify teachers in secondary education and higher education without any distinction in the senior management category? Is it necessary to include education within an industrial context with education within the school context in the estimation of the level of schooling? Finally, as is shown in the example of Durkheim's anomie, we can 'measure' certain variables only from *indicators*. We are also confronted with the problem of choice of and permutations of the indicators: is it necessary to measure 'social status' by considering only the relative prestige of a set of professions, the average income of these professions, and the levels of competence that are presumed for them? Must we combine these different indicators? If yes, how do we weight them? It is obvious that there will never be a single answer to these questions. The notion of social status expresses a social reality: certain professions are associated with higher material and symbolic rewards than others. But it is very difficult to set up a hierarchization that is capable of accommodating the consensus of all the professions that it is possible to identify and it is certainly futile to attempt to deduce such a hierarchization from a theory of stratification, for the simple reason that no general theory of social stratification exists (cf. 'Social stratification'). Let us point out, nevertheless, that some important technical literature (Likert, Lazarsfeld, Duncan, etc.) allows us resolve in a more satisfactory way the problem of selecting the weighting and permutations of indicators as indices.

Let us put utility, in certain cases an indispensable attribute of measurement, on one side, and problems of measurement on the other side. What position is one to take in this dilemma? For some, such as Douglas, the distortions introduced by the statistical record-keeping methods for crime and suicide, for example, are such that it is preferable to refuse any quantitative analysis so long as the recording is not more rigorously controlled. Not only does this type of position forbid the sociologist ever to ask certain types of historic questions (has suicide increased in France between 1850 and 1900?), it has the disadvantage of throwing the baby out with the bath water. If it is true that the record-keeping methods for phenomena such as suicide are socially biased, we still have available certain notions about the nature of this bias. And these notions are sometimes sufficient for us to decide on the validity or the lack of validity of certain conclusions. A simple example can illustrate this point. Suppose that we observe that between such and such dates in such and such country the record of female suicide is increasing and that the distribution of method of suicide remains more or less constant. Suppose in other respects there is no reason to suspect that the record-keeping method is becoming more efficient or more rigorous from the early period to the later period. In this case, a proposition that 'the rate of female suicide has passed from m to n per 1 million' should be taken as false, as it is almost certain that m and n are distortions of the true number of suicides. However, the proposition that 'the number of female suicides has increased' can be held as acceptable until further examination. On the contrary, it would be dangerous to accept the proposition if some change in the distribution of the method of suicide between the two periods had appeared. Similarly, when Durkheim observes that the rate of suicide varies in a regular way with age, there is no reason to interpret this variation as an artefact, as we do not see why the record-keeping method would be more capable of detecting a suicide when the victim is 50 years old than when he is 30. Although the suicide rates for 30-year-olds and 50-year-olds are very likely to be false, the *sign* of the difference does correspond to reality. In short, if the sociologist who is interpreting the data gathered by a non-socially neutral record-keeping method must be constantly on the look-out for the tricks of a cunning genius, he can often detect its presence and protect himself from its effects.

Let us now examine the second type of difficulty mentioned earlier, that is to know how to group certain elements of a population into a hierarchy of categories, or how to assign to certain elements a 'value' based on one variable. This difficulty is both real and general. It is unusual for a sociologist to find himself in a situation where he can without ambiguity classify, arrange, or measure all the individuals in a population. An associated difficulty: certain individuals are more likely to be inadequately classified than other individuals. Consequently, the phenomenon of tax evasion and the unequal ease in getting away with it depending upon the profession being practised results in the incomes of certain categories being more likely to be understated than those of other categories. Here again, the reasonable attitude for the sociologist to take to avoid this pitfall is to ensure that the propositions that he puts forward will usually differentiate between the data that are assumed incorrectly not to contain such distortions and the data that do take them into account. Thus, it would be risky to pretend, by using the data extracted from tax returns, that the income of shopkeepers is on average n times greater than that of school teachers. Even so, we can, after checking the stability of certain institutional data, claim that doctors' incomes have increased (or decreased) faster than school teachers' incomes. By the same token, if we decide to measure the level of educational attainment by using the number of years of instruction, we might be inconsistent in counting a repeated school year as zero or as one year: repeated school years will be recorded inconsistently using this system of measurement. But suppose, as would be reasonable, that a statistical relationship is observed between the level of educational attainment and social origin when we choose to count repeated years as zero, we would also observe a relationship if we decide instead to count them as one. The two relationships will probably give different values. But they will certainly have the same sign and the same order of magnitude. Here again, the sociologist has techniques that allow him to assess the effects of uncertainties and bias that appear when he attempts to classify individuals in a population into a set of categories or to attribute to them values derived from one variable.

Third difficulty: it is generally possible to group several measurements into a single concept. Thus, the level of educational attainment can be measured by the number of years of schooling; also, for example, by the sequence of educational phases taken up to the highest diploma attained (e.g., short secondary, long secondary, higher education). Similarly, we can measure social status using professional prestige as an indicator or by using an indicator based on both prestige and income. Of course, these measurements are not equivalent to a close transformation as are physical measurements such as length or temperature. Two measurements of any lengths m and m' are linked to each other by a transformation of type $m' = am$; two measurements of temperature are linked by a transformation of type $m' = am + b$. A transformation of this type can be defined only when it concerns two measurements of 'anomie', of 'status', or of 'level of schooling'. To get away from this difficulty, we make use of the principle defined by Lazarsfeld of the 'interchangeability of indicators': in many instances, the sign and the order of magnitude of statistical correlation will appear to be identical whatever indicator is used. So, regardless of the method we use to measure the social status of parents and the level of schooling attained by their children, a constant sign relationship will appear. Moreover, the absolute value of the relationship will be maintained within a fairly tight band.

In the preceding discussion, we have mentioned the case of measurements made up of indicators or combinations of indicators (the *accounting indices* of American authors). *Parametric indices* are very important in sociology; their purpose is to summarize information contained in a univariate or multivariate statistical distribution. Thus, we are led to summarize the information which represents the distribution of incomes in such a way as to be able to deduce from it a measurement of *unfairness*. Similarly, we can wish to summarize bivariate distribution giving social status as a function of social origin (a table of social mobility between generations) in such a way as to deduce a measurement of inter-generational social mobility. At first sight, the problem of constructing a measurement is simpler for parametric indices than for accounting indices. In the first case, it involves summarizing finite information. In the second case, it involves drawing from a population that is theoretically undefined by indicators. But any summary represents a loss of information. Moreover, there are always several ways of summarizing statistical information. The different summaries that we can use are generally linked by transformations. But these transformations will not always present the properties of transformations that are typical of physical measurements. Any two measurements of heat m and m' are linked – as we have already stated – by a linear transformation of the type $m' = am + b$. Whatever a and b are, if a measurement $m1$ is strictly superior (or inferior or equal) to $m2$, $m'1$ (an alternative measurement) will then be, in the same way, strictly superior (inferior or equal) to $m'2$: whichever type of measurement is used, either Reaumur or Fahrenheit, the meteorologist will conclude that it was warmer (or colder) at a given time than at another given time. In general, two physical measurements are linked to each other by a *monotonic* transformation.

Unfortunately it is not always so with parametric indices used in sociology. Two indices linked by a transformation can represent two points of view and so result in a different diagnosis. Let us suppose that the GNP of two countries A and B pass from 600 to 1,000 dollars for country A and from 2,000 to 2,500 for country B. We can state that the inequality between the two countries has lessened since the relationship between the GNP of B and that of A has moved from 2,000/600 = 3.7 to 2,500/1,000 = 2.5. But we can just as well show that the inequality has grown since the difference between the GNP of B and that of A has passed from 2,000–600 = 1,400 to 2,500–1,000 = 1,500. Or let us look at two simplified intergenerational social mobility tables (we can assume that we are able to classify a sample of 1,000 observed people into three classes: upper class, middle class, and lower class) and let us imagine that these two tables represent (partially) two sets of observations carried in the two countries A and B.

We are interested only in the mobility of the lower class. If we consider the absolute number of people in an upwardly mobile situation, B appears to be more mobile than A. But we also observe that in A, of 500 people with a lower-class social origin, 300 remain in this category while 200 are upwardly mobile. The rate of upward mobility of the lower class is therefore in this case 2/5 = 40 per cent. In B, this rate is 260/650 = 40 per cent. The indicator allows us this time to conclude that the rates of upward mobility of the lower classes are equal. But we can still see that in B the structure of the social pyramid is such that the maximum theoretical

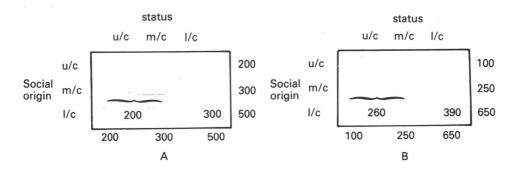

A   B

mobility of the lower class is equal to 350/650. In effect, the maximum size of classes is such that the first two lines and first two columns of table B can contain up to 350 people. It follows from this that the cell corresponding to the number of the individuals coming from the lower class and staying there must contain at least 300 people and that upward mobility cannot be greater than 650−300 = 350. In A, in contrast, the theoretical upward mobility of the lower class is equal to 500. We might be tempted, in order to calculate the mobility of the lower class, to take it to its theoretical maximum. In this case, B appears more mobile than A, since in B the ratio of observed mobility to maximum mobility is equal to 260/350, while in A it is 200/500. Similarly, the difference between 350-260 is less than the difference between 500-200.

Many discussions on the evolution of social mobility, on international differences where mobility is concerned, on the evolution of inequalities, or on international differences in (social) inequality fail to consider that it is generally possible to construct different indicators to represent different points of view which can in consequence result in different diagnoses. Let us consider the case of the Gini index, a classic measurement for inequalities of incomes. This measurement is made up starting with the so-called Lorentz curve which gives the percentage y of the total sum of incomes received by the x per cent less well-off. When equality is perfect, the curve is a straight line. The more convex the curve becomes, the greater the inequality. The Gini index is a measurement of convexity of the curve and is therefore a measurement of inequality. To suppose that this index has a higher value in France than in Germany, for example, would allow us to assume conclusively only that inequality is greater in France. Let us imagine in effect two bureaucratized and egalitarian societies where incomes depend only on age, that is to say where incomes would be identical for all people at a given age. The application of the Gini index to these perfectly egalitarian societies would make a certain level of inequality appear, this inequality resulting simply from the fact that at a given moment everybody does not have the same age. If the two societies appear as different from the point of view of the Gini index, the difference will arise only from a difference in the structure of the demographic pyramid. This theoretical experiment shows that when real societies are involved, before interpreting a difference in the Gini index as the sign of a difference of inequality, it is necessary, among other precautions, to verify that the difference is not due to a simple difference in demographic structure. Similarly, it is evident that a 'social indicator' such as the GNP must be used with great care: if we compare two countries where one is characterized by low personal consumption and the other by high personal consumption, the difference in GNP will give an amplified picture of the difference in the standard of living. Without these precautions, the indices risk becoming effectively ideological weapons. It is so much more important to insist on the need for a critical attitude towards social indicators now that these have, following the work by Ogburn, Raymond Bauer, and others, in the USA at first and then in Europe, acquired an official political existence and a growing political importance to the point that O.D. Duncan could talk in 1969 of a 'social movement' derived from the development of writings on and the passions aroused by social indicators.

Today, the whole of social politics is oriented towards achieving a reduction in the Gini coefficient or its equivalents. But not only is the Gini coefficient to be handled with great care, nothing else shows that a reduction in these coefficients corresponds with a higher level of collective satisfaction. Generally, the significance of indicators and their variations from the socio-political point of view is never obvious or immediate. The suicide rates have no significance in themselves, but only in association with implicit and explicit theories, such as Durkheim's, which use suicide as an indicator of variables such as 'anomie' or 'egoism'. Similarly, measurements of inequalities have significance only in respect to theories that allow us to establish a ratio between inequalities on one side and individual and collective satisfaction on the other side.

Causality, Social Mobility.

Bibliography

BAUER, R. (ed.), *Social indicators*, Cambridge, MIT Press, 1966. – BLALOCK, H.M. Jr (ed.), *Measurement in the social sciences*, Chicago, Aldine, 1974; London, Macmillan, 1975. – BLALOCK, H.M. Jr and BLALOCK, A. (ed.), *Methodology in social research*, New York/London, McGraw-Hill, 1968. – BLALOCK, H.M., AGANBEGIAN, A., BORODKIN, F.M., BOUDON, R., CAPECCHI, V. (ed.), 'Design, measurement and classifications', *in* BLALOCK, H.M., AGANBEGIAN, A., BORODKIN, F.M., BOUDON, R., CAPECCHI, V. (ed.), *Quantitative sociology. International perspectives on mathematical and statistical modeling*, New York/London, Academic Press, 1975, 259–472. – BOUDON, R., *Mathematical structures of social mobility*, Amsterdam/London, Elsevier, 1973. – DEGENNE, A., *Techniques ordinales en analyse des données*, Paris, Hachette, 1972. – DOUGLAS, J., *The social meanings of suicide*, Princeton, Princeton University Press, 1967. – FAVERGE, J.M., FLAMENT, C., GROOT, A. (de), KNOPS, L. (ed.), *Les problèmes de la mesure en psychologie*, Symposium de l'Association de Psychologie scientifique de Langue française, Paris, PUF, 1962. – LAND, K.C. and SPILERMAN, S. (ed.), *Social indicator models*, New York, Russell Sage, 1975. – MARANELL, G.M. (ed.), *Scaling. A sourcebook for behavioral scientists*, Chicago, Aldine, 1974. – NAGEL, E., 'Measurement', *Erkenntnis*, II, 1re partie: Exposés, 1931, 313–335. *in* MARANELL, G.M. (ed.), *Scaling. A sourcebook for behavioural scientists*, Chicago, Aldine, 1974, 3–21. – OGBURN, W.F., *Social change, with respect to culture and original nature*, New York, B.W. Huebsch, 1922. – PAGLIN, M., 'The measurement and trend of inequality: a basic revision', *American economic review*, LXV, 4, 1975, 598–609. – TORGERSON, W.S., *Theory and methods of scaling*, New York, Wiley, 1958. – YASUDA, S., 'A methodological inquiry into social mobility', *American sociological review*, XIX, 1, 1964, 16–23.

Methodology

Contrary to a current misunderstanding, this idea does not describe the *techniques* of empirical investigation and the analysis of data, but the *critical* activity which is applied to various products of research.

In a well-known text, mentioned in the foreword to the first French edition of this *Dictionary*, Bridgman notes that in physics progress results not only from the creation of new theories but at least as much from the *criticism* of existing theories. And Lazarsfeld recalls that the theory of relativity was born less perhaps from the *anomaly* which the experiments of Michelson-Morley indicated than from the carefully worked-out criticism of the *idea* of simultaneity by Einstein. At the time when this idea was being given universal significance, Einstein observed that it had a different meaning according to whether one applied it to two events which both occur on earth or to two events of which one occurs on earth and the other on the moon. Lazarsfeld has forcibly emphasized that Bridgman's distinction applies literally to the social sciences as much as it applies to the natural sciences. And he has many times laid stress on the fact that the very best method is *par excellence* that of *explanation of the text.*

Methodology thus conceived is applicable to all types of research, whether it concerns *quantitative* or *qualitative* studies, work with a theoretical orientation or sociographical studies. It is therefore not necessary to give an inventory of its contributions, but only to illustrate its importance with some examples.

In the field of quantitative work it has produced fundamental results which nowadays are part of the indispensable knowledge of the sociology apprentice. It is even more necessary to emphasize this point because statistical data, like the results of statistical measures and analyses, are often treated as if they are endowed with a kind of immediate objectivity and, as a result, are highly susceptible to doubtful interpretations.

Many illustrations of these comments can be given. A lot of literature uses measurements such as GNP (gross national product) in a non-critical manner to illustrate, for example, the evolution of disparities between nations. But the meaning of such a measurement varies according to the proportion of transactions expressed under a monetary form and, generally, with the proportion of goods and services taken into account. As a result the GNP is often a very uncertain means of measurement. If all Frenchwomen cleaned their neighbours' houses instead of their own, the GNP would increase, but the total of real services performed would not. In another way, the growth of the GNP can be translated as an improvement but also a *worsening* of living conditions: when the frequency of cancer increases, it causes an increase in the expenditure on health services, and, as a result, in the GNP. In another sphere, in France the statistics concerning low wages have long been accepted without question, without it being realized that these statistics lump together the underpaid workman, the student working part-time, and the surgeon's wife who works sporadically.

The analysis of statistical correlations also very often leads to doubtful conclusions, which are seductive because of the apparent objectivity of the statistical tool. Let us suppose that one grades the countries of western Europe, on one hand according to the consumption per capita of pasta and on the other hand according to the relative importance of the communist electorate. Despite the fact that such a correlation has no doubt never been calculated, one could hazard a bet that it would be quite high. Certainly, it would have very little significance and would reveal neither any *structure* nor any hidden *reality*. But in other cases, it is easier to confound good sense. It is not certain that a correlation, even duly calculated in a group of societies, between forms of family organization and types of political regime makes the least sense. But the correlation is likely to be seductive, if only because certain sociologists like Le Play have accorded the family organization the same role of *primum movens* as Marx conferred upon the forces of production.

Lazarsfeld, Simon, and others have emphasized that the interpretation of a correlation could be precisely stated if care was taken to introduce controlled variables. To use a celebrated example of Lazarsfeld's, in the cantons of Alsace there is a positive correlation between the average number of children and the number of storks, but this does not correspond to any causal influence, as good sense would suggest and as one can show by noting it becomes nullified when care is taken to make separate calculations for rural cantons and for urban cantons (cf. 'Causality').

In practice, one rarely encounters statistical structures so marked as this teaching example, but it is true that the taking into account of controlled variables often contributes to the clarification of the interpretation. Thus, in French statistics, secondary teachers are counted as 'higher management' and other teachers as 'middle management'. When one analyses the correlation between the scale of socio-professional categories (CSP) and such and such a dependent variable, it might thus be a good thing to ask oneself how much the variable is affected by this classification: thus, museum visiting is greater when the CSP is highest, but the relationship diminishes considerably when one eliminates secondary teachers from the analysis. Similarly, in the domain of criminal sociology, the theory of stigmatization (labelling theory) claimed to show that prison creates criminals. But it relied on a positive correlation between the number of years spent in prison and the frequency of recidivism, and did not point out that the number of years in prison is itself an indication of the gravity of the crime committed. Similarly, Halbwachs emphasized, on encountering the interpretation given by Durkheim of the fact that Protestants committed suicide more than Catholics, that Protestants more often live in towns than Catholics, and they are differently distributed in socio-professional categories. These classic remarks do not exhaust the question of the interpretation of statistical relationships, which raise problems which vary with the subject of being dealt with (cf. 'Experimentation', 'Causality').

Let us now consider, as a complementary example, another heading, that of the criticism of *theories*. A current methodological approach consists of asking questions concerning the congruence of such and such a theory with the data drawn from observation, because the Popperian principle of 'falsification', even though it is not the only valid criterion of the validity of a theory and though it is not always easy to apply, is relevant for the social sciences as well as for natural science.

Numerous examples can be mentioned in this connection. Thus, during the years 1960–70, many sociologists propounded the thesis that advertising was capable of the creation, from start to finish, of a demand for products. This demand did not correspond to any 'need'. This led them to suggest that advertising was an indispensable accomplice of capitalist mass production. This theory had its hour of glory because it gave scientific authority to the slogans current towards the end of the 1960s and early 1970s, which were summarized by the expression 'the consumer society'. But it was not long before it was pointed out that it was incompatible with well-established data. First, if the consumer is manipulated without mercy, why must market researchers conduct expensive surveys on 'motivation'? Second, surveys on the influence of advertising show that the message is generally treated by a consumer as information, as a signal, which does not mechanically set off the act of buying except in exceptional cases. Most frequently, the consumer tests the advertising message against informants in whose credibility he has confidence (neighbours, friends, etc.). He only buys once he has carried out this complementary research. Finally, if the theory is valid, how does one explain why a considerable proportion of the products launched backed up by great advertising and 'marketing' do not sell, as has been shown by research?

Another theory which was also very popular in the years 1950–60 had it that television favours conformity and uniformity and imposes the values of the 'dominant class' on everybody. But Cazeneuve has rightly observed that in countries that have had television for a long time, public lassitude is produced, which prompts the producers to put on programmes which seek, on the contrary, to attack the viewer's beliefs and shake his prejudices. A programme such as Polac's *The Right to Reply* is thus perhaps an illustration of a general tendency which has been already apparent for some time in the United States, rather than an expression of a non-conformist temperament.

To use an example taken from an entirely different area, the Leninist theory of imperialism, according to which colonization would have been a 'necessary' consequence of the accumulation of a surplus of financial capital which appeared in European societies in the last years of the nineteenth century, is hardly compatible with the fact that the British Empire knew considerable expansion well before, between 1840 and 1870. And the theory of 'dependence' according to which underdeveloped countries must suffer increasing underdevelopment is hardly compatible with the fact that, in the decades following the Second World War, the GNP grew more rapidly in Latin America than in the United States. Nor is it any more compatible with the fact that, in a country such as Nigeria, English colonial rule considerably stimulated the service and agricultural enterprises put under the responsibility of the natives. And it is not consonant with the fact that, in the recent past, Singapore, South Korea, and other countries have enjoyed a remarkable economic development starting with the time when a series of factors, most importantly the lowering of the productivity of advanced industrial societies, contributed to opening up western markets to them.

However, it must be seen that the submission of evidence of data which are incompatible with a theory results in the destruction of the latter only when it is particularly fragile. In other cases, criticism can contribute to the enrichment of the theory, in suggesting variants and allowing its nature to be more exactly perceived. This is what has happened, for example, in the case of the theories of social diffusion. Tarde believed that the processes of diffusion were always the result of the mechanisms of imitation, that is, as we would prefer to say, of *influence*, and from this he drew the conclusion that they were always of an exponential form. Today we know that Tarde's model (cf. 'Diffusion') was only one particular case. Similarly, most of the theories of development have laid claims to generality. But today we see more clearly that they constitute a collection of *idealized* models of which the individual elements can be applied more or less successfully to certain particular cases. In a general fashion, sociology often progresses by the analysis of *cases* which appear as *deviant* compared with such or such a theory. Thus, if Weber was interested by the relationship between capitalism and Protestantism, it was in the particular context of difficulty in equating it with Marxist-inspired theories. If he sought to determine the reasons for the vitality of Protestantism in the United States at the beginning of the century, it is because it contradicted the widely accepted theory according to which 'modernization' must 'necessarily' lead to a destruction of transcendental religions.

Criticism can also have the function of examining the weaknesses of certain concepts. Simmel said that, when we are incapable of seeing the reasons which have caused us to commit a certain act, we have a tendency to speak of *unconscious* motivation. He adds that this does not mean we attach a label to our ignorance. The need to give ourselves an explanation is so great that we allow ourselves to fall into a verbal trap: while to be rigorously correct, it would be necessary to talk of *unknown* motivation, we speak of *unconscious* motivation, by which we lend reality even to the unconscious. In the same way, when a sociologist observes behaviour in others that he does not understand, he will rarely rest with that negative report. On the contrary, he will talk of 'irrational' behaviour, and, instead of considering that expression as a label attached to his ignorance, he will give an objective reality to the idea of irrationality. Such ideas as 'resistance to change' and 'sociological weight' are the product of this type of mechanism. It was in order to break these vicious circles that Weber proposed that the behaviour of the social actor should be considered, by definition, as *rational.*

This criticism lead to important practical consequences and is of immediate utility. In effect, it forces the sociologist to collect supplementary information on the situation of the actor whose behaviour appears obscure to him. Very often this investigation permits him to render intelligible behaviour at first perceived as 'irrational'. Thus studies on the diffusion of innovation in the agricultural milieu have often shown that an innovation which is as advantageous for the peasant as for the collectivity may not be adopted until after a long lapse of time. Often 'resistance to change' or peasant 'traditionalism' are evoked in order to interpret such phenomena. But more attentive observation is likely to reveal that peasants prefer to wait before deciding, and to observe the real effects of innovation on their neighbours. Obviously, when everybody tends to adopt this sort of attitude, the starting of the process can only be very slow.

Generally, the criticism of a theory thus consists of asking oneself questions, on one hand about the structure and the composite parts of that theory, on the other hand about the congruence between the theory and observation. From the first point of view, it is, for example, important to disclose the presence of concepts which lead to tautological explanations ('resistance to change', for example) or to see that such a proposition implies an arbitrary judgement on the part of the observer (the peasant rejects an advantageous innovation; *therefore* he is irrational). From the second point of view, the critic particularly asks questions regarding the existence of facts which are opposed to the theory, or about facts which the theory does not take into account.

Conceived in this way, methodology is an essential dimension of the sociologist's activity. His apprenticeship passes, as Lazarsfeld wished, in a prolonged training in *analysis of the text*. And, if this is essential to the progress of physics, it is perhaps even more so in the case of social sciences, for two reasons.

The first reason is that the social sciences are particularly exposed to the fashion of the time. When, at the end of the great post-war period of growth, the rejection of the consumer society became a popular theme for the 'enlightened' intelligentsia, certain sociologists developed theories demonstrating, or at least claiming to, that consumption *benefited* only the producers, and that one could thus rightly denounce the 'system' and call for 'zero growth'. When the theme of 'imprisonment' was a winner, sociologists undertook to demonstrate that prison contributes *in the aggregate* to an increase in criminality.

The second reason is that social sciences, and sociology in particular, cover very diverse types and styles of research activity. The production system of social sciences is fragmented into a collection of sub-communities between which communication is not always easily established. This results in an 'anomic' division of work and an absence of communication between the holders of different paradigms. But, very often, criticism makes it apparent that a problem cannot be resolved except within the framework of a change of paradigm. Thus, the results of a statistical analysis can be made intelligible only by resorting to non-statistical methods; and the analysis of a case which is abnormal compared to a model can be impracticable within the framework of the model method.

At a time when sociology has often contributed by conferring on chimera the authority of science, it is important to emphasize the role of critical activity which is referred to by the idea of methodology in the development of social sciences. To this evidence, two more things must be added, namely that this critical activity cannot consist of opposing one dogmatism to another, and that, far from being immediately accessible, it assumes on the contrary a training and, consequently, institutions which make that training possible.

Causality, Development, Diffusion, Experimentation, Knowledge, Objectivity, Spencer, Theory.

Bibliography

BAUDELOT, C., *L'évolution individuelle des solaires en France, 1970–75*, coll. de l'INSEE, series M, october 1983. – BÉNÉTON, P., Inégalité des chances et culpabilité sociale, in BÉNÉTON, P., *Le fléau du bien*, Paris, Laffont, 1983, 47–64. – BOUDON, R., *La place du désordre. Critique des théories du changement social*, Paris, PUF, 1984. – BRIDGMAN, P.W., *The nature of physical theory*, Princeton, Princeton University Press, 1936. – CAZENEUVE, J., *La vie dans le monde moderne*, Paris, Seuil, 1982. – CUSSON, M., *Le contrôle social du crime*, Paris, PUF, 1983. – FIELDHOUSE, D.K., *The theory of capitalist imperialism*, London, Longmans & Green, 1967.

Minorities

The term minority conjures up first the division of a group into at least two subgroups, one of which is larger than the other, or, if there are more than two subgroups, then the sum of the others. The majority can add other attributes to the quality of being the largest number; the largest number can also be the most powerful: which is what happens from a strictly political point of view in democratic regimes. Conversely, the less numerous can be reputed to be the best, as in aristocratic regimes, or in societies with an élitist orientation.

In any case, as soon as the distinction is made between majority and minority(ies), two series of questions must be asked. First, does the separation result from a scission? If this is the case, it is because the unity of the group has been broken. To take up the classic distinctions of Hirschman, the minorities are confronted with three possible strategies. They can by 'loyalty' stay in the group and submit to the majority will. If this will appears to them to be a diktat, the only choice left for them is secession ('exit') or protest ('voice'). Each of these strategies permits of more or less refined variants, the examination of which has no place here. What must be underlined is that strategy 1 (loyalty) and strategy 3 (protest) particularly have been formalized by the theoreticians of democratic regimes – so effectively that one can define the democracy as the regime in which the relationships between the majority of the citizens and the rest of the political body have been arranged in a manner to render possible the peaceful coexistence of one with the other.

How is this arrangement established and preserved? One can quote the famous adage: *vox populi, vox Dei*. But as soon as one renounces this religious conception of democracy and of democratic rule, one is led to recognize that, in order to avoid what de Tocqueville and the nineteenth-century liberals called the tyranny of the majority, it is necessary to seek to establish a strict demarcation of its competences. The majority does not only recognize the existence of the 'others' who belong to the political body with the same rights as it. It also recognizes that 'the others' are fully justified in pursuing their own interests, in expressing the opinions typical of them. Two things result. If the majority cannot claim any superiority of value and of dignity, it is only distinguishable from the minority by the nature and extent of its competence, notably the capacity to take decisions which also bind the minority. The second thing is even more interesting. No part of the population is authorized to speak for the whole population. If the majority cannot prevail except through a delegation by which it is entrusted with the task of deciding certain matters of common interest in agreed forms, *a fortiori* a minority cannot boast of speaking for 'the entire population'. This is a restrictive conception of the majority's rights, which guarantees reciprocally, by the rule of alternation or a similar other institutional arrangement, the rights of those citizens who find themselves in the minority. It is taken for one of the fundamental qualities of the constitutional conception of democracy.

The concept of minority is not reducible to that of the opposition, which in pluralist democracies patiently awaits its turn to come to power, as a bastion against the risks of arbitrariness and enslavement. The European history of the nineteenth century was marked by the question of nationality and the paradoxical status reserved to 'non-native' populations in two multinational empires, that of the Turks and that of the Hapsburgs. The Ottoman sovereigns counted among their subjects Christian populations, which were submitted to a discriminatory status which excluded them from a certain number of rights and of advantages. In the Austro-Hungarian Empire, above all after the 1867 compromise, and equally in the Romanoff Empire, the non-native racial groups (Slavs in the Hapsburg Empire, Poles and Jews in the Tsarist Empire) were second-class citizens. Even when they benefited, either as landowners or as heads of families, from basic civil rights, they were excluded from a certain number of jobs, or at least saw themselves admitted only in small numbers – by, for example, the game of *numerus clausus* – and only then at middle or lower levels of the hierarchy. Above all, their national or denominational identity being denied them, these populations were led to demand autonomy to a greater or lesser extent, or at least to claim, if need be by violent means, the right to independence and secession.

By virtue of the social and cultural heterogeneousness of the resident population at the birth of its new republic, and of those large migrations which afterwards came to it from Europe and even the Far East starting from the second half of the nineteenth century, the United States has also found itself confronted with a minority problem. It is true that the black slaves were not citizens before their emancipation by Lincoln, and when they became citizens, they became 'second-class' citizens by virtue of all sorts of discrimination. The idea of minority has never had the same sense in America as in the Austro-Hungarian Empire or the Turkish Empire. First, the Black or Indian 'minorities' have almost never developed an explicit secessionist claim. The menace of secession came not from the black slaves but from their masters. Moreover, even before the Civil War, official ideology always presented conditions of equality as the basis of the American republic. This principle was obviously flouted, at least in the southern states, but the scandal of slavery, presented as a peculiar institution, was excused by accommodating advocates as a temporary and progressively adjustable situation. Even more important, once the 'peculiar institution' had been abolished by Lincoln, and as a result of very rapid economic growth, induced partly in the last third of the nineteenth century by the influx of immigrants, America became the classic country of mixing of races and assimilation – a sort of *melting pot*, in which the original characteristic racial differences are supposed to melt.

But whatever American society offered the new arrivals by way of a chance of individual advancement, the assimilative capacity with which the Americans have long credited their society should not be over-emphasized. Even if it does not present any dangers to 'loyalty' to Uncle Sam, specific ethnic consciousness persists. It is accompanied by a certain number of types of behaviour which have contributed to maintaining the *distance* between the different groups – a distance which has in other respects been hierarchized and developed. Commensual contacts, neighbourhood relationships, marriages are much more frequent inside than outside each group. The new Americans of Italian or Polish origins maintain their loyalty to the Catholic Church. Italian, Polish, and Russian immigrants continue to speak, at least at home, the language of their native country. It is not until the third generation, if one is to believe an opinion which had been generally accepted, that the pot delivers a more or less homogenized cultural product. Even once 'assimilated' the Italo-American will remain distinct from the Germano-American, and attached sentimentally to the 'old country'. This last point has not passed unnoticed by politicians, who make efforts not to rub the minorities up the wrong way – above all in times of international tension.

What is perhaps more important is that each group has found itself continuingly over a long period specialized in very different roles and statuses. Glazer and Moynihan have shown this in the case of New York. Jews, Italians, Irish, and Blacks do not find themselves places on the same rung of the system of stratification – neither from the point of view of political power nor that of cultural influence nor from the point of view of wealth or income. It would be altogether wrong to confuse them in a catch-all category of 'dominated'. There are rich, influential Jews, prosperous Irish; and if, generally, the Blacks do constitute a discriminated against and underprivileged mass, within their group exist *differences* of condition more and more marked in proportion to the improvement in their *average* position. Because of the very diverse types of jobs they do, the Irish and the Italians, who constitute coherent and clearly marked minorities, without being however too far from the WASP model (White Anglo-Saxon Protestant) from which they are excluded by neither race nor colour, have long been held to be *influence brokers* of irreplaceable effectiveness in the municipal life of New York. Jews and Blacks, situated at very distant points from one another in the system of stratification, above all because of the remarkable 'break-through' of the Jewish group into the most prestigious jobs of the intellectual and professional sector, incarnate life styles and projects of mobility which, despite their great differences, have long been rendered politically compatible by the *bosses* of the Democratic Party.

The 'assimilation' of minorities in the melting pot can only be taken for what it is, that is to say a metaphor. But this metaphor conveniently draws our attention to the nature of relationships between the minorities in American society, and to the problematic nature of these relationships. They are certainly not those of equality: discrimination is not absent – it is of a kind which, sometimes openly, sometimes underhandedly, bars access to high status to people from minorities. Discrimination is camouflaged by the confidence displayed by the official ideology (*American creed*) in equality of opportunity ensuring the promotion of the most deserving, and consoling the unlucky and the handicapped by the concession of 'consolation prizes'. Alongside the official ideology, racial prejudices 'rationalize' the failure of underprivileged groups by implying that they are 'naturally' inferior or that their failure can be corrected only by a very slow education process. Thus, the advantages of the well-off are denied or legitimized, and they can with a clear conscience attribute them to their own merits.

A practice of gradual and careful *inclusion* has for a long time been presented as the most adequate way to describe the situation of minorities in American society and history. This interpretation presupposes a certain number of conditions which have largely been, but with a very unequal degree of precision, born out in the case of most of the minorities: Irish, Germans, immigrants from eastern and southern Europe, Jews. The plan of inclusion rests on three conditions. First, it was necessary that the expectations of the newcomers were more or less compatible with what the welcoming society could offer them or agree to give them. This congruence was assured, on the side of the immigrants, by the selective character of the migratory process. The candidates for departure were principally those individuals who, feeling attracted by the utopia of a free society, open and progressive, benefited from an anticipatory socialization. Second, it was necessary that in the receiving society ethnic difference was sufficiently tolerated so that the gradual and prolonged injection of strangers did not result in a reaction, and a rejection of an over-violent, pro-native, and fundamentalist nature. In the case of the Blacks, who had for a long time been slaves, and who because of this had integrated both into the production process and, to a certain extent, the culture of their masters, the risk of a radical repudiation – by expulsion or repatriation – never arose, either before or after the Civil War. On their part, European immigrants could be discriminated against, both for religious reasons and for reasons of their geographical origins. In the eyes of Americans of *old stock*, Protestants, proud of their English or Scottish ancestors, the 'papist' Italian or Pole, the Russian, Polish or German Jew, are not altogether part of the family. Also, the superiority of the *old stock* was not only proclaimed by the WASPS themselves. Certain of the most ambitious individuals belonging to the discriminated-against minorities recognized this superiority in their way, and 'internalized' it by seeking a WASP wife, admission in their clubs, mixing with them socially, and to be treated by them as a 'companion and peer'.

The situation of the Black minority illustrates the limits of the inclusion model, and makes its generality doubtful. First, the handicap suffered by the Blacks in terms of socio-economic status (income and professional qualifications), level of education and training is so great – or at least has been so great until the last few years – that individual mobility strategies can only slightly correct it. It is not sufficient to demand *equal treatment* in order that the rules of competition assure the most gifted and deserving members of the black community their chance. The level of poverty – material and cultural – in which the majority of the Blacks are trapped makes their advancement very difficult. The question has thus come to be asked whether their massive and rapid integration does not presuppose a real rupture with one of the most essential rules of the game. The Irish, Italians, and Jews have been able to become Americans 'entirely on their own' without the 'meritocratic ideal' suffering in an irreparable manner. Is the Americanization of the American Black possible without American society changing its inclusion procedures?

De Tocqueville has already asked this question, which has become more acute since certain activist leaders started to ask whether the 'liberation' of Blacks, the conquest of a cultural identity did not have as a pre-condition a sort of 're-Africanization' which could go as far as a radical 'de-Americanization'. If it continued in this way, the 'recognition' of the minority group by the majority would be problematic. These members of the minority passionately refuse to be assimilated. They do not want to be tolerated, they do not accept the 'liberal and generous' conditions that the majority declare themselves sometimes ready or resigned to give them. To begin with, they want the legitimacy of their revolt or their dissidence to be recognized. One often sees this in the final phase of 'wars of liberation'. In the same way, the most radical black Americans do not wish to be known as black Americans, but as Blacks who are *also* Americans – *not as black Americans, but as American Blacks*.

This identity, understood thus as a radical difference, poses the problem of the hierarchy of loyalties, which affects all the groups which belong to the same society by the simple fact that they belong to it. The same question is asked by the *activist* minorities, who must be distinguished from the ethnic or national minorities of whom we have talked until now. The 'liberation' of women, homosexuals, pot-smokers, ecologists, do they pose different problems to those which are posed by the liberation of Armenians or the fight against anti-Semitism? According to received opinion, it is anti-Semitism which 'makes' the Jew, and flogging fathers who make homosexual sons. The authoritarian projects his own urges on to imaginary objects. What he cannot tolerate in other people is that which his super-ego cannot tolerate in himself. Prejudice is firstly misunderstanding. If the anti-Semite saw the Jew as he is, he would perceive that the negative attributes that he gives him do not exist. This explanation is not entirely without relevance. It implies a relationship between aggression, understood as responses, and a preceding frustration. However, as well as hardly clarifying that relationship, it ignores two essential points. First, this explanation of the anti-minority behaviour of authoritarianism, and of its prejudices, ignores the claims of the minority group. The Jew is something other than the inverted image of anti-Semitism. He attributes to himself, and wishes to have recognized, positive qualities which define his identity. Lastly, these explanations ignore the positive content of the minority's claims, and also ignore the social conditions in which these claims might be made to work. One does not see women, even the most feminist, wishing to make a radical break from the society that they form with men, as the Algerian nationalists proposed to break the legal and political connections which attached their country to 'French colonialism'. In as much as gay or feminist groups, and supporters of drugs, have a less consistent identity than that of ethnic or racial minorities, the problem the 'new minorities' pose for democratic societies seems at first view less difficult than the problems posed latterly to unitarian empires by ethnic or religious foreign groups. Is it not sufficient to invoke the principle according to which everyone is free to do what he wants as long as he does not harm the rights of others?

The claims of the 'new minorities' could be dealt with by the method of toleration if they were all strictly specified and limited. If it were only a question of legalizing certain drugs or of closing one's eyes to the love-making of consenting adults of the same sex, it is probable that the most repressive taboos would gradually perish, in a more or less slow and capricious manner. But the demands of the 'new minorities' are not only turned against certain bizarre superstitions, they also have an overall and diffuse character. Ecologists base their claims on the order, founded on 'profit', of the 'consumer society'; it is the 'repression of sexuality' that is attacked by the feminists and gays. The result is a continuous escalation by the claimants who are led to over-state their demands, whereas on the side of the conservatives or the conformists, a retraction occurs which leads them to reject all concessions from fear of being dragged well beyond the point at which they would be resigned to meet their adversaries.

The behaviour of people in minorities covers a variety of forms as great as the behaviour of people in majorities, or conformists, with regard to the minority. The minorities find themselves faced with a certain number of dilemmas. First, they may seek toleration or recognition. They may seek immediate recognition, *hic et nunc*, of their claims, or partial and deferred recognition. They can play it each for himself or combine their claims. This last option is particularly important. If a minority seeks coalition with other minorities, it enters the game of democratic association. What it aims at is that, in including its own claims on a platform which consolidates them in going beyond themselves, it makes them *acceptable* to the possibly very large sectors of public opinion which are at first partly hostile or reserved. By this strategy, the minority seeks to gain the support of majority opinion. Conversely, if it shuts itself within its own claim, it isolates and radicalizes itself. It isolates itself if it limits itself to itself. It radicalizes itself if it seeks only the support of those groups which, like itself, present their demands in the mode of 'all or nothing'.

The status of minorities is perceived according to two extreme models, each rarely achieved. Minorities can be perceived as a foreign body, made up of drop-outs, who are likely to become abnormal, if not dissidents and rebels: this is the conservative, conformist view. But minorities can, on the contrary, be treated as the salt of the earth. Today misunderstood and persecuted, they show the way to a future of which they will have been the principal builders. It would seem more reasonable to adopt a temperate viewpoint towards minorities. They show the degree of diversity that a society can tolerate within itself without suffering fatal ruptures; or without having to fundamentally rearrange the hierarchy of its value and the hierarchy of loyalties which its members are expected to respect. Thus, the appearance of a minority announces: 1) an acceleration of the process of social differentiation; 2) the emergence or intensification of conflicts; 3) the risk of a break-up of social hierarchies, with the possible violent exit of minorities or foreign ethnic or religious groups; 4) the promise of qualitative leaps and innovations, offering minorities (the ethnic groups at the epoch of the melting pot) and at the same time the entire society the possibility of a higher performance.

Action (collective), Conformity and Deviance, Élite(s), Social Change, Social Mobility, Social Stratification, State, De Tocqueville.

Bibliography

BLAU, P., *Inequality and heterogeneity: a primitive theory of social structure*, New York, The Free Press/London Collier-Macmillan, 1977. – *Daedalus*, 'The Negro American', autumn 1965 – winter 1966; 'American Indians, Black, Chicanos and Puerto Ricans', spring 1981. – EISENSTADT, S.N., *Absorption of immigrants in Israël (with special reference to oriental Jews)*, Jerusalem, 1951; London, Routledge & Kegan Paul, 1954. – FINKELSTEIN, L. (ed.), *The Jews: their history, culture and religion*, New York, Harper, 1949, 2 vol.; New York, Schocken Books, 1970–1971, 3 vol. – FRAZIER, E.F., 'The impact of colonialism on African social forms and personality', *in* STILLMAN, C.W., *Africa in the modern world*, Univ. of Chicago Press, 1955, 70–96. – FRISBIE, W.P., NEIDERT, L., 'Inequality and the relative size of minority populations: a comparative analysis', *American Journal of Sociology*, 1977, LXXXII, 5, 1007–1030. – GLASS, R., *London's Newcomers. The West Indian migrants*, Cambridge, Harvard Univ. Press, 1961; London Centre for

Urban Studies, 1960. – GLAZER, N. and MOYNIHAN, D.P., *Beyond the melting pot*, Cambridge, MIT Press, 1963, 1970. – HIRSCHMAN, A.O., *Exit, voice and loyalty. Response to decline in firms, organizations and states*, Cambridge, Harvard Univ. Press, 1970. – HUGHES, E.C. and HUGHES, H.M., *Where peoples meet: racial and ethnic frontiers*, Glencoe, Free Press, 1952. – KILLIAN, L.M. and GRIGG, C., *Racial crisis in America*, Englewood Cliffs, Prentice-Hall, 1964. – KLOBUS, P.A., EDWARDS, J.N., 'The social participation of minorities: a critical examination of current theories', *Phylon*, 1976, XXXVII, 2, 150–158. – LOUBSER, J.J., 'Calvinism, equality and inclusion: the case of Afrikaner calvinism', *in* EISENSTADT, S.N. *The protestant ethic and modernization*, New York, Basic Books, 1968. – MOSCOVICI, S., *Psychologie des minorités actives*, Paris, PUF, 1979. – MUGNY, H., 'Majorité et minorité ; le niveau de leur influence', *Bulletin de Psychologie*, 1974–1975, XXVIII, 16–17, 831–835. – MYRDAL, G., *An American dilemma: the negro problem and modern democracy*, New York/London, Harper & Brothers, 1944; New York, Harper & Row, 1969. – OBERSCHALL, A., *Social conflict and social movements*, Englewood Cliffs, Prentice Hall, 1973. 'Research among racial and cultural minorities: problems, prospects and pitfalls', *Journal of Social Issues*, 1977, XXXIII, 4 1–178. – ROSE, A.M., ROSE, C.B. (ed.), *Minority problems*, New York, Harper, 1965. – SARTRE, J.-P., *Réflexions sur la question juive*, Paris, P. Morihien, 1946; Paris, Gallimard, 1962. – THOMAS, W., ZNANIECHI, F., *The Polish peasant in Europe and America monograph of an immigrant group*, Boston, P.G. Badger, 1918; New York, Dover, 1958. – TOCQUEVILLE, *Democracy in America* (op cit). – TOURAINE, A., *La voix et le regard*, Paris, Seuil, 1978. – TOURAINE, A. *et al.*, *La prophétie anti-nucléaire*, Paris, Seuill, 1970. – WAGLEY-, C. and HARRIS, M., *Minorities in the New World*, New York, Columbia Univ. Press, 1958.

N

Needs

Any human being is characterized by x number of needs which show his dependence in relation to his external environment. To take animals as an example, 'quest' behaviour appears when they end up short of food, shelter, or sexual partner. Possession of these items is a source of pleasure and satisfaction. Deprivation can be coupled with 'aggressive' behaviour against real or imagined obstacles to their access to these things. Satisfying need is, however, either more or less easy. 'Abundance' describes the situation when the range of available food is adapted to the demands of the starving, when it is sufficient, so that anyone looking for it can have some without taking away a fraction, however small, from anyone else's share. But why is abundance an ongoing promise constantly pushed forward in time in our societies instead of being a natural situation?

The first reason explaining that all the needs of everybody cannot be satisfied is 'scarcity'. Nature is mean. It does not give or produce enough, as it should, to feed everyone. In such an important domain as nourishment, Malthus underlines the serious risk, that population growth might overtake food increase. He includes the possibility that agricultural productivity cannot increase fast enough to balance population increase. If such an essential – primitive – need as food is not satisfied, men will kill each other to take each other's food. The origin of all conflicts would therefore be a 'mean' nature unable to provide for all our needs.

According to Rousseau, this is a 'blasphemous' supposition. Nature is not mean, we are greedy. It does not treat us badly, we are the ones stopping her fulfilling her promises, wasting her resources. Men's needs can be satisfied by nature so long as they have not upset nature by the division of labour. The neolithic experience would show this, when the first farmers were producing basic food and satisfied their needs without becoming the prisoners of luxury.

How does this 'de-naturation' happen? To explain, it must be understood that not all of men's needs are of a material nature. We need food. But in a different

251

way we also need other men or women as co-operators, as sexual partners. Rousseau accepts this but he emphasizes the fragility of such links. He emphasizes the 'independence' of man from nature. Man, before his social corruption, can be fully himself without obtaining other men's recognition. On that point, Rousseau's position is different from that of the philosophers, like Hegel, who make of recognition, through the opposition in the master/slave relation, the condition of self-awareness. I can be myself without needing others. Because of this independence, the primitive relationship with the other would be that of benevolence or pity.

Everything changes with the division of labour, and the creation of property. It is true that the division of labour multiplies everyone's productive efforts. But the sharing out of the surplus products resulting from this improved productivity crystallizes, through unequal contributions, the inferiority of some and the superiority of others. It allows the strongest to establish their domination by seizing the means of production and, in particular, by seizing land. From then onwards, instead of men's needs expressing the dependency of each on nature, they begin to express the 'domination' of some over others. We owe the socialization of our needs to the corrupted society of division of labour and ownership and not to primitive society based on sympathy and pity. But there is in the division of labour an implicit agreement which could prevent its abuse: this association was only begun to improve the fruit of men's efforts. Should there be a fair basis for sharing, our needs could be satisfied equitably in the case of the division of labour.

Two points come out of Rousseau's analysis and they have not lost their validity for contemporary sociologists. First, there is a social conditioning of needs which is both 'revealed' and 'denatured' by society. Veblen put forward this thesis, in his argument about 'the leisure class'. People who have money and nothing to do come to be noticed through the extravagance of their consumption. Not only do they spend a lot (a single meal of one of these nabobs would suffice to feed a Chinese village), but they also buy the strangest of things that they have had imported at great expense from exotic countries. The needs they satisfy are not real 'needs': to use the Stoicist distinction it can be said that such needs are neither 'necessary' nor 'natural'. The logic of this consumption is not the satisfaction of individual preferences, it is the strategy used by the consumer to enforce his power and his prestige towards his partners who also are his rivals. The *nouveaux riches* don't eat caviar because they love it but to show that they can afford to. Their consumption is 'conspicuous'.

Economists have developed two kinds of analyses on the subject. First, their interest concentrated on the 'demonstration effect'. An object or a service is in great demand only when it becomes 'visible' to a large number of potential consumers – even if, to start with, these consumers cannot afford it. It is the function of advertising to ensure this visibility when the mere appearance of the product on the market is not enough for it to be bought. Once part of the population able to afford this luxury is won over, the 'principle of effect' as psychologists call it, i.e., the satisfaction linked to the use or the ownership of the thing, reinforces the first result: 'one can't do without it.' Consumption of this object becomes a kind of habit and only by abusing language can we still talk of need.

The acquisition of any new consuming habit goes through several phases. The potential consumer first realizes that what he is offered is within his reach. The financial constraints are not unbearable, the object is obviously useful, its handling and upkeep seem neither difficult nor costly. In other words, the eventual buyer will not have to fight great battles with himself to decide to buy it. Second, the example of those around him, better off, more sensitive to advertising or themselves convinced by the examples of neighbours and friends, can influence, motivate him, change him from being a potential buyer to being an actual buyer: if the Smiths have a television, why shouldn't I? Finally, if after some time the new object does not cause extra, unplanned costs, the habit will be definitely 'consolidated'. It will have become a need, for, as the saying goes, 'habit is second nature'.

The demonstration effect stops us seeing consumption as a strictly individual behaviour, following the comparison between a scale of preferences and financial constraints. The act of buying, as well as the act of consuming of course, remain quite individualistic, but constraints and preferences are defined in a context of interpersonal comparisons. The notion of 'envious comparison' thus came to be prominent for research. It was first introduced in organization analysis, particularly in the case of paradoxical responses given by soldiers of different ranks about their promotion. They are concerned not first with the rate at which they are promoted, but also with the effect of the general incidence of promotion in relation to other categories of colleagues and friends (cf the notion of 'reference group'). As far as consumption is concerned, the comparison with the other is also at the centre of the buying decision.

Advertising attempts to create another kind of consumer (knowledgeable, modern): the famous actor Y smokes only this brand of cigarettes. This reference is both cognitive and evaluative. It tells us what Y buys, attempting to pass on Y's values and personality to the products that Y uses. If I want to be like Y, I'll do the same as him, I'll buy X cigarettes, which are no more expensive than the others and, besides, such and such persons I know smoke them. My act of buying is subjected to three systems of comparison, Y and myself, X cigarettes and other brands, I who smoke X cigarettes and those of my friends and relatives who smoke (or don't) X cigarettes. This comparison is called 'envious'. But there are no reasons to restrict to envy or jealousy the feelings motivating the comparison. These may include curiosity, the desire to explore a range of possibilities from which we are not for ever excluded. Besides, the accusation of envy or jealousy is very suspect in view of its obviousness. 'If the Smith's have television why shouldn't I have one?' This argument does not necessarily express a feeling of paranoia towards the Smiths. Asking 'if you, why not me?' is in general legitimate since it might lead me to realize that I cannot afford it, that I am not able to buy this object which I don't really need anyway – and that the Smith's, who 'treated themselves', don't either. The comparison, far from containing the subject within a confrontation with a single category of reference, can considerably broaden and enrich the perception of his range of actions. Instead of taking any comparison for 'envious', it has to be examined as a generalization mechanism. Without neglecting 'envious comparison', there can also be an 'identification' comparison, as in the case of the famous actor I want to emulate, and an all-directions comparison by 'combination instinct', making the subject think hypothetically how he would use his resources in the various situations he has experienced or can imagine. Comparing does not only make us face more or less arbitrary referents. It 'uncovers' the extent and the complexity of our preferences.

There is therefore a social genesis of needs, by comparing subject to subject or group to group. The examples discussed above relate to consumer needs, but 'moral' as well as economic needs could be discussed. These moral needs could be described as the assertion and claiming of our rights: rights to be recognized, loved, to 'take part'. We particularly become aware of them when fighting for them against those who would want to deprive us of them. Then we express them by such expressions as 'it is not tolerable that . . .'. Such needs can be said to be social in several ways. First, in the way that they are described and created. Their defence is taken care of by organizations or social movements. Second, these needs can be satisfied only if the accompanying demands are listened to by the public or, eventually by political authorities. Third, they aim at a certain social order they want to change or keep, through the creation of 'public services' which take care of such needs as health, education, housing, security. So they are social in their shape, destination, and content.

The 'moral' character of 'social needs' is essential but not easy to define. What authenticates a claim is the possibility of it being accepted as a social need. A claim then becomes a legitimate demand that society members have a right to expect from the State. A distinction now becomes possible between the two forms of socialization of needs we have just discussed. In the consumption example, socialization of needs affects only private individuals who are supposed to satisfy their needs with their own resources and judgement. In the second case, socialization of needs relates to citizens who intend to obtain their demands from political authorities. But this is a delicate distinction, as in the case of poverty for instance, where having to do with a sub-standard level of existence is seen as a scandal calling for justice to be done.

The social genesis of needs cannot be seen as a simple passing on of a behavioural pattern. 'Society' has so much trouble in imposing its 'tastes' that the goods and services we demand from it most insistently are the ones it does not provide, and many of those provided are neglected and despised by us. There is no question of denying the attempts at flattery and seduction directed at both consumers and citizens. Through advertising, producers are busy feeding us their products. Through demagogy, politicians stir up demands and claims, hoping to be voted in to satisfy them. But needs are not completely 'fabricated' by demagogues or publicists. They are constructed through an awareness – which is not devoid of errors or illusions – by which we gradually discover what we want, what we can expect for ourselves, and what we are owed.

Rousseau clearly saw the risk of corruption resulting from the de-naturation of needs within a social context. This risk cannot be decoupled from the division of labour. Are we protected against this risk if society is able to see what it should and can do for everyone? Such an undertaking appears extremely difficult when the notion of poverty is examined. It seems, however, so simple to describe poverty as the consumption level below which the 'primary needs' of individuals are not 'covered'. But defining these 'primary needs' is problematic. Food will undoubtedly be one. But there are several ways of feeding oneself, some approved, others disapproved, by dieticians. And these choices do not all have the same costs for the community – whether physical or financial. Even 'primary' needs can be satisfied in very different ways and satisfying them costs a different price to society. In the case of the richest countries, even if they devoted all their resources to it, the most deprived could cover their 'primary needs' only if they gave up satisfying others. In a rich country, the poor person is one who gives up satisfying 'superior needs' so as not to feel hungry. Today this is considered to be an unacceptable constraint – the elements constituting the indices designed to track the variations of workers' buying power are there to prove it. Leisure expenditure constitutes a significant part of such an index. As indices are supposed to measure the change in real income of the poorest, 'social needs' are consequently not ordered in an objective and clear hierarchy. But it is, however, what 'Engels' law' suggests at first sight. The change in the structure of workers' budgets would show that needs like health, housing, or leisure are satisfied only after more constraining needs like food and clothing. This is true, but only in general and over a long period of time. Many consumers among the poorest decide between categories of expenses according to very different criteria from those of Engels. Many 'poor' spend more on leisure (entertainment, alcohol, etc.) than would be reasonable, and less on housing or food than they could. Unless there were to be a form of rationing which would take away extras from some to re-distribute them according to an imposed formula, it is difficult to see how the 'poor' could get the maximum out of their resources. It might be possible if this rationing and distribution was done in kind – not in cash – although in some cases, a black market might result.

It might be possible to get round this difficulty by showing that this critique of the objectivity of social needs refers back only to a narrow 'technocratic' conception of these needs – such as is derived from the studies of dieticians, agriculturalists, or architects. But it would not really help to include in the list of social needs, abstract or spiritual needs, like the need for knowledge, individual expression, change, and innovation. A problem already mentioned now appears even more serious. There are many ways to satisfy the need for knowledge or expression; besides, choices made by individuals between such needs and food or clothing needs go so deep into anyone's ultimate preferences than it would be misleading to condemn as 'irrational' the person who chooses to eat less so as to satisfy his need for elegance in his appearance and dress.

The fact that there is no objective hierarchy of social needs does not mean that any hierarchy would be completely arbitrary. Halbwachs, comparing white-collar workers' expenses with those of manual workers, found that with the same income white-collar workers spend less than manual workers on food and more on clothes and leisure. It could be said that the manual worker, a heavy physical worker, needs to eat more meat or drink more wine than the employee behind a counter or desk – unless a manual worker is identified as a heavy worker, it is tempting to follow Halbwachs when he emphasizes how important it is for a white-collar worker to appear respectable so as to be seen as a member of the lower middle class. The hierarchy of their needs is greatly influenced by the conditions in which they work, by their self-image, and by the status they want to project around them.

Social needs are neither objective nor artificial, in both cases for very obvious reasons when we realize the huge difficulties posed for the planner, the producer (it is known – see Lindbeck – that a large proportion of widely advertised goods end up being a failure on the market), or the entrepreneur by the objective of making expected consumption coincide with actual consumption. Although social needs are neither objective nor artificial, it does not mean that they have no reality. They in fact correspond to habits, gradually created and legitimized by references to ideals or, as de Tocqueville says, to 'general and dominant passions'. If in Occidental societies freedom and equality are the criteria distinguishing 'good' social relations, the realization of situations corresponding to these criteria will be seen as a need – or as an ideal over which the individual, as a member of that society, cannot compromise. As for knowing how to succeed in ensuring the realization of these social needs, three main ways have been suggested. Some liberal theoreticians think that social needs are nothing more than the total demand of consumers as optimized by producers. Some utopian thinkers have argued that social needs are demands that society has accepted as legitimate and which it has tried, from its all-knowing and all-powerful position, to satisfy. The third view emphasizes the complex character of social needs, the definition of which would include both forecast or anticipated requirements, as well as the stated views of private individuals and citizens, and as derived from organizational and political leaders. These various groups – which both 'consume' and 'demand' – are led to divert, each to their own advantage, the process of definition, of social needs not only by denaturing them, but by changing the need itself into an instrument of dependency and exploitation, and no longer an attempt to satisfy a requirement. Rousseau saw, more clearly than any other thinkers, the solution to this as lying in changing the need without corrupting it in the process.

Alienation, Capitalism, Development, Egalitarianism, Groups, Rousseau, Socialization.

Bibliography

BAUDRILLARD, J., *La société de consommation; ses mythes, ses structures*, Paris, SGPP, 1970. – CHOMBART DE LAUWE, P.-H., *Pour une sociologie des aspirations; éléments pour des perspectives nouvelles en sciences humaines*, Paris, Denoël, 1969. – Club of Rome, *Beyond the age of waste: a report to the Club of Rome*, by GABOR, D., and COLOMBO, U., Oxford, New York, Paris, Pergamon Press, 1978. – DUESEN-BERRY, J.S., *Income, saving and the theory of consumer behavior*, Harvard Economic Studies, vol. 87; Cambridge, Harvard University Press, 1949. – FRIEDMAN, M., *A theory of the consumption function*, National Bureau of Economics Research, General series n° 63, Princeton Univ. Pres, 1957; Oxford, Oxford University Press 1957. – HALBWACHS, M., *La classe ouvrière et les niveaux de vie. Recherches sur la hiérarchie des besoins dans les sociétés industrielles cotemporaines*, Paris, F. Alcan, 1912. *L'évolution des besoins dans les classes ouvrières*, Paris, A. Alcan, 1933. – HEGEL, G.W.F., *Die Phänomenologie des Geistes*, 1807. – KATONA, G., *Psychological analysis of economic behavior*, New York, McGraw-Hill, 1951, 1963. – KEYNES, J.M., *The general theory of employment, interest and money*, livre III: *The propensity to consume*, London, Macmillan, 1936. – LEBRET, L.J., *Niveaux de vie, besoins et civilisation*, Paris, Éditions Ouvrières, 1956. – LECUYER, B.-P., OBERSCHALL, A., 'The early history of social research', *International Encyclopedia of Statistics*, 1978, 1013–1031. – LEWIS, O.,

Five families: Mexican case study in the culture of poverty, New York, Basic Books, 1959; New York, American Library, 1965; *The children of Sanchez; autobiography of a Mexican family*, New York, Random House, 1961. – LINDBECK, A., *The political economy of the new left: an outsider's view*, New York, Harper & Row, 1971. – MALTHUS, Th. R., *An essay on the principle of population, as it affects the future improvement of society. With remarks on the speculations of Mr Godwin, M. Condorcet, and other writers*, London, J. Johnson, 1798; London, Dent, 1973. – MASLOW, A.H., *Motivation and personality*, New York, Harper, 1954, 1970. – PÉTONNET, C., *On est tous dans le brouillard: ethnologie des banlieues*, Paris, Galilée, 1979. – ROUSSEAU, J.-J., *Discours sur l'origine et les fondements de l'inégalité*. – RUNCIMAN, W.G., *Relative deprivation and social justice*, London Routledge & Kegan Paul, 1966. – SARTRE, J.-P., *Critique de la raison dialectique*, Paris, Gallimard, 1960. – VEBLEN, Th., *An economic study of institutions*, London, Macmillan, 1899; ed. rev., New York, Viking Press, 1967.

O

Objectivity

Can sociology claim to be objective? Since the beginnings of sociology this question has been subject to persistent controversy. It was brought up again by Adorno and Habermas in the context of the dispute about positivism (*Positivismusstreit*) which developed in Germany during the 1960s. Knowledge – especially sociological knowledge – is, according to Habermas, linked to the social interests of social actors. This is why there is necessarily a sociology of the Left, and a sociology of the Right. Thus, sociology is only as valid as the interests which it serves. This conception represents a variant on the principles contained in Marxist sociology since its origins. For Marx, whom Pareto considered to be correct on this point, English political economy was subservient to the interests of the capitalist bourgeoisie. In mind no doubt of Marx's thesis, Dostoyevsky makes the drunkard Marmeladov say, in *Crime and Punishment*, that political economy demonstrates scientifically how it is useless to show mercy towards the poor. By contrast, Marx thought that his own doctrine was destined to serve the proletariat's interests. But Marx did not think that this partial character of his doctrine was incompatible with its pretensions towards objectivity. As the proletariat is destined to replace the dominant bourgeois class, to be on the side of the proletariat was, according to Marx, to be in a position to bring out the scientific laws of history.

There is little doubt that sociologists' conceptions are often affected by their interests, and more generally by the constraints which their position imposes on them, by their social role as well as by the biases or 'preconceptions' (Durkheim) which can result from their location in a specific social and historical context. It is helpful to recall some examples in this regard. Ricardo's 'iron law of wages' states that wages cannot rise permanently above subsistence level. If they do rise above this level, birth rates are pushed up in such a way that after a certain period of time, of variable duration, competition between workers in the labour market becomes more severe, leading to a fall in wages. If wages drop below subsistence level, the birth rate will decline, leading to competition between entrepreneurs for labour. Wages are thus doomed to oscillate around the level of subsistence. It is clear nowadays that this law, as with the majority of 'laws' put forward by the social sciences in the more or less distant past, has been contradicted by events. One of the main reasons for Ricardo's error is that he had not anticipated the phenomenon of unions and the influence that workers' organizations would exert in the process of wage-fixing, at least as regards the *short term*, because in the *long term* the factors are so intertwined that it is difficult to determine their respective contribution to the evolution of wage rates. But during the period when he was writing, the idea of association inevitably evoked the image of the feudal corporations which enlightenment philosophy and economic liberalism maintained had been relegated among fossilized forms of social organization. This parameter, so ideologically characteristic of his time, made it difficult for Ricardo to imagine that the phoenix might rise from its ashes in order to correct the implacable logic of the law of wages.

When the international development agencies were set up at the end of the Second World War, they relied upon the services of experts whose role was to establish the best ways of allocating aid to the Third World. Precisely because of the nature of their role, these experts were encouraged to conceive of development as an external, *exogenous* process (see 'Development'). Indeed, to have thought otherwise would have been to empty the notion of aid or assistance of its meaning. Equally, they were encouraged to assign major influence in the triggering of the development process to factors such as the accumulation of physical and overhead capital – factors which could be directly influenced by external aid. In consequence they were also encouraged to treat Third World countries as basically identical to each other, to minimize their differences – however striking they might have been – and to direct themselves to the discovery of a general theory of development. From the moment when the Third World was constituted as a problem and underdevelopment as an illness, it was necessary to find the cure for a sickness conceived of as a singular disease.

The fact that the social sciences developed within the nations of the industrialized western world is also responsible for the ethnocentrism that may be discerned in much sociological research. Development theorists, for example, have tended to interpret the western type of development process as a preferential model whose logic was thought to be capable of universalization. Thus, Rostow emphasizes the role of advanced industrial sectors in the triggering of development, in mind no doubt of the role played by the textile industry in England, the steel industry in Germany, or the dairy industry in Denmark.

In other cases, the influence of the parameters affecting the social context of the researcher is more insidious. In a classic study of automobile industry workers, Chinoy states that the workers he studied had, in objective terms, only very slight chances of being promoted into the middle levels of the occupation structure. None the less, these workers do not in any way have the feeling that they are caught in a blind alley, as shown by Chinoy's interviews. On the contrary, they think they will be able to get on and even 'make it'. There is no doubt that they have little chance of changing status, but they may expect modest increases in wages or in job prospects. They have few chances of moving up to a higher level of consumption or of changing their way of life; but they do have a good chance of being able to gradually acquire the consumer goods which are most coveted in their milieu. In sum, although they are in a blocked situation, they feel they have opportunities, that the future is open. Chinoy's interpretation of this feeling is that it can only be a *rationalization*. The workers' future *is* blocked. They see it as open. Why? Because society places a pre-eminent value on social success. An individual can thus only accept himself if he has the impression of having 'succeeded' or of being in the process of succeeding. When he is placed in a situation of *impasse*, he has to 'hide' his failure. This is why Chinoy's worker accords an excessive import-ance to the small wage increases which he obtains, and to the modest 'improve-ments' in comfort that he is able to give to his family. But Chinoy's interpretation rests on a very questionable assumption. The situation of the workers which he describes is hardly an enviable one. But such a proposition belongs to the realm of ethics and has nothing to do with the problem in question: to analyse the attitudes and behaviour of these workers. The interpretation provided is based on the egocentrism of the observer. A university professor will generally place little importance on earning a few more cents. If the subject under observation, however, places importance on it, it can only be through a process of rational-ization. But this conclusion is only convincing if it is admitted that the attitudes and evaluations of university professors constitute some sort of universal measure. It would be very easy to cite numerous other examples where the social position of the observer influenced not just certain elements but the heart of the analysis itself. Hence, educational sociologists, who owe their social position to their own degrees and qualifications, tend to consider the absence of 'educational ambition' as an abnormal phenomenon and to explain its appearance as the action of evil social forces. Similarly, the sociologist of the family – who is highly likely to belong to a society where the nuclear family is the dominant type – will tend to set up the nuclear family as the normal model and to overestimate the effects of the industri-alization and development processes on family structures. Incidentally, we may note that socio-centrism may take either a *direct* form, as in the preceding exam-ples, or an *inverted* form. In the latter case the sociologist tends to analyse and eval-uate his own social milieu in relation to the ways in which he sees other milieux.

In addition to the social context of the researcher, his personal context must be included among the factors which are capable of influencing observation and analysis. Durkheim thought that sociology was not worth a quarter of an hour's trouble if it could not demonstrate its social utility. Pareto, by contrast, saw socio-logy as a disinterested cognitive activity: to him, ideologies appeared to be much more socially useful, or in other words more influential, than the effort expended by sociologists in explaining social phenomena. As a result of these fundamental differences of attitude, the two sociologists are not merely concerned with different problems but will also provide different interpretations of the same phenomena. Because he was preoccupied with the integration of the individual in society, Durkheim interpreted social conflicts as pathological symptoms. Since he had no predispositions of this nature, Pareto saw social conflicts as normal phenomena. A sociologist will generally analyse an identical development process in a different way according to whether he conceives of his analysis as either principally cognitive or principally practical. In the first case, the sociologist will be likely to emphasize the singularity of the process. In the second he will tend to see it as an individual manifestation of a general process.

Having established that, under normal conditions, the observations and interpretations of the sociologist are affected by what we have termed his social and personal context, must we conclude in a sceptical fashion that sociology cannot claim objectivity? Or must we conclude, in a Marxist fashion, that certain social and personal contexts are preferable to others, either because they facilitate an easier prediction of the course of history (Marx) or because they are commended by a superior ethical viewpoint (Frankfurt School)? Or indeed, should Feyerabend's ironic suggestion be followed (perhaps inspired by a proposition of Flaubert's in *Sentimental Education*) that the truth of scientific propositions should be decided by universal suffrage? Is it necessary to treat the belief in the possibility of objectivity in the social sciences as a sign of support for the *ideology* generally labelled *positivist* by those who accept this argument and to draw the circular conclusion that sociology can only have one objective, to fight for *legitimate* interests? We do not see, in fact, that any of these conclusions is necessary. On the other hand, it is easy to discern the doubts to which such conclusions lead, and the rhetorical procedures which enable them to be given an apparent foundation.

Why? Because the influence of socio-personal contexts does not prevent a sociological analysis being subjected to rational and critical discussion, nor does it stop such a discussion leading to conclusions which are in principle capable of general acceptance. Nowadays, it seems to be accepted that Ricardo's law of wages is false. Despite the efforts made by Marxists, until the Stalinist era and beyond, to reconcile this observation with Marx's version of the law (relative pauperization) it is now known to be false because it is incompatible with observed data. In addition, it is known why it is false (because it presupposes, among other things, the absence of union power) and why it was able to be formulated at a certain time (because the innovation which the union phenomenon represented could hardly be predicted, for historical reasons which are easily identified, by Ricardo's contemporaries). During the first two decades following the Second World War, a type of general development theory came into force. It conceptualized development as a process of a fundamentally exogenous nature, resulting from chain reactions set in motion by certain favoured 'triggers' such as the accumulation of overhead capital. But monographic studies have shown the weakness of this general theory and drawn attention to the complexity and diversity of development processes. It is not difficult to recognize, to return to one of the earlier examples, that Chinoy's analysis of car workers contains a principle which is both indispensable, since it constitutes the keystone of his argument, and unacceptable. On what basis can the conception of social success created by the observer be used as a criterion of distinction between 'true' and 'false' success? What foundation does the sociologist use as support for considering that families which do not exhibit educational ambition are proved to behave irrationally, unless it is in the use of criteria which are egocentric or sociocentric?

These few examples suggest that the influence of the socio-professional context does not by its nature disqualify sociology's claim to objectivity.

Actually, it is not clear that the 'logic of scientific discovery', contrary to one contemporary view, does not obey the same principles in sociology as in the other domains of scientific activity. In sociology, as elsewhere, it is possible to analyse a theory in order to identify the specific introduction of untenable postulates. Critical analysis of this type, even where it refers to a particular theory, may have a general relevance. Thus the critique of Chinoy outlined above would tend to provoke an attitude of doubt towards all theories which, either explicitly or implicitly, rest upon a comparison between the attitudes and preferences of observer and observed. Economists have for long been wary of the dangers of such interpersonal comparisons. It may be thought that the development of a critical attitude of the same type is called for among sociologists. Admittedly, resistance is considerable, because current sociological concepts such as 'false consciousness' or 'rationalization' as well as numerous sociological theories are based on the right which the observer accords himself to use his own attitudes and preferences as measures of the attitudes and preferences of anyone. But the principle on which such concepts are founded is so unacceptable that critical scepticism should eventually be generalized.

Internal critique of theories (that is, the critique of the propositions which constitute a theory, of the admissibility of the concepts used, etc.) is thus the first path open to sociology, as to any discipline, towards scientific progress. A second path is that of *external* critique, the confrontation of theories, in terms of their premises and consequences, with observed data. On this point, Popper's theories are relevant – after certain modifications – to sociology. The theory which states that economic development presupposes a prior accumulation of overhead capital can no longer be considered as of general validity from the moment when it is clear that in this or that country – for example, Argentina at the turn of the century – the formation of overhead capital accompanied rather than preceded spectacular economic development. The theory according to which development must necessarily be accompanied by a process of 'nuclearization' of the family cannot be considered as unconditionally valid from the moment when it is observed that in such or such a context – as in India, for example – the transition from an exchange economy to a market economy can reinforce rather than weaken traditional family structures. The renowned criteria on which Popper proposes to evaluate scientific theory, in particular the criterion of falsifiability, thus should be admitted into sociology as they are elsewhere. It is not difficult to demonstrate that when a sociological theory is the subject of consensus, in general it can be taken to satisfy the Popperian criteria. A theory, Popper suggests, is the more credible if it explains a larger number of distinct observed data. The more it explains numerous and diverse data, the more it is difficult to find an alternative and different theory which might take account of the same body of data and ultimately of additional data.

Although it may be impossible in the last analysis to demonstrate the truth of a theory, according to Popper, a theory capable of accounting for a large amount of data may give the impression of being true. Such a form of analysis applies perfectly to classic theories such as that of de Tocqueville (*L'Ancien Régime et la Révolution*) which locates French administrative centralization as the principal cause of the many differences observed between France and England in the eighteenth century. French administrative centralization led to greater prestige for civil servants. The State's prestige meant that the offices that it distributed were more numerous and sought after. Landlords were thus encouraged to seek a royal office rather than to exploit their lands. This is one of the reasons which would explain the backwardness of French agriculture by comparison with English agriculture. The proliferation of royal offices led, at the local level, to small-scale urban concentrations which have no equivalent in England. The excessive visibility of the power of the French State oriented political reformers, the '*philosophes*' [philosophers of the Enlightenment, *trans.*] or, as we would say today, the 'intellectuals', towards an abstract vision of political phenomena and towards a revolutionary conception which subordinated all social change to a prior change of institutions and political personnel. In the same way, the Durkheimian theory of suicide, even if it may be criticized in certain of its aspects, is considered as a necessary point of reference because it explains a large number of different forms of data on suicide. By contrast with these examples, the *ad hoc* or *post factum* theories referred to by Merton (in other words theories constructed so as to take account of a specific phenomenon, which do not appear to have sufficient explanatory power to extend to other phenomena) are unlikely to sustain an analogous impression of credibility: only capable of explaining isolated phenomena, they are likely to give the reader the feeling that it is relatively easy to imagine an alternative explanation for the same phenomena. As an example of the hundreds of *ad hoc* theories, the social mobility theory of Lipset and Zetterberg can be cited. Having observed that social mobility is as easy in societies where there is rigid social stratification as in those where this is less pronounced, these authors put forward the hypothesis that, in a society with rigid stratification: 1) social barriers are by definition more difficult to cross; 2) social actors have more incentive to try to cross them. Obviously, although such a theory opens up an interesting line of research, it could only be considered valid if its postulates were *directly* verified or if they allowed the explanation of phenomena other than those by which it was inspired.

The *rapprochement* between Durkheim and de Tocqueville carries a further lesson. The complex logical criteria which confer the trademark of objectivity on a theory are the same, whatever the nature of the questions posed and of the data which has to be accounted for. De Tocqueville's analysis deals with a group of 'qualitative' differences between two countries. That of Durkheim deals with a group of differential quantitative data. But the logical outcome is the same in both cases.

Sociologists are subject to the influence of personal and social contexts. In addition, they approach the reality which they claim to account for, not in the state of innocence that classical empiricist philosophy assigns to the knowing subject, but ready armed with paradigms (cf. 'Theory') from which they construct their theory.

These paradigms constitute styles of *a priori forms* in the Kantian sense. They are adopted, at least initially, on the basis of an act of faith rather than a proof. It is possible, as Feyerabend suggests, that the difference between social and natural sciences is, on these two points, more of degree than of substance. The theories of Lamarck and Darwin are partially the product of their 'social contexts'. Physicists, like sociologists, approach reality and formulate their theories within the framework of paradigms which are themselves unproven. Despite that, the rights of objectivity are preserved by the possibility – available to the sociologist as to the physicist – of carrying out a rational critique of the theories brought to his attention.

Beliefs, Ideologies, Knowledge, Prediction, Social Symbolism, Theory.

Bibliography

ADORNO, T.W. (ed) *The Positivist Dispute in German Sociology* (trans. Adey, G. & Frisby, D.) London, Heinemann, 1976. – ALBERT, H. *Traktat über Kritische Kernunft*, Tübingen, J.C.B. Mohr, 3rd enlarged edition 1975. – CHINOY, E. 'The Tradition of Opportunity and the aspirations of automobile workers' *American Journal of Sociology* LVII, 5, 1952,, pp. 453–459. – FEYERABEND, P.K. *Against Method*, London, NLB, 1975. – HABERMAS, J. *Technik und Wissenschaft als Ideology*, Frankfurt, Suhrkamp, 1968. *Towards a Rational Society*, London, Heinemann, 1971. *Knowledge and Human Interests*, London, Heinemann, 1972. – JACOB, P. (ed) *De Vienne a Cambridge: l'héritage du positivisme logique de 1950 à nos jours. Essais de philosophie des sciences*, Paris, Gallimard 1980. – PARSONS, T. 'Evaluations and Objectivity of Social Science, an interpretation of Max Weber's Contribution', in PARSONS, T. *Sociological Theory and Modern Society*, Glencoe, Free Press 1967, pp. 79–102, and PARSONS, T. 'An Approach to the Sociology of Knowledge' *ibid*, pp. 139–166. – POPPER, K.R. *The Logic of Scientific Discovery*, London, Hutchinson: New York, Harper 1959. *Objective Knowledge: An Evolutionary Approach*, Oxford, Clarendon Press 1973. – RICARDO, D. *On the Principles of Political Economy and Taxation*, London, John Murray 1817. – WEBER, M. *The Methodology of the Social Sciences* New York, Free Press 1969.

P

Power

The term power is overused, and with a great variety of meanings. Very generally, this term refers to three connected notions each of which help to make it explicit. There is no power without *allocation of resources*, of whatever nature these might be. Furthermore there must be some *ability* to use these resources. If we give a computer to a chimpanzee, this implement will not increase his power either in relation to the man who will have given him this resource, or in relation to any of his fellow monkeys. The use of resources implies *a plan of use* and requires minimal information about the conditions and consequences of this use. Finally, to refer to resources which can be used according to the abilities of the person who disposes of them naturally, or who has intentionally assembled them in view of the aims he set himself or which have been proposed to or imposed on him, comes back to recognizing the *strategic* character of power and that ultimately it is exercised not only against the inertia of things, but against the *resistance of opposing wills*.

Whether one considers the resource, the ability to use the resource, or the strategic ability *vis-à-vis* others to mobilize and combine resources, power can be considered either as a relation belonging to the analysis of *interaction*, or as a more complex phenomenon *'emerging' from the aggregation or the composition* of a variety of elementary types of interaction. Max Weber is, among the classical sociologists, the first who most clearly isolated the concept of power and who endeavoured to deal with it from the double point of view of interaction and aggregation. To the second point of view he added a dynamic analysis, or at least a sketch of such an analysis.

In terms of interaction, power is an asymmetrical relation between at least two actors. With Max Weber, it is possible to define it as the ability for A to insist that B does what B would not have done by himself and which conforms to A's intentions or suggestions. Two points are explicit in Weber's definition. First, B's behaviour *depends* on A's: B responds to the initiatives, desires, or even more generally to A's way of being. This kind of relation has been shown in the micro-sociology of discussion groups. Thus, Bale attempted to distinguish *proactive* individuals (those who start the debate, plan it, and then have solutions adopted) from *reactive* individuals, who content themselves with approving or refusing their consent. The second feature of the relation of power is that it increases A's global capacity. But Weber does not make clear whether this increase of capacity is gained by A to the deteriment of B, or whether it can be attributed to the AB pair, on condition that there is a means of distribution between the members of the pair. Second, and Weber is more explicit on this point, one must question the nature of the resources at A's disposal to ensure B's compliance.

There is no reason to limit, as too many hasty readers of Marx have been tempted to do, the relation of power as a zero-sum game of two people. Indeed, if one considers capitalists as one actor, if one makes the same simplifying hypothesis about the proletariat, basing oneself on the community of interests of each class and on the strictly exclusive character of the advantages each class is seeking, one arrives at a situation where: 1) the power of the A class can only be exercised on or rather against the B class; 2) the power of the A class is strictly the same thing as the powerlessness of the B class. Such a situation includes at least two variants: the total and lasting dedendency of one of the actors in relation to the other and the *deadly war* between the two protagonists. Such situations certainly belong to the area of the relations of power, but it is no less certain that there are others which do not conform to the zero-sum model. For example, it is enough for a 'third party' to enter the game (referee, mediator, in brief a neutral (disinterested) intervenor or, on the contrary, cynical exploiter of the possibilities his position offers) for a new distribution of the stakes to become possible. From the opposition of two rivals each of whom wants the other's death, one moves to a regime of *coalition*, where the negotiating ability of a third party, which depends on both relatively stable circumstances and data, can modify the relation of forces deriving from their initial distribution. In the same way, the appearance of a 'surplus' can reduce the opposition between the antagonists, either because the surplus can be cleared away only by means of co-operation between them, or because the surplus improves the situation of one and the other at the same time, without its appearance being attributable to either (*windfall profit*).

To the same extent that power cannot be reduced to a zero-sum game for two, the *resources* of power are not limited only to the exercise of *force*, that is all the physical and material constraints (ability to kill, to starve, to inflict, directly or indirectly, unbearable penalties) which are at A's disposal against B to make him co-operate with the realization of A's own aims. This point has been well perceived by political theorists, and especially by Rousseau when he writes in the *Social Contract* that nobody is strong enough to be certain always to be the strongest. It does not follow that power has nothing to do with strength: it often happens that we are obliged to surrender to the other's will, either because he exercises his greater strength, or even because he just threatens us with it. A's power over B is, then, not always based on a sanction which is *actually* carried out. The threat alone can be sufficient. But it must be, as one says, *credible*. The relations between force and power are therefore extremely complex, and the reduction of one to the other forms only a limiting case – even if the reference to force is constitutive of every power-relation.

The opposite resource to force is *legitimacy*. Weber uses this notion widely, and it seems that for him there is no lasting domination without minimal legitimacy. Legitimate power is power which is able to have its decisions accepted as well as justified; it is, in terms of interaction and behaviour, a power whose directives are adhered to, or at least agreed to by those they are intended for. This resigned agreement, or enthusiastic adhesion, contributes to make of power a moral or juridical obligation which ties the ruled to the ruler or power-holder. But neither one nor the other is alone enough since, in their absence, a legitimate institution can mobilize effective sanctions against the contravener. Weber did not try to distinguish the kinds of acceptance by the 'ruled' of the 'rulers' instructions. However, it is not unimportant that B accomplishes what A has directed him to do by dragging his feet, or, on the contrary that he goes beyond what A has prescribed because he is doing it wholeheartedly. What is especially interesting for Weber about legitimacy are the ideological and institutional bases it gives to the exercise of the different types of power: traditional, charismatic, rational-legal. He seems to have given more importance to the bases of legitimacy than to the process of legitimization. Legitimacy ratifies a complex equilibrium between institutional givens (for example the marginality of the prophet in relation to the religious *establishment*, or, on the contrary, the central position of the traditional chief recognized as the heir of a common ancestor by other chiefs of subordinate descent) and ideological givens (for example, the superiority of inspiration and subjective certainty, or on the contrary, the primacy of methodical and bureaucratic procedures). Unfortunately the Weberian typology does not enable us to understand the relation between force and legitimacy in the maintenance of power systems.

To leave the over-simple opposition between situations of pure constraint and situations of legitimacy, it is necessary to combine an analysis of resources with an analysis of strategies. One can indeed make the hypothesis that the ability – power *lato sensu* – of an individual or collective actor depends not only on the nature and quantity of his resources, but also on the congruence between his resources and his strategies. One can imagine an actor over-provided with resources but lacking any strategy. There is good reason for fearing that he will forego using these resources or that he will waste them. Let us imagine a strategy without resources. It is very unlikely to succeed in achieving its aims. For an actor, maximizing his power assumes that he can adapt his resources to their use with an appropriate strategy.

In very general terms, we can say now that power is an intentional process affecting at least two actors which affects the relative level of capacities of each actor in a way which is at least compatible with the actual formula of legitimacy by a redistribution of resources obtained via various strategies. Power is a general social relation but it goes without saying that resources and strategies can only be understood in relation to a situation and not in the absolute. It also goes without saying that it is possible to refer to power in any social context whatsoever, as much in the largest societies as in the smallest groups – whether they are small groups according to Bales, Lewin, or Moreno. For Bales, groups devote themselves relatively precisely to problem solving or task execution which have some practical importance in their opinion. The observer can see among them individuals who put forward the most pertinent and best received propositions, thus leading the group, at the end of the session, to the solution of the problem it had been given. In Moreno's groups, power is the *attraction* possessed by some people (the stars), their abilities to be 'chosen' or else their popularity. From these intersubjective choices or rejections, sociometrical analysis is in a position to build more or less coherent and solid constellations. As to the Lewinian groups, they are characterized by the 'climate' which is found there (democratic or authoritarian) and by the nature of the control exercised by the group over its members and consequently over its own 'dynamics'. Drawing out a proposition common to these three approaches, we would say that power is the ability exercised by *leaders*, both on one another and on the members of the groups, to make motivations and heterogeneous interests coincide.

What limits generalization of the microsociological analysis of power is that it leaves the genesis of the formula of legitimacy in the dark. Moreno's popularity is a quite ambiguous form of power since it can apply equally well to conformist individuals as to rebels or divergent individuals. In Bales, the ability to solve the problem given to the group is not much clearer since this ability can be placed, according to the way in which the problem has been understood by the group members, either in the category of technical skills or in that of tact and seduction (social skills). Finally, the superiority claimed by the Lewinians in favour of the 'democratic' climate is based on the 'natural' character of consensus and the conciliation of interests and opinions.

Now, any formula of legitimacy is to a large extent an historical artefact. For example, *majority rule* is not a rule whose logical coherence is well founded. The paradoxes of the majority decision, stressed by so many writers from Condorcet to Guilbaud and Arrow, clearly testify to this. Majority rule is a highly artificial and contingent construction, the meaning of which can only be adequately understood by a very tendentious historical and institutional analysis.

Let us inquire now in which situations relations of power appear. They are seen especially when there is a need for *co-ordinating* multiple and potentially divergent activities. The paradigm of the division of labour which we borrow from Hume illustrates this situation: that is, a common task, which involves clearing a road of trees blown down by a storm blocking the access to the adjacent fields of two neighbouring farmers. Collective use of individual resources, supposing that it is more efficient than 'each for himself and God for all', assumes both a *specialization* of tasks, each of which takes its place in the chain of the required means for achieving the collective aim, and a *co-ordination* of effort. The question of power occurs in connection with this co-ordination. Does co-ordination take the form of a contractual association? If so, it leads to two series of consequences. Some concern the relations of the associates and in particular the way in which they share the eventual fruits of their co-operation. The others concern the relations between the associates and the delegates or representatives whom they have designated to lead them and supervise the way they execute their undertaking. Thus the power relation has at least two elements at stake: control of the co-operative process and the share of the resulting benefits. But co-ordination, instead of being associative, can be *hierarchical*. Even if the elements at stake are constituted by the distribution of the product resulting from co-operation and by the assignment of people and roles in the co-operation and do not affect the relative position of the co-operating individuals, the power relation can take at least two forms: associative or hierarchical. In the system of *associative co-ordination*, power takes the form of instructions and programmes. Under the system of *hierarchical co-ordination*, it takes the form of commands. Instructions may leave an important margin of autonomy to the associates, who may have an important part in the elaboration of the programmes. Command proceeds from the top. It aims to establish a strict conformity between leaders' expectations and executants' behaviour. To these two forms one may add a third, which we shall call *competitive power*. It is no longer the task and its optional organization which serve as basic criteria; it is *rank*, the *pecking order*, which is the primary determinant. A characteristic bias of many political scientists (such as Lasswell and Kaplan) is to deal with power as if this social relation was reducible to comparison, rivalry, or confrontation. It may happen indeed that, when we are faced with a co-operative task whose rules we believe are oppressive, iniquitous, or absurd, we would rather suffer loss than let others win. It is the situation described by the Castilian proverb about 'the gardener's dog who does not eat, to stop the others from eating'. This ability to block or sabotage is the power to harm. It seems to be as arbitrary to reduce power to the ability to harm as it is to describe it as the willingness to co-operate governed by the principle of the common good.

Whatever the modalities of power, its exercise is subject to certain conditions which in effect limit the field of action of those who dispose of it. The English Parliament is supposed to be able to do anything – except change a man into a woman. The exaggeration is obvious, since, in default of a written constitution, England enjoys customs which are sufficiently strong and respected to moderate the rival claims of different forces. Those who try to ensure the help of others to realize their aims, through their resources and their strategies, are obliged to justify their claims with the help of very general principles, such as the common good or the general will. The first principle states that the constraints imposed by the powerful have only been imposed 'for the good' of those supporting them. The second stipulates that the obligations have been wanted or at least agreed to by those they bond. If these two principles are respected, legitimacy presupposes that power is not arbitrary and is not exercised in the exclusive interest of its holder.

Power can therefore be treated as a social fact. First, it is not reduced to physical force, even if the use or evocation of force constitutes one of the conditions of the exercise of power. Moreover it is social in the triple sense that it is based on expectations and strategies, that it tends towards the realization of certain common objectives, considered as good by all or part of the collectivity concerned, and finally that it is exercised according to more or less explicit procedures, the rules of competitive or co-operative games. Even with the most strongly individualized power, for instance the power of the charismatic prophet, which is exercised without rules, and which is based on a singular authority ('I tell you that . . .'), society's action is perceptible. The prophet invokes an ideal, calls upon a tradition, addresses a church or a public, proposes a plan to them. The Spirit, that is to say the collective requirement 'may your Kingdom be on earth as in heaven', speaks through him. But the fact that power which is exercised upon us, as with the power which we exercise upon others, goes beyond the frame of interaction, and is exercised with a view to collective aims, within limits and according to norms beyond us, does not mean either that we are always powerless or that this collective power hovers over us, without some specific relation to our own resources, preferences, and strategies.

It is very rare that the resources upon which the exercise of power is based are immediately available without cost. Most often the mobilization of resources is previous to the exercise of power; and this preliminary is sometimes difficult and uncertain. The strategy which is intended to bring them into play must begin by obtaining or negotiating their concession. Except in the case of a monopoly over natural resources which are unsubstitutable, or else in the situation of semi-slavery imagined by Marx, where the owners of the means of production can dominate the proletariat who have only their labour power, access to resources is always the object of some sort of transaction, even if it is very one-sided.

The disposal of resources is therefore problematic, and most problematic of all is the attitude of those involved, especially of those whose contributions must be co-ordinated by the leaders. Thus the negotiation of resources (*inputs*) is as important a stage as the sharing of products (*outputs*). And since these two phases are reciprocally linked, by the mechanism of anticipation, it is also the case that power relations are also controlled to a certain extent by both those who exercise power *and* those over whom it is exercised. Now if power can be considered as a quantity, as for example in treating the highest level of efficiency of a collective organization in relation to the ends which it serves, or the greater or lesser exploitation of one group by another, or even inversely as the propensity of groups or individuals to co-operate, it seems reasonable to say that this quantity is variable, and that political systems in the widest sense – that is, the systems of co-ordination created to make the members of a group co-operate in the realization of common objectives – have a very unequal performance according to the way in which their resources – people, their roles, and obligations – are allocated.

Authority, Bureaucracy, Charisma, Marx, Rousseau, State.

Bibliography

ARON, R., 'Macht, power, puissance', *Archives européennes de Sociologie*, 1964, V, 1. – BALANDIER, G., *Anthropologie politique*, Paris, PUF, 1967; rev.ed. 1978. – BALES, R.F., *Interaction process analysis: a method for the study of small groups*, Cambridge, Addison-Wesley, 1950, Folcroft, Folcroft Editions, 1970. – BARNARD, C.I., *The functions of the executive*, Cambridge, Harvard Univ. Press, 1938, 1968. – BOUDON, R., *Effects pervers er ordre social*, Paris, PUF, 1977. – CROZIER, M., *Le phénomène bureaucratique*, Paris, Seuil, 1963; *La société bloquée*, Paris, 1970. – DAHL, R.A., 'The concept of power', *Behavioral Science*, II, 3, 1957, 201–215; *Modern political analysis*, Englewood Cliffs; Prentice Hall, 1963. – DEUTSCH, K.W., *The nerves of government: models of political communication and control*, New York, Free Press, 1963, 1966; London, Collier Macmillan, 1966. – EASTON, D., *A systems analysis of political life*, New York, Wiley, 1965. – GOLD-HAMER, H., SHILS, E., 'Types of power and status', *American Journal of Sociology*, XLV, 1939, 171–182. – HARSANYI, J.C., 'Measurement of social power, opportunity costs, and the theory of two-person bargaining games', *Behavioral Science*, VII, 1, 1962, 67–80. – JOUVENEL, B., de *Du pouvoir: histoire naturelle de sa croissance*. Geneva, Bourquin, 1947; *De la souveraineté: à la recherche du bien politique*. Paris, M.T. Génin, 1955; *De la politique pure*, Paris, Calmann-Lévy, 1963. – LASSWELL, H., KAPLAN, A., *Power and society*, New Haven, Yale Univ. Press, 1950, 1961. – MARCH, J.G., 'An introduction to the theory and measurement of influence', *American Political Science Review*, XLIX, 2, 1955, 431–451; 'The power of power', in EASTON, D., *Varieties of political Theory*, Prentice-Hall, Englewood Cliffs, 1966, 39–70. – MARCH, J.G. and SIMON, H.A., *Organizations*, New York, Wiley, 1958. – MILLS, C.W., *The power elite*, New York, Oxford Univ. Press, 1956. – MORENO, J.L., *Who shall survive? Foundations of sociometry, group therapy and sociodrama*, Beacon, Beacon House, 1934. – PARSONS, T., 'On the concept of political power', American Philosophical Society, *Proceedings*, CVII, 3, 1963, 232–262. – RIKER, W.H., 'Some ambiguities in the notion of power', *American Political Science Review*, LVIII, 2, 1964, 341–349. – ROUSSEAU, J.-J., *The Social Contract*, op cit. – SIMON, H.A., *Models of man: social and rational; mathematical essays on rational human behaviour in a social setting*, New York, J. Wiley & Sons, 1957. – WEBER, M., *Economy and Society*, vol. I Part 1 Ch. 3.

Prediction

There is no action and especially political action possible without some representation of the future, without prediction. But the paradox is that, the more complex and changing societies are, the more necessary and difficult social prediction or forecasting becomes.

It is not difficult to draw up a long list of failures in social forecasting. Denis de Rougemont recalls, for instance, the definition of the car given in 1880 by the very serious German dictionary, the Brockhaus: 'Car: name which has sometimes been given to curious vehicles moved by explosive engines. . . . This invention, forgotten today, has known only failures and disapproval from scientific authorities.' Although dealing with the present, the definition implicitly involved an obviously mistaken prediction. In the *Cours de philosophie positive*, Comte had taken the risk of predicting that it would be impossible for us ever to know the chemical composition of stars. In 1925, a medical journal judged as 'criminal' the pursuit of research on blood transfusion. In 1941, Professor Campbell demonstrated mathematically the impossibility of sending a rocket to the moon. In 1968, G.R. Taylor predicted that parents would be able to choose the sex of their children from 1975. In 1963, Denis Gabor systematically analysed a series of 'prospective' (or predictive) works by 100 British intellectuals between 1924 and 1932: 'None of these volumes deals with overpopulation, in fact the subject is hardly mentioned; only the theme of the deterioration of human heredity, due to the lower fecundity of the élites is dealt with.' In 1897, Durkheim seemed to believe – although he does not make any clear prediction – that rising suicide rates would ineluctably accompany the increasing complexity of the division of labour. Three decades later, Halbwachs observed that from the turn of the century suicide rates did not any longer show systematic tendencies to increase. Towards 1965 an expert of the Ford Foundation predicted that in 1975 universities would be created in the United States at the rate of one per week. Economists have thought for a long time that inflation and unemployment could only vary in inverse ratio to each other.

These few examples indicate some of the main causes of failure in social forecasting or prediction. When a *statistical tendency* (for instance regular increase of suicide rates as shown through the level of statistical record throughout the nineteenth century) or a *correlation* (for instance the negative correlation between inflation and unemployment) persists, a 'natural' temptation occurs, that of extrapolation. More exactly, the persistence of a tendency or a correlation prompts the production of theories which enable it to be taken into account. Such theories can only be conditional. But it is often difficult to specify the conditions which validate them. This leads to a tendency to hold them as unconditionally true. When an *invention* appears, it can lead to variable predictions according to whether its potentialities are visible or not. The first cars were hardly faster than the horse-driven vehicle and certainly much noisier and smellier. From the aesthetic point of view, they looked like carts with a strange lump where it was necessary to accommodate an engine. Likewise, as Konrad Lorenz observes, the first railway wagons had the curious form of a row of horse-drawn coaches which could have been welded together. It is only many years after the first appearance of the invention that railway engine and car acquire speed, that coaches are transformed into compartments of a carriage, that the car progressively takes forms which no longer recall the cart. But at the time of the invention, technical and aesthetic evolution was difficult to forecast. Hence the appearance of predictions which infer the social rejection of the invention. In an opposite way, the rapid progress of genetic engineering immediately suggests the possibility of choosing the sex of children. This 'potentiality' is immediately understandable. The futurologist may then easily be tempted to neglect both the time necessary for the effective realization of technical potentialities and also the social resistances which would oppose the implementation of these potentialities.

Briefly, predictions about the social diffusion of technical inventions are affected by numerous factors. The degree of visibility of the potentialities of the invention is an essential factor in this respect, but there are others. An invention might be useless in a given context and suddenly take on a crucial importance if characteristics of the context are modified (cf. for example the effects of the energy crisis on the interest in geothermics). In other cases, the prediction's failure is due to the presence of value systems and ideological references. Thus, the Social Darwinism in which part of the British intelligentsia was steeped between the two world wars explains why the 'futurologists' of the time were more preoccupied by the problem of the differential fecundity of the social classes than by the global evolution of population. In other cases still, the prediction's failure is due simply to obstacles which are by nature opposed to the anticipation of innovations. However, it must be noted on this point that if it is always impossible by definition to predict an innovation in all its details, some of its elements can be anticipated almost with certitude. Thus, the expansion of the demand for cotton fabrics and the development of the cotton industry in England at the end of the eighteenth century were sufficient indicators to forecast the appearance of more efficient and productive looms. On the other hand, it was difficult, in 1850, to forecast the invention of aeroplanes. Hence, the numberless 'demonstrations' that history has recorded about the impossibility of making heavier-than-air objects fly. Kuhn has indeed explained why scientists tend to hold on to a paradigm or a theory long after the appearance of the first 'facts' which are not compatible with this paradigm or theory. *A fortiori*, the anticipation of an innovation is by necessity a rare event. In other cases too, predictions are wrong because they lead to consequences which cause their invalidity (self-destroying prediction). If everyone thinks the meeting will be crowded, everyone will abstain from going to it, so that there will be no one there in the end. It is possible that the dramatic description of the effects of over-population has in some cases facilitated the adoption of birth-control policies and consequently contributed to invalidate or at least make them appear as excessive predictions on this matter. Likewise, the prediction of catastrophic effects due to poor hygiene can contribute to improve hygiene and thus avoid the predicted catastrophes. A symmetrical case is the self-fulfilling prophecy made popular by Merton: it is the case of predictions which would be wrong if they did not lead to consequences which make them come true. *Last but not least*, failures in prediction are often due simply to the fact that events or states of affairs are caused by conjunctions of factors which are either unpredictable or unlikely. Thus, in order to predict some decades ago the revival of Islam, it would have been necessary first to know the geographical allocation of oil resources, second to anticipate societies' consumption of fossil fuel, third to forecast the geopolitical division of the earth, as well as numerous other factors, some of which must be held as *contingent*. This is why Herman Kahn admits that his methods would not have enabled him to predict either the First World War, or the growth of Fascism or Communism, or Einstein, Bohr, or Freud.

Ought we then to adopt an attitude of healthy scepticism towards disciplines which undertake to predict or forecast, such as 'futurology' or 'prospective' social sciences? Such an attitude would evidently not be sensible. Because, although we can point to many failures in prediction, it is equally obvious that there are numerous successful predictions. Even more so than it seems, since several remain implicit, precisely because they go without saying. Nobody seriously imagines for instance that the United States will become a totalitarian state before 1990, that the world population will be halved by 2000 or that England will soon become a primarily agricultural society. As examples among thousands of less 'trivial' predictions confirmed by facts, let us refer to the case of Brzezinski who, from 1967, feared that an increase in people's participation in public affairs would make political continuity more precarious in democracies in general, and in the United States in particular (Grambard). Or Daniel Bell's famous argument: as the development of tertiary and quaternary sectors leads to a slowing down of average productivity increase, and salary increases obtained in the sectors with a high productivity increase tend to be diffused in the others, 'post-industrial' societies must be marked by chronic inflationary tendencies.

Naturally, all those professing to make social prediction are more or less aware of the difficulties and risks of failure. Despite these risks and the failures suffered, futurology has progressively and increasingly firmly become institutionalized as a consequence of the efforts of pioneers like Berger and de Jouvenel in France or Kahn in the United States. The reason for this is that predictive disciplines assume important scientific and social functions which are not confined to their most obvious objective, that is to say to attempt to reduce uncertainty about the future. One of these functions could be called the function of 'conceptualization'. Let us take a very simple example. A futurologist claims that if the increase in the number of researchers is maintained at the rate observed between year t and year $t + 1$, half of the population will be composed of researchers in the year $t + K$. There is every chance that he considers the future event thus forecast not only as unlikely, but as almost out of the question. The extrapolation shows in this case the virtue of *conceptualization*: the rate of increase observed between t and $t + 1$ cannot be maintained without leading to intolerable political consequences. The complex extrapolations undertaken by Forrester and Meadows no doubt had the function and perhaps the aim, not of predicting the development of the world system, but of attracting attention to the consequences which would result within certain limits from the maintenance of a certain range of behaviour (energy consumption for example). Hence the method of 'scenarios' developed by the 'futurologists'. This method consists of studying the evolution of complex systems under various hypotheses. By definition, the analyst does not attempt to predict in this case (since, at best, all scenarios except one will be condemned by the future-become-present). But scenario development can guide action by showing up more clearly the consequences of alternative choices.

Second, prediction and forecasting have a methodological function. The consideration of failures in prediction can improve knowledge of social phenomena. Thus failures in demographical prediction have incited researchers not to be satisfied, whenever possible, with the method of extrapolation in current use and to attempt to understand better how demographic phenomena appearing at the aggregate level result from the composition of the microphenomena which make up individual behaviours. Likewise, the failure of extrapolations about suicide statistics led sociologists to a more attentive analysis of suicide phenomena at the individual level. In the same way, the disappointment caused by the failure of some birth-control policies has led researchers to sharpen their analysis of reproductive behaviour. Thus, in India, it was expected that rural people would be easily persuaded to practise birth-control, which apparently *evidently* could only have economic effects beneficial for family unity. The failure of such forecasts prompted the researchers to question this *evidence*, by going back to the field. They observed then that, in some contexts, social and economic structures were such that a farmer had to have on average four sons, two working on the land and two working in a factory, in order to rise above subsistence level. Now, in order to have four sons, one needs an average of eight children.

The drawbacks of forecasting, demonstrated by the limits of summary methods such as extrapolation, have not only led to the improvement of knowledge and better modelling of microsociological phenomena making up aggregate data, they have also led to an awareness of the relevance of system analysis for explaining social phenomena. The cases of the 'self-creating prophecy' or of the 'self-destroying prophecy' are paradigmatic examples of system effects or composition effects. Meadows and Forrester's exercises show the complex effects resulting from the interaction between a great number of variables, effects not easy to see with intuitive methods.

Perhaps, too, the development of forecasting and futurology is not without consequence on the *philosophical* level. It has no doubt helped to sharpen the sense of the circularity of relations between microsociological and macrosociological variables for both researchers in social sciences and politicians together with the sense of the complexity of the social system, the awareness of the gap left by 'structural data', and, correlatively, the sense of the possible. The difficulty of prediction is not due only to ignorance on the part of the researcher. It is caused also by an *objective* indetermination present in various degrees in any social system. This indetermination comes from the fact that the atoms of social systems, individuals, are sources of action. The most able physicist is unable to predict better than the most ignorant the trajectory of a falling leaf. Because, even if he knows the laws of dynamics, he is ignorant of the particular forces at work in the case of *this* leaf which is falling at *this* instant. But the indetermination in this case is quite subjective: it results from the physicist's ignorance about the objective conditions of the leaf's fall. As to the indetermination faced by the sociologist, it is in general partially subjective and partially objective. Because, if social actors act within the frame of constraints imposed by systems, these constraints are not enough generally to determine the course of individual actions. Rather, they have the effect of circumscribing the field of possibilities.

Determinism, Historicism, Ideologies.

Bibliography

BELL, D., *The coming of post-industrial society: a venture in social forecasting*, New York, Basic Books, 1973; London, Heinemann, 1974. 'Twelve modes of prediction. A preliminary sorting of approaches in the social sciences', *in* BENNIS, W.G., BENNE, K.D., and CHIN, R., *The planning of change*, London/New York, Holt, Rinehart & Winston, 1966, 1969, 532–552. – CAZES, B., 'Prévision et planification', *in* DECOUFLÉ, A.C. (ed.), *Traité élémentaire de prévision et de prospective*, Paris, PUF, 1978, 247–265. – FERKISS, V.C., *Futurology, promise, performance, prospects*, London, Sage, 1977. – GABOR, D., *Inventing the future*, London, Pelican, 1963. – GRAS, A., *Sociologie des ruptures: les pièges du temps en sciences sociales*, Paris, PUF, 1979. – GRAUBARD, S.R. (ed.), 'Toward the year 2000', *Daedalus*, LXLVI, 3, 1967, 937–963. – JOUVENEL, B. de, *L'art de la conjecture*, Monaco, Editions du Rocher, 1964. – KAHN, H. and BRUCE-BRIGGS, B., *Things to come: thinking about the seventies and eighties*, New York, Macmillan, 1972. – LORENZ, K., *Die Rückseite des Spiegels. Versuch einer Naturgeschichte menschlichen Erkennens*, Munich/Zurich, R. Piper, 1973. – MATALON, B., 'Les limites de la prévision scientifique', *in* DECOUFLÉ, A.C. (ed.), *Traité élémentaire de prévision et de prospective*, Paris PUF, 1978, 105–130. – MEADOWS, D.H., MEADOWS, D.L., RANDERS, J., BEHRENS, W.W., *The limits to growth*, New York, Universe Books, 1972. – MERTON, R.K., 'The self fulfilling prophecy', *Antioch review*, summer 1948, 193–210, *in* MERTON, R.K., *Social theory and social structure; toward the codification of theory and research*, Glencoe. The Free Press, 1949, rev. ed 1957, 1961, 421–436. – ROUGEMONT, D. (de), *L'avenir est notre affaire*, Paris, Stock 1977. – TÖFFLER, A., *Future shock*, New York, Random House, 1970; Oxford, Pergamon, 1983; New York, Bantam Books, 1970.

Professions

A certain number of activities such as medicine and the legal occupations are designated by the term liberal professions. Although one often refers to the teaching profession, the question is whether teaching is a profession like medicine and law, especially in countries where 'national education' is a large-scale public service managed by public authorities according to bureaucratic forms of financing and staff recruitment.

The sociology of professions is based on three main contributions, those of Weber, Durkheim, and Parsons. Weber stressed the importance of professions in modern western society, and he sees in the process of professionalization the transition from a traditional social order to a social order where everyone's status depends on the tasks he performs and where these are allocated according to 'rational' criteria of ability and specialization. The profession is a 'vocation'. It is not inherited like an ascribed status, but chosen and assumed like a task. Durkheim searched for a legitimate authority able to appease the conflicts of interest which tear apart industrial societies and to re-establish a minimum of cohesion among their members. He believed it would be found in the professional associations or the corporative associations (craft guilds or trade unions), which he does not always clearly distinguish. Each profession is ruled by a special set of rules which develops a discipline among its members and detaches them from individualist egoism.

Parsons enlarged and systematized Weber's and Durkheim's analyses from his paradigm for the therapeutic relation. It was the doctor/patient relationship which he analysed in detail, and that he later tried to generalize. The patient is *dependent* on the doctor. Indeed, the patient cannot regain health on his own; but the doctor, because of his skill, can help him to become healthy again. The doctor's skill rests on a double expertise. He has a certain knowledge of the illness and its causes; he also has the experience of a certain number of intervention techniques. This duality of skills is expressed by saying that medicine is an applied science. Thus, medicine exercises a power over the patient, who is doubly dependent. He is dependent because of his relative incompetence, but also because of the worrying situation in which his illness places him. As there is a relation of power between patient and doctor, there is a risk of exploitation to the prejudice of the former and to the benefit of the latter.

It is from this bilateral relation that the medical value system becomes *understandable*. This imposes obligation on the two parties by institutionalizing their relation of exchange in the context of asymmetry resulting from the unequal distribution of skills between them. The attributes governing the doctor's role are formed by a mixture of interest and detachment (*detached concern*).

This paradigm of the therapeutic relation can be generalized to the other professions: the same combination of technical skill based on knowledge and goodwill towards the client is also found in the case of the teacher who, in principle at least, 'knows more than his pupils' and must exercise his authority 'for their own good' with a view to their education.

Professions are distinguished in other ways from other employments. Even if they ensure substantial incomes, they are not lucrative, in the sense that the priority given to the search for profit is not legitimate for the professional. 'The doctor is not supposed to make money' out of his client. Even in a system of liberal medicine (such as in France or the USA), the doctor does not choose his clients in terms of their potential as a source of income and even less can he abandon patients in danger under the pretext they are not solvent. Second, professionals enjoy a certain autonomy towards the tutelage of hierarchic authorities, or even public authorities. Professional confidence can be invoked by the doctor, even if he works for a 'paying third party'. Likewise, neither the police nor the courts can oblige the lawyer to provide information likely to incriminate his client and the lawyer who would consent to this would be dishonoured.

The professional keeps a certain independence towards his clients but also towards the third parties, political authorities, and even public administrations, financing his services. It is this concern for their independence which characterizes, for example, teachers as professionals, even if they are, as in France, civil servants.

Moreover, the relation between professions and teaching is central but complex, since the competence of most professionals is 'certified' by the teachers who have trained them and who have publicly recognized their knowledge and expertise by delivering grades and diplomas.

Can all activities be 'professionalized'? It is true that an increasing number of activities which were free for a long time are now exercised within the frame of a profession which is officially recognized and provided with more or less statutory powers. The term professionalization is therefore very ambiguous. At one level, it can be held as synonymous with qualification. But this qualification is very far from always being associated with technical competence based on an institutionally guaranteed minimal knowledge. The 'professional' hairdresser is not satisfied any more, like the former village barber, with cutting your hair after the Sunday church service. He has a salon, open at regular hours, where he also sells lotions and creams – luxury products, the rise of which is linked to the rise of 'mass consumption'. But having become a 'trichologist', he is a specialist of the scalp, of hair loss, and even up to a point of skin diseases. Thus understood, does professionalization *really* correspond to upward social mobility? Let us consider now another profession like the physiotherapist's. Its appearance also corresponds to the elevation or the ennobling of a traditional mechanical art, the bone-setter's. But unlike the cosmetician, who has maintained his autonomy towards the health specialists, the physiotherapist has entered the realm of the medical professions. Many of his clients have been referred to him by doctors; and he has typically received some medical training.

In the process of professionalization, many distinct processes are at work. We shall note first a tendency to qualification, which proceeds in parallel with the tendency to academicize professional training. But this process must be related to the search for status and the security linked with it. The level of studies and training required by those practising the trade of hairdresser or tailor is legally guaranteed by a 'certificate' of professional ability. Thus, the general knowledge and the technical skill of the candidate are confirmed. Solicitors, pharmacists, and doctors have always alleged that in order to correctly exercise their responsibilities they first needed to have undertaken a good training, that is to say of a sufficient duration though not necessarily concerned with practice. But the length of training does not guarantee its quality, any more than its academic character is enough to prove its relevance. Furthermore, the qualification requirement does not have the same meaning when we are dealing with a craft or a genuine applied science. Part of the training in the field is different in both cases. The 'latest functions' (Merton) of the politics of training can be studied from two points of view. Indeed, these politics contribute to the *bureaucratization* of many careers and occupations, since these can only be gained now through the exchange of certificates and diplomas. Moreover, it helps each profession to barricade itself in a quasi-corporate group, which defends its status and its privileges in the name of the training undertaken rather than through the services given to its clients.

Sociologists, like Durkheim or Parsons, who had counted on 'professionalization' to 'moralize' industrial societies, should have taken into account these unexpected effects they neglected. Professionalization cannot be analysed merely as a tendency towards qualification. It also contributes to a move towards a tertiarization of the labour market, with low productivity, typically coupled with the defence of narrow corporate interests.

Capitalism, Conformity and Deviance, Social Mobility, Social Stratification.

Bibliography

BELL, D., *The coming of post-industrial society. A venture of social forecasting*, New York, Basic Books, 1973; London, Heinemann, 1974. – COSER, R., 'The complexity of roles as a seedbed of individual autonomy', in COSER, L. (ed.), *The idea of social structure. Papers in honor of Robert K. Merton*, New York, Harcourt Brace, 1975, 237–263. – DURKHEIM, E., *The Division of Labour in Society*, op cit. – HUGHES, E.C., *Men and their Work*, New York, The Free Press of Glencoe, 1958, 1964; 'Professions', *Daedalus, 92*, 1963, 655–668. – HUNTINGDON, S.P., 'Power, expertise, and the military profession', *Daedalus, 92*, 1963, 785–807. – JANOWITZ, M. *The professional soldier: a social and political portrait*, Glencoe, Free Press, 1960, 1965. – MERTON, R.K., *The student-physician. Introductory studies in the sociology of medical education*, Cambridge, Harvard Univ. Press, 1957, 1969. – PARSONS, T., 'The professions and social structure', in PARSONS, T., *Essays in Sociological theory pure and applied*, 1949, 2nd rev. edn, Glencoe, Free Press, 1954; *The social system*, New York, The Free Press, 1951, chap. 10. – POUND, R. *The lawyer from modern times: with particular reference to the development of bar associations in the United States*, Saint-Paul, West, 1953. – VEBLEN, Th., *The engineers and the price system*, New York, B.W. Huebsch, 1921; New York, A.M. Kelley, 1965. – WEBER, M., *Economy and Society* Ch. 2 op cit.

Prophetism

The term *prophetism* designates a group of social activities and roles that concern foretelling the future so far as it relates to some of the essential and most emotionally charged orientations of collective life. The phenomenon of prophetism is associated with the remarkable nature of an exceptional personality. In this respect, it is close to charisma. But it distinguishes itself from this on one point, to which Max Weber draws attention. While charisma is linked to the existence of an 'emotional community' that is more or less stable and which possesses an obvious hierarchical structure, with the chief, or the guide, his lieutenants, and the 'mass' of faithful or partisans, the prophet is an inspired person who isolates himself in tragic solitude away from the public which always begins by being unaware of his message or by rejecting it.

The pathetic or even tragic connotation of prophetism should not be exaggerated. It is tangible above all among the Hebrew prophets of the pre-exile period on which Weber has written pages with such wonderful intelligence. But there are prophets in places besides Israel. Following Erwin Rohde, the same Weber asks himself 'whether the wise men of ancient Greece . . . Empedocles . . . and above all Pythagoras, are not very close to prophetism?' The same can be asked about the gurus of classical India. However, these comparisons, which give rise to the generality if not the universality of prophetism, must not be taken too far. Once we have exhausted all the range of possible comparisons, we must look for the distinguishing characteristic of the phenomenon we are studying.

In as much as he foretells the future, the prophet must be distinguished from the divine or those whom in *Ancient Judaism* Weber also calls the court prophets. This distinction rests on two criteria: the divine often relies on magical techniques. Also, he is dependent on powerful people. The Jewish prophet is a 'prophet of misfortune'. He foretells the punishments that Yahveh will inflict on his people and first on their unworthy leaders. To announce them, he does not base himself on utilitarian knowledge but on explicit learning, the Thorah (the Law) and the Berith (the alliance of Yahveh with his people).

Weber depicts Jewish prophetism on the side of an ethic and theodicy, the one and the other with strongly rationalistic coloration. This interpretation clashes at first sight with the deliberately emotive style of the prophets. Yahveh is in communication with them; some even believe that they can repeat his words literally. But whatever the vehemence of their rhetoric or the strangeness of their behaviour (to proclaim the threat that hangs over his people, Isaiah walks through the streets with a wooden yoke, then an iron one to *announce* the next period of enslavement of the chosen people), the authenticity of the prophesy is attested by the conformity of its message with tradition. What the prophet is preaching has nothing to do with radical rupture or innovation; it is the return of the Levites to instruction that explains the alliance of God and His people. Also, the prophetic message, even if it translates itself by means of disturbing images, is perfectly comprehensible to those whom he is addressing as they have all been educated in the same tradition as the prophet himself. It is also rational, if we make the hypothesis that Yahveh, for whom the prophet is the voice and bearer of the message, always carries out what he has undertaken to do, that he is perfectly trustworthy, and at the same time all powerful. The God in whose name the prophet speaks makes no mystery about his intentions or his desires. He never breaks his Word. What he desires is that the conditions that he has stipulated in their alliance are respected scrupulously by his people. History is thereby foreseeable as it is only the execution of the contract passed between Israel and Yahveh.

This interpretation would not be sustainable if it did not take into account one characteristic dimension of Jewish prophetism. The appeal to traditionalism does not signify the legitimization of the established order. Very much to the contrary, the tradition that he invokes constitutes for the prophet the most redoubtable weapon against the well-to-do. These are then challenged in the name of a tradition of which they are the custodians and which they are accused of betraying. The famous 'he has not put down the mighty from their seat and exalted the humble and meek' does not explain the anger of the prophets against the powerful, but recalls the punishment that they deserve in despising the laws of Yahveh, while the humble remained faithful to their alliance.

But prophetism is not reduced to this moralization of history which gives value to the practices of pious and humble men in a moving style. An eschatological dimension is added to the rational dimension. The confidence of the prophet in the Word of Yahveh who will never abandon his people, even if he punishes mercilessly those who leave the alliance, engenders the *certainty* that, at the end of ends, however imminent it might be, the fulfilment of the promise will come. The 'day of Yahveh' will see the punishment of all iniquities and the fulfilment of all hopes. The relationship between the ethical dimension and the escatalogical dimension of prophesy can only be established thanks to a symbolic compromise on which in the final reckoning, the confidence of the prophet in the rationality and regularity of history rests.

There are other forms of prophetism apart from those that evolved from ancient Judaism. The Buddhist monk is also in his own way a prophet. He bears the promise of an absolutely good life which can be attained if the message imparted by the prophet is taken seriously. But the orientation of the guru is radically different from that of the Hebrew prophet. He is not addressing himself to a people, bonded by a common destiny, which recognizes its identity through its participation in an alliance and a contract. What he brings is his *example*. Moreover, the activism of the ethical prophet corresponds with the detachment of the exemplary prophet. The guru does not pursue the accomplishment of a promise or an engagement but the realization of essential perfection.

Be he 'ethical' as in the Jewish tradition or 'exemplary' as in the Buddhist tradition, the prophet's main characteristic is his vocation, his conviction, but also his singular *grace*. The vocation expresses the way in which the role of the prophet inserts itself among the other social roles. This insertion seems at first sight to be a rupture. But the prophet is not a subversive in a unilateral way. He belongs as much as he is estranged. He conforms as much as he protests. Following the gospel expression, he is 'a sign of contradiction'. The simultaneously subjective and absolute character of his conviction adds to the singularity of the prophet. This exposes both himself and his followers to the risk of being closed up within himself which he faces up to by establishing privileged relationships with the one from whom he draws his mission (as in the case of the ethical prophet) or with his disciples (as in the case of the guru). Grace, the *charisma*, be it personal or institutional, offers a guarantee, if a somewhat fragile one, because it is exposed by the possibility of pseudo-prophets to the risk of imposture and, on the public side, to the hardening of hearts.

Is prophetism a category destined to fade away? The majority of prophetic movements which have become successfully institutionalized have tended to affirm that with the appearance of their founder, the line of prophets is definitively ended. Prophetic hope turns in on itself even before the realization of the promise. It itself creates the conditions needed for its fulfilment (Merton). In lay terms, this affirmation is seen in the thesis of the 'end of history'. Finally, we can ask ourselves whether prophetism as we have characterized it is not a phenomenon that is very much alive today. But to give an adequate description of it, we must add the following characteristics. First, it tends to go beyond the strictly religious field and invades areas of personal intimacy. Second, it has more and more difficulty in becoming institutionalized. Finally, the different conventicles from which it is born die off as rapidly as they appear.

This characteristic instability of prophetism raises the question of 'false' prophets. Imposture is one fundamental category for the analysis of prophetism. Within the notion of imposture we can detect two dimensions. The first is underlined by the rationalist tradition, which makes the imposture into an interested lie. However, the imposture can also be blasphemy. When Jesus affirms that he really is the Messiah, the princes of the priesthood see in this affirmation not only a lie but also a most atrocious attack on divine majesty. Against the imposture of false prophets, the faithful must be put on guard. The evangelist teaches that the tree must be judged by its fruits. Jesus affirms, however, that he did not come to change the law but to accomplish it. Between the prophet and tradition complex links are established which are not adequately explained by the metaphor of rupture or by that of repetition. Prophetism characterizes certain social movements in the sense that they build up around themselves a very acute conscience that a society is in crisis, that its central values are in danger, that it is the time to restore them or replace them.

Authority, Charisma, Ideologies, Power, Prediction, Religion, Role.

Bibliography

BALANDIER, G., 'Messianismes et nationalismes en Afrique noire', *Cahiers intern. de Sociologie*, 1953, vol. XIV. – COHN, N., *The pursuit of the Millennium: revolutionary messianism in medieval and reformation Europe and its bearing on modern totalitarian movements*, Fairlawn, Essential Books, 1957; rev. ed New York, Oxford University Press, 1970; London, Secker & Warburg, 1957. – EISENSTADT, S.N., *Max Weber: on charisma and institution building, selected papers*, Chicago, The Univ. of Chicago Press, 1968. – GELLNER, E., 'Sanctity, puritanism, secularisation, and nationalism in North Africa: a case study', *Archives de Sociologie des Religions, 15*, 71–86. – LODS, A., *Les prophètes d'Israël et les débuts du judaïsme*, Paris, Albin Michel, 1935. – MÜHLMANN, W.E., *Chiliasmus and Nativismus*, Berlin, D. Reimer, 1961. – NEHER, A., *L'essence du prophétisme*, Paris, PUF, 1955. – O'DEA, T., *The Mormons*, Chicago, Univ. of Chicago Press, 1957. – SCHOLEM, G.G., *Major trends in Jewish Mysticism*, New York, Schocken, 1941, 1961.; *The messianic ideology in Judaism and other essays in Jewish spirituality*, New York, Schoken Books, 1971, 1974. – SMITHSON, R.J., *The Anabaptists: their contribution to our protestant heritage*, London, Clarke, 1935. – TALMON, J.L., *Political messianism: the romantic phase*, New York, Praeger, 1961; – WEBER, M., *Economy and Society*, op cit. London, Secker & Warburg, 1960.

R

Rationality

The idea of rationality is used by the social sciences in several senses. In the tradition of economic science, at least as it is expressed by Pareto (*Treatise of General Sociology*), an action is said to be rational when it is objectively well adapted to the goal sought by the subject. Rationality signifies in this case adaptation of the means to the ends. As for the modern economist, he defines rational behaviour as the choice by the individual of the action which he prefers among all those which he has the opportunity of accomplishing, briefly as a choice which conforms to his preferences. This definition tends – let us note incidentally – to introduce an irrefutable hypothesis starting from the moment when the preferences are, as is generally the case, inferred, starting from observed actions. In general, the economist abstains from applying the concept of rationality to the ends themselves. One would however say of an actor that he is irrational if he pursues contradictory ends or if his preferences are incoherent (intransitive). In sociology the concepts of *Zweckrationell* (Weber: rational in connection with the ends), *logical action* (Pareto), *instrumental rationality* (Parsons), *Wozu-Motive* (Schutz) are practically synonymous and describe an action utilizing the means adapted to the desired ends. But Weber also introduces the concept *Wertrationell* (rational in connection with values) to qualify an action adapted to values and not to ends. Thus the hero's sacrifice is *Wertrationell*. Schutz's *Weil-Motive* introduces a concept close to the Weberian notion of *Wertrationalität*.

In the preceding cases, the qualification *rational* is applied to actions. But it can equally be applied to explanatory statements. In this case one would say of a statement (or of a group of statements) that it is rational if it is congruent with the knowledge (in the scientific sense of the term) that one has on the subject or in conformity with the canons of the 'scientific spirit'. The *rational* or *irrational* character of beliefs and myths thrown up in 'archaic' societies, or the myths and ideologies of modern societies, are the object of a classic discussion.

Even in its most simple *praxiological* meaning, the idea of rationality poses numerous problems of definition. Generally, if a specific collection of means exists to arrive at an end, if these means can be totally ordered in relation to one criterion (this criterion could be for example the cost, the difficulty, the accessibility of each means), rational action is that which utilizes the best means in relation to this criterion. But these conditions (overall order in relation to an unique criterion of a finished collection of means) may not all be united (and often are not). If they are objectively united, they may not be so in the consciousness of the actor, who may for example have no knowledge of such and such a means. The notion of rationality, in the praxiological sense of the term, is thus only unequivocally defined in limited situations.

On the other hand, games theory has contributed to showing that one must associate with the idea of rationality multiple definitions from the moment when the relationship between the available means of achieving a certain end are hit by an objective uncertainty. Let us suppose that, in using the means M, I was able to win x francs with the probability p and lose $x1$ francs with the probabiliuty $1 - p$, and that in utilizing $M1$ I was able to win y francs with the probability of $1 - q$. It is obvious that the 'solution' of the game will vary with the values of x, $x1$, y, $y1$, p, and q. If x, y, and $y1$ are small but $x1$ is big, it is only rational to choose $M1$ if $1 - p$ is small, that is to say to minimize the risks or 'regrets' run (Wald's criterion). In effect, the gain which I might hope for in playing $M1$ is small, but the possible loss is also small, whereas M exposes me to a large loss. Conversely, if x is large, and $x1$, y, and $y1$ are small, unless p is small, it is rational to choose M, that is to say to maximize the possible gains (Savage's criterion). In this case M exposes me in effect to a moderate risk, but permits me to hope for large gains if chance is on my side. In these two situations, the form of the rationality (to minimize possible regrets, and to maximize possible gains) results from the structure of the situation of uncertainty. In other words, there is every chance that, faced with the first situation, any gambler would spontaneously adopt a rationality of the Wald type, and faced with the second, a Savage-type rationality. But it is easy to imagine numerous intermediary cases, where the structure of the situation of uncertainty imposes neither the first nor the second criterion. In this case, the criterion implicitly adopted by a gambler would essentially depend on his psychology and his resources, that is to say on variables external to the structure of the situation of uncertainty. In a third case: if one knows the values of p and q and if the choice is repetitive, one can choose the means giving the greatest 'hope of gain' or the least likelihood of loss (Laplace's criterion). But here again, it must be noted that the criterion does not impose itself as a 'natural' definition of rationality, but only for certain values of the parameters p, q, x, $x1$, y, $y1$. For other values, gamblers will hesitate and 'will choose' a different form of rationality according to their psychology or their resources. Certain situations of uncertainty have thus a structure which they 'impose' on every gambler, whatever his psychology and his resources, a particular form of rationality. But this applies to particular cases. Generally, the structure of the situation of uncertainty does not impose one criterion of rationality compared with others in an obvious fashion. In that case, the behaviour of the gambler has every chance of depending upon variables other than those which are defined by the structure of the situation. In the first place it will depend upon the resources of the gamblers and, to some extent, psychological variables. These distinctions are of great importance for the sociologist: they show that the structure of the situation of uncertainty and the social characteristics of the decider (his resources) are, to use statistical language, interactive variables: certain structures of uncertainty impose a particular rationality. In that case the behaviour of the decider may depend a little on his social characteristics. Other structures are compatible with different forms of rationality; the behaviour is likely to depend upon variables such as the resources of the decider.

These observations bear an essential corollary. Let us once again consider the situation of uncertainty mentioned earlier and its structure (that is the parameters $p, q, x, x1, y, y1$). For certain combinations of values of these parameters (that is, for certain structures of the situation of uncertainty) one criterion of rationality imposes itself compared with others, whatever the particular psychology and resources of the deciders. In this case, the model of *homo oeconomicus* (which presupposes interchangeable individuals gifted with an identical rationality) is pertinent. For other structures, no criterion of rationality imposes itself compared with others. The model of *homo sociologicus* (the rationality being dependent upon the social characteristics of the actor, possibly the values in which he believes) is pertinent.

In the foregoing argument, we have considered the case of the solitary decision in conditions of uncertainty. Now it is useful to consider decisions in interactive situations. When the preferences of the deciders are perfectly compatible, the definition of the idea of rationality does not pose any particular problem: the actors are rational if they make the choices which permit them to arrive at the situation which all of them consider to be the best from their point of view. Cases also exist where the actors are committed to compromise: even if I prefer A to B, I see clearly that I must be content with B. In counterpart, my partner agrees to be content with B1 and give up A1 which he prefers. The idea of rationality applies itself without difficulty to the first case (co-operation or convergence) as it does to the second (compromise). But interactive situations also exist, the structure of which is such that, even if one imagines that the subject is conscious of and informed of the parameters of that structure, it is difficult for him to determine the 'rational solution', that is to say to choose the behaviour which will lead to the most favourable result from his point of view. A typical structure in this regard is that called the prisoner's dilemma because of the fable sometimes used by games theorists to illustrate this structure. Imagine that two actors are each able to choose between actions A and B and that the first has the following order of preference: BA, AA, BB, AB (the situation which he prefers is that where he himself would choose B whereas the other person would choose A, afterwards comes, in the order of preference, the situation where each would choose A, etc.). As for the second actor, his order of preferences is AB, AA, BB, BA (that is, he prefers situations where the first having chosen A, he would choose B, followed by the situation where both he and the first actor choose A, etc.). As one can see, both agree to place AA and BB, in that order, at the centre of their scale of preferences, but their preferences are opposed as far as situations AB and BA are concerned. In this case, it is rational for each to choose B, which is a 'dominant strategy' (B is a better choice than A for each of the actors, whatever the choise of the other). But this 'rational' choice by the actors leads to 'solution' BB which is only third in their order of preference. Here one would say that one was dealing with a process with a less than optimum balance. An illustration of this type of figure is the following: two candidates in a presidential election have to decide whether or not they are going to use posters (A) or not use posters (B). The order of preferences has every chance of having the structure above. In fact, the first prefers BA (he uses posters for his campaign, and the other does not; it is to be imagined that if the campaign is effective he will hope to gain votes), then AA (neither of them has such a campaign, no one wins votes or wastes his party's funds), then BB (both have a campaign, no one wins votes and both waste their party's funds), then AB (only the other has a campaign and wins votes). Similarly, the second candidate has the order of preference AB, AA, BB, BA. But for defensive and offensive reasons, it is in each's interest to choose B (to have a campaign). The result is that the finally realized situation will be BB (waste without benefit for anyone). Another classic example of the situation in which the structure could be called equivocal (in that sense where it is difficult to determine the action which constitutes the most 'rational' response) is that where the possible actions A and B cause contradictory consequences in time (cf. the immediate pleasure and the long-term risks run by the smoker, the politics of *'après moi le déluge'*, etc.). Other structures are not only ambiguous, but push the actors into decisions which they are very likely to consider as bad. Let us for example imagine that I sit on a committee and that I have the choice between filling a post today by choosing the best among a collection of mediocre candidates or of leaving the post vacant and waiting until a qualified candidate presents himself. In this case, the norms attached to my role as member of the committee shows me that the rational choice (in this case: this choice which conforms to the implicit norms that I have accepted in agreeing to sit on the committee) consists of deferring the recruitment. But from another point of view, I know that if I demand that the post remains vacant, I have every chance of having the candidates and the personnel representatives from within the committee on my back. In choosing to be lax, I will avoid the disadvantages that I personally will have to put up with in the short term. In the long term, if everyone does as I do, obvious disadvantages result. But the disadvantages are more collective than individual. In addition, they will not be immediately perceptible. Finally, there is a good chance that I will not be personally affected.

These analyses show that the idea of rationality is often difficult to define. In certain situations, one can settle it without hesitation: action A is rational, action B is irrational. But in many situations, it is difficult for the social actor to determine the choice which will result in the consequences closest to his preferences.

Pareto has emphasized that 'logical' actions (which one would nowadays more likely call rational actions), namely those which are characterized by an equivalence between ends and means, occupy a limited place in social life. But it is essential to see that he included in non-logical actions not only actions which could be explained by custom, belief, or impulse (cf. the actions *wertrationell, traditionell,* and *affektuall* of Weber) but also the actions which engender discordant consequences compared with the objectives sought by the actors. Games theory has demonstrated a priori that certain decision-making situations under conditions of interaction marked by oppositions in the preference systems of the actors tend to produce discordances between the objectives sought and the results obtained (cf. the examples above). Sociological theory has shown a posteriori, by the analysis of real situations, that discordance between the objective sought and the result obtained was often the consequence of many interactive situations. It stressed unexpected effects which often go beyond the intentions of the actors. For its part, political theory has stressed the fact that the consequences of an action – and notably of a political decision – always bear unforeseeable results. This observation is the basis of Hayek and Popper's recommendation, according to which piecemeal engineering, limited and gradual adjustment, is always preferable to planned change. This view has been systematized by Braybrooke and Lindblom, who see in gradualism the most general precept of action and finally the only possible definition of rationality. In fact, Braybrooke and Lindblom's recommendation rests on the following reasoning: an action (and above all a political action) always carries unforeseen consequences. It is thus always effected in conditions of uncertainty. In that case, rationality consists of utilizing the strategy which guarantees the minimum risk, that is to say to content oneself with measures of which one feels one can anticipate the results.

Really, it is not certain that one can afford this precept, and the definition of rationality which it includes, a general application. Without doubt many catastrophes are the result of plans or reform by societies inspired by the desire for justice and generosity. But other catastrophes and many processes of degradation of social institutions also result from a succession of gradual decisions (cf. for example the succession of Allied concessions made to Hitler's Germany before the Second World War).

Games theory, sociological theory, and political theory converge therefore towards a fundamental epistemological proposition: a general definition of the idea of rationality cannot exist. In one situation it is more 'rational' to seek to minimize potential losses than to maximise eventual gains, in another it is more rational to seek to maximize gains. In one situation gradual, prudent action will result in happy consequences. In another, it will inaugurate a process of degradation which may become irreversible. The idea of rationality must thus be seen as relative, that is to say as dependent upon the structure of situations. To be sure, it must also be seen as dependent upon the position and generally the characteristics of the actors. It may be rational, if I am rich, and irrational, if I am poor, to risk a modest sum in the hope of a substantial gain. It must be noted on this point that, when an observer interprets the behaviour of the observed as irrational, this often results from the fact that he unduly projects the data characteristic of his own situation on to the situation of the person he observes. Thus he will have a tendency to interpret the behaviour of the observed as the result of a mysterious and irrational 'resistance to change', in a situation where it is rational behaviour if seen from the viewpoint of the person observed.

We will now pass to the complex question raised by the idea of rationality in its cognitive rather than praxiological sense. This question can be summarized in the following manner: are the beliefs and myths observable in archaic societies, but also in modern societies, rational or irrational? In other words, do they correspond to statements or groups of statements of a fundamentally different nature from statements considered as scientific, or are they different from these last in degree rather than in nature?

Three types of response to this question can be distinguished schematically. According to the first type of response, it is by an error in perspective that beliefs and myths are interpreted as cognitive statements: according to this way of seeing it, myths and beliefs should have a significance and a function which is not cognitive but expressive. When the Bororo say that they are the Arara, or when revolutionaries proclaim the arrival of the great day, both express less their belief in the present or future state of things than in feelings – the feeling of belonging to a tribal group in one case or to the group of the damned of the earth in the other. According to the second type of interpretation, traditional since Comte and which may be found for example in the early work of Lévy-Bruhl, myths and beliefs would be statements containing a cognitive value for the subject but lack any value for an observer belonging to a culture impregnated with the scientific spirit or, as Lévy-Bruhl would say, characterized by a 'logical' mentality. Here the illusion would be on the side of the observed subject. According to the third type of interpretation, myths and beliefs are often rational statements with regard to the knowledge within the context where they are observed, and which only appear irrational to the observer when he has a more complete and complex mental equipment. In this sense, the mythical meteorological conceptions that one meets in archaic societies would be neither more nor less irrational than the Cartesian theory of animal-machines. According to that third conception, myths, beliefs, or metaphysical theories are 'rational'. The impression of irrationality which may be felt by the observer is simply the effect, as Piaget would say, of a 'socio-centric' illusion. Here then the illusion is to be found on the side of the observer.

The best way of dealing with this discussion consists, here once more it appears, of taking the viewpoint of the sociological theory of action. Myths and beliefs must be seen as responses to interactive systems. In a society where individuals, whatever their class, tend to think that they would have more to lose than to gain by an overthrow of the class structure, a 'theory' legitimating the social order is likely to be imposed and to last as long as individuals stay in the same situation and consequently have, as Pareto would say, the same 'feelings'. Thus, in a feudal or semi-feudal type of society – such as rural Japan still was at the beginning of the twentieth century – tenants maintained complex relationships with their landlords. The latter no doubt appropriated in part the product of the formers' work, but they supplied them in counterpoint with services equivalent to those offered by banks, insurance companies, and the social security system to their clients in industrialized societies. History shows that, in such a case, it can be difficult to get the tenants to oppose their owners, and to substitute the Marxist mythology of class war for a mythology of the natural order. The 'theory' of natural order to be sure justifies the social order, but it is too summary to see it as an opium by virtue of which the dominant class enslaves the dominated class. More simply, the theory of natural order appears to the tenant to be a more adequate expression of the system of relationships which he keeps up with his owner than the theory of class warfare (cf. 'Beliefs'). This is why Marxist mythology appeared in the Japanese countryside in favour of economic upheaval and the changes accompanying it led to upheavals only in the situation of certain individuals, uprooting them from the traditional system of social relationships. To generalize the lesson of this example, one can, in other words, put forward the hypothesis that when an individual adheres to a belief or persists in a belief, and refuses to adhere to an alternative belief, it is because the first seems to him to express in the most acceptable and useful manner the meaning of his own situation. It is possible that the observer, above all if we are dealing with a committed observer, would have a tendency to perceive the beliefs of the observed as irrational (that is to say in this case as contrary to the interests of the observed, such as the observer conceives them). In most cases, an effort to distance oneself will, however, permit it to be established that the adherence of the observed to a belief is explicable because he sees in it a satisfactory interpretation of the situation he finds himself in and an effective guide for action. To take another example: why did a movement of veneration of culture, of *Bildung* develop in the Germany of the end of the nineteenth century? Essentially it was because the universities, which traditionally wielded considerable influence in the Prussian state, saw their importance menaced by the spectacular economic development of the third part of the century, a development which put the industrialists to the forefront of the stage. Naturally, the universities could not content themselves with bewailing the consequences of industrial development. That would have been ineffective for them. It was necessary for them, to use Pareto's language, to translate their 'feelings' and 'residues' in the form of 'diversions', that is to say by 'theories' demonstrating under the circumstances that the threat to their values threatened society as a whole. This is why they set themselves to lampooning English utilitarianism, to developing untiringly the theme of the opposition between culture and civilization, and to opposing English prosaicness with German *Bildung*. The 'feelings' of German universities and the conceptual and 'theoretical' transpositions (the 'diversions') of these sentiments they produced thus appear fully intelligible as soon as one applies them to their situation.

Of the three types of explanation mentioned above the third is without doubt potentially the most useful, on the condition that it is reformulated in the language of action from that of theory. A belief, a myth, a 'theory' always represents the interpretations developed or, according to the case, accepted by the social actors according to their situation such as they perceive it and interpret it. These interpretations furnish them with effective guides for action. In this sense, one can say that they are 'rational' even if they may appear to the hasty or committed observer as 'irrational'. This point has been brilliantly demonstrated by Durkheim in *Les formes elementaires*: he puts forward the idea that the difference between religion and science is of degree rather than of nature. Both should be interpreted starting from the effort made by the social actor to give himself effective guides to action. By way of consequence, myths and beliefs should be seen as adapted responses, that is to say, fundamentally rational, to situations of variable structure. Modern mythologies, for example socialism, are no more irrational than the theory of natural right, the myth of the noble savage, or the mythology of the Bororo. The theories included in magical practices are perhaps less complex; they are without doubt less effective; they are not more irrational than scientific theories. Both correspond simply to different contexts, but have a common meaning and function: to provide points of reference starting from which objectives and modalities of action may be legitimized in the eyes of the actor. Praxiological rationality and cognitive rationality are thus two dimensions intimately connected to one and the same phenomenon.

Action, Beliefs, Economics and Sociology, Ideologies, Social Symbolism, Utilitarianism.

Bibliography

ALLAIS, M., 'Le comportement de l'homme rationnel devant le risque. Critique des postulats et axiomes de l'école américane', *Econometrica*, XXI, 4, 1953, 503–546. – BRAYBROOKE, D. and LINDBLOM, C.E., *A strategy of decision. Policy evaluation as a social process*, New York, The Free Press London, Collier-Macmillan, 1963. – CAZENEUVE, J., *La mentalité archaïque*, Paris, A. Colin, 1961. – CROZIER, M. and FRIEDBERG, E., *L'acteur et le système. Les contraintes de l'action collective*, Paris, Le Seuil, 1977. – DURKHEIM, E., *The Elementary Forms of the Religious Life*, London, Allen & Unwin, 1976. – DAVAL, R., *La logique de l'action individuelle*, Paris, PUF, 1981. – ELSTER, J., *Ulysses and his sirens: studies in rationality and irrationality*, Cambridge/London/New York, Cambridge University Press / Paris, Editions de la Maison des Sciences de l'Homme, 1979. – GODELIER, M., *Rationalité et irrationalité en économie*, Paris, F. Maspero, 1971. – HARSANYI, J., 'Rational choice models of political behavior vs functionalist and conformist theories', *World politics*, XXI, 4, 1969, 513–538. – HAYEK, F. (von), *Scientism and the study of society*, Glencoe, The Free Press, 1952. – HOWARD, N., *Parodoxes of rationality. Theory of metagames and political behavior*, Cambridge, MIT Press, 1971, – LUCE, R.D. and RAIFFA, H., *Games and decisions. Introduction and critical survey*, New York, Wiley, 1957, 1967. – MAUND, J.B., 'Rationality of belief. Intercultural comparisons', *in* BENN, S.I. and MORTIMORE, G.W. (ed.), *Rationality and the social sciences*, London, Routledge & Kegan Paul, 1976, 34–57. – PARETO, V. *The Mind and Society*, New York, Harcourt, Brace, Jovanovich, 1935; London, Cape, 1935. – SCHÜTZ, A., *in* BRODERSEN, A. (ed.), *Alfred Schütz. Collection papers*. II. *Studies in social theory*, La Haye, Martinus Nijhoff, 1954. – SIMON, H.A., 'A behavioral model of rational choice', *Quarterly journal of economics*, LXIX, 59, 1955, 99–118. Reproduced *in* SIMON, H., *Models of man. Social and rational. Mathematical essays on rational human behavior in a social setting*, New York, Wiley/London, Chapman & Hall, 1957, 241–260; 'From substantive to procedural rationality', *in* LATSIS, S.J. (ed.), *Method and appraisal in economics*, Cambridge, Cambridge University Press, 1976, 129–148. – WEBER, M., 'Fundamental concepts of sociology', in WEBER, M. *Economy and Society*, Ch. 1, op cit.

Religion

In an article published in 1964, Clifford Geertz observes that in the domain of the sociology of religion, the major theoretical contributions at the turn of the century from Durkheim, Malinowski, Weber, and later from Freud in *Totem and Taboo*, have not been extended by later developments of equal calibre. These authors, it is true, are far from defending the same conception of religious fact. But they agreed on at least one point. For all of them except perhaps Freud (who nevertheless takes the greatest pain to point out that religious belief cannot be reduced to a pure delirium and rites to compulsive behaviour), religion is a phenomenon that is a characteristic of all human societies, past, present, and future. In other respects, anthropologists and sociologists claim to give a positive explanation to this pheno- menon. For a long time, theologians insisted that the fact of religion should stay out of the clutches of positive science. They set themselves against the inheritors of rationalist tradition who believed in explaining religion in terms of ignorance or impulses of a blind affectivity. The ignorance that it cultivates, according to Voltaire, among its followers ('Our priests are not that which vain people think/ our credulity is all their science') and the passive sentimentality that it sustains among their people ('the sign of the oppressed creature', as Marx put it) offer the means of manipulation to 'important people' who permit the clergy to make the poor stupid in order to hold them in slavery. The conservative variant of this conception is explained by certain liberals of the nineteenth century, notably French, for whom 'religion is good for the people'; the radical variant is illustrated by the well-known Marxist formula of religion as the 'opium of the masses'. The contributions of sociology and anthropology consist of treating religion as a 'social fact', in other words as a human fact. This results in risks of reductionism that are difficult to control. In this respect, the substitution by Durkheim of the notion of the transcendent for that of the sacred is far from being innocent. We cannot forbid sociologists from concerning themselves with a dimension that is so import- ant in social life by holding against them the accusation of sacrilege.

Religious experience is incarnated in the tissue of social action to which it contributes in giving a sense, although it overflows to the point sometimes of deny- ing it, as in some extreme forms of asceticism and mysticism, all validity if not all reality. Understood in this way, the major religious orientations must be treated not as distant images of an inaccessible ideal nor as the delirious projection of desires that seek in the imagination an illusory reality. This is the approach followed by Max Weber in *The Protestant Ethic and the Spirit of Capitalism*, in which he deals with speculations on the Augustinian and Calvinist theories of grace no longer as if they belong to the universe of ideas but as an essential ingredient in the constitu- tion and maintenance of modern civilization.

For Weber (in particular in the preface to *The Protestant Ethic* . . .), the notion of ethic, that is, to use the strong meaning of the word, of practice, takes first place. What interests him are the normative orientations that define and control the way in which we live our personal and professional lives. It is therefore necessary to explain why a certain number of behaviours become obligatory for us – even if at first sight their demands and their logic become obstacles to the satisfaction of certain of our instincts and our appetites. One of the conditions of this legitimiz- ation is that the so-called obligations appear justified by the set of values that organize the range of our experience – as seen in its most comprehensive dimen- sion.

The weight of puritanism is also very appreciable in the formation of demo- cratic institutions, above all in the case of American democracy. De Tocqueville emphasized the fact that the colonists of the Mayflower were pilgrims who had decided to found a society conforming to biblical teaching in the solitude of the New World. That is why the idea of law is central to the puritan conception. The source of that law is in God. But for the very reason of its origin, the law does not put obligations only upon the governed but also on the governors. They are thus only the ministers of God, and their power is only legitimate in as much as they conform to His will. Puritan theocracy does not necessarily lead to democracy. It can also just as well legitimize conformity and intolerance. In fact, if it does lead to democracy, it is because it substitutes a conception which places governors and governed under the authority of the same one law, impersonal and transcendent, for a democratic conception of sovereignty. But the path that leads from puritan theocracy to pluralist democracy is far from being in a straight line. It is this path that the work of contemporary historians, such as Perry Miller, permits us to reconstitute.

The teachings of Weber, who emphasized the social effectiveness of the religious experience, have unhappily been interpreted as if religious beliefs and practices alone constituted an adequate principle of explanation for the genesis and functioning of modern institutions. Weber never said that Calvinist reform was the 'cause' of capitalist expansion in the Christian West. One might thus be tempted to consider as not pertinent most of the criticisms which have been addressed to his essay. But before going on, it is instructive to compare what Weber in effect said, and what the most sagacious of his critics have said for their part. First, everybody agrees on one point. A correlation exists between religious affiliation and the entrepreneurial quality of the Europe of the sixteenth, seventeenth and eighteenth centuries everywhere where capitalism developed. As for the range and the meaning of that correlation, it is here that difficulties begin. It is first necessary to agree on what one understands by capitalism. Trevor-Roper notes that Weber takes the term capitalist *stricto senso*, in putting the accent on the rationalization of techniques and forms of production rather than on the breadth of exchanges and their mode of finance. If conversely one takes the *lato sensu* interpretation, which sees capitalism essentially as the mode of circulation of wealth (merchandise and capital), a kind of 'economic world' (according to Braudel) which straddles political sovereignties, one starts to talk of capitalism in Flanders and in Italy well before the Protestant Reformation. If one chooses the second interpretation, the spirit of capitalism appears closer to humanism than to the Reformation. In any case, a valorization of mobility enters into the capitalist spirit, whether it concerns the mobility of the factors of production (land, work, capital), the mobility of merchandise and monetary assets, or even the mobility of people and entrepreneurs. How much is this valorization of mobility and consequently of diligence, effort, technological innovation (with the constraints which it introduces in normative systems) connected with the religious beliefs and preferences of the interested parties?

What Weber's analysis does at least establish is the *congruence* (as he called it, elective affinity) between the 'ethic' of Calvinism and the 'spirit' of capitalism. What it does not show is how such a congruence would explain the genesis of capitalist institutions. On this point, historians like Herbert Luthy and Trevor-Roper are much more informative than Weber. Sombart had already validated the fact that the Calvinist ethic is not the 'adequate cause' to capitalist development, by observing that the role Weber assigns to the Protestants had often been held by Sephardic Jews expelled by the Catholic kings. One is thus led to ask whether in the status of entrepreneur the quality of emigrant is not as significant, if not more so, as religious affiliation. To this quality are attached a certain number of traits which can act as advantages to the benefit of exiles. First the victims of persecution find themselves dispersed in different countries. Inside their *diaspora* links of confidence and solidarity are maintained, which, where commercial transactions are concerned, constitute a certain advantage for the members of the dispersed community. It would be the marginality of the Protestants or the Jews and the cohesion of their groups disseminated nearly everywhere in Europe which would have rendered them particularly suitable to be the principal initiators of capitalist development.

This hypothesis is corroborated *a contrario* by a series of data to which Trevor-Roper calls our attention. In the countries and during the periods when the Calvinists established a strict sectarian intolerance, they were no more innovative than the Catholics were in the countries where they were in the majority. But the hypothesis of the marginality of innovators which takes into account the constitution of transnational groups, culturally homogeneous and strongly interdependent, does not allow us to treat as irrelevant Weber's analyses of the congruence between the Protestant 'ethic' and the capitalist 'spirit'. Marginal people have been expelled; and if they have been expelled, it is because of their religious affiliations. Trevor-Roper goes on to tackle a stage which is probably decisive, from which he establishes the weight of religious affinities in the constitution of the first capitalist élite. In effect, the Jewish diaspora, and even that of the Protestants, does not result, as in an 'Exit' in Hirschman's term, from a deliberate calculation by which the people who leave evaluate most accurately the costs and advantages resulting from their decision. It means an *expulsion*, more often than not violent, which bears witness against the society which forces the dissidents to depart. But, among the reasons which are invoked to justify that expulsion, the question of orthodoxy occupies a central position. In the case of the Protestants, Trevor-Roper clearly shows that an alleged pretext was not involved in order to justify the violence and iniquity. What constitutes the nub of the conflict is an authentic conflict of values between the social order with the insupportable weight of monastic sloth and ecclesiastical waste (not to mention the squanderings of princes and their courtiers) and the existential project of merchants, townspeople, and aristocrats who balk at a system that not only obstructs them in their interests but offends them in their sincere and profound adherence to what followers of Erasmus call the 'philosophy of Christ' (Trevor-Roper).

The congruence between the puritan ethic and the spirit of capitalism confirmed by Weber cannot be read like an open book as a group of immediately intelligible relationships between ideas. It results from a complex historical process, where not only more or less stable states of collective consciousness enter into play but also strategies of indoctrination, of dissidence, and of expulsion (connected to economic interests which put the bourgeoisie and the merchants in opposition to the privileged orders). All these things come unexpectedly into conjunctions assigned by historical contingencies (such as the rush of precious metals following the discovery of America). A similar analysis could be pursued on a connected question, that of the relationships between Calvinism, and more generally the 'sectarian' or even Presbyterian forms of Protestantism, and the democratic spirit. The presbyterian organization of Calvinist churches has in many cases suffocated the spirit of investigation, imposed a stifling moral order, and led to a sort of hypocritical dictatorship. It is therefore not Protestantism as such, nor even a category of Protestants, such as the Socinians, the Arminians, or the Unitarians, which is the cause of the development of the democratic spirit. The origin of this development must be sought in a combination of data at once historical and institutional, across which the 'Protestant ethic' has been able to reveal its fertility in the political order as in the economic order.

The teaching of Weberian sociology is twofold. First, it shows the importance of religious trends in the functionings of modern societies. It thus challenges the most naive forms of evolutionary study, which purport to see in religion, so to say, an underdeveloped form of the collective consciousness. Furthermore, Durkheim, who has stressed so much the specificities of primitive religion, for his part always explicitly attributed to all social experience, as long as it is absolute, a properly religious dimension. In as much as he defines religion 'like life taken seriously', he makes of religion a universal component of social life. The second thing taught in the religious sociology of Weber, and we would be tempted to say in all religious sociology, is that it emphasizes the ambiguity of these orientations relative to our ultimate destiny, which to be socially effective must be incarnated in a system of practices and beliefs institutionally defined and sanctioned. In other words, the religious phenomenon is not reduced to the subjective experience of particularly gifted individuals, as 'virtuosos' as Weber would say, of certain existential demands. It would inadequately define the Protestant phenomenon to reduce it to the value system that Weber called 'ascetism in the world' (*innerweltiche Askese*). Protestantism is as much a form of organization of religious society, as a religious project about the organization of lay society.

In one sense, every religion (assuming that we leave out those archaic religions where there is no distinction between priest and congregation, and between properly religious and collective ends) is an organization. We find in them in effect differentiated roles and a hierarchy between these roles. We also find a distinction between the internal surroundings created by religious society, the relationships between the different categories of subjects who participate in it, and the external surroundings, the lay or profane society within which the religious society is established. In comparing the forms that the various religions assume for priest, believers, theologians, and the different disciplinary mechanisms used to control these roles, the sociologist can establish several types of religious organization: sect (in the case of the Dissenters), congregation (either Presbyterian or Episcopalian), assembly of believers or inspired people who, as in the case of the Quakers, await inspiration from the Holy Spirit. These types are made up around criteria such as the nature of the hierarchy, the nature of the control exercised by the clergy or the non-clergy, the cognitive orientations, account taken of the prophets, the legitimacy (or illegitimacy) of charismatic inspiration, the status of orthodoxy, the relationship of orthodoxy with tolerance, the nature of the sanctions invoked against the unfaithful, the non-believers, and the indifferent.

We may take the case of the Catholic religion, following the example of Le Bras and his successors, and ask how the 'faithful' are made up, what percentage of the total population (or from which age group, which profession, or which sex) are said to be practising; what this practice consists of, what is its frequency (daily, weekly, yearly, occasionally); how are the practising localized, how are they distributed between town and country and between the regions of a national territory. We will also examine the recruitment of priests, the composition of this group, the training of ecclesiastics, careers and mobility within the church. Such questions are asked not only of laymen but also of the regular clergy. We can add to this morphology a physiology of clerical society, its recruitment, its financing, the conflicts between the levels of hierarchies (low and high clergy), between the regular and secular clergy. In addition, we can consider the relationships between religious society on one side and civilian society and the State on the other. Under this heading we enter the conflicts of competence in training and education, for research and development of science, confrontations with a public authority which claims sovereignty, at least in its own sphere such as it defines it. We will describe the way in which the church remains present in a lay society: charities, pious associations, confraternities. Since the Catholic Church, as an organization, has a history, we will seek to position it today in relationship to its own trajectory, and we will ask how each organizational form will evolve.

If every religion is an organization, it is an organization that is unlike any other. In any case, less than any other can the analysis of religious organization be reduced to a strictly behaviourist description, however precisely are measured the number of and frequency of certain practices (participation at communion, at confession, etc.). Durkheim, in distinguishing in all religious phenomena the rites of belief in God, recognized the importance of these aspects. We can characterize religious faiths by the nature of the constraint that they hold over the spirit of the believer. We will speak then of dogma, that is to say of propositions worked out by theologians, sanctioned by the hierarchical authorities, which can be discussed only by the believer. Dogmas involve different areas. They can concern historic events. It is a dogma of the Catholic Church that Jesus, son of God, was born at Nazareth, that he was crucified, that he was resurrected three days after entombment. They can embrace metaphysical pronouncements. A single God can embrace three persons; the individual is immortal. They can take the shape also of moral prescriptions: 'Thou shalt love they neighbour as thyself.' In other cases, the dogma concerns the origin of such categories as living creatures, of such a family, or of such a clan, of their place in physical nature, their relationship with man, plants, animals, heavenly bodies, heavenly places. We can then talk of myths, taking care that the term is vague as it designates at the same time legends such as those of the heroes or gods of classical antiquity, tales from the margins of history (such as the Golden Legend), and pseudo-scientific speculations (such as those contained in *Genesis*).

Myths can be treated either as pretexts to be embellished by the artist's imagination, or as the first output of a still rudimentary science.

But whatever the nature of the object on which religious belief is built, it is distinguished by what we would be tempted to call evidence – belief in which is obligatory on pain of blasphemy. Whoever denies the dogma removes himself from the Church. Whosoever, without questioning matters of faith, makes fun of pious traditions risks a more or less pronounced censure. Religion has for a long time confused knowledge with faith. In this confusion, it gives us as for granted a certain experience whose reality it confirms. The questions of existence occupy a primordial place in religious beliefs. It is through this relationship to them that the believers distinguish themselves from the others. For the believers, the holy sacrament attests to the supernatural character of these objects. They are of a different order, even if they show themselves under tangible forms – such a pieces of stone, metal, or wood, for example the Australian aboriginal *churinga* in which it is believed that their ancestors are incarnated.

Apart from dogmas, every religion includes a certain number of precepts and interdicts. We can hence, in the case of religions as in the case of all organizations, speak about a normative system. This, whatever shape it takes during the course of history, distinguishes itself from other normative systems. This last point has been highlighted by authors who insisted on the opposition between religion and magic on one hand and science on the other hand. Even if the believer who accomplishes certain rites does it with a practical intention, the effect that the believer is thus seeking to produce is not controlled as is the technical effect sought after and often obtained by the engineer. The rationalist tradition has long since treated the rite as an act denuded of meaning. But it is not enough, as Malinowski proposed, to seek the meaning of rite in the motivation of *homo religiosus* who seeks to dominate his anguish before an environment that he does not master or before the impenetrable mysteries of his own condition. The meaning of rite must not only be sought after in the psychological needs of the believer. In procuring for us the protection of a substitutive behaviour, rite would lull us into the false security of an 'as if' which transforms on to an imaginary plain a threatening world and an enigmatic destiny. Malinowski himself emphasized the fact that the execution of rite changes the situation of the believer. In practising the propitiatory rites that are designed to make rain, believers do not provoke its coming. But in meeting together in order to carry out the prescribed ceremony, the members of the group mobilize the energies that permit them to bear the ordeal of drought and accompanying poverty better. The meaning of rite is not in its instrumental efficiency. Rite does not procure for the believer only the catharsis of his anguish through its substitutive actions. Execution of rite reinforces and restores the solidarity of the group – on condition that it is taken seriously, and taken as strict obligation.

In themselves absurd and derisory, since they defy all logico-experimental verification, is it the case that beliefs and rites make sense only for those beings who have not yet achieved a really positive development? That evolutionary view hits two difficulties. First, it must be asked if the establishment of positive knowledge and the progress of more and more efficient techniques do not disqualify religion in its double dimension of ritual and dogmatism. Saint-Simon and Comte, who announced with such conviction the coming of the positive age, also prophesied the coming of a 'new Christianity'. The new age would be religious, but the beliefs and practices of the new Christianity would be different from the old. For Durkheim too there was no doubt, both that western religions, and notably Catholicism, had had their time, but also that the sacred would continue to constitute a universal category of human experience. Weber for his part talks of the disenchantment of the world, but carefully fails to announce the end of *homo religiosus*.

The 'perishing' of the religions has been realized only very imperfectly; and, as far as it has occurred, it has not taken the forms predicted. Among the great 'world religions' (*Weltreligionen*, as Weber would say), the Roman Catholic version is probably that which most closely approached the plan outlined by the free thinker and scientist of the last century: decline in practice, crisis of dogmatic beliefs, dispute about hierarchical authority. But apart from the fact that other 'world religions', such as Islam or Judaism, have known a marked renaissance marked by a renewal of dogmas, practice, and loyalties, two principal facts have marked western societies during the twentieth century. First, with the arrival of totalitarian states and parties, in the Soviet Union and in Hitler's Germany, the phenomenon of 'secular religions' has appeared (Aron). This expression is not very clear but, even so, it is worth holding on to. Its paradoxical character comes from the fact that it plays on two opposed terms. Can one describe as 'religious' explicitly anti-religion social movements? Can one associate 'religion' (if this term is taken as synonymous with transcendence) and 'secularization' (which here is manifestly taken as a synonym for laicism)? All the same, Raymond Aron's expression neatly characterizes the formidable reinforcement of their orthodoxies by a 'consecration' of the party apparatuses, by a violent intolerance which goes as far as the physical extermination of adversaries or of dissidents. The paradox of secular religions of the twentieth century is that it is in the name of science, or rather that of a pseudo-science, that the most constraining forms of orthodoxy and of conformism have succeeded. On one hand, the secular religions claim to respond in a form of caricature to the great positivist plan to restore the spiritual unity of the West. But Comte had too high and too accurate a view of intellectual activity to imagine that an ideological dogmatism which relied upon a network of 'work camps' could bring us an authentic 'soul supplement'.

The secular religions of the Hitlerian or Stalinist type do not consistitute the only signs of the religious vitality of the West. But in order to appreciate this clearly, recourse must be had to different indicators from those which have been worked out to describe hierarchical organizations, such as the Catholic Church, and which still have a certain pertinence when one claims to explain the adherence of certain spirits to the most absurd and criminal 'secular religions' as a nostalgia for an integral discipline.

The Protestant Reformation introduced decisive innovations, which invite us to think again about the opposition of the profane to the sacred in terms which no longer permit the sacred to be treated as a collection of dogmatic beliefs and obligatory rites imposed by a hierarchic authority. The direct confrontation of the faithful with the divine message, even when mediated by the Bible, attributes to the conviction of each believer, judging in his heart of hearts, a capacity for authentication which until then had been reserved to agents authorized by tradition. What is significant in order to appreciate the vitality of these new practices engendered by the Reformation is not only the number of believers, the regularity of their meetings, it is the nature of certain engagements, of which the direction is as characteristic as the intensity or the fervour.

During the 1960s in the United States all sorts of social movements developed: for civil rights, for ethnic minorities, against the Vietnam War, against nuclear energy, for women, for homosexuals. One would have difficulty in describing them as religious in the strict sense of that word. All the same, they seem to be marked by a double dimension, charismatic and prophetic. It was an absolute subjective conviction which seized their most active members. Even if they were not directed by heroes or by saints (even though the figure of Pastor Martin Luther King bears comparison with the figure of Gandhi), the message propagated by these movements presented itself as good news, an invitation to the young and the pure to shake the dust of an irremediably corrupt world off their sandals. The fanaticism with which these impassioned minorities proclaim their cause attests to their religious character, since denial or even indifference with regard to their values is held by their followers to be sacrilegious. These movements remain largely ambiguous, both as far as the objectives they pursue are concerned and the style and means of their interventions. One can, all the same, call them secular religions, as long as one states that they belong to decentralized movements (and on this hand as different from the Roman Church as from the Hitlerian and Stalinist type of parties from the organizational viewpoint), because, even if they use violence, they are not totalitarian because they do not claim to reconstitute society from top to bottom according to a sole model integrally legitimized and rationalized.

The recent development of what we have called the 'decentralized secular religions' causes the evolution of the contents of the religious experience to appear retrospectively. This experience perhaps firstly dealt principally with the physical nature of which, by the use of magic rites and mythical stories, it constituted a first and fragile taking of possession. An idea of the tragic destiny of man submitting to combat with the gods and his own passions, both equally incomprehensible, came initially to the Greeks from religion, as did the idea among the Hebrews of a law which founded our obligations upon a pact with God. The Christian synthesis combined these diverse elements in rearranging them, associating them in a theodicy, a philosophy of history, and a morality. Since the Reformation, the dogmatic contents have been eroded by the effect of a great variety of circumstances: the growth of historical criticism and of biblical exegesis, autonomy of positive knowledge compared to theology, differentiation of powers between state and ecclesiastic authorities. But the opposition sacred/profane, if it has changed its contents from the point where engagements which would have been judged worldly now mobilize the ardour of believers, has lost none of its pertinence.

What remains of religion in our societies, despite the enfeebling of the ecclesiastic hierarchy, is the persistence of the charismatic effect, of which three fundamental dimensions can be recognized. First, charisma is the mark which attributes a truly extraordinary importance to a message and to the person who carries it. Second, the charismatic message is a call which is put out to be heard. It is therefore both a principle of responsibility for the message carrier and a source of obligation and of engagement for the receiver (evil be to those . . . who have ears but will not hear). Finally the charismatic message is a project which prepares a way. To be believed, charisma which is in no way the narcissistic expression of desire or of the imaginary assumes on the part of those to whom it is destined an active expectation founded on confidence in history. Because of that constitution, charisma leads to an absolutist vision of social action. The relativist attitude which weighs conditions and circumstances leads to resignation and cowardice, whereas charisma, with the irresistable evidence with which it is invested and the promise of its own realization which it carries with it, demands an unconditional engagement. 'It is necessary to be the lowest of the low' not to put oneself body and soul to the service of the good news. The most exalted forms of militancy, which obviously concern only a very small fraction of party militants and militants of various social movements, illustrate the seduction and the vitality of charisma. It is in this sense that our societies remain, for better or for worse, profoundly religious, or, rather, profoundly exposed to charismatic seduction.

But this interpretation must be clarified on one point. In effect, it carries a risk: that is, of reducing religion to an effusion or even to a compulsive voluntarism. In these two cases, religion would be no more than the absolutism of subjective conviction. Curiously, the traditional religions can accommodate themselves better to this hypersubjectivity than secular decentralized religions, which 'militate' for the achievement of such and such a specific objective. These last find themselves confronted with the choice of ways and means, the appreciation of conjunctions which are often difficult to seize. They are thus led to elaborate cognitive schemes which must both clarify and justify their action. It is thus that ideologies, more or less arbitrary interpretations, crudely sacrilized, are elaborated by our modern secular religions.

The development of sociology and anthropology has produced, in the domain of religious studies, two series of effects apparently divergent but which, on reflection, manifest a certain coherence. On one hand, sociology and anthropology have relativized the religious phenomenon. But, on the other hand, they have disqualified the lay prophet who foresaw the 'decline' of religion. The net result of the work of sociologists is to draw out the specificity and authenticity of the religious phenomenon – without, all the same being able to give it a precise and adequate description. Reductionist theses take very different forms. Some confuse magic and religion, others confuse morality and religion. The former discredit religion in confusing it with utilitarianism and the naivety of popular practice. The latter dissolve it in moral idealism. Others again, like Durkheim in certain texts, draw such a close connection between religion and social life that God and society would be but one and the same thing. Faced with these reductionist orientations, we can put to good account the fact that, in so far as rite is not adequately defined only by its explicit function (healing, the coming of rain, etc.) but also by its latent function (balance restored in the group, health of the sick person who 'feels better' even if he is not cured), we cannot treat it as the derisory substitute for an absent technique. Similarly, morality, if one defines it as obedience to an impersonal law, does not explicitly take into account the relationship between the believer and the All-Powerful who lays down the law (the God of love and of anger). Religion accepts a personalization of the tragic ('This is my blood which I shed for you'), to which moral universality is indifferent. Finally, the correspondence between religion and society – and the reduction of the second to the first – is not any more satisfactory. Either we take society, as Durkheim did sometimes, as the place of ideals and values, and affirm that the only way of giving positive content to religious ideas is to discover the society which will serve as their receptacle and support. But all social ideals are not 'sacred', and the sacred is not carried exclusively in the diverse dimensions of social experience – at least if this term is taken in an entirely indefinite sense. Otherwise, we claim to reduce religion to the projection on the imaginary level of certain primary social experiences, such as working life or family life. But the connection is not convincing. Religion is not always the 'sigh of the oppressed creature'. To the mystic orientation of retreat from the world alluded to by Marx is opposed an ascetic orientation of control and mastery on which Weber was right to lay emphasis. As for the thesis developed by Freud about the universal value of the Oedipus complex which would permit the establishment of a close link between the frustrations which patriarchal authority imposes on the son and the religious theme of culpability, of hope, and of solidarity, as Bellah clearly showed, it does not stand up to comparative analysis: classical China is not less patriarchal than ancient Judaism, but all the same Chinese religion is at the opposite pole from Jewish religion.

The specificity of the religious phenomenon would be established at little cost if, instead of trying to find out of what religious experience is the copy, to which reality it corresponds, we asked in what conditions a regular symbolic communication, by rites and beliefs, can establish itself between believers concerning the fundamental problems of human experience, which Max Weber judges as constituent parts of theodicy. It is not necessary that a 'reality' (nature or society) correponds to religious experience for it to be held to be objective – that is to say other than a rhapsody of hallucinations and projections. It suffices that the collection of rites and beliefs of which it is constituted can be spoken of and lived by the believers who reinforce their community in discovering the sense of this symbolic universe.

Beliefs, Charisma, Durkheim, Ideologies, Prophetism, Social Symbolism, Weber.

Bibliography

BELLAH, R.N., 'Religious evolution', *American Sociological Review*, 1964, *29*, 358–374; *Beyond belief; essays on religion in a post-traditional world*, New York, Harper & Row, 1970, 1976. – BESNARD, P., *Protestantisme et capitalisme. La controverse post-weberienne*, Paris, A. Colin, 1970. – BOULARD, F., *Premiers itinéraires en sociologie religieuse*, Paris, Editions Ouvrières, 1954, 1966. – DURKHEIM, E., *Suicide* (op. cit) *The Elementary*

Forms of Religious Life, (op. cit). – EISENSTADT, S.N., *Modernism: protest and change*, Englewood Cliffs, Prentice-Hall, 1966. – ERIKSON, E.H., *Young man Luther: a study in psychoanalysis and history*, New York, Norton, 1958, 1962. – FREUD, S., *Totem und Tabu*, Leipzig, Vienna, H. Heller, 1913. – *Totem and Taboo*. London, Hogarth Press, 1950. – GAUDEFROY DEMONBYNES, M., *Mahomet*, Paris, A. Michel, 1957, 1969. – GEERTZ, C., 'Religion as a cultural system', *in* BANTON, M. (ed.), *Anthropological approaches to the study of religion*, ASA Monographs, vol. 3, London, Tavistock; New York, Praeger, 1966, 'Ideology as a cultural system', *in* APTER, D.E. (ed.), *Ideology and discontent*, The Free Press of Glencoe, 1964, 47–76. – GIBB, H.A.R., *Mohammedanism*, New York, Galaxy Books, 1962; Oxford, Oxford University Press, 1949. – GRANET, M., *La religion des Chinois*, Paris, Payot, 1980. – JEANMAIRE, H., *Dionysos. Histoire du culte de Bacchus*, Paris, Payot, 1951. – JUNG, C.G., *Einführung in das Wesen der Mythologie: Gottkindmythos; eleusinische Mysterien*, Zurich, Rascher Verlag, 1941. – LE BRAS, G., *Etudes de sociologie religieuse*, Paris, PUF, 1955–1956, 2 vol. – LENSKI, G.E., *The religious factor: a sociological study of religion's impact on politics, economics, and family life*, Garden City, Doubleday, 1961, 1963. – LÜTHY, H., *Frankreichs Uhren Gehen anders*, Zurich, Europa Verlag, 1954, 2 vol. – MALINOWSKI, B., *Magic, science and religion, and other essays*, New York, Doubleday & Co., 1954. – MARX, K., *1844 Manuscripts*, London, Lawrence & Wishart, 1970. – MILLER, P., *Errand into the wilderness*, Cambridge, Cop. by the President and Fellows of Harvard College, 1956; Cambridge, The Belknap of Harvard Univ. Press, 1978. – NIEBUHR, H. and WILLIAMS, D.D. (ed.), *The ministry in historical perspectives*, New York, Harper, 1956. – PARSONS, T., *Sociological theory and modern society*, New York, The Free Press, 1967, chap. 1, 37–78; *Action theory and the human condition*, New York, The Free Press, 1978, 167–322. – POULAT, E., *La naissance des prêtres ouvriers*, Paris, Casterman, 1965. – PIN, E., *Pratique religieuse et classes sociales dans une paroisse urbaine, Saint-Pothin à Lyon*, Paris, Editions SPES, 1956. – RENAN, E., *Le judaïsme et le christianisme; identité originelle et séparation graduelle*, Paris, Copernic, 1977. – RODINSON, M., *Mahomet*, Paris, Seuil, 1961, 1969. – SOMBART, W., *Die Juden und das Wirtschaftsleben*, Leipzig, Duncker & Humblot, 1911. – TILLICH, P., *The courage to be*, New Haven, Yale Univ. Press, 1952. – TOCQUEVILLE, A. de, *Democracy in America*, op. cit. – TREVOR-ROPER, H.R., *Religion, reformation and social change*, London, Macmillan, 1967, 1972. – VON GRUNEBAUM, G.E., *Studien zum Kulturbild und Selbstverständnis des Islams*, Zurich, Stuttgart, Artemis Verlag, 1969. – WEBER, M., *The Protestant Ethic and the Spirit of Capitalism*, op cit.

Reproduction

It is to Marx that we owe the concept of reproduction in its sociological sense. The economic processes described by Marx as simple reproduction processes are characterized by the constancy of the production and the stability of the relationships of production: individuals are replaced in time but the system reproduces itself in an identical fashion. A process is said by Marx to be expanded production when the production is increasing but the economic organization, or, as Marx would say, the production relationships, remain stable: production increases, but the relationship between classes as the relationships of individuals within classes (for example, the competition between capitalists) remains constant.

These ideas and distinctions can be transposed to other areas. Let us look at the example of the replacement of human populations. If the birth and death rates of different age groups remain constant and are such that the pyramid of ages and the size of the population also stay constant, this is a process of simple reproduction. An expanding reproduction process would be that where the constant birth and death rates engender a population of a variable size and possibly a pyramid of variable ages in time. When the birth and death rates change in time, one has a third situation: in Marxist language, one is no longer dealing with a *reproduction* process but with a *transformation* process. But the possible case where the changes in the birth and death rates do not provoke the change of certain *outputs*, such as the size of the population, must be considered apart. In this case, it is proposed that one talks of complex reproduction. One notes in passing that a reproduction process can equally be called a process in *balance*. In fact, the concept of reproduction is hardly more than a double in Marxist vocabulary for the concept of balance.

In order to clarify these distinctions, let us suppose that a process could be translated into a mathematical model. One would take the most simple case, that where the process would be represented by an equation making of a variable yt indexed by relation of time to a function f of a variable xt and of a parameter a. If xt is stable in time ($xt = xt + 1 =$, etc.), yt, being equally stable, one has a simple reproduction process. If xt is unstable (for example $xt, xt+1$, etc.), yt being unstable, one has an enlarged reproduction process. The reproduction is enlarged in the sense that the output yt is unstable. But there is however reproduction in as much as the structure of the process, namely the ensemble constituted by f and a, is stable in time. Let us now suppose that a changes in time. In this case, one has a process, not of reproduction, but of transformation: the structure of the process changes in time. In the particular case where a changes in time according to the change in y, one has a process of endogenous transformation (for example the increase y of the population provokes an overcrowding effect, which in turn affects the birth rate a). But one can also imagine that a and xt change in such a manner that yt is stable. In this case the process of transformation produces an effect of complex reproduction. These distinctions, which are directly suggested by the work of Marx, have an essential methodological importance for the analysis of social change, in so far as they have a general application.

One can find numerous examples of the reproduction process in sociological literature concerning traditional societies or the traditional segments of developed societies or societies in the process of development. Thus, in a study on Western Bengal, Bhaduri asks why, despite the efforts employed by the administration to prompt the peasants to increase the productivity of their land (by the adoption of certain agricultural techniques and practices), they held on to traditional practices which condemned them to a subsistence economy. Here one is really concerned with a simple reproduction process: the production of rice, the abstraction made by seasonal fluctuations staying constant from one year to another, the 'relationships of production' being equally constant. These production relationships are of a semi-feudal type: the share-cropper (*kishans*) are self-employed. But their indebtedness to the owners (*jotedars*) is chronic. That part of the harvest which comes to them (generally about 40 per cent) is in fact insufficient to assure their subsistence during the course of the year. Since their poverty does not permit them recourse to the financial market, they can only borrow from their *jotedar*. In nominal value, the level of interest demanded of the *kishan* is of the order of 40 per cent. In real value it is much higher (in the order of 100 per cent). The interest is in fact increased by the fact that the *kishan* repays after the harvest (at a moment when the price of rice is low) and borrows at a phase in the annual cycle when the price of rice is high. The chronic indebtedness of the *kishans* attaches them to the *jotedar* who assumes towards them a function of *diffuse* protection of a paternalistic nature. In these conditions, an increase in the agricultural yield would eventually have the consequence of increasing the quantity of rice available both to the *kishan* and to the *jotedar*. But at the same time, it would create a serious risk for the *jotedar*: from the moment that the *kishan* did not use up all the surplus which the increase of the yield gave him, his borrowings would diminish. In consequence, the interest paid by the *kishan* to the *jotedar* would lessen. Overall, the additional profit that the *jotedar* would gain from an increase in the yield might be eroded, and more, by the loss which he would sustain because of the reduction of the indebtedness of the *kishan*. The existence of this risk is obvious if the increase in yield is large. It is less so if it is moderate. The risk exists however even in this case, as the mathematical model used by Bhaduri demonstrates. One concludes from the analysis that the 'resistance' to change and to innovation manifested by the *jotedar* results perhaps less from 'weight of tradition' than from the logic of the situation in which he finds himself. As for the *kishans*, they have practically no power of decision as far as the adoption of new agricultural techniques is concerned. In addition, the vertical ties of custom produced by the system make the birth of a 'class consciousness' on the part of the *kishans* difficult. The logic of the situation within which the two categories of actors are placed thus prompts them to immobility. As a result production stays constant and the 'reproduction relationships' reproduce themselves.

When reproduction processes of this type are broken, it generally is the result of exterior forces, either in a voluntary manner, for example by the intervention of political and administrative authority or political entrepreneurs who wish to exploit the market offered by discontent, or in an involuntary manner, by the effect of changes which affect the environment of the system.

Reproduction processes are not exclusively to be observed in traditional societies. For example, the sociology of organizations has shown that an organizational system itself can reproduce itself even if it is inefficient or unsatisfactory from the point of view of the actors who make up the system. It is sufficient for the reproduction of the system that none of the actors should be encouraged to act with a view to transforming the system. Crozier has described a system of this type under the code name of 'Monopoly' in the *The Bureaucratic Phenomenon*. The chart of enterprises which compose the Monopoly is uniform from one enterprise to another. The chart defines a system of roles (director, assistant director, financial comptroller, foremen, production workers, maintenance workers). Naturally, the definition of roles (as is practically always the case) is not sufficiently rigorous to preclude all liberty of interpretation by the actors. This liberty of interpretation results in conflicts between the actors. The remarkable feature is that the points of conflict are practically always the same in the different factories and the 'solution' of conflicts is often identical from one factor to another. All things considered, some actors are prompted (by the structure of their roles) to an interpretation of their role which does not satisfy them, in so far as they find themselves constrained to renounce part of the power and autonomy accorded to them by their role, at least in theory. Meanwhile, for different reasons, actors are not prompted to transform the role system. Certain of them, such as the members of a management team, because their stay in the enterprise is of a relatively short duration, are above all careful not to hold up their transfer to a more central enterprise. Others, such as production workers, avoid any open conflict with the maintenance workers which would threaten workers' solidarity and might harm union efficiency. The system reproduces itself because its structure neutralizes the motives which individuals might have to work towards its transformation. As in the earlier example, it concerns a process of which the transformation can only be exogenous, whether it comes from a modification of the environment (for example, the loss of a monopolistic situation due to the appearance on the market of competing products) or a voluntary modification (the modification of the structures of the role system).

In the domain of the sociology of political organizations, Michels, in his famous *iron law of oligarchy* gave evidence of a readily observable reproductive process: regardless of the efforts which those in charge of organizing a political party deploy to organize it in a 'democratic' manner, or to put it in another way to ensure that the politics of the party should be the expression of the 'will' of its members, the relationship between the organizers and the members has every chance of assuming an oligarchic form. This is because the organizers constitute a small organized group, which can lead with relative ease to collective decisions, whereas the electors constitute an unorganized mass (cf. 'Action (collective)'). If one imagines that the management of Party P are favourable to Policy A and that the electors are, in the majority, in favour of Policy B, generally the electors will have no means of making known their views. It is even possible that this disaccord will not be perceptible at the time of electoral consultation: the electors of P might prefer B to A, but might also prefer by a majority the Policy A proposed by P to the Policy C proposed by P. The iron law of Michels illustrates the blocking effect brought about by the actual structure of certain organizations or social systems.

The enlarged systems of reproduction, in the Marxist sense, are generally much more unstable than simple reproduction processes. In many cases, the change of the 'output' of the process which characterizes enlarged reproduction has, after a certain time, retroactive effects on the structure of the process. Thus, when fixed birth and death rates cause an increase in the population, this increase, above a certain threshold, can have an influence (direct or indirect) on the birth rate. In the same way, continued increase in productivity has complex effects upon the structure of production relationships (for example, industrial concentration, limitation of competition). That is why Marx considers the processes of enlarged reproduction as fundamental in the analysis of historic change: by the retroactive effects they engender, they have a tendency after a time to give birth to processes of transformation.

It is important to note that the stability of certain distributions and more generally of certain social phenomena may not result from the way in which the structure of the system incites social agents to have invariable behaviour. The size and the structure of a population can over a period fail to change even if the birth rate and the death rate change (on condition, to be sure, that they change in a certain way). The reproduction of inequalities, when observed, probably obeys this type of process, which could be called *complex reproduction*: the agents modify their behaviour in time but these microsociological modifications produce no change at the macrosociological level. Thus, one observes that the structure of social mobility between generations in industrial societies is relatively stable over five or six decades: the probability of passing from category *i* of social status to category *j* from one generation to the next varies very little and in a non-systematic manner over time. This is, as Boudon has shown, a complex reproduction effect. The differential evolution of the demand for education according to social origin caused, over a period, a modification in time of the structure of offer of qualifications. As this modification had only a limited effect on the structure of the demand for qualification, the structure of the relationship between the level of education and social status modified in its turn. But the combined change of the structure of the relationship between social origins and educational level on one hand and the educational level and social origin on the other part may not produce, and did not produce in effect in the period studied, more than slight changes in the structure of the relationship between social origin and social status (cf. 'Social mobility'). To be sure, one would not know how to draw from this analysis conclusions which go beyond the spatial-temporal framework within which it was conducted. One can explain, if one falls back on a relatively meticulous statistical and mathematical analysis, the slight changes in the structure of social mobility in industrial societies during the last six or seven decades as an effect of complex reproduction. Clearly it does not follow that such an effect must be observed everywhere and always. A sensitivity analysis shows in effect that, if the effect of complex reproduction appears in a large zone of parametric space defined by the model, it disappears when one leaves that zone.

The phenomena of reproduction – that is to say of balance – are as difficult to explain as the phenomena of change and of instability. They carry a double temptation: that of the teleological explanation (cf. 'Teleology') and that of recourse to the organicist analogy.

Action, Historicism, Marx, Social Change, Social Mobility, Teleology.

Bibliography

BHADURI, A. 'A study of agricultural backwardness under semi feudalism', *Economic journal*, LXXXIII, 329, 1976, 120–137. – BOUDON, R., *L'inégalité des chances. La mobilité sociale dans le sociétés industrielles*, Paris, A. Colin, 1973, 1978. – BOULDING, K., *Ecodynamics. A new theory of societal evolution*, London, Sage, 1978. – BOURDIEU, P. and PASSERON, J.-C., *La reproduction. Eléments pour une théorie du système d'enseignement*, Paris, Minuit, 1970. – BOURRICAUD, F., 'Changement et théories du changement dans la France d'après 1945', *Contrepoint*, 16, 1975, 61–84. – CROZIER, M., *Le phénomène bureaucratique*, Paris, Le Seuil, 1963. – FARARO, T.J. and OSAKA, J., 'A mathematical analysis of Boudon's IEO model', *Social science information/Information sur les sciences sociales*, XV, 2/3, 1976, 431–475. – HARDIN, G., 'The cybernetics of competition: a biologist's view of society', *in* SHEPARD, P. and McKINLEY, D. (ed,), *The subversive science. Essays toward an ecology of man*, Boston, Houghton Mifflin, 1969, 275–296. – HERNES, G., 'Structural change in social processes', *American journal of sociology*, LXXXII, 3, 1976, 513–547. – LANGE, O., *Theory of reproduction and accumulation*, New York, Pergamon, 1969. – MARX, K., in *Capital*, Vol. 1. (op cit) – ROSEN, R., 'Stability theory and its applications', *in* ROSEN, R., *Dynamical system theory in biology*, New York, Wiley Interscience, 1970, vol. 1.

Role

The concept of role, in its sociological sense, is often attributed to Linton, although Nietzsche uses this theatrical term with a sociological meaning ('*Die Lebensfursorge zwingt . . . fast allen mannlichen Europaern eine bestimmte* Rolle auf, ihren sogennanten Beruf': 'The worry about existence imposes . . . on most European males a pre-determined role, their so-called careers', *Le gai savoir*, p. 356). For the sociologist, every organization includes a set of more or less differentiated roles (for example, headmaster, deputy headmaster, bursar, class representative, pupil, etc., in the case of a secondary school). These roles can be defined as systems of boundary conditions (normative constraints), to which the actors who play them are supposed to conform, and of the corresponding rights that these boundaries give. The role defines in this way an area of obligations and constraints that corresponds to an area of conditional autonomy. Because he is obliged to uphold the correct functioning of his establishment, the headmaster has the right, within more or less well defined limits and conditions, to have recourse to certain sanctions should an actor such as a pupil, for example, overstep the bounds which define the role of the pupil. The pupil, for his part, is obliged to conform to these bounds, but he is able, nevertheless, to resist any abuse of power or of authority by the headmaster. The boundary conditions associated with each of the roles being, in the simplest case, more or less known by the set of actors belonging to the organization, thereby create role expectations which have the effect of reducing the uncertainty of interaction: when actor A interacts with actor B, they each have the expectation that the other will behave within the bounds that define his role.

While the notion of role is important, as we will see, in the analysis of certain macrosociological phenomena, it is even more so in *microsociological* analysis. It is a key concept in the sociology of organizations and families. But it is important to stress one point: if the bounds that are imposed on the members of an organization through the definition of their roles are necessary to the analysis of their behaviour, they are not sufficient to determine the behaviour. In effect, the boundary conditions generally include an indeterminacy and an ambiguity that provide the actor with a margin for manoeuvre within which strategic conduct can develop. Goffman insisted on the fact that the person who plays a role recognizes the existence of a distance (that varies according to the case) between himself and his role. Parsons largely insisted on the 'variance' of the boundary conditions associated with roles. Merton underlined their 'ambivalence'. Thus, the role of researcher implies that the holder of this role should be ready to make his results available to his peers as rapidly as possible, but it also implies that he must not show too much haste in publishing an article. He must be impervious to 'intellectual fashions', but he must be receptive to 'new ideas'. He must leave his peers with the task of appreciating his production, but he must also defend his hypotheses and his results. He must know the previous contributions in his subject, but he must also avoid writing them off as 'useless'. He must give value only to the opinions of specialists, but he must also recognize that non-specialists can play a positive role in the orientation of his discipline. He must pay great attention to detail, but avoid pedantry.

Variance and ambivalence of roles are general characteristics of every role system. Even where roles are the object of an a priori definition (in the case of formal organization), it is in effect generally impossible, from a technical viewpoint, to define them sufficiently precisely to account for all possible situations of interaction. The argument is applied *a fortiori* to roles that result only very partially in a priori definitions, as for roles within the family.

The margin of autonomy implied by the variance and ambiguity of roles is a generator of *system effects*, effects that organizational sociologists insist on with vigour. This notion is so important that it is worthwhile illustrating it with a detailed example. The observers of the crisis in the American university system in the 1960s were struck by a surprising finding: the protest against the university system was mainly by students belonging to the best universities. Why? Precisely and mainly because of a system effect resulting from the 'variance' in the role of the university professor. This role contains typically two sub-roles: the role of teacher and the role of researcher. The existence of these sub-roles is the result of the dual function of a university: to produce and to disseminate knowledge. This duality of role gives the individuals who perform it a measure of freedom: they are, within certain limits, free to decide how much of each sub-role it suits them to perform. Let us consider the disadvantages and advantages associated with each of these two sub-roles. By its nature, the system of social compensation of a teacher is local. The 'good' teacher is appreciated by his students. He is seen in a good light by the management of the organization to which he belongs. But it is unlikely that a teacher's reputation will extend beyond the walls of his establishment. By its nature, the system of compensation for a researcher is on the contrary, to use Merton's term, cosmopolitan. The results of a discovery are, in theory, destined to be made available to the whole of the international scientific community. Therefore, by the nature of their roles, the compensation of the teacher is assigned by a local agency, the establishment; that of the researcher is assigned by central agencies. It is necessary to expect therefore that a system that does not accept the separation of the roles of teacher and researcher will make the second sub-role seem much more attractive. Let us now consider the system effect resulting from the variance of roles. The American university system is notable, if we compare it with the French system, for a high degree of mobility. University establishments, being unequal in prestige, are unequally sought after. This has the effect that an individual whose fame is in the ascendant will 'normally' seek to move to a more prestigious establishment. For their part, the prestigious institutions will endeavour to maintain and if possible to enhance their prestige by joining the competition to attract candidates with established reputations. But, by the nature of the sub-roles, reputations are rather more readily established on the basis of the quality of research work than on the quality of the teaching. We must make an exception of the liberal arts colleges, where a certain type of tutoring is highly valued and which have the capacity to offer their teachers a certificate of reputation that is negotiable on the wider university market. But in general, it follows from the special attraction of the compensations that go with the sub-role of researcher that the best universities are also those where the teachers, being more often than not reputable researchers, have the tendency to interpret their role as teacher in the most restricted way possible by seeking to keep to the minimum the time they devote to this sub-role and to spend their energies exclusively in teaching only what is connected with their field of research. We arrive thus at a contradiction which explains the inversion of the correlation between quality and protest: the 'best' universities are those with the 'best' professors and the 'best' students. But these are also the ones whose professors concern themselves the least with the most numerous sector of the student population, the students who are at the beginning of their courses. Numerous, and aware of their quality, since they were admitted only after the most rigorous selection procedures, these students also had the feeling more frequently than students in less prestigious institutions that they were being let down by the teaching staff. This example illustrates in some detail a fundamental case in which we see that role variance can produce system effects with considerable social importance. The analysis of these effects is one of the main objectives of the theory and of the sociology of organizations. The reader who is anxious to go deeper into this point can refer to the works of Deutsch, Crozier, March, and Simon which contain numerous examples of system effect provoked by organizational systems.

Parsons's celebrated *pattern variables* allow us to establish a useful typology of roles and at the same time to illustrate the importance of the notion of role for the analysis of certain questions that are relevant to macrosociology. To introduce Parsons's four variables, let us take the example of the 'bank employee's' role. In performing his role, he must give his customers equal treatment: his role is 'universalist'. By contrast, 'filial respect' is reserved for well-identified individuals (their parents): the role of daughter or son is 'individualist'. Moreover, our employee will deal in and discuss only very precise topics with his customers: his role is 'specific', while that of a daughter or son is 'diffused'. The relationship between the employee and his customers is, on the other hand, unlike that between father and son, 'affectively neutral'. Finally, one becomes a bank employee but one is born a son. The first role is achievement oriented, while the second role is ascribed. Apart from its intrinsic interest, this typology allows us to define precisely the classic opposition between 'traditional' societies and 'industrial' societies. In the case of the former, whose main characteristic is the simple division of labour, roles have the tendency to be individualistic, scattered, not affectively neutral, and ascribed. On the contrary, in the second case, and the more the process of 'rationalization' described by Weber is marked, the roles defined by the system of division of simple labour tend to become universalist in type, specific, affectively neutral, and 'achievement oriented'.

Another consequence of the complexification of division of labour is that it multiplies the roles that fall upon an individual: we can be at the same time daughter, mother of a family, an employee of the Electricity Board, a militant trade unionist, a voter, a pupil's father, etc. This is Merton's *status set*. The complexification of status set goes hand in hand with that of *role set*, in other words the set of role partners. Evolution towards the complexification of role sets and status sets has without doubt, as Coser noticed, important consequences. Just as an individual is obliged to carry out ever more complex and varied roles, he runs greater risks of being exposed to normative demands that are partially incompatible. Consequently, he must turn to his own judgement and ask himself about the best way of interpreting his different roles. In short, the complexification of the division of role sets and the increase of his share of universalist, specific, affectively neutral, achievement-oriented roles without doubt give rise to individuation effects (Coser) and, as Durkheim foretold, to a correlative tendency to the rise of individualism and of 'egoism'.

The notion of role has, as the preceding examples show, an essential importance in macrosociological analysis as it does in microsociological analysis. This is why authors such as Parsons and Dahrendorf proposed considering the role relationships as primitive elements which would be to sociology what particles are to physics. Such a concept comes up against a major objection, that the relationships between social agents are not necessarily role relationships or, as we could say, *interaction* relationships. They can also be relationships which, for the sake of distinguishing them, we can qualify as *interdependence* relationships. Thus a set of consumers must be considered as constituting a system of relationships because the behaviour of each consumer has some effect on the set of his partners. Similarly, the fecundity behaviour of each family in t affects the educational structures in $t + k$, the employment structures in $t + m$, and the demographic structures in $t + n$. The systems of complex interdependence, which, on the evidence, concern the sociologist, are not role systems. In fact, role systems (interaction systems) and interdependence systems form complex entanglements which are often linked by reciprocal causality relationships. Thus, the changes which have affected roles in educational institutions during the last few decades are incomprehensible if we do not consider the growth of 'scholastic demand'. But this growth itself results in competition (a form of interdependence) between families (and individuals) in the market of social status. To give a precise example, let us consider the case of the old *Facultés des Lettres et des Sciences* in France. Traditionally, their principal role was to train secondary school teachers. The increase in 'scholastic demand' on one side, the saturation of the teaching market on the other, resulted in this function being diminished during the 1960s. The universities were therefore motivated to redefine their functions as well as the role of the teachers with the problems that we know about. Whenever the external conditions to which an organizational system is exposed change substantially, the appropriate adjustment can be difficult to identify as the redefinition of roles is very likely to come up against a double obstacle: for the individual, the redefinition of his role can involve not-inconsiderable costs; for the system, there can be a period of latency during which its original functions and roles (derived from functions?) appear as if struck by obsolescence before the new functions can be defined in sufficient detail to make it possible for roles to be given precise redefinitions. This type of situation can conveniently be described with the help of the Durkheimian notion of anomie. We can conclude from this example that organized systems or interactive systems are placed under the influence of facts of interdependence. This proposition obliges us to recognize, first, that types of social relationship exist other than role relationships (by which we mean the relationships we define here by the expression of interdependence relationships), second, that interaction relationships can be affected by interdependence relationships. The reciprocal causality that associates interdependence relationships with interaction relationships or role relationships allows us at last to clarify the link between role and status. This last term defines the actor's hierarchical position in the social group. Now the variation (or constance) of the status associated with a role depends very largely on the effects of interdependence. Thus the spread of education has modified the status of certain types of school teachers.

Contrary to the opinion put forward by Parsons, the 'individual' has, on the whole, a greater calling in composing the irreducible element of sociology than simply that of 'role relationship'. This has the result that, even if organizations can be considered as systems of roles, this does not hold for society.

Conformity and Deviance, Status.

Bibliography

BLAU, P.M., 'Structural constraints of status complements', in COSER, L. (ed.), *The idea of social structure. Papers in honor of Robert K. Merton*, New York, Harcourt Brace, 1975, 117–138. – COSER, R., 'The complexity of roles as a seedbed of individual autonomy', in COSER, L. (ed.), *The idea of social structure. Papers in honor of Robert K. Merton*, New York, Harcourt Brace, 1975, 237–263. – CROZIER, M. and FRIEDBERG, E., *L'acteur et le système. Les contraintes de l'action collective*, Paris, Le Seuil, 1977. – DAHRENDORF, R., 'Homo sociologicus', in DAHRENDORF, R., *Essays in the theory of society*, London, Routledge & Kegan Paul, 1968, chap. II, 19–87. – DEUTSCH, K.W., 'On political theory and political action', *American political science review*, LXV, *1*, 1971, 11–27. – DURKHEIM, E., *The Division of Labour in Society*, op cit. *Suicide*, op cit. – ELRIDGE, J.E.T. (ed.), *Max Weber: the interpretation of social reality*, London, M. Joseph, 1970, 1971. – GOFFMAN, E., *Asylums. Essays on the social situation of mental patients and other inmates*, Garden City, Anchor Books, 1961; Chicago, Aldine, 1961, 1962; Harmondsworth, Penguin, 1968. *Interaction ritual. Essays in face to face behaviour*, Chicago, Aldine, 1967; London, Allen Lane, 1972. – LINTON, R., *The study of man. An introduction*, New York/London, Appleton, 1936. – MARCH, J.G. and SIMON, H.A., *Organizations*, New York, Wiley, 1958. – MERTON, R.K., *Sociological ambivalence and other essays*, New York/London/Glencoe, The Free Press, 1976. – NADEL, S.F., 'Problems of role analysis', 'Conformity and deviance' and 'The coherence of role systems', in NADEL, S.F., *The theory of social structure*, London, Cohen & West, 1957, chap. II, III and IV, 20–44, 45–62 and 63–96. – NIETZSCHE, F., 'Inwiefern es in Europa immer "künstlerischer" zugehn wird', in NIETZSCHE, F., *Die fröliche Wissenschaft*, Chemnitz, E. Schmeitzner / New York, E. Steiger, 1882, § 356. – PARSONS, T. and SHILS, E., *Toward a general theory of action*, Cambridge, Harvard University Press, 1951. – WEBER, M., *The interpretation of social reality*, New York, Scribner, 1971.

Rousseau, Jean-Jacques

Jean-Jacques Rousseau (1712–78) still concerns the modern sociologist because of several aspects of his work, but above all perhaps because of the fundamental question with which his political sociology is concerned, that of the conditions of legitimacy of political institutions.

This question is tackled starting from the second discourse, that is to say the

Discours sur l'origine de l'inégalité parmi les hommes (Discourse on Inequality). The abandonment of natural liberty, that is to say the liberty which 'nartural man' enjoys in the state of nature, is explained there by the perverse effects engendered by interactive systems where each person has the latitude to act according to his own interest alone. In a passage significantly placed at the beginning of the second part of the *Discourse*, at the point where Rousseau undertakes to describe the 'transition' — as one might say in an anachronistic language — from the state of nature to the state of society, he shows that an interactive system of this type can have counterproductive effects for each party:

> See how men can insensibly acquire a certain coarse idea of mutual obligations and of the advantage of fulfilling them, but only as much as present appreciable interest demands; because foresight meant nothing to them; and, far from concerning themselves with a far distant future, they did not even think of tomorrow. If it was a matter of taking a deer, each man understood clearly that he ought to faithfully keep to his post in order to do so; but if a hare happened to pass within the reach of one of them, it is not to be doubted that he would chase after it without scruple, and that having caught his prey that he would give very little thought to having caused his companions to lose theirs.

Rousseau's reasoning can be formalized in the following fashion (see *Table A*). There are three possible 'rewards': D = Deer, H = Hare, 0 = Nothing. If two hunters co-operate, each will get a part of the deer (situation D, D). If the first hunter defects, he catches a hare and the other returns with an empty bag (situation H, 0). If the first hunter keeps a look-out and the second defects, the first returns empty handed and the second catches a hare (situation 0, H). Naturally each prefers D to H and

	2nd Hunter	
	Co-operation	*Defection*
Co-operation	D, D	O, H
Defection	H, O	H, H

1st Hunter (row label)

Table A

H to 0. But there is every chance that the game ends by a 'less than perfect solution' H,H. In effect, each hunter knows that the other, enjoying natural liberty which implies the absence of moral constraint according to Rousseau's own definition, can break off his engagement. Risking returning with nothing if he is the only one to co-operate, he will prefer to choose the strategy of 'defection'. The implicit axiomatic contained in the Rousseauesque idea of 'natural liberty' postulated in effect egotistical and hedonistic individuals. Confronted by a situation such as that of the hunting party, whose structure is summarized in *Table A*, the protagonists are going to have a tendency – to use the language of the theory of games – to utilize the strategy of the *maximum (maximum minimorum)*, that is to say the line of action which preserves with certainty the maximum risk: that of returning empty handed. In doing this they engender the counter-productive result H,H: the prudence which recommends itself to them from the moment when solidarity and the moral constraints that it implies (loyalty) cease to be present means that it is difficult for them ('each understood well . . . but') to achieve the 'optimum solution', D,D. In this regard, one can underline the profound originality of Rousseau compared with another classic theoretician of the social order, Hobbes. Whereas the Hobbesian war is the result of the rivalry of individuals for the conquest of rare possessions, Rousseau shows that, even within a hypothesis of a kindly and generous nature and even if one presumes an absence of mutual hostility between men, they may not be able to realize the objectives they set themselves. The counter-productive effects which the fable of the hunting party illustrates can result – this is its lesson – not from the aggressive nature of man and of the greed of nature, but from the structure of systems of interdependence and of interaction in which the protagonists find themselves engaged.

In the sequel to his mythical story, Rousseau attempts to show that these counter-productive effects are accentuated according to the growth in what Durkheim would have called 'social density'. The absence of constraints causes a state of disorder by which all are affected, even though the 'rich' are to a greater degree than the 'poor'. The rich therefore propose to the poor, who accept it, the abandonment of the state of nature. To avoid the disadvantages of social disorder, each has in fact an interest in accepting a system of constraints which apply to everyone. The better-off merely have a greater interest than the others in the establishment of a social order. Besides, the former have the resources which permit them to abuse the social order, because the establishment of a system of constraints which implies the passage from a state of nature to a state of society cannot be satisfied only by laws. It is also necessary that the laws should be obeyed. But obeying laws presumes the institution of a political power, which is necessarily exercised by men. Despite the inevitable 'abuses' implied by social order, 'even wise men saw that it was necessary to resolve to sacrifice a part of their liberty'.

Far from the *Discours sur l'origine de l'inégalité parmi les hommes* being, as has sometimes been held, contradictory with *Le Contrat Social (The Social Contract)*, the problem posed in the second *Discourse* is in reality systematized in *Le Contrat Social*. *Le Contrat* takes up in a formal manner a demonstration which, in the second

Discourse, was presented as a mythical story. 'Force man to be free', said *Le Contrat*: this formula is only apparently obscure. It only shows that constraint is a means which permits the avoidance of the counter-productive effects of interactive structures which develop in the natural state. Consequently it is in everyone's interest to accept the constraint. Games theory allows convenient formalization of Rousseau's intuitions. Let us imagine an interactive situation in which, if two actors co-operate, the first obtains a remuneration to a value equal to 3 and the second obtains a remuneration to a value equal to 2; that if the first co-operates and if the second defects, the first obtains a remuneration equal to 0, the second a remuneration equal to 4, etc. (see *Table B*). In the hypothesis of the natural state, a remuneration structure such as this leads to the result 1,1.

In effect, each actor does not preserve himself by defecting, at a maximum risk which is represented by the zero value remuneration. In addition, if the other co-operates, he will obtain an advantage from it. Whatever it is, put another way, the choice of the other, co-operation or defection, each has an interest in defection. Naturally such a calculation, although reasonable, will result in an undesirable effect, as in this case; each will have a remuneration equal to 1, that is to say the lowest possible remuneration with the exception of the zero remuneration. How can that effect be eliminated? By associating defection with a negative sanction. Let us suppose in effect that the actors are now exposed to a negative sanction, for example to a fine of the value of 2, if they defect. As *Table C* shows, the introduction of this penalty has the effect of modifying the structure of the system of interaction in a manner which is favourable to the actors. The actors are this time able to obtain the result 3,2, obviously preferable to −1, −1 for the two participants, even although it is unequal.

In effect, in choosing defection, actor 1 exposes himself to a loss: he would only have 2 instead of 3 if the other chose to co-operate. He would have −1 instead of 0 if the other chose to defect. Similarly, actor 2 would have no reason to defect if the other co-operates, and has reason to co-operate if the other defects. The negative sanction has the effect of forcing the individuals to co-operate. Thus it is likely

		2nd Actor	
		Co-operation	Defection
1st Actor	Co-operation	3,2	0,4
	Defection	4,0	1,1

Table B

		2nd Actor	
		Co-operation	Defection
1st Actor	Co-operation	3,2	0,2
	Defection	2,0	−1, −1

Table C

never to be applied and to remain purely potential. Thanks to the threat of sanction, the actors are in a position to obtain the result 3,2 instead of the much less favourable result 1,1 to which the natural state condemned them. Both gain from it. Even though one gains more than the other, it is in the interests of both to accept the threat of sanction. It is thus possible, according to the *Contrat*, to give legitimacy to the passage from natural liberty to civil liberty. The 'wise men' themselves can recognize the utility of this passage, even though it means, according to the expression of *Discours sur l'origine de l'inégalité*, 'cutting off an arm to save the rest of the body'.

Once this essential point has been made, the fundamental problem, already raised by the second *Discourse*, that of the organization of political power, is tackled in a systematic manner in *Le Contrat: Quis custodet ipsos custodes?* Because the threat of sanction cannot remain purely theoretical. Even if it should never be applied, the actors must know that it would be if needs be. It is thus necessary that members of a society accept the existence and the organization of a political power. Rousseau sets off from the principle that, to reply to the old question posed by Plato, it is *useful* to suppose that the 'magistrates', that is to say the political leaders, are utilitarians and egotists. Why such a hypothesis? For obvious reasons which make it unnecessary to have recourse to the hypothesis of Rousseau's pessimism or to that of one's submission to utilitarian values of 'possessive individualism'. If one imagines that political power is held by men who are acting under the general will, its organization can be poor and political theory becomes vain. The essential question is thus to know how political power should be organized if one wishes it to express the general will, even in the situation where the magistrates would be, according to the hypothesis, acting in the first place under their own egotistical will.

We can distinguish three essentially different wills in the person of the magistrate: firstly, the will of the individual, which is only concerned with its own particular advantage; secondly, the common will of Magistrates, which is only to the advantage of the Prince, and which one might call the will of the group, which is generally in connection with government, and particularly in connection with the State, of which the government is part; in the third place, the will of the people or the sovereign will, which is generally as much in connection with the State considered as the whole, as in connection with the government considered as part of the whole. But in the 'natural' order the general will is always the weakest, the will of the group takes second place, and the individual will takes first place of all.

It is thus necessary for the legislator to establish control mechanisms which allow for the reversal of this 'natural' order of wills, exactly as freely consented-to constraint enables the avoidance of counter-productive effects generated by the 'natural state'. How should he do this? Rousseau's response is cautious, complex, and qualified. Undifferentiated societies, those where one sees 'troupes of peasants regulating affairs of state under an oak tree', are the only ones in which the question can receive a satisfactory solution. In this case, the general will is present in each individual, because, each being the same as the others, common interest and individual interest coincide without too much difficulty. As for complex societies, they require mechanisms to control the power of the ruler. But no institutional mechanism can ensure that the 'general will', such as is expressed in the vote count of assemblies, even in a regime of direct democracy, is necessarily identical to the general will, such as is translated by the hypothesis of common interest. The more complex societies are, the more uncertain and doubtful becomes the effectiveness of institutional mechanisms which aim to submit particular wills to the general will. Institutions by themselves cannot thus ensure that the general will imposes itself in all cases. That is why the problem of the education of the citizen is essential (*Emile*). In the end, the legitimacy of the social order depends both on the efficacy of institutions (that is to say their capacity to convert the egotism of the magistrates into altruism) and on the effectiveness of socialization mechanisms. But it depends equally on correcting mechanisms which the holders of political power must introduce pragmatically, with good sense and without a spirit of system, in what Hegel would call the civil society. Thus, social inequalities have, according to Rousseau, an irresistible tendency to grow. It is therefore necessary that the political authority assigns limits to their development, in such a manner 'that the rich are not too rich and the poor too poor'. Everybody having something to lose will thus accept more easily the social order. But it is also necessary that the political authority retains egalitarian illusions (according to Rousseau's theory of inequalities).

The political sociology of Rousseau has given rise to numerous misunderstandings from its own time to our own, because it is of great complexity. The 'natural state' is not a mythical state, a golden age created by Rousseau as an ethical reference point. It should rather be seen as a sort of axiomatic which permits the analysis of the meaning of the mechanisms of coercion or of incentive on which every social order reposes. Like certain modern economists, Rousseau tackles the analysis of political phenomena by the method of models. That is to say by theoretical constructions with simplified, idealized, and consequently necessarily unrealistic designs (cf. the famous *'ecartons les faits'*). The original character of this methodology doubtless explains the admiration of Kant, who saw in Rousseau the Newton of political theory.

But Rousseau was also perfectly aware of the complexity of political systems. Only small societies, where individuals had learnt to be satisfied with little, only societies where face to face dealing is possible and the interpersonal links are dense and inclusive, function in perfect harmony (cf. *La Nouvelle Heloise*). That is why Rousseau's theory powerfully contains the distinction which Tönnies translated by the concepts of *Gemeinschaft* and of *Gesellschaft*. In small, narrow societies coercion is present, but it takes a moral form. Virtue can reign. In complex societies, one can only seek the least ineffective institutional mechanisms to ensure that the individual will does not suffocate the general will and that the will of all is not merely an addition to the particular will. But Rousseau well knew that it is impossible and admitted that it was undesirable to bring a complex society back to a more simple form. At best he hoped that the *Negritie* would be protected from the invader and the predator coming from modern societies. He had no illusions regarding the capacity of complex societies to organize political power and to instruct its citizens in such a way that the mechanisms of collective decisions would be able to reveal the general will. Because for Rousseau, the idea of the general will, too, has principally a methodological function. Like the concept of 'natural state', it describes a logical reference point. It permits Rousseau to pose a fundamental question: under what conditions has the common interest (when it is defined, and Rousseau does not say that it will necessarily be so) a chance of being realized? He replies that it depends on the political institutions, on the systems of values and norms as one would put it later, and those depend in their turn on the history of societies, on their complexity, and on their size. Certainly Rousseau did not see the function of political parties and of representation. But the 'totalitarian' reading of his thought (that is to say the reading which claims to detect in it utopia, that of 'totalitarian democracy' or of the dissolution of the individual in the State) that one sometimes believes it possible to pull out from the idea of the general will is assuredly much less directed at Rousseau than at the interpretation that the French revolutionaries and others (it is reported that Fidel Castro only belatedly exchanged the *Contrat Social* for *Capital*) have made of his thought.

Democracy.

Bibliography

ROUSSEAU, J-J., *Discours sur l'origine et les fondements de l'inégalité parmi les hommes*, Amsterdam, M.M. Rey, 1755. – ROUSSEAU, J.-J., 'Discours sur l'économie politique', written for *l'Encyclopédie* of DIDEROT, D. and d'ALEMBERT, J., Paris, Briasson, 1751–1765, vol. V. – *Discours sur l'economie politique*, Geneva, E. du Villard, 1758. – ROUSSEAU, J.-J., *Contrat social; ou Principes du droit politique*, Paris, Garnier, n.d., Geneva, M.M. Bousquet, 1766. – ROUSSEAU, J.-J., *Du contrat social. Ecrits politiques*, in ROUSSEAU, J.-J., *Œuvres complétes*, Paris, Gallimard, 4 vol., 1959–1969; vol. III, 1964. – BEAUMARCHAIS, J.-P. (de), 'Mathématiques et politique dans le contrat social', in POMEAU, R., *Histoire et littérature. Les écrivains et la politique*, Paris, PUF, 1977. – CASSIRER, E., 'Das problem Jean-Jacques Rousseau', *Archiv für Geschichte der Philosophie*, XLI, 1932, 177–213, 479–513. Trad. angl., *The question of Jean-Jacques Rousseau*, New York, Columbia University Press, 1954. – CASSIRER, E., 'L'unité dans l'œuvre de Jean-Jacques Rousseau', *Bulletin de la Société française de Philosophie*, compte rendu de séance, XXXII, 1932, 46–85. – COBBAN, A., *Rousseau and the modern state*, London, Allen & Unwin, 1934, 1964. – CRANSTON, M. and PETERS, S., *Hobbes and Rousseau: Collection of critical essays*, New York, Doubleday, 1972. – DERATHÉ, R., *Jean-Jacques Rousseau et la science politique de son temps*. Paris, PUF, 1950. – DURKHEIM, É., *Montesquieu et Rousseau, précurseurs de la sociologie*. Paris, M. Rivière, 1953. – MERQUIOR, J.G., *Rousseau and Weber. Two studies in the theory of legitimacy*. London, Routledge & Kegan Paul, 1980. – POLIN, R., *La politique de la solitude: essais sur la philosophie de Jean-Jacques Rousseau*, Paris, Cirey, 1971. – SHKLAR, J., *Men and citizens. A study of Rousseau's social theory*, Cambridge, Cambridge University Press, 1969. – STRAUSS, L., *Natural right and history*, Chicago, Chicago University Press, 1950, 1974. – TALMON, J.B., *The origins of totalitarian democracy*, London, Secker and Warburg, 1952. – WEIL, E., 'Jean-Jacques Rousseau et sa politique', *Critique*, VIII, *56*, 1952, 3–28.

S

Schumpeter, Joseph Alois

It is difficult to describe the works of Schumpeter (1883–1950). *Business Cycles* is the work of an economist, both theorist and historian. *Capitalism, Socialism and Democracy* belongs to political science, and also to economics and sociology. As for the monumental *History of Economic Analysis*, it is a whole where the virtuosity of the historian, the philosopher, and the economist are all equally displayed. There is no author more truly interdisciplinary than Schumpeter. Fortunately, he understands interdisciplinarity very differently from those who claim to be its champions. Interdisciplinarity is not the confusion of all disciplines into a moderated syncretism; nor is it their subordination to one discipline (sociology, history) which would pretend to ensure their 'integration'. The 'interdisciplinarity' in Schumpeter's style organizes the recourse to specific 'hypotheses' to deal with problems not necessarily solvable by the disciplines which set them or in the terms in which they were constituted.

All his life, Schumpeter, attentive reader of Marx, Weber, and Schmoller, took an interest in the evolution of the capitalist economy. However, he cannot be described either as an evolutionist or as an historicist. His research turns on a set of heterogeneous relations (economic, social, and cultural) which do not develop in an abstract period of time, but in the history of three great capitalist countries: England, the United States, and Germany. In his *Business Cycles*, Schumpeter endeavours to restore the continuity of certain time-series data for these three countries: prices, quantities, costs, incomes, monetary aggregates.

Capitalist evolution presents itself as a succession of cycles, or at least of very pronounced fluctuations. Since Schumpeter, statistical information has spread. Moreover, today's economists have more widely varying views on the nature of economic fluctuations than the economists of the 1930s. In the opinion of the more optimistic of the Keynesians, the existence of cycles would no longer be essential to the capitalist process, if it is true that, thanks to the control of demand, the political, fiscal, and monetary authorities were able to control deflation as well as inflation and to ensure at any time the full use of the factors of production.

However, even if the notion of cycle in its strict sense were to be abandoned, Schumpeter's approach would still remain interesting. Fluctuation (and not only cyclic fluctuation) records a divergence between a theoretical state of the economic system (its position of equilibrium/stability according to Walras) and the behaviour through time of the observed variables. Schumpeter starts with the hypothesis that for the system there is a 'state of equilibrium' defined by what he calls a 'theoretical norm' – that provided by the resolution of the equation systems. This norm makes it possible to attribute to the different variables (quantities, prices, costs, interest rates) values which mean they can be compared over time. This is helped if one can assume some data to be constant: size and structure of the population, techniques of production, rules of the institutional game, consumers' tastes, etc.

But if Schumpeter starts from the Walrasian conception of equilibrium, hypotheses about the market of pure and perfect competition are in his opinion incapable of explaining the functioning of any actual economy. However, they form a kind of 'ideal type' which facilitates the comprehension and explanation of the phenomena under observation. Here a parallel between Weber's 'ideal type' and Schumpeter's 'theoretical norm' comes strongly to mind.

Weber, dealing with behaviour considered to be 'irrational', as for example a panic in the Stock Exchange, writes: 'any explanation of "irrational" processes requires above all that one establishes how one would have acted in the borderline case . . . of an absolute rationality by reference to means-ends relationships, and accuracy.' (*Essays on the Theory of Science*, Paris, Plon, 1965, p. 334). Likewise, Schumpeter, in explaining the fact of capitalist cycles, begins by stating the conditions of equilibrium to which the system is subjected if it reproduces itself identically.

In this way, the dilemma between 'empiricism or theory' is avoided. It is not a question of asserting that any interpretation of experience is impossible by arguing that facts do not occur as dictated by the 'theory'. It is a question of working out hypotheses which, when paradoxical facts in relation to the 'theoretical norm' are recorded, account for these paradoxes. Schumpeter, unlike too many economic historians, takes care not to challenge the economic theory on the pretext that Walras's model does not give an immediate and complete explanation of capitalist development. No more is he satisfied with a simple description of essentially institutional data which resist the analysis of 'theoretical' economics. Far from considering them as 'residual', he proposes a theory of institutional factors in terms meaningful to the economist himself.

This is the aim of his theory of innovation. Schumpeter starts from the fact that the 'functions of production' change through time. These functions link 'factors' of production (such as quantities of capital, labour, or land) to products (intermediate or final). They facilitate a comparison of the efficiency by which the different factors which are part of the composition of a given product can be combined. The 'factors of production' are substitutable for each other, but within certain limits: the capitalist can 'arbitrate' between a little more capital and a little less labour (or inversely) according to the increase or decrease of wages costs. But he cannot entirely substitute one of these factors for another.

These constraints, recorded by the function of production, can be observed in the case where the economic system 'reproduces itself' by a circular flow, and the individual exercises his freedom of choice while taking into consideration these constraints. In a stable economic system, consumers and producers choose, but according to constant constraints. Some of these constraints, for example those linked to the indivisibility of factors, generate imperfect equilibria, based on monopolistic competition or imperfect competition. The 'theoretical nórm' of equilibrium does not therefore guarantee stable functioning of the economic system. But it helps us to understand its functioning and especially the tendency of the system to repeat and 'reproduce' its own characteristics.

The functions of reproduction diverge from the 'theoretical norm' in two ways. First, they express the distortions resulting from the imperfection of the markets, which in turn result, at least in part, from capitalists' manipulations. Furthermore, they are likely to change. Schumpeter calls innovation the appearance of a 'new function of production' (*Business Cycles*, p. 87), that is, a new combination of factors.

Innovation is distinguishable from invention. At the beginning of the industrial era, the 'inventor' was the man who made a lucky discovery, largely by trial and error. Very often, the inventor's discoveries were not viable. They disappeared without trace, except in the people's imagination. On the contrary, because he radically changes the structure of costs and profits by introducing new 'functions of production', Schumpeter's innovator propagates original techniques and opens new markets for his products. The example of the car is enough to illustrate this process of 'creative destruction' which destroys whole spheres of the productive system, opening the way for a new generation of captains of industry. Creation and destruction are only two sides of the same coin, and the innovator who launches new products thus hastens the disappearance of obsolete products and inefficient and backward producers.

The innovator-entrepreneur performs a great number of co-ordinated activities. He brings into contact technicians and potential consumers of the new product, the 'organizers' and the 'traders'. He succeeds in doing it because he generates new sources or supplies of credit. In effect he 'creates' credit. The entrepreneur anticipates resources which do not yet exist and which bankers will make available to him. But the 'creation of credit' includes a risk of inflation, as the deferred payment of debts incurred at the beginning of the innovation process involves a risk of deflation for the future.

Capitalism can then be defined as 'this form of economy based on private property in which innovation is realized by means of loans, which themselves result from the creation of credit'. And, a little further: 'The recourse to . . . creation of instruments of credit characterizes an economy as capitalist, as the discovery of arms in a prehistoric economy would characterize it as warlike' (*Business Cycles*, I, p. 223).

For a long time, many historians allowed themselves to confuse the birth of capitalism with the beginnings of the industrial revolution. Against this tendency, challenged today, Schumpeter points out that, if capitalism is characterized by the institutional possibility of 'creating credit', one can find examples of this practice in Italy or the Netherlands from the end of the Middle Ages. Thus, the debate about the relations between the spirit of capitalism and the Protestant ethic loses some of its relevance in Schumpeter's opinion, since he understands capitalism not as a 'spirit' or 'culture', but as a technique of mobilization or creation of credit, without which there would be no room for the innovator.

Schumpeter is not interested only in the process of innovation, he is also interested in the social group of innovators' entrepreneurs. In this respect, his analysis of economic cycles is opposed to that of the economists and historians like Simiand or Labrousse who try to explain such cyclical variations at the level of prices, employment, activity, profit, nominal and real salary by the alternation of 'phases' A (expansion) and 'phases' B (contraction). The 'phases' according to Simiand define a frame strictly constraining the activity of economic agents. With his stress on innovation, Schumpeter puts full attention on initiative, the 'new combination', the decisive weight of innovators and entrepreneurs in economic progress.

Extending his analysis of capitalism, Schumpeter outlined an analysis of the political regime with which this type of organization has been historically associated. He speculated about both the survival chances of the capitalist economy once it reached its 'maturity' and the likelihood of the 'transition to socialism'. He also examined the congruence of the system of values recognized in western countries with the functioning of the capitalist economy. Such are the themes of his last book, *Capitalism, Socialism and Democracy*. In his opinion, the conditions of the 'transition to socialism' are widely independent of the evolution of the capitalist *economy*. Schumpeter's prophecy contains two propositions. As an economic system, capitalism as we have defined it can perfectly well continue to function. However, it is very unlikely that it will survive. According to Schumpeter, it is not the tendency for the rate of profit to decrease, as shown by Marx, or the excess of savings, as feared by Keynes, which condemns capitalism; it is the increasingly apparent discord between the requirements of the capitalist economy and those of the political regime and culture associated with it, especially with regard to initiative, responsibility, and innovation.

What we should remember is the care with which Schumpeter distinguishes the various dimensions of the social system. The economy has its logic which is that of profit through innovation. Politics in modern democracies tends to institutionalize competition between parties or coalitions of parties, which compete to seize power and hold it, before seeking compromises once they have succeeded. Culture and ideology constitute a process of questioning which subjects the various rules of the social game to an endless re-evaluation. The agreement of the three logics (economic, political, and cultural), obeying such different principles, is then neither necessary nor even very likely – nor very lasting once it has been realized.

Durkheim, Methodology, Socialization, Weber.

Bibliography
SCHUMPETER, J., *Theorie der wirtschaftlichen Entwicklung*, Leipzig, Duncker & Humblot, 1912. Trans. *The theory of economic development: an inquiry into profits, capital, credit, interest and the business cycle*, New York, Oxford University Press, 1961. – SCHUMPETER, J., *Epochen der Dogmen- und Methodengeschichte* (1924). Trans. *Business cycles: a theoretical, historical and statistical analysis of the capitalist process*, New York/London, McGraw-Hill, 1939, 2 vol.: abridged edition, New York, McGraw-Hill, 1964. – SCHUMPETER, J., *Capitalism, socialism and democracy*, New York/London, Harper & Brothers, 1942; London, G. Allen & Unwin, 1976. – SCHUMPETER, J., *Ten great economists. From Marx to Keynes*, New York, Oxford University Press, 1951, 1965; – SCHUMPETER, J., *History of economic analysis*, ed. by E. Boody Schumpeter, New York, Oxford University Press, 1954, 1972. – HARRIS, S. (ed.), *Schumpeter, social scientist*, Cambridge, Harvard University Press, 1951. – HEERTJE, A. *et al.*, *Schumpeter's Vision. 'Capitalism, socialism and democracy' after 40 years*, New York/London, Praeger, 1981. – KEYNES, J.M., *The general theory of employment, interest and money*, London, Macmillan, 1936. – PERROUX, F., *La pensée économique de Joseph Schumpeter. Les dynamiques du capitalisme*, Geneva, Droz, 1965. – WALRAS, L., *Eléments d'économie politique pure ou théorie de la richesse sociale*, Lausanne, L. Corbaz, 1874; – WEBER, M., *Gesammelte Aufsätze zur Wissenschaftslehre*, Tübingen, Mohr, 1922, 1951.

Social Change

Philosophers, and after them sociologists, have for a long time been obsessed by the hypothesis that social change follows a privileged, even exclusive pattern: for Marx, who follows Hegel in that respect, and for Marxists, social change is the result of 'contradictions'. The notion of contradictions has several meanings – often uncertain ones in the Marxist tradition (cf. 'Dialectic'). For other authors, such as Nisbet, change results mainly from external causes. Some, following the Saint-Simonians and Comte, maintain that all societies are necessarily heading towards an ideal and better state. Others, following Rousseau, or at least a likely interpretation of Rousseau, tend, by contrast, to interpret change as a regression. Some wish to see in such or such aspects of social systems, or in such or such factors, the determining causes of change: for Montesquieu, the development of international commerce plays a considerable part in it, although less exclusively than does the economic organization of societies for Marx, scientific and technical development for Comte, or religion for Fustel de Coulanges.

In general, if one looks up social change in almost any sociology textbook (cf. for example, Rocher, Moore) on social change, one is likely to find a wide range of 'theories' making ambitious generalizations. Sometimes they search for the prime mover of change, which they identify either as the material conditions of production, technological development, or again in the 'mutations' of the value system. Sometimes they aim to describe the states necessary for the change, to which they implicitly attribute a direction by describing it as an evolution, a development, or a modernization. Other theories look for the driving force of the change (class struggles, conflicts between forward- or backward-looking groups, contradictions between productive forces and cultural models, etc.). Others still look for the forms of the change. Some see it as linear or 'multilinear' (Sahlins). Others see it as a cyclical process (Sorokin) unless it has to take 'necessarily' the form of a succession of blockages and crises. Some see it to be continuous and smooth, proceeding by a succession of progressive maladjustments and adjustments. Others see it to be discontinuous and marked with breaks or 'mutations' – a far-fetched metaphor drawn from the misappropriation of a biological concept. Some theories see in the processes of social differentiation one of the essential forms of change (Parsons), while others insist on the antagonisms and conflicts (Garner). One could easily extend the list.

Modern sociology in its scientific forms tends, however, to repudiate the idea according to which there would be a dominant cause of social change. At the same time, it tends to recognize the plurality of types of change. Some processes of change are endogenous, i.e., determined by internal causes in a social system; others are exogenous; others are mixed. Some processes are linear, others oscillatory. Some processes can be foreseen, others less easily so, especially as they generate a demand for innovations at one stage of their development. As a matter of fact, one may wonder if the expression 'social change theory' still used in sociology is not outdated now because of the evolution of the science itself. To speak of social change, and even more of social change theory, is effectively to suggest either that one can distinguish the main causes of the change or that one can isolate the essential processes of change (for example, processes of differentiation or of class struggle), or else that one can come to a decision about its fundamentally exogenous or endogenous character, or again that one can determine its *form* (evolving, linear cyclic, continuous, or discontinuous). But that is precisely the whole question: can sociology maintain statements of such a general range? Should it not limit itself – at the risk of being used as a cover for ideological concerns – to the analysis of the process of historical and geographical change? This is, one will freely admit, a difficult subject which cannot be exhausted within such a brief entry as this.

So consequently, we shall only suggest that the evident diversity of social change processes is enough to legitimize the question of whether or not one can speak of a 'theory of social changes', and cast some doubts on the importance of theories which claim to discover the main forms, the fundamental processes, or the primordial causes of change. So as not to go back on questions dealt with in other entries ('Historicism', 'Development', etc.), we shall merely succinctly illustrate the diversity of processes while emphasizing the distinction between an *endogenist* theory and as *exogenist* one, and stressing that one should greet theories which tend to represent change (or non-change) as ineluctably governed by 'structures' cautiously.

For example, exogenous change is illustrated by Max Weber's thesis: according to him, the Protestant Reformation would have played a determining role in the development of capitalism by creating a type of *ethics* congruent with the development of the behaviour of investment and savings, which form the condition of capitalist accumulation. On another level, some sociological studies of development, or studies of rural sociology, show that a change or a minor innovation (such as the introduction of hybrid maize in France, in Mendras's work, or of the metal ploughshare, in Lynn White's work) can induce chain reactions leading to a real transformation of the social system. Let us recall briefly Mendras's analysis: the innovation (introduction of hybrid maize) was originally the result of an initiative from the French Ministry of Agriculture. Apparently innocent and introduced in order to increase productivity, it produced complex cumulative effects which could not easily have been foreseen in the initial stages of the process. Hybrid maize cultivation follows a somewhat different cycle from traditional maize cultivation. So it upsets the calendar of the cultivations associated with maize. Moreover, it requires more attentive care and involves different techniques. Thus it needs more fertilizers and insecticides. These differences, minor in themselves, affect however the management of the enterprise: the cost of fertilizers and insecticides is a heavy expense for the family enterprise. To make them profitable, the cultivated areas must be extended. The increase in the maize harvest allows for an increase of poultry. The cash returns increasing, the administration of the farm becomes consequently more complex. The farmer must take out a loan in order to buy a tractor. The increase in takings prompts him to modernize his house. But the debts make him more sensitive to commodity price fluctuations and prompt him to get settled. Returns from poultry breeding themselves contribute to give the farmer's wife greater importance in the system of division of sexual roles. The resort to loans, the increase in returns finally lead to the fuller insertion of the farmer into the economic system. So the transition from a 'traditional' social system to a 'modern' system is, in the case analysed by Mendras, the result of an originally minor fact. Naturally, one must not infer from this example either that any minor change causes a 'structural transformation' or that any 'structural change' is the result of a chain reaction caused by a seemingly harmless measure or change. Against this temptation, it is easy to reveal examples where an exogenous change – even if it is not a minor one – can fail to break a reproductive process (cf. 'Reproduction'). Thus, the injection of physical capital in 'underdeveloped' countries, has not always been sufficient to start a process of development. Mendras's example illustrates a case of transformation with an exogenous origin. One could not infer from it that the process of change is of this type or even that this process is typical.

Other processes are indeed, contrary to the above, *endogenous*. Some of these lead to transformation in the system in which they appear; others to its upholding. One talks about evolutionary processes in the first case, and in the second case about *reproduction* and *repetitive* processes (or, if one wants to use Marx's language, processes of simple reproduction). The systems of 'semi-feudal' organization in agricultural production which are formed in some areas of the world offer an example of this type of process. Some systems are sometimes described in this way, where the farm tenant, while legally a free man, is *de facto* tied to his landlord in so far as: 1) he cannot live upon his own income during the whole of the production cycle; 2) he can only – because of his penury – borrow from his landowner. In such an organization, the landowner often tends to be dissuaded from modernizing his farm, because of the structure of the production returns; indeed, any production increase involves the risk of making him poorer by reducing the interest from his loans.

As in the case above, one must take care not to give too much generality to these examples. Especially, one must not infer from that that the structures govern change or non-change. A semi-feudal structure does not imply, in itself, its self-reproduction. It is true that the landlord might be little encouraged to adopt an innovation which, by reducing the tenant's debts, might well reduce his own income rather than increase it. It would be the case if the productivity yields resulting from innovation were not compensating the loss from the lessening of the tenant's debts. But it is not enough for the structure to be semi-feudal, for the process characterizing such systems to be reproductive. The banks also must not be inclined or encouraged – by political authority for example – to open their door to borrowers who lack the guarantees they consider sufficient. The tenant-farmer must also be culturally forced into consumption spending, chronically increasing his expenses, and no change should occur in this respect. The technical innovations possible at a certain time must promise too a productivity gain such that it is effectively threatening the landowner's income. One could thus multiply the conditions which should necessarily be mentioned in order to give an account of the reproductive process. The outcome of this enumeration is that it is excessive to declare a semi-feudal structure as 'necessarily' generative of self-reproductive mechanisms. If such a necessity effectively prevailed, one would not be able to understand why some semi-feudal agricultural societies (Japan for example) have experienced spectacular development, while others are blocked by self-reproductive mechanisms.

Other processes can be said to be evolutionary (in Marx's language, one would speak of extended reproduction or transformation). In this case, the social system, while functioning, produces a modification of its functioning rules. The development of scientific knowledge, the process of division of labour are simple examples of evolutionary processes. But one must take care – here too – not to make such processes more general and exact than they might be. For example, one knows well today that the process of the division of labour is not as mechanical as it has often been said to be following Adam Smith's famous descriptions of the pin-factory. In France, in Italy, and even the United States, the small business is still alive despite this prediction, and the theme of the recombining of tasks took the place of the spectre of piece work. An evolutionary process which involves dysfunctions or, more prosaically, contributes to the deterioration of the conditions for some categories of actors often leads to retroactive effects which in turn modify the evolution of the process. In other cases, an evolutionary process is stopped temporarily or indefinitely by a modification of the conditions which have accompanied it in the first stages. Thus, the uprisings of 1968 in France and 1969 in Italy led to institutional modifications which tend to limit the margin of autonomy of entrepreneurs in recruiting and sacking staff. Indirectly, this change has caused (cf. Piore and Berger) an increase in subcontracting and consequently an encouragement to the development of small businesses. So, in the case of evolutionary processes as in other cases, one must understand that the evolutionary structure is not the consequence of structural characteristics, but the result of a complex connection of elements forming a system, a connection which it is always rash to hold as eternal or unvarying.

That is why most of the processes can be said to be *exogenous-endogenous* if one observes them over a long period: while developing they produce results which can affect not only the functioning rules of the system in which they occur, but also the system's environment, causing a reaction to it. It is easy to bring forward simple examples of this case: negative consequences of market laws cause a regulative intervention from the state; the powerlessness of a latent group of consumers opposite an oligopolistic group of producers can provoke, and has indeed provoked in numerous actual cases, the intervention of an advocate (such as Ralph Nader) who starts a campaign for the consumers' defence (cf. 'Action'). But there are also some cases where an exogenous change happens to affect an endogenous process without being caused by it, for instance, the continuance of a semi-feudal structure perhaps – to go back to one of the above examples – threatened not only by the 'values' of progress and those supporting them, avant-garde forces and future oriented groups, but in a thousand other ways – the adoption of an innovation leading to chain reaction mechanisms; intervention in the political system even from its host 'reactionary' groups, or, as in some episodes of Colombian history, secondary effects of a cause at first sight as remote as the unequal balance of payments (when it shows a deficit, in a country with essentially agricultural resources, whose organization includes large semi-feudal areas, the 'ruling' class may have an interest in trying to increase land productivity by freeing the exploited peasants).

If all social processes were of the endogenous genre, and of reproductive or evolutionary type, social systems would follow a strict determinism of Laplacian type: by knowing their state in t, one could predict their state in $t + k$(cf. 'Determinism'). In both cases, the change (or non-change) is by definition the result of the very properties of the system structure; as to the environment, it is supposed to remain passive in processes of this type. On the other hand, if all social processes were of exogenous type, social change would always result either from accidents or from voluntary intervention. In reality, the most characteristic processes of change are of exogenous-endogenous type. This type of process, which can imply particularly an innovative reaction of the environment, is generally incompatible with a determinist vision of a Laplacian type. In other words, it is generally within restrictive and definite spatio-temporal conditions that a process can be regarded as endogenous.

Unfortunately the endogenist view of change has in its favour its undeniable seduction. This seduction is both intellectual and ideological. *Intellectual*: necessity and determinism are, according to a widely spread conception of scientific knowledge, always more seductive than contingency. *Ideological*: if the future is contained within the present, the development of the real can be said to be rational, according to Hegel's famous phrase; those who hold themselves to belong to the forces of progress can then regard themselves as the executants of God's plan.

By taking into consideration the complex forms of social change, one consequently dismisses traditions which, like one of the Marxist traditions, hold that change must necessarily take the form of 'breaks' due to the appearance of contradictions. It implies the rejection of the idea that social change results from alleged fundamental 'causes'. It implies also the rejection of variants of 'structuralism' which view the future as contained within the 'structure' of the present. Very often, these so-called 'structures' only designate the elements of the system arbitrarily given primacy by the 'structuralist'.

Cycles, Determinism, Development, Dialectic, Historicism, History and Sociology, Reproduction, Structuralism.

Bibliography

BALANDIER, G. (ed.), *Sociologie des mutations*, Paris, Anthropos, 1970. – COHEN, G.A., *Karl Marx's theory of history: a defense*, Oxford, Clarendon Press, 1978. – DORE, R.P., *Land reform in Japan*, London/New York/Toronto, Oxford University Press, 1959. – EISENSTADT, S.N. (ed.), *Readings in social evolution and development*, New York/London/Oxford, Pergamon Press, 1970. – FUSTEL DE COULANGES, N.D., *La cité antique. Etude sur le culte, les droits, les institutions de la Grèce et de Rome*, Paris, Hachette, 1864, 1963. – GARNER, R. (Ash), *Social change*, Chicago, Rand McNally College Publishing Company, 1977. – HERNES, G., 'Structural change in social processes', *American journal of sociology*, LXXXII, 3, 1976, 513–547. – HIRSCHMAN, A., *Journeys toward progress. Studies of economic policy-making in Latin America*, New York, Doubleday, 1963, 1965; New York, Greenwood Press, 1963, 1968. – JAMOUS, H., *Sociologie de la décision. La réforme des études médicales et des structures hospitalières*, Paris, CNRS, 1969. – LENSKI, G., 'History and social change', *American journal of sociology*, LXXXII, 3, 1976, 548–564 – MENDRAS, H., *La fin des paysans*, Paris, SEDEIS, 1967. Trans *The Vanishing Peasant*. MIT Press, Chicago. 1971. – MOORE, W., *Social change*, Englewood Cliffs, Prentice Hall, 1963. – NISBET, R., *Social change and history*, New York, Oxford University Press, 1969. – PARSONS, T., *Structure and process in modern societies*, Glencoe, The Free Press, 1960; *Societies: evolutionary and comparative perspectives*, Englewood Cliffs/New Jersey, Prentice Hall, 1966. 'The processes of change of social systems', *in* PARSONS, T., *The social system*, Glencoe, The Free Press/London, Collier Macmillan, 1951, 480–535. – PIORE, M. and BERGER, S., *Dualism and discontinuity in industrial societies*, Cambridge, Cambridge University Press, 1980. – ROCHER, G., 'Facteurs et conditions du changement social' and 'Les agents du changement social', *in* ROCHER, G., *Introduction à la sociologie générale*, Paris, HMH, 1968, 3 vol., III, chap. II and III, 33–127 and 128–179. – SAHLINS, M.D. and SERVICE, E.R. (ed.), *Evolution and culture*, Ann Arbor, University of Michigan Press, 1960. – SMITH, A.D., *The concept of social change: a critique of the functionalist theory of social change*, London, Routledge & Kegan Paul, 1973. – SOROKIN, P., *Social and cultural dynamics*, New York, American Books, 1937–1941, 4 vol. abridged ver. 1 vol., Boston, Extending Horizons Books, 1957; Boston, Porter Sargent, 1957, 1970. – WHITE, L., *Medieval technology and social change*, New York, Clarendon Press, 1962, 1966.

Social Control

The idea of social control (and the word itself) comes to us from American sociology. It is also associated with linguistic connotations which do not translate easily into French usage. In English, the word 'control' has a positive sense. To control means to master. Thus Talcott Parsons, in an otherwise questionable translation, translated the German word '*Herrschaft*' (domination), which Max Weber uses constantly, as 'imperative control'. In French, the word 'control' has above all a negative sense. To control means to supervise, possibly to prevent. It is thus that we talk of parliamentary control (Alain defined the member of parliament as a 'controller'), of jurisdictional control, or even of financial control.

In American sociology, interest in social control appeared in the 1920s, principally in two areas. It is to be found in studies concerning deviance and criminality. But we also talk of social control in connection with the apprenticeship of immigrants and members of ethnic minorities to the cultural models practised by Americans belonging to the middle classes, and of the 'hold' that these models had over the newcomers. On the other hand, the existence of criminals or of deviants poses the following problem to society: how can individual conduct be made to conform to the normative system used in the society? The problem of control is thus posed in terms of conformity, and because of that in terms of 'punishments' and 'rewards'.

Social control is the collection of material and symbolic resources which a society has at its disposal to ensure the behavioural conformity of its members to a collection of prescribed and sanctioned rules and principles. For American sociology before 1940, social control comprised those cultural models learned by the individual and the institutional mechanisms which reward and sanction conformity – or deviance – according to those models. Later on, the idea of control was enriched by the progress made in the analysis of the phenomenon of interdependence. Interest was thus brought to bear upon certain liaisons, at once strong and constant, which in the 'biological' order characterize the relationship between the phenotype and the genotype; in the 'economic' order the relationship observable between the economic agencies on the markets and between the different sorts of market; in the 'linguistic' order the connection between the sound and the sense. The hold that these different systems exercise over their elements and the mutual interdependence of the latter suggest a strict determination of the parties by the system to which they belong. In this new acceptance, control is the interdependence of the system and of its component parts.

If we take a common-sense view of it, the control society exercises over its members would be reduced to a system of sanctions by which the sensitive, intelligent, and provident person would adjust his conduct to conform with the expectations of his fellows. But this view remains indeterminate in as much as we are not informed about the manner in which conformity is assured. Can we be content to say that the individual has 'every interest' in conforming to the norm, since, if he goes outside it, he exposes himself to more or less disagreeable sanctions? The idea of interest suffers from the same ambiguity as is attached to that of sanction. At first sight, sanctions can be seen as the positive or negative consequences which accompany certain events. Social control would be of the same nature as that which physical laws exercise on our behaviour. The child who has burnt his finger is put off going too close to the flame. The greedy person who gets indigestion learns the advantages of temperance. Similarly, the imprudent person who takes on something stronger than himself discovers, from the burning correction with which his provocation has been rewarded, that he would have done better to think twice.

This plan of things, born of the combination of a strict determinism and a narrowly utilitarian psychology, is insufficient. First, external stimuli (social and non-social) are often ambiguous. The same event may suggest to me at one time a favourable outcome, at another time an unfavourable outcome; sometimes it will not be followed by any outcome either foreseen or foreseeable. Second, the individual is equipped with a certain capacity for information, and consequently for foresight. He can intervene, and by his intervention reverse the course of events. Third, his scale of preferences is not fixed once and for all. He can accommodate certain eventualities which he initially found unacceptable. He can even, by employing them, judge them to be advantageous. Thus there exists only a limited number of 'absolute' sanctions, positively and negatively effective by themselves and in all circumstances. If the conformity of individual behaviour to the laws of nature, social and physical, was guaranteed only by the play of such sanctions, that conformity would be partial and precarious. Partial, because the area thus covered would be concerned only with instinctive behaviour. For everything else, the actor would escape all control, whether that of the physical environment or that of the social environment. 'Not seen not caught', as popular wisdom has it. If I can escape punishment as long as I ensure that my deviance is unnoticed by, if not unnoticeable to, others, I have no interest in making my behaviour conform to the expectations of others, as long as I can elude their surveillance. Besides, the congruence between my expectations and those of others, if it rests only on an exchange of sanctions between them and me, is precarious, because their expectations can vary independently of mine.

Thus, to be effective, the control exercised by society on individuals cannot be purely external. Classic sociology, for example that of Durkheim, talks of moral education as the most subtle and most effective 'constraint' which society has at its disposal with regard to its members. By a different route, Freud came to an altogether similar view. It is the 'identification' of their members with a common model which assures the symbolic unity of institutions such as the army or the church. But identification is not only a result, which is otherwise never either complete or durable, it is a process regulated by a certain number of mechanisms. The child wishes to become its own father in order to have a certain number of attributes of which it is at present devoid. Identification rests on a series of relationships which establish themselves between the actors, motives which oppose or bring them together, or the super-ego which constitutes the supreme authority to which they defer. Our behaviour is thus not exclusively regulated by the constraints of the exterior environment (physical or social). It is also controlled by internal demands, of which some, impatient of all control, seek to satisfy themselves literally at all costs, and others, tamed, enter into more complex and more long-term strategies. If we now examine Freud's thinking in this direction as it has been interpreted by Parsons, we would say that social control rests upon the capacity of the actor to see his own acts through the eyes of any other actor whatsoever – the 'other' of Mead and of the interactionists. In order that this regard does not appear to the ego as an intrusion, an attempt at violation or seduction (which it is alternatively, according to Sartre), the ego and the other must jointly recognize each other as being relevant to their transactions in the same normative system, equally acceptable to each of them.

In as much as it rests upon an identification by the actor of a solicitation of reciprocity, social control is thus no more reducible to violence, even if only symbolic, than it is to exterior constraint. That is what Durkheim understood when, having made moral education one of the mainsprings of social control, he emphasizes the fact that education, far from being pure learning by heart, calls upon the 'autonomy' of the individual. Durkheim was careful not to set this autonomy up in opposition to all forms of apprenticeship and socialization. It is as much learnt as inculcated or, to put it like Piaget, it results as much from assimilation as from accommodation. What Durkheim understands by autonomy is the capacity of the individual to know himself (get his bearings) in his work and in his projects, to co-operate in the guiding of his own development, to discover in this last a requirement for his own self-realization (all things which are not possible if the social constraint is, in the profound sense of the term, moral, that is to say if it institutes between the ego itself and the other the connections of solidarity and of reciprocity).

No violence, even symbolic, is effective in the long term if the rule that it sanctions institutes between members of the society fundamentally arbitrary relationships, systematically disadvantageous to one party and systematically profitable to the other. It was Freud himself who, coming back to the central intuition of Hobbes, saw in the law a simultaneous and mutual renunciation by all and by each individual of those advantages which can only be acquired to the detriment of others: 'I renounce doing myself good in doing you harm – on the condition that you also renounce it, and on the same terms.' Social control assumes laws that are only effective if they define common and reciprocal obligations.

In the last twenty years, the 'cybernetic analogy' has fascinated many sociologists. On this occasion, as in so many others, more than one has been caught in the trap of analogies. We can start from a very simple example, such as that of the thermostat. A piece of information, the temperature of the room in which the thermostat is, transmitted to the boiler, sets it off without the intervention of an operator, who would have had first to observe the lowering of the temperature, then second to relight the fire in order to bring the temperature back to the desired level. The thermostat permits a direct utilization of the information and commands a series of programme-operations capable of bringing the heating system to the state which has been assigned to it. Various characteristics of the thermostat cannot fail to retain the attention of sociologists: first, the 'automaticness' of the control, by which the fabulous moment can be envisaged when not only will machines work all by themselves, but in addition they will do only that which the engineer who conceived them has ordered them to do; second, the substitution of information for energy as a resource which is predisposed to trigger and fuel the process. Thus is realized, by the means of intelligent organization or programming, an amazing 'economy' of energy, at the same time as a perfect 'yoking' of the process to objectives determined by the user and the beneficiary.

Comparable situations have been observed in biology, which have also in their time fascinated the sociologists. The biologist Cannon observed both the constancy of the natural milieu in living beings (in the case of blood, its temperature and composition) and the existence of mechanisms tending to put things back as they were if they have been put out of order following an exterior disturbance. But homeostasis, as described by Cannon, constitutes only one aspect of the regulation of living beings, and, besides, that regulation, however rigorous it may be, is not, unlike that of machines, under the yoke of an artisan will working according to its own plan and for its own benefit. To the analogy of homeostasis is added that of the genetic programme. It is no longer certain functions of the living being which are strictly controlled, but the collection of properties which define its individual structure and its development.

To what extent do these diverse analogies shed light on the problems of 'social' control? They make us aware of the existence of critical points above and beyond which a system would lose its identity and coherence. They also signal the existence of what one might call a 'strain towards consistency', which more or less durably leads the social system towards certain positions from which it cannot step too far aside without breaking up. The mechanism of price has often been described as a collective regulation – even though it is derived from a large number of individual calculated decisions – which assures the balance and possibly equality between the quantity of merchandise offered and the quantity demanded on a given market. In a regime of pure and simple competition, if the price goes up in a market, the quantities offered by the producers go up until their volume balances the quantities demanded by the consumers. In the situation where balance is broken by excess or insufficiency of offer or demand, the price constitutes a mechanism which 'tends' to equalize the quantities offered and the quantities demanded. One can in the same manner deal with social sanctions, positive and negative, as the mechanism thanks to which the integrity of norms is maintained by the exclusion of deviants – or at least putting them on the fringes of society – and possibly their subsequent reintegration.

But these analogies must be presented with many precautions. First, the automaticness of social mechanisms is not rigorously guaranteed. One sees it in the example of markets where the 'imperfections' have become more and more numerous and more and more serious progressively as observation and theory become more attentive. The existence of these imperfections relates to the importance of individual interactions in social regulation. The denseness of the interaction for the actors themselves thus engenders a series of unexpected and possibly 'perverse' effects which, instead of bringing the social system back towards its position of balance, takes it dangerously further and further away from it. The phenomenon of financial panic, to which great importance has long been accorded in the setting in motion of cyclic crises, is a good example. The anticipation of the crisis serves to render it inevitable. A crisis thus set off can only end in collapse. It is the same plan which underlies the famous 'domino theory'. The fall of the first line of defence, instead of mobilizing the defenders and galvanizing them into action, precipitates the collapse of the whole apparatus. Less extreme states of deregulation exist also, a slow 'drift' where anticipations, instead of controlling the social process so as to lead it back towards the norm when it goes off course, change the norm and erode it to the point of distorting the meaning and the aim.

It is necessary, finally, to use the expression social control only with great care. If one wishes to say that individuals, or at least the most active among them, seek to direct the activity of others and their own in order to make them conform to their objectives, one is absolutely correct; but in doing so, we will scarcely do more than recognize the intentional dimension, or as we still call it, the 'strategic' dimension of social action.

It is only by an entirely excessive extrapolation that we can hold out as equivalent the two expressions *social control* and *controlled society*. The second expression designates an ideal or a utopia likely to take very different forms. In 1949, a Keynesian economist, A.P. Lerner published *Economics of Control*. The thesis supported in this work is that full employment can always be accomplished by techniques of a guaranteed efficacy, which never turn back against the goals sought. The economic system is controllable in as much as we know how to master the factors of production by submitting them to the condition that one among them, the workman, should be 'fully' employed. A second generalization, connected to speculations about the post-industrial age, has taken as a reference concepts such as 'active society' or 'programmed society'. It is necessary in the first place to distinguish the variant according to which social 'activity' would be more and more automatized from the variant according to which the 'programming' finds itself associated with a multiplication and an intensification of the 'conflictivity' – very often understood as if all conflict was by nature 'a carrier of things to come', as if, to borrow from Marx one of his most debatable aphorisms, 'humanity only poses itself problems that it knows how to resolve'.

Two thoughts appear quite forcibly on meeting the two variants of this interpretation. First, they both proceed from an insufficient analysis of the idea of information. In the over-familiar example of the thermostat, the information is regularly associated with the command because the signals on which the regulation reposes are deprived of all ambiguity and they have been defined, then constructed (in the strict sense of the word) by the engineer. The information-command association becomes more complicated when the signals are ambiguous and not completely artificial. In this case, information can find itself invested with a power of inhibition regarding which we can talk of negative power. The 'over-informed' society is also as likely to be an 'inhibited' society as an 'active' society. The active society is likely to be paralysed by the over-abundance of its activity. Similarly, the 'programmed society' can slide towards a sort of chaos by excess co-ordination and forward planning. In addition, we do not clearly see which group in our societies could exercise this second degree of control: to decide not only what there is a good reason to do but, even more radically, if there is a reason to do anything. The supporters of the active or programmed society willingly give this responsibility to the intellectuals or the technicians. But one may doubt their capacity to perform this task.

Briefly, it must be agreed that society can be analysed as a collection of control mechanisms, at once inciting and limiting, which put into play the initiatives and the resources of individuals, collective constraints, and moral obligations; but it is also necessary to watch out for the extent of this control and the nature of the resources that it brings into play. We thus see that it is never total and that the mastery that men have over their society and that which society has over them are both closely and mutually limited.

Conformity and Deviance, Culturalism and Culture, Durkheim, Role, Socialization, System, Teleology.

Bibliography

ALAIN, *Eléments d'une doctrine radicale*, Paris, Gallimard, 1925, 1933. – VON BERTALANFFY, L., *General system theory. Foundations, development, applications*, New York, G. Braziller; London, Allen Lane, 1971. – CANNON, W.B., *The wisdom of the body*, New York, W.W. Norton & Co., 1932; – DEUTSCH, K., *The nerves of government. Models of political communication and control*, New York, The Free Press, 1963. – DURKHEIM, E., *Moral Education* (op cit) – ETZIONI, A., *The active society. A theory of societal and political processes*, London, Collier-Macmillan; New York, Free Press, 1968. – FREUD, S., *Massenpsychologie und Ich-Analyse*, Leipzig, Internationaler psycho-analytischer Verlag, 1921. – GUILDBAUD, G.-Th., *La cybernétique*, Paris PUF, 1954. – JACOB, F., *La logique du vivant*, Paris, Gallimard, 1970. – LERNER, A.P., *The economics of control. Principles of welfare economics*, New York, Macmillan, 1944; New York, A.M. Kelley, 1970. – LEWIN, K., 'Group decision and social change', *in* SWANSON, G.E., NEWCOMB, T.M. and HARTLEY, E.L. (ed.), *Readings in social psychology*, New York, Holt, 1952. – MONOD, J., *Le hasard et la nécessité. Essai sur la philosophie naturelle de la biologie*, Paris, Seuil, 1970. – PARSONS, T., *Social structure and personality*, Glencoe, The Free Press, 1964. – TOURAINE, A., *La société post-industrielle*, Paris, Denoël, 1969. – WEBER, M., *The Protestant Ethic and the Spirit of Capitalism* – THOMAS, W.I., ZNANIECKI, F., *The Polish peasant in Europe and America*, Boston, P.G. Badger, 1918; New York, Dover, 1958.

Social Mobility

This expression describes the movements of individuals or family units within the system of socio-professional categories or – for writers who prefer this expression – the system of social classes. The mobility of individuals is generally described as 'intragenerational'. The mobility of families from one generation to another is called 'intergenerational'. More specifically, 'intergenerational' or 'between generation' mobility studies the relationship between the status or original position of individuals and their actual position in the socio-professional category system. It is above all this last form of mobility that continues to attract the attention of sociologists.

If one omits Pareto's theories on the circulaton of élites, the pioneer work on this subject is Sorokin's book on social mobility. In it Sorokin develops the notion that every society produces complex institutional mechanisms by which individuals are guided from an original social position to an eventual social position. These mechanisms depend on the action of *selection agencies*, the nature of which varies according to period and society. Thus in 'military' societies, in the sense of Saint-Simon or Spencer, the army and possibly the church as well as the family can play an essential role in the process of mobility (for a celebrated literary illustration see Stendhal's *Scarlet and Black*). In modern industrial societies, the main examples of this orientation are given by the family and by the school. These orientation mechanisms have the effect – or 'function' – on one hand of contributing to ensuring a certain permanence in the social 'structure' over and above the continuous stream of individuals who compose it. On the other hand they play a part in ensuring that the statistical distribution of the endeavours and projects of individuals are not too far from the possible objectives offered by the structure. Sorokin's theory can in one sense of the term be described as functionalist, in as much as it investigates the reproductive conditions of social structures. But it is a careful functionalism which does not succumb to teleology. Sorokin clearly saw that nothing guarantees an uninterrupted functioning of the reproductive system: individual examples of orientation can fill their role in an unsatisfactory manner and thus engender a situation of crisis.

The shaking-up of the universities of the 1960s, which in part at least corresponds to a crisis of this type, bears witness to the appeal of Sorokin's theory. Effectively, the arrival of mass education severely disturbed the traditional functioning of that example of orientation represented by the educational system. To be more precise, the years which followed the Second World War were distinguished by a population explosion, which inevitably made its effects felt on the size of the school population after the passage of a certain time. To this effect was added an even more important growth in what it is common to call 'the demand for education', which growth was independent of demographic evolution. Why did this 'demand for education' grow in such an intense manner up until at least the 1970s? Partly, but only partly, it grew as a result of the technological revolution and its effect upon the level of qualification required for jobs. Otherwise, and more importantly, it was the result of competition: investment in education became easier from the time when average resources and standards of living increased; it also appeared desirable to social agencies because extra schooling is a promise of extra status and income. In addition, employers had a tendency to see qualifications as an indicator, or, to speak like the economists, a *signal* of the adaptive capacity of individuals for the tasks they would have to undertake. The combination of the effect of competition and the signal effect engendered overall an inflationary process which was translated, as shown by Ivar Berg in the case of the United States, into a growing discrepancy between the aspirations of individuals leaving the educational system and the possibility of getting a professional job. A qualification became progressively more and more necessary and less and less sufficient in order to obtain a desirable socio-professional position. To what extent was this inflationary spiral fuelled by the unanimously defended ideology in the 1960s, the maxim of education for all? It is hard to know. What this example does show in every case is that, as put forward by Sorokin, the 'orientation agencies', if they have a 'function' of reproducing social structures, do not necessarily fulfil this function in an effective manner. One might even put forward the idea that, on the contrary, an agency such as the school is endemically threatened with dysfunction in as much as it only has a very limited power of regulation over the aspirations and choice of individuals. The 'over-education' crisis of the 1960s is in addition not a unique historical example. Prussia – and equally France – of 1848 knew, for complex historical reasons, a comparable crisis which probably had some connection with the 'events' of 1848.

The years which followed the Second World War are the true point of departure for studies of mobility. The work of Glass in England, Carlsson in Sweden, Lipset and Bendix, Kahl, then Blau and Duncan in the United States, all contribute to make the field of social mobility one of the best nourished areas in sociology. It not only gave rise to numerous observations, but also to continuous theoretical and methodological consideration.

This consideration has to a great extent been stimulated by the unexpected, not to say paradoxical, character of certain results. Thus, many sociologists expected to observe noticeable international differences on the subject of mobility. Certain societies, like America, have never known a system of legal stratification comparable with the German *Stande* or the *Etats* of the France of the *Ancien Régime*. Other societies, such as Sweden, passed abruptly from the agricultural phase to the industrial phase. In certain countries, such as the United States, education was more widespread and more 'democratic'. Intuitively it was felt that such differences must have an effect on the ease with which the barriers between the classes could be surmounted. Lipset and Bendix showed, however, with the support of numerous national surveys, that intergenerational mobility was none the less comparable in countries as different as France, Germany, Japan, Switzerland, Sweden, the United States, etc. It is true that these writers utilized a rough classification (manual/non-manual/agricultural categories). By using finer categories, Miller made certain international differences more obvious. But it does not seem that this analysis or the analyses which followed it have really shaken the general conclusion of Bendix and Lipset. For example, a French study by Darbel shows the great similarity of the structures of mobility in France and in Germany, even though the inequalities in the two countries seem to be of a different intensity.

The second paradox concerns the historical evolution of mobility. Social mobility is without doubt possible, and much more so in industrial societies than in traditional societies. Thus we know, because of studies such as that of Svalastoga, that mobility is much greater in modern Scandinavia than it was in the eighteenth century. All the same – this is the second paradox – despite industrialization, economic growth, and the development of education, the structure of mobility (that is to say the structure of the flow of intergenerational mobility) appeared practically constant for five or six decades in Sweden, as in England or the United States. In France, Thelot observed a weak attenuation of 'social viscosity' between 1953 and 1970. In the case of Denmark, Svalastoga came to the same conclusion. But the general impression is one of invariability. How is this compatible with the change in the factors which appear inevitably to have an effect on mobility?

These paradoxes have directly or indirectly led to abundant 'methodological' research, above all in the measurement of mobility. In fact, to compare two tables of mobility (tables which give the quantitative importance of the flow coming from one social origin i ($i = 1$ to n) to a social situation j ($j = 1$ to n) in time and space, it is practically essential to do so by the construction of an index of mobility (cf. 'Measurement'). To this end, classic statistical tools can be used. But, under the impetus of Yasuda, so-called 'structural' indexes were developed. This type of index aims to understand the relative parts played by *non-structural mobility* and *structural mobility*, or mobility mechanically engendered by the change in the overall size of the different social categories from one generation to another (if, for example, the number of agricultural workers diminishes from one generation to another, some sons of agricultural workers will necessarily be 'mobile'). Yasuda's work suggests that, if the mobility of different industrial nations is similar, the contribution of structural mobility is variable. Duncan and, in his wake, Bertaux have shown the difficulties raised by the idea of 'structural' mobility. Despite its critics, the idea of 'structural' mobility has made a contribution by awakening researchers to the opportunity of interpreting the flow of mobility not overall, as an index of the greater or lesser rigidity of the 'social structures' and of the greater or lesser ease with which they can be surmounted, but as the complex effect of the system of factors resulting from the aggregation of individual behaviour and strategies. Likewise, it can be deduced mathematically from the model that certain factors, which one intuitively reckons should have an effect on the structure of mobility (degree of democratization of the school system, the more or less selective character of educational institutions, etc.), *can* in fact have a limited influence in this respect. Thus the model furnishes a plausible interpretation of the slight difference in the structure of mobility that is observable when one compares different industrialized nations. If this analysis has some relevance, two things result: 1) the constancy of mobility and the statistical relationship between original status and final status that one observes in industrial societies is not the result of a manipulation of the educational system which would permit the 'ruling class' to maintain its position and the life chances of the individuals who issue from it; 2) this invariability is an effect of the complex aggregation which contains nothing inevitable or necessary, but conversely results from the conjunctural combination of a collection of parameters.

The studies conducted by Jencks in the United States, Girod in Switzerland, or Muller and Meyer in Germany are compatible with this strategic and systematic approach to social mobility. They show that, if social origin influences the level of education in a determining fashion, the level of education always affects social status in a moderate manner. All these studies suggest a general hypothesis, namely that the complexity of industrial societies precludes, with certain exceptions, a rigorous functioning of 'selection agencies'. These societies are probably the most mobile known to history. Certainly, they are far from the reference points indicated by the expressions 'perfect' mobility or 'equality of opportunity'. But their very complexity guarantees a margin of autonomy to individuals in relation to the incentives and constraints of structures. This autonomy appears sufficient to preclude a rigid determinism of social status by social origin, or, if more traditional language is preferred, of 'birth' over 'rank'. This type of determinism can only appear in a society where: 1) the distribution of social position can be easily anticipated; 2) the selection agencies and orientation have the capacity of tightly controlling the educational and social path of individuals; 3) these agencies have one major concern (for reasons which it would be thus necessary to explain): that of restricting the social ascendancy of individuals of modest birth. It appears hardly likely that any of these three conditions would be attained even approximately in industrial societies, particularly when they follow a liberal model. It is precisely because they are not attained that the statistical relationships which measure the influence of level of schooling on income or status are generally weak in Switzerland, as in Germany or in the United States, or that, in Great Britain, individuals coming from the higher classes (senior management, the professions) are more likely to lose caste than to maintain themselves in their original position. In France, the fact that the 'polytechnicians' are 'above averagely' of upper-class origin is not on the evidence sufficient to consider French society as being assimilated into the model of a caste society.

In the United States, the influence of egalitarian sociologists was such in the 1960s that the doctrine of self-perpetuation of the ruling class took on the force of gospel there. This is why Jencks caused surprise beyond measure when he showed that, for example, in that country the level of education had an extremely weak influence on income. For similar reasons Girod was poorly received in Europe when he showed – on basis of longitudinal analysis by cohorts – that the inequalities due to contingencies were no less worthy of holding the attention than the inequalities due to structures, in other words that date of birth is a no less interesting factor than original social class. Propositions such as these contradict the dominant theories of the 1960s. In addition, these theories had the 'disadvantage' of registering an 'indefiniteness' the interpretation of which required more subtle theories than that of the self-reproduction of the ruling class.

Egalitarianism, Measurement, Minorities, Professions, Social Stratification, Status.

Bibliography

BERTAUX, D., 'Sur l'analyse des tables de mobilité sociale', *Revue française de Sociologie*, X, *4*, 1969, 448–490. BLAU, P. and DUNCAN, O.D., *The American occupational structure*, New York, Wiley, 1967. – BOUDON, R., *L'inégalité des chances. La mobilité sociale dans les sociétés industrielles*, Paris, A. Colin, 1973, 1978. – CARLSSON, G., *Social mobility and class structure*, Lund, Gleerup, 1958. – DARBEL, A., 'L'évolution récente de la mobilité sociale', *Economie et statistique, 71*, 1975, 3–22. – DUNCAN, O.D., 'Methodological issues in the analysis of social mobility', *in* SMELSER, N. and LIPSET, S.M. (ed.), *Social structures and mobility in economic development*, Chicago, Aldine, 1966, 51–97. – GIRARD, A., *La réussite sociale*, Paris, PUF, 1967. – GIROD, R., *Mobilité sociale*, Paris/Geneva, Droz, 1971; *Inégalité, inégalités*, Paris, PUF, 1977. – GLASS, D., *Social mobility in Britain*, London, Routledge & Kegan Paul, 1954. – GOBLOT, E., *La barrière et le niveau. Etude sociologique sur la bourgeoisie française moderne*, Paris, F. Alcan, 1925; Paris, PUF, 1967. – GOLDTHORPE, J.H., LLEWELLYN, C. and PAYNE, C., *Social mobility and class structure in Britain*, Oxford, Clarendon Press, 1980. – KAHL, J., *The American class structure*, New York, Holt, Rinehart & Winston, 1957. – LIPSET, S.M. and BENDIX, R., *Social mobility in industrial societies*, Berkeley/Los Angeles, University of California Press, 1959; London, Routledge & Kegan Paul, 1966. – MILLER, S.M., 'Comparative social mobility, a trend report and bibliography', 'La mobilité sociale comparée, tendances actuelles de la recherche et bibliographie', *Current sociology/La sociologie contemporaine*, IX, *1*, 1960, 1–89. – MÜLLER, W. and MAYER, K.U. (ed.), *Social stratification and career mobility*, Paris/La Haye, Mouton, 1973. – PESCHAR, J.L., *Chancenungleichheit*, Neuwied/Darmstadt, Luchterhand, 1979. – SOROKIN, P.A., *Social and cultural mobility*, Glencoe, The Free Press, 1959. – SVALASTOGA, K., 'Social mobility: the Western European model', *Acta sociologica*, IX, *1–2*, 1965, 175–182. – THÉLOT, C., 'Origine et positions sociales: faits et interprétation', *Economie et statistique*, 81–82, 1976, 73–88; *Tel père, tel fils*, Paris, Dunod, 1982.

Social Stratification

In any complex society, strata or social classes can be observed, made up of similar individuals with shared characteristics. The idea of stratum being more general than that of class, we chose to use the title 'social stratification' rather than 'social classes' for the following comments. (We deal here only with the phenomena in modern society.) The definition has often been debated. Must classes be seen as representative of a 'total' order (as in the 'American' theory of stratification) or of a 'partial' order, that is as a group of elements only some of which can be ordered? For instance, in Marx's *Capital*, workers and capitalists are neatly differentiated classes but landowners and capitalists are not. Should classes be defined according to one or several criteria, or a combination of them, as suggested by Weber and many other sociologists after him? It has indeed been widely accepted since Weber that it is possible to determine social hierarchy according to 'prestige' (status group), according to 'income' ('class' for Weber), or according to 'power' (élites, management). Should social classes be defined only in terms of their roles in the production process as the Marxist tradition would suggest?

First the problem of the definition and number of classes. Two main traditions exist. The Marxist tradition on one hand, defines the notion of class according to the position of social agents in the productive process and there are as many classes as there are fundamental kinds of position. The theory of 'stratification' on the other hand, is generally inspired by Weber and defines the idea of class or stratum according to status criteria. In spite of the apparent simplicity of the Marxist definition, serious difficulties are found when it is put into practice. If positions are defined in the production system according to 'relationships of production', it will be easy to differentiate capitalists from workers in the nineteenth century, landowners from tenants in the feudal period, but the position of other social agents will be more difficult to assess. Aware of these problems, Marx implicitly suggests that the number of classes to be defined depends on the reason why we want to define them. This is why he mentions three classes in *Capital* (the same number as Ricardo), two in the *Manifesto* and seven in *The Class Struggle in France*. In *Capital*, a study in economics, he could not fail to distinguish three fundamental kinds of social agents that economics always differentiates in relation to the nature of their income: land rent for landowners, 'profits' for industrialists, 'salary' for the 'workers'. These distinctions for economics are different from other types of classifications, like that of Turgot with its physiocratic inspiration (class of farmers or 'productive' class; class of 'skilled men' or 'salaried' class; and class of 'owners' or 'free' class i.e., free to take on public interest duties). In the *Communist Manifesto*, a work of political theory, the picture given by Marx is two-sided. It is easy to understand why. Marx wanted to show that the class struggle is the motor of history; in other words, that social change is the result of class struggles. But the idea of opposition, just as that of 'contradiction' favoured by Marx, like that of war or struggle, implies the idea of duality or duel. In *The Class Struggle in France*, a historical study, the point is to describe a concrete situation in its complexity. This is why more classes are distinguished in this work. In fact, what is sometimes called the Marxist conception of classes does not rely on a well-defined theory but on a multitude of theories based on class struggles and different from each other according to the criteria used to distinguish them and to the number of classes being used. Marx's conceptions of social class appear to vary according not only to the topic discussed but also to the 'public' addressed by the discussion. It is only with some neo-Marxists that the distribution of ownership of such resources as power, income and prestige, is shown to be necessarily 'bi-modal', opposing a 'dominant' class to a 'dominated' class.

Studies of 'social stratification' which began mainly in the US from the 1950s onwards generally tend towards a descriptive model: the point is to re-constitute social hierarchy by characterizing the individual members of one society or one community. Determining social hierarchy is done by criteria such as income, status of job, education, etc. Sometimes, as in Warner's works, there is an attempt to define the social hierarchy that members of one group see as their own. More often, research starts from observable statistical correlations between the various criteria making up a typology which defines a set of classes, also called 'strata' if the elements of the typology are in hierarchical order. Studies of stratification are often descriptive, as previously noted, that is, they do not generally analyse the existence or the reason for these phenomena of stratification.

Let us now discuss the reasons for stratification. Three theories can be put forward. First, the Marxist theory which makes production the agent responsible for class division. This is an historically important theory but difficult to apply to a specific field. It is true to say that industrial revolution created two classes, bourgeoisie and proletariat and that their relationship is largely antagonistic, for some episodes in history can be understood only with this conflict in mind. But the limited validity of the class struggle theory must be noted, even in relation to the first industrial revolution. This Marxist representation can only be applied fully when the conflicting interests develop freely. Thus, the inflexible law of wages, that Marx takes from Ricardo, can apply only if there can be a free and perfect competition between economic forces. After the creation of labour unions, the relationship between capitalists and workers ceases to be completely free and elements of both co-operation and conflict are part of it; unions allow the 'dominated' class to profit from increases in productivity. In the end, union aggressiveness can stimulate productivity and, thus, be of benefit to everyone. The conception of class struggle can thus only correspond to relatively short-lived economic situations in history. On the other hand, it is only because of a relatively scholarly decision that the first industrial revolution can be reduced to a struggle between two sets of actors. Even if the interest is in economic history, even if the focus is on England which was a precursor – in itself quite a debatable proposition – according to Marx, of other societies' industrial history, one cannot put aside the English agricultural revolution and the part played by another 'class', that of rural landowners. It is doubtful that even in the English case, their role can be reduced to that of accomplices whose part was to shed labour so that the capitalist class could use it. When other societies like that of Prussia, are analysed, the antagonistic relation capitalist/workers is almost useless to an explanation of its development. Prussia's industrialization cannot be understood without taking into account the role played by civil servants (*Dienstadel*: service aristocracy), the role of rural migration created by the *Junkers* to modernize their estates which resulted not only from government decrees but from the adaptation of the landowners to their new environment. Even taken in its historical context, the Marxist theory of classes leans strongly upon Marx's view of the destiny of men, i.e., what Marx saw as the future of humanity and of its goal. This involves a pair of propositions according to which: 1) England in the mid-nineteenth century prefigures the evolution of mankind; 2) English history is dominated by the antagonism between two fundamental classes, is only meaningful through – and because of – this 'eschatology' (picture of the world's destiny). Because it is too simple a model to explain the historical process of industrialization, the Marxist theory can even less pretend to describe modern industrial societies in a reliable way. The extension of the State and of its role, the increase in the number of its agents and of their tasks, the increasing complexity of 'organizations' (firms, administrations), the diversification of organizational types, make the socio-professional network impossible to reduce to a small number of 'social classes'. All the more so, the 'social structure' of modern industrial society cannot be described from a model opposing two antagonistic classes. A bi-partite representation can only be reached by multiplying epicycles, making the agents of the State or the agents of 'ideological apparatuses' the obligatory allies of the 'dominant' class, supposing that conflicts of interest or values between fractions of the dominant class are not important or 'concealing' an underlying agreement between the different groups of the 'dominant' classes, or introducing subtle distinctions like that opposing the 'dominant fractions' to the 'dominated fractions' of the ruling class. The result is a fallacious argument used as the thread of some neo-Marxist theories, like that of Althusser for instance – because the State is the instrument of the ruling class, its agents are too, from the postmaster to the teacher – or that of Baudelot *et al.*: because profit can only (?) be generated by the work of a manual worker, the other classes are part of the bourgeoisie; thus teachers belong to the lower middle class because: 1) they earn a share of the money made by industrial workers; 2) this share is smaller than that of administrators and higher and middle executives.

The organization of work and manpower training are seen as having no consequence for production or productivity if this reasoning stands. It is obvious that the making of a complex industrial product can only be the general result of all the workers in a firm's efforts. The theory of surplus value has little meaning in a complex industrial society and Weber's criteria can easily be substituted for Marx's: if everyone – except for a handful of parasites – participates in profit-making, the concept of surplus value becomes useless. On the other hand, social stratification in industrial societies continues to be observed in relation to power, authority, influence, and prestige.

The second type of theory was inspired by 'functionalism', and was formalized by Davis and Moore. For them, stratification is an immediate consequence of work division: as jobs have a more or less important function in the division of labour, they cannot be paid at the same rate (whether in terms of symbolic or real payment). This unequal pay generates competition between individuals, ending in a balancing process, which is more or less satisfactory, between proficiency and function. Added to that, the pay linked to a specific social position is inversely proportional to the number of people who could fill that position. Parsons proposes a different version of the same theory in so far as he makes the 'values' of a society the reference for the pay of socio-professional people. The functionalist theories, in spite of their merits and clear explanations, also present a few draw-backs. First, they unjustifiably apply to the whole of a society mechanisms which characterize social microsystems. It is difficult to imagine that an organization could function normally and acceptably for its agents if the levels of remuneration (real or symbolic) given to its agents were not, in a certain way or measure, related to the importance of the function of their 'contributions' to the efficient functioning of the system. A mistake in product manufacturing is not as serious as a mistake in the production programme. The success of a firm rests more on investments, decisions, or commercial policy than on the skill of one particular worker. It is probably more difficult to find an efficient marketing manager than a good production line worker. Therefore it is understandable that the marketing manager be paid more than the production worker and the latter accepts it so long as the difference is not in excess of the difference of their contributions. But socie-ties are neither firms nor organizations. The latter are always directed to definite objectives, according to which each member's contribution can be assessed more or less precisely. But societies cannot be seen in this light, except in a dubious analogy. Besides, it is difficult to find criteria which would allow the ordering of different kinds of socio-professional positions according to the importance of their 'functions' in society as a whole. Why do barristers, school teachers, doctors, or employees differ in importance in relation to each other?

Parson's version of functionalism is less problematic than Davis and Moore's. According to Parsons, each society is defined by its own set of values with its own hierarchy. Thus, in American society, 'achievement' is a crucial value. Those with great prestige will be scientists or managers who play a vital role in discovering new theories or techniques. In other societies the 'maintenance of cultural models' is of crucial importance. There, those with great prestige will be priests, intellectuals, members of the universities. Unfortunately, Parsons does not explain clearly why the hierarchy of values differs between societies. Finally, it is doubtful that Parson's theory can do much else besides explaining basic aspects of stratifi-cation systems.

A third set of theories makes market mechanisms the catalysts of stratification phenomena. This is hinted at by Adam Smith. Salaries or more generally social remunerations (status) depend on supply and demand relating to a position, according to him. As for supply, it depends on how difficult it is to learn and perform the tasks corresponding to these positions. This is why a doctor's status is higher than a shop assistant's. At the same time, the material and social constraints under which the market operates must be taken into account. Thus, although miners and soldiers have comparable jobs in terms of risks and appren-ticeship, miners will be expected to be paid more, Smith said. Miners cannot indeed be paid like soldiers are, with prestige and glory. Thus the real and symbolic remunerations of miners and soldiers are a result of market laws and of the nature of the tasks to be done. The same reasoning is followed by Dahrendorf. And social system implies a demand, distributed in a certain way, of various kinds of activities to which is linked a supply which is also distributed in a certain way.

Thus, an idle community of women will have a great demand for gossips. The women with most prestige in the group will be the ones generating the most gossip. Similarly, an ideocratic state (just as a non-ideocratic state which is being shaken by sudden change) will generate a demand for new ideologies: ideologists will be remunerated highly, symbolically or materially. But the market of social stratification is not a perfect one. Differences of income and differences of prestige cannot be explained only by the simple process of supply and demand. Differences also depend on complex institutional variables. For instance, the power of unions can have a more or less important influence on income differentials. Since unions have a different strength in different places of work, incomes may differ without any relation to supply and demand or to the 'functional' importance of the job. Differences between skilled workers' and engineers' incomes are slightly less in Germany than in France, partly because unions are more powerful in Germany. Unions are more powerful there for complex reasons, not least of which is that they are less politicized. The small relative difference of income between manual workers and others is also due to the presence in Germany of a technical training programme in direct competition with the general education programme. In the same way, the market of prestige is not perfect, and depends on institutional variables. The prestige of university staff and students in Prussia, and later in Germany in the nineteenth century was not due only to the fact that German science was so successful and to the fact that industrial development generated a great demand for scientists and technicians, but also to the fact that the universities used to be the cradle of the ruling-class civil servants. These examples show that differences of remuneration (in the general sense) cannot be completely explained without mentioning the 'specific' institutions of each system or social micro-system.

Sociology is not ready yet to put forward a 'general theory' of stratification and it may be that such an attempt can only lead to failure. Stratification systems cannot be completely explained by the functional importance of social positions or by the hierarchy of shared values or by the organization of relationships of production. Only some aspects can be explained by one or the other. The idea of functional importance can only be understood clearly in the case of organizations. Even in this case, it cannot establish an order, complete or partial, for the whole system of positions or status. Shared values are – at the most – capable of accounting for some differences between stratification systems. Production relationships can only clearly define a total or partial 'order' in specific cases. In fact, power, prestige, and status differences between groups are the result of a set of variables or rather the result of a system of variables whose composition and structure differ from one social system to another. The market paradigm might be the only one which could pretend to general application: prestige, income, authority, influence, and power are always remunerations corresponding to a specific social demand. This demand of course itself depends on the characteristics of the system within which it is operating. Thus, ideological demand, to use Dahrendorf's example, depends on the type of political power. Besides, the market of stratification must be seen as an imperfect one.

The superiority of the market paradigm appears to be because the fundamental notions defining it, i.e., supply and demand, seem clearer and more easily applicable than the notions of 'functional' importance, 'shared values', or 'relationships of production'.

Élite(s), Power, Role, Social Mobility, Status.

Bibliography

ARON, R., *La lutte des classes. Nouvelles leçons sur les sociétés industrielles*, Paris, Gallimard, 1964. – BAUDELOT, C., ESTABLET, R., MALEMORT, J., *La petite bourgeoisie en France*, Paris, F. Maspero, 1975. – BENDIX, R. and LIPSET, S.M. (ed.), *Class, status and power. A reader in social stratification*, New York, The Free Press, 1953; *Class, status and power. Social stratification in comparative perspective*, 2nd Edition, London, Routledge & Kegan Paul, 1966. – BLAU, P.M., *Inequality and heterogeneity: a primitive theory of social structure*, New York, The Free Press/London, Collier-Macmillan, 1977. – BLAU, P.M. and DUNCAN, O.D., *The American occupational structure*, New York, Wiley, 1967. – DAHRENDORF, R., 'On the origin of inequality among men', in BÉTEILLE, A. (ed.), *Social inequality. Selected readings*, Harmondsworth, Penguin Books, 1969, 16–44. – DAVIS, K. and MOORE, W., 'Some principles of stratification', *American sociological review*, X, 2, 1945 242–249. – LAUTMAN, J., 'Mais où sont les classes d'antan?', in MENDRAS, H., (ed.), *La sagesse et le désordre*, Paris, Gallimard, 1980, 81–99. – MARION, G., 'Les théories de la répartition hiérarchique des revenus de Adam Smith à nos jours', *Revue économique*, XIX, 3, 1968, 385–410. – PARSONS, T., 'An analytical approach to the theory of social stratification', *American journal of sociology*, XLV, 6, 1940, 841–862. in PARSONS, T., *Essays in sociological theory pure and applied*, New York, The Free Press, 1949; London, Collier Macmillan, 1964; *Essays in sociological theory*, rev.ed. 1954, 1964, 69–88; 'A revised analytical approach to the theory of social stratification', in BENDIX, R. and LIPSET, S.M. (ed.), *Class, status and power. A reader in social stratification*, New York, The Free Press, 1953; *Class, status and power. Social stratification in comparative perspective*, 2nd edition, London, Routledge & Kegan Paul, 1966, 92–129. 'Equality and inequality in modern society, or social stratification revisited', *Sociological inquiry*, XL, 2, 1970, 13–72. – STOETZEL, J., 'Les revenus et le coût des besoins de la vie', *Sondages*, 1, 1976. – TUMIN, M.M., *Social stratification. The forms and functions of inequality*, Englewood Cliffs, Prentice Hall, 1967. – TURGOT, A.R.J., *Réflexions sur la formation et la distribution des richesses*, Paris, 1766, in TURGOT, A.R.J., *Ecrits économiques*, Paris, Calmann-Lévy, 1970, 121–188. – WARNER, L., *Social class in America*, Chicago, Science Research Associates, 1949, New York, Harper, 1960. – WEBER, M., 'Orders and Classes', in WEBER, M. *Economy and Society*, op. cit, Ch 4.

Social Symbolism

The word 'symbolic' is used to describe the most various aspects of social life. It is fashionable today to criticize 'symbolic politics' or 'the State as a showpiece'. Used in this way, 'symbolic' describes an activity which substitutes compensatory satisfactions in the absence of planned and promised real results. 'Symbolism' can lead to trickery and manipulation. It misleads us when we take for granted what should be preceded by 'as if'. It promotes lies and deceit when confusion is deliberately created between what is real and what is imagined through discourse, stories, or myths which describe a quite hypothetical state of affairs 'as if you were there', and through rites and practices which make us behave as if the desired situation was real.

In the vocabulary of the classic French sociologists like Durkheim and Mauss, the word 'symbolic' is used to talk about myths and rites, sacrifices and prayers. The famous '*Essai sur le don*' by Mauss is based on a conception of social symbolism which stresses the social consequences of the symbolic function. When describing the chain of complex offerings and counter-offerings made in Polynesian society and in certain Indian tribes of the north-west coast of Canada, Mauss shows this ceremonial – taking place over several years – as the setting for 'reciprocity' which binds the different categories of protagonist without them consciously realizing it. There is 'reciprocity' when the offerings received from an associate A are seen as equivalent to those given by his associate B, in one way or another. But this equivalence is not always obvious immediately. According to micro-economic theory, there may be equivalence in a market when the exchanging partners hold enough of the goods and services to satisfy both demand and supply requirements. If there is not a balance, the exchange will cease or the exchanging partners will modify the exchange contract, or will allow each other 'credit'. The situation as Mauss sees it is different. What the Melanesians engaged in the 'Koula exchange' hope for are not short-term satisfactions like exchanging apples for pears: they hope to create an 'alliance', i.e., durable and extended connections. This is why the cycle of offerings and counter-offerings takes place over a very long period of time and involves a large number of people. Moreover, it involves each of them in depth and 'completely': not in the metaphysical sense of a 'concrete wholeness', with which they would identify themselves, but in the sense that they acquire or impose their status in that exchange process. But if the reciprocity does not reduce itself to the equivalence of discontinuous and *ad hoc* exchanges, if it constitutes a system of positions and statuses, the system which controls the differentiated, complementary, or even antagonistic roles of the exchange partners, this system must be capable of being clearly understood by the people involved. Status is personified by the characters who play their roles in the ceremonies. Parts and characters take the form of images and symbols.

Durkheim develops a similar view of symbolism in *The Elementary Forms of Religious Life*. He deliberately interprets beliefs and totemic rites not literally but symbolically, which is the only way, according to him, to give them a meaning. It is not animals and plants that primitives worship, but 'something' -society that these animals and plants are only here to represent. Here as elsewhere, the difficulty is to understand what Durkheim means by 'society' – a word that he tends to use in a substantialist sense.

However, we will not expand upon this last difficulty. What is interesting here is the link between two propositions which are simultaneously stated by Durkheim: 1) society is symbolical in its essence; 2) social life is the basis of man's rational activity. For these two propositions to be compatible, symbolism and the imaginary must be clearly distinct. This distinction is, at least implicitly, maintained in the works of the classical French sociologists. Indeed, three propositions emerge from their writings. For them, social symbolism is a set of phenomena (practices and beliefs) which can be described as 'objective', in the sense that they create an authentic community between the members of the society. A second, and inverse, proposition can be deduced from this first proposition: no society will be established or continue unless it is a symbolic community. A third proposition must be added to the first two: since social symbolism is inseparable from the communication process, social symbolism varies according to the shape and content of the communication process itself. Thus, in societies of a 'mechanical' type (small close units, strongly integrated, where the expression of individual differences is strictly controlled), ritual and ceremonial are the characteristic shapes of symbolism. In societies of an 'organic' type (with division of labour, differentiated roles, and integration of actors by impersonal mechanisms such as that of the market), not only the share of beliefs in relation to the myths gets modified, but the link between the two changes its nature – while the nature of each of these elements is itself transformed. The development of science, by modifying the status of myths, questions the value of ritual. But neither Durkheim nor Mauss draws the conclusion from these transformations that the symbolic dimension of the social community is ultimately destroyed.

The main difficulty in their conception is that is does not clearly define what the 'objectivity' of symbolism means. Even if a myth is something other than a delusion, even if a rite cannot be reduced to an obsessional neurosis, the conclusion must not be drawn automatically that they are 'rational', simply because we are talking about social activities. One of the great obscure areas of Durkheim's sociology is that it confuses rationality, objectivity, and society. Any social phenomenon can be called 'objective' if more or less standard predictions can be made from it for observers as well as for actors. But it is quite different to say on the basis of this phenomenon, which through its regularity becomes part of one's thoughts, that it is rational. This word has a various number of meanings. It can define the 'adaptation' of one group to its environment, but also the 'legitimacy' of the values that it accepts. The only meaning which could fit in with the case of symbolism is that any society, seen as symbolic system, can define an understandable order of phenomena, i.e., meaningful. By closely linking, to the point of confusion, rationality and society, Durkheim went far beyond what experience could suggest – and also far beyond what he needed to establish his own theories on the 'reality' of what is social and on 'objectivity' in sociology.

This weakness in his thought is brought to light in discussions of the theory of 'collective representations', on which Durkheim based his notion of 'consensus'. These representations constitute a very complex set of practices and beliefs which 'symbolize' society, in a dual sense in that by helping us to intellectualize it, they ensure its existence, since they allow its members to communicate with each other. The flag represents the nation, it is the 'emblem', as Granet defined it when he used the concept for Chinese ideograms. But nobody would say that the tricolour 'is' France. At the most, when it is heading a regiment or hoisted on the front of a public building, it suggests to us a set of behaviours and attitudes: 'take off your hat, it is 14 July' or 'take a firm hold on your purse' if it is the Inland Revenue building, and in both cases enjoy a feeling of exaltation if we are patriots. But these collective representations do not belong to the field of 'logical-experimental thought'. Solidarity is not a 'fact' like the phenomenon of gravity, whether the Durkheimians like it or not. It is a non-logical notion like most ideals and values in our societies, which we manage to understand only by treating it as a synthesis of beliefs and practices.

Expressions like logical and non-logical are borrowed from Pareto. Although sociology has often been presented as 'irrationalistic' and instinctive, the connections made by Pareto between *residues* and *derivations* exclude this interpretation completely, and at the same time shed some light on the notion of symbolism, at least indirectly, although he in fact never recognized the concept as such. According to Pareto, there is in social action a vast domain which is neither logical (logico-experimental) or illogical (irrational). The non-logical is made up of beliefs and practices. These beliefs cannot be shown to be true but are not to be confused with delusions. Ideologies and religious dogma belong to this category. They 'may' become 'delusions' when they are taken as scientific propositions. This delusion increases the more ambiguous are these beliefs, especially when they are given a sacred value. Thanks to this quality, they are not submitted to examination or question and are sometimes associated with clearly false premises which are nevertheless dogmatically accepted. Some variants of egalitarian ideology would be a good example of this. For Pareto, equality is a religious dogma; indeed, to call it in question is felt by many as a blasphemy, which puts anyone questioning this principle outside the 'democratic' community. The logico-experimental justification of this dogma is impossible – as is, in fact, the opposite proposition. To make it acceptable is possible only with rhetoric and dialectic 'derivations'. It then becomes acceptable, thanks to the necessary manipulations which reactivate culturally defined and sanctioned sentiments. It is the role of symbolism to ensure a synthesis (however precarious) between 'residues' and 'derivations'.

On the condition that we do not push this latter theory towards the irrational and the unconscious, psychoanalysis appears to offer to sociologists a very seductive theory of symbolism but one which is very unproductive for them in the end. The *Traumdeutung* (science of dreams) gave Freud the opportunity to develop his theory of symbolism. Although the dream acts on the day's events as much as on very old memories, the dream image is distinct from both the perceptive image and from memory. Freud's perspective is to treat the dream not as the residue of a dead past or the anticipation of an undecipherable future, but as the expression of desires that the dreamer has been unable to satisfy, because in between desire and satisfaction is a moral barrier which pushes desire away from the conscious level. The return of these suppressed drives and desires is only possible thanks to a compromise, and under a borrowed dress. Dream images 'symbolize' repressed desires. If in some way they satisfy it, it can only be in substitutive fashion. They express it, but only by masking it.

Symbolism, understood like that, offers some characteristics incompatible with the qualities given to it by the Durkheimians. Freudian symbolism is a process of substitution and of compromise which treats the conflict between unconscious drives on one side and social constraints and more generally the demands of the reality principle on the other. Unlike the symbolic function which ensures communication between society members for the Durkheimians, the link between unconscious drives and dreams is neither stable nor constant for Freud. It is not stable since the same drive can change both vector and expression. (Freud describes the connection between dream and desire as 'labile'.) It is not constant since the same dream scenario has different meanings for two dreamers. Two bed companions dreaming next to each other dream 'each for himself' while two believers attending the same mass in the same church understand in approximately the same way, the ceremony they are attending: if there is a community of dreamers it is made up of people who are awake. But it has to be added that this community is some way away and begins on the surface of individual drives. 'Dream science' is, according to Freud, something other than a key to dreams which are outdated stock, and almost meaningless, as sayings and standard stories. The traditional psychoanalyst does not look for archetypes, like Jung does. He is not interested in transindividual or cultural stereotypes which tell us little more about the individual psyche or about society's functioning. He tries to sort out the conflict dynamics of one particular 'case', a conflict which prevents the individual from obtaining what he wants while he cannot at the same time give it up. So, as Lévi-Strauss says, the sociologist or the ethnologist must beware of confusing the myths which are always associated with rituals also found in a historically and geographically defined institutional setting, with archetypes or stereotypes.

It is true to say that *Totem and Taboo* offers us a symbolic grid to understand the fate of humanity. But do these extrapolations make up a theory of *social* symbolism? They offer us a few myths (Oedipus, death of the father, reaction of the sons against his despotic authority, then, after his death, their association). These myths can be subjected to a certain number of criticisms. First, Freud's Hobbesian inspiration makes him radicalize the conflict between nature and culture. Second, no matter how attractive are Freudian myths, and particularly Freud's version of the Oedipus 'myth', they treat the symbolic function only from the perspective of the conflict between the psychological mechanisms (id, ego, super ego), but neglect almost completely the objective and cognitive aspects of symbolism which have interested, quite rightly, the Durkheimian sociologists who were so curious about the connections between mythology and science and so eager to base 'collective representations' on a well-controlled communication network. Psychoanalysis does not offer a conception which would allow the sociologist to tackle the fundamental problem of the institutionalization and the objectivization of the interaction process.

As soon as symbolism is close to the communication function, it is its cognitive dimension which is emphasized, as in G.H. Mead – provided of course that the word 'cognitive' is understood properly. Mead sees in the symbol the mediation through which individuals can understand and communicate with each other. Communication is first defined as an interaction. But the latter does not mean to Mead a connection between individuals who would remain superficial and indifferent to each other. Moving balls are interacting since the opposition and movement of each of them can be affected by the position and movement of others. Applied to human relations, this model, which inspires traditional behaviourism, is not acceptable to Mead. This is why he calls his own behaviourism 'social' behaviourism. For him, interaction between social actors is defined as a process through which each actor is able to take the other's place, an imaginary deed in a way since I shall never be anyone else but myself. But this deed is not arbitrary since the substitution is only one of 'roles' which are controlled in their opposition as well as in their complementarity. 'To take the role of the other' – this famous formula underlines the link between the notion of role and that of symbolic inter- action. The role is a set of rights and of obligations given to the ego or even demanded and earned by ego and that in any case it acts for the other – and under the control of the other. There is therefore no interaction without a minimum of understanding between the actors. This understanding for Mead is only in excep- tional cases empathic and intuitive and rests on a set of hypotheses and antici- pations, i.e., more or less justified expectations through which ego and other try to determine their reciprocal positions through more or less precise adjustments. Interaction according to Mead is a set of strategies through which ego and other adjust to each other.

Mead describes this adjustment as *symbolic*. To understand this formula, it is necessary to dwell on the adjustment itself and on the nature of the means and resources that it uses. Let us examine first the ability of each actor to 'take the role of the other'. Literally understood, this formula suggests that the interaction process between properly socialized individuals tends towards a reciprocity, the mastery and manipulation of which each actor could potentially achieve. There would be communication with the other only if each actor could substitute himself for the other, at least in his thoughts.

Has Mead erroneously reduced interaction to its ideal limits, reciprocity? This question touches on the objectivity of social roles and allows us to glimpse what distinguishes them from both the inconsistencies and incommunicability of fanta- sies and the ideal rigour of norms. It still remains to ask what the social symbol must be to ensure an authentic communication between the actors without limit- ing interaction to the sole form of reciprocity.

Symbolic communication is neither strictly conceptual nor even strictly verbal. Conceptual communication is not without misconception or misunderstanding. The concept inscribed in a word can be taken for what it denotes or what it connotes. The word 'woman' can mean a human being of the opposite sex to mine, with differences of chest, hair, voice, and clothes. But it can also refer to a partner with whom I have pleasure or trouble. In addition, there are other symbols than words. Mead clearly distinguished the gesture from the word. Finally, the relation between gesture, sign, and symbol is far from clear. Gesture can be a succession of signs 'started-starter', which must not be confused with a sequence of movements which follow each other mechanically. A gesture can also be an anticipation, an insinuation – a 'strategy'.

Mead did very little to illuminate the notion of communication but Saussure with his distinctions of 'speech', (*langue*) language, and discourse sheds some inter- esting light on it. Saussure argued for a frankly interactionist conception of linguis- tic communication or rather of the 'speech', that he distinguishes from language and discourse. To talk is an action which presupposes at least two individuals between whom begins a process activating an act of phonation (emitting a meaningful sound, an 'acoustic image', as Saussure calls it) and an act of audition which 'associates this image in the brain with the corresponding meaning'. But speech seen in this way is of a much broader type, 'multishaped and irregular': it is *language* that can be taken as synonymous with 'symbolic function', taken in its broadest aspect. Moreover, speech is different from *discourse* which is a personalized expression of the individual who is speaking whereas *speech* is a system of vocabulary and syntactic rules whose field applies to all individuals speaking the same idiom.

Saussure's proposed distinctions have two merits. First, they facilitate the challenge to easy assimilations between 'language facts' and 'social facts'. Speech is a social fact but social communication takes place between individuals not only thanks to speech but also thanks to all the forms of language – verbal and non-verbal. Moreover, since it is spoken by individuals, speech rests on the support provided by the 'speaking mass'. So, for Saussure, the communication taking place between the members of a society can never be reduced strictly to a system of arbitrary 'signs' which are non-motivated and strictly prescribed but has an 'aura' or a symbolic cloud which concentrates around a 'rough' natural link between the sign (*signifier*) and the meaning (*signified*). Social communication cannot therefore be reduced to just speech. It also has a variety of symbolic dimensions called 'semiology' by Saussure.

The extreme vagueness of the term symbol can now be appreciated. To clarify matters there is normally a distinction made between sign and symbol, following Saussure. A sign is characterized by the arbitrary link between the *signifier* and the *signified*: it is only through a convention that a red circle in a street warns a driver that he cannot drive into it. The meaning attached to the sign, besides being arbitrary, is also explicit and constant. For the red circle to stop meaning 'no entry', the responsible authority must let us know in prescribed ways. Is a word a sign or a symbol? When we manage to distinguish between the defined object and what defines it, it is possible to talk of the latter term as a sign. But in many cases we do not take the word for a pure and simple lexical sign. When a humorous man 'makes a pun', when he chooses to make a calculated mistake, the word is surrounded with an 'aura' which goes further than the strict field of its definition.

Even in the case where ego, anticipating correctly the other's game, gets ready for it and prepares the other to respond to his own expectations, communication is something other than an exchange of information. Sometimes gesture contradicts speech. Sometimes it reinforces it; sometimes it weakens it. Actors can think something other than what they say. There is in symbolic communication a shady zone which spreads from a hard core of relatively stable meanings unequivocally understood by anyone (the 'generalized Other' of Mead). Let us take a trivial example from Leach which will show that the diversity of 'cognitive interest' – borrowing one of the favourite expressions of ethnomethodologists – is itself incapable of creating the objectivity of communication in the sense that Mead himself defines this expression. Let us see what is happening in a concert hall where a famous conductor is directing Beethoven's 5th Symphony. The interaction between the conductor, the soloists, the orchestra, and the audience is mediated by the score. But for the conductor, the score is a constraining 'text' which he must strictly follow, whereas for the music lover who is not always a very expert musician the score is a 'pretext' which helps his enjoyment. The conductor is not the author of the score. Being only the interpreter, he is in a similar position to the music-lover in relation to his own interpretation of the work.

Leach further notes that during the Second World War, the first three bars of the Symphony were linked to the two-finger gesture, that of index and the second finger with which Churchill announced victory – a gesture which besides can suggest obscene images in some milieux: horns or worse. The first bars of the 5th Symphony are thus seen as metaphorically representing the victory of the Allies. But in so far as the symbol is a metaphor, it is confused by largely idiosyncratic associations and called a 'floating signifier' by Lévi-Strauss.

The same music by Beethoven which evokes the triumph of democracy for the BBC European service listener will prefigure a theme which will be repeated so many times by such or such an instrument, by all or part of the orchestra, in one form or another for the musician reading the score. It is the systematic part of the 'code' which enables the replacement of one element back into the set of signi-fications of which it is part. Without a code, or if the syntactic rules are incomplete, confused or contradictory, this element 'floats'. Faced with a derivation which eventually takes all meaning away from it, it is excluded from the communication system but can feed reverie or free association in individuals. it is only as a meto-nymy that a symbol constitutes a system of communication.

The theory of social symbolism is pulled in two opposing directions. On one side, symbol is the imaginary, the departure from reality. The symbolical is then the realm of 'as if' but in a way that the dreamer does not attempt to control. In the social order, this symbolism is no longer rite or ceremony, it is an explosive and capricious celebration. Symbolism then no longer has anything to do with the meaning that Mauss gave it in *The Gift* or the way Durkheim used the term *The Elementary Forms of Religious Life*. To give symbolism its social dimension it must be linked closely to code and coding. These terms define a set of given elements which control the appearance and the occurrence of an anticipated and regulated chain of events – even if the link between the given elements of the first situation and the given elements of the second is not understood by those using the code.

Which kind of social events can possibly be 'coded' – and inversely which ones cannot be coded, or only in an approximate, ambiguous, and superifical way? Circumstances allowing coding are those called 'ritual' by Leach: marriage, birth, initiation, purification, sacrifice. These 'ritual circumstances' make up a chain of events called for and generated by each other, according to a constraining model which allocates each participant to a role and a rank. Codes which control 'ritual circumstances' can be called 'markers': they indicate a place for everyone in the hierarchy; they distinguish between or associate individuals; they express appro-val, censure, denigration, submission, and prerogative. These 'markers' are built upon elementary units of behaviour, whether intentional or not, like body position – sitting down, standing up, lying down – like body movement and the speed at which it is done. Markers are also built upon the showing off or the concealment of certain parts of the body, of certain products, or by-products of organic activity.

The notion of coding can be extended beyond ritual situations. Relations of distance, hierarchy, co-operation do not express themselves only within 'ritual situations'. Anthropologists study them in the context of sacrifice or rites of 'passage'. However Goffman is right to describe it as coding when talking about casual meeting; when for instance, on a platform a foreigner asks a native of the society he is visiting the time of the next train, he is speaking to someone he has never seen before and will never see again. The clothing, beard, walk, signal a 'hippy' to the observer; this one, thanks to some clues which identify him in the hurrying crowd as the person capable of giving him the information he needs. Symbolic coding creates a process of recognition and identification – tattoos are an extreme and complete case of this since they are designed to assure our identity both for ourselves and for others.

The notion of social symbolism elaborated by the Durkheimians can be associated with the notion of 'code' understood as a set of 'markers' which, by defining social hierarchy, allow individuals to recognize the sex, age, and above all the status of their partners. All codes, however, use both a lexical pool and a set of syntactic rules. In the codification of status, the vocabulary is made up of gestures and verbal formulae about which it is important to know whether they are natural or conventional. This is a very difficult question; tears do not invariably go with sadness or sorrow, even if ontogenesis allows us to say, as Leach does, that crying is a behaviour common to all children of all cultures when they express sadness and pain. But the coding of tears as expressing sorrow has to do with an original elaboration which differs according to the culture coded.

A pool of images, gestures, and words is not sufficient to constitute a code. A set of directional and compositional rules is also necessary. The recourse to syntactic rules is all the more important if the material referred to in the code is intrinsically more ambiguous. Nowhere is it difficult to distinguish an old man from a child or a man from a woman. But someone's rank, the age group to which a person belongs, the kinship between individuals are not inscribed on their faces. It is thanks to a code (clothes, posture, level and style of consumption, vocabulary, accent, diction) that the information to do with this individual status can be deciphered. Thus codification of status is never perfectly coherent. Status indeed has several dimensions. I can hold a high status on a certain dimension, wealth for instance, and yet have little prestige or power. Coding is more or less difficult depending on the dimension used. It is easier to develop indicators of wealth than of power. It is simpler to assess an individual's power in his organization than his power in the community where he lives.

In a society there are at least as many codes as there are dimensions of social activity. Because of this pluralism should one exclude the possibility of a code of codes? The integration function is often fulfilled by the notion of value system, seen as the sum of collective preferences which all individuals and social categories have to share. But this is an incoherent and hardly operational category which has more to do with lexical variety then with syntactic rigour. Also, the social symbolism in which collective representations come to life is not really a code and this is why the qualifying term 'cognitive' often used by Mead's followers to describe social symbolism must be used carefully. It is no more than the matrix from which both collective representations and the sociologist's critical thought take their inspiration.

Beliefs, Durkheim, Ideologies, Knowledge, Religion, Socialization, Status, Values.

Bibliography

BLUMER, H., *Symbolic interactionism. Perspective and method,* Englewood Cliffs, Prentice-Hall, 1969. – CASSIRER, E., *Philosophie der Symbolischen Formen,* Berlin, B. Cassirer, 1923–1929, 3 vol. – CHOMSKI, N., *Cartesian linguistics; a chapter in the history of rationalist thoughts,* New York, Harper & Row, 1966. – CICOUREL, A.V., *Cognitive sociology: language and meaning in social interaction,* Harmondsworth, Penguin Books, 1973. – DURKHEIM, E., *Elementary Forms of Religious Life,* London, Allen & Unwin, 1915. – ELIADE, M., *Traité d'histoire des religions,* Paris, Payot, 1949; rev ed. Paris, Payot, 1968. – FREUD, S., *Die Traumdeutung,* Leipzig, Vienna, F. Deuticke, 1900. – GOFFMAN, E., *The presentation of self in every day life,* London, Allen Lane, 1969. – JUNG, C.G., *Psychological reflections: an anthology of writings,* New York, Harper, 1953, 1961. – LAPLANCHE, J. and PONTALIS, J.B., *Vocabulaire de la psychanalyse,* Paris, PUF, 1967, 1971. – LEACH, E.R, *Rethinking anthropology,* London, Athlone Press, 1961. – LÉVI-STRAUSS, C., *Le totémisme aujourd'hui,* Paris, PUF, 1962; *Anthropologie structurale deux,* Paris, Plon, 1973. – MAUSS, M., 'Essai sur le don', in *Sociologie et anthropologie,* Paris, PUF, 1950. – MEAD, G.H., *Mind, self and society. From the standpoint of a social behaviourist,* The Univ. of Chicago Press, 1934. – PARETO, V., *Traité de sociologie.* – SAUSSURE, F. de, *Cours de linguistique générale,* Paris, Payot, 1916, 1974.

Socialization

The history of the word 'socialization' has been erratic. It seems that the word is the result of a misinterpretation by Giddings in his translation into English of the notion of *Vergellschaftung* ('coming into a social relationship', 'as-sociation') that is central in the works of Georg Simmel. Whatever the mistake may have been, the word has been part of the classical vocabulary of sociology ever since the 1937 publication of Sutherland and Woodward's sociological textbook. It refers to the assimilation process of individuals into social groups. Even though it is a recent word, it describes a classic problematic for sociology and particularly for Durkheim (cf. 'Durkheim').

Today, the notion of socialization has become a convenient label. It covers studies dealing with the different learning experiences the individual goes through, especially when he is young (linguistic, cognitive, symbolic, normative, etc., learning experiences). Some of these studies attempt to describe the stages of the fundamental socialization processes that are conceived as being independent from particular cultures and social contexts. This is the case, for instance with Piaget's studies on the formation of moral judgement in the child, or with some of Kohlberg's works. But the great majority of works dealing with socialization adopt a comparative perspective. The comparison may be international as in the works of Hagen, Inkeles, Pye, McCelland, or Almond and Verba. These studies, which were mostly conducted in the 1960s, discuss the effect of the values transmitted by educational practices on adults' behaviours and representation. They often appear as being motivated by an hypothesis which was popular in that time of growth, when 'developmentalism' had an important role: the Weber-inspired hypothesis according to which social, economical, and political development depends on values interiorized by individuals and, therefore, on socialization processes (cf. 'Development'). Thus, in an explosive way, specialities sprang up and started to become institutionalized: 'political socialization' became a favourite research subject.

In the next decade, there was a shift in the interests of researchers. The social-ization processes were considered worthy of examination mostly because they seemed to provide the key to the permanence of classes and more generally to understanding social differentiation. Comparisons now dealt mostly with social groups (social classes, socio-professional categories, sexes). To take an example among many others, the English sociologist Bernstein endeavoured to show that the learning process of what he calls 'formal language' – i.e., the kind of language characterized by a clear distinction between subordinate and co-ordination func-tions, by an easy and subtle use of adjectives and adverbs and by a complex syntax – was exclusively spoken by the middle and upper classes, providing them with a significant advantage in the competitive school system even if the 'formal language' obviously cannot, in absolute terms, be considered as richer than the 'popular' language.

It is by no means our purpose to present here an evaluation of the studies deal-ing with socialization, on the one hand, because these countless studies – lacking homogeneity – provide answers to changing motivations and preoccupations, do not always have convergent results, and are not easily integrated in a theoretical framework; on the other hand, because the most interesting proposals concerning socialization phenomena are not necessarily to be found in the literature officially placed under that label. One can easily understand why. Every social process involves acting subjects. The action of these subjects cannot usually be analysed if one disregards the learning experience – in socialization – they went through. Consequently, every sociological study may possibly include more or less interest-ing news or proposals on socialization phenomena.

Rather than attempting to give an impossible evaluation of studies on social-ization, it may be of more use to discuss certain general questions that are impli-citly or explicitly raised by the very notion of socialization, as well as by the literature on socialization. The two essential questions to be asked may be the following ones:

1. What is the most appropriate representation of socialization processes? Can they be primarily regarded as conditioning processes through which the social actor under the influence of his environment would record and internalize the 'answers' that must be given to the various situations he might encounter? We will discuss this question in detail later on. But it is important to notice from the start that the conditioning pattern can only provide the key to the behaviour of social actors if one supposes that they are confronted by a limited number of repetitive situations.

2. What role do socialization effects play in the explanation of social pheno-mena? As this question is only meaningful when made specific, we will attempt to

answer it by a quick overview of particular phenomena (reproductive behaviour, educational inequalities, attitudes towards innovation).

The first question is all the more important because a permanent temptation for sociology – sometimes referred to as 'sociologism' – consists precisely, in the most extreme cases, in treating socialization as some kind of training through which the young person is led to internalize norms, values, attitudes, roles, knowledge of facts, and know-how that will make up a kind of syllabus designed to be achieved later on, more or less mechanically. This conception is, implicitly, to be found in a great deal of the literature on socialization. It is partly the result of a methodological artefact. One if perfectly entitled to question whether such or such a value, such or such a type of ability is more or less frequent in the individuals belonging to such or such a group, for instance, to such or such social class, or whether the need for achievement is stronger in Athens during Pericles' time or in Athens during the decadent period (McCelland). Whenever a correlation is then observed, for instance between social classes and values, the researcher may be tempted to draw conclusions about the mechanistically causal action of social structures in the internalization of values. But the causal interpretation is only possible because it was decided to isolate two variable factors inside a complex process (cf. 'Causality').

To the conditioning paradigm, one may oppose the interaction paradigm (cf. 'Action') of which an exemplary application is found in the works of Piaget on moral judgement. The formation of moral judgement in the child, just as his progressive mastering of logical operations, depends, according to Piaget, on an autonomous process of developing cognitive structures. But it also depends on the nature of the interaction system in which it is included: as long as the child's interactions are limited to his parents, he tends to reify moral rules and to behave in an egocentric way. The sense of mutual respect, of justice, of reciprocal attitudes, and of contracts only appears between 8 and 11 years old when the control exerted by parents diminishes and the child finds a place in peer groups. Internalizing the sense of reciprocity and of justice comes from the fact that the child growing up is more and more frequently confronted by situations in which he can gain respect for his own rights only by showing respect for the right of others.

It is not altogether difficult to find out the reasons for which the interaction paradigm seems to be much more realistic and much more flexible than the conditioning paradigm.

1. To start with, it helps to think of socialization as an *adaptive* process. Facing a new situation, the individual is guided by his cognitive resources and by the normative attitudes resulting from the socialization process he has been exposed to. However, the new situation will finally lead him to enrich his cognitive resources or to modify his normative attitudes.

2. The interaction paradigm is in no way incompatible with – and can include – the fundamental hypothesis of *optimization* according to which, in a given situation, a person tries to adjust his behaviour as closely as possible to what he likes best and to his interests as he sees them. This hypothesis is of course a very general one, but at the same time it is specific enough to exclude the mechanical kind of

behaviour and, in the end, the remote-controlled or *extradetermined* behaviour implied by the conditioning paradigm in its pure form. Optimization behaviour or, to use a word he prefers, *equilibrium* behaviour is a constant theme in Piaget's works. For this author, the individual, generally speaking, tends to look for the solution which, in accordance with his resources and attitudes as well as with the situation as he sees it, seems to him to be the best one. The optimization hypothesis – it should actually be called the optimization postulate instead – does not imply that a person will necessarily choose the best solution *per se*, i.e., the solution which an outside observer would be likely to describe as the best solution for that person. Previous socialization can be the reason behind an inadequate perception of the situation; normative attitudes can exert constraint which is detrimental to the social actor. *Video meliera prologue, deteriora sequor* (I see what is good, I approve of it, and I do what is bad) as the saying goes; this aphorism can easily be analysed in the framework of the interaction paradigm. And this paradigm helps to avoid reaching the conclusion the conditioning pattern often leads to; this conclusion, which is not readily acceptable, reads that the 'social structures' and the socialization process that results from them may lead the members of some social categories to comply with what other people prefer, rather than with what they prefer, or to form preferences opposed to their interests, in short to comply as if they were masochistic and altruistic. Thus, some neo-Marxist theories inspired by central notions in the tradition, such as theories of *alienation* and *false consciousness*, imply that: 1) the internalized value mechanisms that are set in action by the socialization processes are efficient enough; and 2) the power of the ruling class on the definition of common values is great enough for individuals belonging to the ruled class to serve obligingly and correctly the interests of the ruling class which are naturally opposed to theirs (according, of course, to the doctrine of class struggle).

3. Within the framework of the interaction paradigm, it is easier – and essential – to take into account the *degree of internalization* of normative and cognitive frameworks produced by socialization. It is obvious that different learning experiences are more or less long and difficult. One learns more quickly how to ride a bicycle than how to play the piano. Some deep structures of a personality are largely irreversible. On the other hand, everyone has felt for himself that some types of attitudes or of opinions are more easily reversible. When facing a new situation or a new environment, an actor will have, generally speaking, the ability to alter certain effects of the previous socialization he has been exposed to. The 'big business leaders' described by Warner and Abegglen are, with almost no exception, individuals whose fathers (often alcoholics or away from home) were indifferent towards them: this initial situation led them to be more cynical towards others than the average person. This element, largely irreversible, gave them a high degree of adaptability that helped them to go up the social ladder with ease. On the contrary, Keniston's studies show that young people who come from a united, harmonious, and 'respectable' family environment tend to demonstrate and to maintain a very strong conformism in relation with the values of their milieu. But in both cases, we are talking about 'deeply' internalized values so that the very structure of the personality is affected. Obviously, there are also instances when

the internalization of norms and values is more superificial.

4. The interaction paradigm also helps to distinguish each of the internalized elements according to its *constraining power*. Socialization makes you internalize norms, values, cognitive structures, and practical knowledge. Some learning experiences involving the mind or the body lead you to acquire specific aptitudes; others (cf. Bateson's deutero-learning) lead you to master general operating procedures, more or less indefinitely adaptable to the diversity of concrete situations. Some norms are precise and in no way ambiguous ('thou shalt not kill'); others might be interpreted in a variety of contradictory ways, as we are reminded by Pareto's sarcasm towards Kant's categorical imperative:

> Kant states his formula in yet another way: 'May your actions be guided by a maxim only if you would like it to become a universal law.' These formulas usually have such a vague character that one may draw anything out of them, therefore, it would be quicker to say: 'May your actions please Kant and his disciples', since, in any case, the 'universal law' will end up being abolished. (*Treatise of General Sociology*: 1514.)

While some values or norms can be interpreted unequivocally, others are indeed very versatile. See, for example, the classical discussions on 'social mobility'. Here is a notion generally considered to be positive value. But the criteria for success given by different individuals vary a lot and depend partly on their social position (see 'Objectivity'). In the same way, Keniston showed that the young American 'radicals' of the 1960s did not clash with their parents so often because they were attracted by opposite values as because they had different views on the degree of achievement in American society of values which their parents had taught them and which they fully regarded as their own.

5. The interaction paradigm helps to give an effective content to the distinction between *primary socialization* and *secondary socialization* on which Berger and Luckman rightly insist. Part of the primary socialization – corresponding to the childhood period – is questioned again by the secondary socialization to which the teenager, and later the adult, is exposed during his whole life. The notion of secondary socialization is of course incompatible with the conception according to which the effects of primary socialization would be rigorous and irreversible in every case.

6. Generally speaking, thanks to the interaction paradigm, one can include the socialization process in a theoretical framework, that of *action analysis*. Many of the divergent, contradictory, and clashing opinions found in the empirical studies of socialization phenomena probably come from the fact that their authors seldom care about reconstructing the microsociological data responsible for any likeness or difference one can observe at the appropriate level. That authoritarian education methods seem to be more widely used by lower classes than by upper classes becomes an *understandable* fact as soon as one notices that 'permissive' methods involve more complex cognitive and linguistic abilities than authoritarian methods do, and the upper classes are more likely to have such resources. That representations dealing with the ideal size of family vary according to the cultural

and social context can be explained immediately when one is able to show that the context may influence individuals to have a small or a large family. It is well known, for instance, that when infantile mortality is high, it is customary to have a large family as it represents a guarantee of descent.

Let us now tackle the second question, that concerning the role of socialization in the explanation of social phenomena. It is, of course, impossible to give a precise answer to such a general question. But one can point out that sociologists often have a tendency to give excessive weight to socialization phenomena. Frequently, a sociologist observing a *dysfunctional* phenomenon will first attribute its presence and its persistence to an effect of socialization. How can 'resistance' to a change, considered by the observer as being favourable to the actor, be explained, if not because socialization led the actor to internalize dysfunctional norms? How can it be explained that disadvantaged families are less inclined to benefit from the education system, while income and status are positively linked to education level, if not as the effect of a functional socialization in relation to the 'ruling class', but dysfunctional in relation to the 'ruled class' itself? How can it be explained that peasants in India maintain 'dysfunctional' reproductive behaviour if not through the effect of tradition and the rigour of socialization. In fact, it is easy to show from these examples and many more than it is most often debatable to attempt to explain a 'dysfunctional' phenomenon exclusively as an effect of socialization. Indian peasants maintain a high reproduction rate in a case where the structure of the economic environment is such that they are objectively more likely to be raised above the subsistence level with eight children than with two. Disadvantaged families have a lower demand for education. Why? Because, at least partly and for obvious reasons, they are more concerned with the risk implied by the fact of placing a child, whose achievement at school may currently be mediocre, on a long road which he might have to leave halfway. Studies of the spread of innovation in agricultural milieux generally prove that, when peasants avoid adopting innovative methods, it is because they have good reasons to do so. The fact that a new kind of seed produces more than the 'traditional' one does is not enough to persuade peasants to adopt the new one immediately. Is 'resistance to change' due to the effects of socialization and to the weight of traditions? In some cases perhaps. But in most cases, resistance rather comes from the fact that adopting a new seed results in costs which the hurried and prejudiced observer may not think of, but which are immediately perceived by the peasant (cf. HYV rice, for instance).

The uncertainties in studies relating to socialization phenomena largely result from the fact that these studies stick to what Wrong calls an 'oversocialized conception of man': the effects of socialization constitute only one of the parameters of action. Moreover, the notion of secondary socialization suggests that, in varying degrees of intensity, they can be themselves subjected to retroactive effects produced by the structure of the *interaction field* in which the actor is immersed.

Action, Conformity and Deviance, Culturalism and Culture, Role, Values.

Bibliography

ALMOND, G.A. and VERBA, S., *The civic culture; political attitudes in five nations. An analytic study*. Princeton, Princeton University Press, 1963. Abridged ed. Boston, Little, Brown & C°, 1965. – BATESON, G., 'Social planning and the concept of deutero-learning', *in* BATESON, G., *Steps to an ecology of mind*, New York, Chandler, 1972, 159–177; London, Granada, 1972. – BERGER, P. and LUCKMAN, T., *The social construction of reality*, London, Doubleday, 1966. – BERNSTEIN, B., *Class, codes and control*, London, Routledge & Kegan Paul. 1971–1973, 2 vol. – BOURRICAUD, F., *L'individualisme institutionnel*, Paris, PUF, 1977. – CLAUSEN, J.A. (ed.), *Socialization and society*, Boston, Little & Brown, 1968. – GIDDINGS, F.H., *The theory of socialization. A syllabus of sociological principles*, New York/London Macmillan, 1897. – GRILICHES, Z., 'Hybrid corn: an exploration in the economics of technological change', *Econometrica*, XXV, *4*, 1957, 501–522. – KENISTON, K., *Young radicals: notes on committed youth*, New York, Harcourt Brace & World, 1968. – KOHLBERG, L., 'Stage and sequence: the cognitive developmental approach to socialization', *in* GOSLIN, D.A. (ed.), *Handbook of socialization theory and research*, Beverley Hills, Russel Sage, 1969, 325–473. – McCLELLAND, D., *The achieving society*, Princeton, Van Nostrand, 1961. – PADIOLEAU, J.G., 'La formation de la pensée politique: développement longitudinal et déterminants socio-culturels', *Revue française de sociologie*, XVII, *3*, 1976, 451–484. – PIAGET, J., *Le jugement moral chez l'enfant*, Paris, F. Alcan, 1932, Paris, PUF, 1957, 1969. – PYE, L.W., *Politics, personality and nation building. Burma's search for identity*, New Haven/London, Yale University Press, 1962. – SKINNER, B.F., *Science and human behaviour*, New York, Macmillan, 1953. – SUTHERLAND, R.L. and WOODWARD, J., *Introductory sociology*, New York, Lippincott, 1937. – WARNER, W.L. and ABEGGLEN, J.C., *Big business leaders in America*, New York, Atheneum, 1963. – WRONG, D., 'The oversocialized conception of man in modern sociology', *American sociological review*, XXVI, *2*, 1961, 183–193.

Sociobiology

What this term describes is not new. But this particular activity, as a defined field of study can be dated from the publication of *Sociobiology: A New Synthesis* by E.O. Wilson. In any case, it is with that book that this field of study first gets on the agenda for social scientists and is discussed by them. In Flaubert's *Dictionnaire des idées reçues* a definition of 'Sociobiology' would probably have read 'oppose violently'!

The aim of sociobiology, according to those who study the field, is to explain the appearance of a number of social structures through the modern theory of evolution, from Darwin onwards to today's neo-Darwinism and to the 'synthetic' theory of evolution. By so doing, this field leans on accepted facts in modern genetics, the beginnings of which traditionally date back to Mendel's works and which has been considerably revived with the progress of molecular biology.

The main research field for sociobiologists is the animal world. Wilson himself is an expert in insect societies. However, at the same time, a number of biologists, among them Wilson, are convinced that sociobiology can contribute to the analysis of phenomena relating to human behaviour. It is this 'daring idea' which has made sociobiology the object of serious ideological debate.

Let us start with some examples which are aimed at making the methods and objectives of animal sociobiology more concrete. A general sphere of interest is to explain aggressive behaviour in its various forms. In most animal species two kinds of aggressive behaviour have been observed. One in which aggressive behaviour intensifies and might go as far as death battles, another in which aggressive behaviour is controlled and ends up with the retreat of one of the parties involved.

Using games theory, John Maynard Smith showed that, when the behaviour of individuals is defined by a particular distribution of the different kinds of aggression, one gets a 'stable strategy as far as evolution is concerned' (Evolutionary Stable Strategy), so that any individual different from the norm, with a completely different ESS, would have little chance of being selected. To illustrate this idea, a simple analogy could be used. Imagine that a group is made up of 'falcons' and 'doves' (these two labels used as metaphors describing two kinds of individuals); moreover, suppose that one could quantify gains and losses in each kind of fight, deriving these from their effect on the capacity of reproduction of each individual. Thus, in the case of a fight pushed to the extreme, we'll decide on a loss of -100 for the loser and on a gain of $+50$ for the winner. More specifically, a falcon would gain $+50$ if he fights till death with another falcon and wins; and the loser falcon will get -100; also, when a 'falcon' fights a 'dove', the falcon, also the winner according to our definition, gains 50 and the dove 0. A 'dove' (controlled aggressive behaviour) will improve its score by 50 in the case of victory against another dove (a dove can only of course win over another dove, not over a falcon) but will loose -20 in the case that it loses. Therefore a falcon meeting another falcon could hope to gain $(50-100) \times 1/2 = -25$. Whereas the dove fighting another dove could gain $(50-20) \times 1/2 = +15$. Let's imagine now that a 'new' (different from the norm) dove arrives in a group made up exclusively of 'falcons': the 'dove' will hope to make higher gains than the 'falcons'. Its capacity for reproduction will be higher than that of the average falcon. The selection process should then help the mutation until a balance is reached between the relative numbers of the two kinds of individuals. In the same way, a 'new' falcon would be favoured by the process of selection if it arrived among a group of 'doves'. This theoretical analogy (which could easily be made more complicated so as to be more realistic) illustrates a 'conceivable' explanation for the emergence of the two kinds of aggression and for the relative balance of their persistence in some cases. This analogy is seen to use, as is generally the case with sociobiologists (but not with all animal biologists, since Lorenz disagrees specifically on this point), the assumption according to which any process of selection operates on an individual basis. In other words, natural selection is supposed never to retain a mutation which would be in theory favourable to the group but unfavourable or inconsequential for the individual. Also, it is usually postulated that there is no group selection. Games theory allowed us to show that in effect a 'stable strategy as far as evolution is concerned' could correspond to a 'sub-optimal' balance.

Let's go back to the previous numerical example: a population exclusively made up of 'doves' would be in an 'unbalanced' situation, since an arriving 'falcon' would be in a favourable situation and would be in a position to be selected. For a population to reach equilibrium, a specific proportion of 'doves' and 'falcons' will be necessary (or, according to another interpretation of the example, a situation in which each individual will demonstrate the two kinds of behaviour within specific conditions and not at random). But it is clear that this balance is 'sub-optimal' if, in a group exclusively made of 'doves', each individual would, on average, hope to gain more than the necessary coefficient to guarantee the group an equilibrium position. This last example is, formally, to be compared to Schelling's analysis put forward in *The Tyranny of Minor Decisions*. In this work indeed, numerous examples of interrelating systems leading to 'sub-optimal' equilibrium like the one above are to be found. In opposition to a too-literal interpretation of individual selection, it is important to emphasize what happens when a mutation occurs in a small group which is also isolated ecologically. If it is in a positive situation, this mutation can win more easily than in a large group of the same species. The first element can then, in view of its superiority, eliminate the second one.

It is also with a model (taken straight from neo-Darwinism) of 'natural individual selection' that sociobiologists explain the disparity of sexual roles in the animal world. Let us agree, for a moment, with the general postulate of sociobiology, that individuals 'want' to reproduce themselves or, to be more specific, want to transmit their genes. Naturally, it is quite unnecessary to give this postulate an anthropomorphic interpretation. The postulate is in fact the unnecessarily symbolic translation of the evidence: an individual without a genetic need to reproduce would not reproduce and would not be able therefore to transmit its genetic traits. In the case of sexual reproduction, this principle leads to a competition between parents. This competition for instance means that each of the partners would win by letting the other take care of their offspring while they went on to find another partner elsewhere. But if the two parents behave in the same way, the result becomes 'undesirable' since their offspring are then condemned to die for lack of care. Competition between parents cannot, therefore, be a trait of selection. Moreover, the female is generally in a weaker position in this competition (gestation time, etc.). Hence the appearance of two fundamental 'reproduction strategies' in the female, not provoked by a conscious choice but by the selection process. The first of these strategies is the 'domestic bliss strategy'. It is where the female forces the male to invest heavily before copulation (building a nest, courting, etc.). 'Knowing' that he would have to invest in the same way with another female, the male can only benefit (in the reproductive sense) if he takes care of his offspring rather than seduce another female. The other strategy is that of the 'he-man': selection favours females who are attracted by males carrying genes which are complementary to theirs. It is in the female's own interest indeed that her offspring should be healthy.

These two examples illustrate the way sociobiologists explain the presence in the animal world of phenomena such as showing-off or 'courting', having agreed on the principle of individual selection and 'reproductive need'.

Let us talk a little more about the 'altruism' which often appears in the essays of the sociobiologists. Starting from the principle according to which each individual is selfishly driven by its 'self-reproductive interest', how can one explain altruistic behaviour? As in the case of controlled aggression sociobiologists explain this behaviour through the notion of 'well-understood selfishness' (WUS). The presence of WUS behaviour must obviously also be explained as resulting not from 'choice' but from the natural selection process. These altruistic actions appear when an individual's 'reproductive interest' leads him to encourage the reproductive interest of others similar to himself. This way, he will in fact contribute to the transmission of his own genes (in the specific proportions found in Mendelian theory). Using the WUS principle, sociobiologists explain, for instance, why some species produce sterile individuals (hymenoptera, white ants). This phenomenon occurs because, with hymenoptera, females are 'diploids', that is to say they have a father and a mother whereas males are 'haploids' (only have a mother). Two females coming from the fertilization of the queen by the same male are genetically closer to each other than they would be to their own daughter. Quite so, since two females who have the same father have 50 per cent of the same genes, because the father, a haploid, transmits exactly the same genes to his daughters, to which one adds 25 per cent of the same genes from the diploid mother. On the other hand, mother and daughter will share only 50 per cent of the same genes. Hence the 'reproductive interest' that some females have in not reproducing and helping other females to reproduce instead. This hypothesis allows us to understand why, for instance, there are no male 'workers' within hymenoptera. Indeed, a male is no closer to his siblings than to his female offspring (he cannot have sons). These examples illustrate the part played by 'parental selection' in the observation of the phenomenon of altruism. In other cases, sociobiologists explain altruism by the development of mechanisms of 'parental manipulation', understood as the result not of a deliberate choice but of a re-affirmation by the process of natural selection. These mechanisms make the parents force one of their children to serve the other. In other cases still, sociobiologists explain altruism by the principle of reciprocity.

'Human' sociobiology tries to apply the methods and principles which have just been explained to the analysis of phenomena present in the human species. This extension comes from the fact that sociobiologists are convinced that a number of behaviours – reproduction in particular – are genetically determined and are the result of the selection process. Thus, they are convinced that the general phenomenon of 'courting' which comes before copulation has to be partly explained by mechanisms similar to those postulated for the animal world. Different cultures of course generate different patterns of the phenomenon in relation to various contexts. However, these cultural variations, due to the passing down of certain behaviours through education and socialization, are not inborn, and come to add themselves to the 'biological' acts, that is to say to a transmission of the 'phenotype to the phenotype' through the 'genotype' transmission.

Sometimes, the ambitions of sociobiologists go beyond the level of understanding of behavioural reproduction and bring them into the realm of anthropology. Thus, Alexander endeavours to explain with the principle of 'reproductive interest' the fact that in many 'archaic' societies the mother's brother substitutes himself for the father. Such societies could also be ones where fatherhood is generally unspecific. The 'reproductive interest' of the mother's brother towards the child is therefore much greater than any of the presumed father's interests. But, just as it is important to note that the mother's brother takes the father's place, particularly in societies where fatherhood is not clear, it is also important to note that the sociobiological hypothesis appears as an unnecessarily complex and fragile interpretation of the correlation. Similarly, sociobiologists try to explain the different ways that some societies treat their 'parallel' cousins and their 'cross' cousins (the first being considered closer than the second) by the principle of 'reproductive interest'. According to Alexander, the asymmetrical treatment of these two types of cousins would be observed especially within societies of 'sororal' polygeny. And, in this kind of society, parallel cousins can be genetically closer to each other than 'cross' cousins since, in opposition to 'cross' cousins, they can also be half-brothers.

The difference of treatment of these two types of cousins is known to be precisely one of the main arguments used by some anthropologists to give the prohibition of incest a cultural meaning. Thus, Lévi-Strauss explains the prohibition of incest as a way to ensure the movement of women across social units. But it must be said that, if Alexander's analysis is putting forward a valuable and interesting hypothesis, it does not reject a cultural interpretation of incest. In fact, Alexander's hypothesis, that is to say the correlation he shows between 'sororal polygeny' and the treatment of cousins, is not incompatible with Lévi-Strauss's views.

The war phenomenon, as observed in archaic societies, also interests sociobiologists who try here to combine biology and culture. Why is a violent and unprovoked aggressiveness observed among the Mundcuru and not among Eskimo's Durham wonders? Because in the first case, and not in the second, the general environment and the scarcity of animal proteins in particular make the individuals' reproductive interest better served by the elimination of competitors than, for instance, the impossible development of animal breeding. This is why the warrior who comes back with an enemy's head is given the title of 'mother of the pecari' which demonstrates the 'nutritional' function of murder. Harris's studies (1971) of the prohibition of cow's meat in India reach the same conclusions. Although such a tradition could appear irrational, such is not in fact the case. Cows produce manure which is indispensable to the country's agriculture; considered sacred, they keep Indians from giving up their vegetarian traditions and thus ensure a better adaptation of man to his environment. Besides, old cows supply meat for that society's outlaws. In fact, with analyses like these of Alexander, Durham, or Harris, we go beyond the sphere of sociobiology as such. Indeed, their analyses imply in no way whatsoever that the described selective mechanisms are 'natural'. These mechanisms can just as well – if not more easily – be understood as 'cultural'. Why should the 'interest' projected in the Mundcuru's institutions be interpreted by the 'instinct of reproduction' rather than by 'the will to survive'?

These examples are enough to show that human sociobiology cannot be compared without some distortion to the Social Darwinism introduced by Spencer in the nineteenth century. There is no question of sociobiology reducing man exclusively to his biological factors and even less of finding a 'scientific' basis to a doctrine favouring the survival of the fittest. There is also no attempt to deny the complexity of the complicated interaction between nature and culture. Sociobiology's objective is rather to attempt to integrate the biological factor with the human sciences, as far as it can be observed. As far as the animal is concerned, 'crucial' experiments prove that an extreme environmental theory like that of

Pavlov cannot explain some learning phenomena (Garcia). It is not wholly proven that one can explain human sexual attraction more easily by an environmentalist theory than by a sociobiological theory.

There is no doubt that sociobiology is only at its beginnings now and it does sometimes put forward some excessive theories. It certainly carries occasionally (like all sciences) some ideological elements and fails to realize that some phenomena which it is anxious to account for with the concept of 'natural mechanisms' can be explained more obviously by mechanisms of natural selection. Wilson may have a tendency to come to conclusions about other less clear-cut species after observing simple insects' behaviour. He may have a tendency to observe units of behaviours rather than the units within their complex structure. But it is not proved either that those criticizing sociobiology have no element of ideology in their own critique. If sociobiologists have talked a little too lightly about a 'new synthesis', Sahlin's hypothesis, according to which sociobiology would be simply a new form of the utilitarianism normally concocted by a competitive capitalist society, seems too simple. One thing has however become clear; it is the eagerness of sociobiologists to take scientific knowledge into account. It may be that sociobiology ends here and disappears. It might have to limit itself to simple animal societies. It is too early to say. We must remember that although it is built upon a scientific paradigm, the neo-Darwinist evolution theory, which has been disputably documented, has some weaknesses in its logical aspects, and might be open to abuse. Popper – maybe due to his bias towards Lamarck – had already observed the tautological characteristics of Darwinism. The same critique can be made of neo-Darwinism and of sociobiology which stems from it: observed behaviours are those that have been favoured by selection because they were the most successful in terms of reproduction. This basic principle of neo-Darwinism implies that any observed behaviour is by definition the most successful. A careful use of neo-Darwinist theory would be to use it as a hypothesis to validate a proposition empirically rather than as a general theory. Such use would eliminate the risks and pitfalls of tautology. But it leads to great practical difficulties, as it presupposes that it is possible to evaluate precisely the reproductive costs and benefits of such and such a type of behaviour, instead of accepting that the observed behaviour is by definition the most successful for the species rather than another postulated one. The success of sociobiology can be explained by.

1. the documented value of the neo-Darwinist theory of evolution on which it is built;
2. its attractiveness and its clarity when it is taken on a general level;
3. the theoretical and practical problems which prevent it from being used in an empirical fashion (i.e., as an hypothesis which can be proved or disproved), problems which allow its use on a speculative basis;
4. perhaps also because it allows the introduction of a little understanding of 'historical' developments depending partly on contingency (meeting of one specific species with one specific niche), the full understanding of which would presuppose the knowledge of facts which are impossible to have;

5. maybe also – but it is not certain that this aspect is essential and that it could in any case be put before any of the previous ones – because it sends us back to the typical myth of the best possible world.

The case of sociobiology thus illustrates a fundamental proposition of epistemology and of the sociology of knowledge, which is, as Durkheim remarked, that the frontiers between science and ideology can be very thin.

Action, Culturalism and Culture, Historicism, Ideologies, Rationality, Social Change, Teleology.

Bibliography

ALEXANDER, R.D., 'Evolution, human behaviour, and determinism', *in* SUPPE, F. and ASQUITH, P. (ed.), *PSA 1976*, Michigan, PSA, 1976, 3–21. – BARASH, D.P., *Sociobiology and behavior*, New York/Oxford/Amsterdam, Elsevier, 1977. – CHAUVIN, R., 'Sur le néodarwinisme dans les sciences du comportement', *Année biologique*, XIX, 2, 1980, 203–216. – DARWIN, C.R., *On the origins of species by means of natural selection, or the preservation of favoured races in the struggle for life*, London, Murray, 1859. – DURHAM, W.H., 'The adaptive significance of cultural behaviour', *Human ecology*, IV, 2, 1976, 89–121. – GARCIA, J., McGOWAN, B.K., and GREEN, K.F., 'Biological constraints on conditioning', *in* BLACK, A.H. and PROKASY, W.F. (ed.), *Classical conditioning. II: Current research and theory*, New York, Appleton, 1972. – HAMILTON, W.D., 'The genetical theory of social behaviour. I', *Journal of theoretical biology*, VII, 1964, 1–16; 'The genetical theory of social behaviour. II.', *Journal of theoretical biology*, VII, 1964, 17–32. – HARRIS, M., *Culture, man and nature: an introduction to general anthropology*, New York, Crowell, 1971. – MAYNARD SMITH, J., 'The theory of games and the evolution of animal conflict', *Journal of theoretical biology*, XLVII, 1974, 209–221. – RUSE, M., *Sociobiology: sense or nonsense?*, Dordrecht/Boston/London, Reidel, 1979. – SAHLINS, M.D., *The use and abuse of biology. An anthropological critique of sociobiology*, Ann Arbor, The University of Michigan Press, 1976; London, Tavistock, 1977.

Spencer, Herbert

Who killed Herbert Spencer (1820–1903)? This contemporary of Marx attracted the cream of American society when he gave lectures in the USA; as early as 1854, in *Social Statics*, he proposed the hypotheses of evolution found again in 1857 in Darwin's *Origin of Species*. With Comte, he is the only sociologist listed in both philosophy and sociology textbooks. His main work is a *Treatise of Philosophy* in ten volumes, four of which deal with *Principles of Sociology*. Many terms, ideas, and concepts that he used or that he offered to use are still found in contemporary sociology.

In favour of limiting the power of the State, convinced that an 'industrial society' cannot flourish if the State takes over powers which are not its right, Spencer's influence on the élites of industrial societies has not survived the continuous growth of the State in democratic regimes from the 1920s until today. Neither did it survive among professional sociologists, particularly in France, especially because of the successful critique of Durkheim. Like Weber, Simmel, or Tarde, Spencer, in France, is a victim of the orthodoxy of Durkheim and his followers, an orthodoxy which they succeeded in imposing on French sociology over a long period of time. But in England, Germany, and the US, Spencer still counts among the great names of classical sociology.

In the *Principles of Sociology*, Spencer writes that the presence of sects and schools of thought is a specific trait of centralized societies, where the competition of ideas is problematic, and where some have the power to operate a quiet censorship over opinions that they find unconformist. He pointed out that there were more different schools of thought in England than in France. This idea can almost be seen as divinatory since Spencer's influence was great enough in France for all but a few of his works to have been translated while he was alive or shortly after his death. However, he was later carefully kept under constant scrutiny by France's own schools of thought.

Spencer is known mostly as a pioneer of evolutionary or evolutionist sociology: through differentiation and through grouping, societies tend to progress from simple to complex structures. When social density increases (an idea which appears often in Spencer's works and which will later play a central part in Durkheim's *Division of Labour* as we know), social roles tend to differentiate and split, and the division of labour to increase. But differentiation is not the only mechanism which characterizes the trend from simple to complex. The conquest of territory, integrating one population with another, brings a process of differentiation into the new society that is being created. Spencer here puts forward an idea which will play an essential role in the nineteenth century, an idea whose history was studied carefully by Hannah Arendt in *Imperialism*: the idea that distinctions between 'classes' are often the result of conquest. However Spencer does not put forward this idea as one-sidedly as Thierry for instance, and for Spencer, 'classes' can be the result of either differentiation or aggregation: the two can be observed in history and there are no reasons to favour either 'exogenous' (Thierry) or 'endogenous' theories (Durkheim) on this point.

In general, what is striking about Spencer's evolutionism is its great caution. Three points best illustrate this caution. First, if there are laws of evolution or rather – since Spencer prefers to use the singular – a law of evolution, the latter depends on the 'diverse conditions' which promote it or hinder it. 'The living conditions of a particular society' can be 'favourable or unfavourable to the maintenance of a large population', 'inter-relationships can be made more or less difficult inside a territory thus promoting or hindering co-operation'. Therefore, evolution does not appear as an inevitable happening. In short, Spencer's law of evolution is a 'model' (using a new sociological word here) which should not be interpreted too realistically.

The second point is extremely important, for the types of societies defined by Spencer must not be taken too literally. One of the constant traits of sociology is an opposition described by different words but found in many works: societies with mechanical co-operation/societies with organic co-operation (Durkheim), *Gemeinschaft/Gesellschaft* (Tönnies), folk/urban society (Redfield), 'traditional' societies/'modern' societies. Before that, Spencer had offered 'military' societies against 'industrial societies'. But the distinction between the two does not sound as utopian as *Gemeinschaft/Gesellschaft*, nor is it as materialistic as that of Durkheim or the conventional dichotomy of traditional/modern societies. A new concept can be used here to describe this opposition of 'military' and 'industrial' using Weber's notion of 'ideal types'.

What favours this interpretation is first that Spencer reiterates the fact that one society can have traits of both 'industrial' and 'military' types. So, there is nothing to say that armed battles between 'industrial' societies will ever cease and that an industrial society will never need to make the decisions of 'coercion' which characterize a 'military' society. Similarly, competition between industrial societies can lead to a policy of protectionism, and to the coercive power of the State being increased, and thus constitute a movement towards a 'military' type of society (this is one of the theories that Schumpeter will expand on in his theory of imperialism). The words 'military' and 'industrial' are very abstract notions in Spencer's vocabulary and describe two idealistic limits of an ongoing process characterized by the degree of coercion, maximal or minimal, that a social system, through its various structures and institutions, exerts upon its members.

The hypothesis that these famous notions must be seen as 'idealistic' rather than 'descriptive' notions is confirmed by a second point Spencer emphasizes, that is to say that the two types – military and industrial – are not easy to isolate in a process of ongoing evolution. Evidently, Spencer thinks that the 'industrial' type is bound to increase. But both types are found in the most remote historical times, as well as in the most recent. Classical Sparta like modern Russia (Spencer here leans particularly on Custine's accounts) belongs more to the 'military' type. So the laws of evolution cannot be applied in a systematic fashion and nothing precludes the creation in the modern world of 'military' societies.

> What shows that the ideal state of people condemning competition is a military one is first that communism existed in primitive societies, which were mainly war orientated, and secondly that nowadays, plans for communism are mainly found in military societies and find a fertile ground there.

Just as they are found in the modern world, the two types are also found in 'traditional' societies. Here Spencer gives many examples that he takes from ethnography, of small tribes submitting themselves to a decentralized state since they do not need to fight their neighbours. They benefit from a non-coercive regime and are thus illustrating 'some species of industrial society'. Such is the case, according to Spencer, of the 'Pueblos' in New Mexico.

A third point that makes Spencer's evolutionism 'prudent' is that he is very aware of the complexity of social determinisms. Individuals tend to adapt themselves to the social system to which they belong. In a 'military' regime they tend to have the submissive behaviour characterizing the whole system. On the contrary in an 'industrial' regime, they are encouraged to show their inventive qualities and their initiative. In each case, individual behaviour either helps or hinders the creation or the preservation of such a social system. But the link is not a necessary one. Individual behaviour and social structures can both vary without following strict mechanical rules, for other elements come into them: the correlation between social system and environment, how large the particular society is, diversity, etc. Finally, these variations make up a very complex system with unpredictable regressive effects: individuals' actions depend on the social structures, but these actions then affect these structures and these echoing effects depend on other 'variables' – as we would say today – which characterize the system's structure and its relations to its environment.

Finally, Spencer thinks that, in a complicated system, the consequences of a change, because they can happen fast, are difficult to predict. He prefers to leave enough room for western theories, like that of Millar, on the birth of freedom in England. He also stresses that the form of the political regime is not the consequence of a rigid determinism.

There can be no doubt that Spencer's evolutionism is much more complex and subtle than Comte's or Durkheim's for instance. Like Marx, Spencer realizes that the change or preservation of a structure depends on relations of causality between the individual and the system. But he sees more clearly than Marx the difficulties of prediction in sociology and goes further than simply acknowledging the fact that laws in sociology can apply only to 'tendencies'. He clearly accepts – although he does not use the word which had not then appeared in the vocabulary of social science – that evolutionary laws are like ideal 'models' and that they do not enable us to predict history, since the process in reality depends on facts and circumstances that one can observe but hardly anticipate. The world, in its concrete variety and history, in its complexity, plays a greater part in Spencer's work than in Marx's or especially in Durkheim's. And the system's 'spirit' – since this nineteenth-century thinker certainly allots a role to the 'spiritual' aspect the system – is counterbalanced by the trouble he takes to base his theories on a considerable body of literature, particularly ethnographic, and to a small degree historical. This painstaking method of basing theories upon as wide a range of sources as possible reminds us of Montesquieu and Weber.

Ironically, and Spencer could have been either disappointed or encouraged by this, the trouble he took to refer to facts, the huge work of research he did to write *Principles of Sociology* are also the reasons why his influence faded since his sources became obsolete. For Spencer's sources play a much greater part in his works than they do in, for example, Durkheim's *The Division of Labour*.

The use of induction leads in any case to one fundamental consequence: Spencer was driven to a form of evolutionism with traces of relativism. The same inductive method is seen in many pages of *A Study of Sociology*, a methodological study where Spencer describes and classifies the various traps encountered by a sociologist, as a citizen as well as a politician, when he attempts to interpret or make conclusions. First, he might not be able to measure the part played by his own prejudices. There are class prejudices and 'socio-centric' prejudices, political and religious ones, too. Moreover, he might have some technical problems, called by Spencer 'objective' problems so as to differentiate them from the 'subjective' problems which deal with prejudices.

One of these problems is today, for instance, that of drawing unjustified causal conclusions from a 'statistical correlation'. Thus, Bertillon observed that more unmarried people died early than married ones and concluded that marriage was good for you (by the way, Spencer, who died at 83 in spite of health problems – the famous 'mischief' – was not married). The difference is true for all ages and the protection that marriage offers – as Durkheim would later write – appears stronger for men. Spencer, using reasoning similar to Durkheim's in *Suicide*, shows this conclusion to be a fallacy. The correlation does not prove the causality. Those who have money have more chance of getting married than others. They are also more likely to lead a healthier life mentally and physically. Here Spencer was using a type of analysis later called 'multivariate'. It is not impossible that Durkheim, who had read Spencer extensively, had been directly inspired by him in the subtle statistical methodology that he uses in *Suicide*.

Without falling into an over-used interpretation, we might inquire whether Durkheim attacked Spencer so much precisely because he owed him so much. It is a typical rule of the intellectual game to become well known by opposing another well-known figure. Of course Durkheim opposed Spencer on ideological grounds as well. But the ideas of 'social function' and 'social regulation', the organicist analogies which are so important in Durkheim's works, are also found in Spencer's. Theories of differentiations and of the division of labour, the idea of 'density' also come from Spencer. Durkheim's criticism of Spencer's artificiality in the division of labour has little foundation. Of course, Spencer notes that the division of labour has its advantages. But he does not ever say that the anticipation of these advantages is the reason for the division of labour. He rather hypothesized that, when 'circumstances' or an endogenous evolution create beneficial conditions, providing new opportunities for instance, as we would say today, it can lead to a modification and an intensification of the division of labour which might persist because of the advantages it brings for everyone. This is indeed Spencer's recurring theme, i.e., the aggregation of many actions lead to 'unplanned' effects, which can then be changed voluntarily should they not be desirable. Spencer also notes that then a 'planned' change can lead in its turn to 'unplanned' effects. This explains why law, a sign of these interferences, is always developing. In any case, Spencer was well aware that a contract rests on 'pre-contractual' elements. This formula, both attractive and obscure, is not only a figure of speech, but its meaning is explained clearly and at length in *Principles of Sociology*, and Spencer often criticizes directly the 'artificiality' of the theoreticians of the contract. No more than Durkheim did Spencer realize that the constructions of classical contractual political philosophy could be seen, not as realistic description, but as models on which to base analysis and reasoning.

Spencer clearly inspired Durkheim on another issue. In his sociology of religion, he attempts to show that beliefs, far from being superstitutions are schematic interpretations developed by human beings to master their environment. As societies develop, as sciences and techniques progress, these religious representations change. In a complex society God can no longer rule over everyday life and cannot rule every circumstance. Religion's potential for intervention is then limited and no longer has the power to dictate to 'non-religious' bodies. However, even in modern societies, the power of governments extends only into spheres of life that are not yet regulated by tradition. Religion is not a super-stition for Spencer but it is not either, as Durkheim will later understand, the worshipping of *society*. Although Spencer's analyses inspired Durkheim, they are here closer in spirit to those of Max Weber.

So, Spencer had realized, much more clearly than Durkheim, that the laws of evolution could only be projective 'models' which could be constantly overthrown by contingencies and 'circumstances'. But he did not realize as clearly as the class-ical German sociologists will realize later (Max Weber and Simmel in particular) that theoretical constructions of social sciences are 'ideal' as Weber puts it, or 'for-mal' as Simmel does. Spencer is however perfectly aware of the difference between realism and nominalism and of its relevance to sociology. He asks explicitly in his study of the principles of sociology whether 'society' exists or whether it is rather a reasoning being. His answer to that is not nominalist, but is on the other hand very different from that of Durkheim. 'Society' as defined by Durkheim and his follow-ers is nonsensical for Spencer; never does Spencer use phrases such as 'society aspires to . . .', 'society highly regards . . .', 'society formally expresses its inter-est in . . .' found in their works. For Spencer there is not 'one' society, so this concept cannot be materialistically portrayed, but 'many' societies. These societies being 'teleonomic' and not 'teleological' as we would say now. They 'exist' in so far as they are more or less permanent 'groupings', more or less stable systems of relationships between individuals, which persist in spite of the constant change in their constituent elements – human beings.

If Spencer is aware of the trap of 'realism' and if he notices that the laws of evolution apply only if the 'circumstances' are right, his theory of social evolution contains nevertheless an ambiguity: evolution goes through specific processes, linked to specific contexts. Thus, social evolution reached a new stage when money brought people's freedom, since the fact of paying the landlord with money rather than with products gave the farmer a certain leeway in his farm manage-ment. But if some of these mechanisms tend to become popular, either because they give a society where they happen a competitive advantage or because their advantages are obvious to that society, their generalization is by no means typical, even as a tendency. On the contrary, Spencer says that adverse tendencies could appear and gain strength progressively thanks to the process of 'self-maintenance' which makes 'social growth stagnate'. Thus, evolution leads, as we have seen before, to societies of 'military' or 'industrial' types. However, when a society becomes more complex, the 'regulation function' could become overwhelming. The corresponding parts of that society tend then to fix themselves in a particular form. When a government takes on tasks which are not in its proper sphere and which could be done more efficiently by private enterprise, there is an increase in the number of civil servants. Since all social categories develop an *ésprit de corps* and tend to defend this body of interest and its values (interests and opinions being seen here as depending on each other), civil servants will push for the government to acquire new domains of responsibility, thus again increasing the number of their members. Spencer has been thinking of nineteenth-century France, of course.

Spencer does not say that, according to the law of evolution, French society should become less bureaucratic; quite the opposite. If a system lasts, it tends to generate adaptation behaviours which in their turn contribute to the persistence of the system. This is why Spencer can see Comte's reorganization plan as an ideal type of 'military' society in line with the traditional French bureaucracy. He also notes with disquiet that in Prussia, and then in Germany, Bismarck gave the State social responsibilities and he fears there too the appearance of self-generated mechanisms leading to an excessive development of the sections corresponding to these social functions. when such excessive development occurs, situations such as that of Egypt under the Roman Empire are reached where taxes were so high that the State had to give special grants to farmers so that they could buy their seed. Spencer has therefore little sympathy with the German socialists 'who are thought to want and think they ought to re-organize society entirely' and who suggest 'a system where life and work are ruled by public authorities'. Incapable 'of rejecting the type of society in which they have been brought up . . . they put forward a system which is in fact nothing but the same system under a different order'.

The beneficial functioning of the laws of evolution is therefore not guaranteed: many evolutionary processes can be described, but a move back towards the 'military' type of society is never ruled out.

In spite of this, Spencer believed in evolution. The law of evolution seems to govern not only societies but the universe, not only the 'supra-organic' but also the organic. This is why the 'principles of sociology' come after the 'principles of biology'. In the *Principles of Sociology*, Spencer constantly talks of analogies between biological and sociological phenomena, the notions of balance, differentiation, organism can be applied to both spheres of study. But although they can be used in both cases, Spencer stresses that we are only talking of analogies and a demarcation must be clearly made. A society is an 'organism' but only in an analogical way. Here too he is careful to avoid 'realistic' interpretations of the intelligible schemes that he creates and his 'functionalism' is much more relative than that of Durkheim or of Radcliffe-Brown for instance.

In the *First Principles* introducing the *Treatise* of which *Principles of Sociology* forms a part, Spencer says that the law of evolution is comparable to a little window through which the unknown, although unknown, shows its existence. He has a completely different view of the relationship between sciences and religion than Comte has: the development of sciences does not lead at all towards the disappearance of religion, although evolution leads to a modification of the representation of the divine man. First coming from the world itself, what is godly tends to lose its humanity, then become transcendent and finally have the shape of the unknown.

'Who now reads Spencer?' says Parsons in the first sentence of *The Structure of Social Action*, but is it certain that he is entirely buried?

Durkheim, Historicism, Social Change, Teleology.

Bibliography

SPENCER, H., *The principles of sociology: a quarterly serial*, New York, D. Appleton, 1874–1875. – SPENCER,

H., *Principles of sociology*, London, Macmillan, 1969, 1 vol. – SPENCER, H., *First principles*, London, Williams & Norgate, 1862. – ARENDT, H., *L'imperialisme*, Paris, Fayard 1982. – BIERSTEDT, R., 'Theories of progress, development, evolution', *in* BOTTOMORE, T. and NISBET, R. (ed.), *The history of sociological analysis*, New York, Basic Books, 1978, 39–79; London Heinemann, 1979. – CAMPBELL, D., 'Variation and selective retention in socio-cultural evolution', *General Systems*, XIV, 1969, 69–80. – COSER, L., 'Spencer' *in* COSER, L., *Masters of sociological thought*, New York/Chicago/San Francisco/ Atlanta, Harcourt Brace, 1971, 89–127. – DURKHEIM, E., *De la division du travail social*. – HOFSTADTER, R., *Social darwinism in American thought*, New York, Braziller, 1944, 1959. – MILLAR, J., *An historical view of the English government*, London, J. Maruman, 1812. – PARSONS, T., *The structure of social action*, Glencoe, The Free Press, 1937, 1964; London, McGraw Hill, 1937. – SCHNEIDER, L., 'Dialectic in sociology', *American sociological review*, XXXVI, 4, 1971, 667–678.

State, The

To define the State is an almost impossible task. At least three types of difficulty are encountered. First, it associates in an arbitrary manner the normative viewpoint and the descriptive viewpoint. For example, when we speak of a constitutional state – the *Reichsstaat* of the Germans, the *constitutional government* – is an ideal political organization being put forward? Or is the practice of moderate governments being aimed at? Second, the State can designate an historically defined political form. The evolutionists and the Marxists, in the otherwise arguable sense that Marxism is evolutionary, have emphasized the fact that the appearance of the State is linked to certain circumstances which can be dated, and that its 'decline' cannot fail to occur once the conditions have disappeared – notably in the area of production – which preceded its coming into being. Finally, the definition of the State poses a problem concerning the listing and morphology of its organs: by State, should only government be understood? Must the bureaucracy, the judiciary also be included in its definition? What relationship do these specialized organs have between themselves? What relationship do they have with civil society? Even if the State is claimed to be only the entirety of governors, and of the resources which they can mobilize to serve their power, should it be said that the State is nothing more than a 'repressive apparatus' with the help of which the 'dominant' exploit the 'dominated'? Whatever the situation, whatever answers can be given to these questions, we must take the greatest care to avoid ideological stereotypes about the State such as 'rational providence', or of the State as reduced in certain texts by Nietzsche to being 'the coldest of cold monsters'.

To start with the *morphology of the modern state*. Among the activities which it exercises, certain seem to be appropriate to it alone. It is difficult to imagine national defence, the organization of the police, the establishment and the recovery of taxes being the concern of an authority other than that of the State. All the same, many European states relied for a long time on mercenaries for their defence. Thus, it could also be imagined that policing could be put in the hands of private, paid companies. To a great extent the collection of the taxes of the French monarchy was assigned to the *Fermiers Generaux*. Finally, even if the king of France was a judge, justice was rendered in his name by magistrates whom he did not appoint, and, even though they were state servants, the judges saw their independence from the government affirmed and, theoretically at least, guaranteed by their security of tenure. Therefore the State does not always *itself* accomplish all the tasks which result from its sovereignty. Besides, particularly today, among the tasks with which it is charged, certain could be done as well, and even sometimes much better, by private individuals. There is no reason why the education of the young should be a state monopoly or even that the activities of teaching and research should benefit from financial aid from the State only if the teachers are recruited by, and the teaching programmes fixed, by it. In many countries, private schools and universities exist which are also partly maintained by state funds. It should not be concluded from this that in these countries the State is indifferent to the training of the young. Even in this domain, it can abstain from direct management, by fixing by way of law or rules, by incentive, dissuasion, or prohibition, certain objectives and procedures to which it attaches value.

The demarcation between the activities which can manifestly depend only on the State – and on it alone – and activities which in no situation fall within its competence is very uneasy, as can still be seen by the debates on the spread of the nationalized sector in industry. According to the preamble to the 1946 Constitution in France, monopolies and public services are 'cut out' to be nationalized. But the opposition between competition and monopoly is no more enlightening than the idea of public service. It is true that imperfect markets exist, with oligopolies and monopolistic competition. In order to correct these imperfections, should these activities be placed under state control? 'Nationalize' them? Put them under 'state control'? Control them by 'anti-trust' legislation under the supervision of the courts? And above all, what meaning should these expressions be given?

The State, which we believe to be so easily enclosed in repressive institutions (barracks, prisons, courts), conceals itself from our pursuit. The jailer disguises himself as a philanthropist. The sums which are taken from the individual market in the form of duties and taxes constitute an impressive and altogether burdensome amount for the taxpayers. But these deductions are often only the counterpart of his benefits. What it takes from us with one hand, it gives back to us with the other – at least, what it has taken from me, it returns, in whole or in part, to others. On one hand, the State cuts off. In this respect, it is punitive – even more so because it can oblige us to pay, if we evade. But on the other hand, it increases our resources, either directly by transfers and redistributions, or by putting at our disposition a certain number of common assets such as security, liberty, protection from strangers and enemies.

The development of social services (health, education, the generalization of insurance), which, without all being always and everywhere directly managed by the State, are financed by it in a growing proportion, has often been interpreted as a calculation, or a trick, by which the 'dominant class', thanks to certain concessions which are more symbolic than real, purchases the resignation of the dominated class. The social services would be the spoonful of honey which would surround the bitter pill of 'repression'. It was believed that this picture could be refined by treating all the ideologies of redistribution, even the most radical, as a supplementary trick by which 'the dominant faction of the dominant class', abusing the ingenuousness of the 'dominated faction of the dominant class' (the intellectuals), and, above all, exploiting their appetite for upward social mobility, 'reproduces' indefinitely and identically the 'structure of domination'. The politics of employment, of Keynesian inspiration, the programmes of educational action, both training and schooling, would only be a trap by which the modern state, under a new disguise, would continue to fulfil its repressive function. These interpretations are not acceptable. First, we might ask ourselves if the *welfare state* does do the business of capitalism so well. The debate remains open between the upholders of interventionism and their liberal and neo-liberal critics. Second, the historical conditions in which the welfare state was introduced in our western societies are very far from justifying the Machiavellianism so generously imputed to capitalists. Keynes complained of their blindness, of their inability to see that their interest, if clearly understood, must lead them to accept a certain redistribution of income, incidentally more prejudicial to *rentiers* (persons of independent means) than to 'speculators' or 'entrepreneurs'. As for the hypothesis of 'reproduction' deliberately pursued by state apparatus, this has two essential weaknesses. First, it ignores incontestable facts such as the changes which occurred in the structure of the working population and in the social origins of the users of the school and university systems. Following de Tocqueville, Jouvenel showed that the growth of the power of the State occurs to the detriment of the traditional élites and to the advantage of those categories, if not the most underprivileged, at least the most active and the most ambitious. The alliance of the crown and the urban middle-class against the nobility is a commonplace of French historiography. The present situation created by the multiplication of public interventions can be characterized by three traits: the increase in the number of bureaucrats and agents of the State, the creation of clienteles connected to the great public services, the increase in the share of the national product and income deducted by the State. It is difficult to present these three effects as necessarily contributing to reinforce capitalist 'domination'. Decidedly, it is no simpler to say 'what is the State for?' than to identify its organs.

What makes our difficulty even greater is that under the description of State, we include the governed as well as the governors, that is to say all the people who are concerned by political activity, as much in their capacity of 'bourgeois' as that of 'citizens'. All who are governed are both citizen and bourgeois. By *bourgeois* is understood private individuals in as much as they mainly occupy themselves with their businesses, their profits, their unearned income as well as their salaries, but also everything which in public life affects their well-being and that of their families. By *citizens* is understood the same persons, but in so far as they concern themselves with what affects them in as much as they constitute a political body. It must be added that if the bourgeois are subject to orders coming from on high, in our capacity as citizens, we participate in the exercise of sovereignty, since by our votes we are the creators of the laws which we obey. On the other hand, the governors have authority over the governed – and in this respect they are commanders; but their authority is not arbitrary. Even among absolutist theoreticians, the king has to account to God, to his people, to history. Hobbes elaborates a very subtle interpretation of the interests of the 'public person' which, in the monarch, are not confused with those of the private individual who has assumed the crown.

The State can be defined by the interdependence that is established between rulers and ruled, and its action is likely to affect all dimensions of social life – whether it concerns civil society or the 'republic of the mind'. Even if it does not involve itself with spiritual power, the State plays its part in the exercise of that power, as can be seen by the often delicate relationship with the churches, because of the responsibilities which it assumes in the area of education, by its interventions, and possibly the censorship which it exercises in the domain of 'morality'. The action of the State is diffused among all of society. According to a constant tradition, the 'governors' are supposed to act only for the good of the 'governed', and not in their private interest. But a very serious difficulty is raised when, as is the case in modern regimes, the same people are both governors and the governed. Furthermore, among the governors, we have no difficulty in recognizing very different categories: politicians, higher civil servants, the leaders of parties – those of the majority, certainly, but also those of the opposition, above all when the demarcation line between government and opposition is rather vague – leaders of pressure groups, unionists, and at the limit the persons of note of all kinds. Nor do the 'governed' constitute a more amorphous and undifferentiated mass. They take an interest and they participate in a very unequal manner in the life of the State. The famous distinction between 'active citizens' and 'passive citizens' does not only have a meaning in a censitory regime (where suffrage is based on property qualification). It casts light equally upon the differences of behaviour, of motivation, and of intention, between the citizens who are content to vote and those who do not vote, between the electors and the militants.

However, whatever the obscurity which affects the distinction between 'governors' and 'governed', it remains probably the most pertinent for taking a view of the totality of questions relative to the State. It has been elaborated in a methodical manner in the *contractualist tradition*. In effect, the explicit ambition which the contractualist theoreticians set out is to outline in a manner as precise as possible the rights and duties of citizens towards the State, to assign to it defined limits of its legitimate intervention. Without doubt Hobbes, Locke, Rousseau have strongly divergent ideas on the nature of the social contract. The first sees in the State the reward given to each of us in return for the renunciation of our rights, that is to say the power that we hold from nature. The second sees in government the extension and the consolidation of peaceful exchanges between men in the state of nature.

But these theoreticians are, despite everything, in agreement on a certain number of essential points. First, the State possesses the capacity of possibly obliging individuals to conform to the rules of conduct which it has decreed. But it does not exercise this power in an *arbitrary* manner, according to caprice and in the interests of the governors, or in an *absolute* manner, that is to say without taking into account the rights and interests of the governed. Even if it is seen as sovereign, by Rousseau for example, the modern state is *constitutional*, in the sense that its functioning is subordinate to explicit rules of functioning and also, more radically, in the sense that the governors are only, as Rousseau again says, *the assistants* of the sovereign. The modern state can thus be characterized, in so far as it has been fashioned by the contractualist tradition, with the aid of three characteristics. It has force at its disposal as a last resort over a given territory and a given population. It exercises this last resort power, that one can call sovereignty, over individuals and groups which fall within its jurisdiction, but it also exercises it against other states. However, sovereignty can be called absolute only in a clearly defined sense. It cannot be confounded with the arbitrariness of governors. 'Such is our pleasure' does not signify that the king acts only at his caprice. This expression signifies that in certain domains no authority can be opposed to his and that he is not obliged to account for himself to anyone. Sovereignty is not an absolute power strictly speaking; it is a discretionary power. Finally, the power of the State is not all-absorbing compared with the power of private individuals. It does not annul this any more than it renders it infinite. The distinction between the public and the private is variable, but a reserved area always survives, a *heart of hearts*, which no citizen is in a position to renounce. The possibility of a critical judgement by the citizens does not constitute a very effective guarantee against despotism or tyranny. But it obliges the governors to be reasonable, or at least to seek to pass as being so, in putting their power to the proof of legitimation.

As soon as we examine them with a little care, the formulas which define the relationship between the governors and the governed seem to be of an impenetrable obscurity. According to Rousseau, the governors are *delegates* but not *representatives*, while, in the liberal tradition, representation is spread out in a sufficiently extensive manner to allow the governors, under the control of the governed, an altogether appreciable margin of initiative. All the same, a point which is common to Rousseau as to Montesquieu, to Hobbes as to Locke survives, that is, that the State *must* not constitute a reality in itself, that the sources, the methods, and the limits of its action cannot be sought elsewhere than in the same characteristics of interaction between individuals which make it up. Hobbes stresses in particular the *artificial* character of the State, which excludes the possibility that a self-sustaining entity might be made of it. This is what is expressed by the very image of *Leviathan*, a monster created by individuals themselves, of which the all-powerful nature is only the counterpart of their impotence. Rousseau stresses the 'denaturalization' which the attachment of individuals to the Republic presupposes, which means both that the existence of the State creates specific obligations on private individuals, but also that the obligations of citizens to the State are in the final analysis no more than their obligations to each other. Thus obedience to law, that is to the general will, would be the highest expression of individual liberty. These formulas have the merit of seeking to express, even if in an obscure fashion, a certain *consubstantiality* of the Republic and of citizens or, if we wish, the immanence of the citizens in the State. But this relationship. like all immanent relationships, is extremely ambiguous. I am not the French republic, any more, incidentally, than Louis XIV was the State. However I am, as a French citizen, *partially* identified, in my interests, in my opinions, in my personal destiny, with that Republic. What must be seen clearly is that, despite its obscurity, this formula is again the least inadequate for explaining the phenomenon of civil obedience in societies like our own where the modern conception of the State is in the profound sense of the term a secular and relativist conception. Secular because at its limits the State has no transcendent ends, or at least that its ends, if it has any, are no more than *emergent* combinations of those of private individuals, and, in this respect, they are always *relative* to the latter.

From the point of view of the governors, the image which best sums up this idea of the State is that of an *arbitrator*, in the strongest meaning of that term. Three things should be understood by the arbitrator. It means a person who has the ability to lay down the law. In this respect, the arbitrator is distinct from the mediator. Unlike the latter, he does not wait to offer his services until the litigants ask him to help them reach a mutually acceptable compromise. Second, the arbitrator has direct or indirect means of enforcing his sentence: he does not depend upon the acquiescence and the goodwill of parties who can always refuse to put into effect the compromise proposed by the mediator. Finally, the arbitrator acts according to the principle of reciprocity. He does not seek arrangements where 'each puts a little of what he has'; he decides according to the principle of 'to each according to his due'. On all the evidence, the modern state is not an arbitrator in the strict sense of the word, as the often unfair distribution of public resources shows, as does the bias of much legislation in favour of the 'privileged'. Furthermore, the metaphor of the arbitrator is hardly compatible with what history teaches of the origins of the modern state. It has often been advantageous to the king of France to put himself forward as a judge. But the fact that the French monarchs have come to impose themselves by holding the balance equal between the nobles and the middle class does not allow us to forget the legal inferiority in which most of those subject to the judicial system were maintained. Even so, it is as both judge and arbiter that the modern state, even when it takes the form of a so-called 'absolute' monarchy, presents itself in order to claim the title of legitimacy to which it might otherwise be doubted that it fully had the right. This conception of the State as a dispenser of justice, if we dare say so, is met with again among positivist lawyers. According to Leon Duguit, for example, what founds the power of the State is the capacity to redistribute in an equitable manner, by means of public services, a part of the collective resources.

The rule of reciprocity appears to be the principle which is likely to rationalize and universalize social relationships, between which the State exercises its arbitrating authority. The 'disadvantages of the natural state', to which, according to Locke, 'civil government must provide a remedy', arise because each individual is inclined to act in an exaggerated fashion in his own interest. In order to avoid the clashes which inevitably result from the excessive attachment of each person to himself, the intervention of an 'impartial and disinterested third party', capable of rendering to each party his due, to assure to individuals who have been robbed the goods of which they have been deprived by violence or trickery, is advisable, and even perhaps necessary. But the analogy between the arbiter and the governor is of limited relevance. The authority of the arbiter in private law can only be exercised in specific areas, and generally only for a fixed period. Besides, nothing guarantees that an all-powerful arbitrator will always behave as an 'impartial and disinterested third party'. This risk becomes more serious depending upon how closely the vital interests of the litigants are involved in the matter upon which the arbitrator is exercising his authority. The abuses for which the government can be responsible, if we entrust ourselves to it, do not only concern its power to punish, and more generally to repress deviations from the social norm; they also concern its power to redistribute resources for the benefit of certain members of society and to the detriment of others. How can the risk of an improper redistribution be avoided, if by putting the pseudo-arbitrary authority of governors above private interests, we give them the power, under the protection of law, to take from some to give to others? This menace is very imperfectly controlled in the modern state. Rousseau's famous fable shows that hunters have an interest in accepting a common discipline if they prefer not to return empty-handed to the house. But a condition is necessary: which is that everyone gets his share at the moment of the distribution of the catch. Without doubt restitutions exist, redistributions and sanctions which cause the prejudices, egotism, and bad faith of the arbitrator to burst out, rather than the detachment which we have the right to expect of an 'impartial and disinterested third party'.

The only way to protect ourselves against the risk of a corruption of the arbitration function would be to arrange it so that the services rendered by the State could never be imposed upon private individuals by force, but that they would always have the option of refusing them or, if they wished to use them, possibly to obtain them from agencies other than the State. This is the meaning of the idea put forward by Robert Nozick, of an *ultra-minimal state* or a *hyperminimal state*, which must not be confused with the *night watchman state*. In effect, in this last metaphor, what is taken into consideration is the spread of the domain in which the State exercises its functions, much more than the manner in which these services are rendered to private individuals and financed by them. What mattered to Nozick is to preserve the contractual and non-constraining character of the relationship between the State and the citizens. The references to certain anthropological data (Clastre) enable this idea of a hyperminimal state to be grasped, which would provide, if one can say so, on request, the 'public benefits' which are procured in a peremptory and obligatory manner by the modern state – whether socialist or liberal.

The path taken by Nozick and the anarcho-liberals – and which Nozick himself qualifies as utopian – is that of a state which would agree systematically to offer its own services in competition with those who would also offer voluntary associations to private individuals. Can the State renounce *all* privileges in the provision of *all* services? This is what the anarcho-liberal 'utopia' would affirm. It is doubtless true for certain public services that it would be altogether possible to 'denationalize' them or, rather, to 'take them out of state control'. There can be great advantages in giving the state a monopoly of the services of health, transport, or education. But nobody would say that this solution is the only possible one and that a state would cease to be a state if it gave up the management of them. Would it be the same if the State accepted that *its* police, *its* army enter into competition with police forces or armies recruited, paid, and employed by associations of private individuals?

A positive response meets with the scepticism of those who, like Max Weber, see in the State the authority which, in a given country, has a monopoly as far as the employment of legitimate force is concerned. Max Weber's formula, it is true, is not entirely convincing. What should be understood by 'legitimate force'? If we wish to say that, in a given country, a certain number of authorities are in a position to oblige, possibly by force, individuals who are recalcitrant about paying their taxes, serving in the army, serving prison sentences imposed by a judge, we can agree in calling these authorities the State, and we can also observe that, as long as they are not effectively put into check by organized resistance, they really benefit from a monopoly in the use of force. It can even be added that this employment of force is, except for a minority of anarcho-liberals, generally held to be 'legitimate'. But many activities which are the concern of the State require neither the employment nor even the threat of force. They only imply it in a very indirect and very derivative manner. Or rather, they only imply it as far as their conclusions and their procedures are conflictive and find themselves effectively disputed. Rigorously to accept Weber's formula thus does no more than beg the question. The State, in so far as it is not of a contractual nature, is based upon force. The weakness of the Weberian formula is perceptible if instead of the expression 'employment of legitimate force' that of 'employment of power' is substituted – which at first sight appears to be equivalent to the former. However, it is very clear that the State cannot be adequately defined by the monopoly of *power*. It is in effect only too obvious that in every society, powers exist – legitimate, if not effective – other than that of the State.

Even so, it is altogether impossible to be content with Nozick's hyper-contractualism. In effect, when we claim to limit the State to a voluntary association like others, which would agree to offering all its services in competition with those of other voluntary associations, we meet with a fundamental difficulty which it is easy to analyse in the light of Olson's paradox: how could public resources (in particular security from violent people from the interior and the exterior) be effectively and regularly furnished by institutions which could not mobilize any force faced with citizens who showed themselves to be recalcitrant in paying for the services of which in other respects they would be the beneficiaries? The number of people who in effect suffer the assaults of thieves is limited. Will those who have not yet suffered in this way, and who estimate, rightly or wrongly, that their chances of being robbed are small, voluntarily accept paying the sum for the police required to assure their security?

There is only one way of getting out of the vicious circle between contractualism and absolutism, and that is to treat the state phenomenon as the result of a process of emergence. It is the very structure of the interactive process which explains phenomena such as delegation, representation, the dispossession of private individuals for the benefit of authorities charged with giving effect to certain norms of co-ordination and of co-operation. They are never given in the pure state. This is why the claim to reduce the state process to a single dimension – constraint or contract – leads to difficulties which become even more serious as the modern state emerges as a requirement of contract on a basis of violence and of force. The second difficulty is that such processes, even if they result from the interaction of individuals, are not immediately and adequately perceived by them. Because of their composite and partly unconscious character, these processes cannot be the object of either a precise localization or dating. Nevertheless, the advantage of the step which we propose is double. First, it permits us to identify certain elementary interactive structures which can be presented as fables or parables before being dealt with under an analytical and abstract form. The second advantage of this method is to save us from a pointless question concerning the *date* of the appearance of the State. Was it born in Greece? In the fourteenth century? At the time of the French Revolution? At such a level of generality and abstraction, the question does not have much meaning; and whatever one says about his empiric naïvety, Rousseau is right here, when he warns us that, to understand what Bertrand de Jouvenel would later call 'the mystery of civil obedience', it is necessary to 'start by throwing away all facts, even if it entails reintroducing them in a selective and controlled manner as and when theoretical schemes capable of casting light upon them are worked out.

The extreme difficulty of grasping the nature of the State becomes clear if it is noticed that the state form is, at least today, the most accomplished expression of the effort to organize the relationships between men in a rational (or reasonable) manner. Such at least is the teaching of the classical teachers, from Aristotle to Hegel. But this effort remains fundamentally 'unsatisfactory'. Our dissatisfaction faced with the state organization (oblige men to be free, as Rousseau said) poses a problem both of hierarchy and of co-ordination. We perceive this difficulty when we reflect on the opposition of State/Nation, or rather State/Civil Society. Certain readers of Hegel see in the State an idea which constrains civil society and does not know the diversity of its intermediary bodies, which claims to be like a rational will in the face of the 'needs' and the aspirations of the 'masses'. In the second place, the connection between the country, the nation, and the State remains problematic. In as much as it claims to rationalize social relationships, the State is cut out for universality, it 'goes beyond' the 'particularism' of interests and of needs. In other respects, whatever have been the failures and crimes which have marked the various attempts to build a universal state, the idea of a single sovereignty regulating the allocation of the resources of the planet according to the needs of humanity seen in its entirety cannot be purely and simply challenged as the interested speech of any old imperialism. As Montesquieu saw very clearly, there is a human community, which is not reducible either to that of nations or to that of states. But these, whatever is the tendency of national states to go beyond the particularity of interests and of opinions by the institution of law and of a constitution, remain despite everything enclosed in their particularism since they are not sovereign, that is to say capable of making themselves obeyed, except for a space and for a time, since they have a beginning, a peak, and a decline. It is therefore as difficult to say that the State embodies the reasonable nature of man, as it is to refuse to see there an attempt to rationalize social relationships by universalizing them, at least partially.

Bureaucracy, Elections, Power, Rousseau.

Bibliography

BADIE, B. and BIRNBAUM, P., *Sociologie de l'Etat*, Paris, Grasset, 1979. – CASSIRER, E., *The myth of the state*, New Haven, Yale Univ. Press, 1946, 1966. – CLASTRE, P., *La société contre l'Etat*, Paris, Minuit, 1974. – DOWNS, A., *An economic theory of democracy*, New York, Harper, 1957, – DUGUIT, *Traité de droit constitutionnel*, Paris, Fontemoing, 1911, 2 vol.; 1923–1927, 5 vol. – EISENSTADT, S.N., *The political systems of empires*, Glencoe, The Free Press, 1963, 1967. – HAURIOU, M., *Précis de droit administratif et de droit public*, Paris, L. Larose & Forcel, 1892; 12th edn, Paris, Sirey, 1933. – HOBBES, T., *Leviathan, or the matter, form and power of a common wealth ecclesiastical and civil*, London 1651; Harmondsworth, Penguin, 1968. – HOFSTADTER, R., *The American political tradition and the men who made it*, New York, A. Knopf, 1948. – JOUVENEL, B. de, *Du pouvoir: histoire naturelle de sa croissance*, Geneva, Bourquin, 1947; *De la souvèraineté: à la recherche du bien politique*, Paris, M. T. Génin, 1955; *The pure theory of politics*, Cambridge, Univ. Press, 1963. – KEYNES, J.M., *Essays in persuasion*, London Macmillan & Co., 1931; *How to pay for the war; a radical plan for the chancellor of the exchequer*, London Macmillan & Co., 1940. – LASKI, H.J., *The state in theory and practice*, London Allen & Unwin, 1935, 1956. – LIJPHART, A., *The politics of accommodation; pluralism and democracy in the Netherlands*, Berkeley, Univ. of California Press, 1968; Cambridge, Cambridge University Press, 1968. – LOCKE, J., 'Essay concerning the true original, extent and end of civil government', in *Two treatises of government*, London 1690. – LOWI, T., *American government. Incomplete conquest*, New York, Holt, Rinehart & Winston, 1977. – MONTESQUIEU, C. de, *De l'esprit des lois*. – MOORE, B. Jr., *Social origins of dictatorship and democracy. Lord and peasant in the making of the modern world*, Boston, Beacon Press, 1966; London, Penguin, 1967. – POULANTZAS, N., *Pouvoir politique et classes sociales*, Paris, Maspero, 1968. – ROUSSEAU, J.-J., *Du contrat social*. – SKOCPOL, T., *States and social revolutions*, Cambridge Univ. Press, 1979. – TOCQUEVILLE, A. de, *De la démocratie en Amérique*. – WEIL, E., *Hegel et l'Etat*, Paris, J. Vrin, 1950.

Status

This word describes the position that an individual holds in a group or that a group holds in a society (defined as a group of groups). This position has two dimensions, of which one could be called horizontal and the other vertical. Horizontal represents the network of contacts and of real exchanges or possible ones with other individuals on the same level as himself or the reciprocal from them to him. Vertical represents contacts and exchanges the individual has with others above or below his levels or reciprocally from them to him. These two sets of information can be combined to define status as the sum of equal and hierarchical relationships that an individual has with the other members of his group.

In the notion of status there is something more than the notion of real or possible contacts and exchanges. These are part of status in so far as they define the position of the individual in a stable way and this position does not depend only on the way the individual's relationships develop at one specific time. My status in a discussion group is affected by the shrewdness and pertinence of my answers, the quality of my strategy towards my opponents, the seriousness and honesty with which I face counter-arguments. But it also depends on permanent elements which were previous to the discussion and will remain after it. I am a man, and not a woman. I am middle-aged, not too old or too young. I am a teacher and not a student. These attributes (sex/age/occupation) do not only contribute to mould the other's perception of myself, they also affect the way I play certain parts in so far as these parts are linked to these attributes. My role is made easier or more difficult according to whether my status's attributes are compatible with each other or whether, globally, this status is compatible with my role. Poise, an attribute of age, caution, of a teacher, help me to be accepted as the chairman of the debate. These attributes would be weaker if I played the part using liveliness, charm, or seduction.

Status can be defined as a sum of real or virtual resources, which an actor can use to interpret and play his parts with more or less eccentric variations. But the relationship between status and role is not one-sided. Status is not only a resource for an actor to play his parts. It is also the appraisal of the way it has been played. This appraisal can be negative or positive. Thus status is not a simple sum of rights and duties. It is not enough to be old to be respected, to have a qualification to be seen as educated. The relationship between the particular status's attributes and the process of being given the status itself is quite problematic. The network of contacts and exchanges which should theoretically give me access to the 'middle-aged' status might not do so if others think that I do not behave the way I should and 'put my white hair to shame'.

Are the criteria for the attribution of status dichotomic? Linton, and following him Parsons, said that a status can be allocated according to natural and objective criteria: age and sex belong to that category. But socio-professional status can be obtained or gained thanks to effort, ambition, or merit. The first kinds of criteria will be called 'ascribed' (Parsons also mentions 'equality' in this case). The second kind will be called 'prescribed': the status-attribution involves an 'achievement'. This achievement is of a particularly complex nature, and involves a confirmation linked to achievement that is 'merit'. But merit can be intellectual or moral, or a combination of both. Also, signs of merit are not to be confused with those of success which does not always go with effort and morality on one side, or brilliance and talent on the other.

The problems which appear in the attribution of status have often been outlined by the theoreticians of organizations. These problems make it difficult to read an organization chart, for example. In an organization, hierarchy of status must be easily available. This is the only way communication will be made possible, messages and orders be made authentic, without which communication might be lost among the different status positions of the network. However, the 'formal' structure of the organization is often very different from the 'effective' structure or 'informal' structure. This split between formal and informal hierarchies, one of them clear and highly artificial, the other hidden and more or less self-made, can be observed when comparing the schematic network with the structure of status as it appears from sociometric observations or from analyses based on the 'reputation' of given individuals. Indeed, the status of the head of an organization is not linked only to his decision-making capacity and to the responsibilities that he carries, but also to his image and popularity. To establish a hierarchy of status is not only to answer: 'Who decides?' but also other questions such as: 'Who in the group is seen as the most competent?' 'The most popular?' 'The most devoted?' Finally, a third way, often used by historians, is to look for what is attributed to such or such individual formally in charge or not in a given process.

The ambiguities in the hierarchy of status call for several comments. First, we should ask at what level it is particularly visible. Modern theories have noted a kind of discord because of the opposition between hierarchical and functional status as far as the communication of messages and orders is concerned. The line of authority often appears to be broken, the power to decide is no longer so clearly allocated as it floats, so to speak, between those in charge of day-to-day activities on one hand and the headquarters in charge of the more or less near future on the other. Once this ambiguity has been observed, cause and effect must be investigated. It can appear to be the result of partial and unspoken compromise which, by leaving some management connections vague, gives employees a kind of 'free zone' and the most aggressive heads of department 'private domain' where they can use their discretionary powers. As for the effects of this well or badly used ambiguity, they can contribute to the flexibility of an organization or, on the contrary, they can slow down and hinder its efficient functioning.

The hierarchy of status can be measured according to its degree of clarity and its efficiency. These two characteristics are particularly emphasized in Weber's conception of bureaucracy. But no bureaucratic organization – not even a military one – is perfectly protected against risks of duplication and confusion when messages and orders are transmitted through its varied strata. This problem of hierarchy of status does not affect only organizations and those in charge of them. It also affects the characters of actors and the 'culture' of their group. The confusion of status is a criterion of social disorder and probably the source of deviance.

This problem is the heart of the discussion of anomie, as Durkheim indicates, at least in his early works (*De la division du travail social*). For Durkheim the presence of anomie is linked to the break-down of the hierarchy of status. In an industrializing society it occurs in two forms. First, the expectations of a person towards their own position and that of others towards that person are no longer pre-determined. Whereas in the traditional cycle everyone knew what to expect and also knew his rights and duties, we are now facing situations for which we are not prepared, because of a more and more complex division of work and of the instability of the productive network on which we have become dependent. Second, this instability effects both the structure of rewards and the level of our contentment.

On what was the hierarchy of status based in traditional or pre-industrial societies? When considering only modern western societies – thus excluding tribal societies – three main points are seen to affect the hierarchical position of an individual: sex, age, the membership of an 'estate' (social group). Of these points the most distinctive in pre-industrial societies is the estate (lord, peasant, serf, etc.) movement between which is made difficult by a series of legal and symbolic restrictions. The system of 'estates' differs from the tribal system in that hierarchy is not given a sacred value (Louis Dumont). Even in societies which are predominantly traditionalist (Weber: status is legitimated by a reference to ancestors' custom), which defined themselves by the important part played by 'ascriptive' elements (such as family ancestry, honour, the paternal line), status is also defined by the spirit of enterprise and the access to wealth. The protection of a prince who distributes titles is also accepted, though in a restrictive manner, as a quite acceptable criterion of recognition. The hierarchy of status is based on elements which are partly practical and not linked to religion. However, 'ultimately' the recognition of status hierarchy in traditional societies has been based on religion for a long time. Such was the case for the Catholic Europe of the Counter-Reformation and also, as Weber notes, in several countries where Protestantism became dominant. Even in Calvinist countries, where the economy was less in the hands of the clergy, a link still remained between status hierarchy and godly power. This power indeed forced the faithful to abide by God's laws, even if the principles and their consequences remain buried in the mystery of God's will. In such a context, the ultimate guarantee of status remains 'metasocial' (Touraine).

Status hierarchy can be thought of either according to the categories of meritocratic ideology or according to the categories of holistic sociology. The attribution of status would depend, in the meritocratic hypothesis, on my talents and efforts; and in the holistic hypothesis on a social process of which it would be a strictly conditioned result. These two positions can be seen as 'ideological' because both give us an apparently simple if not naïve picture of a phenomenon which is obviously complex, and also because they do not take into account a number of paradoxical and inexplicable facts within both the meritocratic and the holistic system. The observed factors called 'status incongruities' are particularly interesting for the sociology of organization, and also for the study of stratification. In the case of organization the difference between knowledge and ability on one side and power on the other (such as the observer sees it through the participation of the expert when decisions are made) shows more or less clear incongruities in different forms which are found at various levels of hierarchy. Instead of decisions being made by competent and selfless people, they are made by 'capitalists' who know only the 'logic of profit' or by 'soulless' technocrats. As for the system of stratification, the mismatch between income and consuming power on one hand and professional qualification on the other often comes under attack. Abnormalities in this case can be attacked in the name of the meritocratic ideal. They can also be attacked in the name of a more general conception of morality, after comparing what a 'decent family man' should earn and what he does in fact earn. The abnormalities of status are seen not only because of envy but also within a more or less coherent feeling of justice, which is also kept going by envious comparisons showing that we do not get what we deserve whereas our neighbours 'working no harder than we do' earn more than us.

As stratification systems become more complex, and change rapidly, the attribution of status becomes more insecure. First, the list of determining criteria is growing. And these are often incongruous or redundant or quite contradictory. It become difficult to sum up the pack of so many diverse attributes linked to one person's social label, when in traditional societies it was enough to say 'he is the son of so and so' to know the rank of the said person, his/her fortune, his/her friends, relatives, and dependants. In traditional rural communities, person, character, and status were narrowly dependent. Today, person and status do not automatically intermingle. Personal identity is no longer inherited: it is built by a lifetime of effort. This way we hold on to an identity which we are constantly in danger of losing because of the multiple dimensions under which our status appears. At the same time, personal identity is derived less from the feeling of belonging to a single group for one and for all, and more from the fragility of this feeling of belonging.

Bureaucracy, Conformity and Deviance, Durkheim, Groups, Role, Social Mobility, Social Stratification.

Bibliography

BENDIX, R. and LIPSET, S.M., (ed.), *Class, status and power; a reader in social stratification*, Glencoe, Free Press, 1960; *Class, status and power: social stratification in comparative perspective*, 2nd edition, London, Routledge & Kegan Paul, 1966. – BOURDIEU, P., 'Condition de classe et position de classe', *Archives Européennes de Sociologie, 7*(2), 1966, 201–223. – CHAPIN, F.S., *The measurement of social status by the use of the social status scale*, Minneapolis, The Univ. of Minnesota Press, 1933. – DUMONT, L., *Home heirarchicus. Essai sur la systeme des castes*, Paris, Gallimard, 1967. – DURKHEIM, E., *The Division of Labour in Society*, op. cit. – GOLDTHORPE, J.H. and HOPE, K., *The social grading of occupations. A new approach and scale*, Oxford, Clarendon Press, 1974. – HOMANS, G.C., *Social behavior: its elementary forms*, New York, Harcourt, 1961; London, Routledge & Kegan Paul, 1961. – HUGHES, E.C., 'Dilemmas and contradictions of status', *American Journal of Sociology*, 1945, *50*, 353–359. – HYMAN, H.H., 'The psychology of status', *Archives of Psychology*, 1942, *38*, n° 269. – KAHL, J.A. and DAVIS, J.A., 'A comparison of indexes of socioeconomic status', *American Sociological Review*, 1955, *20*(3), 317–325. – KORNHAUSER, R.P., 'The Warner approach to social stratification', *in* BENDIX, R. and LIPSET, S.M., (eds), *Class, status and power*, London, Routledge & Kegan Paul, 1966. – LENSKI, G.E., 'Status crystallization: a non-vertical dimension of social status', *American Sociological Review*, XIX, 4, 1954, 405–413. – LINTON, R., *Cultural background of personality*, New York, London, D. Appleton-Century Co.; London, Routledge & Kegan Paul, 1958. – MERTON, R.K., 'Continuities in the theory of reference groups and social structure', *in* MERTON, R.K., *Social theory and social structure*, Glencoe, The Free Press, 1959, 281–286. – MORENO, J.L., *Who shall survive? Foundations of sociometry, group psychotherapy and sociodrama*, New York, Beacon House, 1934. – MOSER, C.A. and HALL, J.R., 'The social grading of occupations', in GLASS, D.V., *Social mobility in Britain*, London, Routledge & Kegan Paul, 1954. – PITT RIVERS, J.A., *The fate of Shechem, or the politics of sex. Essays in the anthropology of the mediterranean*, Cambridge Univ. Press, 1977, chap. 2. – SPEIER, H., 'Honor and the social structure', in SPEIER, H., *Social order and the risks of war: papers in political sociology*, New York, Stewart, 1952, 36–52. – TREVOR-ROPER, H.R., 'The gentry: 1540–1640', *Economic History Review*, Supplement 1, Cambridge Univ. Press, 1953. – WEBER, M., *Economy and Society*, op cit., volume 1.

Structuralism

This word describes a complex and dispersed thread of ideas which saw the light in the social sciences mainly in the 1960s and more or less exclusively in France.

Originally, structuralism seemed like a methodological attempt to extend to other social sciences the benefits of the 'structuralist' revolution which had been happening in linguistics. Classical philology had mainly applied itself to the 'historical' description of languages in their different elements (vocabulary, syntax, etc.). On the other hand, 'structuralist' linguistics aimed to analyse the 'structure' of language. The example of phonology allows us to illustrate simply what is meant by the notion of structure (cf. 'Structure') in this context. 'Classical' phonology aims at distinguishing different phonemes (elementary sounds in a language). Eventually, it attempts to describe the evolution of these phonemes historically and their variation from one part of a country to the other; for example, to compare a set of German phonemes with French ones, etc. 'Struct-uralist' phonology aims on the other hand to prove that the whole set of a language's phonemes makes up a coherent 'system', able to offer a 'convenient' and economical framework to the communication process. Let us take English phonemes. According to Jakobson, they are all made from the combination of twelve 'distinct' binary and elementary 'traits': 'vocalic/not vocalic', 'consonantal/non-consonantal', 'flat/sharp', 'nasal/oral', 'long/short', etc. These twelve dual traits can in theory allow $2^{12} = 4,096$ combinations of possible phonemes. In prac-tice, most languages (one of them English) use only a few dozen phonemes alto-gether. Of course, the real phonemes are not a haphazard 'selection' of possible phonemes: they represent a 'system' of combinations of elementary distinctive traits, the structure of which structural phonology sets out to analyse precisely. (cf. 'Structure', 'System').

The distinction between 'classical' and 'structural' phonology and more gener-ally, 'classical' and 'structural' linguistics, rediscovers in the domain of language studies old and familiar distinctions, familiar to several social sciences. Thus, social institutions can be simply described whereas the structure of the system making up the whole of a society's institutions can be studied too. This last method, which can be called 'structural' is the one used by Montesquieu for instance in *L'Esprit des lois* (*The Spirit of the Laws*). Political framework, juridicial organization, social and family organization, according to Montesquieu, tend to make up a coherent whole, 'structures' as we say now, excluding many possible combinations because they are not conceivable in that particular social structure. However, Montesquieu does not say that different social elements necessarily imply each other. The fact that some combinations are excluded does not mean that the finite and observable ones are systematically coherent. The same idea appears in de Tocqueville: *L'Ancien Régime et la Revolution* explains how the centralized character of French administration made the French social and political 'system' very different from the English system. Even modern authors, like Murdock, may be found to have the same ideas. In *Social Structure*, Murdock explains, using elements belonging to a set of archaic solutions, how residence rules (mother or father orientated, etc.), inheritance rules, filiation rules (mother or father orientated, etc.), incest prohibi-tion rules, the vocabulary used to describe different types of kinship, etc., how all these are made-up 'structures', in the sense that combinations are not random, and where a type of residence rule is more likely to be associated with a particular kind of descendency rule and to a particular marriage alliance rule than to another. But Murdock, like Montesquieu views this coherence of institutional system from a 'minimalist' rather than 'maximalist' point of view: for example, statistic correlations derived from his data are rarely strong. Reciprocal impli-cations of relations are comparable not to 'strict' implications of a logical kind (A implies B) but to 'weak' implications of a stochastic kind (A often implies B). Also, the typical social opposition – which is not without its problems – of 'traditional society'/ 'modern society' can be seen as an example of 'structural' analysis: the two types of societies are defined or supposed to be defined by a set of traits which oppose each other.

These studies are part of what can be called 'structural' analysis. In any case the point is to show that a set of institutions describing a society makes up a 'structure' so that this set must be seen as a dependable (not random) combination of elements. In phonology, 'structural' analysis has to go as far as showing that a language set of phonemes offers co-ordinated, interdependent, distinctive traits. 'Structural' linguistics, following the 'structural' steps, is not therefore a radical innovation in methodology. If we can talk of 'revolution', it is more in the domain of 'language' studies, as this method had been traditionally used in sociology and economics before. In the same way as Jourdain was 'speaking prose without knowing it', Montesquieu and de Tocqueville had unwittingly applied 'structuralism' to sociology or, one might say, used a 'structural' sociology. The fact that the terms 'structural linguistics' or 'structural anthropology' are used as opposed to 'structural economics' or 'structural sociology' might prove that structural analysis had been traditionally followed in economics and sociology.

The same does not apply to anthropology. In the *Structures elementaires de la parente* (*The Elementary Structures of Kinship*), Lévi-Strauss applies the 'structural' view as defined above to a field of ethnology which had traditionally been viewed in a descriptive manner. Until Lévi-Strauss, ethnologists had to face a difficult problem: to explain the wide diversity of incest prohibition rules. Why is marriage between parallel cousins forbidden when any marriage between crossed cousins is tolerated in some societies, yet in other types of societies, certain types of marriage between crossed cousins is tolerated (marriage of *Ego* with the daughter of his mother's brother) and others forbidden (marriage of *Ego* with the daughter of his father's sister)? Lévi-Strauss set out to solve these questions using a similar methodology to 'structural' phonology. The phonologist aims to show that any phonetic system can be seen as the particular answer to a general problem: it gives the process of communication an economical sound support. Similarly, Lévi-Strauss aimed to show that the systems of marriage rules found in archaic societies are the specific solutions to a general problem: to ensure the circulation of women between the various sections of societies. Once this general problem has been considered, it is possible to show, for instance, that a coherent answer (from a certain point of view) consists, among other rules, in forbidding marriage between parallel cousins and allowing marriage between crossed cousins, while another coherent system consists in forbidding marriage between parallel cousins and allowing marriage between some crossed cousins (*Ego* marrying the daughter of his mother's brother).

Lévi-Strauss's theory faced serious criticisms. Omans, for instance, emphasizes its teleological character (marriage rules are there to ensure group solidarity). Also, he notes that the preferred marriage with the daughter of the mother's brother is preferably found in 'patrilinear' societies, where *Ego* has distant relations with his brother and his brother's sister, while his relations with his mother and her brother are warm and close-knit. According to Lévi-Strauss, emphasizing such 'facts' is coming back to the 'past wanderings' of 'psychologism'. As for Leach, he was to emphasize, using the analysis of Kachin's systems in particular, that it is impossible to isolate marriage contracts from a larger context (economic exchanges, politics) to which they belong.

It must be said that, while the 'structural' revolution (adoption of a 'structural methodology') in linguistics and anthropology must be seen as local rather than general, in the sense that these disciplines are spreading new ideas to old fields, they have brought in new methodologies which go beyond the spectrum of linguistics or ethnology. Thus, structural phonology, structural syntax (Chomsky), the studies of Weil and Lévi-Strauss, those of Bush on kinship, all use a new mathematical methodology which contributed to their public acclaim and to their prestige.

This prestige is one of the reasons for what has proved to be a slip towards metaphysics, in what was at first a methodological concept. Although some writers like Piaget, mix the notions of 'structural perspective' and 'structuralism' it is for that slip itself that one should keep the use of the word 'structuralism'. This is a gross generalization, or rather a reaffirmation of postulates that linguists and anthropologists had come to introduce naturally in their own fields, but where their use and generalization raise a problem of legitimacy in other fields. Thus, the ethnologist studying societies without a written tradition or the phonologist studying a language are therefore forced to follow a 'synchronic' perspective: they can look at an existing system, with marriage rules, a set of mythical stories, but they do not have facts or data allowing them to study the genesis or the evolution of these 'systems'. Indeed, the nature of the facts in effect prevents them carrying out a 'diachronic' analysis. The prestige of structural analyses in linguistics and anthropology at that time (the 1960s), the prestige accorded to Lévi-Strauss's epistemological aphorisms led some sociologists to conclude that 'synchronic analysis' was mysteriously loaded with unconditional advantages in comparison with 'diachronic' analysis. Althusser and Balibar, for instance, began to read Marx generally and *Capital* in particular, again. They attempted to discover a typology of social formations and of production modes starting from simple elements. Marx was, in fact, only a convenient excuse. The point was to show that 'social formations' are structured combinations of simple elements (like the forms of surplus value, etc.), exactly in the same way as phonetic systems are structured combinations of distinctive traits. Marx thus appeared disguised as a structuralist eager to study the 'synchronic' structure of social groupings and, indeed as practically indifferent to the analysis of social change. The 'structuralist' interpretation of Marx, emphasizing the possibility of building various combinatory systems, had the useful advantage of bringing 'flexibility' into the infrastructure–superstructure relationships to 'show' that capitalist and socialist 'social formations' could correspond to a certain diversity of structure. This is why it had some success. The structuralist treatment given by Althusser and his followers to Marx enabled them to drag 'vulgar' Marxism out of the ditch into which it had fallen, and to give it back an academic respectability and a certain flexibility that Marxist thinkers could not fail to appreciate. The same taste for the 'synchronic' can be seen in *Words and Things* by Michel Foucault, in which the history of the social and natural sciences is explained as a sequence of structural disequilibria: the great 'eras' of this history are dominated by epistemic 'structures' which Foucault analyses in terms of an infallible internal coherence. As for the sequencing of these structures, Foucault sees it as having no intelligence and lacking in interest. The brilliant construction found in *Les Mots and les choses* is nothing more, from a logical point of view, than a typology; this typology, on top of that, has little concern for the history of sciences. For example, no historian of the social sciences would agree that Adam Smith prefigured an epistemic change when he proposed, 'for the first time', endogenous evolutionary models for social change.

By singling out 'synchronic' analysis as opposed to 'diachronic' analysis, in fields where the nature of the given facts does not demand it, the structuralists considerably reduced their ambitions: most often to developing typologies, but ignoring the reason for which they exist. This can be seen as a doubtful progress compared to investigations such as those of Marx or de Tocqueville, who always interpreted synchronic differences in social types as the result of a diachronic process. The different 'systems' observed in France and England or in France and America are explained by de Tocqueville as the result of a cumulative process resulting from initial differences. Marx is the same: the differences between observed social types at a synchronic level are always explained by him as a result of a 'diachronic' process. The unconditional importance given to the synchronic not only succeeds in making unintelligable the differences between types but also exaggerates and re-affirms these differences. Thus, the opposition 'modern/ traditional' societies greatly helped simplify and falsify conceptions of evolution. The sociology of modernization often accepts that 'traditional societies', for instance, are necessarily unchanging or that 'modernization' is bound to create progress on all fronts (cf. 'Development'). Such propositions, which cannot stand up to even a superficial survey, arise from the fact that the typology opposing traditional to modern societies is seen, not as an heuristic tool, but as the expression of a 'reality' of an 'underlying structure'.

The constraints imposed on an anthropologist studying archaic myths or on the phonologist also constrain them to analyse myths or phonetic systems as products of 'human activity' (which they obviously are). Structuralist metaphysics, again using generalization and crystallization, draws methodological and ontological propositions from these special conditions. 'Methodological' proposition: social phenomena are the result or the manifestation of structures and cannot be seen as the result of man's actions. Ontological 'proposition': only the structures have a 'real' existence; individuals are simple appearances or 'support structures'. They are of interest only in so far as they allow the structure to be visible. And when individuals are not reduced to support structures and described by the structuralist sociologist as being capable of 'strategic' behaviour (incorrectly using 'strategic' as meaning 'intentional'), these intentional behaviours are soon discovered to lead only to the reproduction of structures or, according to the sociologist's ideological fad, to their development in a direction predetermined by historical meaning. Adam Smith and Darwin, according to Foucault, are nothing but specific manifestations of the 'epistemic' structure of their time. The 'ego' which had a fundamental part to play in Freud's classical trilogy (ego, super-ego, id) disappears, as

Turkle showed, in the structuralist interpretation give of psychoanalytic doctrine by Lacan. With Lacan, the individual becomes the simple support of the unconscious structures he is made of (the id). The social agents of structuralist sociology are also simple supports or, at best, willing or blind *ersatz* through which social structures are made up, express themselves, reproduce, and change. As for 'social structures', they are generally reduced to a few arbitrarily chosen variables, and are seen to dominate the set of variables which make up the social system. There again, the contrast with an author like de Tocqueville must be noted: 'administrative centralization' is not seen a priori as an essential variable. Its importance is in fact demonstrated a posteriori. On the contrary, the stratification variables, themselves reduced in the simple leading/led classes opposition, are seen as the essential variables a priori by structural sociologists. The existence of the State can be ignored since it is accepted that it is necessarily in the hands of the leading class (cf. 'State').

Structuralism (not, as Piaget defines it, that of 'structural analysis' but in the meaning defined here as a metaphysical slip from 'structural analysis') is an exchange of diffuse ideas which took place mainly in France, as mentioned previously. Why? Because, in the late-twentieth century, the decline of existentialism left some room for a new intellectual fashion, because the Parisian intellectual jet-set seems to crave permanently for new philosophies, and there is no similar intellectual jet-set structure in England, or in Germany, Italy, or in the US (Clark). Perhaps, also, because structuralism could take on a scientific prestige which derived from the discoveries of linguistics and anthropology for a time. Finally, because a number of talented writers were able to make up a skilled verbal synthesis (re)interpreting into the structuralist vocabulary the sacred texts of Freud, Marx, Nietzsche, and a few others. If structuralism is a local speciality which has not spread and could be described by Alberoni, an Italian familiar with the French culture, as an illustration of the '*arroganza della cultura francese*' (arrogance of French culture), it is because, in spite of the verbal skill which made its success and of its devotion to the value of 'depth', it is, in its metaphysical formula, an intellectual throwback. By eradicating the margin of autonomy left to the agent or to the social actor by structures, by substituting rough typologies for the diversity of social types, by reducing the structural complexity of interdependent and interacting systems to a few variables seen as arbitrarily important (stratification variables for instance), by giving an unconditional priority to the 'synchronic' over the 'diachronic', how can one expect to advance the knowledge of social process and system?

Function, Functionalism, Social Change, Structure, System.

Bibliography

ALTHUSSER, L., *For Marx*, London, New York, Random House, 1969. – ALTHUSSER, L. and BALIBAR, E., *Reading Capital*, London, Pluto Press, 1979. – CHOMSKY, N., and MILLER, G.A., 'Introduction to the formal analysis of natural languages' and 'Formal properties of grammars', *in* LUCE, D., BUSH, R., and GALANTER, E., (ed.), *Handbook of mathematical psychology*, New York, Wiley, 1963–1965, 3 vol., vol. II, chap. XI and XII, 269–321 and 323–418. – CLARK, T., *Prophets and patrons: the French university and the emergences of the social sciences*, Cambridge, Harvard University Press, 1973. – COLIN, C., *On human communication*, New York, Wiley, 1957. – DUMÉZIL, G., *Mitra-Varuna. Essai sur la représentation indo-européene de la souveraineté*, Paris, Gallimard, 1948. – FOUCAULT, M., *Les mots et les choses. Une archéologie des sciences humaines*, Paris, Gallimard, 1966. – HÉRITIER, F., *L'exercice de la parenté*, Paris, Le Seuil, 1981. – HEYDEBRAND, W.V., 'Marxist structuralism', *in* BLAU, P.M., and MERTON, R.K., *Continuities in structural inquiry*, London, Sage, 81–119. – HOMANS, G., 'Marriage, authority and final causes', in HOMANS, G., *Sentiments and activities*, Glencoe, Free Press, 1962, 202–256; 'Bringing men back in', *American sociological review*, XXIX, 5, 1964, 809–818. – JAKOBSON, R., and HALLE, M., *Fundamentals of language*, Paris/La Haye, Mouton, 1956, 2nd rev. edn, 1971. – LEACH, E.R., 'British social anthropology and levi-straussian structuralism', *in* BLAU, P.M., and MERTON, R.K., *Continuities in structural inquiry*, London, Sage, 1981, 27–49; *Rethinking anthropology*, London, Athlone, 1961. – LÉVI-STRAUSS, C., *Anthropologie structurale*, Paris, Plon, 1958, 1974; *Anthropologie structurale deux*, Paris, Plon, 1973; *Les structures élémentaires de la parenté*, Paris, PUF, 1949, Paris/La Haye, Mouton, 1967; *Mythologiques*. I: *Le cru et le cuit*, Paris, Plon, 1964; II: *Du miel aux cendres*, Paris, Plon, 1964; III: *L'origine des matières de la table*, Paris, Plon, 1968; IV: *L'homme nu*, Paris, Plon, 1971. – LEVI-STRAUSS, C., *Structural Anthropology*, London, Allen Lane 1968; *The Elementary Structure of Kinship*, Boston, Beacon Press, 1969; *The Raw and the Cooked*, New York, Harper & Row, 1969. – MULLER, J.C., 'Straight sister-exchange and the transition from elementary to complex structures', *American Ethnologist*, 1980, 518–529. – MURDOCK, G.P., *Social structure*, New York, Macmillan, 1949; London, Collier Macmillan, 1965. – NEEDHAM, R., 'The formal analysis of prescriptive patrilateral cross-cousin marriage', *Southwestern Journal of Anthropology*, XIV, 1958. – PIAGET, J., *Le structuralisme*, Paris, PUF, 1968, 1974. – SEBAG, L., *Marxisme et structuralisme*, Paris, Payot, 1964. – TURKLE, S., *Psychoanalytic politics, Freud's French revolution*, New York, Basic Books, 1978; London, Burnett Books, 1979.

Structure

The concept of structure has so many meanings in sociology that it is difficult if not impossible to make an exhaustive list. Some reference points only will have to be explained here.

For Murdock, the concept of 'social structure' describes the coherence of social institutions: institutions are not arbitrary and random conglomerates; they have a 'structure'. Murdock rediscovers in the field of archaic societies a fundamental idea that Montesquieu had systematically studied in *L'Esprit des lois* (cf. 'Structuralism'). This idea is sometimes taken as a form of structural–functional analysis. One of the objectives of this type of analysis is precisely to explain coherence and to show the interdependence of social institutions. Thus, Parsons attempted to show that the industrial 'structure' of professions is not compatible with family institutions of a traditional type (extended family with residence unity) (cf. 'Functionalism').

More generally, the concept of structure, particularly for functionalists and structuralists, has meant something similar to the concept of type. Making up a typology consists of:

1. establishing a list of variables considered as relevant;
2. showing that these variables are characterized by 'structured' correlations which are weaker or stronger, i.e., are not random;
3. using these intercorrelations to distribute the observed data into types or classes.

Take a simple case: four variables are given with two traits $(+/-)$; all the elements under observation are either $++++$ or $----$: in this case, two types of elements will be said to be found or two kinds of 'structures' will be said to have come to light. In this case, the intercorrelations between variables are perfect. Sorting out types of 'structures' can be attempted when the intercorrelations are not haphazard although not perfect.

In other intellectual contexts, the concept of structure is used in opposition or in relation to other words. Gurvitch for instance distinguishes structured groups from organized groups. Social classes can, according to him, be 'structured' without being 'organized'. This distinction in fact recalls a familiar distinction: Gurvitch simply emphasizes that groups and grouping can be following a kind of continuum, one end of which represents groups of which the 'interests' are represented by one or several organizations and the other end represents groups corresponding to simple statistical categories. Between the 'organized' groups and the groups which can be called 'nominal', Dahrendorf's 'concealed' groups could be placed, these 'concealed' groups being made up of people sharing common interests. Gurvitch, more a partisan of continuum than Dahrendorf, thinks that between nominal and organized groups can be placed a more or less structured ladder of groups.

Sometimes, the concept of structure is opposed to that of contingency. In the same way, 'structure' often defines the stable elements of a system (cf. 'System') as opposed to its variable elements. Then, a model's 'structure' represents either the parameters of this model or the whole of the functions linking the variables to each other, or again the whole of the functions' parameters. Thus, if we take three variables x_1, x_2, x_3 linked together by the following system: $x_2 = f(x) = ax_1 + b$; $x_3 = g(x_1, x_2) = cx_1 + dx_2 + q$: in some cases, it will be said that the parameters a, b, c, d, q, represent the system's structure. Sometimes, 'structure' will more likely represent the form f and g of the variable's relations. At other times, it will represent the whole of the forms f and g and of the parameters a, b, c, d, and q.

'Structure' is also used more or less vaguely to sort out the fundamental from the secondary, the essential from the inessential, the basic from the contingent. Thus, Mannheim uses 'social structure' to mean 'the thread of interacting social forces which generates various modes of observation of thought.' Here, social structure represents implicitly the whole of the elements of a social system which the sociologist assumes to dominate and produce the others. For Mannheim, it is material elements (vaguely named 'social forces') which explain ideological elements. This recalls of course the famous Marxist distinction of base and superstructure. The influence of the Marxist tradition explains why sociologists frequently use the concept of 'social structure' as another version of 'stratification system', where the variables of stratification are considered basic and determining. If some classes of variables are not taken as determining a priori, 'social structure' then becomes another version of concepts like that of social organization or system of social relations; Kroeber, Evans-Pritchard, and Radcliffe-Brown made this point clear in their own different ways.

Sometimes, 'social structure' represents the system of constraints which individual action faces. If to this perfectly acceptable definition is added a somewhat contested proposition according to which structures suffice in all cases to determine individual action, i.e. generally leave no autonomy to the subject, a widely spread species of concept of the 'structuralist' type is obtained (cf. 'Structuralism').

In other contexts, structure becomes almost synonymous with 'distribution' in the statistical sense of the word. 'Socio-professional structure' is then used to describe the distribution of individuals of a population into the different kinds of socio-professional positions. In the same way, Lazarsfeld speaks of 'structural' variables when talking about variables characterizing collective units. Also, Blau talks of 'structural' effect when a variable appears like a function of a distribution. Thus, according to Blau, there is a 'structural' effect when the tendency of manual workers to vote for the Left appears to be determined by the proportion of manual workers in the environment.

'Structure' is also used as an equivalent to the German word *Gestalt* and the English one 'pattern'. This then calls for the concept of configuration. In that sense, a sociogram is said to represent a group 'structure', and group 'structural analysis' is used to describe the graphic or matrix representation of the attraction and repulsion relationships between members of a group. 'Structure' is also used to describe the matrix of correlations between variables to indicate that the coefficients of correlation values are not distributed randomly.

Thus, the concept of 'structure' can be seen in correlation with that of 'system' if system is taken to mean a set of 'interdependant elements'. It can also be taken as being defined by opposition or contiguity with an important set of other concepts, in various meanings which the context alone will determine its more or less precise meaning.

Aggregation, Function, Functionalism, Methodology, Social Change, Structuralism, System.

Bibliography

BLAU, P.M., 'Formal organizations: dimensions of analysis', *American journal of sociology*, LXIII, *1*, 1957, 58–69. – BLAU, P.M., and MERTON, R.K. (ed.), *Continuities in structural inquiry*, London, Sage, 1981. – BOUDON, R., *A quoi sert la notion de structure? Essai sur la signification de la notion de structure dans les sciences humaines*, Paris, Gallimard, 1968. – COSER, L.A., (ed.), *The idea of social structure. Papers in honor of Robert K. Merton*, New York, Harcourt-Brace, 1975. – GURVITCH, G., 'Le concept de structure sociale', *Cahiers internationaux de sociologie*, XIX, *2*, 1955, 3–44. – LAZARSFELD, P.F., and MENZEL, H., 'On the relation between individual and collective properties', *in* ETZIONI, A. (ed.), *Complex organizations*, New York, Holt, Rinehart & Winston, 1961, 422–440. – LÉVI-STRAUSS, C., 'La notion de structure en sociologie', *in* LÉVI-STRAUSS, C., *Anthropologie structurale*, Paris, Plon, 1958, 1974, Trans. *Structural Anthropology*, London, Allen Lane 1968. – MURDOCK, G. P., *Social structure*, Glencoe, The Free Press, 1949, 1965. Trad. Franç., *De la structure sociale*, Paris, Payot, 1972. – NADEL, S.F., *The theory of social structure*, London, Cohen & West, 1957. – RADCLIFFE-BROWN, A.R., *Structure and function in primitive societies. Essays and addresses*, Glencoe, The Free Press, 1952; London, Cohen & West, 1959.

Suicide

A familiar theme in sociology. Touched on by 'moral' statisticians like Guerry and Morselli for instance, it is also the theme of a well-known 'sociological study' by

Durkheim, *Suicide* (1897). Durkheim's ideas were then remodelled several times, especially by Halbwachs in *Les Causes du suicide* (1930) or by Henry Short in *Suicide and Homicide* (1964). All these studies can be situated in the field of *moral statistics* since they all deal with the regularities, changes, and differences of suicide rates as they are observed in official statistics. More recently, the rationale of this quantitative perspective has been criticized, if not by denying the facts at least in a radical way, notably by Douglas (1967).

The interest of moral statisticians in suicide phenomena can be explained in three ways. First, because official suicide statistics are available in many countries, sometimes from the beginning, but more often from the second half of the nineteenth century: these statistics form a rare statistical data base allowing comparisons in time as well as space. Second, suicide rates appear to have been generally increasing during the whole of the nineteenth century: they therefore constitute a privileged field for thinking about the consequences of the 'industrial revolution'. Third, suicide is above all an individual act, but the statistics show remarkable regularities. The second half of the nineteenth century is in fact dominated, as far as the history of sociology is concerned, by a strong 'naturalist' flow of ideas (i.e., there is no difference between human and natural phenomena) and a 'positivist' flow of ideas (i.e., human phenomena must be studied like other scientific phenomena in sciences and particularly the science of physics). The study of suicide (like that of crime) was therefore interesting from an epistemological viewpoint: it made it possible to show that the most individual of actions could be seen quite rightly as the product and the manifestation of collective forces (as moral statisticians call them, intentionally using a key concept in physics).

Durkheim's *Suicide* is the master-work generated by the ideas of moral statistics. Using a considerable database, Durkheim attempts to show that suicide cannot be reduced to a physiological or psychopathological phenomena: there is no statistical correlation between suicide rates and indicators of frequency of mental illness. But Durkheim's demonstration of this point is not very convincing. It passes lightly over the difficulty of interpretation, very clearly shown by the quantitative ecological analysis, of correlations worked out on collective units (cf. Selvin). Suicide cannot, according to Durkheim, be reduced to the physiological consequence of weather or climatic factors, in spite of seasonal suicide cycles. Indeed, seasonal suicide cycles are coupled with weekly and daily cycles. The first alone could be attributed to an effect of this kind. But this hypothesis must be rejected, because for one thing the seasonal cycles in suicide are much greater in rural than in urban areas. Variations in suicide cannot be reduced either to individual causes or 'natural' causes and must, according to Durkheim, be seen as the consequence of social variables.

Durkheim develops on this basis his famous theory of four types of suicide: the adaptation of the individual to society presupposes an 'individuation' which is neither too weak nor too strong. If it is too strong, it generates an excessive individualism that Durkheim called *egotism*. The individual tends then to be cut off from his environment and isolated, and the *egoistic* type of suicide occurs. If the process of individuation is too crude, *altruistic* suicide is more frequent. On the other hand, the balance individual–society presupposes social norms to be neither too demanding nor too undemanding and vague: too-demanding norms provoke suicide of a *fatalistic* type. A later example of that type, post-Durkheim, would be the kamikaze suicide. Too undemanding norms are coupled with the occurrence of the *anomic* type of suicide. Because the individual is not guided by a clear vision of objectives or socially valued means, he becomes disoriented. Durkheim's demonstration is made with great methodological skill, and well explained in an important article by Selvin. Ahead of his time, Durkheim invented what methodologists were to call 'multivariate analysis' (cf. 'Causality') and quantitative 'ecological' analysis, the principles of which he sometimes (as has been shown) forgets when they lead him to undesirable conclusions. To show for instance that suicide increases with egotism, Durkheim looks for a number of indicators of this variable which are 'invisible' as such. In so far as Protestantism gives more room to 'self-criticism', it is more likely to lead to egotism than is Catholicism. It is demonstrated that suicide rates in Protestant countries are generally higher and that they vary (in German provinces or Swiss provinces, for instance) in direct correlation with the proportion of Protestant believers. Also, individual data show that Protestants have a higher suicide rate than Catholics. Because egotism tends to decline (according to Durkheim) in times of war or political crisis, the egotistic type of suicide also declines. The same demonstration is used for the other types of suicide (however the fatalistic type is explained only by a short passage). Thus Durkheim uses what we will later call 'correlations' between suicide rates and the indicators of anomie. Suicide is, for example, more common in a period of economic boom; it is more frequent in the typical professions of modern industrial societies than among traditional professions. It also increases with divorce, etc.

Thirty years later, Halbwachs studied Durkheim's theory and confirmed some of his conclusions. Thus, variations in suicide after the Dreyfus and Boulanger crisis in France show, in fact, that suicide tends to decline in times of political crisis. At the same time, the supplementary data available to Halbwachs by comparison with Durkheim, and a detailed appraisal of Durkheim's text, make the fragility of some conclusions of *Suicide* apparent, particularly in the case of the opposition of Catholics/Protestants: Denmark, Sweden, and especially Norway have, from 1900 onwards for the first of these countries and from 1840 for the others, a much lower rate of suicide than France for instance. Is it because Sweden and Norway are then 'rural' countries? Difficult to say. Also, Halbwachs shows clearly that Durkheim's conclusions about Germany are doubtful: Protestants are not merely Protestants; generally they are more likely to live in towns than Catholics; their distribution on the socio-professional hierarchy is different from Catholics; also, the East German provinces have important Polish minorities. Halbwachs's criticisms come to this: many of Durkheim's conclusions would have demanded a more in-depth 'multivariate' analysis. A larger number of controlled variables should have been used. But, on crucial points, such a control is impossible because of the correlations that there are between 'explanatory' variables. It is a fact that Catholics are represented more in some professions than in others. How in this case to distinguish the effects of faith from that of profession? Are suicide rates among Protestants higher because they are Protestants or because they more often hold stressful positions? In some cases Durkheim is aware of the problem raised by the possibility of a correlation between explanatory variables. But in other cases he does not realize that this 'co-linear' phenomenon – as it is later to be called – can make it difficult to decide between very different hypotheses. Facing this problem, Durkheim rather tends to opt for the interpretations which fit better with his general theory on suicide, as Halbwachs shows.

Besides this, Halbwachs's work emphasizes a further three important points. First, he shows clearly the difficulties of interpreting suicide statistics which differ in the time and the location of their collection. Second, he underlines the importance of taking into account failed suicides as well as 'successful' suicides; both appear to be distributed differently in terms of variables such as age and sex, which often differ quite strongly. 'Successful' suicides are, for instance, more numerous among men, but suicide attempts are more numerous among women. Third, Halbwachs, working more than twenty-five years after Durkheim, was able to show that suicide rates, which had generally increased in the second half of the nineteenth century, tended to stabilize, even decrease in some countries from the beginning of the twentieth century to the time when he wrote. Following Halbwachs, it is useful to note that evolution is then very different from one context to another: between 1903–13 and 1970, suicide is stable in Hanover, in Hesse, and in Baden-Wurtenberg, but it increases in Bavaria and Westphalia; it is stable in London from 1900 to 1970, but strongly decreased in Paris during the same period. Such variations preclude an immediate crude explanation. Today it is not certain either that another of Halbwachs's conclusions can be confirmed, that of a tendency for suicide rates to standardize, although they seem to be on the increase over the last decade.

After the critical examination of Durkheim by Halbwachs, the impression is given that if the multivariate analysis used by Durkheim is to be an efficient one for suicide data analysis, it must include a very large number of control variables, and this impression is all the stronger when later suicide data are given and used by Halbwachs. Because in many cases, important variables are not available in statistical data, these should be accompanied by sample surveys where these unobserved variables could be introduced and where the effects of these variables could be differentiated from statistical data from which they are not usually broken down. Even today, case studies, sample studies, and statistical studies are analysed in un-coordinated fashion. The result is that the causes of suicide and its variations in time and space are still largely unexplained, in spite of the results pointed out by Durkheim and corrected by Halbwachs. We realize today how complex are the causes of suicide. How it can be explained for instance that from 1830 to Halbwachs's work, suicide and alcoholism both regularly increased in France, both went down in Norway but in Sweden alcoholism decreased while suicide increased? These complex developments make one consider with circumspection those theories which pretend to discover the effects of certain cultural traits on suicide rates. Even if these culturalist hypotheses contain some truth, it is difficult to believe – one should in any case prove it with the sort of multivariate analysis of which Durkheim had seen the fundamental value in the analysis and interpretation of statistics – that suicide rates are particularly high in France and Germany because in these countries there is an important *petite bourgeoisie* particularly fond of asceticism.

The difficulties met by applying statistical methods to the analysis of suicide provoked radical criticisims: that of Douglas in the USA and later of Baechler in France, Pushing Halbwachs's doubts about the credibility of suicide statistics to the extreme, Douglas advocates an analysis of a biographical and qualitative type: the sociologist's objective can only be to show the meaning of the suicide in relation to the individual who commits it. It is difficult to imagine a more extreme position than Douglas's compared to Durkheim's. Durkheim tried to show that the motivations of suicide victims are very difficult to analyse and of minor scientific interest. Douglas sees motivations alone as being scientifically interesting but also alone to be really accessible, since statistical data are seen as useless. Baechler brilliantly developed the programme proposed by Douglas: from an historical corpus of suicide, Baechler tried to show that, when you have enough information, it is always possible to interpret suicide as an answer to a situation: all suicides would result from a trapped situation into which the actor has fallen. Suicide must therefore be understood as a 'strategy' used by the individual to solve existential problems. Although such a theory has an important element of truth it is too general in its scope, just as that of Durkheim which it is set to oppose. It is difficult to accept, as Durkheim wanted to, that suicide is always a result of social context. Difficult also to agree that a 'strategic' theory of suicide could have a general application. By rejecting the effect of factors that Durkheim qualified as 'psychopathologic', the two theories show a sociological imperialism likely to gain little ground as far as the analysis of suicide is concerned.

The study of suicide can really only go deeper, as Halbwachs suggested, if it is possible to analyse the motivations for suicide, an objective which Durkheim had dogmatically refuted. Ideally, motivations, social reasons affecting the distribution of these motivations as well as the variation of this distribution in time and space should be known. This implies giving up the sociological perspective according to which neither suicide *motivations*, nor more generally the *causes* of suicide linked to personality structure can represent pertinent 'social facts' and also giving up the atomist perspective according to which a sociologist should be content with making out a typology of individual progressions leading to suicide.

Anomie, Conformity and Deviance, Crime, Durkheim, Measurement.

Bibliography

BAECHLER, J, *Les suicides*, Paris, Calmann-Lévy, 1975. – BESNARD Ph., 'Anti ou ante-durkheimisme? Contribution au débat sur les statistiques officielles du suicide', *Revue française de sociologie*, XVII, 2, 1976, 313–341. – CHESNAIS, J.-C., *Les morts violentes en France depuis 1826. Comparaisons internationales*, Paris, PUF, 1976. – CHESNAIS, J.-C., and ZBORILOVA, J., 'Le suicide en Europe centrale, en France et en Suède depuis un siècle', *Revue français des affaires sociales*, XXXI, 1, 1977, 105–137. – DOUGLAS, J., *The social meanings of suicide*, Princeton, Princeton University Press, 1967 – DURKHEIM, E., *Suicide, op cit.* – FERRI, E., *L'omicidio-suicidio, responsabilità giuridica*, Turin, Bocca, 1884, 1925. – GUERRY, A. M., *Essai sur la statistique morale de la France*, Paris, Crochard, 1833. – HALBWACHS, M., *Les causes du suicide*, Paris, F.

Alcan, 1930. – HENRY, A.F., and SHORT, J.F., *Suicide and homicide*, New York, The Free Press, 1954. – MORSELLI, E.A., *Il suicidio: saggio di statistica morale comparata*, Milan, Dumolard, 1879. Trans. *Suicide: an essay on comparative moral statistics*, New York, Arno Press, 1975. – ŒCONOMO, J.-C., 'Le comportement suicide et le problème de la tentative (en France et plus particulièrement dans la Seine, à partir de sources statistiques inédites)', *Revue de Science criminelle et de Droit pénal comparé*, XIV, *4*, 1959, 805–828. – SELVIN, H.C., 'Durkheim's 'suicide' and problems of empirical research', *American journal of sociology*, LXIII, *6*, 1958, 607–619. – TODD, E., *Le fou et le prolétaire*, Paris, Laffont, 1979.

System

Take a solvable 'system' of n linear equations with n unknowns. By modifying any value of any 'one' of the coefficients, the value of all the unknown quantities will be affected. By excluding one of the unknowns the system will become unsolvable. By adding one unknown quantity, the system will have an endless number of solutions. Therefore, the set of equations makes up a system in the sense that any modification of one of the elements affects all the others. Bertalanffy writes: 'a system is a set of interdepending elements, i.e. linked together by correlations such as if one is altered, so are the others and the whole set is then changed.' This definition is similar to that of Condillac: 'a hierarchy where all the different parts are mutually related.'

Often the word 'system' in sociology is used with only a slightly different meaning. For instance, an organization will be defined by a system of roles. In this case, modifying one element could affect the whole system. In the chapter entitled 'Bureaucratic phenomena' in his essay on 'Monopoly', Crozier uses the case of an organization made up of a number of roles. The management team is made up of a manager, a deputy manager, a finance manager, a technical engineer. The manager and his deputy have – at least in France – a good academic background but often a limited practical experience of production problems. The technical engineer, often a long-standing factory employee, is superior to them on the technical side. These facts describe a complex system of interactions. The formal authority of the manager and his deputy is threatened by the technical knowledge of the engineer. In the same way the financial adviser has a right of veto on the manager's decisions when they appear risky to him. The role system creates 'zones of uncertainty' in very specific areas inside which repeated conflicts, of which the end result is generally predictable, are generated: the technical engineer always wins over the manager, the financial adviser confines himself to a formal behaviour. The structure of this interacting system would be completely changed should one of the elements be modified: for instance, if deputy managers stayed longer in one single factory, if the manager has had direct experience of production techniques or if the financial adviser was independent of the manager's authority.

We could take another example: that of the education market. It is a system because the behaviour of each educational 'client' can have effects on all the others. Hence, if n people choose to study medicine rather than physics they will increase the intensity of the competition between candidates for medicine while reducing it for physics. These people might eventually ease the process of finding a job for physicists. These people may also contribute to a fall in the average income for doctors. The choices of each individual have of course only a marginal, negligible effect. But the sum of choices generates collective or system effects.

The first example describes a role system or 'interaction system'. The second one describes a system of relations which are clearly not role relations. In this case, individuals can be said, however, to be in relation because the choice of each affects the consequences that each is expecting from their choice. Such an effect is sometimes called 'external effect' or more briefly, 'externality'. A system which generates external effects because of the lack of individual interaction can be defined by the notion of interdependent system. Most concrete social systems are composed simultaneously of interdependent sub-systems and interactive sub-systems, and the links between them are quite complex. Thus, if an interdependent sub-system provokes negative effects in relation to some actors (for instance over-production of low-quality doctors), the political system can intervene to attempt to correct them (cf. 'Role').

When analysing a social system, exchanges between the system and its environment have to be studied. In this way the population of a nation state can be seen as a system. Its structure and dimensions are effected by the behaviour of individuals belonging to the system (in terms of reproduction, hygiene, etc.). In the case of where there is no immigration or emigration, this system can be called a 'closed system'. The concept of a 'closed system' could also be applied to a rural community engaged in self-sufficient economy and not involved in economic or demographic exchanges with its environment. But examples of 'closed systems' are few. Most systems can be described as 'open' in so far as they have exchanges with their environment. Examples would be population affected by migratory phenomena or a rural community engaged in a cash economy. When there are exchanges with the environment, they can either have no effects or have different kinds of effects on the system structure. To take a famous example, the system of the boiler, radiator, and thermostat is open: the thermostat is sensitive to the water temperature and the cooling of the water depends on the outside temperature. According to the outside temperature the mechanisms which start the boiler again are going to be more or less frequent. But the changes at the level of the environment (outside temperature) affect neither the radiator temperature nor, of course, the functioning mechanisms of the system.

Exchange between a system and its environment can also provoke a modification in the system through a retroactive effect from the environment to the system. Using an example dear to Malthus for instance, a growing population might exhaust the natural resources which are vital for its survival. The result is negative 'feedback' – a check on population growth. Le Roy Ladurie (*Les Paysans de Languedoc*) notes a similar process in Languedoc in the fourteenth century: an increasing number of males leads to the dividing of land, leading to a fall in income which creates a demographic reverse. In other cases, exchanges between system and environment can produce more complex effects: take for instance a rapidly increasing population leading to a severe housing shortage. This process can have a dual effect. System-wise, it is possible that individuals adapt their behaviour and produce less children. Environment-wise, the authorities will no doubt try, if they can afford to, to enact decisions aimed at limiting the housing crisis.

These examples show that notions of system and environment correspond to distinctions of convention, rather than substantive difference. In other words, the line between system and environment is decided for each particular case in view of the problem faced and begins according to the level of analysis required. The notion of environment is not automatically based on a topographical connotation and can have a more abstract sense. In the same way, the employment market can be taken as the environment of the education market. But the education market and the employment market can also be seen as one single system and the possibility of state intervention in this system can be localized as an environmental factor.

The previous examples also show, contrary to common belief, that the notion of system does not go hand in hand with that of balance and stability. This belief probably derives in some ways from misuse of examples such as the thermostat in the didactic presentation of the notion of system. This belief probably also derives from a tendency, not just since the beginnings of sociology but since the beginnings of the study of societies, a tendency to conceive of social systems as capable, in the same way as living systems, of restoring their stability in fluctuating conditions. And when social systems appear to be unbalanced, following the biologically-derived comparison, they will be said to be in a developing or growing state. A population can certainly make up a stable system when its structure and size remain the same from one era to another. But there are populations growing or in decline as well. Similarly, an organization can be a stable system. But it too can experience an evolution which will affect the role-system defining it. The organization can also have effects on its environment which in turn will generate a retroactive effect on that organization. A market can be stable, in decline, or expanding, and the expansion can produce complex active or reactive effects between that market and its environment. Take for instance the case of the expanded education market between 1950 and 1970. Following this expansion, social expectations linked to qualifications were consequently modified. An increase in educational resources offers people a hope of gaining more in terms of income and status during the period. But the average income and status linked with each level of education are decreasing. The behaviour of educational 'clients' is then affected in a complex retroactive way: because of differential earnings these clients try to get the highest possible qualification after taking into account the various constraints limiting their ambitions; but the fall of the average gain of educational investments encourages individuals to try to obtain their qualifications at the least cost and occupy part of their time with paid activities. The growth of the education market also led to a complicated modification of the relationship between education and work.

Modern sociology, acknowledging the diversity of dynamics which can affect a system and its environmental relations, is leaving behind the elementary paradigms to which nineteenth-century social sciences were attached. Ricardo,

Malthus, and Marx tended to reduce these processes to a few central types: processes of reproduction and 'explosive' processes tending to provoke a break-up or negative feedback effect from the environment. For Ricardo, when salaries grow past the subsistence level, the population increases which leads in turn to the increase of what Marx would later call a reserve army of labour. Because of increasing competition between workers, wages are brought back down to the level of subsistence. The mechanical recurrence of negative feedbacks changes the potentially 'explosive' process into a cyclical process for both Malthus and Ricardo. For Marx, 'explosive' process can lead to cyclical process but also to breaking-point and to radical change. It is clear today that change processes cannot be reduced to these few typical and idealistic patterns (cf. 'Social change'). The complexity of the effects of a system, the creative ability of the actors belonging to the system, and its environment set very narrow margins of validity to the perspectives which view the process of social change as a mechanical process like the patterns present in eco-systems analysis. Balance, variations around the equilibrium, and break-up are not privileged patterns in the case of social systems. Analysing systems as if they were eco-systems can be of only a slight interest for the sociologist.

Realizing the complexity of processes affecting social systems, modern sociologists tend to look sceptically at any attempt to represent societies as systems. One of Parson's books is still entitled *The Social System*. Easton and Etzioni, whatever their differences, also wish to apply the categories of system analysis to societies seen as a whole. It can be objected that attempts to describe the 'social system' in a general way have rarely succeeded in keeping away from teleological temptation. The fundamental examples of the thermostat in physics and of the organism in biology help to associate the notion of system with that of adaptation to a changing environment, with that of maintaining fundamental balance in the face of changing internal and external conditions. But with systems like markets, or even more so the social system in general, clear and fundamental differences emerge. If it is obvious that a market can provide some equilibrium, it is difficult to explain its effects in a teleological way. Such a view as Parson's four functions model or schema (AGIL) (adaptation, goal attainment, integration, latency) is a more accurate description of interaction systems than of interdependent systems. Societies cannot be taken for interactive systems in the way we have used this expression; societies are, in other words, of a higher level of complexity than organizational systems. The fact that political power tries to maintain a balance, that public opinion reacts against it, and that it is more or less successful according to its means, is obvious and incontestable. But it is not enough to base analogies more or less openly on society as organism. It is not unreasonable to imagine a society as a system providing the notion of system is taken in such a general way that it no longer means anything. In this case there will be little to say about social systems in general.

There is a tendency today to represent societies as a complex network of sub-systems maintaining more or less vague and changing links with each other (see the complexity of the link between education and employment markets or between sub-political and sub-economic systems). Therefore, the analysis of 'the' social system is reaching the limit of sociological knowledge. When Wallerstein and Braudel propose notions like 'World-System', apparently even more ambitious than Parsons's notions of social system, they in fact do not pretend to study the world as a system as such. They note that 'some particular processes' can only be understood on a world scale. The fact that international relations, for instance, can be studied today only on a world scale does not imply that any social process has to be studied on a world scale. The scale is determined by the particular process studied.

Up until now, it is the 'diachronic' analysis of social process that has been considered here. An important sociological tradition stretching from Montesquieu to so-called structural anthropology is involved in the 'synchronic' analysis of social institutions and systems. For these approaches it is a question of explaining the coherence of a set of institutions observed in a specific society at a specific time. Presupposing that institutions are coherent is the same as presupposing that they imply each other reciprocally and therefore make up a system.

The notion of 'system' derives from a simple observation, i.e., that in the physical or biological or social world, sets of interdependent elements can be found. After such an observation, one step forward is to identify types of systems. The thermostat is one of them. But it is not certain that the taxonomy of systems can be taken very far. On the other hand, one must certainly be careful not to conclude too rapidly that there are analogies between systems belonging to different realms of reality. This explains why the general 'theory' of systems sometimes gives a fragmented impression, with, on one side, a series of concepts useful to the description of concrete systems and their processes and, on the other hand, a collection, which keeps growing, of case studies taken from different realms of reality. The set boiler-radiator-thermostat makes up a system, but so does any mathematical equation 'system'! These systems have little more in common than the fact that they constitute sets of interdependent elements. On a general level, little more can be said. The general notion of a system is really helpful only as guidance. It begins to mean something specific only when it is used to analyse concrete process and systems, i.e., when they are singled out.

Function, Functionalism, Reproduction, Role, Structuralism, Structure.

Bibliography

BERTALANFFY, L. (von), *General system theory. Foundations, development, applications*, New York, G. Braziller, 1968; London, Allen Lane, 1971. – BUCKLEY, W., *Sociology and modern systems theory*, Englewood Cliffs, Prentice Hall, 1967. – CONDILLAC, E. (Bonnot de), *Traité des systèmes; où l'on démêle les inconvéients et les avantages*, La Haye, Neaulme, 1749; Paris, Libraires associés, 1749. – DEUTSCH, K., *The nerves of government*, New York, The Free Press, 1963, 1966. – EASTON, D., *A systems analysis of political life*, New York, Wiley, 1965. – EMERY, F.E., *Systems thinking*, London, Penguin modern management readings, 1965, 1970. – ETZIONI, A., *The active society*, New York, The Free Press, 1968. – LAPIERRE, J.W., *L'analyse des systèmes politiques*, Paris. PUF, 1973. – MARUYAMA, M., 'The second cybernetics: deviation amplifying causal processes', *American scientist*, LI, 1963, 164–179. – PARSONS, T., *The social system*, Glencoe, The Free Press/London Collier–Macmillan, 1951. – WALLERSTEIN, I., *The modern world system, capitalist agriculture and the origins of the European world economy in the sixteenth century*, London, Cambridge University Press, 1979.

T

Teleology

Aristotle identifies four types of causes. One of these is 'final' causes. Thus, the reason for this person's behaviour seen entering a tobacco shop is that he wants to buy cigarettes. The purpose of his behaviour is also its justification or cause. A teleological explanation for a phenomenon is therefore one which is based on explaining it through the goal aimed at by an individual, a group, or a system.

Let us first take the individual level. Some sociologists, like Durkheim, tend to think that the motivations and intentions of social actors must be removed from sociological analysis. The famous proposition, put forward in *Suicide*, according to which the suicide victim's motivations are of no help whatever in the sociological analysis of suicide (cf. 'Durkheim'), is well known. Such is the case, according to Durkheim, because, on the one hand, motivations can only be observed with difficulty and indirectly and, on the other hand, the statistical regularities as far as suicide is concerned reveal 'social' causes which are specifically the interest of the sociologist. This view has been widely criticized. It certainly is not the view of Max Weber for whom intentional actions have a privileged place in sociological analysis, together with three other types of actions (value-oriented actions, tradition and emotion-oriented actions). (cf. 'Action'). Nor is the view of Pareto, who identifies 'logical' actions (means and ends are proportionate) as against 'non-logical' actions some of which (second and fourth types) are intentional. The others (first and third types) are non-intentional but of limited interest to the sociologist according to Pareto. Intentional 'non-logical' actions are defined by the lack of relation between what is wished for by way of subjective ends and the objective consequences produced. Modern sociologists tend to follow Max Weber and Pareto rather than Durkheim on the subject. Many social phenomena can clearly be properly analysed only if actors' final ends are taken into account. It must be added immediately however: 1) that there can be a dissonance between the pursued ends and the resulting consequences; 2) that all actions are not always intentional; 3) that consequently they are not always rational as economists define it (cf. 'Rationality').

Let us now turn to the group level. Can one explain teleologically a group or collective action, using this group's ends? The answer depends on the kind of group considered. Taking the simplest case, that of the organized group, with institutionalized, collective decision-making, an 'idiomorphic' interpretation of its actions can be given. In other words it can be treated as if it were an individual. Thus, there is nothing shocking in talking about the intentions, wishes, beliefs, or decisions as far as, say, the German government or a union is concerned in such and such a way. However one has to specify: 1) that the collective ends are defined and acted on by a managing team with constitutional authority; 2) that the probability of reaching these ends depends on the relationship between the officials and other members of the group, for in this case using a vocabulary borrowed from individual psychology for a collective entity does not lead to a major ambiguity. It is quite different when the 'idiomorphic' vocabulary (i.e., assimilating the group to an individual) is used for non-organized groups or groups which cannot be 'institutionally represented', such as social classes or groups described as latent (cf. 'Action (collective)') by Dahrendorf, groups with members who share a common interest (i.e., apart from social classes, such as consumers, taxpayers, etc.). Take, for instance, the expression: 'the will of the working class'. Here, either this 'will' is voiced by a particular organization with a mechanism for collective decision-making like the Communist Party and such an expression – even if sociologically arguable – has no logical ambiguity, or such a formulation is untenable. The expression then becomes either a simple metaphor or a short-cut to express the idea that each of the members of a hidden group (or a majority of them) are showing the 'will' talked about. At this point comes what has sometimes been called the paradox of collective action (cf. 'Action (collective)'). Marx drew attention to this paradox: in the *Eighteenth Brumaire* he shows that peasant smallholders do not appear to be class conscious and are not in any case capable of achieving their class interest, i.e., the interest of the 'possible group' that they make up, or even the common interests of each of the smallholding peasants. Pareto also explains how the actions of directors of a monopolistic firm are generally of a logical kind, but actions of directors in a perfect competition system are often of a non-logical kind (fourth kind), actions where subjective ends and objective consequences do not correspond. Generally, an enterprise's director aims to increase his profits by increasing productivity. But in a perfect competition climate, since all the entrepreneurs aim to do the same, they will only make prices go down to the consumer's benefit without any additional profit to the firms. On the other hand, a monopoly or an oligopoly can increase their profits (*Treatise of General Sociology*: 159). Thus, in 'some cases', a latent group may not be able to serve its own interests. Thus, it cannot then be analysed idiomorphically. This pattern appears when there is a contradiction between the individual and collective interests of the latent group. Of course there are also cases when individual and collective interest coincide. An idiomorphic analysis is then possible and it is also possible to talk of 'conscience' or 'class consciousness'. Thus, while Marx showed that smallholding peasants have contradictory individual and collective interests, it is not the same for other classes.

Lastly, there is the 'system level'. Some social systems seem to be guided by a goal. Some systems appear to 'advance' in a continuous direction. Others appear to 'aim at' their own reproduction. In complex societies a process of linear progress can be observed (the process of increasing 'individuation' which Simmel, Durkheim, and Parsons emphasized; the process of nuclearization of the family which has become a traditional theme since Parsons; the process of increasing societal interdependence and complexity; the process of the extension of individual rights, described by T.H. Marshall, etc.). Reproductive processes are also found (i.e. reproduction of social hierarchies). Some social processes recall in other terms the evolutionary and reproductive phenomena observed at the level of the living entity. Following Monod, these phenomena can be called 'teleonomical': the system as such appears to aim at an end or goal (*telos*).

Teleonomic phenomena can be explained in two ways. In the first kind of explanation (type 1), the teleonomic character of the system is shown as being part of a goal inscribed in the constituting elements of the system. This kind of explanation is found in Comte. The 'progress' of humanity, summed up by the 'law of the three states', would come from the fact that men follow 'a tendency to perfect their nature', according to Comte. We find the same point emphasized by Bossuet too: in *Discours sur l'histoire universelle*, men are supposed to act following the laws defined by the hand of Providence. Some modern historians conceive historical development as the result of the direction of history, apparent either to individual consciousness in general or only to the most enlightened. For Touraine, intellectuals, technicians, and experts are the modern carriers of historicity. In the second type of explanation (type 2), the teleonomic character of the system is seen as an emergent effect resulting from the aggregation of elementary mechanisms while logic is *not in any way* guided by the ends towards which the system as such seems to lead. The most obvious of such examples in the field of natural sciences is represented by Darwinism, or more exactly by neo-Darwinism: according to this theory, evolution is the result of natural selection that operates through environmental interaction with random mutation. In the sociological field, numerous examples of this second type are found. Both Simmel and Parsons's explanations of the individuation process specific to complex societies are of this type. Merton also uses this type of explanation when he analyses the development of anti-black racism among American manual workers between the First and Second World Wars: economic problems and general conditions at the time forced many Blacks to come to the North to find work. As the black workers had no unionized tradition, white workers preferred to favour white workers for recruitment (not because of racism but because they wanted to preserve the union institutions). Blacks then became an easy prey for strike-breaking bosses. Hence, Whites now had 'factual' confirmation of their suspicions: Blacks cannot be 'good union men'. Racism then appears as an emergent effect coming from the aggregation of the behaviours of different classes of individuals as they are introduced into the social context. For an overall view of emergent effects and for an introduction to logical problems facing the analysis of the aggregation of individual actions, Hirschman, Merton, and Schelling can be consulted (see 'Bibliography').

Sometimes, type 1 explanations are called 'finalist' or 'teleological' and type 2 explanations are described as 'mechanistic'. This vocabulary is acceptable when applied to biology. But it is a source of confusion when applied to sociology. Thus, in type 2 explanations, actors' behaviours can often be seen as intentional or teleological. Union members in Merton's case do act in relation to a goal: to avoid weakening union power. But it is in fact a type 2 explanation because the new racism is seen as an *emergent* effect, not a goal set by the actors. Similarly, the nuclearization of families in complex societies derives from the aggregation of teleological behaviour, and is not something specifically sought after by the actors themselves. It is thus an emergent effect.

In the case of biology, it would seem undeniable that Darwin's 'mechanistic' interpretation is a step forward compared to the 'finalist' interpretation like Cuvier's. In Marx's works, 'mechanistic' analysis (type 2) of some linear historical processes is a step forward compared with the 'teleological' analysis used by Bossuet, Comte, or certain historicists (type 1). Marx and Engels were perfectly aware of what they owed to Darwin on this point and of their convergence with him, as a letter from Engels to Marx points out in November, 1859: 'Besides, this Darwin that I am reading now is first class. On one level, teleology has not been demolished yet, it is still being done.' But it is not true that type 2 explanations are unconditionally and generally preferable to type 1 explanations. This point is shown well by Pareto's distinction referred to earlier: a monopoly, a cartel, or an oligopoly can generally obtain what it wants (for example, the petrol price increase in 1973 was due to the fact that the oil producers' cartel thought that such an increase was desirable and could be imposed). In that case the goals of the system are directly inscribed in the actors' motivations. On the other hand, the fall in prices which could result from the increase in productivity in a context of perfect competition is an emergent effect which has not been intended by the actors.

In the same way some revolutionary processes are unleashed by groups aiming to start a revolution. These processes can also result from the aggregation of behaviours which *do not* have a revolution as their objective. Both de Tocqueville and Cochin emphasize this point. They propose an analysis of the causes of the French Revolution mixing both type 1 and 2 interpretations. The contrast with the common conception found from Aulard to Souboul and including Mathiez, when type 1 explanations are used, seeing the revolt as the product of the discontent of some groups and of the desire for change that it implied, is striking.

This is an interesting example, as it shows that it is possible to waver between a type 1 and a type 2 explanation in some circumstances or, more exactly, points to the possibility of combining both types. In the example of the French Revolution, both types probably hold a part of the truth. De Tocqueville and Cochin showed that lawyers unwittingly played an important part in the starting of the Revolution (type 2). But the discontent of some social groups, like the peasants, naturally had an influence (type 1). But it is fair to point out that the peasants probably did not wish for such an uncontrollable revolution as the one that followed. In some cases only type 2 explanations are acceptable. Traffic jams are not the deliberate product of drivers' actions or their unconscious desire. Similarly, reproductive or evolutionary processes taking place over a long period of time (such as nuclearization of the family, individuation, complexification, reproduction of social differentiation) cannot be seen as type 1 patterns. Except if the hand of Providence is reintroduced in a roundabout and somewhat mysterious way, (not in the sense of de Tocqueville's introduction to *Democracy in America* but in the sense of Bossuet's *Discours sur l'histoire universelle*), it is difficult for the above processes to be the products of conscious intentions or unconscious motivations which would make social actors look for these effects. In reality, these processes come from the aggregation of motivations orientated towards individual ends which are unconnected with the consequences that they produce. They are thus more akin to type 2 explanations.

Action, Cycles, Determinism, Historicism, Reproduction, Social Change.

Bibliography

BOUDON, R., 'Introduction, Sociologie et liberté', 'Effets pervers et changement social', and 'Déterminismes sociaux et liberté individuelle', *in* BOUDON, R., *Effets pervers et ordre social*, Paris, PUF, 1977, chap. I, II and VII, 5–15, 17–58 and 187–252. – COCHIN, A., *L'esprit du jacobinisme. Une interprétation sociologique de la Révolution française*, Paris, PUF, 1979, from *Les sociétés de la Pensée et de la Démocratie*, Paris, Plon, 1921. – HIRSCHMAN, A.O., *Exit, voice and loyalty. Responses to decline in firms, organizations and states*, Cambridge, Harvard University Press, 1970. – MERTON, R.K., 'The unanticipated consequences of purposive social action', *American sociological review*, I, 6, 1936, 894–904. – MONOD, J., *Le hasard et la nécessité. Essai sur la philosophie naturelle de la biologie moderne*, Paris, Le Seuil, 1970. – POPPER, K.R., *The poverty of historicism*, London, Routledge & Kegan Paul, 1957, 1963; New York, Basic Books, 1960; New York, Harper and Row, 1961, 1964. – SCHELLING, T., *Micromotives and macrobehaviour*, Toronto, Norton, 1978. – STARK, W., 'Society as an organism', *in* STARK, W., *The fundamental forms of social thought*, London, Routledge & Kegan Paul, 1962, 15–106. – TOCQUEVILLE, *The Ancien Régime*, op cit. (II). – TOURAINE, A., *Production de la société*, Paris, Le Seuil, 1973.

Theory

To open any work on sociological theory (e.g., Parsons and Shils's *Theories of Society* or Gross's *Symposium on Sociological Theory*) is to realize that the notion of theory means many things in sociology and that these meanings are even more diverse than in the natural sciences. Merton indicated this diversity very clearly in a classical text in his *Social Theory and Social Structure*. He writes that sociologists tend to use the word theory as synonymous with 1) methodology; 2) general sociological orientations; 3) conceptual analysis; 4) post factum sociological interpretations; 5) empirical generalizations; 6) 'derivations' (deductions from consequences derived from already established propositions) and 'codifications' (the search for general propositions through induction, permitting the sociologist to subsume already established propositions); 7) sociological theory (in the strict sense).

If theory (in the strict sense) means a set of propositions comprising a system, from which justifiable conclusions can be drawn from a confrontation with observed data, Merton then is right: the concept of theory as used in sociology cannot be reduced to that meaning. The concept might however be less varied than Merton suggests. In sociology, theory appears to have two fundamental meanings. That of 'theory in the strict sense' on one hand and that of 'paradigm' on the other. Paradigm is here used as meaning a set of propositions or meta-theoretic hypotheses aiming less at social reality than at the language used to study this social reality. Let's clarify this point. In *Social Mobility*, Sorokin uses theory in a strict sense. The following propositions summarize it: 1) any society is stratified, stratification is due to the division of labour; 2) the persistence of this stratification is ensured from one generation to another by a certain number of selection mechanisms; 3) in industrial societies, there are two main selecting agents, family and school; 4) if these agents do not operate efficiently, young people will develop social aspirations that society will not be able to satisfy; 5) in this case revolutionary ideologies will appear. A theory in the strictest sense appears here: a set of linked propositions from which it is possible to infer consequences which in principle can be confronted with reality. Let us take as a counter-example the 'paradigm of functional analysis' which Merton proposes in *Social Theory and Social Structure*. To explain a social phenomenon, like an institution, it is generally useful to consider its manifest and latent functions. Having said that, some institutions can be a-functional, others functional in relation to some groups, and dysfunctional in regard to other groups. The Mertonian theory of the political machine is a typical example of the paradigm of functional analysis: the reason for the political machinery of the American democratic party is its 'latent function' as 'social security' for the most deprived part of its electorate. 'Functional analysis' is a paradigm rather than a theory because it is composed of a set of propositions dealing with the steps the sociologist must follow to build a theory aiming to explain such or such an aspect of society, rather than dealing directly with such or such an aspect of society. Propositions defining 'functional analysis' are really of a meta-theoretical nature: they are not a discourse on social reality but on the theories relative to social reality. This definition of paradigm is notably different from Kuhn's definition, although not incompatible with it (cf. 'Knowledge').

It is useful to attempt a rough classification of paradigms found in sociological theory (in a wide sense) without pretending to be exhaustive. A first set of paradigms can be referred to under the heading of 'conceptual paradigms' so-called 'classificational paradigms', since they are often based on a classification or an implicit or explicit typology. For instance: the opposition between *Gemeinschaft* (community) and *Gesellschaft* (society) analysed by Tönnies. This opposition suggests that the different forms of association between men can be described as a continuum, the ends of which are represented by associations of a contractual type on one hand and by the primary group (for instance the family) on the other. In the first case, individual relationships are mainly of a utilitarian type; they are the consequence of the manifestation of a well-understood self-interest; interactions between the members of society are designed to very definite goals. In the second case, relationships are mainly of an affective type; they are guided by altruism; interactions have numerous functions (members of a family can gather for a council session or simply because they enjoy meeting each other). These distinctions, according to Tönnies, not only can be used as a guide to describe and analyse different kinds of small groups, but can also provide a (metaphorical) frame for the analysis of organizations or of whole societies. The well-known distinction, derived from Redfield, between traditional societies and modern societies, and the opposition between industrial societies and post-industrial societies are other examples very close in their shape and epistemological function to Tönnies's distinction. In any case, the paradigm appears as an opposition between concepts, the virtue of which is to seize fundamental differences and distinctions at all levels of analysis the sociologist might deal with: at a microsociological level, community or well-defined group level, or macrosociological level. Parsons's theory of 'pattern variables' is another well-known example of a conceptual paradigm. It is shaped as four conceptual oppositions and Parsons endeavoured to show that they were useful to the analysis of extremely diverse social phenomena (i.e., analysis of professions, processes of professionalization and de-professionalization, comparative analysis of stratificiations systems).

A second set of paradigms can be classified as 'analogical paradigms'. In this case the 'theoretician' suggests that a set of more or less circumscribed but numerous social phenomena can be seen as directed by analagous mechanisms which characterize either other types of social phenomena, or phenomena typically dealt with by other fields than sociology. Sociology of migration provides a good example of an analogous paradigm. Names like Zipf, Dodd, or Stouffer are part of the research tradition but their 'theories' (in the narrow sense) are all built on a paradigm postulating an analogy between migratory phenomena and the mechanisms of attraction described by Newtonian mechanics. Also, many works to do with the sociology of diffusion postulate an analogy between social diffusion and epidemic phenomena (cf. 'Diffusion'). A 'theory' such as Homans's exchange theory also belongs to the analogous paradigm category. In an article which was to inspire many studies, 'Social behaviour as exchange', Homans suggests that social interaction mechanisms can generally be seen as analogous to those of economic exchange. In the simplest case of exchange, two protagonists X and Y come into interaction. They own two things x and y. So that the exchange will take place, what it will cost X to transmit x to Y must be seen as lower than the benefit he will get from Y in exchange. In the same way, Y will also want to see himself as benefiting from the exchange. So as to show that this mechanism can be applied by analogy to many kinds of social interaction, Homans shows that several studies are made clearer if the exchange paradigm is used to explain them. One of these studies dealt with the behaviour of inspectors in charge of assessing the management efficiency of certain companies. These inspectors had to report to a controller. The exchange paradigm can easily be applied to the interactions between inspectors and controllers. If these inspectors need to make an unfavourable report, they have to pay a price: to be disowned if their conclusions are wrong. Asking the controller's point of view beforehand is a benefit, the value of which has to be weighted against the possibility of being disowned. The controller can see his role in different ways. If he asks his inspectors too high a price (for instance by showing off his superiority), he will discourage consultation. The controlling part will be less efficient and the controller will be responsible for that. He will then

eventually pay a higher price than the satisfaction he has in enjoying his superiority. If he asks too low a price, he will expose himself to a 'loss', by other mechanisms which are easily analysed. He will waste part of his time advising his
inspectors and end up doing their work. So as to reduce the price to pay, it was
observed that inspectors often asked for their colleagues' opinions. This leads us to
analyse the system 'as' an exchange system between three partners. Many other
analogous paradigms can be mentioned. Parsons, in a well-known essay, set out to
conceptualize the social function of power in a similar way to money. Some
variants of functionalist 'theory' consider social systems as analogous to biological
systems. The interactionist sociological 'theory' (role, actor, etc.) uses an analogy
with the actor who 'plays' his part on the stage and the social actor who 'plays' his
part against the background of a particular institution or organization. Some
analogous paradigms are more implicit but widely represented in sociological
literature. Thus, many actors agree that global societies can be 'considered' as
organizations of a highly complex level. Others accept that social conflicts can
always be 'conceived as duels' where the winner's gain equals the loser's loss.

A third set of paradigms can be listed under the heading of 'formal paradigms'.
Unlike the two previous paradigms, formal paradigms carry indications which are
more syntactic than semantic about the way sociological theories (in the narrow
sense) should be built or analysis of social phenomena should be guided. The
Mertonian paradigm of 'functional analysis' is of this type (cf. 'Functionalism').
According to Merton, the sociological explanation of social institutions must
devote an essential role to the analysis of the needs and demands to which institutions respond, and he proposed to call this response 'function'. The sociological
analysis of institutions must bring their functions to light, must see that the manifest functions (if there are any) do not necessarily coincide with the latent functions, that dysfunctional institutions can persist if they have functional elements for
some groups, etc. Another example of formal paradigm is the analysis of 'systems'.
This paradigm (cf. 'System') depends on the interdependence of variables and on
the circular character of the relationships of causality that link them. Structural
analysis, aiming to illuminate the relations of interdependence between the institutions of a social system or between the linguistic characteristics of a text, is another
example of a formal paradigm, similar to systems analysis (cf. 'Structuralism').
Another example could be the dialectic that lends fundamental explanatory power
to the analysis of contradiction and conflict in social systems and social processes
(cf. 'Dialectic').

Often, research practices are based on implicit formal paradigms. A good deal
of empirical sociology aims to establish the relative influence of a set of explanatory
variables (still described as independent) on a set of variables which are still to be
explained (usually described as dependent). The researcher uses an implicit
formal paradigm, whether he uses multivariate analysis, a regression analysis with
multiple equations, a correlation analysis, or indeed any statistical device. This
paradigm can be summarized by the proposition according to which the explanation of a dependent variable y (concerned with, for example, electoral behaviour,
with level of education, with individual social status, or with $\overline{GDP}$) is intended to

determine the influence of various 'factors' on this variable (cf. 'Causality'). In regression analysis with multiple equations, these factors are identified a priori. In correlation analysis and other forms of factorial analysis, these factors are identified a posteriori, more or less successfully. But the implicit formal paradigm is identical in both types of statistical technique.

The three types of paradigms already mentioned share some common traits. Some concepts are inspired by metaphors (cf. architectural origin of the notion of 'structure' or the geometrical origin of the notion of 'social distance'). Therefore they have a base in analogy. Some formal paradigms (like system analysis) postulate a structural analogy between different zones of reality.

The paradigms of sociological 'theory' largely follow the dynamic processes described by Kuhn for natural sciences. In sociology, as in natural science, specific theories are formulated from a metatheoretical frame used as a guide for their establishment. Some of these paradigms are of an analogical character (i.e., corpuscular theory on light, 'survival' theories, 'artificial intelligence' theories), others are of a formal character (cf. the use of systems analysis in ecology), others are of a conceptual character (cf. taxonomies used by paleontologists). As in natural science, paradigms in sociology seem to present either great vitality or great inertia depending on how you look at it. Because they constitute the intellectual frame for the work of research sub-communities, they tend to persist long after they have been challenged by observation and other theories.

There are three reasons for this inertia. First, it is nearly always possible to manipulate a theory based on a paradigmatic frame so as to make it uniform with observations which are hardly compatible with it at first sight. Second, for a paradigm to be abandoned a more convincing and useful paradigm has to be found. Otherwise, the researcher finds himself in a situation of anomie: lacking guidance of a paradigm, his activity becomes confused, he cannot decide what to look for. Third, abandoning a paradigm is generally done at high social cost for the researcher (cf. 'Knowledge'). This is why paradigms are a kind of 'Janus-faced' entity. Indispensable to research, they tend to take on too great an efficiency and generality. In some cases they can become a hindrance.

Redfield's distinction between traditional and modern societies, the opposition proposed by Tönnies between 'community' and 'society' have had similar and considerable influence. They have inspired much research and given it a conceptual and methodological frame. But these paradigms have also provoked the appearance of undesirable conceptions. Sociologists of development often accept that underdeveloped societies are generally stagnant, essentially due to the weight of traditions and to a greater interdependence than in modern societies between the economic and cultural aspects of social life, and that development must therefore be an exogenous process. Accepting this they derive inspiration from the paradigms of Tönnies and Redfield but take them too far. Neither Japan nor Prussia in the nineteenth century was a stagnant society before it took off. In both cases development appears historically to be more endogenous than exogenous. In the same way, role theory has led to 'hyper-functionalist' theories of society. Sometimes, the class position of actors is seen as a kind of partition that they would inevitably enter. Formal paradigms like structural analysis have led to theories where actors and social agents disappear from the analysis and are merely seen as 'supports' for the structure. The underlying factorial paradigm in statistical instruments like regression analysis or correlation analysis sometimes led researchers to a debatable and implicit postulate i.e., that all individuals and societies can be represented by a list of variables, the purpose of the analysis simply being able to establish the influence of these variables on each other. Although it is probably useful to find out the statistical weight of such or such variable, for instance the differential coefficients of fertility (or of schooling), a statistical analysis of this kind can represent in general only one stage of the analysis. To explain fertility coefficients (or educational ones) always in the end means explaining the behaviour of actors in terms of fertility (or of schooling). To do this means rejecting the paradigm, 'the individual in a list of variables' and replacing it with the paradigm, 'the individual as acting subject'.

Can sociological theory (in the widest sense), i.e. paradigms used by sociologists, be seen as progressing? The answer seems positive. Paradigms like systems analysis, structural analysis, Homans's exchange paradigms have explained phenomena which are less clearly understood with less powerful paradigms. The structural analysis of kinship in archaic societies helps us to understand the apparently anarchical rules of incest prohibition. The exchange paradigm, as presented by Olson, helps to explain obscure aspects of the sociology of union institutions and, more generally, of the sociology of voluntary group participation. Also, with time, the limits and zones of validity of paradigms are more clearly seen. It is clearer today than yesterday that the traditional/modern opposition must be used with care. The risks of a slide from structural analysis to structuralism or from functional analysis to functionalism are the more clearly seen. The limits of validity of an analogous paradigm like role theory are better understood. Generally, the dangers of analogous conceptual paradigms, when they are given too wide a relevance or too literal a meaning or too realist an interpretation, are well understood. Sociological theory (in the widest sense) finally appears as capable of advance. It might well be that the variety of paradigms described above is less diverse than it is made to appear. Many of the above paradigms in fact share a common paradigm: that social phenomena are seen as the product of the aggregation of individual actions, whether it is a question of events, statistical regularity, differences or similarities between groups or societies. Awareness of this shared paradigm re-translates in a clear way the intuitions contained in paradigms which at first sight are paradoxical, like functional analysis and dialectic, for instance. However the history of sociology which would attempt to study the development, mutations, convergence, and divergence of sociological paradigms has still to be written. Although several authors have taken that direction, i.e., Stark, Nisbet, Eisenstadt, there is still no equivalent in sociology to Schumpeter's *History of Economic Analysis*.

The notion of theory as such in sociology includes entities that it might be better to call paradigms on one hand and 'theories in the narrow sense' on the other. As far as sociological theories in the narrow sense are concerned, some epistemological questions might be asked. How far is the structure of these theories different from the theories proposed by the natural sciences? How far can they be verified? How far can the conceptions of writers like Popper, Lakatos, or Feyeraband about the rationality criteria of scientific theories be applied to sociological theories? In which way does the 'interpretative' characteristic of the sociologist researcher make the theories different from the ones found in other fields of scientific research? These questions, with others, are considered in the articles on 'Objectivity' and 'Knowledge'.

Action, Functionalism, Knowledge, Objectivity.

Bibliography

BOTTOMORE, T., and NISBET, R., *A history of sociological analysis*, New York, Basic Books, 1978; London, Heinemann, 1979. – EISENSTADT, S.N., and CURELARU, M., *The form of sociology, paradigms and crises*, New York/London, Wiley, 1976. – GROSS, L., (ed.), *Symposium on sociological theory*, New York/Evanston/London, Harper, 1959. – HEATH, A., 'Review-article: exchange theory', *British journal of political science*, I, *1*, 1971, 91–119. – HOMANS, G.C., 'Social behavior as exchange', *American journal of sociology*, LXIII, *6*, 1958, 597–606. – KUHN, T.S., *The structure of scientific revolutions*, Chicago, Chicago University Press, 1962, 1970. – LAKATOS, I., 'Falsification and the methodology of scientific research programmes', *in* LAKATOS, I., and MUSGRAVE, A. (ed.), *Criticism and the growth of knowledge*, London, Cambridge University Press, 1970, 91–196. – NISBET, R., *The sociological tradition*, New York, Basic Books, 1966; London, Heinemann, 1967. – PARSONS, T., 'On the concept of political power', *Proceedings of the american philosophical society*, CVII, *3*, 1963, 232–262. – PARSONS, T., SHILS, E., NAEGELE, D., PITTS, J.R. (ed.), *Theories of society. Foundations of modern sociological theory*, New York, The Free Press/London, Collier-Macmillan, 1961. – SCHUMPETER, J., *History of economic analysis*, London, Allen and Unwin, 1954, 1972. – STARK, W., *The fundamental forms of social thought*, London, Routledge & Kegan Paul, 1962.

Tocqueville, Alexis de

Although he was widely praised and respected by his contemporaries as one of the most perceptive observers of his time, Alexis de Tocqueville was almost completely forgotten in France until after the Second World War, despite some references to his work by Durkheim. However, his prestige was never eclipsed in the United States, where his *Democracy in America* was widely thought to be one of the most pertinent studies ever to have been written on American society.

None the less, de Tocqueville was not to be admitted as a full member of the sociological pantheon until Raymond Aron drew attention once more to his work. His somewhat eccentric and marginal contemporary Auguste Comte still stands as 'founder' of sociology. Karl Marx, another character whom de Tocqueville was unlikely to encounter in everyday life at the *Academie Française*, or at the Chamber of Deputies (French equivalent of the House of Commons or Congress – (ed.)), is also thought of today as one of sociology's founding fathers. Perhaps in waiting so long for recognition de Tocqueville pays the price of being neither a radical nor the founder of a sect, but instead a lucid observer who always kept at a suitable distance from the object of his study.

De Tocqueville offers a coherent and original interpretation of the nature, functioning, and development of modern – or, as we like to say now, industrial – society. It concerns the movement from a traditional society, of orders and estates, to modern society characterized by competition between relatively mobile and statutorily equal individuals. In his work certain alternative models are used. On the one hand, where he deals with the administrative history of France, he offers us a model of reproduction. The Revolution is not a break with the past: both the imperial and the republican administrations reinforce bureaucratic tendencies already strongly evident in the offices and institutions of the *Ancien Régime.* But on the other hand, the Revolution, with its affirmation of the principle that citizens are formally equal, constitutes a real break with a conception of law based on equality, or in other words on differences and privileges. In the case of America, it is possible to observe the same contrast. From one point of view American society – at least that which developed on the coast of New England – is the offspring of English society, or at least of the puritan variant of that society. But from the other side, purged of all *Tory* influence, American society is a radical experiment in social and political organization, pursued with incomparable and unique vigour. The United States is, in the precise sense of the expression given to it by Lipset, *the first new nation.*

De Tocqueville is also sensitive to what we would nowadays call cumulative effects. This aspect of his work is most clear-cut in the third part of *The Ancien Régime and the Revolution.* De Tocqueville's insistence on emphasizing how the characteristics of administrative organization of France in the nineteenth century were already present in the royal bureaucracy does not make the dramatic rupture of the late-eighteenth century immediately understandable. De Tocqueville adds to the two models of reproduction and reinforcement presented in the first two parts of the study, a final part which analyses two types of cumulative process, one of relatively short duration, the other conjunctural. The first concerns the process of de-legitimation of the traditional order by the *philosophes.* The second concerns what could be called the self-stabilization of *Ancien Régime* society by the king, his counsellors, and senior civil servants – which achieved its apogee in Calonne's disastrous project of administrative reform of 1786.

De Tocqueville practised comparative method spontaneously, but carried it out quite rigorously. He had direct experience, although by different routes, of the three great societies of his time in process of democratization: the USA, England, and France. But he had a very fine understanding of national differences. None the less, when discussing Tocquevillian comparison, we should steer clear of two hazards. First, anecdotes always had a general significance for de Tocqueville. They were not quoted so as to provide a picturesque ethnographic effect but in order to invoke certain differences in the institutional structure which de Tocqueville sought to explain. Second, the differences which serve so often as points of departure for his reflections are never reduced to historical particularities, although he attached great importance to the history of the peoples which he studied. For example, the differences in attitudes towards political authority – defiance among the French, deference among the English – is explained in part by the role of public adminstration in France, in England, or in America. But these attitudes are not treated as irreducible givens which evoke a mysterious national character.

De Tocqueville's comparativism is based on a logic of institutional differences. The analysis of the political radicalism of *Ancien Régime* intellectuals is a classic. De Tocqueville contrasts the turbulence of the French *philosophes* of the Enlightenment with the practical approach of English and American intellectuals. But he is careful to explain these differences by reference simply to the nature of the 'general and dominant passion' for liberty and equality that is so closely associated with the heritage of Voltaire and the Encyclopaedists. Indeed, these 'passions' are not confined to French intellectuals. They are the property of democratic man. The only thing specific to the French case is a certain cultural tradition – the primacy of the humanities, but especially a certain location within the social structure, which brought the intellectuals close to the powerful of eighteenth-century society (through the institution of the *salon*), and at the same time kept them far from the decision-making centres which continued to be monopolized by the king and his people.

De Tocqueville offers us an interpretation of the political societies of the modern West, combining finesse and rigour unequally as part of a project whose objectives were fairly well circumscribed: how do three societies which inherited the same tradition, France, England, and the United States, move towards the creation of a democratic society? What directions do they follow? What institutional specificities ensure the originality of each in relation to the others?

Action, Democracy, Experimentation, History and Sociology, Objectivity, Weber.

Bibliography

TOCQUEVILLE, Alexis de; *Democracy in America* ed Philips Bradley, New York, Alfred A. Knopf, 1945; *The Old Régime and the French Revolution*, trs. Stuart Gilbert, London, Mayflower, 1960. – ARON, R., *Main Currents in Sociological Thought, Vol 1*, London, Weidenfeld and Nicolson, 1965. – TOCQUEVILLE, Alexis de, *De la démocratie en Amérique*, 1835; *L'Ancien Régime et la Révolution*, 1856, in *Œuvres complètes*, Paris, Gallimard, 1952–1970, 13 vol. – ARON, R., 'La définition libérale de la liberté: Alexis de Tocqueville et Karl Marx', *Archives européennes de Sociologie*, V, 2, 1964, 159–189; *Les Grandes étapes de la pensée sociologique*, Paris, Gallimard, 1967, 1974. – BIRNBAUM, P., *Sociologie de Tocqueville*, Paris, PUF, 1970. – BOURRICAUD, F., 'Cotradition et traditions chez Tocqueville', *The Tocqueville Review*, Winter 1980, 11, 1, 25–39; *Le bricolage idéologique. Essai sur les intellectuals et les passions démocratiques*, Paris, PUF, 1980, 37–67. – DRESCHER, S., *Dilemmas of democracy, Tocqueville and modernization*, Pittsburg, Univ. of Pittsburg Press, 1968. – FURET, F., *Penser la Révolution française*, Paris, Gallimard, 1978. – GAUCHET, M., 'Tocqueville, l'Amérique et nous. Sur la genèse des sociétés démocratiques', *Libre*, VII, 1980. – JARDIN, A. and PIERSON, G.W., (eds.), *Gustave de Beaumont, Lettres d'Amérique, 1831–1832*, Paris, PUF, 1973. – LAMBERTI, J.-C., *La notion d'individualisme chez Tocqueville*, Paris, PUF, 1970. – LIVELY, J., *The social and political thought of Alexis de Tocqueville*, Oxford, Clarendon Press, 1962. – SCHLEIFER, J.T., *The making of Tocqueville's Democracy in America*, Univ. of North Carolina Press, 1980.

U

Utilitarianism

The term was invented by Bentham and reinvented by John Stuart Mill, two authors for whom it was initially a philosophical doctrine, the discussion of which is beyond the scope of this *Dictionary*. Outside these particular doctrines, utilitarianism is a movement of thought and a complex reflection on the role of interests in social order and social change.

The fact that England did not experience a regime of absolute and centralized monarchy in modern times, and also the fact that social change there assumed the shape of economic upheavals that seemed to result from the encounter between so many individual initiatives and enterprises, probably explain to a great extent why interest in utilitarian thought is largely an English phenomenon. Apart from Bentham and John Stuart Mill, the main figures of utilitarianism are Adam Smith, Ricardo, James Mill, Alfred Marshall, Henry Sidgwick, and Herbert Spencer. The concept of the 'invisible hand' in Adam Smith's work states in a shorthand way a type of general theorem of order and social progress: the pursuit of particular interests works to the advantage of the general interest. Smith comes back to the proof contained in the *Fable of the Bees* by Mandeville, a book published in the earlier part of the eighteenth century, but which was extremely popular for many decades. Rousseau refers to it and so does Marx. The central theorem of the *Fable* reads: 'Private vices make public virtue.' Similarly, Smith attempts to show that the juxtaposition of selfish behaviours generates unintentional altruism. By bringing down his prices to attract his rival's customers, a butcher thinks he serves his own interest. In fact, he is only serving the consumer's interest since his rival will do the same. With Smith and Ricardo, the movement of utilitarian thought results in the creation of a new discipline: economic theory. That economics is anchored in the utilitarian tradition is historically indisputable, even if modern economics is sometimes presented as being freed from its utilitarian origin through the simple fact that it tends to substitute the notion of *preference* for the traditional notion of interest. But the utilitarian paradigm was not limited to the analysis of economic phenomena only. Thus, for Spencer, the endless development of co-operation entails a process of continuous differentiation in societies. With Spencer, the interplay of individual interests results in an evolutionist theory of societies. This process of growing differentiation suggests, according to Spencer, an analogy between the development of the embryo and the development of society. But this is only an analogy. The cause of this differentiation lies in the interplay of individual interests.

English utilitarianism was always considered, in German-speaking countries and in France, with some kind of repulsion, at least from the twentieth century. For the philosophy of Enlightenment is impregnated with utilitarianism, not only in Helvetius's work but also in Rousseau's. *The Social Contract* is based on the observation that conflicting interests under the regime of natural liberty lead to counterproductive effects as far as these very interests are concerned. But from the twentieth century, the utilitarian paradigm appears to French and German thinkers as incapable of taking social phenomena properly into account. The French Revolution had proved how important political conflicts were in social change. The excesses of that same Revolution had, according to authors such as Bonald and de Maistre, demonstrated the paradox of how important traditions were in the analysis of social order and social change. As Nisbet showed, Bonald's and de Maistre's major intuitions reappear in Durkheim's work ('collective consciousness') and Weber's technical rationality. In Prussia, the role played by the monarchy in the modernization of society suggested that social change is not exclusively the result of anonymous 'social forces' as the partisans of utilitarianism thought it was. Hence the role attributed by Hegel to the State in the *Grundlinien*. The 'sphere of needs' being, according to him, a generation of anarchy rather than order, the movements of 'civil society' must be prescribed by the State.

Generally speaking, in the same way that economics has been defined as an extension of the movement of utilitarian thought and found favourable ground in England, sociology has been defined in reaction to the same movement and developed mainly in France and in Germany where, for complex historical reasons some of which are suggested above, the anonymous 'social forces' represented by the interplay of interests did not seem to be enough to explain social change. De Tocqueville insists on the role of collective passions (for instance the passion for equality) in the analysis of social developments. Through the notion of class consciousness, Marx suggests that social actors may not recognize their own interest in some circumstances. Durkheim does not give much credit to interests and certainly disputes the fact that the phenomenon of the division of labour results from their interplay. Weber insists on the fact that individual actions may be not only *zweckrationell*, but also *traditionell* and *wertrationell*. Pareto only attributes a minor role to interests and regards the 'residues' as essential. Incidentally, one will notice that the widespread repulsion which the concept of *interest* inspired, reached the economists themselves who have a tendency nowadays to define utilitarianism in a very restrictive manner, as the normative conception according to which the maximization of individual utilities would represent the only possible collective ideal. Moreover, the same economists have a tendency, nowadays, to define *homo oeconomicus* as a man who follows not his interests but his preferences.

Looking back, it appears that the contrast between the two traditions of thought must not be over-emphasized. Perhaps sociology, not as it is often presented but as it really is, is based less on the categorical rejection of the utilitarian paradigm than on the refusal to narrowly define and apply that paradigm.

Let us examine some classical examples of sociological analysis. *The Class Struggles in France* or *Eighteenth Brumaire* of Marx are obviously studies in which change is interpreted as a result of the conflict of the particular interests of a group of social categories. Marx refuses to accept the concept of some pre-established harmony of interests and insists, on the contrary, on their conflicting nature. The conflicting nature of interests is due to the dependence of the latter upon the position of individuals in class structure. When social actors act against their interests, it is because a contradiction between their individual interests and their collective interests appears. It would naturally lie in the advantage of the smallholding peasants to defend the interests of their category, but their boundary problems make them opposed to each other. Likewise, capitalists are doomed to a fierce competition that makes their individual interests and their class interests incompatible. Collective passions certainly play a fundamental part in de Tocqueville's work, but so do interests. French landowners of the *Ancien Régime* abandon their estate to buy a royal practice because, when settling in town, they can escape land tax and because holding a public office entails benefits in prestige and power. Therefore, interests depend on 'structures'. The interests of English landowners are not the same as those of the French. But the category of interests plays a fundamental part in de Tocqueville's sociological analysis. The *wertrationell* and *traditionell* actions are considered as fundamental by Weber. But traditions and values are only maintained for as long as they can adapt, i.e., for as long as they are compatible with interests. The cultural revolution represented by Protestantism allows industrial and commercial entrepreneurs to escape the afflictions the old cultural order exposed them to and consequently facilitates their enterprises. In the nineteenth century, one of the reasons for the vitality of Protestant sects in the United States lay in the fact that belonging to a Protestant sect provided traders, merchants, and commercial travellers with a certificate of respectability that allowed them to establish a relationship based on trust with their partners. It may not be exaggerated to regard the dialectics between values and interests as one of the major themes of Weber's sociology. As for Durkheim, it is true that he firmly rejects the theory in which Spencer states that the division of labour could be explained by the advantages it creates. But his main objection is methodological. Spencer's analysis appears to him teleological, and perhaps rightly so. The fiction according to which people might have decided to co-operate by relying on the anticipated benefits of co-operation cannot be taken as an acceptable description of the division of labour. Rather, the latter must be considered as the result of a complex process: the growth of 'material and moral density' facilitates the appearance and institutionalization of specialized roles. But Durkheim's analysis is not incompatible with that of utilitarians. Portugal does not expand its wine production following a co-operation contract with England. To return to a famous analysis by Ricardo, the division of labour between these two countries at the beginning of the nineteenth century is the result of the interplay of the law of comparative costs: it is less costly for England to buy wine than to produce it. The division of labour in this case is indeed the result of a mechanical process but it necessitates – as Durkheim rightly implied – the growth of moral and material density, as in this case the development of means of transport and of trust between the trading partners.

In other words, sociological analysis tends to correct and soften the utilitarian paradigm rather than to reject it. Sociologists first contributed to a refutation of the myth of harmonious interests and of the necessary transmutation of egotism into altruism. Particular interests serve the common interest in some ideal cases only. Occasionally, the meeting of interests, even if they conflict, can benefit all parties. A game that is presented at static level as a zero-sum game may well be turned into a game with a positive sum. Coser analysed this type of process with meticulous care in his theory of conflicts. It is well known for instance that, in some cases, the aggressive behaviour of trade unions may result in stimulating innovation in particular and productivity in general. But interests have no more of a natural propensity to converge than to diverge and to assume the shape of a zero-sum game. It all depends on the structure of the system of interaction or of interdependence within which these interests are expressed. Sociological analysis led here to a second point: the interests of social actors are not interchangeable. They depend on the position of individuals in the social structure but also on complex contextual factors. The interests of French landowners in the *Ancien Régime* are not the same as those of English landowners in the same period. A third point is that the same actor can have contradictory interests. It can be in my interest if the situation of the category I belong to improves, but it is also in my interest to improve my own position within that category. Both interests can be compatible but are not necessarily so: the union activist can incur risks for his own career. In certain structures of interaction interest may be difficult to define (thus the 'rebel' is trapped when everybody starts behaving like him).

Finally, sociological analysis exposes the complex interaction between values, beliefs, and interests. It may be in my interest to pursue objective A rather than objective B because A is more positively valued in society. It is clear, as Weber showed, that it is easier to be an entrepreneur in a cultural context where individual enterprise is positively valued. To reach A, I can make use of means P or Q and choose P, not because of its efficiency but because its value in society is greater. I can also choose P because I *believe* in its efficiency, not because this efficiency was proved but because P is the object of a collective belief. Thus, a government may *believe* that *tax* measures (P) or *social* measures (Q) are the best instruments for a good agrarian policy. But this belief may result from the relative influence of such or such a pressure group.

The fact that sociology defined itself partly against the movement of utilitarian thought has sometimes led, in the words of Wrong, to an 'oversocialized view of man' or, in other words, to a hyperculturalist conception in which the individual behaviour of social actors is interpreted as the simple manifestation of affective beliefs and values. In India, the pariahs's submission is often interpreted as the result of their internalization of cultural order that is percieved to be unchangeable. The following observation, recounted by Epstein, is enough to show the limits of such interpretation:

> a member of parliament who came from the city offers to pariahs – for whom an inconvenient well is reserved on the edge of the village – to gain access for them to the well that is reserved for the peasant caste. The pariahs refuse, not so much – if one is to believe their allegations – out of submission to a social taboo as because, by going to draw water from the same well as the peasants with whom they maintain a patron-client relationship, they would be liable to arguments and quarrels which they regard as undesirable. Wherever a hurried observer tends to see the product of cultural determinism in behaviour he does not fully understand, a more careful observer often perceives the presence of interests.

Beliefs, Dialectic, Economy and Sociology, Ideology, Rationality.

Bibliography

BARRY, B., *Sociologists, economists and democracy*, New York, Collier-Macmillan, 1970. – BENTHAM, J., *An introduction to the principles of morals and legislation*, London, T. Payne, 1789; Oxford, Clarendon Press, 1876, 1929; New York, Hafner Pub. Co., 1948; London, Athlone, 1970. – DURKHEIM, E., *The Division of Labour in Society*, Glencoe, Free Press, 1933. – EDGEWORTH, F.Y., *Mathematical psychics; an essay on the application of mathematics to the moral sciences*, London, Kegan Paul, 1881, 1961; New York, A.M. Kelley, 1961, 1967. – MARSHALL, A., *Principles of economics*, New York, Macmillan, 1890, 1948. – MILL, J. (Stuart), *Utilitarianism*, London, Parker & Bourn, 1863. – NISBET, R.A., *The sociological tradition*, London, Heinemann/New York, Basic Books, 1966. – SIDGWICK, H., *The methods of ethics*, London, Macmillan, 1874, 1930. – SMITH, A., *An inquiry into the nature and causes of the wealth of the nations*, London, W. Strahan & T. Padell, 1776; London, Ward Lock, 1812; Oxford, Clarendon Press, 1976; *The theory of moral sentiments; or an essay toward an analysis of the principles by which men naturally judge concerning the conduct and the character, first of their neighbours, and afterwards themselves*, London, A. Millar, 1759; New York, Kelley, 1966; Oxford, Clarendon Press, 1976. – SPENCER, H., *The principles of sociology: a quarterly serial*, New York, D. Appleton, 1874–1875, Abridged as: *Principles of sociology*, London, Macmillan, 1969.

Utopia

The term 'utopia' refers to a literary genre – a sort of political fiction – as well as to the often constraining and sometimes brutal attempt to achieve some form of social organization in which an ideal, that is reputed to be of absolute good, is supposed to be embodied.

The utopian tendency appears almost everywhere in history but, however diverse in content it may be, it always has some easily recognizable characteristics. First, utopia is constituted in opposition to the prevailing values of the society within which it was born. Moreover, it stands out because of its absolutism, which may lead the followers of the 'utopian sect' to the utmost intolerance – both towards a corrupted world and towards those who are known to prevent the coming of the new order. Absolutism and authoritarianism are two attributes of utopian behaviour that may, indeed, vary in intensity – ranging from the most uncompromising fanatacism to the kind of egotistic satisfaction that grows freely within those small, closed societies where happiness consists of living in a close and confined group. Being enclosed protects the utopian society, both from outside corruption and from the threat of strangers. The enclosure may be either dictated – as in the case of convents – by an authority in the hierarchy, or desired – as is the case in the Fourierist utopia – by the Phalansterians themselves.

However close the various forms of utopia that we can document may seem, they can be classified into a few clearly distinct types. The city imagined by Plato in *The Republic* is in clear contrast with the Thelene abbey Rabelais tells us about in his first book. It is true that if one tries to characterize these two forms of utopia by comparing them, it would also be necessary to wonder whether Plato was really serious when he told us about his totally just city and whether the description of Thelene was not, to a certain extent, providing sheer entertainment for Rabelais and his readers. To characterize the different types of utopia, it is not enough to stick to the differences that define their contents; one must also take into consideration the function that each of them is supposed to fulfil for its author and for the audience the author is writing for.

Utopias differ because of their contents. Some propose a society of plenty, others a society of strict parsimony; a society of saints for some, a society of heroes for others. But utopian thinking has some common features. It arises from fundamental dissatisfaction with the present conditions of social existence. This dissatisfaction must not be reduced to an individual and rather transient feeling. It is the source of a movement that incites us to restore harmony between what we consider fair (a just and free society, a society of equals) and life as it is for us here and now. We can try to make up with the old order (of things) by changing those elements that shock or hurt us. But we can just as well deny it any legitimacy, and even take any reality out of it – and since it should not exist, act as if it did not exist – by creating from scratch a new order in which we will be able to see a reflection of ourselves.

What is socially desirable is being constructed in terms of a deconstruction of some aspects of everyday life, and also by projecting or idealizing other aspects of everyday life. The issues over which the discontinuity between society as it is perceived and as it *should* be, are presented, and can be found, at the point of articulation between the normative system and frustrated expectations. In our societies income is distributed unequally: a small percentage of the population monopolizes a very high percentage of collective resources. And what is worse, this distribution is unfair: the relation between taxation and remuneration is broken down. Those who work least get most. Those who are in positions of authority are not the best qualified. Those who should be allowed to speak are condemned to silence. The power-holders interfere with the people they command in a much tighter way than is required for the smooth running of society. Social order generates hardships and frustrations that are not so much proofs of the intrinsic rarity of wealth and services as they are proofs of human sadism and malice; literally, society is set up the wrong way round, since hierarchy contradicts the most legitimate expectations and the highest requirements.

Utopian thinking does not remain at that negative stage, especially if the image of a possible society that acts as a reference is considered by it as being an ethical requirement. As for the conditions required to achieve the possible society, utopian thinking rejects incremental or gradual ones, or at least attaches only a limited importance to them. It prefers to assert, but in an ideal sense, that what is negated here and now is being achieved, and to take this assertion as the necessary counterpart of the negation of what is presently given. How does this jump into the ideal happen? One can recognize there at least three main directions. In the first version, utopian thinking turns directly to the advent of a social state in which, all 'contradictions' being solved, our desire to be fully ourselves would be fulfilled without any interference. The young Marx, in his commentaries on Hegel, talked about that time when man would be finally reconciled with himself, with nature, and with his fellow-men. This utopia may well assume the form of an ecological movement, such as the Green 'back to the land' movement. What animates it is the *naturalism* that ignores or rejects the biblical curse according to which, since his 'fall', man is condemned to earn his bread by the sweat of his brow.

From that first version, which may be called *millennarian*, one must distinguish the *ethical utopia*, which considers some values with such absolute seriousness that it is totally involved in their preservation or their promotion, whatever the cost of their realization may be. In the same way as we made a distinction between an ecological expression and a Rousseauist, ascetic expression of the first form of utopia, two versions of the ethical utopia may also be distinguished. In the first one, the ideal is dealt with as if, on account of its legitimacy, we were obliged to realize it. The ethical utopia is then in danger of drifting towards *terrorism*, since no value can be opposed to utopia and the realization of that utopia is virtually a legal imperative. The ethical utopia can also assume a non-violent and non-cosmic dimension. This term, which Max Weber applied to gurus, indicates retreat from the world that may go as far as refusing any contact with other people, as is characteristic of hermits, and which is coupled with a radical renunciation of all sensual pleasures. But this anti-cosmic form may be either made of pessimism and absolute renunciation or, on the contrary, made of reception of and identification with life under all its aspects, even the most orgiastic ones.

In any type of utopian thinking, all the following elements are to be found in various combinations: millennarianism, ethical absolutism, anti-cosmic values (terrorist). The ethical dimension is present in the Renaissance utopians' works as well as in the works of the nineteenth-century socialists. In all these works, it counterbalances the millennarian orientation. The anti-cosmic orientation is the greatest resort for any utopian thinking since the 'renouncer' who retires from the world enjoys at least the fruit of his own wisdom, of which no power in the world can deprive him. Utopian thinking is confronted by series of choices made up of alternatives: either changing the world or making a social order come that is to conform to the ethical ideal, either through activism or exemplary behaviour. Each of these terms is itself ambiguous. Activism can assume the form of political terrorism or that of missionary proselytism. Exemplary behaviour can go far beyond obedience to an external discipline, as far as the search for perfection beyond all compulsion or sanction.

Of all the ambiguities of utopian thinking, the most significant deals with the role of violence in the realization of utopia. Terrorism may appear as a necessary condition for the realization of the ethical utopia. But terrorism may also be considered as incompatible with the ethical ideal it brings dishonour on. The refusal of violence is then established as being one of the essential components of utopian behaviour. As for non-violence, its forms differ widely, from Jesus Christ's to Gandhi's.

Utopian thought is embodied in differentiated institutional versions. The millennarian utopia and the ethical utopia admit very different institutional expressions. The citizens of the Platonic Republic will be compelled to be just. The members of Fourier's Phalanstery will be able to go out as they please and to choose their partners according to their preference and their attractions. The anti-cosmic utopia suggests that individuals should isolate themselves, or at least keep the servitudes of the division of labour limited to the minimal requirements of the communication between the guru and his followers. But variations are possible between the types we distinguished, as the case of classical India proves, where, to quote Max Weber once again, the orgiastic orientation and the anti-cosmic orientation reinforce each other.

Utopian thinking deals with a certain number of presently given constraints as if they could or should be suppressed. It therefore constitutes a very special form of change since it is involved in an object towards which it suppresses all critical distance, while at the same time it finds itself short of means to intervene on the environment in which it is being developed – either out of contempt, as in the case of the anti-cosmic utopia, or because, as in the case of the ethical utopia, it considers this environment as a totally manageable substance that can be handled to fit its purpose. Therefore, utopian thinking settles in an 'as if' type of situation out of which it can come only through ethical voluntarism, which leads to an authoritarian and sometimes terrorist conception of society, or through an aesthetic and orgiastic value-system which leads to more or less clandestine associations, like secret societies.

Utopian thinking, like utopian society, is essentially unstable and ambiguous. But one must not reach the conclusion that it is inefficient at all times and in all places. It has inspired projects that were finally embodied in some lasting organizations. The utopian desire to escape impiety and corruption produced the monastic flowering which had extremely important consequences for the economy of the Christian West. The same desire was also the driving force behind the Mayflower pilgrims who went across the Atlantic to look for the Promised Land on the American shores. The mission settlements of the Jesuits in Paraguay were some sort of community in which the Good Fathers tamed the native Indians, and illustrate how serious they were in their project of creating a society and making it live according to the plans of Providence.

But utopia does not only refer to a *project* to be used by intransigent founders and reformers. It can also make up a theoretical *model* that helps us to understand how concrete societies evolve. It is not at all certain that Plato seriously wanted to build a republic exactly true to the utopia he presents in his famous treatise. But his tripartite society (philosophers, warriors, and craftsmen) sheds light on the way western societies functioned before the industrial revolution. It is absolutely clear that Rousseau never seriously thought that the European monarchies were going to change to fit the models of Geneva or Corsica. But the paradigm of the 'social contract' throws light on the problem of legitimacy in democratic societies.

The fecundity of the concept of utopia can be appreciated from three different angles. First, it can ensure the existence and survival of 'small circles' or, as is said today, of 'communities'. Second, it helps maintain the hope that a certain harmony can be achieved between the ideal requirements and the real conditions of life in society, even if it can also produce every possible deception or crime. But utopia is not only one of the sources of social change; it also provides food for theoretical thinking or a working-out of plans. The 'as if' of utopian thinking may lead to the exploration of *possible*, but not presently given, types of organization. Then, one has good reasons to speak about the utopia of competition, of 'liberal utopia', or 'socialist utopia'. What characterizes this last process is the fact that it tries to state fairly precisely what are the requisites of a social condition known to be desirable. Therefore, this process constitutes a hypothetical exercise. But it is possible to build a normative system thanks to which the relations that are recognized as desirable can be operationalized (for instance, in the case of liberal utopia, the notion of a multiplicity of independent producers, i.e., incapable of co-ordinating production to the detriment of consumers, can be specified in terms of production coefficients, or matrices of product-factors, which provide an estimate of the inter-dependence of firms). Thus, the watchword '*laissez-faire, laissez-passer*' can, after suitable modification, be transformed into a *model* of general balance. The market of pure and perfect competition is a utopia, in the sense that relations of production have at no time and in no place ever been strictly controlled by the impersonal confrontation of individual and independent supplies and demands. Moving from utopian thinking to methodical thinking requires two conditions: an effort of precision in explaining what is desirable and a realistic examination of the conditions and the circumstances in which what is desirable is being inscribed, to specify what is possible and what is not, as well as the various degrees of likelihood.

Utopian thinking is often in danger of autism. It closes itself up by becoming indifferent to whatever is not itself, to the point of not having anything to say any more on the conditions of its own achievement (I believe it because I hope it is so, I hope it is so because I believe it). Yet it happens that, even when caught up in that circle, utopian thinking may succeed, through a sublimation process, in producing artistic works which express, in a symbolic manner, the desirable state it carried in its womb but did not succeed in personifying. The religious architecture of the Middle Ages can be regarded as the realization of a double desire to cut oneself off from the world at the same time as creating a closed society.

It is just as difficult to evaluate the impact of utopian orientations in a society as it is to tell precisely where they are to be found. Karl Mannheim thought he discovered the avant-garde of utopia in the radicalized intelligentsia – the *freischwelende Intelligenz*. This opinion which, in a slightly different form, was later adopted by Marcuse, must be considered with great caution. First, while it is true that utopia criticizes the existing social order, it assumes, as we saw, different shapes. In its ethical form it can be monopolized by intellectuals who, as de Tocqueville observed so accurately, are more than willing to substitute the alleged evidence of abstract principles for the diversity, and possibly the incoherence, of concrete situations. But utopia cannot be confined to the political sphere. In its orgiastic form, or in its anti-cosmic form, it gets closer to art or religion. Nor can it be presented as necessarily conservative, whether or not it is a political utopia. There are libertarian utopias and authoritarian ones. There would be no purpose in claiming, as Mannheim does, that authoritarian pseudo-utopias are no more than disguised *ideologies*, i.e., justifications of the *status quo* or invitations to restore the *status quo ante*. Nazism, for instance, hawks back to a pre-industrial social order that lost its way due to the perversions of History, and which has to be re-established or established by all the means available to a merciless fanaticism. Yet, Hitler was not working for the *Junkers*. The restoration or the strengthening of traditional order was not a priority objective for him. There is no reason either why every utopia should necessarily contribute to the realization of a 'better future' nor why utopians should be regarded with reverence as being the driving force of history, the salt of the earth. The central question asked by Mannheim can be stated as follows: 'What's the use of utopias?' Unfortunately, this question does not have a precise answer. In less crudely functionalist terms than those used by the neo-Marxist Mannheim, we will say that utopia is the expression, if not the embodiment, of the desire to fill the gap between what social order is and what it should be, if it could be made 'satisfactory'.

Alienation, Beliefs, Ideologies, Marx, Religion, Rousseau, Social Symbolism.

Bibliography

BUBER, M., *Paths in utopia*, New York, Macmillan, 1950. – COHN, N., *The pursuit of the Millennium: revolutionary messianism in medieval and reformation Europe and its bearing on modern totalitarian movements*, Fairlawn, Essential Books, 1957; New York, Oxford University Press, 1970. – MANNHEIM, K., *Ideologie und Utopie*, Bonn, F. Cohen, 1929. Trans. *Ideology and Utopia*, London, Routledge & Kegan Paul, 1963. – MANUEL, F.E., *The new world of Henri Saint-Simon*, Cambridge, Harvard Univ. Press, 1956; *The prophets of Paris*, Cambridge, Harvard University Press, 1962. – MANUEL, F.E. (ed.), *Utopias and utopian thought*, Boston, Houghton Mifflin, 1966, London, Souvenir Press, 1973. – MARCUSE, H., *One dimensional man. Studies in the ideology of advanced industrial society*, Boston, Beacon, 1964; London, Routledge & Kegan Paul, 1964; *Das Ende der Utopie*, Berlin, V. Maikowski, 1967. – MARX, K., *Economic and Philosophical Manuscripts of 1844*, London, Penguin, 1974. – PARETO, V., *Les systèmes socialistes*. – ROUSSEAU, J.-J., *Discours sur l'origine de l'inégalité*. – WEIL, E., *Hegel et l'Etat*, Paris, J. Vrin, 1950.

Weber, Max

The work of Max Weber (1864–1920) emphasizes a certain number of tensions inherent in any form of sociological thought. But its significance is not simply due to the rigour with which each of these central issues of sociology is discussed, if not resolved. For more than a half-century, the Weberian heritage has furnished a series of continually relevant landmarks to those researchers who have not given up the association of both a wide-ranging historical-comparative perspective with careful institutional analysis and personal commitment with methodological detachment. Through its contained violence and energy, its tone of condescension, combined with an empathy which at some points achieves almost the status of pure mimicry, by both its strong points and those which sound a more dissonant tone, the work of Weber leaves an impression of true aesthetic prowess or *virtuosity* (the *virtuoso* being a figure to whom, in the sociology of religion, Weber frequently returns). In this brief entry we can only point to some of the essential perspectives of this work, either Weberian solutions which have retained their pertinence to the present day, or the unresolved questions left to us which retain their *provocative* value.

To begin with, Weber well understood the importance of the concept of action, and was the first to do so. He indicated its two aspects very clearly in his definition of sociology as a 'science concerning itself with the interpretive understanding of social action and thereby with causal explanation of its course and consequences'. Social action or conduct (*soziales handeln*) is that in which the subjective meaning involved relates to another individual or group. Action is clearly differentiated from mere behaviour (in the sense used by the behaviourists), for, as Weber says, it includes 'all human behaviour when and in so far as the acting individual attaches a subjective meaning to it'. The Weberian conception of action is immediately qualified by that of interaction, since 'action is social insofar as, by virtue of the subjective meaning attached to it by the acting individual (or individuals), it takes account of the behaviour of others and is therefore oriented in its course'. Social action thus must be seen as including the meaning that actors attach to it. This meaning may be of two types, *subjective* and *intersubjective*, since I cannot assign a meaning to my own action if I do not also take into account the response that I may anticipate from my co-actors. Such *anticipation* is more or less well-founded, it may be more or less adequately verified, but without it my action is deprived of meaning.

As Weber understands it, sociology is an interpretative discipline (*deuten verstehen*). But this interpretation is not a liberating methodology or a hermeneutic device. Its purpose is not to liberate the imagination or to bring to the surface the lived experience of the social 'imprisoned' in the mould of convention. It requires us, not to laboriously describe the respective positions of actors in society, but simply to take account of the meanings that actors assign to their own positions. At the same time as 'understanding' should not be confused with a hermeneutics of social unconsciousness, the 'subjectivity' which Weber describes should not be taken as the singular essence of an individual. Weberian method has analytic and generalizing ambitions. It is not the singular individual at which it is aimed, it is the actor in the constraints of his situation, where of course the intentions of other actors have the greatest importance.

Weber's insistence on talking about 'action', and 'subjective meaning' led him to qualify his sociology not just as individualist but also as 'rationalist'. In their essential aspects these two qualifications are closely linked. In effect the Weberian individual is provided with a certain number of attributes – notably those of combining means and ends, and of evaluating the eventualities which present themselves. It is in this sense that he or she is rational. Naturally this term does not mean for Weber that social actors are always and everywhere equipped with a scale of explicit preferences, or that they have complete information available to them, or complete mastery over their resources or environment, or that the sum or result of their individual actions will satisfy the demands of collective rationality. Weber's sociological 'rationalism' consists simply of the supposition that the meaning of our actions is determined in relation to our intentions and activities, concerning the intentions and activities of others. Any sociology which neglects these hypotheses finds itself condemned to an infinity of paralogisms, from which derive the tendency to treat society as a substantial reality – whether the 'substance' is spiritual or material.

Among the 'founding fathers' of modern sociology, Weber is the figure most insulated against the propensity for 'totalitarian realism' – as Piaget called it – which treats 'society' as a transcendent entity distinct from individuals. For Weber, the frame of social life is constituted by the actions of individuals capable of anticipation, evaluation, and the situation of themselves *vis-à-vis* others. By contrast, with the 'individualists' and the 'idealists' criticized by Durkheim, Weber saw very clearly the 'emergent' character of social facts. He established a clear distinction between the intentions and motivations of actors on the one hand and the aggregate effect of their action at the social and cultural level on the other hand. Thus the Puritans believed that by conforming to the letter of divine commandments they would express their submission to an almighty god who would judge or condemn them according to his immense and unfathomable justice. However, from the point of view of the historian or sociologist, such beliefs contributed to the legitimation of secular values such as saving, abstinence, hard work, which constitute indispensable ingredients of the work discipline of industrial societies. 'Interpretive sociology' is not any way a psychologism which *reduces* social conduct to the 'subjective meaning' which social actors attribute to it. It is better defined as an attempt to seize the processes of combination and composition from which social types and historical particularities *emerge*.

The term 'ideal-type' has led to as much debate as the term 'understanding'. But to the extent that the term 'understanding' is clear, although sometimes the debate has made it more obscure, the concept of 'ideal-type' has appeared highly resistant to exegesis. We will attempt to make the concept a little clearer, while recognizing the polemical dimension given to it by Weber, who thereby sought to distance himself from the German historicist tradition. We should begin by grasping why Weber talks about 'ideal-types' to designate the 'concepts' which sociologists make use of when they distinguish the diverse range of societies which they study. These concepts are not copies of the social forms which they seek to represent. Interpretative sociology proceeds not by *reproduction*, but by *construction*. It is this aspect of his method that Weber was emphasizing when he wrote about 'ideal-typical' concepts. But it is necessary to ensure that these types or models are not taken as arbitrary constructions. They may be assessed according to proper *evidence* which reconstitutes not simply the content of a single intention, but the *link* between the different aims of this intention and its results. For example, what provides evidence for the ideal-type of economic or technical action is the nature of the relationship between the ends pursued and the means utilized.

Classical economics provides the most easily understood examples (for example, types of markets) of what can be meant by 'ideal-type'. But there are other ideal-types than those illustrated by economics. The famous typology of domination (*herrschaft*) is an effective way of illustrating the Weberian method. On the basis of a definition of power, Weber attempts to characterize the resources required by an actor to ensure, ultimately through the use of force, the compliance or agreement of his partners. The assessment of the resources available to each actor, as well as their aims and the constraints to which they are subjected, enables him to distinguish a group of clearly differentiated situations: tradition, charisma, rational-legal authority.

Certain concepts, such as capitalism, feudalism, industrial society, post-industrialism, modern, or post-modern society, can also be represented as ideal-types. But they associate purely abstract relationships, such as types of markets or forms of rationality, with historical processes or events. On the one hand, they utilize abstract social relations, universal characteristics of social action, (what Parsons called 'pattern variables'); on the other hand, they place these abstract forms in the context of historically defined conjunctures. In order to understand capitalist society, the historian and the sociologist must have recourse to concepts such as choice, optimization, etc. But they cannot ignore the circumstances, the social framework, the institutional complex in which the enterpreneur exercises his choice.

The ideal-type is thus a mixture of abstract relations and of historical and contingent data. Problems arise however where the sociologist has to control the level of abstraction of the types that he constructs. The distinction between charismatic and rational-legal authority is 'obvious' if we mean by that the ability to identify each type of authority according to its own logic. But on what basis can these 'obvious' distinctions be 'relevant' for the historian or comparativist? It is essential to realize that ideal-types are not simply definitions and hypotheses. For example, Weber provides definitions of economic activity which involve the notion of scarcity, and of authority in relation to the ability of a person to have his wishes fulfilled despite the objections of others. These notions are, however, closer to concepts than to types: the notion of authority is wider than the ideal-type of charismatic power. The notion of authority is also more abstract than the ideal-type of charismatic domination – and is even more obviously abstract than the concept of capitalist society or imperialist domination. The construction of ideal-types has to satisfy two requirements: the apprehension of simple relations – obvious but abstract – between aims, constraints, and resources of actors, and the *compatibility* of these elementary relations within the complexes thus created.

Even if these requirements are met, the ideal-type remains no more than a hypothetical representation. The same reality may suggest a plurality of types and therefore of representations. There is perhaps a 'total social fact' – but there surely is not a 'total' vision of social reality. Weberian sociology is radically pluralist to the extent that it recognizes in both actor and observer a plurality of orientations: all understanding or interpretation is a choice that the actor or observer makes at his own risk, among the intentions of the other. Because of its pluralism, Weberian sociology represents the most efficient antidote to the diverse variants of scientistic sociology.

The construction of ideal-types would run the risk of being nothing but a worthless exercise, if no means were available to assess their *relevance*. The most abstract types have much in common with the axiomatic constructions of the sort outlined by Parsons in 'pattern variables'. Weber did not go far down this road, either because he saw that it might lead to a dead-end or because his attention was diverted to other tasks. In effect, the ideal-types whose relevance Weber sought to test were 'middle-range'. For example, he was less directly and systematically interested in the problem of the relation between 'values' and 'interests' than in the relations between puritan 'values' and the 'interests' of capitalist producers and merchants.

The relevance of an ideal-type, such as that of the Protestant ethic, may be established in two ways. Weber initially shows the congruence (or *elective affinity*) between puritan values and the norms which regulate the conduct of capitalist entrepreneurs. But such a congruence is not entirely adequate. The puritan and the capitalist do not speak the same 'language'. But they *understand* each other in the sense that what one does (or should do) in his sphere is compatible with what the other does (or should do) in his. The congruence between their types of activity goes further. For example, the work of the capitalist appears to the puritan as a wholly acceptable way, if not the only legitimate one, to prepare for the kingdom of heaven on earth, by obeying strictly to the letter God's commandments.

The second stage consists of showing that the congruence between the orientations of the puritan and the capitalist thus established through interpretative sociology takes 'adequate' account of the emergence of capitalist institutions. Weber never claimed that he had *demonstrated* such a connection. It is moreover impossible to do so. It derives as much from historical as sociological analysis. Now the historical material is not homogeneous. It comprises movements of a very long duration, virtually static, in which any development in relation to the institutional or physical environment is hardly perceptible. But it also contains cyclical phenomena and events which to a considerable extent are accidental: the battles of Marathon or Salamis, Columbus's voyage, and the subsequent discovery of silver and gold in the Americas. According to Max Weber, the historic importance of an event can only be a matter of 'a retrospective judgement of probability'. What would have happened if the triremes of Athens had been beaten by the Persian galleys at Salamis in 480 BC? How would international commerce have been funded if South American silver had not flooded into Western Europe via Spain? Calculations of retrospective probability can be more or less precise; they can take into account a larger or smaller number of variables, by going either further back in terms of antecedents or further forward in terms of consequences. In any case, the researcher attempting to evaluate the adequacy of an ideal-type to explain historical processes is required to examine – quite apart from the logical coherence of the model and the evidence for the propositions which form its base – the probability that the events would have taken the course that they did if the relationships stated by the ideal-type were taken as hypotheses. The higher is this probability, the greater is the explanatory value of the ideal-type.

Did Weber always strictly follow the requirements of his own method? As he set it out, it frequently lacks clarity – particularly where the extent of the field over which the 'judgement of retrospective probability' should be exercised is concerned. In fact, Weberian method has a practical relation with the needs of the researcher whose interests lie in historical and comparative sociology. Weber was as passionately interested in contemporary as historical societies. Paul Lazarsfeld has suggested, with some justification, that there is in Weber's work a part which qualifies him as a great empirical sociologist of daily life. It is tempting to wonder if Weber would not have clarified some of the problems related to the conception of the ideal-type if he had continued along such a road. In many ways, Weber is the Montesquieu of the twentieth century. Like the great French thinker, he was immensely erudite. Similarly, he had a very lively sense of the variety of factors determining – as causes – 'morals, manners, and laws'. Weber was no less sensitive to the variety of civilizations which were for him expressed in the most striking manner by the variety of religious traditions. And, a little like Montesquieu's search for invariants which constitute the basis of legislative activity across all circumstances and traditions, Weber sought the common features of the 'rationalization' of human conduct, which solicited the reflection of the historian and comparativist.

Weber's relativism is more radical than that of Montesquieu for whom, in the last analysis, 'laws are the necessary relationships which flow from the nature of things'. Is there a concept of nature in Weber – either of things or men? Weberian relativism is affirmed with a particular force where it concerns individual or collective values. The influence of Nietzsche, as Mommsen's analysis has shown, seems most likely here. But this relativism is tempered in two ways. First, as it concerns the individual actor, Weber insists on the responsibility which is the counterpart of freedom of choice. Such a responsibility is particularly required of politicians who cannot use the excuse of the respectability of their intentions to excuse the catastrophic consequences of their commitment to a particular ideology. Scientists and thinkers, for their part, are subject to the obligation of verifying their assertions and making them understandable. Ethical relativism does not involve epistemological relativism, and so *a fortiori* neither does it imply scepticism. The second limitation imposed on the relativism of values follows from their espousal by protagonists who, in seeking to put them into practise, face problems of *legitimation* and *realization*. The legitimation process takes the purely arbitrary character away from the affirmation of values. In one way or another, they have to be *founded*: either on a tradition or via a more complicated process of 'certification' that Weber analyses in relation to the puritans and the Hebrew prophets. In respect of the requirement for realization, it controls the introduction of values into an efficient and differentiated normative system. This double problematic ensures that values have at least a minimal rigour, which means that they cannot be treated as purely arbitrary preferences. In short, Weber is on his guard against confusing 'values' with 'tastes'.

Have values any foundation apart from the society which recognizes and sanctions them? Leo Strauss has raised a very strong objection against Weberian method in this regard. In affecting a very strong axiological 'neutrality', Weber ends up with a sort of indifference in which 'anything goes', which not only prevents him choosing between different types of societies, and notably between libertarian and tyrannical societies, but also leads him to neglect the specificity of the tyrant, to the extent that such a figure is characterized by the intention of negating and destroying. Axiological neutrality here leads 'interpretative sociology' to a sort of voluntary blindness.

It is possible to make two responses to such a critique. First, axiological neutrality – which is not a metaphysical device, but a methodological procedure – does not lead to cynicism or indifference. In fact, Weber says only two things, very different from those attributed to him by Strauss. First, it is not necessary to condemn or approve in order to understand or explain. Second, even if we condemn or approve, it is not against the rules to wonder what actors understand by what the moralist approves or condemns – and how things have come to the point where the person making the judgement sees them. Moral judgement does not mean dispensing with the effort of understanding or the effort of explanation; and, whatever its importance, will not mean a great deal in these two tasks which are closer to specifically intellectual methods. To go beyond this polemic and grasp the importance of Weberian relativism, it is important not to allow values to be enclosed in a cultural circle where they do not communicate among themselves but are defined in relation to religious movements and traditions, which are ultimately co-extensive with historical processes themselves. Throughout his career Weber was attentive to – and perhaps this was the cherished object of his intellectual interest – the great world religions (*Weltreligionen*) through which the great singular experiences of individuals and groups are opened up to the requirements of universalization.

Action, Bureaucracy, Capitalism, Charisma, Durkheim, Methodology, Prophetism, Rationality, Religion, Schumpeter.

Bibliography

WEBER, M., *Gesammelte Aufsätze zur Religionssoziologie*, Tübingen, Mohr, vol. I, 1920, vol. II, 1921, vol. III, 1921. Trans. *The Protestant Ethic and the Spirit of Capitalism*, London, George Allen & Unwin, 1930; *The religion of China*, Glencoe, The Free Press, 1951; London, Macmillan, 1963. *The religion of India: the sociology of hinduism and buddhism*, Glencoe, Free Press, 1958; London, Collier Macmillan, 1961. – *Wirtschaft und Gesellschaft*, Tübingen, Mohr, 1922, 1925, 1947, 1956, Trans. *Economy and Society*, New York, Bedminster Press, 1968. – *Gesammelte Aufsätze zur Wissenschafslehre*, Tübingen, Mohr, 1922, 1951. *From Max Weber*, ed. GERTH, H.H. and MILLS, C.W., London, Routledge & Kegan Paul, 1945. – ARON, R., *La sociologie allemande contemporaine*, Paris, F. Alcan, 1935; Paris, PUF, 1966; *Les étapes de la pensée sociologique*, Paris, Gallimard, 1967, 1974. – BENDIX, R., *Max Weber, an intellectual portrait*, New York, Doubleday, 1960; London, Methuen, 1966. – EISENSTADT, S.N. (ed.), *Max Weber: on charisma and institution building, selected papers*, Chicago, The Univ. of Chicago Press, 1958. – FREUND, J., *Sociologie de Max Weber*, Paris, PUF, 1966. – FREUND, J., and LÜTHY, H., 'Controverse sur Max Weber', *Preuves*, September 1964, CLXIII, 85–92. – LAZARSFELD, P.F. and OBERSCHALL, A.R., 'Max Weber and empirical social research', *American Sociological Review*, 1965, XXX, 185–199. – MARTINDALE, D., 'Sociological theory and the ideal type', *in* GROSS, L. (ed.), *Symposium on Sociological Theory*, Evanston, Row Peterson, 1959, 57–91. – MOMMSEN, W., *Max Weber und die deutsche Politik, 1890–1920*, Tübingen, Mohr, 1959, 1974. – PARSONS, T., *The structure of social action: a study in social theory with special reference to a group of recent European writers*, Glencoe, Free Press, 1937, 1949, part III, chap. 14 to 17; *Sociological theory and modern society*, New York, The Free Press, 1967, chap. 1, 79–101. – STRAUSS, L., *Natural Right and history*, Chicago, University of Chicago Press, 1950.

Thematic Index

436